AF689750

Max-Planck-Institut für ausländisches öffentliches Recht und Völkerrecht

Beiträge zum ausländischen öffentlichen Recht und Völkerrecht

Begründet von Viktor Bruns

Herausgegeben von
Armin von Bogdandy · Rüdiger Wolfrum

Band 230

Roland Otto

Targeted Killings and International Law

With Special Regard to Human Rights and International Humanitarian Law

Springer
the language of science

ISSN 0172-4770
ISBN 978-3-642-24857-3 e-ISBN 978-3-642-24858-0
DOI 10.1007/978-3-642-24858-0
Springer Heidelberg Dordrecht London New York

Die Deutsche Nationalbibliothek verzeichnet diese Publikation in der Deutschen Nationalbibliografie; detaillierte bibliografische Daten sind im Internet über http://dnb.d-nb.de abrufbar.

© by Max-Planck-Gesellschaft zur Förderung der Wissenschaften e.V., to be exercised by Max-Planck-Institut für ausländisches öffentliches Recht und Völkerrecht, Heidelberg 2012
Dieses Werk ist urheberrechtlich geschützt. Die dadurch begründeten Rechte, insbesondere die der Übersetzung, des Nachdrucks, des Vortrags, der Entnahme von Abbildungen und Tabellen, der Funksendung, der Mikroverfilmung oder der Vervielfältigung auf anderen Wegen und der Speicherung in Datenverarbeitungsanlagen, bleiben, auch bei nur auszugsweiser Verwertung, vorbehalten. Eine Vervielfältigung dieses Werkes oder von Teilen dieses Werkes ist auch im Einzelfall nur in den Grenzen der gesetzlichen Bestimmungen des Urheberrechtsgesetzes der Bundesrepublik Deutschland vom 9. September 1965 in der jeweils geltenden Fassung zulässig. Sie ist grundsätzlich vergütungspflichtig. Zuwiderhandlungen unterliegen den Strafbestimmungen des Urheberrechtsgesetzes.
Die Wiedergabe von Gebrauchsnamen, Handelsnamen, Warenbezeichnungen usw. in diesem Werk berechtigt auch ohne besondere Kennzeichnung nicht zu der Annahme, dass solche Namen im Sinne der Warenzeichen- und Markenschutz-Gesetzgebung als frei zu betrachten wären und daher von jedermann benutzt werden dürften.

Gedruckt auf säurefreiem Papier

Springer ist Teil der Fachverlagsgruppe Springer Science+Business Media (www.springer.com)

Acknowledgements

The present treatise is an updated version of the thesis which was accepted by the Faculty of Law of the Humboldt University of Berlin in March 2009 in partial fulfilment of the requirements for the degree of Dr. iur. The research for the treatise was started while I was working as a research fellow at the Göttingen Institute of International and European Law. The topic of "targeted killings" was chosen as the outcome of one of many fruitful discussions with Prof. Dr. Georg Nolte, then director of the said institute. The main research – as well as the update to December 2010 – was done there.

I would like to express my sincere appreciation to all those who have directly or indirectly contributed to this thesis.

I would like to thank my "Doktorvater" Prof. Dr. Georg Nolte for his academic supervision, professional guidance and personal support and for reviewing the thesis in very short time. I would also like to thank Prof. Dr. Dr. h.c. Christian Tomuschat for quickly reviewing the thesis as the secondary referee.

I would like to thank Prof. Dr. Dr. h.c. Rüdiger Wolfrum and Prof. Dr. Armin von Bogdandy, editors of the series "Beiträge zum ausländischen öffentlichen Recht und Völkerrecht" of the Max Planck Institute for Comparative Public Law and International Law, for accepting the publication of the treatise in the series.

I would like to thank the whole staff – scientific and non-scientific – of the Göttingen Institute of International and European Law for (not only) providing the best conditions for research.

I would like to thank Meghan Gray and Dr. Michael Stuart (Jim) Bolton for proofreading an earlier version of the text.

I would like to thank my parents for rendering possible the education I enjoyed. Finally, I would like to thank my wife Kerstin for continuously and patiently supporting me in every phase of the work on this treatise. I dedicate the treatise to her.

Göttingen, December 2010 Roland Otto

Summary of Contents

Table of Contents

Introduction

The topic of "targeted killings" is strongly – but by no means exclusively – related to the State of Israel. Since the 1970s, dozens of alleged "terrorists"[1] are reported to have been assassinated by Israeli security forces in Israel and abroad.[2] In the early 1990s a number of human rights associations alleged that the Israel Defence Forces had set up units of "pseudo-Arabs" whose official mission was to catch wanted terrorists, but whose operation procedures *de facto* allowed the forces to kill their targets in many cases rather than arrest them.[3] However, such a practice was vehemently denied by Israel and is thus at least not the official beginning of a policy of targeted killings.[4]

A. The Recent Situation in Israel

The topic became more prominent when Israel, as a consequence of the sharp escalation of the Israeli-Palestinian Conflict in October 2000, officially adopted a strategic military policy aimed at "neutralizing terrorist organizations" by "targeting wanted terrorists" suspected of initiating, planning, and executing terrorist activities against Israeli citizens.[5] The Israeli Deputy Minister of Defence stated:

---

1 The term "terrorism" will be examined thoroughly *infra*, Introduction, Chapter F) II.

2 Gal Luft, 'The Logic of Israel's Targeted Killing: It's Worked – Most of the Time', in: 10 *Mid. E. Q.* (2003), pp. 3-14, at 3-7.

3 *Compare* Emanuel Gross, *The Struggle of Democracy Against Terrorism: Lessons from the United States, the United Kingdom, and Israel*, Charlottesville 2006, p. 222.

4 *See* UN General Assembly, Special Committee to Investigate Israeli Practices Affecting the Human Rights of the Palestinian People and other Arabs of the Occupied Territories, Report of October 21, 1992, UN Doc. A/47/509 (1992), paras. 48-49; B'Tselem, 'Activities of the Special Units in the Territories', Report of May 1992, pp. 27-52.

5 Gross, *Struggle of Democracy*, p. 222.

> I can tell you unequivocally what the policy is. If anyone has committed or is planning to carry out terrorist attacks, he has to be hit ... It is effective, precise, and just.[6]

In the context of the al-Aqsa Intifada,[7] within less than two and a half years, 1,828 Palestinians are reported to have been killed by the Israeli Forces. At least 128 of them are reported to have lost their lives as a result of the Israeli policy of targeted killings, including 42 bystanders in such operations.[8] Presently,[9] these numbers have risen to 4,396 Palestinians killed by Israeli Forces. This number includes 372 persons reported to have been killed during targeted killings, 147 persons of whom are reported to having been bystanders.[10] According to these numbers, innocent people make up about 39% of the persons killed in Israeli targeted killings.[11]

---

6 Statement by Israel's Deputy Minister of Defence *Ephraim Sneh*, quoted in: UN Comm'n H.R., *Question of the Violation of Human Rights in the Occupied Arab Territories, including Palestine – Report of the Human Rights Inquiry Commission established pursuant to Commission Resolution S-5/1 of 19 October 2000*, UN Doc. E/CN.4/2001/121 (March 16, 2001), p. 17 (para. 54).

7 The 2000-2005 al-Aqsa Intifada is also referred to as the Second Intifada, as opposed to the 1987-1993 First Intifada, *compare infra*, Part Five, Chapter A) II. 1. d).

8 Orna Ben-Naftali; Keren R. Michaeli, 'Justice-Ability: A Critique of the alleged Non-Justiciability of Israel's policy of Targeted Killings', in: 1 *J. Int'l Crim. Just.* (2003), pp. 368-405, at 370 with further references. During the same period, 460 Israeli civilians and 216 Israeli security personnel are reported to have been killed by Palestinians, *see ibid.* This thesis is in no way meant to relativise any violent action taken by either side. Also killings of Israelis by Palestinians raise issues of international responsibility, *see e.g.* Demian Casey, 'Breaking the Chain of Violence in Israel and Palestine: Suicide Bombings and Targeted Killings under International Humanitarian Law', in: 32 *Syracuse J. Int'l L. & Com.* (2005), pp. 311-344, at 330-336.

9 Including the period of September 29, 2000 till December 31, 2007.

10 *See* B'Tselem, 'Statistics: Fatalities 29.9.2000-31.12.2007'. During the whole period, 705 Israeli civilians and 325 Israeli security personnel are reported to have been killed by Palestinians, *see ibid.*

11 Casey, 32 *Syracuse J. Int'l L. & Com.* (2005), at 316 refers to at least 30-35%. According to Helen Keller/ Magdalena Forowicz, 'A Tightrope Walk between Legality and Legitimacy: An Analysis of the Israeli Supreme Court's Judgment on Targeted Killing', in 21 *Leiden J. Int'l L.* (2008), pp. 185-221, at

The most prominent cases under this policy, among others, were the eliminations of Sheikh *Ahmed Ismail Yassin*,[12] the founder of the Hamas[13] organisation and *Salah Shehade*, the commander of the military wing of the Hamas[14]. After many eliminations had taken place, Israel finally officially accepted responsibility for the policy both through notices issued by Israel Defence Forces' spokesmen[15] and through interviews given by senior political figures and defence officials.[16]

Until now, these operations have been executed by using three main techniques, namely sniper shooting, bomb laying (especially placing bombs in cars and phone booths) and pinpoint air strikes by fighter planes and helicopter gunships. Almost all operations have taken place in the Occupied Palestinian Territory[17] and most targets have been mid-

---

186, some 38 per cent of those killed in total were bystanders, and only 62 per cent of them were accurately targeted.

12 Margot Dudkevitch, 'Sheikh Ahmed Yassin killed in Airstrike', in: *Jerusalem Post*, Online Edition, March 22, 2004.

13 The word "Hamas" means "strength and bravery". The full Name of the organisation is "Harakat al-Muqawama al-Islamiyya" or "Islamic Resistance Movement".

14 Luft, 10 *Mid. E. Q.* (2003), at 7-8; Gross, *Struggle of Democracy*, p. 238; Sharon Weill, 'The Targeted Killing of Salah Shehadeh: From Gaza to Madrid', in: 7 *J. Int'l Crim. Just.* (2009), pp. 617-631, especially on the criminal investigations in Spain concerning the killing of *Shehadeh*.

15 *See e.g.* the November 9, 2000 statement by Major General *Yitzhak Eitan*, Chief of the Army's Central Command issued shortly after the attack on *Hussein 'Abayat*: "You have to understand that such actions are taken by high levels of the IDF and by high levels of the Israeli government, and I would say that it was the same this time and I would prefer not to add anything about it. ... The action was based on intelligence information. It was performed with accuracy by the Israeli air force.", quoted in: Amnesty International, *Israel and the Occupied Territories, State Assassinations and Other Unlawful Killings*, AI Doc. MDE 15/005/2001 (February 21, 2001), p. 7.

16 *See e.g.* the statements by Prime Minister *Ariel Sharon*: "The goal of the plan is to place the terrorists in varying situations every day and to knock them off balance so that they will be busy protecting themselves.", quoted in: Deborah Sontag, 'Israelis, Suspecting Mortars, Raid Camp; 2 Arabs Die', in: *New York Times*, April 12, 2001; *compare also* Gross, *Struggle of Democracy*, p. 222.

17 On this terminology "Occupied Palestinian Territory" *compare infra*, Introduction, Chapter F) I.

to high-level officials of various Palestinian militant organizations involved in violent operations against Israeli targets.[18]

A petition brought before the Israeli Supreme Court against targeted killings was first rejected by reasoning that "choice of means of warfare" was not justiciable.[19] The Court ruled that

> the choice of means of war employed by respondents in order to prevent murderous terrorist attacks before they happen, is not among the subjects in which this Court will see fit to intervene.[20]

Obviously, the policy became the subject of intense public, political, and legal controversy in domestic and in international fora. In that discussion, the policy of targeted killings has been labelled as "unlawful killings" by the U.K. Foreign Secretary *Jack Straw*[21] and as a "summary execution that violates human rights" by *Anna Lindh*,[22] then the Foreign Minister of Sweden. It has been described as being "contrary to

---

18 Yuval Shany, 'Israeli Counter-Terrorism Measures: Are they "kosher" under International Law?', in: Michael N. Schmitt/ Gian Luca Beruto (eds.), *Terrorism and International Law: Challenges and Responses*, San Remo 2003, pp. 96-118, at 103.

19 Supreme Court of Israel, *Barakeh v. Prime Minister ("Targeted Killings" Admissibility I)*, H.C.J. 5872/01, Judgment of January 29, 2002, in: 56 *Piskei Din* (2002), Issue 3, p. 1; *compare also* Eyal Benvenisti, 'Ajuri et. al. – Israeli High Court of Justice, 3 September 2002', in: 9 *Eur. Pub. L.* (2003), pp. 481-491, at 487 (footnote 18).

20 Supreme Court of Israel, *"Targeted Killings" Admissibility I*; *also quoted in*: Supreme Court of Israel, *The Public Committee Against Torture in Israel and LAW (Palestine Society for the Protection of Human Rights and the Environment) v. The State of Israel* et al. *("Targeted Killings" Merits)*, H.C.J. 769/02, Judgment of December 11, 2006, para. 9, English translation reprinted in: 46 *ILM* (2007), pp. 375-408, at 378.

21 Matthew Tempest, 'UK condemns "unlawful" Yassin killing', in: *Guardian*, March 22, 2004.

22 The then Swedish foreign minister, *Anna Lindh*, told the Swedish news agency TT with reference to the United States dropping a bomb on six al-Qaeda terrorists in Yemen: "If the USA is behind this with Yemen's consent, it is nevertheless a summary execution that violates human rights. If the USA has conducted the attack without Yemen's permission it is even worse. Then it is a question of unauthorised use of force.", *see* Brian Whitaker/ Oliver Burkeman, 'Killing Probes the Frontiers of Robotics and Legality', in: *Guardian*, November 6, 2002.

international law" by UN Secretary-General *Kofi Annan*,[23] and the issue was *inter alia* considered by the United Nations Human Rights Committee in its 2003 review of the report submitted by Israel. The Committee stated that

> The State Party should not use 'targeted killings' as a deterrent or punishment. The State party should ensure that the utmost consideration is given to the principle of proportionality in all its responses to terrorist threats and activities. State policy in this respect should be spelled out clearly in guidelines to regional military commanders, and complaints about disproportionate use of force should be investigated promptly by an independent body. Before resorting to the use of deadly force, all measures to arrest a person suspected of being in the process of committing acts of terror must be exhausted.[24]

In late 2006, the Israeli Supreme Court finally considered whether the policy of targeted killings of the Israeli government was lawful under international law. The Court held that hostilities were taking place in the context of an international armed conflict but that the "terrorists" who are targeted by Israeli forces do not have combatant status under international humanitarian law.[25] Therefore, the Court considered them to be civilians, but as civilians taking a "direct part in hostilities". The Court stated that a person who is belonging to an armed group and "in the framework of his role in that organization he commits a chain of hostilities" is loosing his immunity from attack.[26] However, after taking this "law of war" approach, the Court introduced human rights elements well know from the European Court of Human Right's *McCann* judgment[27] such as a general test of proportionality to the question.[28]

---

23 *See* UN Secretary General *Kofi Annan*, Statement at the UN Headquarters, in: *Off the Cuff – Remarks to the Press and the Public*, March 22, 2004 (unofficial transcript).

24 H.R. Committee, *Concluding Observations on Israel*, UN Doc. CCPR/CO/78/ISR (August 21, 2003), para. 15.

25 Supreme Court of Israel, *"Targeted Killings" (Merits)*, H.C.J. 769/02, Judgment of December 11, 2006, para. 24, English translation reprinted in: 46 *ILM* (2007), pp. 375-408, at 386.

26 *Id.*, para. 39, 46 *ILM* (2007), at 393.

27 Eur. Ct. H.R., *McCann, Farrell and Savage v. United Kingdom*, Appl. No. 18984/91, Judgment (Grand Chamber) of September 27, 1995, Series A, No. 324.

B. The Further International Context

Beside Israel, it is foremost the U.S. which has an – albeit not official – practice of targeted killings.[29] In the past, this mostly concerned assassination plots by the Central Intelligence Agency (CIA).[30] A prominent recent example which is part of the so called "war on terror" is the killing of six alleged terrorists in their car by a U.S. Predator drone in Yemen:

> On 3 November 2002, over the desert near Sanaa, Yemen, a Central Intelligence Agency-controlled Predator drone aircraft tracked an SUV containing six men. One of the six, Qaed Salim Sinan al-Harethi, was known to be a senior al-Qa'ida lieutenant suspected of having played a major role in the 2000 bombing of the destroyer USS Cole. He 'was on a list of "high-value" targets whose elimination, by capture or death, had been called for by President Bush.' The United States and Yemen had tracked al-Harethi's movements for months. Now, away from any inhabited area, the Predator fired a Hellfire missile at the vehicle. The six occupants, including al-Harethi, were killed.[31]

---

[28] *Compare especially* Supreme Court of Israel, *"Targeted Killings" (Merits)*, para. 40, 46 *ILM* (2007), at 393.

[29] *See also* Heiko F. Schmitz-Elvenich, *Targeted Killing: Die völkerrechtliche Zulässigkeit der gezielten Tötung von Terroristen im Ausland*, Frankfurt am Main 2008, pp. 14-15; *compare also* Michael N. Schmitt, 'Targeted Killings in International Law: Law Enforcement, Self-Defense and Armed Conflict', in: Roberta Arnold/ Noëlle Quénivet (eds.), *International Humanitarian Law and Human Rights Law: Towards a New Merger in International Law*, Leiden 2008, pp. 525-553, at 525-526; Kenneth Anderson, 'Targeted Killing in U.S. Counterterrorism Strategy and Law', in: Benjamin Wittes (ed.), *Legislating the War on Terror: An Agenda for Reform*, Washington, D.C. 2009, pp. 346-400, at 365-375. For further examples concerning Russia, France and the United Kingdom, *see* Stefanie Schmahl, 'Targeted Killings – A Challenge for International Law?', in: Christian Tomuschat/ Evelyne Lagrange/ Stefan Oeter (eds.), *The Right to Life*, Leiden 2010, pp. 233-266, at 235-236.

[30] *See* William C. Banks/ Peter Raven-Hansen, 'Targeted Killing and Assassination: The U.S. Legal Framework', in: 37 *U. Rich. L. Rev.* (2003), pp. 667-749, at 702-705; Schmahl, in: Tomuschat *et al.* (eds.), at 235.

[31] Gary Solis, 'Targeted Killing and the Law of Armed Conflict', in: 60 *Nav. War C. Rev.* (2007), pp. 127-146, at 130 (footnotes omitted). *See also* 72 *Archiv*

Four years later, in June 2006, the targeted killing of *Abu Musab al-Zarqawi*, the leader of al-Qaeda[32] in Iraq, was celebrated as a strategic and political victory by the U.S.[33] Since September 11, 2001 a series of at least nineteen targeted killings by the U.S. via Predator fired Hellfire missiles is reported to have taken place, killing at least four senior al-Qaeda leaders and also many civilians.[34] This practice is continued. On January 28, 2008, senior al-Qaeda commander *Abu Laith al-Libi* and several other persons were reportedly killed by a Predator fired Hellfire missile in Pakistan.[35]

But also democracies which are less involved in the so called "war on terror" do not necessarily decline targeted killings as a means. Such States which have not been directly affected by transnational terrorism sometimes offer what has been termed as "nice recipes ... that have little practical relevance" and "seem to be blind to real life hard choices".[36] On the other hand, for example, Germany's Federal Minister of the Interior, *Otto Schily*, in a 2004 interview took into account

---

der Gegenwart (2002), p. 45987; Walter Pincus, 'U.S. Strike Kills Six in Al Qaeda', in: *Washington Post*, November 5, 2002, p. 1; James Risen, 'Threats and Responses: Hunt for Suspects – C.I.A. is reported to kill a Leader of Qaeda in Yemen', in: *New York Times*, November 5, 2002, p. 1; *c.f.* Amnesty International Press Release, 'Yemen/USA: Government must not sanction Extra-Judicial Executions', November 8, 2002, AI Index AMR 51/168/2002; Chris Downes, '"Targeted Killings" in an Age of Terror: The Legality of the Yemen Strike', in: 9 *J. Confl. Sec. L.* (2004), pp. 277-294; Gross, *Struggle of Democracy*, p. 243; Anderson, in: Wittes (ed.), at 362-363.

[32] The group's name is frequently also spelled as "al-Qaida", "al-Qa'ida" or "al-Qa'idah", which is Arabic and means "the base".

[33] Solis, 60 *Nav. War C. Rev.* (2007), at 134.

[34] These examples include the December 2005 killing of senior al Qaeda operative *Abu Hamza Rabi'a* in Pakistan and the unsuccessful effort to kill al Qaeda co-leader *Ayman al-Zawahiri* in January 2006, also in Pakistan, which killed eighteen civilians. *See* Josh Meyer, 'CIA Expands Use of Drones in Terror War', in: *Los Angeles Times*, January 29, 2006, p. A1; W. Jason Fisher, 'Targeted Killing, Norms, and International Law', in: 45 *Colum. J. Transnat'l L.* (2007), pp. 711-758, at 712 with further references.

[35] *See* Eric Schmitt, 'Senior Qaeda Commander Is Killed by U.S. Missile', in: *New York Times* (February 1, 2008).

[36] Rein Müllerson, '*Jus ad Bellum* and International Terrorism', in: 32 *Isr. Yb. Hum. Rts.* (2002), pp. 1-51, at 18.

the possibility of killing suspected terrorists.[37] His successor, *Wolfgang Schäuble*, recently addressed the topic in relation to *Osama Bin Laden*:[38]

> Imagine someone knew what cave Osama bin Laden is sitting in. A remote-controlled missile could then be fired in order to kill him.[39]

Schäuble criticised that the question of legality of such an action was not regulated under German national law[40] – based on the fact that such an action is not explicitly rendered legal under German national law.[41] It is questionable whether the latter was possible at all if not only national but international standards are taken into account. In trying to answer this question, the emphasis is put on State behaviour and responsibility and not on individual criminal liability. However, before going into the question of legality, a word about terminology is in order:

C. Defining "Targeted Killings"

> During World War II, in April 1943, Admiral Isoroku Yamamoto, commander in chief of the Japanese Combined Fleet, was on an in-

---

[37] German Federal Minister of the Interior *Otto Schily*, Interview, 'Wer den Tod liebt, kann ihn haben', in: *Der Spiegel* (2004), No. 18 (April 26, 2004), p. 44.

[38] The full name "Osama bin Muhammad bin Awad bin Laden" is most often mentioned as "Osama bin Laden" or "Usama bin Laden".

[39] German Federal Minister of the Interior *Wolfgang Schäuble*, Interview, 'We Could Be Struck at Anytime', in: *Spiegel Online* (July 9, 2007). For the original German version *see* German Federal Minister of the Interior Wolfgang Schäuble, Interview, 'Es kann uns jederzeit treffen', in: *Der Spiegel* (2007), No. 28 (July 9, 2007), pp. 31-33.

[40] *Schäuble* stated: "The legal questions involved would be completely open, especially if Germans were involved. We should try to clarify such questions as precisely as possible in constitutional law, and create legal bases that give us the necessary liberties in the struggle against terrorism. I think nothing of citing a supra-legal state of emergency, in accordance with the motto: 'Necessity knows no law'." *See id.*

[41] On the situation under German national law *see* Winfried Bausback, 'Terrorismusabwehr durch gezielte Tötungen? Assassination als Mittel des (deutschen) demokratischen Rechtsstaates?', in: 24 *NVwZ* (2005), pp. 418-420.

> spection tour hundreds of miles behind the front lines. Having broken the Imperial Japanese Navy's message code, U.S. forces knew his flight itinerary and sent sixteen Army Air Forces P-38 Lightning fighter aircraft to intercept him. Near Bougainville, in the northern Solomons, the American pilots shot down their target, a Betty bomber, killing all on board, including Admiral Yamamoto. Was this a 'targeted killing'?[42]

The answer to this question depends on the definition of "targeted killings" and has no prejudice on the question concerning the legality of such an act.[43] The focus is on killings by State actors of singled out individuals. The context in which these killings take place is generally non-penal – be it at war or in times of peace. However, any penal aspect involved in such a killing does not automatically exclude it form the definition of "targeted killings".[44] Nevertheless, the death penalty is not the subject of the present considerations. While non-penal in that context means preventive, this term has to be understood in the widest sense possible, as many killings labelled as preventive turn out to be penal, if looked at closely. It will be shown infra that this distinction has a strong influence on the question of the legality of a given "targeted killing".

I. Different Terms Frequently Used

Different terms are used for what will be referred to here as targeted killings. The use of such terms is often value-laden and already includes a legal prejudice. The terms frequently used are the following: "assassination policy",[45] "assassination",[46] "defensive assassination",[47] "elimi-

---

42 Solis, 60 *Nav. War C. Rev.* (2007), at 128.

43 *But see* Solis, 60 *Nav. War C. Rev.* (2007), at 128 and 130, stating that a "combatant taking aim at a human target and then killing him is not what is meant by the term 'targeted killing'" on the basis that such an action would be legal in the context of an armed conflict. On this question *see infra*, Part Two.

44 *See also* Anderson, in: Wittes (ed.), at 356.

45 Jacques Pinto, 'Sharon's assassination policy sparks controversy in Israel', in: *Agence France Presse*, February 5, 2002.

46 Michael L. Gross, 'Fighting by Other Means in the Mideast: A Critical Analysis of Israel's Assassination Policy', in: 51 *Pol. Stud.* (2003), pp. 1-19, at 1-

nation policy",[48] "extra judicial executions",[49] "extra-judicial killings",[50] "extra judicial punishment",[51] "interception",[52] "liquidation",[53] "liquidation operation",[54] "liquidation policy",[55] "long-range hot pur-

---

2; Amnesty International, AI Doc. MDE 15/005/2001 (February 21, 2001); Asaf Zussman/ Noam Zussman, *Targeted Killings: Evaluating the Effectiveness of a Counterterrorism Policy*, Jerusalem 2005, e.g. at p. 23.

47 Brenda L. Godfrey, 'Authorization to Kill Terrorist Leaders and Those who Harbour Them: An international Analysis of Defensive Assassination', 4 *San Diego Int'l L.J.* (2003), pp. 491-512.

48 *See e.g.* Emanuel Gross, 'Thwarting Terrorist Acts by attacking the Perpetrators or their Commanders as an Act of Self-Defense: Human Rights versus the State's Duty to protect its Citizens', in: 15 *Temp. Int'l & Comp. L.J.* (2001), pp. 195-246, at 196.

49 Amnesty International, *Broken Lives: A Year of Intifada – Israel, Occupied Territories, Palestinian Authority*, London 2001, pp. 32-33.

50 *See e.g.* International Committee of the Red Cross, 'International Humanitarian Law and the Challenges of contemporary armed Conflicts: Excerpt of the Report prepared by the International Committee of the Red Cross for the 28th International Conference of the Red Cross and the Red Crescent Geneva, December 2003', in: 86 *Int'l Rev. Red Cross* (2004), No. 853, pp. 213-244, at 217 and 233.

51 Luft, 10 *Mid. E. Q.* (2003), at 3.

52 Samantha M. Shapiro, 'Announced Assassinations', in: *New York Times*, December 9, 2001, p. 54; Steven R. David, *Fatal Choices: Israel's Policy of Targeted Killing*, Ramat Gan 2002, p. 2.

53 Political correspondent Qeren Neubach on Israel TV Channel 1, Jerusalem (in Hebrew), at 16.30 gmt, on June 20, 2001, according to *BBC Worldwide Monitoring*, June 20, 2001.

54 Voice of Palestine, Ramallah (in Arabic), at 6.00 gmt, on March 7, 2002, according to *BBC Monitoring International Reports*, 'Palestinian Radio says death toll rises to 18', March 7, 2002.

55 Statement by the Palestinian Minister of Local Government *Sa'ib Uray-quat* in Voice of Palestine, Ramallah (in Arabic), at 11.33 gmt, on August 20, 2001, according to *BBC Monitoring International Reports*, 'Palestine Minister slams Israeli "War Crimes", criticizes US role', August 20, 2001; Voice of Israel, Jerusalem (in Hebrew), at 8.00 gmt and 12.00 gmt, on February 2, 2002, according to *BBC Monitoring International Reports*, 'Israeli PM's Meeting with Palestinian Leaders had Arafat's Approval', February 2, 2002.

suit",[56] "physical liquidation",[57] "pinpoint liquidation",[58] "pinpointed prevention",[59] "pinpointed preventive actions",[60] "pinpointed preventive operation",[61] "planned liquidation",[62] "pre-emptive killings",[63] "preventive actions",[64] "preventive killings",[65] "preventive liquidation",[66] "selective targeting",[67] "sikul memukad",[68] "specifically directed liquidation",[69] "summary execution",[70] "targeted killing",[71] "tar-

---

56 Luft, 10 *Mid. E. Q.* (2003), at 3.

57 MENA news agency, Cairo (in English), at 11.00 gmt, on March 15, 2001, according to *BBC Summary of World Broadcasts*, 'Palestinian Security Heads says Intifadah "Message of Peace"', March 17, 2001.

58 *Compare* Peter Hirschberg, '"Pinpoint Liquidations" to Continue', in: *Irish Times*, August 3, 2001, p. 13.

59 Voice of Israel, February 2, 2002.

60 Amnesty International, *Broken Lives*, pp. 32-33.

61 Qeren Neubach on Israel TV Channel 1, June 20, 2001.

62 ITAR-Tass News Agency, 'ITAR-Tass News Digest' of September 27, 2002.

63 *C.f.* Mordechai Kremnitzer, 'Präventives Töten', in: Dieter Fleck (ed.), *Rechtsfragen der Terrorismusbekämpfung durch Streitkräfte*, Baden-Baden 2004, pp. 201-222, at 201, based on a speech given at the February 2004 Conference on "Rechtsfragen der Terrorismusbekämpfung durch Streitkräfte" by the German Society for Military Law and the Law of War in Bonn.

64 Qeren Neubach on Israel TV Channel 1, June 20, 2001.

65 Kremnitzer, in: Fleck (ed.), *Rechtsfragen*, at 201.

66 *Compare* Georg Nolte, 'Preventive Use of Force and Preventive Killings: Moves into a Different Legal Order', in: 5 *Theo. Inq. L.* (2004), pp. 111-129, at 114.

67 Luft, 10 *Mid. E. Q.* (2003), at 3.

68 Hebrew for "targeted prevention", used by the Israel Defense Forces (IDF) according to Joseph Croitoru, 'Nach Liquidierung Scheich Jassins: Moraldebatte unter israelischen Philosophen', in: *FAZ*, March 24, 2004 (No 71), p. 43.

69 Yoram Gabbai, 'The American Way', in: *Israel's Business Arena*, October 7, 2001.

70 Swedish foreign minister *Anna Lindh* on US Yemen attack: Downes, 9 *J. Confl. Sec. L.* (2004), at 278; *c.f.* Whitaker; Burkeman, *Guardian*, November 6, 2002.

geted personnel elimination",[72] "targeted preventive elimination",[73] "targeted thwarting"[74] or "targeting terrorists".[75]

These different terms include similar but also different connotations. Some of them stress a certain character of the killing, i.e. its punishing or preventive function. The differentiation between these two aspects has an important influence on the legality of the act.[76] Especially Israeli officials refer to "targeted thwarting", "interception"[77], and "elimination policy"[78], whereas the terms "extra-judicial killings" and "assassination"[79] are not used by Israel itself.[80] As will be shown below in detail, for example the term "assassination" has a connotation that the action is illegal.[81] With a similar connotation,[82] an "extra judicial execution" has been defined by Amnesty International as

---

[71] *See e.g.* Shany, in: Schmitt/ Beruto (eds.), at 103; Amos Guiora, 'Targeted Killing as Active Self-Defense', in: 36 *Case W. Res. J. Int'l L.* (2004), pp. 319-334; Nils Melzer, *Targeted Killing in International Law*, Oxford 2008, p. 3 *et seqq.* An earlier version of *Melzer's* treatise was published as his doctoral thesis: Nils Melzer, *Targeted Killing under the International Normative Paradigms of Law Enforcement and Hostilities*, Zürich 2007. The term is also used in Dutch as "gerichte executie", *see* Tom Ruys, 'Inter arma non silent leges: Israëlisch Hooggerechtshof spreekt zich uit over "targeted killings"', in: *Juristenkrant* (January 17, 2007), at para. 9.

[72] Emanuel Gross, 'The Laws of War waged between Democratic States and Terrorist Organizations: Real or Illusive', in: 15 *Fla. J. Int'l L.* (2003), pp. 389-480, at 393.

[73] Gross, *Struggle of Democracy*, pp. 220-246.

[74] Shapiro, *New York Times*, December 9, 2001, p. 54; David, *Fatal Choices*, p. 2.

[75] IDF according to Kremnitzer, in: Fleck (ed.), *Rechtsfragen*, at 201.

[76] *Compare infra*, Part One, Chapter B) II. 1.

[77] Shapiro, *New York Times*, December 9, 2001, p. 54.

[78] Gross, 15 *Temp. Int'l & Comp. L.J.* (2001), at 196.

[79] Gross, 51 *Pol. Stud.* (2003), at 1-2; Amnesty International, AI Doc. MDE 15/005/2001 (February 21, 2001); Voice of Palestine, March 7, 2002.

[80] Israel, Ministry of Foreign Affairs, 'Targeting Terrorists', Background Paper, August 1, 2001; *see also* Shapiro, *New York Times*, December 9, 2001, p. 54; David, *Fatal Choices*, p. 2; Luft, 10 *Mid. E. Q.* (2003), at 3.

[81] *See infra*, III. *See also* Downes, 9 *J. Confl. Sec. L.* (2004), at 279.

> an unlawful and deliberate killing carried out by order of a government or with its acquiescence. Extra judicial killings are killings which can reasonably be assumed to be the result of a policy at any level of government to eliminate specific individuals as an alternative to arresting them and bringing them to justice. These killings take place outside any judicial framework.[83]

Thus "targeted killings" as a more neutral descriptive term and the term that also the Israeli government itself has used to refer to such actions will be used in this treatise, but not exclusively. It has been defined in the following manner:

> A targeted killing is a lethal attack on a person that is not undertaken on the basis that the person concerned is a 'combatant', but rather where a state considers a particular individual to pose a serious threat as a result of his or her activities and decides to kill that person, even at a time when the individual is not engaging in hostile activities.[84]

But the understanding of the term will be reduced to the following aspects herein: "Targeted killing" means the intentional slaying of a specific person by a state official. It refers to the Israeli policy and other cases with a minimum of semantic baggage implying approval or disapproval of the corresponding actions.[85] "Targeted killing" is also chosen in order to differentiate it from the term "preventive killing". Not all

---

82 *Compare* Orna Ben-Naftali/ Keren R. Michaeli, 'We Must Not Make a Scarecrow of the Law': A Legal Analysis of The Israeli Policy of Targeted Killings', 36 *Cornell Int'l L.J.* (2003), pp. 233-292, at 235 (footnote 6).

83 Amnesty International, *Israel and the Occupied Territories: Israel must end its Policy of Assassinations*, AI Doc. MDE 15/056/2003 (July 4, 2003), p. 1 (footnote 1); *see also* Guiora, 36 *Case W. Res. J. Int'l L.* (2004), at 329.

84 Louise Doswald-Beck, 'The Right to Life in Armed Conflict: Does International Humanitarian Law provide all the Answers?', in: 88 *Int'l Rev. Red Cross* (2006), No. 864, pp. 881-904, at 894; *compare also* University Centre for International Humanitarian Law, 'The Right to Life in Armed Conflict and Situations of Occupation', Report of the Geneva Expert Meeting, September 1 and 2, 2005, pp. 5-6.

85 *See also* Steven R. David, 'Israel's Policy of Targeted Killing', in: 17 *Ethics & Int'l Aff.* (2003), No. 1, pp. 111-126, at 112; Melzer, *Targeted Killing*, p. 8; Schmitz-Elvenich, *Targeted Killing*, p. 12, even though *Schmitz-Elvenich's* understanding of the term is narrower in only capturing targeted killings by foreign forces.

targeted killings are preventive in character and not all of them merit a label with a connotation of being legitimate.[86] The main differentiation has to be made between true "targeted killings" and those which are really preventive in character. This differentiation is based on the intention with which the act is performed.

II. Aspects of Intention

Before the standards of human rights and international humanitarian law relevant to the present topic are examined, it is important to look into the possible categories of actions that can lead to the death of a person. In doing so, the question of whether the death of a person is intended plays a decisive role. A short formula on the meaning of intention could be: "Things done as means and ends are intended, side-effects are not."[87] It remains to be seen if this very general understanding of "intention" suffices to address the specific questions concerning the deprivation of life. Even though terminology deriving from criminal law is used in this context, the following considerations are meant to be value-free. They shall solely clarify the foundation upon which the examination of the human rights and humanitarian law rules is based *infra*.

1. Intention in Relation to the Targeted Person

The first and most important question relates to the person that is actually targeted. While innocent third persons may also be affected,[88] the targeted person will always be affected and thus is the focus of the considerations. A person can be executed due to penal considerations or to preventive considerations. The former is capital punishment while the latter, as will be shown *infra*, can be divided into different categories. It must be kept in mind that it is not the reason or motive for a killing that

---

[86] Ben-Naftali/ Michaeli, 36 *Cornell Int'l L.J.* (2003), at 235 (footnote 6); *but see* Guiora, 36 *Case W. Res. J. Int'l L.* (2004), at 322 and 330.

[87] Andrew P. Simester/ G. Robert Sullivan, *Criminal Law: Theory and Doctrine*, 2nd ed., Oxford 2003, p. 128.

[88] *Compare infra*, Introduction, Chapter C) II. 2.

is considered here, but the degree of intention concerning the death of the person subject to this killing.

a) Capital Punishment

The death penalty coincides with the strongest intention concerning the deprivation of life. The execution of a death sentence as a matter of course aims at the death of the convicted person. This is the purpose, objective or aim for its own sake.[89] Speaking in criminal law terminology, this kind of intention is called "direct intention",[90] "intention in its core sense",[91] "*dolus directus* of the first degree", "Absicht"[92] or "dol général".[93] Would the person acting regard himself as having "failed" in some sense, if the result is not achieved?[94] If the answer is in the affirmative, then the result was intended in the above mentioned sense. This is true for the death penalty. Further aims such as deterrence of others,[95] prevention of further deeds by the perpetrator etc. are rather

---

89 William Wilson, *Central Issues in Criminal Theory*, Oxford 2002, p. 149; Simester/ Sullivan, *Criminal Law*, p. 127; T. J. McIntyre/ Sinéad McMullan, *Criminal Law*, Dublin 2001, p. 38.

90 Wilson, *Criminal Theory*, p. 150.

91 Simester/ Sullivan, *Criminal Law*, pp. 127-130 and 135.

92 Johannes Wessels/ Werner Beulke, *Strafrecht Allgemeiner Teil: Die Straftat und ihr Aufbau*, 37th ed., Heidelberg 2007, p. 81 (para. 211); Adolf Schönke/ Horst Schröder/ Theodor Lenckner (eds.), *Strafgesetzbuch: Kommentar*, 27th ed., München 2006, § 15, paras. 65-67 (pp. 277-278).

93 Xavier Pin, *Droit pénal général*, Paris 2005, para. 168 (p. 123), although the concept of *dol général* comprises more factors than the will to achieve the result.

94 R. Antony Duff, *Intention, Agency and Criminal Liability: Philosophy of Action and the Criminal Law*, Oxford 1990, pp. 61-63; Simester/ Sullivan, *Criminal Law*, p. 128.

95 On the discussion concerning the question of deterrence and its empirical analysis *see* John Donohue/ Justin J. Wolfers, 'The Death Penalty: No Evidence for Deterrence', in: 3 *The Economists' Voice* (2006), No. 5, Article 3; Paul H. Rubin, 'Reply to Donohue and Wolfers on the Death Penalty and Deterrence', in: 3 *The Economists' Voice* (2006), No. 5, Article 4, each with further references.

motives that give the basis for the decision to apply the death penalty. The actual aim of the execution itself is the death of the person.

b) Targeted Killings

The situation is the same concerning targeted killings. The death of the targeted person is the goal, irrespective of the reasons or motives that are the basis for such killings. Such reasons or motives may be the prevention of deeds by the targeted person in (remote) future. It may be general prevention, deterrence or the protection of any other legally protected abstract interest or against an abstract danger. However, in the specific situation of the targeted killing, its performers would regard their action as having failed if the targeted person survived. The death of the targeted person is thus intended directly. It is again covered by "*dolus directus* of the first degree".[96]

Even though many aspects of capital punishment and targeted killings are identical, the terms may not be used interchangeably. Capital punishment takes place in the execution of a judgment by a court of law while targeted killings lack such a judgment.

c) Preventive Killings

Again, the situation may be the same concerning preventive killings. An offender who is in the process of committing a deed is killed. The death of the offender might have been intended; however, if examined thoroughly, the actual aim is not to kill him but to prevent his deed. One would not regard the intervention as having failed in the case that the offender survives if the deed is nonetheless prevented. Thus, only preventing the deed is the actual aim of the intervention. The death of the offender may be inevitable to achieve this aim. In that case, the death is also intended, as it is a means or necessary precondition to achieve an-

---

[96] *See also* Melzer, *Targeted Killing*, p. 4; Nils Melzer, 'Targeted Killings in Operational Law Perspective', in: Terry D. Gill/ Dieter Fleck (eds.), *Handbook of the International Law of Military Operations*, Oxford 2010, pp. 277-301, at 277 (para. 17.01.1), albeit *Melzer* does not expressly distinguish direct intention of first and second degree.

other purpose, objective or aim.[97] This kind of intention is also part of "direct intention"[98] and "intention in its core sense",[99] but of a lesser degree. It is thus also called "*dolus directus* of second degree", "Wissentlichkeit", "unmittelbarer Vorsatz"[100] or "dol indéterminé".[101]

d) Preventive Use of Force Presumably Lethal

It is also possible that the death of the offender is not inevitable to prevent his deed, i.e. if the offender is not shot in the head but in the torso or a limb. The offender's death is still possible and would be accepted by the performers in order to prevent the deed. However, it is not certain that the offender will die. In the event that the offender does die, the death is still intended as it is a virtually certain consequence of achieving the purpose, objective or aim.[102] This is the case if it is a practically or morally certain side-effect of what is desired, or if it is clear that the death would ordinarily result from the actions carried out to achieve that aim.[103] The law enforcement personnel know that their action may kill the offender, but do not care, or accepts that this may be the result of their behaviour in order to reach their aim. This kind of intention is called "the second category of intention"[104] "bedingter Vorsatz", *dolus eventualis*[105] or "dol éventuel".[106]

---

97 Wilson, *Criminal Theory*, p. 149; McIntyre/ McMullan, *Criminal Law*, p. 38.

98 Wilson, *Criminal Theory*, p. 150.

99 Simester/ Sullivan, *Criminal Law*, pp. 127-130 and 135.

100 Wessels/ Beulke, *Strafrecht Allgemeiner Teil*, p. 82 (para. 213); Schönke/ Schröder/ Lenckner (eds.), *Strafgesetzbuch*, § 15, paras. 68-69 (p. 278).

101 Pin, *Droit pénal général*, para. 181 (p. 134).

102 Simester/ Sullivan, *Criminal Law*, p. 127; McIntyre/ McMullan, *Criminal Law*, p. 39.

103 Wilson, *Criminal Theory*, p. 153.

104 Simester/ Sullivan, *Criminal Law*, pp. 132-136.

105 Wessels/ Beulke, *Strafrecht Allgemeiner Teil*, p. 82 (paras. 214-215); Schönke/ Schröder/ Lenckner (eds.), *Strafgesetzbuch*, § 15, para. 72 (p. 278).

106 Pin, *Droit pénal général*, para. 183 (p. 136); Gaston Stefani/ Georges Levasseur/ Bernard Bouloc, *Droit pénal général*, 18th ed., Paris 2003, para. 237 (p. 269); the French concept of "dol éventuel" is not absolutely identical with the

e) Preventive Use of Non-Lethal Force

Furthermore, the death of an offender may be neither inevitable nor reasonably probable if the action to prevent the deed is performed by the law enforcement personnel. This includes examples like overpowering the offender without shooting at him. Nevertheless, it is possible even in that context that a lethal injury is caused and the offender dies eventually. While the aim to prevent the deed is reached, the death of the offender is a side-effect. *In contrast* to the cases above, it would not be the intention but could still be recklessness,[107] conscious negligence, *luxuria*[108] or "l'imprudence consciente"[109] if the probability of the side-effect is lesser than practically certain. Then, the acting persons do not intend to bring about the particular result, but they run a risk of bringing that result about, while they hope or believe that nothing will happen.[110]

Taking these considerations into account, the formula that "[t]hings done as means and ends are intended, side-effects are not"[111] has to be extended; practically or morally certain side-effects are also covered by intention.[112] Only those side-effects that are less probable are not intended, but could be caused negligently.

2. *Intention in Relation to Innocent Third Persons*

Beside the person that it is aimed at, the use of force in the manners described above may also affect innocent third parties. Regarding the intention concerning such "collateral damage", the same principles as shown above apply. While it is excluded conceptually that a third per-

---

German concept of *dolus eventualis*, *see* Tonio Walter, *Betrugsstrafrecht in Frankreich und Deutschland*, Heidelberg 1999, p. 273.

107 Wilson, *Criminal Theory*, p. 153.

108 Wessels/ Beulke, *Strafrecht Allgemeiner Teil*, pp. 82-83 (para. 216).

109 Pin, *Droit pénal général*, para. 184 (p. 138).

110 McIntyre/ McMullan, *Criminal Law*, p. 39; Wessels/ Beulke, *Strafrecht Allgemeiner Teil*, pp. 82-86 (paras. 216-230) with further references.

111 Simester/ Sullivan, *Criminal Law*, p. 128.

112 Wilson, *Criminal Theory*, p. 153.

son is targeted with the aim to kill him or her, i.e. with *dolus directus* of the first degree,[113] all other degrees of intention are possible:

It may be that a person who is targeted can only be reached at the inevitable cost of innocent lives. If this is accepted, the innocent third persons are killed with direct intention, however, with *dolus directus* of second degree. It is not the aim of the action to hit them, but it is a means or necessary precondition to achieve another purpose, namely to hit the targeted person.

If the death of an innocent third persons is not inevitable, but a side-effect that is practically certain and is accepted, they may have been killed with *dolus eventualis*. It is known that the action will very likely kill third parties and that fact is not taken in account or accepted in order to reach the goal of the action, i.e. to hit the targeted person. If the probability of such a side-effect is less than practically certain and it is hoped that it will not occur, then it is not intended but may be caused negligently.

III. "Assassination"

"Assassination"[114] is generally regarded as being prohibited under international law.[115] It is roughly understood as murder, usually of a po-

[113] A possible exception could be an *error in persona*, concerning the identity of the targeted person. Such an confusion of persons has no influence on the intention concerning the person actually targeted, *compare e.g.* Wessels/ Beulke, *Strafrecht Allgemeiner Teil*, p. 92-93 (paras. 247-249).

[114] The word originates from the order of the "Assassins", a Muslim sect of the eleventh and twelfth centuries, whose members furthered their own political interests by murdering high officials, Daniel B. Pickard, 'Legalizing Assassination? Terrorism, the Central Intelligence Agency, and International Law', in: 30 *Ga. J. Int'l & Comp. L.* (2001), pp. 3-35, at 3 (footnote 1).

[115] Louis René Beres, 'Assassination and the Law: A Policy Memorandum', in: 18 *Stud. Confl. Terror.* (1995), pp. 299-315, at 299; David, 17 *Ethics & Int'l Aff.* (2003), at 112; Downes, 9 *J. Confl. Sec. L.* (2004), at 279; W. Hays Parks, 'Memorandum of Law: Executive Order 12,333 and Assassination', in: 19 *Army Lawyer* (December 1989), No. 204, pp. 4-9, at 4; Pickard, 30 *Ga. J. Int'l & Comp. L.* (2001), at 21; Michael N. Schmitt, 'State Sponsored Assassination in International and Domestic Law', in: 17 *Yale J. Int'l L.* (1999), pp. 609-690, at 627-268.

litical or other public person, for political reasons.[116] Early western scholars – such as *Hugo Grotius*, *Alberico Gentili* and *Emerich de Vattel* – defined the term "assassination" as an illegal act most commonly associated with targeting and killing enemy leaders in peacetime or war. They all recognised the lawfulness of targeting and killing an enemy leader in war, although some considered killing the enemy leader in a treacherous manner off the battlefield as an act of assassination.[117]

Today, some use the terms "targeted killing" and "assassination" interchangeably to describe the killing of a singled out individual or a "named killing".[118] Assassination involves the targeting of a specific individual,[119] often – but not necessarily – of a public figure who is assassinated for political reasons.[120] According to these aspects of the meaning of "assassination", the term is still independent of the legality or illegality of the act:

In an armed conflict, the term "assassination" is applied to killings where the death of one person is accomplished by means expressly prohibited by international humanitarian law.[121] However named, such

---

[116] Parks, 19 *Army Lawyer* (December 1989), No. 204, at 4; *compare also* Asa Kasher/ Amos Yadlin, 'Assassination and Preventive Killing', in: 25 *SAIS Review of Int'l Aff.* (2005), pp. 41-57, at 41-44.

[117] Jefrey F. Addicott, 'Proposal for a new Executive Order on Assassination', in: 37 *U. Rich. L. Rev.* (2003), pp. 751-785, at 767.

[118] *Compare e.g.* Michael L. Gross, 'Assassination and Targeted Killing: Law Enforcement, Execution or Self-Defence?', in: 23 *J. Applied Phil.* (2006), pp. 323-335, at 323-324.

[119] *See also* Schmitt, 17 *Yale J. Int'l L.* (1999), at 627.

[120] David, 17 *Ethics & Int'l Aff.* (2003), at 113; Parks, 19 *Army Lawyer* (December 1989), No. 204, at 4; Albert Sydney Hornby/ Jonathan Crowther (eds.), *Oxford Advanced Learner's Dictionary of Current English*, 5th ed., 3rd impression, Oxford 1995, p. 58; *see also* Nathan Canestaro, 'American Law and Policy on Assassinations of Foreign Leaders: The Practicality of Maintaining the Status Quo', in: 26 *B.C. Int'l & Comp. L. Rev.* (2003), pp. 1-34, at 11; Schmitt, 17 *Yale J. Int'l L.* (1999), at 627; Kenneth W. Watkin, 'Humans in the Cross-Hairs: Targeting and Assassination in Contemporary Armed Conflict', in: David Wippman; Matthew Evangelista (eds.), *New Wars, New Laws? Applying the Laws of War in 21st Century Conflicts*, Ardsley, N.Y. 2005, pp. 137-179, at 169-178.

[121] Schmitt, 17 *Yale J. Int'l L.* (1999), at 632; Canestaro, 26 *B.C. Int'l & Comp. L. Rev.* (2003), at 4.

killings are not prohibited because they are – by definition – "assassinations". They are prohibited for other reasons, and additionally referred to as "assassination". This concerns mostly killings of persons who may be targeted – due to their combatant status – by resort to perfidy or treacherous means.[122] Thus, in the context of armed conflicts, the term "assassination" does not have a particular status.[123] The situation is similar outside armed conflict. Here, the "assassination" of officials of other states is regarded by some to represent "the crime of aggression and/or the crime of terrorism"[124] or "intervention"[125] or is regarded as illegal as it violates an international treaty.[126]

Thus, while not every illegal killing is an "assassination", every "assassination" is an illegal killing. Any killing which is legal cannot be referred to as assassination. But "[s]imply because a killing is not assassi-

---

122 Gross, *Struggle of Democracy*, p. 242. An example referred to in that context is the May 1942 assassination of SS Obergruppenführer Reinhard Heydrich, the SS chief of security police, deputy chief of the Gestapo, and the person largely responsible for "the final solution." He was killed in Prague by two British-trained Czech soldiers disguised as civilians. "Although Heydrich was a lawful combatant target, his combatant killers engaged in perfidy by disguising themselves as civilians. His killing was an assassination." *see* Solis, 60 *Nav. War C. Rev.* (2007), at 129.

123 Watkin, in: Wippman/ Evangelista (eds.), at 138 and 169-178.

124 Louis René Beres, 'The Newly Expanded American Doctrine of Preemption: Can it include Assassination?' in: 31 *Denv. J. Int'l L. & Pol'y* (2002), pp. 157-178, at 160; *compare also* Kenneth W. Watkin, 'Canada/United States Military Interoperability and Humanitarian Law Issues: Land Mines, Terrorism, Military Objectives and Targeted Killing', in: 15 *Duke J. Comp. & Int'l L.* (2005), pp. 281-314, at 309 who regards it as a form of terrorism.

125 Beres, 18 *Stud. Confl. Terror.* (1995), at 300.

126 For example Article 2 of the (New York) Convention on the Prevention and Punishment of Crimes Against Internationally Protected Persons, Including Diplomatic Agents, adopted by the UN General Assembly on December 14, 1973, Resolution 3166 (XXVIII), Annex, UN GAOR 28th Sess., Supp. No. 30, pp. 146-149, UN Doc. A/RES/3166 (1973), entry into force on February 20, 1977, reprinted in: 1035 *UNTS* (1977), No. 15410, pp. 167-247; Article 1 of the European Convention on the Suppression of Terrorism, adopted at Strasbourg, France on January 27, 1977, entry into force on August 4, 1978, *European Treaty Series* No. 90, reprinted in: 1137 *UNTS* (1979), No. 17828, pp. 93-111. *See e.g.* Beres, 31 *Denv. J. Int'l L. & Pol'y* (2002), at 162; David, 17 *Ethics & Int'l Aff.* (2003), at 112; Schmitt, 17 *Yale J. Int'l L.* (1999), at 618-619.

nation does not mean that it is legal, or even justified."[127] The fact that a certain killing can be referred to as assassination does not have any effect regarding its legality. The term "assassination" does not have specific legal effects. A killing that is regarded as an assassination is examined according to the same legal standards as any other killing.

IV. Conclusion: Targeted Killings and Preventive Killings

Throughout this treatise, the term "targeted killings" will be used in two ways. First, it is the most common and frequently used term to refer to the said policies of eliminating certain persons. In that regard, it will be used as the generic term, including killings with different motives and intentions. Second, where appropriate, the term "targeted killings" will be used as opposed to "preventive killings" for those cases, in which the main aim and purpose is the death of the targeted person. The death of the targeted person is thus intended directly, with *dolus directus* of the first degree, irrespective of the further motivation for the specific killing. In opposition to this, concerning "preventive killings", the main aim and purpose of the action is to prevent a specific deed by this person, while the death of the targeted person may only be a necessary side-effect in order to achieve this aim. The question of how immediate the prevented deed must be will be one of the central issues addressed *infra*. These considerations shall serve as a basis for the following examination concerning the human rights protection of the right to life and the corresponding international humanitarian law rules.

D. Moral Legitimacy and Effectiveness of Targeted Killings

> Before dismissing, morally and legally, an attempt to thwart acts of terrorism by killing terrorists, it should be remembered that such measures can and do save many lives.[128]

Alongside the difficult legal issues, the topic of targeted killings also involves numerous moral questions.[129] It is not the scope of this treatise

---

[127] Schmitt, 17 *Yale J. Int'l L.* (1999), at 628.

[128] Gross, *Struggle of Democracy*, p. 244.

to find answers to these questions. However, some of them should be addressed and are, as will be shown, strongly interrelated with the legal questions coming throughout the examination of this topic. In many regards, international law tries to give answers to moral questions as well. According to *Gross*,

> [e]ven though we are considering the elimination of a terrorist who seeks the death of innocents, such killing still involves the death of a human being.[130]

This statement is based on two presumptions: First, the killing is a true preventive killing, i.e. it is aimed at saving another person's life. Second, it is based on the presumption that the targeted person is the right person. This is probably the most difficult moral question. Is the targeted person really the one who is expected? Is the information, from which the decision to target this person is based on, correct and can it be trusted? These issues are of overwhelming practical relevance. The most important prerequisite from a moral point of view is that of certainty.

Even if the identification of the targeted person is taken for granted, the question of moral legitimacy is still not solved. It is a general political and moral question whether or not a State – presupposing that it is legal – follows a policy of targeted killings.[131] Motivations for such a policy can be found in revenge, retribution and the feeling that justice is done to certain perpetrators.[132]

The moral legitimacy of such a policy is mostly based on the somewhat simplistic calculation that the killing of one person will prevent the death or serious injury of many persons and is thus possible according

---

[129] *Compare e.g.* Eric Patterson/ Teresa Casale, 'Targeting Terror: The Ethical and Practical Implications of Targeted Killing', in: 18 *Int'l J. Intell. & Counterintell.* (2005), pp. 638-652.

[130] Gross, *Struggle of Democracy*, p. 232.

[131] *For a discussion of these moral aspects compare e.g.* Daniel Statman, 'Targeted Killing', in: 5 *Theo. Inq. L.* (2004), pp. 179-198; Kasher/ Yadlin, 25 *SAIS Review of Int'l Aff.* (2005), at 45-53; Asa Kasher/ Amos Yadlin, 'Fighting Terror: A View from Israel', in: 8 *Pacem* (2005), pp. 41-48; Avery Plaw, 'Fighting Terror Ethically and Legally: The Case of Targeting Terrorists', working paper prepared for the CPSA Conference, June 2006; Yael Stein, 'By Any Name Illegal and Immoral: Response to "Israel's Policy of Targeted Killing"', in: 17 *Ethics & Int'l Aff.* (2003), pp. 127-137, at 132-133.

[132] David, 17 *Ethics & Int'l Aff.* (2003), at 121-126.

to the "principle of moral utilitarianism".[133] First, such considerations cannot justify true targeted killings but only justify preventive killings. Second, it may be doubted whether such a justification can be as unrestricted as *Gross* formulates it:

> If the good result ensuing from the performance of the act outweighs the bad ensuing from it, then it must be performed, irrespective of whether the act entails killing, torture, or the like.[134]

The – absolute – prohibition of torture under human rights law immediately shows that such an appreciation of values cannot be unrestricted. It will be influenced by questions of immediacy and proportionality – as will be shown *infra* – as an integral part of human rights law and may be subject to limits.[135]

Thus, for example *Eliezer Raz*, a leader of the Israeli Meretz Party, is reported to have referred to the targeted killing of *Salah Shehade* and 14 other Palestinians as immoral even though he acknowledged that "This man was a murderer". Nevertheless, *Raz* stated, the death penalty cannot be applied even in cases of trial and conviction of murder, lest without any process. Furthermore, the "death penalty does not stop the terror, and may make it worse."[136]

Statman, on the other hand, draws parallels to the law of war in assessing the question of moral legitimacy:

> [I]f one accepts the moral legitimacy of the large-scale killing of combatants in conventional war, one cannot object on moral grounds to targeted killing of members of terrorist organizations in wars against terror. If one rejects this legitimacy, one must object to all killing in war, targeted and non-targeted alike, … .[137]

It will be examined infra whether this comparison can stand scrutiny.[138] Additionally, the killing of one person may affect other persons who may or may not be involved in the deeds of the targeted persons.

---

133 Gross, *Struggle of Democracy*, p. 233.

134 *Id.*, *compare also id.*, pp. 238-239.

135 *See infra*, Part One, Chapter B) II. 2.

136 Charles A. Radin, 'In Israel, Support, Concerns on Attack some say that Nation must press the Fight', in: *Boston Globe*, July 25, 2002, p. A1.

137 Statman, 5 *Theo. Inq. L.* (2004), at 197.

138 *See infra*, Part Two.

> The difficult question that arises, therefore, is whether, in certain circumstances, it is possible from a moral point of view to attack terrorists even though doing so entails endangering the population that is affording them cover.[139]

International law provides some guidance concerning these moral questions. As will be shown *infra* the latter situation *Gross* is referring to raises issues of collateral damage and human shielding at least under international humanitarian law.[140]

Alongside with the question of moral legitimacy comes the question of effectiveness.[141] This question is relatively easy to answer in connection with preventive killings which prevent an immediate violent act. Their direct success is obvious, even though such an action can have side effects on an ongoing conflict. The problem is more complex when it comes to true targeted killings:

> Killing senior terrorists, expert bomb makers, and those who provide philosophical guidance for terrorists may spare countless noncombatant victims while, at the same time, forgoing risk to friendly combatant forces. A successful targeted killing removes a dangerous enemy from the battlefield and deprives the foe of his leadership, guidance, and experience. The targeted killing of terrorist leaders leaves subordinates confused and in disarray, however temporarily. Successors will feel trepidation, knowing they too may be in the enemy's sights. Targeted killing unbalances terrorist organizations, making them concerned with protecting their own membership and diverting them from their goals.[142]

Pursuant to these considerations, targeted killings generally seem to be a rather effective means in fighting "terrorism" and saving lives, but also in "providing retribution and revenge for a population under siege".[143] But can these effects be measured? According to a study on the basis that stock markets should react positively to effective counter

---

139 Gross, *Struggle of Democracy*, p. 233, *compare also id.*, pp. 238-239.

140 *See infra*, Part Two, Chapter D) II.

141 *See e.g.* Daniel Byman, 'Do Targeted Killings Work?', in: 85 *Foreign Aff.* (2006), pp. 95-112.

142 Solis, 60 *Nav. War C. Rev.* (2007), at 140.

143 David, *Fatal Choices*, p. 2; *compare also* Schmahl, in: Tomuschat *et al.* (eds.), at 265-266.

terrorism measures but negatively to counterproductive ones, interesting differences are existing:

> The market does not react to assassinations of low ranked members of Palestinian terrorist organizations. The market does react strongly, however, to the assassination of senior leaders of terrorist organizations: it declines following assassinations targeting senior political leaders but rises following assassinations of senior military leaders. This implies that the market perceives the first type of assassination as counterproductive but the second as an effective counter-terrorism policy.[144]

This outcome corresponds with the following considerations. Especially in larger terrorist groups, a killed person can be supplemented easily, at least if it is not an eminently charismatic person with outstanding abilities that is targeted.[145] On the other hand, the pressure created by targeted killings may deter sympathisers and complicate the recruitment of such groups. It may force the members of these groups to use much of their energy in order to hide and avoid targeted strikes and could ultimately lead to the readiness of the group to accept a ceasefire.[146] But it has to be kept in mind that deterrence is not a useful tool concerning suicide bombers. The knowledge that death will be inevitable can lead to totally unrestricted fighting.[147] Such considerations are *inter alia* the reason behind the prohibition of a "no quarter" policy in international humanitarian law.[148]

An empirical analysis of three years of suicide bombing data in Israel revealed an increase in such attacks through March 2002 followed by a steep decline through the end of 2003. The model developed based on this data suggests that the targeted killings of terror suspects sparks estimated recruitment and thus increases rather than decreases the rate of suicide bombings. Surprisingly, only the deaths of suspected terrorists, and not Palestinian civilians, are associated with such estimated re-

---

144 Zussman/ Zussman, *Targeted Killings*, p. 23.

145 Kremnitzer, in: Fleck (ed.), *Rechtsfragen*, at 211.

146 *Id.*, at 211-212.

147 *Id.*, at 212; *compare also* Andrew C. McCarthy, 'Terrorism on Trial: The Trials of al Qaeda', in: 36 *Case W. Res. J. Int'l L.* (2004), pp. 513-522, at 518.

148 *See infra*, Part Two, Chapter C) III. 1.

cruitment. The reduction of suicide bombings over time is, according to the study, an effect of preventive arrests rather than targeted killings.[149]

Thus, while a policy of targeted killings can deter, it can also lead to a vicious circle of violence and counter violence in revenge. Instead of deterrence, it can even motivate terrorist groups in order to *a fortiori* show that these killings will not be successful in the long run.[150] The use of superior technique such as helicopters or other air strikes to target a single person may also foster sympathy for the targeted person and ultimately lead to additional motivation to further engage in activities against the adversary.[151]

Targeted killings can thus prove counterproductive, in that they can instigate greater violence in revenge or retaliation.[152] In so far, an overreaction by a State acting outside accepted standards of human rights and international humanitarian law is a real danger.[153] Then, responses to threats and attacks can do more damage than the threats and attacks themselves.[154] Thus,

> many past and present military and intelligence officials have expressed alarm at the Pentagon policy about targeting Al Qaeda members. Their concerns have less to do with the legality of the program than with its wisdom, its ethics, and, ultimately, its efficacy. Some of the most heated criticism comes from within the Special Forces.[155]

---

[149] Edward H. Kaplan/ Alex Mintz/ Shaul Mishal/ Claudio Samban, 'What Happened to Suicide Bombings in Israel? Insights from a Terror Stock Model', in: 28 *Stud. Confl. Terror.* (2005), pp. 225-236.

[150] *Compare* Kremnitzer, in: Fleck (ed.), *Rechtsfragen*, at 212.

[151] *Id.*

[152] Solis, 60 *Nav. War C. Rev.* (2007), at 141; Müllerson, 32 *Isr. Yb. Hum. Rts.* (2002), at 18-19.

[153] David Kretzmer, 'Targeted Killing of Suspected Terrorists: Extra Judicial Executions or Legitimate Means of Defence?', in: 16 *Eur. J. Int'l L.* (2005), pp. 171-212, at 212.

[154] Mark A. Drumbl, '"Lesser Evils" in the War on Terrorism', in: 36 *Case W. Res. J. Int'l L.* (2004), pp. 335-348, at 345.

[155] Seymour M. Hersh, 'Manhunt: The Bush Administration's new strategy in the war against terrorism', in: *New Yorker*, December 23 and 30, 2002, p. 66.

However, the question of legality must generally be considered independently from the question of efficiency and moral legitimacy.[156] If a policy is lawful, efficiency is an important argument concerning the question of whether a State should resort to that policy. If this policy is inefficient and – despite its legality – causes considerable damage, it is true that it probably should not be used. This is, however, not a legal argument, but a mere political question. An exception to the latter statement exists in international humanitarian law, as will be shown *infra*. There, the question of effectiveness of an operation plays a role in connection with "military necessity"[157] and "collateral damage".[158] On the other hand, if a policy is not lawful, the question of efficiency has no influence concerning the use of that policy. It simply is prohibited.

> The nobility of ends is no guarantee against resort to evil means: indeed, the more noble they are, the more ruthlessness they can endorse.[159]

E. The State of Research: Different Approaches

The topic of targeted killings was not in the focus of discussion of international law until recently. In consequence, little attention was paid to it in legal literature. Related questions were mainly dealt with earlier by U.S. military lawyers in the context of the question of legality of assassination following the famous 1989 memorandum of *W. Hays Parks*.[160]

---

[156] *But see* Kremnitzer, in: Fleck (ed.), *Rechtsfragen*, at 212.

[157] *See infra*, Part Two, Chapter B) I.

[158] *See infra*, Part Two, Chapter D) II. 2.

[159] Michael Ignatieff, *The Lesser Evil: Political Ethics in an Age of Terror*, Edinburgh 2004, at 119.

[160] *See* Parks, 19 *Army Lawyer* (December 1989), No. 204, pp. 4-9; *compare* Patricia Zengel, 'Assassination and the Law of Armed Conflict', in: 134 *Mil. L. Rev.* (1991), pp. 123-155; Louis René Beres, 'On Assassination as Anticipatory Self-Defense: The Case of Israel', in: 20 *Hofstra L. Rev.* (1991), pp. 321-340; *id.*, 'Assassinating Saddam: A Post-War View from International Law', in: 19 *Denv. J. Int'l L. & Pol'y* (1991), pp. 613-623; *id.*, 'The Permissibility of Statesponsored Assassination During Peace and War', in: 5 *Temp. Int'l & Comp. L.J.* (1992), pp. 231-249; *id.*, 18 *Stud. Confl. Terror.* (1995), pp. 299-315; *id.*, 'Assassinating Sad-

I. The Topic's Perception in Legal Writing

Only due to the official Israeli statements since late 2000 that it pursued a policy of targeted killings, has legal writing started to deal with the topic. Following these statements, the policy was first condemned by human rights organisations[161] but also defended by some authors.[162]

While the Supreme Court of Israel rejected a petition brought against targeted killings on the basis that it regarded "choice of means of warfare" as not justiciable,[163] the topic was discussed on the Begin-Sadat

---

dam Hussein: The View from International Law', in: 19 *Ind. Int'l & Comp. L. Rev.* (2003), pp. 847-869; Thomas C. Wingfield, 'Taking Aim at Regime Estates: Assassination, Tyrannicide, and the Clancy Doctrine', in: 22 *Md. J. Int'l L. & Trade* (1998), pp. 287-317; Schmitt, 17 *Yale J. Int'l L.* (1999), pp. 609-690; Jami Melissa Jackson, 'The Legality of Assassination of Independent Terrorist Leaders: An Examination of National and International Implications', in: 24 *N.C. J. Int'l L. & Com. Reg.* (1999), pp. 669-697; Michael Ashkouri, 'Has United States Foreign Policy towards Libya, Iraq & Serbia violated Executive Order 12333: Prohibition on Assassination?', in: 7 *New Eng. Int'l & Comp. L. Ann.* (2001), pp. 155-175; Pickard, 30 *Ga. J. Int'l & Comp. L.* (2001), pp. 3-35.

[161] *See e.g.* Amnesty International, AI Doc. MDE 15/005/2001 (February 21, 2001); Yael Stein, 'Israel's Assassination Policy: Extra-Judicial Executions', in: *B'Tselem Position Paper* (January 2001); *compare also* Michael Eisenstadt, '"Preemptive Targeted Killings" as a Terror Tool: An Assessment of Israel's Approach', in: *Peacewatch*, No. 342 (August 28, 2001).

[162] *See e.g.* Steven R. David, 'The Necessity of Targeted Assassinations – The Israeli Reply to Terror is Moral and Appropriate', in: *Los Angeles Times*, July 25, 2002, p. 13; David B. Rivkin, Jr./ Lee A. Casey/ Darin R. Bartram, 'Suicide Attacks are War Crimes, Targeted Killings aren't', in: *Jerusalem Post*, November 7, 2002; Benjamin A. Gorelick, 'The Israeli Response to Palestinian Breach of the Oslo Agreements', in: 9 *New Eng. J. Int'l & Comp. L.* (2003), pp. 651-677, at 668-671.

[163] Supreme Court of Israel, *"Targeted Killings" Admissibility I*. The decision reads in its entirety: "We read and widely listened to the claims of the Applicant's representative. It seems to us that the announcement given on behalf of the Respondents supplied an exhaustive response to the Applicant's claims. The choice of means of warfare, used by the Respondents to preempt murderous terrorist attacks, is not the kind of issue the Court would see fit to intervene in. This is the case *a fortiori* when the appeal lacks a firm factual foundation and seeks a sweeping redress." Translation by Ben-Naftali/ Michaeli, 1 *J. Int'l Crim. Just.* (2003), at 368.

Center for Strategic Studies June 2002 conference on *Democracy and Limited War* and the December 2002 Minerva Center for Human Rights conference on *Liberty, Equality, Security*, both resulting in various publications.[164] At the same time, the first articles were published in international law journals.[165] Since 2003, the topic has been dealt with in conferences and in legal literature more often[166] and the first more comprehensive analyses were published.[167]

In the aftermath of the 2004 U.S. Yemen strike, more publications followed.[168] This included *David Kretzmer's* important article[169] and a study on the effectiveness of targeted killings.[170]

---

164 David, *Fatal Choices*; Nolte, 5 *Theo. Inq. L.* (2004), pp. 111-129, based on a speech given at the Minerva Center for Human Rights International 2002 Conference. For the German translation *see* Georg Nolte, 'Weg in eine andere Rechtsordnung – Vorbeugende Gewaltanwendung und gezielte Tötungen', in: *FAZ*, January 10, 2003, p. 8; Statman, 5 *Theo. Inq. L.* (2004), pp. 179-198, based on a speech given at the said conference.

165 *See e.g.* Nicholas J. Kendall, 'Israeli Counter-Terrorism: "Targeted Killings" under International Law', in: 80 *N.C. L. Rev.* (2002), pp. 1069-1088; Joshua Raines, 'Osama, Augustine, and Assassination: The Just War Doctrine and Targeted Killings', in: 12 *Transnat'l L. & Contemp. Probs.* (2002), pp. 217-243.

166 *See e.g.* Luft, 10 *Mid. E. Q.* (2003), pp. 3-14; David, 17 *Ethics & Int'l Aff.* (2003), pp. 111-126; Stein, 17 *Ethics & Int'l Aff.* (2003), pp. 127-137; Steven R. David, 'If Not Combatants, Certainly Not Civilians: Response to Yael Stein', in: 17 *Ethics & Int'l Aff.* (2003), No. 1, pp. 138-140; Robert F. Turner, 'It's not really "Assassination": Legal and Moral Implications of intentionally targeting Terrorists and Aggressor-State Regime Elites', in: 37 *U. Rich. L. Rev.* (2003), pp. 787-810. Concerning the situation under US national law, *see* Banks/ Raven-Hansen, 37 *U. Rich. L. Rev.* (2003), pp. 667-749 and Matthew C. Wiebe, 'Assassination in Domestic and International Law: The Central Intelligence Agency, State-Sponsored Terrorism, and the Right of Self-Defense', in: 11 *Tulsa J. Comp. & Int'l L.* (2003), pp. 363-406, at 374-386.

167 *See* Ben-Naftali/ Michaeli, 36 *Cornell Int'l L.J.* (2003), pp. 233-292; Kremnitzer, in: Fleck (ed.), *Rechtsfragen*, pp. 201-222.

168 *See e.g.* Downes, 9 *J. Confl. Sec. L.* (2004), pp. 277-294; Guiora, 36 *Case W. Res. J. Int'l L.* (2004), pp. 319-334; Ralph Alexander Lorz, 'Sind gezielte Tötungen mit dem internationalen Recht vereinbar?', Commentary, April 7, 2004; Christian Tomuschat, 'Gezielte Tötungen (Targeted Killings) – Zugleich ein Kommentar zum Gutachten des Internationalen Gerichtshofs vom 9. Juli 2004', in: 52 *VN* (2004), pp. 136-140; Philip B. Heymann/ Juliette N. Kayyem,

Many recent publications on the topic are related to the case brought before the Israeli Supreme Court – including *Antonio Cassese's* expert opinion written at the request of the petitioners[171] – and to the Court's December 2006 judgment.[172]

Preserving Security and Democratic Freedoms in the War on Terrorism – Final Report of the Long-Term Legal Strategy Project, Cambridge, Mass. 2004, p. 5 and pp. 59-68; Bausback, 24 *NVwZ* (2005), pp. 418-420; Casey, 32 *Syracuse J. Int'l L. & Com.* (2005), pp. 311-344; Vincent-Jöel Proulx, 'If the Hat Fits Wear It, If the Turban Fits Run for Your Life: Reflection on the Indefinite Detention and Targeted Killings of Suspected Terrorists', in: 56 *Hastings L.J.* (2005), pp. 801-900; Tom Ruys, 'Licence to Kill?: State-sponsored Assassination under International Law', in: 44 *Rev. dr. mil.* (2005), pp. 13-49; Watkin, 15 *Duke J. Comp. & Int'l L.* (2005), pp. 281-314; Byman, 85 *Foreign Aff.* (2006), pp. 95-112; Gross, 23 *J. Applied Phil.* (2006), pp. 323-335; Fisher, 45 *Colum. J. Transnat'l L.* (2007), pp. 711-758; Solis, 60 *Nav. War C. Rev.* (2007), pp. 127-146.

169 Kretzmer, 16 *Eur. J. Int'l L.* (2005), pp. 171-212.

170 Zussman/ Zussman, *Targeted Killings*.

171 Antonio Cassese, 'Expert Opinion on Whether Israel's Targeted Killings of Palestinian Terrorists is Consonant with International Humanitarian Law', written at the request of the Petitioners in: Supreme Court of Israel, *The Public Committee Against Torture* et al. *v. The Government of Israel* et al. H.C.J. 769 /02.

172 *See e.g.* Orna Ben-Naftali, 'A Judgment in the Shadow of International Criminal Law', in: 5 *J. Int'l Crim. Just.* (2007), pp. 322-331; Antonio Cassese, 'On Some Merits of the Israeli Judgment on Targeted Killings', in: 5 *J. Int'l Crim. Just.* (2007), pp. 339-345; Amichai Cohen/ Yuval Shany, 'A Development of Modest Proportions: The Application of the Principle of Proportionality in the Targeted Killings Case', in: 5 *J. Int'l Crim. Just.* (2007), pp. 310-321; Anthony Dworkin, 'Israel's High Court on Targeted Killing: A Model for the War on Terror?', in: *Crimes of War Project* (December 15, 2006); William J. Fenrick, 'The Targeted Killings Judgment and the Scope of Direct Participation in Hostilities', in: 5 *J. Int'l Crim. Just.* (2007), pp. 332-338; Joanne Mariner, 'The Israeli Supreme Court Rules on "Targeted Killings"', in: *FindLaw's Writ* (December 22, 2006); Marko Milanovic, 'Lessons for human rights and humanitarian law in the war on terror: comparing Hamdan and the Israeli Targeted Killings case', in: 89 *Int'l Rev. Red Cross* (2007), No. 866, pp. 373-393; Ruys, *Juristenkrant* (January 17, 2007); Roy S. Schondorf, 'The Targeted Killings Judgment: A Preliminary Assessment', in: 5 *J. Int'l Crim. Just.* (2007), pp. 301-309; Kristen F. Eichensehr, 'On Target? The Israeli Supreme Court and the Expansion of Targeted Killings', in: 116 *Yale L.J.* (2007), pp. 1873-1881; Keller/ Forowicz, 21 *Leiden J. Int'l L.* (2008), pp. 185-221; Nils Melzer, 'Targeted Killing or Less

Finally, in 2008 – after the main research for the present treatise was finalised – two monographs were published which discussed the topic of targeted killings with different foci: *Schmitz-Elvenich* mainly addressed questions concerning *jus ad bellum*,[173] whereas *Melzer* comprehensively examined the topic under the paradigms of "law enforcement"[174] and "hostilities".[175]

II. Different Approaches

The perspective which is taken as a starting point in assessing the legality of a targeted killing has vast consequences on the result. Possible approaches depend on a wide variety of factors, such as the status of war or peace, the status of the targeted person as a civilian or combatant, the character of a conflict as internal or international and the level or intensity of the conflict. But they also depend on more general con-

---

Harmful Means? – Israel's High Court Judgment on Targeted Killing and the Restrictive Function of Military Necessity', in: 9 *Yb. Int'l Hum. L.* (2009), pp. 87-113.

[173] Schmitz-Elvenich, *Targeted Killing*, pp. 25-164. Interestingly, *Schmitz-Elvenich* focuses on the "US approach, as the Israeli cases, in part, cannot be generalised", *id.*, p. 15.

[174] Melzer, *Targeted Killing*, pp. 83-239.

[175] *Id.*, pp. 241-419. Further recent publications concerning the topic are: Alexandre S. Wilner, 'Targeted Killings in Afghanistan: Measuring Coercion and Deterrence in Counterterrorism and Counterinsurgency', in: 33 *Stud. Confl. Terror.* (2010), pp. 307-329; Elisabeth Strüwer, *Zum Zusammenspiel von humanitärem Völkerrecht und den Menschenrechten am Beispiel des Targeted Killing*, Frankfurt am Main 2010; Yutaka Arai-Takahashi, 'So-called Targeted Killings in Volatile Occupied Territories – Critical Appraisal through the Concept of Direct Participation in Hostilities and the Principle of Proportionality', in: 108 *J. Int'l L. & Dipl.* (2009), pp. 1-47; Celso Eduardo Faria Coracini, 'Targeted Killing of Suspected Terrorists during Armed Conflicts: Compatibility with the Rights to Life and to a Due Process?', in: Stefano Manacorde/ Adán Nieto (eds.), *Criminal Law between War and Peace: Justice and Cooperation in Criminal Matters in International Military Interventions*, Cuenca 2009, pp. 387-402; Tatiana Waisberg, 'The Colombia-Ecuador Armed Crisis of March 2008: The Practice of Targeted Killing and Incursions against Non-State Actors Harbored at Terrorist Safe Havens in a Third Party State', in: 32 *Stud. Confl. Terror.* (2009), pp. 476-488.

siderations. The fundamental question of whether the rule of law should apply at all to certain situations has come up in the aftermath of September 11, 2001:

> I have been struck by how many Americans – and how many lawyers – seem to have concluded that, somehow, the destruction of four planes and three buildings has taken us back to a state of nature in which there are no laws or rules.[176]

If such far-reaching considerations are not accepted, according to some authors, the present international law cannot provide adequate guidance on the topic. "[I]nternational law as it currently exists appears to be ill-equipped to deal with terrorism".[177] *Fisher*, in his Article on targeted killings concludes that

> international law is not currently in a position to guide State behavior with respect to targeted killing. At present, the international legal community is divided over the legality of the use of targeted killing as a counter-terrorism tactic. The international legal community is so fractured with regard to the targeted killing question that there is not even agreement on which legal regime – IHR, the law of belligerent occupation, or IHL – should apply to an assessment of the tactic's legality.[178]

He thus shows which legal regimes have to be taken into consideration, namely international human rights law, international humanitarian law and the law of occupation as part thereof, but at the same time is of the opinion that the international law on targeted killings still has to be developed by States.[179]

---

[176] Harold Hongju Koh, 'September 11, 2001 – Legal Response to Terror: The Spirit of the Laws', in: 43 *Harv. Int'l L.J.* (2002), pp. 23-40, at 23.

[177] Guiora, 36 *Case W. Res. J. Int'l L.* (2004), at 324. *Compare* David Wippman, 'Do New Wars call for New Laws? Introduction', in: David Wippman/ Matthew Evangelista (eds.), *New Wars, New Laws? Applying the Laws of War in 21st Century Conflicts*, Ardsley, N.Y. 2005, pp. 1-28.

[178] Fisher, 45 *Colum. J. Transnat'l L.* (2007), at 575.

[179] *See also* Anne-Marie Slaughter/ William Burke-White, 'September 11, 2001 – Legal Response to Terror: An International Constitutional Moment', in: 43 *Harv. Int'l L.J.* (2002), pp. 1-22, at 2, who state: "Article 2(4)(a) [of the UN Charter] should read: 'All states and individuals shall refrain from the deliberate targeting or killing of civilians in armed conflict of any kind, for any purpose'."; *compare generally* Kenneth W. Watkin, 'Controlling the Use of Force: A Role

In opposition to this, non-governmental organisations and human rights institutions generally object to the perception that existing international law rules are not adequate to face domestic and transnational terrorism. They fear that over-reaction to terror and the adoption of measures incompatible with human rights and humanitarian law rules poses the real threat in the present situation.[180] This fear cannot be dismissed easily.[181] However, those authors, who regard parts of the existing international law as being applicable to targeted killings, take several main approaches to the topic:

First, authors regard the international human rights law as the decisive legal scheme in assessing the question of legality of targeted killings.[182] As part of this assessment, the question of immediacy is crucial.[183] In consequence, law enforcement and criminal liability are rather regarded as the means which should be employed in situations in which targeted killings are discussed.[184] This includes that an arrest, as an alternative to targeted killings, must be taken into account,[185] also in a situation of occupation.[186] According to this assessment, targeted killings – or rath-

---

for Human Rights Norms in Contemporary Armed Conflict', in: 98 *Am. J. Int'l L.* (2004), pp. 1-34.

180 *See e.g.* International Commission of Jurists, *The Berlin Declaration: The ICJ Declaration on Upholding Human Rights and the Rule of Law in Combating Terrorism*, adopted August 28, 2004.

181 *Compare e.g.* Kretzmer, 16 *Eur. J. Int'l L.* (2005), at 174.

182 *See e.g.* Amnesty International, AI Doc. MDE 15/005/2001 (February 21, 2001), pp. 26-30; Stein, *B'Tselem Position Paper* (January 2001), pp. 6-8.

183 *See* Nolte, 5 *Theo. Inq. L.* (2004), pp. 111-129.

184 *Compare e.g.* Wolfgang S. Heinz, 'Zu Auslandseinsätzen der Bundeswehr in der Terrorismusbekämpfung: Analysen und Empfehlungen aus der Sicht des internationalen Menschenrechtsschutzes', in: Dieter Fleck (ed.), *Rechtsfragen der Terrorismusbekämpfung durch Streitkräfte*, Baden-Baden 2004, pp. 67-99, at 96; *compare also* Dominic D. McAlea, 'Post-Westphalian Crime', in: David Wippman/ Matthew Evangelista (eds.), *New Wars, New Laws? Applying the Laws of War in 21st Century Conflicts*, Ardsley, N.Y. 2005, pp. 111-134, at 133.

185 *Compare e.g.* Casey, 32 *Syracuse J. Int'l L. & Com.* (2005), at 340; Gross, 15 *Fla. J. Int'l L.* (2003), at 468-471. Although *Gross* also argues that targeted killing can be justified as self-defence according to Article 51 UN Charter.

186 Gerd Seidel, 'Die Palästinafrage und das Völkerrecht', in: 44 *AVR* (2006), pp. 121-158, at 144-145.

er preventive killings – are not generally illegal, but must be the *ultima ratio*.[187] If "a war between a terrorist organization and a state is not a conventional war" the situation demands for a restriction to the mildest means – i.e. human rights rather than "law of war" considerations – like capture, extradition and trial.[188]

Second, some authors are of the opinion that targeted killings are legitimate acts of self-defence.[189] While some of these authors refer to individual self-defence and thus rather belong to the first group,[190] most authors refer to self-defence in the meaning of the UN Charter in response to an international armed attack by non-State actors.[191] This includes anticipatory self-defence prior to such an attack[192] and is also discussed in the context of the just war doctrine.[193]

---

[187] Roman Schmidt-Radefeldt, 'Die Menschenrechtsverpflichtungen von Streitkräften bei antiterroristischen Maßnahmen im Ausland', in: Dieter Fleck (ed.), *Rechtsfragen der Terrorismusbekämpfung durch Streitkräfte*, Baden-Baden 2004, pp. 101-123, at 118; *similarly, but less strict* Drumbl, 36 *Case W. Res. J. Int'l L.* (2004), at 345-346.

[188] Gross, 15 *Fla. J. Int'l L.* (2003), at 468-471 and 479-480.

[189] *See e.g.* Godfrey, 4 *San Diego Int'l L.J.* (2003), at 507-509; Gross, 15 *Temp. Int'l & Comp. L.J.* (2001), pp. 195-246; Kendall, 80 *N.C. L. Rev.* (2002), at 1070 and 1078-1082; Matthew J. Machon, *Targeted Killing as an Element of U.S. Foreign Policy in the War on Terror*, Fort Leavenworth 2006, pp. 47-48.

[190] *See e.g.* Lorz, Commentary, April 7, 2004, who states that Israeli targeted killings of suicide attackers on the way to commit the attack ("ticking bomb") could be justified as self-defence.

[191] *See e.g.* Guiora, 36 *Case W. Res. J. Int'l L.* (2004), at 323-326; Peter Rowe, 'Response to Terror: The New "War"', in: 3 *Melb. J. Int'l L.* (2002), pp. 301-321, at 304-311; Schmitz-Elvenich, *Targeted Killing*, pp. 50-161, in particular pp. 104-121; Solis, 60 *Nav. War C. Rev.* (2007), at 130-131; Wiebe, 11 *Tulsa J. Comp. & Int'l L.* (2003), at 386-401; Schmitt, in: Arnold/ Quénivet (eds.), at 530-542. *Compare also* Jackson Nyamuya Maogoto, 'Walking an International Law Tightrope: Use of Military Force to Counter Terrorism – Willing the Ends', in: 31 *Brook. J. Int'l L.* (2006), pp. 405-462, at 405; Daniel Janse, 'International Terrorism and Self-Defence', in: 36 *Isr. Yb. Hum. Rts.* (2006), pp. 149-180.

[192] *See e.g.* Beres, 20 *Hofstra L. Rev.* (1991), pp. 321-340; Gorelick, 9 *New Eng. J. Int'l & Comp. L.* (2003), at 668-671; Gross, *Struggle of Democracy*, pp. 225-226; Kendall, 80 *N.C. L. Rev.* (2002), at 1078-1088.

[193] *See* Raines, 12 *Transnat'l L. & Contemp. Probs.* (2002), at 233-243.

This approach naturally leads to the question of the existence of an armed conflict as the context of a given targeted killing, which would lead to the application of international humanitarian law rules.[194] Thus, many authors examine the policy of targeted killings in the context of an ongoing armed conflict,[195] partly identified as a "war on terror".[196]

Third, other authors deny such an approach concerning either the "war on terror" or the situation in Israel.[197] Some authors do not make an absolute decision between the war paradigm and the law enforcement paradigm. These authors use mixed approaches[198] or strictly differentiate between different contexts.[199] This is partly due to the opinion that neither the law-enforcement model, as reflected in standards of international human rights, nor the armed conflict model, as reflected in stan-

---

[194] Casey, 32 *Syracuse J. Int'l L. & Com.* (2005), pp. 311-344; Kathleen A. Cavanaugh, 'Rewriting Law: The Case of Israel and the Occupied Territories', in: David Wippman/ Matthew Evangelista (eds.), *New Wars, New Laws? Applying the Laws of War in 21st Century Conflicts*, Ardsley, N.Y. 2005, pp. 227-258, at 250-254; Watkin, 15 *Duke J. Comp. & Int'l L.* (2005), at 309-314; Noëlle Quénivet, 'The Applicability of International Humanitarian Law to Situations of a (Counter-)Terrorist Nature', in: Roberta Arnold/ Pierre-Antoine Hildbrand (eds.), *International Humanitarian Law and the 21st Century's Conflicts: Changes and Challenges*, Lausanne 2005, pp. 25-59, at 27.

[195] *See e.g.* Ben-Naftali/ Michaeli, 36 *Cornell Int'l L.J.* (2003), at 255-262, who regard the situation in the Occupied Palestinian Territory as a non-international armed conflict; Casey, 32 *Syracuse J. Int'l L. & Com.* (2005), pp. 311-344; Fenrick, 5 *J. Int'l Crim. Just.* (2007), pp. 332-338; Gross, 23 *J. Applied Phil.* (2006), at 325-332; Proulx, 56 *Hastings L.J.* (2005), pp. 801-900; Solis, 60 *Nav. War C. Rev.* (2007), pp. 127-146; Tomuschat, 52 *VN* (2004), at 137-140, albeit *Tomuschat* argues that the situation in the Occupied Palestinian Territory does not represent an armed conflict, *see ibid.*, at 138; Watkin, 15 *Duke J. Comp. & Int'l L.* (2005), at 309-314.

[196] *See e.g.* David, *Fatal Choices*, p. 22; David, 17 *Ethics & Int'l Aff.* (2003), at 116; Downes, 9 *J. Confl. Sec. L.* (2004), at 281-283; Luft, 10 *Mid. E. Q.* (2003), pp. 3-14; Statman, 5 *Theo. Inq. L.* (2004), pp. 179-198.

[197] *See e.g.* Stein, 17 *Ethics & Int'l Aff.* (2003), at 128; Schmahl, in: Tomuschat *et al.* (eds.), at 237.

[198] *Compare e.g.* Kretzmer, 16 *Eur. J. Int'l L.* (2005), at 175.

[199] Casey, 32 *Syracuse J. Int'l L. & Com.* (2005), pp. 311-344; Cavanaugh, in: Wippman/ Evangelista (eds.), at 250-254; Kremnitzer, in: Fleck (ed.), *Rechtsfragen*, pp. 201-222; Watkin, 15 *Duke J. Comp. & Int'l L.* (2005), at 309-314.

dards of international humanitarian law, provided an adequate framework for the issue of transnational terror. Therefore a framework that combines elements of both models is suggested by some authors.[200]

The present treatise does not follow any of these approaches in an absolute manner. Its aim is – so to speak – to take no special approach, at least none that could anticipate a certain result. Thus, all fields of law discussed above will be examined in relation to the topic of targeted killings. In doing so, the starting point is human rights law, and especially the right to life.[201] Further major fields of law are international humanitarian law, including the law of occupation.[202] A section on the question of other justifications follows,[203] and most importantly, a section discussing the question of applicability of these different schemes of law will.[204] Finally, the specific situation in Israel will be discussed, including the judgment by the Supreme Court of Israel on targeted killings.[205]

F. Terminology

Beside the terms of "targeted killings" and "preventive killings", some phrases will often be used throughout this treatise, which demand some clarification. This concerns the terms "Occupied Palestinian Territory" and "Terrorism".

---

200 *Compare e.g.* Kretzmer, 16 *Eur. J. Int'l L.* (2005), at 175.

201 *See infra*, Part One. On this assessment, *compare also* Kremnitzer, in: Fleck (ed.), *Rechtsfragen*, pp. 201-222; Melzer, in: Gill/ Fleck (eds.), at 278-281 (paras. 17.02.1-17.02.6); Schmahl, in: Tomuschat *et al.* (eds.), at 237.

202 *See infra,* Part Two.

203 *See infra,* Part Three.

204 *See infra,* Part Four.

205 *See infra,* Part Five.

I. Occupied Palestinian Territory

The West Bank, the Gaza Strip and East Jerusalem have been referred to by a number of different names since 1967. Official Israel refers to those areas as either "Judea, Samaria, and Gaza" or the "administered territories" (neither of which include East Jerusalem). The Palestine Liberation Organization and the international community through such bodies as the UN Security Council, the UN General Assembly, and the International Committee of the Red Cross, have referred to those areas as the "Occupied Palestinian Territories", presumably with the intention to regard these areas as the territory where the Palestinian people are legitimately entitled to exercise their right to self-determination. Recently, the UN began to refer to the areas collectively as the "Occupied Palestinian *Territory*", deliberately using the singular form, apparently for the purpose of underscoring the contiguous nature of what is regarded as the self-determination unit of the Palestinian people. The West Bank, including East Jerusalem, and the Gaza Strip, will be referred to collectively as the Occupied Palestinian Territory throughout this treatise in accordance with the UN practice.[206]

II. Terrorism

> Increasingly, questions are being raised about the problem of the definition of a terrorist. Let us be wise and focussed about this. For the most part, terrorism is terrorism. It uses violence to kill and damage indiscriminately to make a political or cultural point and to influence legitimate governments of public opinion unfairly and amorally. There is common ground amongst all of us on what con-

---

[206] *See e.g.* UN GA Res. ES-10/2 (April 25, 1997), *Illegal Israeli Actions in Occupied East Jerusalem and the Rest of the Occupied Palestinian Territory*, UN Doc. A/RES/ES-10/2 (May 5, 1997); UN Secretary-General, *Report Submitted in Accordance with General Assembly Resolution ES-10/2*, Report of June 26, 1997, 10th Emergency Special Sess., Agenda Item 5, UN Doc. A/ES-10/6 (June 26, 1997). *See also* Ardi Imseis, 'On the Fourth Geneva Convention and the Occupied Palestinian Territory', in 44 *Harv. Int'l L.J.* (2003), pp. 65-138, at 67 (Fn. 20).

> stitutes terrorism. What looks, smells and kills like terrorism is terrorism.[207]
>
> In the Israeli terminology, a Palestinian is forever a terrorist, never a combatant, even if the objects of his attack are Israeli soldiers advancing into his hometown.[208]

The two quotations above tell a lot about the problem of defining terrorism. Terrorism is a phenomenon that is plagued by lack of definition, let alone an agreed universal definition.[209] There is certainly some aspect of "I know it when I see it"[210] to it: To describe small boys who throw stones – whether in Ramallah or in Belfast – as terrorists invites ridicule. To refer to a car bomber or to a group deliberately attacking a school bus as terrorist seems to fit obviously. To distinguish an Argentinean soldier on the Falklands and a member of the IRA in Northern Ireland, both firing on a British patrol again might be obvious to some and less clear to others.[211] "[W]hat is terrorism to some is heroism to others."[212] It thus becomes clear that it depends highly on the position of the observer whether he regards something as "terrorism" or not. The whole question is highly political and using the term "terrorist" is

---

[207] United Kingdom, Permanent Representative to the United Nations (Sir Jeremy Greenstock, KCMG), Statement at the General Assembly Debate on Terrorism, October 1, 2001, in: UN General Assembly, 56th Sess., 12th Plenary Meeting, Official Records, UN Doc. A/56/PV.12 (October 1, 2001), pp. 17-19, at 18.

[208] Ben-Naftali/ Michaeli, 36 *Cornell Int'l L.J.* (2003), at 235 (footnote 6).

[209] Kevin Boyle, 'Terrorism, States of Emergency and Human Rights', in: Wolfgang Benedek/ Alice Yotopoulos-Marangopoulos (eds.), *Anti-Terrorist Measures and Human Rights*, Leiden 2004, pp. 95-116, at 97; Alex Peter Schmid, *Political Terrorism: A Research Guide to Concepts, Theories, Data Bases and Literature*, Amsterdam 1984, p. 585 identifies 109 definitions; *compare also* Louis René Beres, 'The Meaning of Terrorism: Jurisprudential and Definitional Clarifications', in: 28 *Vand. J. Transnat'l L.* (1995), pp. 239-250.

[210] U.S. Supreme Court, *Jacobellis v. Ohio*, Judgment of June 22, 1964, 378 *U.S.* (1964), pp. 184-204, Concurring Opinion by Justice Potter Stewart, at 197.

[211] Christopher Greenwood, 'Terrorism and Humanitarian Law – The Debate over Additional Protocol I', in: 19 *Isr. Yb. Hum. Rts.* (1989), pp. 187-207, at 189-190.

[212] M. Cherif Bassiouni, 'Terrorism: The Persistent Dilemma of Legitimacy', in: 36 *Case W. Res. J. Int'l L.* (2004), pp. 299-306, at 299 and 306 referring to a 1973 conference in Siracusa, Italy, where he first coined this phrase.

dangerous insofar as everybody will have a different perception of what is covered by that term. It has been stated that "[a]n objective definition is not only possible; it is also indispensable to any serious attempt to combat terrorism."[213]

I disagree: Luckily, and this might be surprising, it is possible not to fundamentally rely on the term "terrorism" in examining the legality of targeted or preventive killings. As long as no legal consequences are attached to the fact that someone "is" a terrorist or not, but instead to his behaviour, the examination will manage to do without a definition of "terrorism".[214] And as will be shown *infra*, the question of whether a person is referred to as a "terrorist" or not, has no influence on the question of whether this person may be targeted:[215] Concerning human rights, it is not a "status" of a person but his personal behaviour which is decisive in assessing his targeting. Concerning international humanitarian law, persons do have a status, e.g. as civilian or as combatant, but "terrorist" is no such status. Thus, the question of targeting – even though it depends *inter alia* on the status of the person – is not related to the fact that this person is referred to as a "terrorist" or not, or most likely both, depending on the position of the observer. Thus, any attempt to define "terrorist" or "terrorism" has no specific impact on the questions addressed in this treatise.

---

213 Boaz Ganor, 'Terrorism: No Prohibition Without Definition', in: The International Policy Institute for Counter-Terrorism, *Articles by ICT-Staff* (October 7, 2001).

214 *Compare similarly,* Quénivet, in: Arnold/ Hildbrand (eds.), at 26-27.

215 *See also* Schmitz-Elvenich, *Targeted Killing*, p. 10.

Part One – Human Rights

Human Rights rules are laid down in numerous human rights treaties and also exist as customary international law. The human rights treaties examined here are the International Covenant on Civil and Political Rights,[1] the African Charter on Human and Peoples' Rights,[2] the American Convention on Human Rights[3] and the European Convention on Human Rights.[4]

The right to life is the right in the focus of this examination. It is laid down in Article 6 of the International Covenant, in Article 4 of the African Charter, in Article 4 of the American Convention and in Article 2 of the European Convention. It is furthermore included in Article 3 of

---

1 International Covenant on Civil and Political Rights, adopted by the UN General Assembly on December 16, 1966, Resolution 2200 A (XXI), annex, UN GAOR, 21st Sess., Supp. No. 16, pp. 49-60, at 52-58, UN Doc. A/6316 (1966), entry into force on March 23, 1976 for all provisions except those of Article 41, and on March 28, 1978 for the provisions of Article 41, reprinted in: 999 *UNTS* (1976), No. 14668, pp. 171-301 and 1057 *UNTS* (1977), p. 407 (corrigendum).

2 African Charter on Human and Peoples' Rights, adopted by the Organization of African Unity Summit at Nairobi, Kenya, on June 27, 1981, OAU Doc. CAB/LEG/67/3/Rev. 5, entry into force on October 21, 1986, reprinted in: 1520 *UNTS* (1988), No. 26363, pp. 217-292 and 21 *ILM* (1982), pp. 59-68, also known as the "Banjul Charter on Human and Peoples' Rights".

3 American Convention on Human Rights, also referred to as the "Pact of San José", adopted by the Inter-American Specialized Conference on Human Rights at San José, Costa Rica, November 22, 1969, entry into force on July 18, 1978, reprinted in: *OAS Treaty Series* No. 36, 1144 *UNTS* (1979), No. 17955, pp. 123-212.

4 European Convention on Human Rights, formally entitled "Convention for the Protection of Human Rights and Fundamental Freedoms", adopted at Rome, Italy, on November 4, 1950, entry into force on September 3, 1953, reprinted in: *Council of Europe Treaty Series* No. 5 and 213 *UNTS* (1955), No. 2889, pp. 222-261.

the Universal Declaration of Human Rights[5] and is regarded as part of general international law.

A. Human Rights Conventions and the Right to Life

Human Rights Conventions are, like all international treaties and conventions, subject to the general principles of interpretation as laid down in Articles 31-33 of the Vienna Convention on the law of Treaties.[6] Principles of interpretation reflect customary international law.[7] The interpretation is thus based on the ordinary meaning of the terms used, the subject and purpose of the treaty and subsequent practice, supplemented, if necessary, by the *travaux préparatoires* of the treaty.[8] These

---

5 UN GA Res. 217 (III) A (December 10, 1948), *International Bill of Human Rights – Universal Declaration of Human Rights*, UN GAOR, 3rd Sess., Part 1, UN Doc. A/810 (1948), pp. 71-77.

6 Vienna Convention on the Law of Treaties, adopted at Vienna, Austria, on May 23, 1969, entry into force on January 27, 1980, reprinted in: 1155 *UNTS* (1980), No. 18232, pp. 331-512; *see e.g.* H.R. Committee, *J. B. et al. (Alberta Union of Provincial Employees) v. Canada*, Communication No. 118/1982, U.N. Doc. CCPR/C/28/D/118/1982 (July 18, 1986), para. 6.3; Eur. Ct. H.R., *Golder v. United Kingdom*, Appl. No. 4451/70, Judgment of February 21, 1975, Series A, No. 18, p. 14 (para. 29); Manfred Nowak, *U.N. Covenant on Civil and Political Rights – CCPR Commentary*, Kehl am Rhein 1993, Introduction, para. 17 (p. XXIII); Louis Henkin, 'Introduction', in: Louis Henkin (ed.), *The International Bill of Rights: The Covenant on Civil and Political Rights*, New York 1981, pp. 1-31, at 25-26; Scott J. Davidson, *The Inter-American Court of Human Rights*, Aldershot 1992, p. 130; Scott J. Davidson, *The Inter-American Human Rights System*, Aldershot 1997, pp. 67-69 and 265.

7 *Compare* ICJ, *Kasikili/Sedudu Island, Botswana v. Namibia*, Judgment of December 13, 1999, I.C.J. Reports 1999, pp. 1045-1237, at 1059 (para. 18), applying the rules of the Vienna Convention whereas neither party to the dispute was a party to that convention; *compare also* ICJ, *Territorial Dispute, Libyan Arab Jamahiriya v. Chad*, Judgment of February 3, 1994, I.C.J. Reports 1994, pp. 6-41, at 21-22; ICJ, *Oil Platforms, Islamic Republic of Iran v. United States of America*, Judgment (Preliminary Objections) of December 12, 1996, I.C.J. Reports 1996, pp. 802-900, at 812 (para. 23).

8 On the corresponding customary rules of treaty interpretation *compare* Arnold Duncan McNair, *The Law of Treaties*, Oxford 1961, pp. 364-431; Ru-

principles of interpretation have been affirmed and applied by the Inter-American Court of Human Rights,[9] the European Court of Human Rights,[10] the United Nations Human Rights Committee[11] and are also deemed applicable to the African Charter on Human and People's Rights.[12]

Furthermore, some special rules of interpretation apply to human rights treaty regimes. Unlike other international treaties, human rights conventions comprise more than mere reciprocal engagements between the contracting States. They create, over and above a network of mutual, bilateral undertakings, objective obligations.[13] Due to this objective char-

---

dolf Bernhardt, *Die Auslegung völkerrechtlicher Verträge*, Köln 1963, pp. 58-133.

9 *Compare e.g.* Inter-Am. Ct. H.R., *Viviana Gallardo et al.*, Advisory Opinion No. G 101/81, Decision of November 13, 1981, Series A, No. G 101/81 (1981), para. 20; Inter-Am. Ct. H.R., *"Other treaties" subject to the advisory jurisdiction of the Court (Art. 64 American Convention on Human Rights)*, Advisory Opinion No. OC-1/81 of September 24, 1982, Series A, No. 1 (1982), paras. 33 and 45; Inter-Am. Ct. H.R., *Restrictions to the Death Penalty (Arts. 4(2) and 4(4) American Convention on Human Rights)*, Advisory Opinion No. OC-3/83 of September 8, 1983, Series A, No. 3, at para. 48; Inter-Am. Ct. H.R., *Enforceability of the Right to Reply or Correction (Arts. 14(1), 1(1) and 2 American Convention on Human Rights)*, Advisory Opinion No. OC-7/86 of August 29, 1986, Series A, No. 7 (1986), para. 21.; on the means of interpretation of the Inter-American Court *compare generally* Davidson, *Inter-American Court*, pp. 130-142.

10 The European Court of Human Rights refers to Articles 31 to 33 as "in essence generally accepted principles of international law to which the Court has already referred on occasion.", *see Eur. Ct. H.R., Golder*, Series A, No. 18, p. 14 (para. 29).

11 *See e.g.* H.R. Committee, *J. B. et al. (Alberta Union of Provincial Employees)*, UN Doc. CCPR/C/28/D/118/1982, at para. 6.3.

12 *See e.g.* Fatsah Ouguergouz, *La Charte africaine des droits de l'homme et des peoples – Une approche juridique de droits de l'homme entre tradition et modernité*, Paris 1993, pp. 263, 391-392.

13 *See e.g.* Eur. Ct. H.R., *Ireland v. United Kingdom*, Appl. No. 5310/71, Judgment of January 18, 1978, Series A, No. 25, p. 90 (para. 239); Inter-Am. Ct. H.R., *The Effect of Reservations on the Entry into Force of the American Convention on Human Rights (Arts. 74 And 75)*, Advisory Opinion OC-2/82 of September 24, 1982, Series A, No. 2, paras. 29-30; Inter-Am. Ct. H.R., *Restrictions to the Death Penalty*, Series A, No. 3, para. 50; H.R. Committee, CCPR

acter, it is argued that the rights protected have to be interpreted rather extensively,[14] i.e. *in dubio pro libertate*, and restrictions have to be interpreted narrowly.[15] The aim of such an interpretation is to achieve effective protection.[16] Human rights treaties also have to be seen "in the

---

General Comment No. 24, *Issues relating to Reservations made upon Ratification or Accession to the Covenant or the Optional Protocols thereto, or in Relation to Declarations under Article 41 of the Covenant*, 52nd Sess., November 4, 1994, UN Doc. CCPR/C/21/Rev.1/Add.6 (1994), reprinted in: Compilation of General Comments and General Recommendations adopted by Human Rights Treaty Bodies, U.N. Doc. HRI/GEN/1/Rev.7 (May 12, 2004), pp. 161-167, at 165-166 (para. 17); *compare* the similar reasoning in ICJ, *Reservations to the Convention on the Prevention and Punishment of the Crime of Genocide*, Advisory Opinion of May 28, 1951, I.C.J. Reports 1951, pp. 14-69, at 23.

[14] *See e.g.* Nowak, *CCPR Commentary*, Introduction, para. 20 (p. XXIV); Franz Matscher, 'Methods of Interpretation of the Convention', in: Ronald St. John Macdonald/ Franz Matscher/ Herbert Petzold (eds.), *The European System for the Protection of Human Rights*, Dordrecht 1993, pp. 63-81, at 66; Pieter van Dijk/ Godefridus J. H. van Hoof, *Theory and Practice of the European Convention on Human Rights*, 3rd ed., The Hague 1998, pp. 33-34; Katja Wiesbrock, *Internationaler Schutz der Menschenrechte vor Verletzungen durch Private*, Berlin 1990, pp. 10-12. Critically on an apparent new tendency *see* Alexander Orakhelashvili, 'Restrictive Interpretation of Human Rights Treaties in the Recent Jurisprudence of the European Court of Human Rights', in: 14 *Eur. J. Int'l L.* (2003), pp. 529-568, esp. at 567-568.

[15] *See e.g.* H.R. Committee, CCPR General Comment No. 6, *The Right to Life (Article 6)*, 16th Sess., April 30, 1982, reprinted in: Compilation of General Comments and General Recommendations adopted by Human Rights Treaty Bodies, U.N. Doc. HRI/GEN/1/Rev.7 (May 12, 2004), pp. 128-129, at 129 (para. 7); Nowak, *CCPR Commentary*, Introduction, para. 20 (p. XXIV); Henkin, in: Henkin (ed.), at 24; Rudolf Bernhardt, 'Thoughts on the Interpretation of Human Rights Treaties', in: Franz Matscher/ Herbert Petzold (eds.), *Protecting Human Rights: The European Dimension – Studies in Honour of Gérard J. Wiarda*, Köln 1988, pp. 65-71, at 70; *see generally* Bernhardt, *Auslegung*, pp. 182-185.

[16] *See e.g.* Inter-Am. Ct. H.R., *Angel Manfredo Velásquez-Rodríguez v. Honduras*, Judgment of July 29, 1988, Series C, No. 4, paras. 59-68; H.R. Committee, CCPR General Comment No. 7, *Torture or cruel, inhuman or degrading Treatment or Punishment (Article 7)*, 16th Sess., May 30, 1982, reprinted in: Compilation of General Comments and General Recommendations adopted by Human Rights Treaty Bodies, U.N. Doc. HRI/GEN/1/Rev.7 (May 12, 2004), pp. 129-130, at 129-130 (para. 1); H.R. Committee, *Carlton Reid v. Jamaica*, Communication No. 250/1987, Views adopted on July 20, 1990, UN Doc.

light of present day conditions".[17] They are thus subject to dynamic or evolutive interpretation.[18] Furthermore, human rights treaty provisions are interpreted autonomously, i.e. independently of the respective national understanding of a party to a human rights treaty.[19] For this pur-

---

CCPR/C/39/D/250/1987 (August 21, 1990), para. 10.5; Eur. Ct. H.R., *Airey v. Ireland*, Appl. No. 6289/73, Judgment of October 9, 1979, Series A, No. 32, p. 15 (para. 26); Eur. Ct. H.R., *Artico v. Italy*, Appl. No. 6694/74, Judgment of May 13, 1980, Series A, No. 37, p. 16 (para. 33); Eur. Ct. H.R., *Soering v. United Kingdom*, Appl. No. 14038/88, Judgment of July 7, 1989, Series A, No. 161, p. 34 (para. 87); Eur. Ct. H.R., *Lala v. Netherlands*, Appl. No. 14861/ 89, Judgment of September 22, 1994, Series A, No. 297-A, p. 14 (para. 34); Florian Reindel, *Auslegung menschenrechtlicher Verträge am Beispiel der Spruchpraxis des UN-Menschenrechtsausschusses, des Europäischen und des Interamerikanischen Gerichtshofs für Menschenrechte*, München 1995, pp. 82, 113 and 139-141; Mark E. Villiger, *Handbuch der Europäischen Menschenrechtskonvention (EMRK) unter besonderer Berücksichtigung der schweizerischen Rechtslage*, Zürich 1993, para. 155 (pp. 97-98); Matscher, in: Macdonald *et al.* (eds.), at 67; Walter Kälin, 'Die Europäische Menschenrechtskonvention als Faktor der europäischen Integration', in: Walter Haller/ Alfred Kölz/ Georg Müller/ Daniel Thürer (eds.), *Im Dienst an der Gemeinschaft: Festschrift für Dietrich Schindler zum 65. Geburtstag* Basel 1989, pp. 529-538, at 534.

17 Eur. Ct. H.R., *Tyrer v. United Kingdom*, Appl. No. 5856/72, Judgment of April 25, 1978, Series A, No. 26, pp. 15-16 (para. 31).

18 *Compare e.g.* Inter-Am. Ct. H.R., *Restrictions to the Death Penalty*, Series A, No. 3, para. 50; Eur. Ct. H.R., *Marckx v. Belgium*, Appl. No. 6833/74, Judgment of June 13, 1979, Series A, No. 31, p. 19 (para. 41); Eur. Ct. H.R., *Soering*, Series A, No. 161, p. 40 (para. 102); Eur. Ct. H.R., *Loizidou v. Turkey (Preliminary Objections)*, Appl. No. 15318/89, Judgment of March 23, 1995, Series A, No. 310, pp. 26-27 (para. 71); Reindel, *Auslegung*, pp. 53-55, 81, 108-113, 138-139 and 150-151; Bernhardt, in: Matscher/ Petzold (eds.), at 68-69; Rudolf Bernhardt, 'Evolutive Treaty Interpretation, Especially of the European Convention of Human Rights', in: 42 *German Yb. Int'l L.* (1999), pp. 11-25, at 17-20; Søren C. Prebensen, 'Evolutive Interpretation of the European Convention on Human Rights', in: Paul Mahoney/ Franz Matscher/ Herbert Petzold/ Luzius Wildhaber (eds.), *Protection des droits de l'homme: la perspective européenne: Mélanges à la mémoire de Rolv Ryssdal*, Köln 2000, pp. 1123-1137.

19 *See e.g.* Inter-Am. Ct. H.R., *The Word "Laws" in Article 30 of the American Convention on Human Rights*, Advisory Opinion OC-6/86 of May 9, 1986, Series A, No. 6, para. 19; H.R. Committee, *Gordon C. Van Duzen v. Canada*, Communication No. 50/1979, UN Doc. CCPR/C/15/D/50/1979 (April 7, 1982), para. 10.2; Eur. Ct. H.R., *König v. Germany*, Appl. No. 6232/73, Judgment of June 28, 1978, Series A, No. 27, p. 29 (para. 88); Eur. Ct. H.R.,

pose, cross-reference to other international instruments is common.[20] However, States are granted a certain margin of appreciation,[21] subject to the principle of proportionality.[22]

I. The Scope of Protection of Human Rights

Classically, civil and political rights were perceived as freedoms from arbitrary interference of the State.[23] The obligations placed on a State which is party to a human rights instrument is now considered to have

---

Engel and others v. Netherlands (Just Satisfaction), Appl. Nos. 5100/71; 5101/71; 5102/71; 5354/72 and 5370/72, Judgment of November 23, 1976, Series A, No. 22, p. 34 (para. 81); Jean Allain/ Andreas O'Shea, 'African Disunity: Comparing Human Rights Law and Practice of North and South African States', in: 24 *Hum. Rts. Q.* (2002), pp. 86-125, at 86-87; Walter Jean Ganshof van der Meersch, 'La caractère "autonome" des termes et la "marge d'appréciation" des gouvernements dans l'interprétation de la Convention eurropéenne des Droits de l'Homme', in: Franz Matscher/ Herbert Petzold (eds.), *Protecting Human Rights: The European Dimension – Studies in Honour of Gérard J. Wiarda*, Köln 1988, pp. 201-220, at 201-206; Reindel, *Auslegung*, pp. 75-78, 102-104, and 136.

20 *See e.g.* Inter-Am. Ct. H.R., *Proposed Amendments of the Naturalization Provisions of the Constitution of Costa Rica*, Advisory Opinion OC-4/84 of January 19, 1984, Series A, No. 4, para. 56; Eur. Ct. H.R., *Soering*, Series A, No. 161, pp. 34-35 (para. 88); Henkin, in: Henkin (ed.), at 27-28.

21 *See e.g.* Inter-Am. Ct. H.R., *Proposed Amendments*, Series A, No. 4, para. 56; Eur. Ct. H.R., *Case "relating to certain aspects of the laws on the use of languages in education in Belgium"*, Appl. Nos. 1474/62, 1677/62, 1691/62, 1769/63, 1994/63 and 2126/64, Judgment of July 23, 1968, Series A, No. 6, pp. 34-35 (para. 10); Eur. Ct. H.R., *Handyside v. United Kingdom*, Appl. No. 5493/72, Judgment of December 7, 1976, Series A, No. 24, p. 22 (para. 48); Ganshof van der Meersch, in: Matscher/ Petzold (eds.), at 206-220.

22 Matscher, in: Macdonald *et al.* (eds.), at 79; Yutaka Arai-Takahashi, *The Margin of Appreciation Doctrine and the Principle of Proportionality in the Jurisprudence of the ECHR*, Antwerp 2002, p. 193.

23 Sarah Joseph/ Jenny Schultz/ Melissa Castan, *The International Covenant on Civil and Political Rights: Cases, Materials, and Commentary*, 2nd ed., Oxford 2004, para. 1.71 (p. 33); Dominic McGoldrick, *The Human Rights Committee: Its Role in the Development of the International Covenant on Civil and Political Rights*, Oxford 1991, para. 1.16 (p. 11).

four components: to respect, to protect, to promote and to fulfil the rights recognised. In this context, 'respect' generally refers to the classical negative obligation on the part of the State and its agents not to interfere with the rights.[24] This vertical obligation[25] is of utmost importance for the examination at hand, as targeted killings are conducted by State agents in the vast majority of cases. 'Protect' refers to the State's positive duty to ensure that other individuals do not violate a person's rights.[26] This positive obligation on the horizontal level becomes relevant in cases in which a State does not act via its agents directly, but merely supports or only approves killings performed by private actors. However, these duties are overlapped by the obligations of States party to human rights instruments to take affirmative steps to promote the observance of the substantive provisions.[27]

II. The Special Status of the Right to Life

The right to life has been referred to as "the most important and basic of human rights. It is the foundation from which all human rights spring. If it is infringed, the effects are irreversible."[28] It has also been

---

24 Christof Heyns, 'Civil and Political Rights in the African Charter', in: Malcolm Evans/ Rachel Murray (eds.), *The African Charter on Human and Peoples' Rights: the System in Practice, 1986-2000*, Cambridge 2002, pp. 137-177, at 138; in the opinion of other authors, the word 'respect' also refers to a positive dimension, *c.f.* Bertrand G. Ramcharan, 'The Concept and Dimensions of the Right to Life', in: Bertrand G. Ramcharan (ed.), *The Right to Life in International Law*, Dordrecht 1985, pp. 1-32, at 17; Daniel D. Nsereko, 'Arbitrary Deprivation of Life: Controls on Permissible Deprivations', *id.*, pp. 245-283, at 246; Scott N. Carlson/ Gregory Gisvold, *Practical Guide to the International Covenant on Civil and Political Rights*, Ardsley, N.Y. 2003, p. 61.

25 *Compare e.g.* Joseph/ Schultz/ Castan, *International Covenant*, para. 1.76 A (p. 35).

26 *C.f.* Nowak, *CCPR Commentary*, Art. 6, paras. 3-6 (pp. 105-107); Heyns, in: Evans/ Murray (eds.), at 138; Carlson/ Gisvold, *International Covenant*, p. 61; Joseph/ Schultz/ Castan, *International Covenant*, para. 1.77 (p. 36).

27 *Compare e.g.* Carlson/ Gisvold, *International Covenant*, p. 61.

28 UN Comm'n H.R., *Summary or Arbitrary Executions: Report by the Special Rapporteur (S. Amos Wako)*, UN Doc. E/CN.4/1983/16 (January 31, 1983), para. 22; *see also* UN Comm'n H.R., Resolution 1982/7, UN Doc. E/CN.4/

referred to as "a sacred right in the sense that it was given to man by the creator himself."[29] The "supreme"[30] status of the right is emphasized by its positioning in the human rights treaties. The right to life is the first subjective right in the International Covenant on Civil and Political Rights and in the European Convention on Human Rights.

The focus of the following considerations will be on the question of permissible deprivation of life according to the standards of the conventions mentioned above. Questions concerning the beginning of life as well as those concerning the decisive factors defining the end of life can remain out of consideration.[31]

B. The International Covenant on Civil and Political Rights

The International Covenant on Civil and Political Rights (ICCPR) is part of the United Nations' Human Rights System. The text of the Covenant was adopted by the United Nations General Assembly in

---

RES/1982/7 (February 19, 1982); UN Comm'n H.R., Resolution 1984/43, UN Doc. E/CN.4/RES/1984/43 (March 9, 1984); *compare also* Hélène Tigroudja; Ioannis K. Panoussis, *La Cour interaméricaine des droits de l'homme: Analyse de la jurisprudence consultative et contentieuse*, Bruxelles 2003, para. 138 (p. 184).

29 Nsereko, in: Ramcharan (ed.), at 245.

30 H.R. Committee, CCPR General Comment No. 6, at 128 (para. 1); Nowak, *CCPR Commentary*, Art. 6, para. 1 (p. 104); Karl Josef Partsch, 'Die Rechte und Freiheiten der europäischen Menschenrechtskonvention', in: Karl August Bettermann/ Franz L. Neumann/ Hans Carl Nipperdey (eds.), *Die Grundrechte – Handbuch der Theorie und Praxis der Grundrechte*, Berlin 1966, Vol. 1.1, pp. 235-492, at 339; on the status of the General Comments *see* Eckart Klein, 'General Comments – Zu einem eher unbekannten Instrument des Menschenrechtsschutzes', in: Jörn Ipsen/ Edzard Schmidt-Jorzig, *Recht – Staat – Gemeinwohl: Festschrift für Dietrich Rauschning*, Köln 2001, pp. 301-311.

31 On these questions *compare e.g.* Nowak, *CCPR Commentary*, Art. 6, paras. 34-37 (pp. 122-125).

1966[32] and entered into force on March 23, 1976[33] after the required number of 35 ratifications was reached.[34]

The right to life is stipulated in Article 6 of the Covenant. Article 6 para. 1 reads:

> Every human being has the inherent right to life. This right shall be protected by law. No one shall be arbitrarily deprived of his life.[35]

The protection of the right to life is supplemented by the Second Optional Protocol, which aims at the abolition of the death penalty.[36]

The significance of the right to life is stressed first by the use of the term "inherent":[37] Article 6 is the only article of the Covenant referring

---

[32] UN GA Res. 2200 A (XXI), annex, December 16, 1966, *International Covenant on Economic, Social and Cultural Rights, International Covenant on Civil and Political Rights and Optional Protocol to the International Covenant on Civil and Political Rights*, UN GAOR, 21st Sess., Supp. No. 16, pp. 49-60, at 52-58, UN Doc. A/6316 (1966).

[33] For all provisions except those of Article 41 and on March 28, 1979 for the provisions of Article 41, after the 10th declaration was deposited, *see* 999 *UNTS* (1976), No. 14668, pp. 171-301 and 1057 *UNTS* (1977), p. 407 (corrigendum).

[34] *Compare* Article 49, para. 1 of the Covenant. To date, the Covenant has 156 State parties and 6 remaining Signatories, *see* UN High Commissioner for Human Rights, *Status of Ratifications of the Principal International Human Rights Treaties as of July 14, 2006*; on the history of the Covenant *see* Arthur Henry Robertson/ John G. Merrills, *Human Rights in the World: An Introduction to the Study of the International Protection of Human Rights*, 4th ed., Manchester 1996, pp. 30-34.

[35] The remaining part of Article 6 is devoted to the regulation and abolition of the death penalty in those states which maintain it. On the legislative history of the article *see* Bertrand G. Ramcharan, 'The Drafting History of Article 6 of the International Covenant on Civil and Political Rights', in: Bertrand G. Ramcharan (ed.), *The Right to Life in International Law*, Dordrecht 1985, pp. 42-56.

[36] Second Optional Protocol to the International Covenant on Civil and Political Rights, aiming at the Abolition of the Death Penalty, adopted by the UN General Assembly on December 15, 1989, Resolution 44/128, annex, UN GAOR 44th Sess., Supp. No. 49, pp. 207-208, UN Doc. A/RES/44/128 (1989), entry into force on July 11, 1991, reprinted in: 1642 *UNTS* (1991), No. 14668, pp. 414-471.

to the inherency of a right,[38] and thus revisits one of the fundamental statements of the Preamble.[39] Second, the term "*has* ... the right to life" is used instead of "shall have": Present tense is only used in two other articles of the Covenant, i.e. Articles 1 and 9.[40]

This wording can be traced back to a proposal *inter alia* by Colombia and Uruguay.[41] It was meant to express the natural law basis that the right to life had in the understanding of the majority of delegates in the 3rd Committee of the General Assembly.[42] Hence, the Committee concluded that the right to life must not be interpreted restrictively and is not only a negative right, but calls for positive measures by States to ensure it.[43] The importance of the right to life within the Covenant's framework can also be gauged by the fact that it is the first right that is subject to two general comments by the Human rights Commission.[44]

---

[37] *C.f.* Yoram Dinstein, 'The Right to Life, Physical Integrity, and Liberty', in: Louis Henkin (ed.), *The International Bill of Rights: The Covenant on Civil and Political Rights*, New York 1981, pp. 114-137, at 114-115.

[38] *See also* Bertrand G. Ramcharan, 'The Right to Life', in: 30 *Nether. Int'l L. Rev.* (1983), pp. 297-329, at 316.

[39] The Preamble in its second paragraph reads: "Recognizing that these rights derive from the inherent dignity of the human person, ...".

[40] Article 1 para. 1 reads: "All peoples have the right of self-determination. ..."; Article 9 para. 1 reads: "Everyone has the right to liberty and security of person. ...".

[41] UN General Assembly, Third Committee (Social, Humanitarian and Cultural), 12th Session (1957), UN. Doc. A/C.3/L.644. Other proposals that contained this phrase were those by Panama, UN. Doc. A/C.3/L.653, and by Belgium, Brazil, El Salvador, Mexico and Morocco, UN. Doc. A/C.3/L.654. *C.f.* Marc J. Bossuyt, *Guide to the "Travaux Préparatoires" of the International Covenant on Civil and Political Rights*, Dordrecht 1987, p. 119.

[42] Karl Doehring, 'Zum "Recht auf Leben" aus nationaler und internationaler Sicht', in: Rudolph Bernhardt/ Wilhelm Karl Geck/ Günther Jaenicke/ Helmut Steinberger (eds.), *Völkerrecht als Rechtsordnung – Internationale Gerichtsbarkeit – Menschenrechte: Festschrift für Hermann Mosler*, Berlin 1983, pp. 145-157, at 147; *see also* Nsereko, in: Ramcharan (ed.), at 245; William A. Schabas, *The Abolition of the Death Penalty in International Law*, 2nd ed., Cambridge 1997, p. 95.

[43] H.R. Committee, CCPR General Comment No. 6, at 129 (para. 5).

[44] Id. and H.R. Committee, CCPR General Comment No. 14, *Nuclear Weapons and the Right to Life (Article 6)*, 23rd Sess., November 9, 1984, re-

I. The Scope of Protection of Article 6

Concerning the question at hand, the most relevant part of the right to life is its defensive function.[45] This function corresponds to its vertical dimension,[46] the *status negativus* or *status libertatis*[47] of the right's holder in relation to the State, i.e. the State's negative obligation not to interfere with the right.[48] The extent of the article's scope of protection in this sphere depends on the concept of "arbitrary deprivation":

1. The Defensive Function (status negativus)

The part of Article 6 reading "No one shall be ... deprived of his life" would provide for absolute protection from any execution or murder.[49] The true scale of protection is based on the meaning of the word "arbitrarily". This term is also used in the American Convention and the Af-

---

printed in: Compilation of General Comments and General Recommendations adopted by Human Rights Treaty Bodies, U.N. Doc. HRI/GEN/1/Rev.7 (May 12, 2004), p. 139; on General Comment 14 *compare also* McGoldrick, *Human Rights Committee*, para. 8.13 (pp. 335-336).

45 German legal doctrine calls this an "Abwehrrecht" or *status negativus*. The term can be translated as "Rights of Defence" as opposed to rights of benefits ("Leistungsrechte") or *status positivus*, *see* Bernd Holznagel, 'Function and Interpretation of Fundamental Rights', in: Albrecht Weber (ed.), *Fundamental Rights in Europe and North America*, The Hague 2002, pp. GER 81-94, at 81.

46 Cordula Dröge, *Positive Verpflichtungen der Staaten in der Europäischen Menschenrechtskonvention*, Berlin 2003, p. 379.

47 Georg Jellinek, *System der subjektiven öffentlichen Rechte*, 2nd ed., Tübingen 1905, pp. 94-114.

48 The more controversial economic and social component that may or may not be part of Article 6 of the Covenant, i.e. a right to food and medical care etc. has no relevance for the examination. On this Question compare e.g. Vernon Van Dyke, *Human Rights, the United States, and World Community*, New York 1970, pp. 52-59; Carlson/ Gisvold, *International Covenant*, p. 69.

49 *Compare e.g.* Dyke, *Human Rights*, pp. 9-10; Dinstein, in: Henkin (ed.), at 115.

rican Charter,[50] as well as in the Universal Declaration of Human Rights.[51]

a) "Arbitrary Deprivation" as "Unlawful Deprivation" of Life

"[A]rbitrariness and lawlessness are twin brothers",[52] but are these terms also interchangeable? The ordinary meaning of "arbitrarily" and "arbitrairement"[53] in the likewise authentic French text,[54] comprises a legal connotation. It can mean *inter alia* bound by no law,[55] illegal,[56] irregular,[57] lawless,[58] unconstitutionally,[59] unjust[60] or unjustified.[61] This forms the basis for one possible interpretation of the term "arbitrarily" as used in Article 6 of the Covenant: It can be interpreted as "unlaw-

---

50 *See infra*, Part One, Chapters C) and D).

51 Articles 9, 12, 15, and 17 Universal Declaration of Human Rights. For the text of these Articles *see infra*, Part One, Chapter B I. 1. b) (3).

52 Nsereko, in: Ramcharan (ed.), at 276.

53 Article 6, para. 1 ICCPR reads: "Le droit à la vie est inhérent à la personne humaine. Ce droit doit être protégé par la loi. Nul ne peut être arbitrairement privé de la vie."; The roots of the English words "arbitrary" and "arbitrarily" can possibly be traced back to the French words "arbitraire" and "arbitrairement" respectively, *see* Charles Talbut Onions; G. W. S. Friedrichsen, *The Oxford Dictionary of English Etymology*, Oxford 1966, p. 47.

54 *See* Article 53, para. 1 ICCPR. It is assumed that the terms used in the authentic texts have the same meaning.

55 Christian Gerritzen, *Synonyms: Sinnverwandte Ausdrücke der englischen Sprache*, Eltville am Rhein 1988, p. 30.

56 Paul Robert, *Dictionnaire alphabétique et analogique de la langue française: les mots et les associations d'idées*, Casablanca 1951, p. 215.

57 Robert, *Dictionnaire alphabétique*, p. 215 ("irrégulier").

58 Elizabeth MacLaren Kirkpatrick, *Roget's Thesaurus*, London 1998, para. 954 (p. 653).

59 John Andrew Simpson/ Edmund S. C. Weiner/ James Augustus Henry Murry, *The Oxford English Dictionary*, Vol. 1, 2nd ed., Oxford 1989, p. 602.

60 Robert, *Dictionnaire alphabétique*, p. 215 ("injuste").

61 Henri Bertaud du Chazaud, *Dictionnaire des synonymes*, Paris 1983, p. 41; Henri Bénac, *Dictionnaire des synonymes: Conforme au dictionnaire de l'Académie Française*, Paris 1956, p. 55 ("injustifié").

ful", "illegal"[62] or "without due process of law".[63] Thus, Article 6 is understood as encompassing the obligation "to prevent unlawful deprivations of the right to life" by State agents.[64] According to this approach, any action sanctioned by statute would qualify as arbitrary.[65] The same holds true for deaths on the grounds of, or in accordance with procedures other than those established by law.[66]

This notion of the term "arbitrary" would leave room for the narrow interpretation that the deprivation of a life permitted by any national law, irrespective of that law's content, could not qualify as arbitrary. However, such a limited understanding finds little contextual support in the Covenant. The words "arbitrary" and "arbitrarily" are not only used in Article 6 but in three further articles of the Covenant: Article 9,[67] Article 12[68] and Article 17.[69]

Article 12 para. 4 is phrased very similarly to Article 6 and gives no further definition to the meaning of "arbitrary". Concerning another right, Article 12 para. 3 prohibits "restrictions except those which are provided by law".[70] This formulation seems to have a different meaning from "arbitrarily", which is used in para. 4 of the same article.

---

62 *Compare e.g.* Paul Sieghart, *The International Law of Human Rights*, Oxford 1983, para. 8.0.3 (p. 88), referring to "prescribed by law".

63 Nowak, *CCPR Commentary*, Art. 6, para. 13 (p. 110); Ramcharan, 30 *Nether. Int'l L. Rev.* (1983), at 317; *Compare also* Bossuyt, *Travaux Préparatoires*, pp. 122.

64 Ramcharan, in: Ramcharan (ed.), at 17.

65 *Id.*

66 *Id.*, at 20.

67 Article 9 of the Covenant reads in its relevant part: "No one shall be subjected to arbitrary arrest or detention. No one shall be deprived of his liberty except on such grounds and in accordance with such procedure as are established by law."

68 Article 12 para. 4 of the Covenant reads: "No one shall be arbitrarily deprived of the rights to enter his own country."

69 Article 17 of the Covenant reads: "1. No one shall be subjected to arbitrary or unlawful interference with his privacy, family, home or correspondence, nor to unlawful attacks on his honour and reputation."

70 Article 12 para. 3 of the Covenant reads: "The above-mentioned rights shall not be subject to any restrictions except those which are provided by law, are necessary to protect national security, public order (ordre public), public

Article 9 at first sight might support the interpretation that "arbitrary" means "unlawful". The declaration that no one shall be subjected to arbitrary arrest or detention is supplemented by the illustration that "[n]o one shall be deprived of his liberty except on such grounds and in accordance with such procedure as are established by law". This statement clarifies that in the context of Article 9, "arbitrary" at least comprises "unlawful". However, it does not exclude the possibility that "arbitrary" is broader in its meaning than "unlawful".

The assumption that arbitrariness and unlawfulness are concepts that are not congruent finds further support in Article 17 of the Covenant. According to Article 17, no one shall be subjected to "arbitrary *or* unlawful interference" (my emphasis) with the rights protected in that article. In Article 17, both terms are used as alternatives, while they are not used as exclusive alternatives in Article 9.

Hence, in the Covenant, the word "arbitrary" is used as encompassing "unlawful", but also as a broader concept than "unlawful" that has to be further defined. It furthermore has to be kept in mind that the test of arbitrariness in relation to the right to life may be stricter than in the context of other rights including the term "arbitrary", as a consequence of the right's inherency and the primordial nature of the value protected.[71]

b) "Arbitrary Deprivation" as a Broader Concept than "Unlawful Deprivation" of Life

As shown above, the term "arbitrary" in the Covenant encompasses "unlawful" but still leaves room for a more comprehensive interpretation:

(1) Text and Context

Beside the legal connotation referred to earlier, the ordinary meaning of "arbitrary" has four aspects which are partly interrelated:

---

health or morals or the rights and freedoms of others, and are consistent with the other rights recognized in the present Covenant." *See also* Article 18 para. 3, Article 19 para. 3 and Article 22 para. 2.

71 Ramcharan, in: Ramcharan (ed.), at 19.

First, concerning an arbitrary action, the position of the person acting is absolute,[72] authoritarian,[73] autocratic[74] or dictatorial.[75]

Second, this enables that person to act in a manner that is capricious,[76] despotic,[77] fanciful,[78] high-handed,[79] imperious,[80] insolent,[81] irresponsible,[82] tyrannical,[83] unthinking[84] or wilful.[85] "Despotical power is an absolute, arbitrary power one man has over another, to take away his life, whenever he pleases."[86]

---

72 Gerritzen, *Synonyms*, p. 30; Simpson *et al.*, *Oxford Dictionary*, p. 602; Bertaud du Chazaud, *Synonymes*, p. 41; Bénac, *Synonymes*, p. 55.

73 Kirkpatrick, *Roget's Thesaurus*, para. 735 (p. 493).

74 Gerritzen, *Synonyms*, p. 30; Marc McCutcheon, *Roget's Superthesaurus*, 3rd ed., Cincinnati, Ohio 2003, p. 39; *compare also* Laurence Urdang (ed.), *Longman Synonym Dictionary*, Harlow 1986.

75 Charlton Grant Laird/ Michael Agnes, *Webster's New World Roget's A-Z Thesaurus*, 4th ed., New York 1999, p. 40; Gerritzen, *Synonyms*, p. 30; McCutcheon, *Superthesaurus*, p. 39.

76 Barbara Ann Kipfer/ Robert L. Chapman, *Roget's International Thesaurus*, 6th ed., New York 2001, para. 364.05; Kirkpatrick, *Roget's Thesaurus*, para. 604 (p. 385); Laird/ Agnes, *Webster's Thesaurus*, p. 40; Gerritzen, *Synonyms*, p. 30; Simpson *et al.*, *Oxford Dictionary*, p. 602; McCutcheon, *Superthesaurus*, p. 39.

77 Laird/ Agnes, *Webster's Thesaurus*, p. 40; Gerritzen, *Synonyms*, p. 30; Simpson *et al.*, *Oxford Dictionary*, p. 602; *compare also* Robert, *Dictionnaire alphabétique*, p. 215.

78 Gerritzen, *Synonyms*, p. 30; McCutcheon, *Superthesaurus*, p. 39.

79 Urdang (ed.), *Synonym Dictionary*.

80 Kipfer/ Chapman, *International Thesaurus*, para. 417.16; Laird/ Agnes, *Webster's Thesaurus*, p. 40; Gerritzen, *Synonyms*, p. 30.

81 Kirkpatrick, *Roget's Thesaurus*, para. 878 (p. 596).

82 Gerritzen, *Synonyms*, p. 30.

83 Laird/ Agnes, *Webster's Thesaurus*, p. 40; Gerritzen, *Synonyms*, p. 30; Simpson *et al.*, *Oxford Dictionary*, p. 602.; *see also* Robert, *Dictionnaire alphabétique*, p. 215.

84 Kipfer/ Chapman, *International Thesaurus*, para. 365.10.

85 Kirkpatrick, *Roget's Thesaurus*, para. 602 (p. 384); Gerritzen, *Synonyms*, p. 30.

86 John Locke, *Two Treatise of Government*, London 1698, Vol. 2, para. 172.

Third, the arbitrary action itself lacks an objective basis and predictability; it is discretionary,[87] illogical,[88] irrational,[89] personal,[90] random,[91] summary,[92] unpredictable,[93] unreasonable,[94] unrelated,[95] unscientific,[96] varying[97] or volitional.[98]

Fourth, due to the dependence of the act upon the actor's will, pleasure[99] or discretion,[100] there is no control or instance to control the act. It is unconditional,[101] unlimited, unrestrained[102] or subject to uncontrolled power.[103]

In short, aspects of arbitrariness are the unrestrained exercise of will[104] based on personal opinion or impulse, subject to personal whims or prejudices. This entails the lack of any reason or system and of any adequate determining rule or principle.[105]

---

87 Laird/ Agnes, *Webster's Thesaurus*, p. 40; McCutcheon, *Superthesaurus*, p. 39.

88 Kirkpatrick, *Roget's Thesaurus*, para. 477 (p. 292).

89 Laird/ Agnes, *Webster's Thesaurus*, p. 40.

90 McCutcheon, *Superthesaurus*, p. 39.

91 Laird/ Agnes, *Webster's Thesaurus*, p. 40; McCutcheon, *Superthesaurus*, p. 39.

92 Urdang (ed.), *Synonym Dictionary*.

93 Laird/ Agnes, *Webster's Thesaurus*, p. 40.

94 *Id.*

95 Kirkpatrick, *Roget's Thesaurus*, para. 10 (p. 6).

96 McCutcheon, *Superthesaurus*, p. 39.

97 Simpson *et al.*, *Oxford Dictionary*, p. 602.

98 Kirkpatrick, *Roget's Thesaurus*, para. 595 (p. 378).

99 Simpson *et al.*, *Oxford Dictionary*, p. 602.

100 Onions/ Friedrichsen, *English Etymology*, p. 47.

101 Kirkpatrick, *Roget's Thesaurus*, para. 744 (p. 501).

102 Gerritzen, *Synonyms*, p. 30.

103 Onions/ Friedrichsen, *English Etymology*, p. 47; Simpson *et al.*, *Oxford Dictionary*, p. 602.

104 Simpson *et al.*, *Oxford Dictionary*, p. 602; Laird/ Agnes, *Webster's Thesaurus*, p. 40.

105 Laird/ Agnes, *Webster's Thesaurus*, p. 40; Gerritzen, *Synonyms*, p. 30.

The lack of an objective basis and predictability corresponds with the connotation "illegal" mentioned above, and could be resolved easily by any national law. It has no substantial requirements regarding that law's content. The same holds true for the absence of an instance of control; such an instance is futile if the standards applied by it lack substance.

But "arbitrary" does not only correspond to the absence of objective rules, it also comprises the deliberate improper application of existing rules:[106] Even if an objective basis, i.e. a legal regulation, exists, the fact that an decision is reached according to personal opinion or impulse and not in application of objective criteria constitutes an abuse of discretion and is arbitrary none the less. However, these requirements for a decision to be in accordance with certain rules remain a mere "technicality" without adding any substantial definition to the term "arbitrary".

Thus, the literal meaning of the word "arbitrary" cannot encompass just "illegal" or "in accordance with national law". It must have a connotation that refers to superior standards.[107]

(2) Object and Purpose

The object and purpose of the Covenant also demands a substantial protection with regard to international standards:[108] The Preamble in its fourth paragraph refers to "universal respect for, and observance of, human rights and freedoms" as the duty agreed on by the Member States to the United Nations Charter.[109] Such a universal aim cannot be reached if the substance of single provisions depends on national legislation. This would not establish international standards and would run

---

106 *See e.g.* Ramcharan, in: Ramcharan (ed.), at 20.

107 Thomas Desch, 'The Concept and Dimensions of the Right to Life (as defined in International Standards and in International Comparative Jurisprudence)', in: 36 *ÖZöRV* (1985), pp. 77-118, at 104-105.

108 *Compare e.g.* H.R. Committee, CCPR General Comment No. 16, *The Right to Respect of Privacy, Family, Home and Correspondence, and Protection of Honour and Reputation (Article 17)*, 32nd Sess., April 8, 1988, reprinted in: Compilation of General Comments and General Recommendations adopted by Human Rights Treaty Bodies, U.N. Doc. HRI/GEN/1/Rev.7 (May 12, 2004), pp. 142-144, at 142 (para. 4).

109 Nowak, *CCPR Commentary*, Preamble, para. 6 (p. 3).

counter to the principle that human rights provisions are interpreted autonomously, i.e. independently from the respective national understanding by a party to a human rights treaty.[110]

A first step to interpreting the term "arbitrary" in this manner was taken by the Human Rights Committee.[111] Even though its decisions are not binding, the entire case law on individual communications and the General Comments by the Human Rights Committee are regarded as authoritative interpretation of the Covenant.[112] The Committee clarified in its first General Comment on the right to life that "the law must strictly control and limit the circumstances in which a person may be deprived of his life by such authorities" of a State.[113] Thus, acts pursuant to a law that does not satisfy these requirements are arbitrary.[114] This approach was affirmed in *Maria Fanny Suarez De Guerrero*. The Committee came to the conclusion that despite the legal defence under domestic law that had been adjudged constitutional by the Colombian Supreme Court, the killing in question violated Article 6.[115]

---

[110] *Compare supra*, Part One, Chapter A) I.

[111] The Human Rights Committee was established to review and consider complaints according to the optional protocol. It is not a United Nations body *per se*, rather it is an independent expert committee. While the Committee has no power to "enforce" the Covenant, it has an essential role in further defining human rights protections and holding states accountable for violations of the Covenant. *Compare* Optional Protocol to the International Covenant on Civil and Political Rights, adopted by the UN General Assembly on December 16, 1966, Resolution 2200 A (XXI), annex, UN GAOR, 21st Sess., Supp. No. 16, pp. 49-60, at 59-60, UN Doc. A/6316 (1966), entry into force on March 23, 1976, 999 *UNTS* (1976), No. 14668, pp. 302-346; *see also* Carlson/ Gisvold, *International Covenant*, pp. 3-5.

[112] Nowak, *CCPR Commentary*, Introduction, para. 21 (p. XXIV); Carlson/ Gisvold, *International Covenant*, p. 9.

[113] H.R. Committee, CCPR General Comment No. 6, at 128-129 (para. 3); *see also* H.R. Committee, *Maria Fanny Suárez de Guerrero v. Colombia ("Camargo Case")*, Communication No. 45/1979, UN Doc. CCPR/C/15/D/ 45/1979 (March 31, 1982), at para. 13.1. The case was submitted by *Pedro Pablo Camargo* and is thus sometimes referred to as the "Camargo Case".

[114] *See e.g.* Joseph/ Schultz/ Castan, *International Covenant*, para. 8.04 (p. 165); Ramcharan, 30 *Nether. Int'l L. Rev.* (1983), at 317.

[115] H.R. Committee, *Maria Fanny Suárez de Guerrero ("Camargo Case")*, at paras. 13.2-13.3.

This principle was confirmed in relation to Article 17 of the Covenant; here, the term "arbitrary interference" has been interpreted by the Human Rights Committee as possibly extending "to interference provided for under the law. The introduction of the concept of arbitrariness is intended to guarantee that even interference provided for by law should be in accordance with the provisions, aims and objectives of the Covenant and should be, in any event, reasonable in the particular circumstances."[116]

(3) Preparatory Work

"Arbitrarily" was one of the most excessively debated terms in the drafting process of the Covenant.[117] The debates show that the word "arbitrary was chosen with the intention to provide the highest possible level of protection and to confine permissible deprivations to the narrowest of limits."[118] Several indications can be found in the debates that a term covering more than mere "illegality" was searched for.[119]

The same problem had already been considered in connection with the Universal Declaration of Human Rights,[120] which served as an archetype for the Covenant: In the Universal Declaration, the word "arbi-

---

[116] H.R. Committee, CCPR General Comment No. 16, at 142 (para. 4).

[117] *Compare* the proposals and discussions reprinted in Bossuyt, *Travaux Préparatoires*, pp. 121-124; *see also* Ramcharan, 30 *Nether. Int'l L. Rev.* (1983), at 316; Laurent Marcoux Jr., 'Protection From Arbitrary Arrest and Detention Under International Law', in: 5 *B.C. Int'l & Comp. L. Rev.* (1982), pp. 345-376.

[118] Ramcharan, 30 *Nether. Int'l L. Rev.* (1983), at 316; *see also* Ramcharan, in: Ramcharan (ed.), at 19; David Weissbrodt, 'Protecting the Right to Life: International Measures against Arbitrary or Summary Killings by Governments', in: Bertrand G. Ramcharan (ed.), *The Right to Life in International Law*, Dordrecht 1985, pp. 297-314, at 298.

[119] *Compare* the statements by delegates given in the Third Committee's 5th, 9th and 12th Session (1950, 1954 and 1957 respectively), reprinted in Bossuyt, *Travaux Préparatoires*, pp. 123-124.

[120] UN GA Res. 217 (III) A (December 10, 1948), *International Bill of Human Rights – Universal Declaration of Human Rights*, UN GAOR, 3rd Sess., Part 1, UN Doc. A/810 (1948), pp. 71-77. There is no difficulty in employing the preparatory work of the Universal Declaration in interpreting "arbitrary" as used in the Covenant because the main drafters of both texts were generally the same, *see* Desch, 36 *ÖZöRV* (1985), at 106.

trary" is used in four Articles, i.e. in Article 9,[121] Article 12,[122] Article 15[123] and Article 17.[124] It was first introduced to Article 9 in an attempt to protect individuals against unjust laws. Earlier versions had excluded cases "established by pre-existing law" from the prohibition of detention. The term "arbitrary" was chosen because "[r]ights should not derive from law, but law from rights." The drafting of Article 9 of the Universal Declaration shows that protection from illegal as well as unjust arrest was desired.[125] Thus, regarding Article 9 of the Universal Declaration, actions that are legal under national laws can still be arbitrary, if they violate international law.

In Article 12 of the Universal Declaration the word "unreasonable" was replaced by "arbitrary", because there was a consensus within the third Committee that the word "arbitrary" had a broader meaning than "illegal" and included the concept of "unreasonableness".[126] Concerning Article 17 of the Universal Declaration, ICJ Judge *Levi Carneiro* interpreted the term "arbitrarily" in a way that covers "violations of the principles of international law".[127]

---

[121] Article 9 of the Universal Declaration reads: "No one shall be subjected to arbitrary arrest, detention or exile."

[122] Article 12 of the Universal Declaration reads: "No one shall be subjected to arbitrary interference with his privacy, family, home or correspondence, nor to attacks upon his honour and reputation. Everyone has the right to the protection of the law against such interference or attacks."

[123] Article 15 of the Universal Declaration reads: "1. Everyone has the right to a nationality. 2. No one shall be arbitrarily deprived of his nationality nor denied the right to change his nationality."

[124] Article 17 of the Universal Declaration reads: "1. Everyone has the right to own property alone as well as in association with others. 2. No one shall be arbitrarily deprived of his property."

[125] Parvez Hassan, 'The Word "Arbitrary" As Used in the Universal Declaration of Human Rights: "Illegal" or "Unjust"?', in: 10 *Harv. Int'l L.J.* (1969), pp. 225-262, at 236-242; David Weissbrodt/ Mattias Hallendorff, 'Travaux Préparatoires of the Fair Trial Provisions: Articles 8 to 11of the Universal Declaration of Human Rights', in: 21 *Hum. Rts. Q.* (1999), pp. 1061-1096, at 1083-1089, both with further references.

[126] Hassan, 10 *Harv. Int'l L.J.* (1969), at 243-246 with further references.

[127] ICJ, *Anglo-Iranian Oil Co., United Kingdom v. Iran (Preliminary Objections)*, Judgment of July 22, 1952, I.C.J. Reports 1952, pp. 93-171, Dissenting Opinion of Judge Levi Carneiro, pp. 151-171, at 166-168 (paras. 19-20).

However, beside the fact that "arbitrary" in the Universal Declaration, as well as in the Covenant, refers to superordinate, international standards rather than national laws, the *travaux préparatoires* of the Covenant leave a vast flexibility to interpret the term[128] and give little guidance to achieve results beyond those developed above.

c) Guiding Principles

The general conclusions that can be drawn from the interpretation at this point are the following:

Whether the deprivation of a life is arbitrary or not must be determined by reference to international human rights norms and is not subject to national legislation.[129] Conversely, the deprivation of a life that does not violate international human rights standards *per se* but is in violation of national legislation, is arbitrary none the less.

Even though the term "arbitrarily" is used elsewhere in the Covenant and in other international instruments, the test of arbitrariness in relation to the right to life may be more stringent than in the context of other rights, as a consequence of the right's inherency and the primordial nature of the value protected.[130]

The deprivation of a life can be arbitrary irrespective of whether it is enforced with direct intention, with *dolus eventualis* or negligently.[131]

However, the term "arbitrarily" aims at the specific circumstances of an individual case and their legality and predictability[132] as well as their reasonableness or proportionality, making it difficult to comprehend the term *in abstracto*.[133]

---

[128] McGoldrick, *Human Rights Committee*, para. 8.21 (p. 342).

[129] *Compare supra*, Part One, Chapter A) I.; *see also* Ramcharan, 30 *Nether. Int'l L. Rev.* (1983), at 316.

[130] *See e.g.* Ramcharan, in: Ramcharan (ed.), at 19.

[131] Walter Gollwitzer, *Menschenrechte im Strafverfahren – MRK und IPBPR*, Berlin 2005, Art. 2 MRK/Art. 6 IPBPR, para. 8 (p. 157); Nowak, *CCPR Commentary*, Art. 6, para. 12 (footnote 35).

[132] *Compare* the cases enumerated by Nowak, *CCPR Commentary*, Art. 6, para. 15.

[133] Nowak, *CCPR Commentary*, Art. 6, para. 14 (p. 111).

Nsereko tries to capture these aspects in his definition:

> Deprivation of life would be arbitrary if: (a) it is made without due regard to the rules of natural justice or the due process of law; or (b) it is made in a manner contrary to the law; or (c) it is made in pursuance of a law which is despotic, tyrannical and in conflict with international human rights standards or international humanitarian law.[134]

d) Specific Examples

Others are of the opinion that the term "arbitrary" has to be defined on a case by case basis[135] and refer to examples that are regarded as being arbitrary deprivations of life:[136]

(1) Genocide, Mass Killings and Other Acts of Mass Violence

Killings which qualify as genocide are arbitrary deprivations of life under the Covenant,[137] even though the definition of genocide given in the Genocide Convention[138] and the corresponding rule of customary[139] law does not necessarily comprise the actual death of human be-

---

[134] Nsereko, in: Ramcharan (ed.), at 248.

[135] Gollwitzer, *Menschenrechte*, Art. 2 MRK/Art. 6 IPBPR, para. 8 (p. 157).

[136] Ramcharan, in: Ramcharan (ed.), at 19-20.

[137] H.R. Committee, CCPR General Comment No. 6, at 128 (para. 2); Nowak, *CCPR Commentary*, Art. 6, para. 14 (p. 111); Ramcharan, 30 *Nether. Int'l L. Rev.* (1983), at 317. On history and examples *compare* Leo Kuper, 'Genocide and Mass Killings: Illusions and Reality', in: Bertrand G. Ramcharan (ed.), *The Right to Life in International Law*, Dordrecht 1985, pp. 114-119.

[138] Convention on the Prevention and Punishment of the Crime of Genocide, adopted by the UN General Assembly on December 9, 1948, Resolution 260 (III) A, annex, UN GAOR, 3rd Sess., Part 1, U.N. Doc. A/810 (1948), pp. 174-177, entry into force on January 12, 1951, 78 *UNTS* (1951), No. 1021, pp. 277-323.

[139] *See e.g.* ICJ, *Legality of the Threat or Use of Nuclear Weapons*, Advisory Opinion of July 8, 1996, I.C.J. Reports 1996, pp. 225-593, at 240 (para. 26); *c.f.* Ross Garland, 'The international Court of Justice and Human Rights in the 1990s – linking Peace and Justice through the Right to Life', in: Sienho Yee/

ings. The *actus reus* may also be: Imposing measures intended to prevent birth within a group as well as forcibly transferring children of the group to another group.[140] However, it is clear that killings which qualify as genocide are arbitrary deprivations of life.[141] This is the case if the *actus reus* was committed with the "intent to destroy, in whole or in part, a national, ethnical, racial or religious group".[142]

The same holds true for mass killings that correspond to the *actus reus* of genocide, but lack the specific *mens rea*, the genocidal intent,[143] and for deaths resulting from mass violence. Due to their random and unrestrained character and their lack of any objective basis or predictability, such killings also constitute arbitrary deprivations of life under the Covenant.[144]

(2) Killings that Contradict International Humanitarian Law

Killings that contradict international humanitarian law and thus may, *inter alia*, constitute crimes against humanity or war crimes are arbitrary deprivations of life under the Covenant.[145] States have been criticized by the Human Rights Committee for their use of illegal means of combat or disproportionate force in armed conflicts.[146] The standards

---

Wang Tieya (eds.), *International Law in the Post-Cold War World: Essays in Memory of Li Haopei*, London 2001, pp. 398-408, at 406-407.

140 *Compare e.g.* Article II of the Genocide Convention; Antonio Cassese, *International Law*, 2nd ed., Oxford 2005, p. 444.

141 H.R. Committee, CCPR General Comment No. 6, at 128 (para. 2).

142 *Compare e.g.* Article II of the Genocide Convention; William A. Schabas, 'Developments in the Law of Genocide', in: 5 *Yb. Int'l Hum. L.* (2002), pp. 131-165, at 147-150; Cassese, *International Law*, p. 444.

143 ICTY, *Prosecutor v. Jelisić*, Case No. IT-95-10-T, Judgment of December 14, 1999, at para. 108, holding that *Jelisić* "killed arbitrarily rather than with the clear intention to destroy a group".

144 *See e.g.* Ramcharan, 30 *Nether. Int'l L. Rev.* (1983), at 317; *compare also* H.R. Committee, CCPR General Comment No. 6, at 128 (para. 2).

145 Ramcharan, 30 *Nether. Int'l L. Rev.* (1983), at 317; Nowak, *CCPR Commentary*, Art. 6, para. 9.

146 *See e.g.* H.R. Committee, *Concluding Observations on the Russian Federation*, UN Doc. CCPR/C/79/Add.54 (July 26, 1995), para. 28; H.R. Commit-

set by the corresponding humanitarian law and their applicability will be examined *infra*.[147] However, this relation between the standards of the Covenant itself and international humanitarian law already gives a glimpse of the *lex specialis* nature of the humanitarian law concerning the protection of life in relation to the corresponding human rights rules.[148]

(3) Deaths Resulting from Acts of Aggression

Deaths resulting from acts of aggression or other wars contrary to the UN Charter are regarded as arbitrary deprivations of life by some authors.[149]

However, such a broad approach mixes aspects of *jus ad bellum* with those of *jus in bello*. From an international humanitarian law point of view, the overall legal nature of an armed conflict has no consequence concerning the standards applicable in that conflict.[150]

This strict distinction should not be circumvented by recourse to human rights standards. These standards can rather be allocated to *jus in bello*:

> The test of what is an arbitrary deprivation of life, however, then falls to be determined by the applicable *lex specialis*, namely, the law

---

tee, *Concluding Observations on the Federal Republic of Yugoslavia (Serbia and Montenegro)*, UN Doc. CCPR/C/79/Add.16 (December 28, 1992), paras. 5-7.

147 *Compare infra*, Part Two.

148 *Compare infra*, Part Four, Chapters C) and D); *see generally* Hans-Joachim Heintze, 'On the Relationship between Human Rights Law Protection and International Humanitarian Law', in: 86 *Int'l Rev. Red Cross* (2004), No 856, pp. 789-814, at 796-798.

149 Ramcharan, 30 *Nether. Int'l L. Rev.* (1983), at 317; *see also* Karima Bennoune, 'Toward a Human Rights Approach to Armed Conflict: Iraq 2003', 11 *U.C. Davis J. Int'l L. & Pol'y* (2004), pp. 171-228, at 215; *but see* Dinstein, in: Henkin (ed.), at p. 120; Hans-Joachim Heintze, 'Las Palmeras v. Bamaca-Velasquez und Bakovic v. Loizidou? Widersprüchliche Entscheidungen zum Menschenrechtsschutz in bewaffneten Konflikten', in: 18 *HuV-I* (2005), pp. 177-182, at 182.

150 For example, whether a target is a legitimate one depends on the same standards for all parties to a conflict, irrespectively of their responsibility for the conflict as such, *compare infra*, Part Four, Chapters C) and D).

applicable in armed conflict which is designed to regulate the conduct of hostilities.[151]

If all deaths resulting from an act of aggression would by definition constitute arbitrary deprivations of life, the humanitarian law standards applicable to that conflict would be irrelevant for the aggressor, as any death caused by this party to the conflict would *per se* be illegal, irrespective of whether the victims were combatants or civilians. This would not only contradict the principle of distinction,[152] it might even lead to a "no quarter" policy.[153]

While the Human Rights Committee has confirmed that States are obliged to minimize armed conflicts,[154] it has never criticized a specific State in a comment for participating in an armed conflict.[155] States have only been criticized for their use of illegal means of combat or disproportionate use of force *in* an armed conflict.[156]

If analysed carefully, this distinction corresponds the system of the prohibition of aggression as well as the prohibition of the use of force. Even though these prohibitions shall "save succeeding generations from the scourge of war", they exist in relation to other States and do not confer rights on individuals. Their scope of protection is not the life of single human beings. This can be well established if the exceptions to the prohibition to use force are taken into account: Neither self-defence nor collective security aim at the protection of single individuals and their lives. Life is taken in unlawful wars of aggression as well as in lawful wars of self-defence.[157] The only exception of the prohibition to use

---

[151] ICJ, *Legality of the Threat or Use of Nuclear Weapons*, Advisory Opinion of July 8, 1996, I.C.J. Reports 1996, pp. 225-593, at 240 (para. 25).

[152] *Compare infra*, Part Two, Chapter B) IV.

[153] *C.f.* Ingrid Detter de Lupis Frankopan, *The Law of War*, 2nd ed., Cambridge 2000, p. 297; Jean-Marie Henckaerts/ Louise Doswald-Beck (eds.), *Humanitarian Law*, Vol. 1, Rules, Cambridge 2005, pp. 161-163 (Rule 46).

[154] H.R. Committee, CCPR General Comment No. 6, at 128 (para. 2).

[155] Joseph/ Schultz/ Castan, *International Covenant*, para. 8.50 (p. 187).

[156] *See e.g.* H.R. Committee, *Concluding Observations on the Russian Federation*, UN Doc. CCPR/C/79/Add.54 (July 26, 1995), para. 28; H.R. Committee, *Concluding Observations on the Federal Republic of Yugoslavia (Serbia and Montenegro)*, UN Doc. CCPR/C/79/Add.16 (December 28, 1992), paras. 5-7.

[157] Dinstein, in: Henkin (ed.), at 120.

force that aims at the protection of the individual's life would be the humanitarian intervention. Humanitarian intervention is, however, far from being a recognised exception from the prohibition of the use of force.[158]

In consequence, the loss of life as the result of an act of aggression is not automatically an arbitrary deprivation of life. From the moment of an act of aggression onwards, international humanitarian law is applicable[159] and thus killings that contradict humanitarian law are considered arbitrary under the Covenant.[160]

(4) Deaths Resulting from Torture or Other Ill-Treatment

Deaths resulting from torture or other ill-treatment, especially in prison or detention, constitute arbitrary deprivations of life.[161] Such deaths are the result *per se* of illegal treatment of persons and can thus never be lawful, particularly as States bear a higher responsibility for the life of

---

[158] *See* Georg Nolte, 'Kosovo und Konstitutionalisierung: Zur humanitären Intervention der NATO-Staaten', in: 56 *ZaöRV* (1999), pp. 941-960, at 945-955; *compare also* Petr Valek, 'Is Unilateral Humanitarian Intervention Compatible with the U.N. Charter?', in: 26 *Mich. J. Int'l L.* (2005), pp. 1223-1256, at 1229-1231 and 1255 ("illegal, but legitimate"); Jim Whitman, 'Humanitarian Intervention in an Era of Pre-emptive Self-Defence', in: 36 *Security Dialogue* (2005), pp. 259-274; Ralph Zacklin, 'Beyond Kosovo: The United Nations and Humanitarian Intervention', in: Lal Chand Vohrah *et al.* (eds.), *Man's Inhumanity to Man – Essays on International Law in Honour of Antonio Cassese*, The Hague 2003, pp. 935-951, at 948-951, who proposes six pre-conditions for a humanitarian intervention.

[159] The exact relationship of human rights law and international humanitarian law will be dealt with *infra*, Part Four.

[160] *Compare supra*, Part One, Chapter B) I. 1. d) (2); *see also* H.R. Committee, CCPR General Comment No. 6, at 128 (para. 2); Ramcharan, 30 *Nether. Int'l L. Rev.* (1983), at p. 317; Nowak, *CCPR Commentary*, Art. 6, para. 9.

[161] *See e.g.* UN Comm'n H.R., *Extrajudicial, Summary or Arbitrary Executions: Report of the Special Rapporteur Philip Alston*, UN Doc. E/CN.4/2005/7 (December 22, 2004), para. 19 (p. 8); Nowak, *CCPR Commentary*, Art. 6, para. 14 (p. 111); Ramcharan, 30 *Nether. Int'l L. Rev.* (1983), at 317.

persons in detention due to the dependency characterizing the relation of these persons to the State.[162]

(5) Enforced or Involuntary Disappearances

The same holds true for enforced or involuntary disappearances:[163] In such cases the dependency of the victim is even greater, as he or she is not in official custody but detained without any contact with the outside. Since the responsibility of State agents for killings taking place under such circumstances is extremely difficult to prove, the emphasis is on the duty to protect. A State violates its duty to protect under Article 6 of the Covenant if it does not take reasonable measures to hinder involuntary disappearances or fails to investigate the responsible persons effectively.[164]

(6) Deaths Resulting from Excessive Use of Force by Law-Enforcement Personnel

Deaths resulting from excessive use of force by law-enforcement personnel also constitute arbitrary deprivations of life under the Covenant.[165] Actions of law-enforcement agents which result in death have to be proportionate to the requirement of law enforcement in the circumstances of the case in order to be non-arbitrary.[166] "If a law enforcement agent uses greater force than is necessary to achieve a legitimate objective and a person is killed that would amount to an 'arbitrary

---

[162] *See e.g.* Gollwitzer, *Menschenrechte*, Art. 2 MRK/Art. 6 IPBPR, para. 12 (p. 161).

[163] Ramcharan, 30 *Nether. Int'l L. Rev.* (1983), at 317.

[164] Gollwitzer, *Menschenrechte*, Art. 2 MRK/Art. 6 IPBPR, para. 12a (p. 161); *compare also* H.R. Committee, CCPR General Comment No. 6, at 129 (para. 4); *see infra*, Part One, Chapter B) I. 2.

[165] Nowak, *CCPR Commentary*, Art. 6, para. 14 (p. 111); Ramcharan, 30 *Nether. Int'l L. Rev.* (1983), at 317.

[166] H.R. Committee, *Maria Fanny Suárez de Guerrero ("Camargo Case")*, para. 13.3; Ramcharan, 30 *Nether. Int'l L. Rev.* (1983), at 318.

execution'."[167] Examples discussed include the shooting of suspected offenders or those attempting to escape from lawful custody where the life or limb of the arresting officer or that of a third party is not in peril.[168] The Human Rights Committee has censured measures taken by States combating terrorism,[169] *inter alia* extra judicial executions.[170] Further cases will be discussed in length *infra*.[171]

(7) Executions Carried Out without Due Process of Law

Executions carried out without due process of law constitute arbitrary deprivations of life under the Covenant.[172] As regards penal executions, the standards applicable are laid down in the Covenant itself.[173] Regarding preventive executions, the standards will be developed *infra*.[174]

e) Characteristics of the Examples Discussed

The examples discussed above have certain characteristics in common that can be roughly divided into two groups: killings of numerous persons that are arbitrary due to the lack of predictability, and the killings of single persons that are arbitrary due to the lack of an objective basis. The emphasis of the further analysis will be on the second group, concerning the killing of specific single persons that are targeted.

---

[167] UN Comm'n H.R., *Summary or Arbitrary Executions: Report by the Special Rapporteur (S. Amos Wako)*, UN Doc. E/CN.4/1983/16 (January 31, 1983), para. 60.

[168] Nsereko, in: Ramcharan (ed.), pp. 254-255.

[169] *See e.g.* H.R. Committee, *Concluding Observations on Yemen*, UN Doc. CCPR/CO/75/YEM (July 26, 2002), para. 18.

[170] H.R. Committee, *Concluding Observations on Peru*, UN Doc. CCPR/C /79/Add.8 (September 25, 1992), para. 8.

[171] *See infra*, Part One, Chapter B) II.

[172] Ramcharan, 30 *Nether. Int'l L. Rev.* (1983), at 317.

[173] *See infra*, Part One, Chapter B) II. 1.

[174] *See infra*, Part One, Chapter B) II. 2.-4.

2. *The Beneficiary Function* (status positivus)

The ability to enjoy most rights protected by the Covenant would be undermined if States had no duties to control the abuses of such rights by private actors. Therefore, Article 2 para. 1 of the Covenant establishes duties, including the duty to protect individuals from abuses of all Covenant rights by others.[175] These duties are not progressive duties as laid down in Article 2 para. 1 of the International Covenant on Economic, Social and Cultural Rights (ICESCR),[176] even though the Human Rights Committee has confirmed that Article 6 ICCPR has a socio-economic aspect.[177] Beside those "moral soft law obligation[s]",[178] the Covenant imposes immediate obligations.[179] These obligations do not exclusively concern the legislator, but all State authorities, including the executive, the police and the military.[180]

Regarding the right to life, the Human Rights Committee made it clear that "the protection of this right requires that States adopt positive

---

[175] Joseph/ Schultz/ Castan, *International Covenant*, para. 1.84 (p. 38); Thomas Buergenthal, 'To Respect and to Ensure: State obligations and Permissible Derogations', in: Louis Henkin (ed.), *The International Bill of Rights: The Covenant on Civil and Political Rights*, New York 1981, pp. 72-91, at 77.

[176] International Covenant Economic, Social and Cultural Rights, adopted by the UN General Assembly on December 16, 1966, Resolution 2200 A (XXI), annex, UN GAOR, 21st Sess., Supp. No. 16, pp 49-60, at 49-52, UN Doc. A/6316 (1966), entry into force on January 3, 1976, reprinted in: 993 *UNTS* (1976), No. 14531 pp. 3-106; *compare also* Franciszek Przetacznik, 'The Right to Life as a Basic Human Right', in: 9 *Rev. dr. hom.-Hum. Rts. J.* (1976), pp. 585-609, at 585-586, who differentiates between "the right to life" as protected by the ICCPR and "the right to living" as protected by the ICESCR in that regard.

[177] H.R. Committee, CCPR General Comment No. 6, at 129 (para. 5); *compare* McGoldrick, *Human Rights Committee*, para. 8.4 (p. 329-330).

[178] H.R. Committee, CCPR General Comment No. 6, at 129 (para. 5); *see also* Joseph/ Schultz/ Castan, *International Covenant*, para. 8.45 (p. 185); Nowak, *CCPR Commentary*, Art. 6, para. 5 (p. 107, esp. footnote 17).

[179] Carlson/ Gisvold, *International Covenant*, p. 18.

[180] Inter-Am. Ct. H.R., *Juan Humberto Sánchez v. Honduras*, Judgment of June 7, 2003, Series C, No. 99, para. 110; *see also* Ramcharan, in: Ramcharan (ed.), at 17; Przetacznik, 9 *Rev. dr. hom.-Hum. Rts. J.* (1976), at 586.

measures"[181] both to prevent arbitrary State killings as well as arbitrary killings by other individuals.[182] This includes the recognition of such executions as offences under criminal law,[183] the training of the relevant personnel such as police officers and prison guards in order to minimize the chance of their violations of the right to life and the special protection of detainees.[184]

a) Effects on the Burden of Persuasion

In the sphere of human rights protection by international organs, these organs have the authority to investigate and the subjective burden of proof is not borne by either party.[185] This is a result of the objective character of human rights treaties.[186] Contrary to this, the objective

---

[181] H.R. Committee, CCPR General Comment No. 6, at 129 (para. 5); *see also* Halûk A. Kabaalioğlu, 'The Obligation to 'respect' and to 'ensure' the Right to Life', in: Bertrand G. Ramcharan (ed.), *The Right to Life in International Law*, Dordrecht 1985, pp. 160-181, at 164-165; *c.f.* Nowak, *CCPR Commentary*, Art. 6, paras. 3-6 and 17; Eckart Klein, 'The Duty to Protect and to Ensure Human Rights Under the International Covenant on Civil and Political Rights', in: Eckart Klein (ed.), *The Duty to Protect and Ensure Human Rights*, Berlin Verlag, Berlin, 2000, pp. 295-318, at 306-310; Dinstein, in: Henkin (ed.), at 115.

[182] H.R. Committee, CCPR General Comment No. 6, at 128-129 (para. 3); Carlson/ Gisvold, *International Covenant*, p. 67; Ramcharan, in: Ramcharan (ed.), at 17.

[183] UN Economic and Social Council, Resolution 1989/65 (May 24, 1989), Annex, *Principles on the effective Prevention and Investigation of extra-legal, arbitrary and summary Executions*, 1989 UN ESCOR, Supp. No. 1 (UN Doc.E /1989/89), pp. 52-53, at 52 (para. 1).

[184] Joseph/ Schultz/ Castan, *International Covenant*, paras. 8.39-8.40 (p. 181).

[185] *See e.g.* Eur. Ct. H.R., *Ireland v. UK*, Series A, No. 25, p. 64 (para. 160); Eur. Ct. H.R., *Artico*, Series A, No. 37, p. 14 (para. 30); Juliane Kokott, *Beweislastverteilung und Prognoseentscheidungen bei der Inanspruchnahme von Grund- und Menschenrechten*, Berlin 1993, pp. 383-385; Beate Rudolf, 'Beweislastprobleme in Verfahren wegen Verletzung von Art. 3 EMRK', in: 23 *EuGRZ* (1996), pp. 497-503, at 499.

[186] *Compare supra*, Part One, Chapter A) I.; *see also* Wiesbrock, *Verletzungen durch Private*, p. 233.

burden of proof, i.e. the burden of persuasion[187] or "burden to convince",[188] in human rights cases rests with the applicant. In human rights cases, as in criminal law cases, the decision is whether or not a binding rule has been violated. If the facts that constitute an alleged violation cannot be proved, the application will generally be dismissed.[189] This fact entails difficulties in showing the responsibility of a State, due to the imbalance of power between the State and the individual, especially if evidence beyond a reasonable doubt is necessary.[190]

Due to the beneficiary function, difficulties in proving the responsibility of a State for a human rights violation decrease if the responsibility is based on the fact that the State did not fulfil its duty to protect. It is of minor importance whether or not the State has actively and directly caused the violation of the rights in question.[191] If it is not possible to establish such active violation, it might still be possible to prove that the State did not fulfil its duty to protect.[192] This aspect played a decisive role in the case of *Hugo Dermit*:

> While the Committee cannot arrive at a definite conclusion as to whether Hugo Dermit committed suicide or was killed by others while in custody; yet, the inescapable conclusion is that in all the circumstances the Uruguayan authorities either by act or by omis-

---

[187] Kokott, *Beweislastverteilung*, p. 390.

[188] Wiesbrock, *Verletzungen durch Private*, p. 243.

[189] *See e.g.* Inter-Am. Ct. H.R., *Angel Manfredo Velásquez-Rodríguez*, Series C, No. 4, para. 123; Inter-Am. Ct. H.R., *Godínez-Cruz v. Honduras*, Judgment of January 20, 1989, Series C, No. 5, para. 129; Inter-Am. Ct. H.R., *Fairén-Garbi and Solís-Corrales v. Honduras*, Judgment of March 15, 1989, Series C, No. 6; para. 126; Hans Christian Krüger, *Probleme der Beweiserhebung durch die Europäische Kommission für Menschenrechte*, Saarbrücken 1996, p. 7; Wiesbrock, *Verletzungen durch Private*, pp. 233-234.

[190] Kokott, *Beweislastverteilung*, p. 383.

[191] *Compare* Wiesbrock, *Verletzungen durch Private*, p. 231.

[192] Gordon A. Christenson, 'Attributing Acts of Omission to the State', in: 12 *Mich. J. Int'l L.* (1991), pp. 312-370, at 348; Joachim Wolf, 'Zurechnungsfragen bei Handlungen von Privatpersonen', in: 45 *ZaöRV* (1985), pp. 232-264, at 236; Wiesbrock, *Verletzungen durch Private*, p. 231.

sion were responsible for not taking adequate measures to protect his life, as required by article 6(1) of the Covenant.[193]

b) The Duty to Investigate as Part of the Right to Life

The situation described above still entails problems for applicants. For an individual applicant it may be difficult – if not impossible – to prove violations that may have taken place in custody or comparable situations. These difficulties can be circumvented due to the *duty to cooperate* in human rights cases:[194] The Human Rights Chamber for Bosnia and Herzegovina admitted circumstantial and presumptive evidence in regard to the disappearance of a person from official custody and created a presumption of responsibility on the part of the Government in question for that person's fate.[195] This was based on jurisprudence concerning the European Convention on Human Rights[196] and the American Convention on Human Rights.[197]

"The [Human Rights] committee has, in its past jurisprudence, made clear that circumstances may cause it to assume facts in the author's favour if the State party fails to reply or address them."[198] It presumes allegations as true, if the State in question does not fulfil its duty to coop-

---

[193] H.R. Committee, *Guillermo Ignacio Dermit Barbato and Hugo Haroldo Dermit Barbato v. Uruguay*, Communication No. 84/1981, UN Doc. CCPR/C/17/D/84/1981 (October 21, 1982), para. 9.23.

[194] Kokott, *Beweislastverteilung*, p. 393.

[195] Bosnia and Herzegovina, Human Rights Chamber for Bosnia and Herzegovina, *Josip, Božana and Tomislav Matanović v. Republika Srpska*, Case No. CH/96/1, Decision (Merits) of July 11, 1997, para. 35; Bosnia and Herzegovina, Human Rights Chamber for Bosnia and Herzegovina, *Ratko Grgić v. Republika Srpska*, Case No. CH/96/15, Decision (Merits) of August 5, 1997, para. 6.

[196] *See e.g.* Eur. Comm'n H.R., *Koçeri Kurt v. Turkey*, Appl. No. 24276/94, Report of December 5, 1996, *ECHR* 1998-III, pp. 1203-1232, at 1218 (para. 202); Eur. Ct. H.R., *Koçeri Kurt v. Turkey*, Appl. No. 24276/94, Judgment of May 25, 1998, *ECHR* 1998-III, pp. 1152-1202, at 1186 (para. 128).

[197] Inter-Am. Ct. H.R., *Angel Manfredo Velásquez-Rodríguez*, Series C, No. 4, para. 131.

[198] H.R. Committee, *William Eduardo Delgado Páez v. Colombia*, Communication No. 195/1985, UN Doc. CCPR/C/39/D/195/1985 (August 23, 1990), at para. 5.6.

erate and provide information on the case.[199] The Committee has emphasized that,

> denials of a general character do not suffice. Specific responses and pertinent evidence (including copies of the relevant decisions of the courts and findings of any investigations which have taken place into the validity of the complaints made) in reply to the contentions of the author of a communication are required.[200]

This approach has earlier been explained theoretically as an *implicit approval* by the State of the allegations.[201] Such a strict interpretation would amount to a subjective burden of proof on the part of the responding State and thus is in contradiction to the objective character of human rights cases.[202] However, insufficient cooperation by the responding State is taken into account.

The substantive provisions of the Covenant are understood to include a duty "to ensure an effective protection through some machinery of control. Complaints about ill-treatment must be investigated effectively by competent authorities."[203] The Committee established violations of the Covenant on the basis that the State party failed to effectively investigate the responsibility for deaths. For example, in the case of *José Herrera* and *Emma Rubio de Herrera* it ruled: "State parties should ... establish effective facilities and procedures to investigate thoroughly, by an appropriate impartial body, cases of missing and disappeared persons in circumstances which may involve a violation of the right to life."[204]

---

[199] *Compare* Joachim Wolf, *Die Haftung der Staaten für Privatpersonen nach Völkerrecht*, Berlin 1997, p. 276; Wiesbrock, *Verletzungen durch Private*, p. 241.

[200] H.R. Committee, *Maria Fanny Suárez de Guerrero ("Camargo Case")*, at para. 15; *c.f.* McGoldrick, *Human Rights Committee*, para. 8.7 (pp. 331-332).

[201] Joseph-Charles Witenberg, 'La théorie des preuves devant les juridictions internationales', in: 56 *RdC* (1936-III), pp. 1-105, at 50.

[202] Kokott, *Beweislastverteilung*, pp. 395-396.

[203] H.R. Committee, CCPR General Comment No. 7, at 129-130 (para. 1).

[204] H.R. Committee, *Herrera Rubio v. Colombia*, Communication No. 161/1983, UN Doc. CCPR/C/31/D/161/1983 (November 2, 1987), para. 10.3.

A State thus also violates its duty to protect under Article 6 of the Covenant if it fails to investigate quickly and effectively, and punish the persons responsible for involuntary disappearances and State killings.[205]

3. Limits of the Scope of Protection: The Socio-Economic Aspect

The scope of protection of the right to life has limits concerning the extent of the concept of "life". Article 6 does not protect the freedom to live as one wishes.[206] The right to life is first and foremost a civil right, as opposed to the rights protected in the International Covenant on Economic, Social and Cultural Rights. Whether it has a socio-economic aspect[207] or does not give guarantees against death from famine, cold or lack of medical attention[208] can remain open for the purpose of this treatise.

II. Exceptions: Non-Arbitrary Deprivations of Life

Neither the International Covenant nor other human rights instruments guarantee the right to life in an absolute manner. Article 6 para. 1 in its first sentence confirms the existence of every human being's right to life. But the prohibition of deprivations of life is limited to "arbitrary deprivations". Those are not lawful under the Covenant.[209] Implicitly, by using this formulation, the Covenant accepts that "non-arbitrary deprivations" of life are possible. This is confirmed in paras. 2-6 of Article 6, which refer to the death-penalty. It is legal, subject to the condi-

---

[205] *Compare* H.R. Committee, CCPR General Comment No. 6, at 129 (para. 4); H.R. Committee, *Herrera Rubio*, para. 12; H.R. Committee, *Eduardo Bleier v. Uruguay*, Communication No. 30/1978, UN Doc. CCPR/C/15/D/30/1978 (March 29, 1982), paras. 13.3-14; *see also* Gollwitzer, *Menschenrechte*, Art. 2 MRK/Art. 6 IPBPR, para. 11c (p. 160) and para. 12a (p. 161); Joseph/ Schultz/ Castan, *International Covenant*, para. 8.09 (p. 162); Nsereko, in: Ramcharan (ed.), at 265.

[206] Dinstein, in: Henkin (ed.), at 115.

[207] *Compare* H.R. Committee, CCPR General Comment No. 6, at 129 (para. 5); McGoldrick, *Human Rights Committee*, para. 8.4 (p. 329-330).

[208] *Compare* Dinstein, in: Henkin (ed.), at 115.

[209] Ramcharan, 30 *Nether. Int'l L. Rev.* (1983), at 317.

tions imposed in Article 6, in States which have not ratified the Second Optional Protocol.

State practice tends to reveal considerable agreement over certain cases in which legitimate deprivation of life may be possible. These cases, beside the death penalty where not abolished, include law enforcement actions such as arresting suspected offenders or preventing the escape of lawfully arrested persons; quelling riots or disbanding unlawful assemblies; defending security zones; and military actions in times of armed conflict.[210] Whether these cases are examples of non-arbitrary deprivation will be examined *infra*:

1. *The Death Penalty*

The judicial imposition of a death sentence is an exception to the general norm protecting the right to life that is recognised by international law.[211] The imposition of the death penalty is prohibited in States party to the Second Optional Protocol, which states in its Article 1:

> (1) No one within the jurisdiction of a State Party to the present Protocol shall be executed. (2) Each State Party shall take all necessary measures to abolish the death penalty within its jurisdiction.

This abolition of the death penalty is only binding upon the Parties to the Protocol itself and not upon all States party to the Covenant. It furthermore permits reservations concerning the death penalty in times of war.[212] Thus while Article 6 of the Covenant itself does not outlaw capital punishment, it only authorises it in restrictive terms.

---

[210] Nsereko, in: Ramcharan (ed.), at 258.

[211] Joseph/ Schultz/ Castan, *International Covenant*, para. 8.19 (p. 166); Nsereko, in: Ramcharan (ed.), at 246.

[212] Article 2 para. 1 of the Second Optional Protocol reads: "No reservation is admissible to the present Protocol, except for a reservation made at the time of ratification or accession that provides for the application of the death penalty in time of war pursuant to a conviction for a most serious crime of a military nature committed during wartime."

a) General Limitations

A death sentence may be imposed only for the most serious crimes. It must be in accordance with the law in force at the time of the commission of the crime and may not be contrary to the provisions of the present Covenant and to the Convention on the Prevention and Punishment of the Crime of Genocide.

The limitation of capital punishment to the most serious crimes emphasizes the fact that the death penalty is "a quite exceptional measure".[213] The Human Rights Committee confirmed that the following crimes are not "most serious" under Article 6: abduction not resulting in death, abetting suicide, adultery, apostasy, corruption, crimes of an economic nature, drug-related offences, embezzlement by officials, multiple evasion of military service, piracy, property offences, robbery, committing a third homosexual act, theft by force, traffic in toxic or dangerous wastes, and treason.[214] The Committee implied that non violent infringements are not serious enough to attract capital punishment.[215] The general concept seems to be that crimes which do not result in the loss of life do not attract the death penalty.[216] Thus, only intentional killings or attempted killings and perhaps the intentional infliction of grievous bodily harm can justify the imposition of the death penalty.[217] However, retribution cannot be legally accepted as a ground for the imposition of capital punishment.[218]

Article 6 para. 2 reiterates the principle *nullum crimen, nulla poena sine lege* that is also contained in Article 15 of the Covenant and prohibits retroactive legislation as a basis for capital punishment.

The death penalty must not be imposed in a discriminatory manner, e.g. on the basis of race, religion of other grounds contrary to Article 2 pa-

---

213 H.R. Committee, CCPR General Comment No. 6, at 129 (paras. 6-7).

214 *Compare* Joseph/ Schultz/ Castan, *International Covenant*, para. 8.22 (p. 167) for further references.

215 H.R. Committee, *Concluding Observations on Iraq*, UN Doc. CCPR/C/ 79/Add.84 (November 19, 1997), para. 10.

216 H.R. Committee, *Concluding Observations on the Islamic Republic of Iran*, UN Doc. CCPR/C/79/Add.25 (August 3, 1995), para. 8.

217 Joseph/ Schultz/ Castan, *International Covenant*, para. 8.22 (p. 167).

218 H.R. Committee, *Concluding Observations on the Libyan Arab Jamahiriya*, UN Doc. CCPR/C/79/Add.101 (November 6, 1998), para. 8.

ra. 1 of the Covenant. The same holds true for other procedural rights protected by the Covenant. Additionally, the Covenant stresses the limits set by the Genocide Convention: massive use of the death penalty could result in a disguised genocide and therefore be unlawful as such.[219]

b) Due Process Requirements

According to Article 6 para. 2, capital punishment can only be carried out pursuant to a final judgement rendered by a competent court. However, this is not the only procedural requirement that has to be taken into account. Article 6 para. 2 prohibits violations of other provisions of the Covenant in connection with the death penalty. Thus, violations of the fair trial guarantees of Article 14 of the Covenant constitute at the same time violations of Article 6 para. 2.[220]

Under Article 14 of the Covenant, a sentence of death may only be imposed by a competent, independent and impartial tribunal provided for by law. The decision must be reached after a fair and public hearing that pays regard to the prohibition of discrimination, the presumption of innocence and the minimum rights of the accused guaranteed by Article 14 para. 3 of the Covenant. These minimum guarantees of Article 14, para. 3 include the right of the accused to be informed promptly and in detail of the nature and cause of the charges against him (*lit.* a); the right to defend himself in person or through legal assistance (*lit.* d), to have adequate time and facilities for the preparation of the defence (*lit.* b) and to examine the witnesses against him (*lit.* e); and the right not to be tried *in absentia* (*lit.* d).

In the case of a targeted killing, these rights are violated *per definitionem*. While the targeted person my be informed of the fact that a deci-

---

219 R. Sapienza, 'International Legal Standards on Capital Punishment', in: Bertrand G. Ramcharan (ed.), *The Right to Life in International Law*, Dordrecht 1985, pp. 284-296, at 286.

220 H.R. Committee, *Daniel Monguya Mbenge v. Zaire*, Communication No. 16/1977, UN Doc. CCPR/C/18/D/16/1977 (March 25, 1983), para. 17; H.R. Committee, CCPR General Comment No. 6, at 129 (para. 7); *see also* Weissbrodt, in: Ramcharan (ed.), at 298.

sion on his targeting is imminent in some situations,[221] the absence of the other criteria is part of the concept of targeted killings: The targeted person has no possibility to defend himself as the decision on whether he shall be targeted is taken elsewhere, in his absence and clandestine.

This is why *Tomuschat*, arguing on the basis that no death penalty may be based on mere suspicions and that the accused has the right to defend himself, concludes that targeted killings are a clear violation of the Covenant.[222] This is undoubtedly true in the case of targeted killings of a penal character. Those targeted killings will violate the due process requirements and thus cannot be accepted as killings under the capital punishment exception of the Covenant. However, this outcome does not necessarily mean that all targeted killings are illegal under the provisions of the Covenant. The legality of those killings without a penal character still has to be examined:

2. Deprivation of Life in Self-Defence or in Defence of Another Person

An explicit rule on non-penal deprivations of life is not included in Article 6 of the Covenant.[223] Specific exceptions were discussed in the course of the Article's drafting: The killing of a person by officials in self-defence or in defence of another person, killings in the course of the attempt to effect lawful arrest or to prevent escape of a person lawfully in custody, and death resulting from actions lawfully taken to suppress an insurrection, rebellion or riot. However, any enumeration was opposed: "a clause providing that no one should be deprived of his life 'arbitrarily' would indicate that the right was not absolute and obviate the necessity of setting out the possible exceptions in detail."[224] Such a detailed list, it was feared, could have appeared as giving more weight to the limitations than to the right to life itself. On the other

---

[221] Here, the example of a hostage taker who is threatened to be shot in case he will not release the hostage comes to mind.

[222] Tomuschat, 52 *VN* (2004), at 137.

[223] On the limitation clauses concerning some of the other rights protected by the Covenant *see* Alexandre Charles Kiss, 'Permissible Limitations on Rights', in: Louis Henkin (ed.), *The International Bill of Rights: The Covenant on Civil and Political Rights*, New York 1981, pp. 290-310.

[224] UN Comm'n H.R., 5th Session (1949), UN Doc. A/2929, Chapter VI, para. 3, reprinted in: Bossuyt, *Travaux Préparatoires*, pp. 121-122.

hand, the drafters were also worried that cases could arise that were not included in such a list but might nevertheless be fully justified.[225] In consequence, the Covenant does not give specific guidance as to which cases of non-penal deprivation of life might be non-arbitrary.

Other instruments list specific non-penal cases that may allow for the lethal use of force. The European Convention on Human Rights includes explicit exceptions such as force that is absolutely necessary to defend any person from unlawful violence, force to effect a lawful arrest or to prevent the escape of a person lawfully detained, or in actions lawfully taken for the purpose of quelling a riot or insurrection.[226] These categories of exception are closed and no derogation is permissible outside of the permitted categories. The UN Basic Principles on the Use of Force and Firearms by Law Enforcement Officials[227] in Principle 9 state:

> Law enforcement officials shall not use firearms against persons except in self-defence or defence of others against the imminent threat of death or serious injury, to prevent the perpetration of a particularly serious crime involving grave threat to life, to arrest a person presenting such a danger and resisting their authority, or to prevent his or her escape, and only when less extreme means are insufficient to achieve these objectives. In any event, intentional lethal use of firearms may only be made when strictly unavoidable in order to protect life.

These possible limits aim at the protection of the rest of the members of the community.[228] Hence, the use of force that is absolutely necessary in the defence of a person from unlawful violence is widely considered as not "arbitrary" in the meaning of Article 6 of the Covenant.[229] This

---

[225] *Compare* Nsereko, in: Ramcharan (ed.), at 248, with further references.

[226] Article 2 para. 2 European Convention on Human Rights; see *infra*, Part One, Chapter E).

[227] UN General Assembly, Conference 144, *UN Basic Principles on the Use of Force and Firearms by Law Enforcement Officials*, UN Doc. A/CONF.144/28/Rev.1 (1990), pp. 112-116.

[228] Nsereko, in: Ramcharan (ed.), at 257.

[229] Dinstein, in: Henkin (ed.), at 119; David J. Harris, *Cases and Materials on International Law*, 5th ed., London 1998, p. 654; Arthur Henry Robertson, 'The United Nations Covenant on Civil and Political Rights and the European Convention on Human Rights', in: 43 *Brit. Yb. Int'l L.* (1968-69), pp. 21-48, at 30;

can only hold true if such action has a legitimate aim and abides by the standards of proportionality.[230] The aim of a killing in self-defence or in defence of another person is saving the life of a person. This represented a legitimate aim[231] and even a duty of States.[232] It does not have any punitive aspect and its goal is at the prevention of harm.

> On its face, prevention is a neutral term. Lawyers use it when they deal with possible harm. Harm should be prevented. At the same time, lawyers know that harm may not be prevented at any price. Therefore, prevention is about methods and about the balancing of competing values.[233]

As the right to life of the person targeted will most likely be taken, the very core of the right is touched. Indeed, the right to life is not protected absolutely, but the Human Rights Committee has stressed in connection to the death penalty that exceptions from the right to life have to be interpreted restrictively.[234] The same applies to preventive

---

Anthony Dworkin, 'Military Necessity and Due Process: The Place of Human Rights in the War on Terror', in: David Wippman/ Matthew Evangelista (eds.), *New Wars, New Laws? Applying the Laws of War in 21st Century Conflicts*, Ardsley, N.Y. 2005, pp. 53-73, at 69; Nowak, *CCPR Commentary*, Art. 6, para. 14 (p. 111); H.R. Committee, *Maria Fanny Suárez de Guerrero ("Camargo Case")*, para. 13.2.

230 *See e.g.* Ramcharan, 30 *Nether. Int'l L. Rev.* (1983), at 319; Ramcharan, in: Ramcharan (ed.), at 21; Jaime Oraá, *Human Rights in States of Emergency in International Law*, Oxford 1996, pp. 140-141; Principle 5 of the UN Basic Principles on the Use of Force and Firearms by Law Enforcement Officials reads: "Whenever the lawful use of force and firearms is unavoidable, law enforcement officials shall: (a) Exercise restraint in such use and act in proportion to the seriousness of the offence and the legitimate objective to be achieved; ...".

231 Nowak, *CCPR Commentary*, Art. 6, para. 14 (p. 111); Nolte, 5 *Theo. Inq. L.* (2004), at 120-121.

232 *Compare e.g.* Kabaalioğlu, in: Ramcharan (ed.), at 167-179; Klein, in: Klein (ed.), at 306-307; Nowak, *CCPR Commentary*, Art. 6, paras. 3-6; *Compare also* Gross, 15 *Fla. J. Int'l L.* (2003), at 463; Gross, 15 *Temp. Int'l & Comp. L.J.* (2001), at 215.

233 Nolte, 5 *Theo. Inq. L.* (2004), at 111.

234 H.R. Committee, CCPR General Comment No. 6, at 129 (para. 7).

action, which must adhere to the principle of proportionality.[235] Disproportionate action is arbitrary in the meaning of Article 6 of the Covenant.[236] Thus, such measures must be capable of furthering their legitimate goal. They must be the least intrusive means,[237] and they must be reasonably related to their goal.[238]

a) Capability of Furthering the Goal

The requirement that is partly referred to as "suitability" suggests that an action interfering with a right must be at least "theoretically capable of contributing to achieving its aim".[239] To kill the person who threatens the life of another person is conducive to saving the latter person's life.

b) Necessity of the Means

However, the requirement of necessity demands that the authorities must choose the least restrictive means from among those equally effective.[240] It is thus necessary to review the possibility of milder means

---

[235] Nowak, *CCPR Commentary*, Art. 6, para. 14 (p. 111); Nsereko, in: Ramcharan (ed.), at 261-263; Jost Delbrück, 'Proportionality', in: , in: Rudolf Bernhardt (ed.), *EPIL*, Vol. 7, Amsterdam 1984, pp. 396-400, at 398; *Compare also* Article 2, para. 2 ECHR ("the use of force which is no more than absolutely necessary") and Principle 9 of the UN Basic Principles on the Use of Force and Firearms by Law Enforcement Officials ("...only when less extreme means are insufficient to achieve these objectives. In any event, intentional lethal use of firearms may only be made when strictly unavoidable in order to protect life.").

[236] H.R. Committee, *Maria Fanny Suárez de Guerrero ("Camargo Case")*, para. 13.3.

[237] *Compare Id.*, para. 13.2; Nsereko, in: Ramcharan (ed.), at 254.

[238] Georg Nolte, 'General Principles of German and European Administrative Law – A Comparison in Historical Perspective', in: 57 *Mod. L. Rev.* (1994), pp. 191-212, at 193.

[239] Nolte, 57 *Mod. L. Rev.* (1994), at 193.

[240] Arai-Takahashi, *Margin of Appreciation*, p. 192; Nolte, 57 *Mod. L. Rev.* (1994), at 193; Nsereko, in: Ramcharan (ed.), at 254; Principle 5 of the UN Basic Principles on the Use of Force and Firearms by Law Enforcement Officials reads: "Whenever the lawful use of force and firearms is unavoidable, law en-

which could be equally effective in attaining the aim. This "hard core of the principle of proportionality"[241] is also applied by the Human Rights Committee: "Before resorting to the use of deadly force, all measures to arrest a person suspected of being in the process of committing acts of terror must be exhausted."[242] The persons targeted pose a threat by their behaviour. This implies that they can change this behaviour and terminate the threat.[243] Thus, possible milder means may include warning the persons targeted and giving them an "opportunity to surrender ... or to offer any explanation of their presence or intentions."[244] Furthermore, the use of non-lethal force has to be considered.[245] However, these means must be equally effective:

(1) Self-Defence

Self-defence in reaction to an unlawful assault gives the person defending his life and limb the right to use the force necessary to repulse the assault.[246] Giving a warning to the attacker will prove ineffective once the attack is underway. Obviously, if non-lethal force is effective in terminating the assault, it is not necessary to kill the offender. Possible

---

forcement officials shall: ... (b) Minimize damage and injury, and respect and preserve human life; ...".

[241] Nolte, 57 *Mod. L. Rev.* (1994), at 193.

[242] H.R. Committee, *Concluding Observations on Israel*, UN Doc. CCPR/CO/78/ISR (August 21, 2003), para. 15.

[243] *Compare e.g.* Karsten Baumann, 'Das Grundrecht auf Leben unter Quantifizierungsvorbehalt: Zur Terrorismusbekämpfung durch "finalen Rettungsabschuß"', in: 57 *DÖV* (2004), pp. 853-861, at 859-860.

[244] H.R. Committee, *Maria Fanny Suárez de Guerrero ("Camargo Case")*, para. 13.2; *c.f.* McGoldrick, *Human Rights Committee*, para. 8.19 (pp. 340-341); *see also* Nsereko, in: Ramcharan (ed.), at 254.

[245] Nsereko, *id.*

[246] It is less clear whether this is also true in defence of property, *see* C. K. Boyle, 'The Concept of Arbitrary Deprivation of Life', in: Bertrand G. Ramcharan (ed.), *The Right to Life in International Law*, Dordrecht 1985, pp. 221-244, at 221-222. However, this question can remain open for the present examination, as targeted killings are constantly explained as reaction to life-threatening situations.

means can be chemical irritant agents,[247] audible and optical distraction devices,[248] kinetic impact munitions,[249] electrical incapacitation devices[250] or microwave incapacitation devices.[251] These means are more likely to be at the disposal of law enforcement personnel than to be available to private persons. Thus, Article 6 may be violated by a definition of the right to self-defence which is too broad, e.g. concerning police officers that are granted a general statutory presumption of justification for combating certain offences.[252] However, the person defending himself does not have to choose means that do not terminate the attack for sure. This is at least questionable concerning chemical irritant agents, which have relatively rapid effects, but do not take effect instantaneously. They are not appropriate to stop someone from firing a weapon, detonating a bomb or taking other deadly actions in the time between exposure and onset of effects.[253] Thus, once the attack has actu-

---

[247] Commonly referred to as "tear gas".

[248] Such as diversionary devices, stun grenades, flash-bangs or smoke munitions, *compare* William P. Bozeman/ James E. Winslow, 'Medical Aspects of Less Lethal Weapons', in: 5 *Internet J. Resc. & Disaster Med.* (2005), No. 1; Klaus-Dieter Thiel, 'Non-Lethal Weapons: An alternative Option facing unconventional Threats', in: 42 *Rev. dr. mil.* (2003), pp. 379-393, at 388.; Friedhelm Krüger-Sprengel, 'Non-Lethal Weapons – a Humanitarian Perspective in Modern Conflict', in: 42 *Rev. dr. mil.* (2003), pp. 357-377, at 362; *compare generally* Gerard A.J.M. van Vugt, 'Juridische aspecten van niet-letale wapens', in: 44 *Rev. dr. mil.* (2005), pp. 39-64.

[249] Such as non- or less penetrating projectiles, e.g. rubber bullets, plastic baton rounds or bean bags, *compare* D. Hughes, K. Maguire, F. Dunn, S. Fitzpatrick and L. G. Rocke, 'Plastic Baton Round Injuries', in: 22 *Emergency Medicine Journal* (2005), pp. 111-112; Thiel, 42 *Rev. dr. mil.* (2003), at 386-387; Krüger-Sprengel, 42 *Rev. dr. mil.* (2003), at 362.

[250] So called "Tasers", *see* Thiel, 42 *Rev. dr. mil.* (2003), at 388; Bozeman/ Winslow, 5 *Internet J. Resc. & Disaster Med.* (2005), No. 1; on the risks of "Tasers" *see* Amnesty International, *United States of America: Excessive and Lethal Force? Amnesty International's Concerns about Deaths and Ill-treatment involving Police Use of Tasers*, AI Doc. AMR 51/139/2004 (November 30, 2004).

[251] Comparable to so called "phasers", *see* Thiel, 42 *Rev. dr. mil.* (2003), at 389-390; Krüger-Sprengel, 42 *Rev. dr. mil.* (2003), at 362.

[252] H.R. Committee, *Maria Fanny Suárez de Guerrero ("Camargo Case")*, paras. 1.6 and 13.3.

ally started,[254] the preventive killing of the offender may be necessary if non-lethal force or even the use of force that is presumably lethal will not be of the same efficiency.

Applying the categories of intention developed above further clarifies the possibilities the options available to person defending himself. This person's aim is to terminate the assault. The death of the attacker may be inevitable in reaching this aim, but it should never be the goal of the action in itself. The latter could be the case due to comprehensible motives such as revenge. The aim of the action is the termination of the attack. Thus, the person defending himself may not kill the attacker with direct intention of the first degree, but only accept the attacker's death as an inevitable side-effect and thus act with direct intention of second degree.[255] Strictly speaking, if the use of force which is presumably lethal is equally effective, strictly speaking this kind of force would have to be preferred, as it includes the possibility of preventing the assault and sparing the offender's life. However, the standards of behaviour demanded of the victim defending himself against an assault cannot be too high. Self-defence gives this person a right to choose a means that is definitely efficient and it is not possible to expect too detailed a consideration of the necessity for that means in such a stressful situation.[256] Admittedly, in the case of self-defence these are considerations of a merely theoretical character; the result of any means may be the death of the attacker. The intention of the person defending himself cannot be distinguished from the perspective of an objective observer. The benefit of the doubt will thus lead to the assumption that the person did not kill the offender with direct intention of the first degree, but aimed to prevent the assault.

---

[253] Bozeman/ Winslow, 5 *Internet J. Resc. & Disaster Med.* (2005), No. 1.

[254] On the question of immediacy compare *infra*, Part One, Chapters B) II. 2. b) (3)-(6).

[255] *Compare supra*, Introduction, Chapter C) II. 1.; *see also* G.E.M. Anscombe, 'War and Murder', in: Larry May/ Eric Rovie/ Steve Viner (eds.), *The Morality of War: Classical and Contemporary Readings*, Upper Saddle River, N.J 2005, pp. 203-212, at 206.

[256] As Justice *Oliver Wendell Holmes, Jr.* memorably said in the United States Supreme Court: "Detached reflection cannot be demanded in the presence of an uplifted knife.", *see* U.S. Supreme Court, *Brown v. United States*, No. 103, Judgment of May 16, 1921, 256 *U.S.* (1921), pp. 335-344, at 343.

(2) Defence of Another Person

The possibility of finding a milder means of defending another person's life which are equally effective may vary in different situations. The following situations may serve as examples, albeit they are strongly simplified:

In the first situation, an offender directly threatens to kill his victim. He cannot proceed if he is interrupted by use of lethal force against him. In the second example, an offender who is on the way to his victim is killed at this early point and thus cannot kill the victim either. And in the third case a person is just about to instigate an offender to kill a victim. The agitator cannot proceed if he is killed at that point. In all three cases, the means is effective in achieving the goal of saving the victim's life. It is, however, questionable whether the use of lethal force is the least intrusive means in such cases.

The first case equals a situation of self-defence except for the fact that the person threatened is not identical with the person taking action against the offender. A warning or arrest of the offender would most likely not have the same effect as the use of force: Giving a warning to the offender leaves him with the possibility of surrendering but also with the possibility of killing his victim. An attempt to arrest the offender might have the same result. If non-lethal force is effective in preventing the assault, it is not necessary to use force that is presumably lethal or even to kill the offender. But the important characteristic of this case is that the realisation of the threat only depends on one further step by the offender. In a situation of such a high degree of danger the decision on whether force is used is exclusively based on the prognosis regarding the offender's will to take that ultimate step and kill his victim. On this basis, preventively killing the offender is likely to be the only reliable means of saving the victim's life. This includes, as shown above, direct intention of second degree concerning the death of the offender, as the aim of the interference exclusively is to prevent the assault. If the use of force that is presumably lethal would be equally effective, then this kind of force has to be preferred, as it includes the possibility of preventing the assault and of sparing the offender's life.

In this situation, it may be doubted whether the person acting in defence of another person deserves the same benefit as a person defending himself, i.e. the possibility of choosing a means that is definitely efficient without too detailed considerations concerning its necessity. At least in the case where law enforcement personnel are acting it seems to be appropriate to demand more specific considerations than those that can be expected of private persons in an exceptionally stressful situation.[257] To accept that deadly force is the only effective means in such a situation could amount to a presumption of justification similar to the one criticized by the Human Rights Committee.[258] Furthermore, it is more likely that law enforcement personnel can resort to "less lethal weapons" such as chemical irritant agents, distraction devices, kinetic impact munitions or electrical incapacitation devices.[259] On the other hand, once force is used, too strict requirements concerning the intention appear academic if the action in question is a shot in the head: If this action is the only effective means, the intention it is performed with is not visible. Independently of whether the sharp shooter hopes that the offender will survive or knows that he will die, the result of his shot will be the same.

In the second example proposed above, more possibilities are apparent: The targeted person must still find his victim and then "pull the trigger". This situation has been described by an Israeli general in the context of the 2000 killing of a Palestinian Fatah leader and deputy of *Yasir Arafat* as follows: "He's not shooting at us yet, but he's on his way."[260]

This means that at least two steps have to be taken by the offender before the threat might be realised. Thus, the offender might be arrested before he reaches his victim. In this situation, an arrest is more promising than in the first case, because it takes place at a time when the threat for the victim is less immediate. Additionally, the victim might be secured before the degree of danger becomes as high as in the first case. Whether such measures are practically possible remains to be established. However, they show that the instant use of lethal force against the offender is not necessary in all cases, at least not before the offender has taken the penultimate step to the realisation of his goal. This assessment is supported by the Human Rights Committee, which refers to persons "suspected of being in the process of committing" assaults

---

[257] *See also* Kremnitzer, in: Fleck (ed.), *Rechtsfragen*, at 203.

[258] H.R. Committee, *Maria Fanny Suárez de Guerrero ("Camargo Case")*, paras. 1.6 and 13.3.

[259] *See* Bozeman/ Winslow, 5 *Internet J. Resc. & Disaster Med.* (2005), No. 1.

[260] *Quoted by* Deborah Sontag, 'Israelis Track Down and Kill a Fatah Commander', in: *New York Times*, November 10, 2000, p. A 1.

who may be targeted under certain conditions.[261] The wording "in the process" implies that an attack by the targeted persons must be so imminent that it cannot be halted by arresting the perpetrator. This degree of imminence is a precondition for preventive killings.[262] It is not yet reached in the second case, as the offender has not yet reached his victim. The preventive killing of the offender (implying direct intention of second degree) is thus not proportionate at this early point. The same holds true for the use of force that is presumably lethal: Since the realisation of the threat is still at some distance, the possibility exists to overpower the offender and spare his life. Thus, any action directed against the offender at this early point must not include intention towards his death. Whereas the possibility exists that the offender is fatally injured, this has to be the absolute exception and may only be the result of negligence. Fatal injuries may not even be caused with *dolus eventualis*.

In the third case used as an example above, the threat is even less imminent: The agitator must first convince the offender, the offender must then decide to commit the deed, find his victim and finally kill him. This means that at least four additional steps have to be taken before the danger is put into effect. This may provide for the possibilities mentioned above: the offender may be arrested or the victim may be secured. However, it is the agitator who is in the focus of these considerations. In that respect, this situation differs from the second case: From the perspective of the agitator, one of the steps necessary to realise the threat depends on the autonomous decision of a third person. The offender must decide to commit the deed. The behaviour of the agitator does not automatically cause the death of the victim. Only if the offender decides to commit the deed and is *en route* to the victim, is the scenario comparable to the second case shown above. Then it may be necessary to use force against the offender, if he cannot be overpowered by other means early enough. The situation of the agitator is a different one. The prognosis forming the basis for the use of force against him depends on the decision of the offender. In the case that the offender decides not to commit the deed, the use of force against the agitator would not have been required at all. Even in the case that the offender

---

261 H.R. Committee, *Concluding Observations on Israel*, UN Doc. CCPR/CO/78/ISR (August 21, 2003), para. 15.

262 Kretzmer, 16 *Eur. J. Int'l L.* (2005), at 180.

decides to commit the deed, he may still be stopped before committing it. Thus, in this example it is a milder means to wait and observe whether or not the offender decides to commit the deed and to then direct any measures to prevent the deed against him. Persons in the background are responsible as agitators and thus they are indeed criminally responsible. They are, however, too far away from the deed itself to be the addressee of preventive force. Penal aspects that may, on the surface, justify such targeting morally may not influence preventive action.[263] If these persons are targeted, the use of force is neither justified as penal, as the procedural requirements are not fulfilled,[264] nor as preventive, as it is not the least intrusive means to stop the assault. A means less intrusive is to direct preventive measures against the offender once he has decided to commit the deed and pursues that aim. Hence, the use of force against the agitator is not necessary and thus not proportionate. He has to be overpowered in order to hold him accountable in criminal procedure, but his life has to be spared in doing so.

The cases above demonstrate that the number of steps necessary before the threat is realised reflects on the possibility of using significantly less intrusive means to obstruct the threat. These steps can serve as an instrument to assess the degree of danger, i.e. the immediacy of the situation. The more steps the alleged offender has to take to reach his victim and commit his deed, the more possibilities are open to the authorities to stop him. These possibilities encompass most likely an arrest of the offender before he reaches his victim or the use of non-lethal force against him. Thus, as long as the offender has not had the possibility of assaulting his victim at any time, milder means are most likely at the disposition of the authorities. These considerations do not mean that authorities have to wait until the danger is as imminent as described above before they act at all. They are obliged to act as early as possible by the means least intrusive.[265] Only if these milder means are not available may lethal force be used, but not before the required degree of imminence is reached.

---

[263] *See also* Gross, *Struggle of Democracy*, pp. 221 and 229.

[264] *See supra*, Part One, Chapter B) II. 1. b).

[265] This is the decisive consideration in the context of the European Convention based on the decision of the Eur. Ct. H.R., *McCann*, Series A, No. 324.

(3) New Concepts of Immediacy?

On the other hand, it has been argued that in some cases "the unlawful violence might not be imminent, but the need to use lethal force in order to prevent that violence might be immediate, since if such force is not used now, it may not be possible to prevent violence later."[266] This assessment refers to what has been termed the "last window of opportunity"[267] Such a concept goes beyond the traditional concept of immediacy; it covers situations in which a person who is difficult to overpower can be targeted even though in that situation he does not pose a direct threat to anyone. If such a situation is still regarded as proportionate, the concept of immediacy has to be stretched:[268] Traditionally, the decisive question is the imminence of the threat to the victim. The new link would have to be the possibility of the State authorities of overpowering the offender. This means that not the concrete danger for the potential victims is decisive, but a rather abstract danger that an offender could do harm in future if he is not targeted now. This kind of prevention differs as it has aspects of mere risk prevention. If regarded thoroughly, this shift of immediacy from the concrete threat posed by an offender to the possibility of overpowering him is not only a gradual extension of the concept of immediacy; it is rather "a move into a completely different kind of legal system."[269]

(4) Dismissal of the Concept of Immediacy?

Another possibility to cover situations that fall outside the traditional concept of immediacy would be to abandon that concept altogether. Such an assessment is based on the argument that the "new threat" by international terrorism is of such a diffuse quality and the possible harm of such great a quantity that immediacy in the classical sense cannot be applicable any more. An example for this assessment could be

---

[266] Kretzmer, 16 *Eur. J. Int'l L.* (2005), at 182.

[267] Michael N. Schmitt, 'Counter-Terrorism and the Use of Force in International Law', in: 32 *Isr. Yb. Hum. Rts.* (2002), pp. 53-116, at 110.

[268] Nolte, 5 *Theo. Inq. L.* (2004), at 115-116.

[269] *Id.*, at 117.

the strike by U.S. agents in Yemen:[270] On November 3, 2002 a missile fired by a U.S. Predator drone killed six suspected al-Qaeda terrorists in a vehicle, including Senior al-Qaeda leader Qaed Salim Sinan al-Harethi and five lower-level operatives.[271] This first strike outside the conflict in Afghanistan which was not based on any immediate threat these persons posed[272] was

> authorized under the same set of classified presidential findings, legal opinions and policy directives ... that have set the rules for the administration's campaign to prevent terror. These orders gave the C.I.A. wide powers to pursue Qaeda terrorists anywhere in the world.[273]

It was thus based on a certain quality or characteristic of the targeted persons (as "terrorists") and not on a specific deed these persons were about to commit.

Up to now, the term "terrorist" did not denote an inherent quality of a person. It expressed rather the relationship of a person to a certain terrorist act. Thus, "terrorists" must be punished for past acts they have committed or are related to in other ways. This falls into the ambit of

---

[270] *Id.*, *Nolte* also draws parallels to the U.S. Supreme Court's strategy to justify the relaxation of the standard of "clear and present danger" for the restriction of the freedom of speech in the 1950s. Since the threat posed by the worldwide communist movement was regarded diffuse and since it put the whole U.S. system of government at risk, the requirement of "clear and present danger" was abandoned in that context, *compare* U.S. Supreme Court, *Dennis v. United States*, No. 336, Judgment of June 4, 1951, 341 *U.S.* (1951), pp. 494-517, at 508-509; *compare also* Norman L. Cantor, 'On Clear and Present Danger, Clear Probability, and Free Speech Standards in Israel', in: 16 *Isr. Yb. Hum. Rts.* (1986), pp. 260-290.

[271] *See* Pincus, *Washington Post*, November 5, 2002, p. 1; Risen, *New York Times*, November 5, 2002, p. 1; *c.f.* Amnesty International Press Release, AI Index AMR 51/168/2002; Downes, 9 *J. Confl. Sec. L.* (2004), pp. 277-294; Gross, *Struggle of Democracy*, p. 243.

[272] *See also* Carsten Stahn, '"Nicaragua is dead, long live Nicaragua" – The Right to Self-Defence under Art. 51 UN Charter and International Terrorism', in: Christian Walter/ Silja Vöneky/ Volker Röben/ Frank Schorkopf (eds.), *Terrorism as a Challenge for National and International Law: Security versus Liberty?*, Berlin 2004, pp. 827-877, at 874-876.

[273] David Johnston/ David E. Sanger, 'Yemen Killing Based on Rules set Out by Bush', in: *New York Times*, November 6, 2002, p. A 16.

criminal prosecution and may not be inflicted by an executive decision to kill the person.[274]

But there may be reasons to change this assessment: Besides the desire (and duty) to protect the life of innocent people it is the quasi military means that are used by terrorist groups and the fear that they will use weapons of mass destruction in the future that may call for a new appraisal of the situation. If this "new threat" calls for a "global war on terror", it may imply that the targeted killing of alleged terrorists is comparable to the killing of enemy combatants in an armed conflict. Such killings, subject to the principles of international humanitarian law, are *per se* legal independently of any immediate threat the combatants pose.[275] Whether such a new assessment of the situation is justified will be examined in-depth *infra*.[276]

(5) The Classical Concept of Immediacy

There are, however, good reasons to retain the classical concept of immediacy in human rights law:[277] As shown above, the right to life is among the supreme values in international law and may only be compromised in the most compelling circumstances. These circumstances must either satisfy high procedural standards or pay regard to the fact that the use of force is the last resort in situations in which other means are not available. Reducing or even abandoning this standard would widen extensively the exception to the right to life.

Furthermore, to the degree the threshold of immediacy is lowered, the probability of error or even abuse will rise. The threshold of immediacy implies that the potential offender is rather close to the deed regarding time and place when the authorities intervene. This means that it is comparably easier to target the right person and that the facts upon which that decision is based are at least potentially obvious to the community. If the offender poses a visible threat to a victim, it is certain that the right person is targeted. Without such an aspect of public con-

---

[274] Nolte, 5 *Theo. Inq. L.* (2004), at 120.

[275] These principles include *inter alia* the prohibition of perfidy and treacherous killings, *see infra*, Part Two, Chapter C) III. 1).

[276] *See infra*, Part Two, Chapter E).

[277] *See also* Stahn, in: Walter *et al.* (eds.), at 874-876.

trol, the danger of mistake or abuse increases and could put everybody at risk.[278]

Additionally, the use of lethal force in cases of lowered or even no immediacy runs the risk of being motivated by the wish to deter others instead of preventing a concrete danger.[279] Such considerations have to be exclusively part of the criminal law sphere. They should not play any role in the decision on a preventive action, which must be limited to addressing the threat which is posed:[280] They do not aim at the prevention of a threat in the situation at hand, but at the general prevention of general dangers in the future.[281]

The risk exists for aspects of retribution or retaliation to influence decisions on the use of force. Such considerations are part of the traditional concept of punishment but should not play a role in preventive actions. While preventive actions may, to a certain degree, take into account the targeted person's earlier behaviour, the decisive factor is not what he did, but what he is just about to do. Past deeds may give clues as to the likelihood of a further deed. But they may not be the sole basis for the preventive use of lethal force. The less immediate a future deed is the more influence is likely to be gained by aspects of retaliation or revenge.

Until now, the international legal order has accepted the risks connected with the classical understanding of immediacy. Human rights law prohibited the preventive killing of an alleged offender before he "raised his gun", even though that may mean that the State could miss the last opportunity. This concept is not sacrosanct, but the consequences of a possible change have to be taken into account. If the threshold is lowered or even abandoned, not only are the targeted per-

---

[278] Nolte, 5 *Theo. Inq. L.* (2004), at 118.

[279] *Compare e.g.* the statement by the Israeli Prime Minister *Ariel Sharon*: "The goal of the plan is to place the terrorists in varying situations every day and to knock them off balance so that they will be busy protecting themselves.", quoted in: Sontag, *New York Times*, April 12, 2001.

[280] University Centre for International Humanitarian Law, Report of the Geneva Expert Meeting, September 1 and 2, 2005, p. 8.

[281] According to the Human Rights Committee, "deterrent or punishment" raise issues under Article 6 in connection with preventive use of lethal force, *see* H.R. Committee, *Concluding Observations on Israel*, UN Doc. CCPR/CO/78 /ISR (August 21, 2003), para. 15.

sons put in jeopardy, but everybody is at risk. The classical requirement of immediacy also serves the confidence of the legal community that preventive force is always used appropriately and without ulterior motives.[282]

If it is not the future deed which is the determining principle of a preventive action, but exclusively the past behaviour, the border between preventive and penal action is blurred, even though it has to be admitted that the past behaviour is one of the foundations for predicting the future behaviour. But persons stigmatised exclusively according to their past behaviour or according to a certain group membership are thus treated like combatants in an armed conflict or even as outlaws who can be subject to forcible action at any time. Such force can easily be the result of unrestrained exercise of will based on personal opinion or impulse or subject to personal whims or prejudices. It lacks reliable reasoning and an adequate determining rule or principle. The use of force in absence of immediacy is thus arbitrary.

(6) Consequences

If these considerations are taken into account, the consequences are as follows: the decisive factor in assessing whether a threat is immediate is the contiguousness of the deed, not the possibility of the authorities to act. While interference by milder means is demanded as early as possible, lethal force may not be used unless the offender is in a position to assault his victim at any time. While he is still *en route*, milder means are probably at the disposition of the authorities. As soon as more than one person is involved (i.e. an agitator and an offender), the forcible action has to be directed against the person that is responsible for the last steps leading to the assault. The use of lethal force against agitators is not necessary as milder means do exist, and thus not proportionate.

c) Proportionality in the Narrow Sense

Cases that necessitate the use of force to reach a legitimate goal may still be disproportionate if no proper balance is struck between the injury caused to the individual by the interfering action and the desired aim. Those measures for which the disadvantage to the individual outweighs

---

282 Nolte, 5 *Theo. Inq. L.* (2004), at 119 and 122.

the purported aim are unduly burdensome and thus disproportionate.[283]

In the case of self-defence, the aim – for instance to save a life – has to be balanced with the cost of a life taken. It is generally accepted that this is in proper balance in the event that the person illegally attacked can save himself at the cost of the offender's life.[284] Only in exceptional cases, e.g. if the assault was intentionally provoked by the person defending himself, can this balance be lacking.[285] The same holds true for the first case considered above, concerning the defence of another person. As the use of lethal force in the second and third example described above is not the mildest means or least-injurious alternative and thus not necessary, the question of proportionality in the narrow sense does not arise in those cases.

3. Deprivation of Life in Order to Effect an Arrest or Prevent the Escape of a Person Detained

The use of force that is absolutely necessary to effect a lawful arrest or to prevent the escape of a person lawfully detained is also not considered "arbitrary" in the meaning of Article 6 of the Covenant.[286] This in-

---

[283] Arai-Takahashi, *Margin of Appreciation*, pp. 192-193; Nolte, 57 *Mod. L. Rev.* (1994), at 193 and 202; H.R. Committee, *Maria Fanny Suárez de Guerrero ("Camargo Case")*, para. 13.3.

[284] *See e.g.* Nowak, *CCPR Commentary*, Art. 6, para. 14 (p. 111); Robertson, 43 *Brit. Yb. Int'l L.* (1968-69), at 30; Dinstein, in: Henkin (ed.), at 118-119. The same situation is accepted in many national legal systems, *compare e.g.* Jochen Abraham Frowein, 'Im Zweifel für den vielleicht tödlichen Schuß?' in: Erhard Denninger/ Manfred O. Hinz (eds.), *Kritik und Vertrauen: Festschrift für Peter Schneider zum 70. Geburtstag*, Frankfurt am Main 1990, pp. 112-121; Heike Witzstrock, *Der polizeiliche Todesschuß*, Frankfurt am Main 2001.

[285] *See e.g.* Schönke/ Schröder/ Lenckner (eds.), *Strafgesetzbuch*, § 32, paras. 55-61.

[286] Dinstein, in: Henkin (ed.), at 119; Robertson, 43 *Brit. Yb. Int'l L.* (1968-69), at 30; Nowak, *CCPR Commentary*, Art. 6, para. 14 (p. 111); *similarly*, H.R. Committee, *Maria Fanny Suárez de Guerrero ("Camargo Case")*, para. 13.2; Nsereko, in: Ramcharan (ed.), at 246.

terpretation finds support in the *travaux préparatoires*.[287] Again, this exception to the protection of the right to life has to pursue a legitimate aim and adhere to the standards of proportionality in order to be legal. The arrest of an alleged offender or the prevention of the escape of a person legally detained are legitimate aims. To be proportionate, the use of force must be capable of furthering these aims; it must be the least intrusive means, and it must be reasonably related to the aim.[288]

a) Capability to Further the Aim

The use of force must be at least "theoretically capable of contributing to achieving its aim",[289] i.e. to effect an arrest or prevent an escape. As far as the prevention of an escape is concerned, the capability of the use of force to reach this aim is rather clear: If a detainee tries to escape, he cannot proceed if he is injured or even killed.

The same question is more problematic concerning the use of force in order to arrest a person: If the person is injured and thus cannot flee, the use of force is capable of attaining the arrest. However, in the event that the targeted person is killed, he cannot be "arrested". Strictly speaking, force causing the death of a person can never be capable of furthering that person's arrest. Thus, the death of the person may neither be intended directly nor be an inevitable or practically certain side-effect that is accepted of the action taken.[290] This does not mean that the use of lethal force is absolutely prohibited whenever a person is being arrested: The law-enforcement agents are of course allowed to use lethal force in self-defence and in defence of other persons that are threatened by the alleged offender, subject to the immediacy of this threat. Such a use of lethal force is, however, not justified as force necessary to effect an arrest. It is justified to defend the life of another person.

---

[287] *See e.g.* the Netherlands proposal to amend Article 6 and include the exceptions known from the European Convention on Human Rights, UN Doc. A/C.3/L.651, reprinted in: Bossuyt, *Travaux Préparatoires*, p. 124.

[288] Nolte, 57 *Mod. L. Rev.* (1994), at 193.

[289] *Id.*

[290] *But see* Kremnitzer, in: Fleck (ed.), *Rechtsfragen*, at 203.

In consequence, the use of force that will inevitably or practically certainly lead to the death of the alleged offender is not capable of furthering that person's arrest. "The shooting to kill of suspected offenders ... where the life or limb of the arresting officer or that of third parties is not in peril is arbitrary."[291] Law enforcement personnel may thus only shoot to injure a person in order to effect an arrest. As a result of the employment of such force some individuals may be fatally injured nevertheless.[292] Such deaths are not automatically arbitrary as long as they are unwanted side effects.

Thus, the use of force that will not fatally injure an alleged offender is capable of furthering his arrest, whereas the use of any force up to the level that will inevitably be lethal is capable of preventing the escape of a detainee.

b) Necessity of the Means

The use of these different categories of force must furthermore be necessary, i.e. the least intrusive means among equally effective means to achieve these aims.[293]

(1) Effecting an Arrest

Concerning an arrest, possible milder means may include warning the offender and giving him the opportunity to surrender as well as overpowering him without using force of arms. These means have to be equally effective. This may be doubtful concerning a warning. However, such a warning is generally required before force is used.[294] Over-

---

291 Nsereko, in: Ramcharan (ed.), at 254-255; *see also* Christoph Grabenwarter, *Europäische Menschenrechtskonvention*, 3rd ed., München 2008, § 20, para. 14 (p. 137) in the context of the European Convention.

292 Nsereko, in: Ramcharan (ed.), at 246.

293 Arai-Takahashi, *Margin of Appreciation*, p. 192; Nolte, 57 *Mod. L. Rev.* (1994), at 193; Nsereko, in: Ramcharan (ed.), at 254.

294 *See e.g.* H.R. Committee, *Maria Fanny Suárez de Guerrero ("Camargo Case")*, para. 13.2; *c.f.* McGoldrick, *Human Rights Committee*, para. 8.19 (pp. 340-341); Nsereko, in: Ramcharan (ed.), at 254; Principle 10 of the UN Basic Principles on the Use of Force and Firearms by Law Enforcement Officials reads: "...law enforcement officials shall identify themselves as such and give a

powering the offender without using weapons is equally effective as long as the person subject to the arrest is not armed, and even if that person is armed but can be overpowered in a manner so surprising that he cannot use his weapon. Furthermore, the use of distracting devices or electrical incapacitation devices may give the law enforcement personnel several seconds in which the targeted person is not able to react and can thus be overpowered.[295] Only if this is not possible, should there be resort to firearms to effect his arrest, and then in a way that will not fatally injure him. However, it has to be kept in mind that the law enforcement personnel may use more extensive force to defend themselves.

(2) Preventing an Escape

Concerning the prevention of an escape, possible milder means may also include warning the offender and giving him the opportunity to surrender, overpowering him without using weapons as well as the use of non-lethal force.[296] These means have to be equally effective.

Regarding a warning, the same standards apply as above. Such a warning is generally required before the use of force. Overpowering the detainee without using weapons is equally effective as long he is not armed, and even if he is armed but can be overpowered by surprise before he can resort to force himself.

Only if the detainee is armed and ready to use his weapon, the use of force possibly lethal is necessary at all. The aim of preventing his escape

---

clear warning of their intent to use firearms, with sufficient time for the warning to be observed, unless to do so would unduly place the law enforcement officials at risk or would create a risk of death or serious harm to other persons, or would be clearly inappropriate or pointless in the circumstances of the incident."

[295] Distraction devices explode with a brilliant flash of light and a loud report and, beside the surprise they cause, impair the vision of persons subjected to them briefly. Electrical incapacitation devices usually cause tetany of large muscle groups for the duration of the electrical flow and thus prevent any action by the person subjected to them for that period of time. *See* Bozeman/ Winslow, 5 *Internet J. Resc. & Disaster Med.* (2005), No. 1; Thiel, 42 *Rev. dr. mil.* (2003), at 388.

[296] Nsereko, in: Ramcharan (ed.), at 254.

could probably be achieved by the use of non-lethal force. If a person is injured in a way that makes it impossible for him to continue his escape, the aim is reached and the person can easily be overpowered. If the person is still capable of resisting in a way that endangers the law enforcement personnel, the use of further force may be necessary to overcome that resistance. This may include lethal force if that is justified as self-defence or the defence of another person. Thus, it is argued that "[t]he shooting to kill of suspected offenders or those attempting to escape from lawful custody ... where the life or limb of the arresting officer or that of third parties is not in peril is arbitrary."[297]

Only in the case where it is not possible to stop the person by non-lethal force is use of force that is presumably lethal the only means of preventing the escape. However, it has to be kept in mind that the aim is to prevent the escape and not to kill the detainee. It is sufficient to incapacitate him in a way that prevents him from escaping but spares his life. It is not necessary to kill the detainee with direct intention even though his death might be a side effect of the action. Thus, the intention concerning the death of the detainee may not go beyond *dolus eventualis*. Such cases are probably the absolute minority, but they cannot be excluded absolutely. It is rather unlikely, but nevertheless possible that the use of presumably lethal force is necessary to prevent the escape of a legally detained person.

c) Proportionality in the Narrow Sense

Even if the use of force which is presumably lethal is the only promising means to stop the escape of a person, it may be disproportionate if no proper balance is struck between the injury caused to the individual and the desired aim.[298]

At this point, the aim "to prevent an escape" has to be examined in depth. A first impulse may be to differentiate between the escape of a thief and that of a mass murderer. According to this view, the seriousness of the offence with which the targeted person is charged or has

---

[297] *Id.*, at 254-255.

[298] *Compare* Arai-Takahashi, *Margin of Appreciation*, pp. 192-193; Nolte, 57 *Mod. L. Rev.* (1994), at 193 and 202; H.R. Committee, *Maria Fanny Suárez de Guerrero ("Camargo Case")*, para. 13.3.

been convicted of must be considered. "Shooting an individual charged with or convicted of a petty offence may not be justified."[299]

This assessment does not only take the escape into account, but seems to regard the potential harm that can be done by the person in question as the decisive factor.[300] This harm is assessed according to the past deed the offender is convicted or accused of.

If the potential harm such a person might cause in the future is decisive, the threat posed by him has to be imminent to justify the use of lethal force. Unless the offender poses a threat to the law enforcement personnel (which could then act in self-defence) or to a third person, i.e. a hostage (which could justify the use of lethal force to save that person), the threat the offender poses is not immediate if the standards developed above are applied:[301] Neither is a convicted thief who is fleeing just about to steal anything, nor is a murderer who tries to escape, automatically just about to kill someone.

As a consequence, the use of lethal force against escaping persons cannot be exclusively based or depend on such vague future threats. The reason to use such force must be to prevent the escape of a person lawfully detained. The fact that a person lawfully detained tries to escape has to be regarded as a threat *per se*, irrespective of the offences the person is accused or convicted of. Only when it comes to the severity of that threat, can factors such as the past deeds of the person be taken into account if an inequitable result is to be avoided: the authorisation to avoid any escape at any price could result in a general policy of shooting to kill in such cases.

Yet, a limitation that takes account of the specific threat posed by the escaping person is not easily feasible: it may be doubted whether law enforcement personnel would have the necessary information and would be able to take the severity of a past deed into account in a stressful situation like the escape of a detainee. Additionally, if a past deed was the decisive fact concerning the use of lethal force in case of an escape, offenders accused or convicted of minor offences could trust

---

299 Nsereko, in: Ramcharan (ed.), at 254; concerning the same question with regard to the European Convention *see also* Dijk/ Hoof, *European Convention*, p. 305

300 *See* Kremnitzer, in: Fleck (ed.), *Rechtsfragen*, at 202.

301 *Compare supra*, Part One, Chapter B) II. 2. b) (5).

in the fact that the use of lethal force against them would not be proportionate. They could thus try to escape with a very limited risk.

Thus, if the acting authorities are aware of the very low danger that a detainee would present if he were to escape, should they not resort to force which is presumably lethal but only to non-lethal force. Their intention has to be to prevent the escape, while hoping or believing that the detainee will survive.

4. Deprivation of Life for the Purpose of Quelling a Riot

The use of force necessary to suppress an insurrection or quell a riot is considered as not "arbitrary" in the meaning of Article 6 ICCPR.[302] As for all exceptions to the protection of the right to life, the use of force in such a situation has to pursue a legitimate aim and adhere to the standards of proportionality in order to be legal. States have a right and also a duty to protect the lives of innocent persons.[303] The aim of quelling a riot or insurrection is to re-establish a status of security and thus avoid possible harm to individuals. If the dangers resulting from mass violence are taken in into account, it becomes clear that the suppression of insurrections and the quelling of riots are generally legitimate aims. To be proportionate, the use of lethal force has to be capable of furthering this aim while being the least intrusive means and it must be reasonably related to its aim.

a) Capability to Further the Aim

The use of lethal force has to be capable of quelling a riot or insurrection. Force against a single person taking part in a riot is capable of stopping that person. It is, however, not clear whether such force is capable of stopping the riot as a whole, i.e. not only the targeted person but more importantly, the other persons. The force may shock the oth-

---

[302] Dinstein, in: Henkin (ed.), at 119; Nowak, *CCPR Commentary*, Art. 6, para. 14 (p. 111); Nsereko, in: Ramcharan (ed.), at 247-248. *See also* the Netherlands proposal to amend Article 6 and include the exceptions known from the European Convention on Human Rights, UN Doc. A/C.3/L.651, reprinted in: Bossuyt, *Travaux Préparatoires*, p. 124.

[303] *Compare e.g.* Kabaalioğlu, in: Ramcharan (ed.), at 167-179; Klein, in: Klein (ed.), at 306-307; Nowak, *CCPR Commentary*, Art. 6, paras. 3-6.

er participants and deter them from further acts. On the other hand, the use of lethal force, e.g. by utilising fire arms, brings a new quality of violence into the situation. This may also spin the cycle of violence further and lead to an escalation of the situation rather than calming it down.

If all persons taking part in a riot are targeted, the use of such force is definitely capable of stopping an insurrection, even though such an extensive use of force will clearly fail to meet the requirements of necessity *infra*. Thus, the use of lethal force against persons taking part in a riot is capable of quelling that riot, but it is not *per se* clear how many persons have to be targeted in order to have an impact on the whole group.

b) Necessity Regarding the Quelling of a Riot or Insurrection

The use of lethal force must be necessary, i.e. the least restrictive means among means equally effective in ending a riot.[304] In such a situation, milder means are palpable: Anti-riot forces which are equipped with protective gear such as riot shields and can resort to truncheons, water cannons, chemical irritant agents, distraction devices, kinetic impact munitions or electrical incapacitation devices can fight a riot very efficiently,[305] a fact that might lead to a duty to equip forces with such or comparable gear.[306] These milder means might even prove more effective: The better the law enforcement personnel are protected, the greater is their opportunity to act defensively and avoid any escalation.

If a fire arm is used by a single rioter, obviously a situation of self-defence exists *vis-à-vis* that person. This situation justifies the use of lethal force subject to the conditions developed above.[307] Nevertheless, this does not mean that the general use of firearms is then justified

---

304 Arai-Takahashi, *Margin of Appreciation*, p. 192; Nolte, 57 *Mod. L. Rev.* (1994), at 193; Nsereko, in: Ramcharan (ed.), at 254.

305 On the different means that could be employed and the risk they involve *see* Bozeman/ Winslow, 5 *Internet J. Resc. & Disaster Med.* (2005), No. 1 (with further references); *compare also* 42 *Rev. dr. mil.* (2003), at 385-393.

306 On this question in connection with the European Convention on Human Rights, *compare infra* Part One, Chapter E) II. 2. d).

307 *Compare supra*, Part One, Chapters B) II. 2. b) (1) and (2).

against the whole group. This does not automatically change when several rioters use fire arms: Still each person has to be regarded individually. It is still the single person that poses a threat to limb or life of the law enforcement personnel, and not the group as such.

This general assessment will only change in the case of a violent internal unrest of such severity that the application of international humanitarian law is triggered:[308] In such situations the question of who may be targeted is treated differently.[309] States of emergency in the meaning of Article 4 CCPR do not necessarily entail such a change, as the right to life is one of the non-derogable rights excepted in Article 4.[310] States of emergency may have the quality of an armed conflict, but may also stay beneath that threshold.[311]

Thus, according to the author's view, the use of lethal force exclusively to suppress a riot or insurrection is not necessary. Single cases of self-defence may necessitate such force, but only against those persons who pose a specific threat. The general use of force against a whole group of rioters is not acceptable under the Covenant unless such force is justified under international humanitarian law.

The use of lethal force to quell a riot is permitted by Article 2 para. 2 European Convention and is thus regarded by many authors as a non-arbitrary under the Covenant.[312] Some authors are even of the opinion that cases of deprivation of life permitted by the Covenant "go far beyond" those permitted by Article 2 para. 2 of the European Convention.[313] However, if the possibilities of quelling a riot by non-lethal means are taken into account and cases of self-defence are separated

---

[308] *Compare infra*, Part Four, Chapter C).

[309] *Compare infra*, Part Two, Chapters C) and D).

[310] *Compare* ICJ, *Legality of the Threat or Use of Nuclear Weapons*, Advisory Opinion of July 8, 1996, I.C.J. Reports 1996, pp. 225-593, at 240 (para. 25); Nowak, *CCPR Commentary*, Art. 4, para. 21.

[311] Nowak, *CCPR Commentary*, Art. 4, para. 12.

[312] Robertson, 43 *Brit. Yb. Int'l L.* (1968-69), at 30-31; Dinstein, in: Henkin (ed.), at 119; Joseph/ Schultz/ Castan, *International Covenant*, para. 8.05 (p. 156); Nowak, *CCPR Commentary*, Art. 6, para 14; Gollwitzer, *Menschenrechte*, Art. 2 MRK/Art. 6 IPBPR, para. 8 (p. 157).

[313] Heinz Guradze, 'Die Menschenrechtskonventionen der Vereinten Nationen vom 16. Dezember 1966', in: 15 *Jb. Int. R.* (1971), pp. 242-273, at 255.

carefully, the use of lethal force is not necessary to quell a riot. This corresponds the following view: "Certain rights are not protected by the European Convention, or are defined more broadly or expressively in the International Covenant. Such rights include ... the right to life ... . Although the texts of both conventions immediately admit of limitations on the enjoyment of rights, the International Covenant permits narrower State discretion in imposing limits."[314]

c) Proportionality in the Narrow Sense?

Still, according to Robertson, the use of lethal force for the purpose of quelling a riot of insurrection might "nevertheless be considered 'arbitrary' within the meaning of the Covenant on the ground that the objective of the demonstration was just and that the quelling of a resultant riot was 'unjust'."[315] This assessment indicates that *Robertson* acquires the proportionality in the narrow sense of such force. This "marginal case", as *Robertson* calls it, does not even arise in the author's opinion, as the use of lethal force is not necessary to quell a riot or insurrection as long as the situation is governed by human rights and not by international humanitarian law.

5. Absolute Limits and Non-Derogability of Article 6

As shown above, the exceptions to the right of life exclusively apply to persons that give reason for the use of lethal force by their own behaviour. The use of such force may solely be directed against a person that causes a threat. The death of third persons has to be considered individually for each person and is not justified if these persons did not pose an immediate threat themselves. As seen in the example of quelling a riot, human rights in contrast to international humanitarian law[316] do not tolerate "collateral damage": The right to life does not leave room for the killing of innocent persons even if the overall aim is to save life.

---

[314] Liz Heffernan, 'A Comparative View of Individual Petition Procedures under the European Convention on Human Rights and the International Covenant on Civil and Political Rights', in: 19 *Hum. Rts. Q.* (1997), pp. 78-112, at 89-90.

[315] Robertson, 43 *Brit. Yb. Int'l L.* (1968-69), at 31.

[316] *Compare infra*, Part Two, Chapter D) II. 2.

This even applies if several persons could be saved at the cost of one innocent person's life.[317] Possible exception to this principle can only derive from humanitarian law standards[318] and cannot be "deduced from the terms of the Covenant itself."[319]

Additionally, the right to life is part of those rights that may not be derogated from. Article 4 of the International Covenant provides for the possibility of derogations:

> In time of public emergency which threatens the life of the nation and the existence of which is officially proclaimed, the States Parties to the present Covenant may take measures derogating from their obligations under the present Covenant to the extent strictly required by the exigencies of the situation, provided that such measures are not inconsistent with their other obligations under international law and do not involve discrimination solely on the ground of race, colour, sex, language, religion or social origin.[320]

---

[317] *Compare* Georg Nolte, 'The *Bundesverfassungsgericht* on the German Aerial Security Law: A *Sonderweg* from the perspective of international law?', in: Christian Tomuschat/ Evelyne Lagrange/ Stefan Oeter (eds.), *The Right to Life*, Leiden 2010, pp. 83-94, at 88-91; see also German Federal Constitutional Court (Bundesverfassungsgericht), Case No. 1 BvR 357/05 (Luftsicherheitsgesetz/"Aviation Security Act"), Judgment of February 15, 2006, reprinted in: 59 *NJW* (2006), pp. 751-761, at 757-760 (paras. 119-139); *compare also* Helmut Philipp Aust, 'German Constitutional Law Cases 2004-2006', in: 13 *Eur. Pub. L.* (2007), pp. 205-222, at 205-209; Oliver Lepsius, 'Human Dignity and the Downing of Aircraft: The German Federal Constitutional Court Strikes Down a Prominent Anti-terrorism Provision in the New Air-Transport Security Act', in: 7 *German L. J.* (2006), pp. 761-776, at 766-774; Nina Naske/ Georg Nolte, 'International Decisions – "Aerial Security Law"', in: 101 *Am. J. Int'l L.* (2007), pp. 466-470; *see also* Baumann, 57 *DÖV* (2004), at 858-860. The same reasoning was adopted by the Polish Constitutional Court, *see* Nolte, in: Tomuschat *et al.*, at 83 (with further references). On the comparable question within the framework of an armed conflict *see* Eyal Benvenisti, 'Human Dignity in Combat: The Duty to Spare Enemy Civilians', in: 39 *Isr. L. Rev.* (2006), pp. 81-109.

[318] *Compare infra*, Part Two, Chapter D) II. 2. b).

[319] ICJ, *Legality of the Threat or Use of Nuclear Weapons*, Advisory Opinion of July 8, 1996, I.C.J. Reports 1996, pp. 225-593, at 240 (para. 25).

[320] On the definition of this concept compare Section (A) 1 of the International Law Association, *Minimum Standards of Human Rights Norms in a State of Emergency*, adopted on the conference from August 26 to September 1, 1984, in Paris, France, also referred to as "Paris Standards", reprinted in: 79 *Am.*

Such derogations are subject to an official proclamation and the requirement of proportionality.[321] They have to be in conformity with international law and must be non-discriminatory.[322] Article 5 further limits the possibility of derogation: It calls for a subjective inquiry into the aims and objectives of a State's derogation from the Covenant, be it pursuant to Article 4 or Article 22 para. 2.[323]

While these derogations are accepted as a "necessary evil",[324] the most basic rights protected by the covenant are non-derogable:[325] According to Article 4 para. 2 ICCPR, the right to life may never be suspended.[326] "Exceptional circumstances including a state of war or threat of war, internal political instability or any other public emergency may not be invoked as a justification of ... [arbitrary] executions."[327] This, however, does not mean that any deprivation of life in an armed conflict is contrary to the Covenant:

J. Int'l L. 1985, pp. 1073-1081; *see also* Joseph/ Schultz/ Castan, *International Covenant*, para. 25.51 (pp. 824-825); Buergenthal, in: Henkin (ed.), at 79-80.

[321] *Compare* H.R. Committee, CCPR General Comment No. 29, *Derogations during States of Emergency (Article 4)*, 72nd Sess., August 31, 2001, UN Doc. CCPR/C/21/Rev.1/Add.11 (2001), reprinted in: Compilation of General Comments and General Recommendations adopted by Human Rights Treaty Bodies, U.N. Doc. HRI/GEN/1/Rev.7 (May 12, 2004), pp. 184-191, at 185-186 (paras. 4-6); Oraá, *States of Emergency*, pp. 140-170; Boyle, in: Benedek/ Yotopoulos-Marangopoulos (eds.), at 104.

[322] *Compare* H.R. Committee, CCPR General Comment No. 29, at 186-187 (paras. 8-10); Oraá, *States of Emergency*, pp. 171-189; Buergenthal, in: Henkin (ed.), at 82-83.

[323] Carlson/ Gisvold, *International Covenant*, p. 26.

[324] Joseph/ Schultz/ Castan, *International Covenant*, para. 25.49 (p. 824).

[325] Oraá, *States of Emergency*, pp. 87-97.

[326] Nowak, *CCPR Commentary*, Art. 6, para. 1 (pp. 104-105); H.R. Committee, CCPR General Comment No. 6, at 128 (para. 1).

[327] UN Economic and Social Council, Resolution 1989/65 (May 24, 1989), Annex, *Principles on the effective Prevention and Investigation of extra-legal, arbitrary and summary Executions*, 1989 UN ESCOR, Supp. No. 1 (UN Doc. E/1989/89), pp. 52-53, at 52 (para. 1).

6. Deprivation of Life in the Course of an Armed Conflict

According to Voltaire, "killing a man is murder unless you do it to the sound of trumpets."[328] But not all killings in the course of an armed conflict are legal due to the fact that they take place in that context. Concerning the deprivation of life in course of an armed conflict, two different approaches do exist: Generally, international humanitarian law is applied as the standard to assess the legality or arbitrariness of a deprivation of life. Additionally, the overall legality of the conflict in the context of which such a deprivation takes place could also be included into the considerations.

According to the International Court of Justice, international humanitarian law constitutes the *lex specialis* in the context of armed conflicts concerning the interpretation of the term "arbitrarily" in Article 6 ICCPR:

> In principle, the right not arbitrarily to be deprived of one's life applies also in hostilities. The test of what is an arbitrary deprivation of life, however, then falls to be determined by the applicable *lex specialis*, namely, the law applicable in armed conflict which is designed to regulate the conduct of hostilities. Thus whether a particular loss of life, through the use of a certain weapon in warfare, is to be considered an arbitrary deprivation of life contrary to Article 6 of the Covenant, can only be decided by reference to the law applicable in armed conflict and not deduced from the terms of the Covenant itself.[329]

This statement has recently been referred to and confirmed by the Court.[330] It is not necessary at this point to exhaust the general relationship of human rights law to international humanitarian law.[331] However, there is agreement that acts of war are not prohibited by Article 6 ICCPR, "if they do not violate internationally recognized laws

---

[328] *Compare* Schmitt, 17 *Yale J. Int'l L.* (1999), at 610.

[329] ICJ, *Legality of the Threat or Use of Nuclear Weapons*, Advisory Opinion of July 8, 1996, I.C.J. Reports 1996, pp. 225-593, at 240 (para. 25).

[330] ICJ, *Legal Consequences of the Construction of a Wall in the Occupied Palestine Territory*, Advisory Opinion of July 9, 2004, I.C.J. Reports 2004, pp. 133-271, at 177-178 (paras. 104-106).

[331] On this question compare *infra*, Part Four.

and customs of war."[332] Such lawful acts of war have to be distinguished from deprivation of life as an act of retribution[333] and war crimes, which are obviously arbitrary.[334] The international humanitarian law rules governing such acts will be examined *en detail infra*.[335]

7. *Means of Control*

The standards developed above can only be of sustainable effect if their application is controlled by any means at all. This proves difficult in situations of dependency, especially regarding detention: The Human Rights Committee has therefore lowered the procedural requirements in such cases.[336] Control also proves difficult in situations in which decisions have to be made by law enforcement personnel in a short amount time, under stress and based on limited knowledge of the facts. Nevertheless it is of utmost importance to prevent killings that are not necessary in such situations.

---

[332] UN Secretary-General, *Respect for Human Rights in Armed Conflicts*, Report of September 18, 1970, 25th Sess., Agenda Item 47, UN Doc. A/8052 (September 18, 1970), p. 104 (Annex I, para. 46); *compare also* Buergenthal, in: Henkin (ed.), at 83; Yoram Dinstein, *The Conduct of Hostilities under the Law of International Armed Conflict*, Cambridge 2004, pp. 23-24; Jochen Abraham Frowein/ Wolfgang Peukert (eds.), *Europäische Menschenrechtskonvention – EMRK-Kommentar*, 2nd ed., Kehl am Rhein 1996, Art. 15, para. 12 (p. 484); Theodor Meron, *Human Rights in Internal Strife: Their International Protection*, Cambridge 1987, p. 24; Fausto Pocar, 'Human Rights under the International Covenant on Civil and Political Rights and Armed Conflicts', in: Lal Chand Vohrah *et al.* (eds.), *Man's Inhumanity to Man – Essays on International Law in Honour of Antonio Cassese*, The Hague 2003, pp. 729-740, at 734; Ramcharan, 30 *Nether. Int'l L. Rev.* (1983), at 308-309.

[333] Meron, *Internal Strife*, p. 24; UN General Assembly, Third Committee (Social, Humanitarian and Cultural), *Government of the Netherlands proposal*, GAOR 10th Sess., Annexes (X), 28 – I, p. 24, A/C.3/L.460 (September 20, 1955).

[334] Ramcharan, 30 *Nether. Int'l L. Rev.* (1983), at 317; *c.f.* H.R. Committee, CCPR General Comment No. 6, *at* 128 (para. 2).

[335] *See infra*, Part Two.

[336] *Compare supra*, Part One, Chapter B) I. 2. a).

a) Perspective of a Third Person as Standard?

One possibility to secure that the theoretical considerations on immediacy can bear the practical requirements is to use the perspective of a third person as standard, i.e. "the requirement of visible immediacy":[337] Only if the situation obviously demands the use of lethal force to stop the offender and hinder his deed, as the offender's distance to the victim is to small for alternative means to be promising, may such force be used. The obvious nature of the situation according to this approach must be compelling.[338] If an objective observer would not come to this conclusion, as the danger is not yet visible, then most likely other possibilities to hinder the deed exist.

Can this standard be reasonably applied to the situations examined above? In a situation of self-defence and of in the defence of another person, an observer sees the threat the offender poses to his victim, i.e. the gun that is raised, and thus the imminence of the situation is evident. If the situation is not yet as imminent[339] this will most likely not be true, as the offender and the victim are still in different places. However, not all dangers are as obvious as a raised gun. The case might be difficult concerning suicide attacks. In such cases, the danger cannot be spotted if the explosives remain hidden until the trigger is pulled. Thus, the "visible immediacy" is a strong indication to assess a situation as imminent, but cannot be an exclusive means.

b) Procedural Safeguards *ex post factum*

A more comprehensive means of safeguarding that necessity and immediacy are considered adequately are a procedural safeguard *ex post factum*. Each country has to have an effective system of checks and controls with regard to permissible deprivations of life.[340] Each case in-

---

337 Nolte, 5 *Theo. Inq. L.* (2004), at 119.

338 *Id.*, at 118.

339 *Compare* the second and third examples used above, *supra* Part One, Chapter B) II. 2. b).

340 Ramcharan, in: Ramcharan (ed.), at 21.

volving the preventive use of lethal force should thus be investigated by an impartial body.[341]

The source of a duty to conduct such investigations is the Covenant itself: Beside the general duty to actively protect laid down in Article 2 of the Covenant,[342] the right to life itself "requires that States adopt positive measures"[343] to prevent arbitrary killings.[344] If such measures include the recognition of arbitrary executions as offences under criminal law,[345] it is a matter of course that investigations have to take place in order to assess whether the deprivation of a life qualifies as arbitrary. Such "killings are the more arbitrary when the authorities fail to bring recalcitrant law enforcement officials to justice."[346] However, the investigations cannot be identical to criminal prosecution, as the latter's realisation depends on a certain degree of suspicion. There have to be standard procedures that are performed in each and every case, irrespectively of whether it is suspicious or seems clearly legal. This investigation would then show whether criminal proceedings are due.

Such an investigation has consequences not only for the examined case, which is considered retrospectively, but more importantly for future cases: It shows which standards are applied and clarifies that investiga-

---

[341] *Compare e.g.* H.R. Committee, *Concluding Observations on Peru*, UN Doc. CCPR/C/79/Add.8 (September 25, 1992), para. 8: "It [the Committee] is troubled by the great number of complaints of extrajudicial executions and disappearances attributed to the security forces. In this respect, the Committee is deeply concerned with the absence of civilian control ...".

[342] *Compare supra*, Part One, Chapter B) I. 2.

[343] H.R. Committee, CCPR General Comment No. 6, at 129 (para. 5); *see also* Kabaalioğlu, in: Ramcharan (ed.), at 164-165; *c.f.* Nowak, *CCPR Commentary*, Art. 6, paras. 3-6 and 17; Klein, in: Klein (ed.), at 306-310; Dinstein, in: Henkin (ed.), at 115.

[344] H.R. Committee, CCPR General Comment No. 6, *at* 128-129 (para. 3); Carlson/ Gisvold, *International Covenant*, p. 67; Ramcharan, in: Ramcharan (ed.), at 17.

[345] UN Economic and Social Council, Resolution 1989/65 (May 24, 1989), Annex, *Principles on the effective Prevention and Investigation of extra-legal, arbitrary and summary Executions*, 1989 UN ESCOR, Supp. No. 1 (UN Doc. E/1989/89), pp. 52-53, at 52 (para. 1).

[346] Nsereko, in: Ramcharan (ed.), at 255, referring to excessive use of force during arrest or the prevention of escape.

tions and eventually prosecution will take place. This compels the law enforcement authorities to act in a responsible manner.

Additionally, such investigations must, at least generally, be public. It is a "cardinal rule of procedural justice that requires judicial tribunals to open their proceedings to public scrutiny so that justice is not only done but also manifestly appears to be done."[347] Thus, in a parallel argument to the "requirement of visible immediacy", public control can help to maintain the standards developed above. Furthermore, public perception of the investigations provides a basis for the trust of society into its law enforcement authorities.

The exigency of *ex post* investigations in cases of preventive deprivation of life has been developed *en detail* by the European Court of Human Rights concerning the protection of the right to life by the European Convention.[348]

III. Conclusion: Killings Under the International Covenant

The right to life under the ICCPR offers a high, albeit not absolute standard of protection: The death penalty is a possible exception but must adhere high procedural standards. Beside that, targeted killings, i.e. killings which aim at the death of the person with "*dolus directus* of the first degree", are clearly arbitrary deprivations of life under the covenant.

In preventive action, lethal force may only be used to address immediate threats. In this context, the classical concept of immediacy applies: Lethal force may only be used if the realisation of a threat can be immediately triggered by the alleged offender without any further steps in between. At an earlier time, milder means are available. The decision on the use of preventive force may not be influenced by aspects of retaliation or punishment.

In these situations, the death of the targeted person may only be a side-effect and not the aim of the action. This side-effect should theoretically be probable at the most, i.e. intended with *dolus eventualis*. However,

---

347 *Id.*, at 250.

348 *See* Eur. Ct. H.R., *McCann*, Series A, No. 324, p. 49 (para. 161); *compare infra*, Part One, Chapter E) I. 2. b).

in practice, the differentiation between *dolus eventualis* and direct intention of second degree will most likely be impossible and may even appear cynical: It is accepted that the death of the offender can be an inevitable side-effect in order to save another person's life.

Concerning an arrest, the death of the person may never be intended: The force used may only injure the targeted person. Regarding the prevention of an escape, the detainee's death may, at the most, be intended with *dolus eventualis*. In exceptional cases, even this may be disproportionate. In quelling a riot or insurrection, lethal force may not be used at all. However, the law enforcement personnel may act in self-defence if necessary in each of these situations. Finally, the human right to life does not accept "collateral damage": The death of innocent third persons cannot be justified under the Covenant.

These principles may not be derogated from, but grant one exception: If international humanitarian law is applicable, the arbitrariness of the deprivation of a life is assessed according to humanitarian law standards. Lawful acts of war are not arbitrary under Article 6 of the Covenant.

C. The American Convention on Human Rights

The American Convention on Human Rights,[349] also referred to as the "Pact of San José",[350] was adopted by the Organization of American States on November 22, 1969 and entered into force on July 18, 1978, after it received the required number of eleven ratifications.[351] Accord-

---

[349] American Convention on Human Rights, also referred to as the "Pact of San José", adopted by the Inter-American Specialized Conference on Human Rights at San José, Costa Rica, November 22, 1969, entry into force on July 18, 1978, reprinted in: *OAS Treaty Series* No. 36 and 1144 *UNTS* (1979), No. 17955, pp. 123-212.

[350] *See e.g.* Thomas Buergenthal, 'The Inter-American System for the Protection of Human Rights', in: *Annuario Jurídico Interamericano* (1981), pp. 80-120, partly reprinted in: Thomas Buergenthal/ Robert Norris/ Dinah Shelton, *Protecting Human Rights in the Americas – Selected Problems*, 2nd ed., Kehl 1986, pp. 3 *et seqq.*, at 12-13.

[351] *Compare* Article 74 para. 2 American Convention on Human Rights. On the history of the Inter-American System *compare* Christina M. Cerna, 'The In-

ing to Article 1, the States party to the American Convention have an obligation both to "respect" the rights guaranteed and to "ensure" the free and full exercise of these rights. This comprises "necessarily ... the concept of the restriction of the exercise of State power"[352] in order to respect the rights, and also appropriate means by which violations are prevented, punished, or compensation is paid in order to ensure the rights.[353] This duty concerns all civil and political rights contained in the Convention.[354] Thus the convention places positive and negative duties on the parties to it.[355]

I. Article 4 American Convention on Human Rights' Scope of Protection

The right to life is protected in Article 4 of the American Convention on Human Rights. Article 4 paragraph 1 reads:

---

ter-American System for the Protection of Human Rights', in: 16 *Fla. J. Int'l L.* (2004), pp. 195-212, at 196-203; Robertson/ Merrills, *Human Rights*, pp. 197-202.

[352] Inter-Am. Ct. H.R., *The Word "Laws" in Article 30*, Series A, No. 6, para. 21; *compare also* Inter-Am. Ct. H.R., *Angel Manfredo Velásquez-Rodríguez*, Series C, No. 4, para. 165; Inter-Am. Ct. H.R., *Godínez-Cruz*, Series C, No. 5, para. 174; on the Court's authority to issue advisory opinions and judgments in contentious cases *see* Robertson/ Merrills, *Human Rights*, pp. 218-226 and 226-230 respectively.

[353] Inter-Am. Ct. H.R., *Angel Manfredo Velásquez-Rodríguez*, Series C, No. 4, paras. 166-167.

[354] Cecilia Medina Quiroga, *The Battle of Human Rights: Gross, Systematic Violations and the Inter-American System*, Dordrecht 1988, p. 98.; concerning economic and social rights *compare* Article 26: "The States Parties undertake to adopt measures, both internally and through international cooperation, especially those of an economic and technical nature, with a view to achieving progressively, by legislation or other appropriate means, the full realization of the rights implicit in the economic, social, educational, scientific, and cultural standards set forth in the Charter of the Organization of American States as amended by the Protocol of Buenos Aires."

[355] Buergenthal, in: Buergenthal *et al.*, at 14.

> Every person has the right to have his life respected. This right shall be protected by law and, in general, from the moment of conception. No one shall be arbitrarily deprived of his life.[356]

The protection is supplemented by the "Protocol to Abolish the Death Penalty", which is not ratified by all State Parties.[357] The wording of Article 4 para. 1 is very similar to that of Article 6 para. 1 ICCPR,[358] apart from the concept of inherency.[359] Nevertheless, also in the context of the American Convention the right to life is regarded as, "without a doubt, the foundation and sustenance of all the other rights."[360] A difference exists in the clarification that duties to protect already arise in the moment of conception,[361] a topic that is controversial concerning the ICCPR.[362] The core sentence that is in the focus of this examination is, however, literally identical; like the ICCPR, the American Convention states: "No one shall be arbitrarily deprived of his life."

---

356 The remaining part of Article 4 is devoted to the regulation and abolition of the death penalty in those states which maintain it. On the drafting history of the article *see* J. Colón-Collazo, 'A Legislative History of the Right to Life in the Inter-American Legal System', in: Bertrand G. Ramcharan (ed.), *The Right to Life in International Law*, Dordrecht 1985, pp. 33-41.

357 Protocol to the American Convention on Human Rights to Abolish the Death Penalty, adopted at the 20th Regular Session of the OAS General Assembly at Asunción, Paraguay, by Res. 1042 of June 8, 1990, entry into force on August 28, 1991, *OAS Treaty Series* No. 73, reprinted in: 29 *ILM* (1990), pp. 1447-1448.

358 Article 6 para. 1 ICCPR reads: "Every human being has the inherent right to life. This right shall be protected by law. No one shall be arbitrarily deprived of his life."

359 *Compare supra*, Part One, Chapter B).

360 Inter-Am. Comm'n H.R., *Ten Years of Activities, 1971-1981*, Washington, D.C. 1982, p. 339, reprinted in: Colón-Collazo, in: Ramcharan (ed.), at 41; *compare also* Davidson, *Inter-American System*, p. 261; Tigroudja/ Panoussis, *La Cour interaméricaine*, para. 138 (p. 184).

361 *But see* Davidson, *Inter-American System*, p. 263.

362 *Compare e.g.* Nowak, *CCPR Commentary*, Art. 6, paras. 35-36; Joseph/ Schultz/ Castan, *International Covenant*, paras. 8.55-8.57; Gollwitzer, *Menschenrechte*, Art. 2 MRK/Art. 6 IPBPR, para. 3a (p. 154).

1. The Defensive Function (status negativus)

The States party to the convention have the obligation not to violate an individual's rights.[363] Concerning the right to life, this is especially made clear by the sentence "No one shall be arbitrarily deprived of his life." The scope of protection thus depends on the word "arbitrarily". This word is used in four Articles of the Convention: Article 4, Articles 7, 11[364] and 20[365] include the term arbitrary.

Whereas Articles 11 and 20 do not give clear indications as to the concept of arbitrariness, Article 7 is more fertile. Its Paragraph 3 reads: "No one shall be subject to arbitrary arrest or imprisonment." If Article 7 para. 2 is taken into account, it becomes clear that the term "arbitrary" goes beyond the meaning of "unlawful" or "illegal". Para. 2 reads: "No one shall be deprived of his physical liberty except for the reasons and under the conditions established beforehand by the constitution of the State Party concerned or by a law established pursuant thereto." As the mere legality of a deprivation of liberty is already guaranteed by para. 2, para. 3 has to have an additional scope. This result is supported by the fact that Article 30 explicitly limits restrictions of convention rights to those "in accordance with laws".[366] Thus, in the context of the American Convention, the term "arbitrary" must go beyond "illegal" or "unlawful". According to the Inter-American Court of Human Rights, a State "is subject to law and morality" in its actions.[367] This system corresponds to that of the ICCPR.[368] Hence, the

---

363 Buergenthal, in: Buergenthal *et al.*, at 14; Davidson, *Inter-American Court*, p. 148.

364 Article 11 para. 2 reads: "No one may be the object of arbitrary or abusive interference with his private life, his family, his home, or his correspondence, or of unlawful attacks on his honor or reputation."

365 Article 20 para. 3 reads: "No one shall be arbitrarily deprived of his nationality or of the right to change it."

366 Article 30 reads: "The restrictions that, pursuant to this Convention, may be placed on the enjoyment or exercise of the rights or freedoms recognized herein may not be applied except in accordance with laws enacted for reasons of general interest and in accordance with the purpose for which such restrictions have been established."

367 Inter-Am. Ct. H.R., *Godínez-Cruz*, Series C, No. 5, para. 168; Inter-Am. Ct. H.R., *Angel Manfredo Velásquez-Rodríguez*, Series C, No. 4, para. 154; on

considerations concerning the meaning of the word arbitrary in Article 6 ICCPR also apply to the use of that term in Article 4 of the American Convention. Arbitrary comprises aspects such as the unrestrained exercise of will based on personal opinion or impulse, subject to personal whims or prejudices. It entails the lack of any reason or system and of any adequate determining rule or principle.[369] The object and purpose of the Convention require that whether the deprivation of a life is arbitrary or not must be determined by reference to international human rights norms.[370] Thus "arbitrary" includes examples like genocide, deaths contrary to international humanitarian law, deaths resulting from torture and involuntary disappearances and the further examples dealt with above.[371] However, the cases concerning the right to life that were brought before the Inter-American Court and Commission were mostly so clear and unambiguous that they did not give those bodies the option of elaborating on details of that right.[372] Extra judicial executions, assassinations and enforced disappearances have been classified without further analysis as distinct breaches of the right to life.[373]

2. *The Beneficiary Function* (status positivus)

Beyond this negative duty, the adoption of affirmative measures necessary and reasonable under the circumstances may be required by the positive obligation "to ensure the full enjoyment of the rights guaranteed."[374] Concerning the right to life, the Inter-American Court was ve-

---

the competence of the Court *see* Robertson/ Merrills, *Human Rights*, pp. 216-218.

[368] *Compare supra*, Part One, Chapter B) I. 1. a).

[369] *Compare supra*, Part One, Chapter B) I. 1. b) (1).

[370] *Compare supra*, Part One, Chapter B) I. 1. c); *see also* Ramcharan, 30 *Nether. Int'l L. Rev.* (1983), at 316.

[371] *Compare supra*, Part One, Chapter B) I. 1. d).

[372] An exception to this is the extensive consideration of international humanitarian law influences to the right to life, *compare infra*, Part One, Chapter B) II. 6.

[373] Davidson, *Inter-American System*, p. 266.

[374] Buergenthal, in: Buergenthal *et al.*, at 14.

ry reluctant on this subject when it first arose[375] and provoked a dissenting opinion by three judges who argued for a strong positive obligation:

> The right to life and the guarantee and respect thereof by States cannot be conceived in a restrictive manner. That right does not merely imply that no person may be arbitrarily deprived of his or her life (negative obligation). It also demands of the States that they take all appropriate measures to protect and preserve it (positive obligation).[376]

Even though the Court never explicitly advanced an opinion on that conflict, it later ruled that States have the obligation "to guarantee the creation of the conditions required in order that violations of this basic right do not occur and, in particular, the duty to prevent its agents from violating it."[377] The Court even repeatedly referred to General Comment No. 6 concerning Article 6 ICCPR as an example[378] and thus made clear that it accepts positive duties arising from Article 4 of the Convention:

> The State has a legal duty to take reasonable steps to prevent human rights violations and ... to identify those responsible, to impose the appropriate punishment and to ensure the victim adequate compensation.[379]

---

[375] Inter-Am. Ct. H.R., *Asok Gangaram-Panday v. Suriname*, Judgment of January 21, 1994, Series C, No. 16, paras. 61-62.

[376] *Id.*, dissenting opinion of Judges Picado-Sotela, Aguiar-Aranguren and Cançado Trindade, para. 3.

[377] Inter-Am. Ct. H.R., *Villagrán-Morales et al. v. Guatemala ("Street Children")* Judgment of November 19, 1999, Series C, No. 63, para. 144; *compare also* the joint concurring opinion of Judges Cançado Trindade and Abreu-Burelli, *ibid.*

[378] Inter-Am. Ct. H.R., *Villagrán-Morales*, Series C, No. 63, para. 145; Inter-Am. Ct. H.R., *Efraín Bámaca-Velásquez v. Guatemala*, Judgment of November 25, 2000, Series C, No. 70, para. 172.

[379] Inter-Am. Ct. H.R., *Angel Manfredo Velásquez-Rodríguez*, Series C, No. 4, para. 174.

Thus, a State's failure to "protect" individuals under its jurisdiction can thus also constitute a violation of the Convention, and eventually of Article 4.[380]

a) Effects on the Standards of Proof Applicable

Generally, in the Inter-American system the objective burden of proof rests with the applicant; if the circumstances of the case cannot be clarified, the application will generally be dismissed.[381] However, in the context of forced disappearances, the Inter-American Court has developed a presumption that the person was killed in cases where no corpse was found.[382] It declared as inadmissible the argument that "the body of the crime ... would be missing" in the case that a person's whereabouts are not known.[383] The Commission even went further; according to Article 42 of its Regulations it presumes allegations as true, if the State in question does not fulfil its duty to cooperate and provide information on the case:

> The facts reported in the petition whose pertinent parts have been transmitted to the government of the State in reference shall be presumed to be true if ... the government has not provided the pertinent information, as long as other evidence does not lead to a different conclusion.[384]

---

380 *See also* Heyns, in: Evans/ Murray (eds.), at 148.

381 *See e.g.* Inter-Am. Ct. H.R., *Angel Manfredo Velásquez-Rodríguez*, Series C, No. 4, para. 123; Inter-Am. Ct. H.R., *Godínez-Cruz*, Series C, No. 5, para. 129.

382 *See e.g.* Inter-Am. Ct. H.R., *Angel Manfredo Velásquez-Rodríguez*, Series C, No. 4, para. 188: "The context in which the disappearance of Manfredo Velásquez occurred and the lack of knowledge seven years later about his fate create a reasonable presumption that he was killed." *Compare also* Tigroudja/ Panoussis, *La Cour interaméricaine*, para. 143 (p. 191); Davidson, *Inter-American System*, p. 267.

383 Inter-Am. Ct. H.R., *Castillo-Páez v. Perú*, Judgment of November 3, 1997, Series C, No. 34, para. 73.

384 *See e.g.* Inter-Am. Comm'n H.R., *Masacre Las Hojas v. El Salvador*, Case 10.287, Report No. 26/92 of September 24, 1992, in: *Annual Report* (1992-93), OEA/Ser.L/V/II.83 Doc. 14, Corr. 1 (March 12, 1993), Chapter III, at para. 7; Inter-Am. Comm'n H.R., *Juan Carlos Abella v. Argentina ("La Tablada")*, Ca-

This presumption is based on the assumption that a silent State has something to hide.[385] Such a low level of proof is partly understood to be a sanction of the Inter-American Commission, as it is not a tribunal giving binding decisions.[386] It also emphasizes a special responsibility of States with regard to persons within custody.[387] The jurisprudence regarding the disappearance of persons from official custody and the creation of a presumption of responsibility on the part of the Government in question for that person's fate is referred to by other Human Rights bodies.[388]

b) The Duty to Investigate as Part of the Right to Life

As early as 1980, the Inter-American Commission recommended that States should order a full and impartial investigation to determine the responsibility for the violations of the right to life and inform the Commission of the measures taken.[389] As an effect of the positive obli-

---

se 11.137, Report No. 55/97 of November 18, 1997, in: *Annual Report* (1997), OEA/Ser.L/V/II.98 Doc. 6 rev. (April 13, 1998), Chapter III, para. 216; *see also* Inter-Am. Ct. H.R., *Angel Manfredo Velásquez-Rodríguez*, Series C, No. 4, para. 139; Inter-Am. Ct. H.R., *Víctor Neira-Alegría, Edgar Zenteno-Escobar and William Zenteno-Escobar (El Frontón) v. Peru*, Judgment of January 19, 1995, Series C, No. 20, para. 65; *compare also* Wolf, *Haftung für Privatpersonen*, p. 276; Wiesbrock, *Verletzungen durch Private*, p. 241; Davidson, *Inter-American Court*, pp. 83-86.

[385] Kokott, *Beweislastverteilung*, pp. 392-393; Rudolf, 23 *EuGRZ* (1996), at 503.

[386] Rudolf, 23 *EuGRZ* (1996), at 503.

[387] Juliane Kokott, 'The Duty to Protect and to Ensure Human Rights Under the Inter-American System of Human Rights', in: Eckart Klein (ed.), *The Duty to Protect and Ensure Human Rights*, Berlin 2000, pp. 235-276, at 242.

[388] *Compare e.g.* Human Rights Chamber for Bosnia and Herzegovina, *Josip, Božana and Tomislav Matanović v. Republika Srpska*, Case No. CH/96/1, Decision (Merits) of July 11, 1997, at para. 35; Human Rights Chamber for Bosnia and Herzegovina, *Ratko Grgić v. Republika Srpska*, Case No. CH/96/15, Decision (Merits) of, August 5, 1997, at para. 6.

[389] Inter-Am. Comm'n H.R., *Bolivia ("Community of Caracoles")*, Case 7481, Report No. 30/82 of March 8, 1982, in: *Annual Report* (1981-1982), OAS Doc. OEA/Ser.L/V/II.57, Doc. 6, rev. 1 (September 20, 1982), pp. 36-40; *c.f.* Weissbrodt, in: Ramcharan (ed.), at 300.

gation described above, a government might be deemed to have violated a right protected under the convention if it fails to take measures reasonably calculated to protect individuals. This may be the case even if the responsibility of State agents for the violation cannot be proven.[390] As a consequence, the State's duty to hinder violations includes investigations of such violations.[391] This establishes the responsibility of the State even if the deeds themselves were committed by private persons.[392] It has to use the means at its disposal to carry out a serious investigation of violations committed within its jurisdiction:[393]

> The State is obligated to investigate every situation involving a violation of the rights protected by the Convention. If the State apparatus acts in such a way that the violation goes unpunished and the victim's full enjoyment of such rights is not restored as soon as possible, the State has failed to comply with its duty to ensure the free and full exercise of those rights to the persons within its jurisdiction. The same is true when the State allows private persons or groups to act freely and with impunity to the detriment of the rights recognized by the Convention.[394]

This duty was taken as an example by the European Court of Human Rights.[395]

---

390 Buergenthal, in: Buergenthal *et al.*, at 14.

391 Kokott, in: Klein (ed.), at 257-266.

392 Inter-Am. Ct. H.R., *Angel Manfredo Velásquez-Rodríguez*, Series C, No. 4, para. 182; Inter-Am. Ct. H.R., *Godínez-Cruz*, Series C, No. 5, para. 191.

393 Inter-Am. Ct. H.R., *Angel Manfredo Velásquez-Rodríguez*, Series C, No. 4, para. 174.

394 *Id.*, para. 176; *Davidson* refers to this concept as "Drittwirkung", *see* Davidson, *Inter-American Court*, p. 150. The decisive factor of the jurisprudence referred to above is, however, the responsibility of the State for private actions and not the binding effect of the convention rights on private actors.

395 *Compare e.g.* Eur. Ct. H.R., *Mehmet Kaya v. Turkey*, Appl. No. 22729 /93, Judgment of February 19, 1998, *ECHR* 1998-I, pp. 297-361, at 324-326 (paras. 86-92); on further examples of mutual influence of the two regional systems *see* Thomas Buergenthal, 'The European and Inter-American Human Rights Courts: Beneficial Interaction', in: Paul Mahoney/ Franz Matscher/ Herbert Petzold/ Luzius Wildhaber (eds.), *Protection des droits de l'homme: la perspective européenne – Mélanges à la mémoire de Rolv Ryssdal*, Köln 2000, pp. 123-133.

II. Exceptions – Non-Arbitrary Deprivation of Life

Like the ICCPR, the American Convention on Human Rights does not protect the right to life in an absolute manner.[396] The Convention only prohibits arbitrary deprivations of life and thus accepts that non-arbitrary deprivations of life are possible under the Convention. This system is confirmed in Article 4 paras. 2-6 which refer to the death penalty. Thus, under certain circumstances, capital punishment as well as the use of force by law enforcement personnel is legitimate under the Convention. The Inter-American Court has developed some strict standards for both actions.[397] However, the violations of the right to life have largely been so clear and straightforward that the Commission and Court could only consider a few issues concerning the interpretation of Article 4.[398]

1. The Death Penalty

The only literal exception to the right to life as protected in Article 4 of the Convention is the death penalty.[399]

> The expression 'arbitrarily' excludes ... the legal proceedings applicable in those countries that still maintain the death penalty.[400]

It is implied as generally legal but the Convention strictly regulates its application: Article 4 paras. 2 and 3 prohibit its extension to offences to which it did not apply at the time the Convention was signed and forbids States which had abolished the death penalty from re-introducing it. The Commission made clear that a new introduction of the death penalty based on the goal of fighting terrorism is a violation of the right to life.[401] Capital punishment may only be enforced pursuant to a final judgment rendered by a competent court and in accordance with a law

---

396 Davidson, *Inter-American System*, p. 262.

397 Tigroudja/ Panoussis, *La Cour interaméricaine*, para. 139 (p. 185-186).

398 Davidson, *Inter-American System*, p. 266.

399 Tigroudja/ Panoussis, *La Cour interaméricaine*, para. 140 (p. 186).

400 Inter-Am. Ct. H.R., *Víctor Neira-Alegría*, Series C, No. 20, para. 74.

401 Inter-Am. Comm'n H.R., *Status of Human Rights in Peru*, in: *Annual Report* (1993), OEA/Ser.L/V.85, Doc. 9 rev. (February 11, 1994), Chapter IV.

establishing such punishment.[402] According to para. 4, it may not be inflicted for political offences or related common crimes.[403] It shall not be imposed upon persons under the age of 18 or over 70 years, and not upon pregnant women (para. 5). Additionally, the right to apply for amnesty, pardon or commutation of sentence is guaranteed in para. 6.[404] Finally, the right to a fair trial as guaranteed in Article 8 of the Convention is also part of these standards.[405]

The fact that capital punishment may not be re-established once it is abolished shows the general tendency to abolish capital punishment:

> [W]ithout going so far as to abolish the death penalty, the Convention imposes restrictions designed to delimit strictly its application and scope, in order to reduce the application of the penalty to bring about its gradual disappearance.[406]

---

402 Article 4 paras. 2 and 3 read: "2. In countries that have not abolished the death penalty, it may be imposed only for the most serious crimes and pursuant to a final judgment rendered by a competent court and in accordance with a law establishing such punishment, enacted prior to the commission of the crime. The application of such punishment shall not be extended to crimes to which it does not presently apply. 3. The death penalty shall not be reestablished in states that have abolished it."

403 *Compare also* Inter-Am. Ct. H.R., *Restrictions to the Death Penalty*, Series A, No. 3, para. 10; Davidson, *Inter-American System*, p. 273.

404 Article 4 paras. 4, 5 and 6 read: "4. In no case shall capital punishment be inflicted for political offenses or related common crimes. 5. Capital punishment shall not be imposed upon persons who, at the time the crime was committed, were under 18 years of age or over 70 years of age; nor shall it be applied to pregnant women. 6. Every person condemned to death shall have the right to apply for amnesty, pardon, or commutation of sentence, which may be granted in all cases. Capital punishment shall not be imposed while such a petition is pending decision by the competent authority."

405 Schabas, *Death Penalty*, p. 281; Matthias Maslaton, *Notstandsklauseln im regionalen Menschenrechtsschutz – Eine vergleichende Untersuchung der Art. 15 EMRK und Art. 27 AMRK*, Frankfurt am Main 2002, p. 106.

406 Inter-Am. Ct. H.R., *Restrictions to the Death Penalty*, Series A, No. 3, para. 57; *see also* Inter-Am. Ct. H.R., *The Right to Information on Consular Assistance in the Framework of the Guarantees of the due Process of Law*, Advisory Opinion OC-16/99 of October 1, 1999, Series A, No. 16 (1999), para. 134.

This tendency, that is also evident in other international documents,[407] translates into the principle whereby those States that still have the death penalty must exercise the most rigorous control for the observance of judicial guarantees in these cases. Thus, the non-observance of a detained foreign national's right to information, recognised in Article 36 para. 1 *lit.* b of the Vienna Convention on Consular Relations, is prejudicial to the guarantees of the due process of law. In such circumstances, imposition of the death penalty would be an "arbitrary" deprivation of life and violates Article 4 of the Convention.[408]

2. Deprivation of Life in the Course of Administrative Police Action

Interestingly, the view has been expressed that the death penalty is the only case of justified deprivation of life under the American Convention. While it is clear from the wording "arbitrarily" that the Convention envisages circumstances in which a non-arbitrary deprivation of life would be permissible, the fact that the right to life is non-derogable under Article 27 para. 2 of the Convention,

> provides the context within which Article 4(1) must be read. ... since the only exception to the right to life is the exercise of the death penalty ... a proper reading of the provision would seem to suggest that there can be no other justification for deprivation of right to life.[409]

Neira-Alegría et al. v. Peru [410] is cited in support of this thesis. However, in this case the Court does not maintain that the death penalty is the only possible exception to the right to life. It is true that the Court regards "the right of the State to use force, even if this implies depriving people of their lives to maintain law and order, [as] an issue that currently is not under discussion."[411] However, the following remarks by

---

[407] *See e.g.* UN Economic and Social Council, Resolution 1984/50 (May 25, 1984), Annex, *Safeguards Guaranteeing Protection of the Rights of Those Facing the Death Penalty*, 1984 UN ESCOR, Supp. No. 1 (UN Doc. E/1984/84), p. 33.

[408] Inter-Am. Ct. H.R., *The Right to Information*, Series A, No. 16 (1999), para. 137.

[409] Davidson, *Inter-American System*, p. 262.

[410] Inter-Am. Ct. H.R., *Víctor Neira-Alegría*, Series C, No. 20.

[411] *Id.*, para. 74.

the Court strongly resemble proportionality considerations: "Although it appears from arguments previously expressed in this judgment that those detained ... were highly dangerous and, in fact armed, it is the opinion of this Court, those do not constitute sufficient reasons to justify the amount of force used in this and other prisons where riots had occurred."[412] It has to be noted that the Court did not base its findings simply on the fact that the killings did not constitute capital punishment but elaborated on "the disproportionate use of force"[413] as the reason for the conclusion that the persons in question were arbitrarily deprived of their lives. Thus, the view is accepted that other exceptions to the right to life do in fact exist: Those grounds for the use of force listed in the European Convention on Human Rights and in Principle 9 of the Basic Principles on the Use of Force and Firearms by Law Enforcement Officials are accepted as non-arbitrary under the American Convention.[414] The Inter-American Commission has stated that

> in situations where a state's population is threatened by violence, the state has the right and obligation to protect the population against such threats and in so doing may use lethal force in certain situations. This includes, for example, the use of lethal force by law enforcement officials where strictly unavoidable to protect themselves or other persons from imminent threat of death or serious injury, or to otherwise maintain law and order where strictly necessary and proportionate.[415]

These and other exceptions, i.e. self-defence, the defence of another person, the use of force in order to effect an arrest or prevent an escape as well as in order to quell a riot are subject to proportionality.[416] In the

---

412 *Id.*

413 *Id.*, para. 76.

414 *See e.g.* University Centre for International Humanitarian Law, Report of the Geneva Expert Meeting, September 1 and 2, 2005, p. 13; *compare also* Tigroudja/ Panoussis, *La Cour interaméricaine*, para. 142 (p. 190), referring to "Le droit à l'autoprotection de l'Etat".

415 Inter-Am. Comm'n H.R., *Report on Terrorism and Human Rights*, OEA/ Ser.L/V/II.116 Doc. 5 rev. 1 corr. (October 22, 2002), para. 87 (footnotes omitted).

416 Inter-Am. Ct. H.R., *Víctor Neira-Alegría*, Series C, No. 20, paras. 74 and 76; Inter-Am. Comm'n H.R., *Armando Alejandre Jr., Carlos Costa, Mario de la Peña, and Pablo Morales v. Cuba ("Brothers to the Rescue")*, Case 11.589, Re-

context of emergency situations justifying the derogation of convention rights, the Court specified: "The lawfulness of the measures ... will depend, moreover, upon the character, intensity, pervasiveness, and particular context of the emergency and upon the corresponding proportionality and reasonableness of the measures."[417] Elsewhere, the Court has spelled out the need for applying the standard of proportionality and the doctrine of less restrictive alternatives when limiting rights protected by the Convention: "[I]t must be necessary, which means that it must be shown that it cannot reasonably be achieved through a means less restrictive of a right protected by the Convention."[418] Thus, generally the same considerations concerning the capability of furthering these aims that were developed in relation to the ICCPR apply, i.e. necessity and proportionality, as well as those concerning the immediacy of a threat.[419]

a) A Different Concept of Immediacy?

On the other hand, the Commission has been interpreted as using, at least to some extent, another concept of immediacy than the one developed above. The Commission explained in its "Report on Terrorism and Human Rights":

> [I]n peacetime situations, state agents must distinguish between persons who, by their actions, constitute an imminent threat of death or serious injury, or a threat of committing a particularly serious crime

---

port No. 86/99 of September 29, 1999, in: *Annual Report* (1999), OEA/Ser.L/V/II.106 Doc. 6 rev. (April 13, 1999), Chapter III, at para. 37.

[417] Inter-Am. Ct. H.R., *Habeas corpus in Emergency Situations (Arts. 27(2), 25(1) and 7(6) American Convention on Human Rights)*, Advisory Opinion OC-8/87 of January 30, 1987, Series A, No. 8, para. 22.; *c.f.* Maslaton, *Notstandsklauseln*, pp. 167-169.

[418] Inter-Am. Ct. H.R., *Compulsory Membership in an Association Prescribed by Law for the Practice of Journalism (Arts. 13 and 29 American Convention on Human Rights)*, Advisory Opinion OC-5/85 of November 13, 1985, Series A, No. 5; *see also* Arai-Takahashi, *Margin of Appreciation*, p. 191.

[419] *Compare supra*, Part One, Chapter B) II. 2.

> involving a grave threat to life, and persons who do not present such a threat, and use force only against the former.[420]

This statement has been interpreted as showing that the Commission "takes the clear stand that when there is a threat of a particularly serious crime involving a grave threat to life, the use of force may be justified even if the threat is not imminent."[421] This assessment is not convincing. The context of the statement cited above is the distinction between "armed conflict situations", that require the application of the principle of distinction "between military objectives and civilians or civilian objects"[422] and peacetime situations, in which the imminence of any threat constituted by an individual is decisive for the use of force. Read in that context, it becomes clear that the word "imminent" refers to "threat of death of serious injury" as well as to "threat of committing a particular serious crime". It is the classical concept of immediacy that the Commission is referring to, and it stresses that this concept applies in all peacetime situations.

b) A Different Concept Concerning the Quelling of a Riot?

The Inter-American Commission has stated that a State has the right to use lethal force "to protect themselves or other persons from imminent threat of death or serious injury, or to otherwise maintain law and order where strictly necessary and proportionate."[423] The last example given by the Commission seems to refer to riots or other disturbances and not to the targeting of a specific individual.[424] However, the further considerations of that issue are somewhat confusing:

> In such circumstances, the state may resort to the use of force only against individuals that threaten the security of all, and therefore the state may not use force against civilians who do not present such a threat. The state must distinguish between the civilians and those individuals who constitute the threat. Indiscriminate uses of force

---

420 Inter-Am. Comm'n H.R., *Report on Terrorism*, para. 111; *but see* Maslaton, *Notstandsklauseln*, p. 178.

421 Kretzmer, 16 *Eur. J. Int'l L.* (2005), at 181 (footnote 45).

422 Inter-Am. Comm'n H.R., *Report on Terrorism*, para. 111.

423 *Id.*, para. 87 (footnotes omitted).

424 Kretzmer, 16 *Eur. J. Int'l L.* (2005), at 181.

> may as such constitute violations of Article 4 of the Convention and Article I of the Declaration.[425]

The terminology "distinguish between the civilians and those individuals who constitute the threat" resembles international humanitarian law considerations, as it seems to refer to some status that a person has. In the sphere of human rights, it is not a status, but exclusively the behaviour and thus the threat presented by which an individual person is assessed.[426] However, at another point the Commission clarifies the topic: "[S]tate agents must distinguish between persons who, by their actions, constitute an imminent threat ... and persons who do not present such a threat, and use force only against the former."[427] This statement shows that the Commission considers the quelling of a riot in the same way as shown in connection with the ICCPR; force may only be applied to prevent harm by single individuals, i.e. in self-defence or defence of another person. "[U]nder no circumstances can persons be executed to restore public order".[428]

3. Non-Derogability of Article 4

Similarly to the International Covenant, the American Convention on Human Rights also allows the suspension of rights. According to Article 27, para. 1:

> In time of war, public danger, or other emergency that threatens the independence or security of a State Party, it may take measures derogating from its obligations under the present Convention to the extent and for the period of time strictly required by the exigencies of the situation, provided that such measures are not inconsistent with its other obligations under international law and do not involve

---

425 Inter-Am. Comm'n H.R., *Report on Terrorism*, para. 90 (footnotes omitted).

426 *See also* Kretzmer, 16 *Eur. J. Int'l L.* (2005), at 181.

427 Inter-Am. Comm'n H.R., *Report on Terrorism*, para. 111.

428 Inter-Am. Comm'n H.R., *Areas in which Steps need to be taken towards full Observance of the Human Rights set forth in the American Declaration of the Rights and Duties of Man and the American Convention on Human Rights*, in: *Annual Report* (1986-1987), OEA/Ser.L/V/II.71, Doc. 9 Rev. 1 (September 22, 1987), Chapter V.I; Davidson, *Inter-American System*, p. 286.

> discrimination on the ground of race, color, sex, language, religion, or social origin.

Article 15 of the European Convention on Human Rights is regarded as the origin for part of this provision[429] although the wording "life of the nation", that is also used by the ICCPR, is substituted by "independence or security of a State Party".[430] Another difference in comparison to the International Covenant is the express reference to war.[431] However, Article 27, para. 2 makes numerous exceptions to the possibility of derogation. It excludes, *inter alia*, the right to live from any suspension,[432] even in times of war. This does not mean that any killing in the course of an armed conflict is contrary to the convention:

4. Deprivation of Life in the Course of Armed Conflict

The Inter-American Commission on Human Rights addressed the question of deprivation of life in armed conflict comprehensively:

> The American Convention, as well as other universal and regional human rights instruments, and the 1949 Geneva Conventions share a common nucleus of non-derogable rights and a common purpose of protecting human life and dignity. These human rights treaties apply both in peacetime, and during situations of armed conflict. Although one of their purposes is to prevent warfare, none of these human rights instruments was designed to regulate such situations

---

429 Medina Quiroga, *Battle of Human Rights*, p. 106; Oraá, *States of Emergency*, p. 91; *compare infra*, Part One, Chapter E) II. 3.

430 For further details *compare* Carlos Ruiz Miguel, 'The States of Emergency in the American Convention on Human Rights', in: 33 *Isr. Yb. Hum. Rts.* (2003), pp. 105-122.

431 For a critical note on that fact *compare* Medina Quiroga, *Battle of Human Rights*, p. 108.

432 Article 27 para. 2 reads: "The foregoing provision does not authorize any suspension of the following articles: Article 3 (Right to Juridical Personality), Article 4 (Right to Life), Article 5 (Right to Humane Treatment), Article 6 (Freedom from Slavery), Article 9 (Freedom from Ex Post Facto Laws), Article 12 (Freedom of Conscience and Religion), Article 17 (Rights of the Family), Article 18 (Right to a Name), Article 19 (Rights of the Child), Article 20 (Right to Nationality), and Article 23 (Right to Participate in Government), or of the judicial guarantees essential for the protection of such rights."

> and, thus, they contain no rules governing the means and methods of warfare. ... the Commission's ability to resolve claimed violations of this non-derogable right [to life] arising out of an armed conflict may not be possible in many cases by reference to Article 4 of the American Convention alone. This is because the American Convention contains no rules that either define or distinguish civilians from combatants and other military targets, much less, specify when a civilian can be lawfully attacked or when civilian casualties are a lawful consequence of military operations. Therefore, the Commission must necessarily look to and apply definitional standards and relevant rules of humanitarian law as sources of authoritative guidance in its resolution of this and other kinds of claims alleging violations of the American Convention in combat situations.[433]

Thus, parallel to the ICCPR, killings in the course of armed conflict are assessed according to standards of international humanitarian law.[434] Killings that are "legitimately combat related [do] not constitute violations of the American Convention"[435] whereas killings that violate international humanitarian law rules such as common Article 3 of the 1949 Geneva Conventions do also violate the right to life under the Convention.[436]

While the Inter-American Commission on Human Rights grants itself broad competences to apply international treaties other than the Con-

---

[433] Inter-Am. Comm'n H.R., *Juan Carlos Abella ("La Tablada"), Annual Report* (1997), at paras. 158 and 161.

[434] *See e.g.* Inter-Am. Comm'n H.R., *Arturo Ribón Avilán v. Colombia*, Case 11.142, Report No. 26/97 of September 30, 1997, in: *Annual Report* (1997), OEA/Ser.L/V/II.98, Doc. 6 rev. (April 13, 1998), Chapter III, at para. 202; *compare also* Inter-Am. Comm'n H.R., *Juan Carlos Abella ("La Tablada"), Annual Report* (1997), at paras. 176-189; Inter-Am. Comm'n H.R., *Hugo Bustíos Saavedra v. Perú*, Case 10.548, Report No. 38/97 of October 16, 1997, in: *Annual Report* (1997), OEA/Ser.L/V/II.98, Doc. 6 rev. (April 13, 1998), Chapter III, at paras. 60-61 and 88; Inter-Am. Ct. H.R., *Efraín Bámaca-Velásquez*, Series C, No. 70, paras. 204-214; the referral to international treaties beside the American Convention is also supported by the Court, *compare* Inter-Am. Ct. H.R., *"Other treaties"*, Series A, No. 1, para. 43.

[435] Inter-Am. Comm'n H.R., *Juan Carlos Abella ("La Tablada"), Annual Report* (1997), at para. 188.

[436] *See e.g.* Inter-Am. Comm'n H.R., *Hugo Bustíos Saavedra, Annual Report* (1997), at para. 88.

vention,[437] the Inter-American Court seems to be more reluctant when it comes to the direct application of international humanitarian law:

> Although the Court lacks competence to declare that a State is internationally responsible for the violation of international treaties that do not grant it such competence, it can observe that certain acts or omissions that violate human rights, pursuant to the treaties that they do have competence to apply, also violate other international instruments for the protection of the individual, such as the 1949 Geneva Conventions and, in particular, common Article 3.[438]

The Court thus interprets the American Convention with reference to international humanitarian law, but does not directly apply it.[439] Nevertheless, Court and Commission agree that killings that constitute lawful acts of war are regarded as non-arbitrary deprivations of life under the American Convention. If killings violate international humanitarian law rules, they are also arbitrary under Article 4 of the Convention. So far, these rules are regarded as *leges speciales* in relation to the human rights rules.[440] The merits of these rules will be examined in depth *infra*.[441]

---

[437] *Compare* Lindsay Moir, 'Decommissioned? International Humanitarian Law and the Inter-American Human Rights System', in: 25 *Hum. Rts. Q.* (2003), pp. 182-212, at 191-198; Theodor Meron, 'The Humanization of Humanitarian Law', in: 94 *Am. J. Int'l L.* (2000), pp. 239-278, at 271-272.

[438] Inter-Am. Ct. H.R., *Efraín Bámaca-Velásquez*, Series C, No. 70 para. 208.

[439] Inter-Am. Ct. H.R., *Las Palmeras v. Colombia (Preliminary Objections)*, Judgment of February 4, 2000, Series C, No. 67, paras. 32-33; Inter-Am. Ct. H.R., *Efraín Bámaca-Velásquez*, Series C, No. 70, para. 209. The Commission apparently has adopted the same approach following the *Las Palmeras* Judgment of the Court, *compare* Inter-Am. Comm'n H.R., *Monsignor Oscar Arnulfo Romero y Galdámez v. El Salvador*, Case 11.481, Report No. 37/00 of April 13, 2000, in: *Annual Report* (1999), OEA/Ser.L/V/II.106 Doc. 6 rev. (April 13, 1999), at para. 72; and more explicitly in Inter-Am. Comm'n H.R., *Riofrío Massacre (Colombia)*, Case 11.654, Report No. 62/01 of April 6, 2001, in: *Annual Report* (2001), OEA/Ser./L/V/II.111 Doc. 20 rev. (April 16, 2001), at paras. 53-54; *but see* Heintze, 18 *HuV-I* (2005), at 178-179.

[440] ICJ, *Legality of the Threat or Use of Nuclear Weapons*, Advisory Opinion of July 8, 1996, I.C.J. Reports 1996, pp. 225-593, at 240 (para. 25); *compare supra*, Part One, Chapter B) II. 6.

[441] *Compare infra*, Part Two.

III. Conclusion: Killings Under the American Convention

The Protection of the right to life under the American Convention on Human Rights is very similar, if not identical to the one under the International Covenant on Civil and Political Rights. The decisive phrase for the topic this examination focuses upon is identical: "No one shall be arbitrarily deprived of his life." The Inter-American Court accepts the same exceptions to the right to life as are accepted under the ICCPR; besides the death penalty with its high procedural standards and further limits, the loss of life in administrative action is not generally prohibited, but must adhere to a strict standard of proportionality. Here, the Court applies the same classical concept of immediacy as was developed above. Both, the Commission and the Court are progressive in developing procedural safeguards, which have served as examples for other human rights protection systems. Whereas most cases before the Inter-American Court were so clear-cut that the court did not have the possibility of elaborating on many details of the right to life, both Court and Commission are ready to apply international humanitarian law standards when necessary to define the Convention's scope of protection.[442] In that respect, both bodies accept the *lex specialis* character that the International Court of Justice has referred to and are very willing to actively apply those standards.

D. The African Charter on Human and Peoples' Rights

The African Charter on Human and Peoples' Rights, commonly referred to as the "Banjul Charter", was adopted in 1981 at the Eighteenth Conference of Heads of State and Government of the Organization of

---

[442] This is partly due to the extensive jurisdiction of the Court to give advisory opinions on the interpretation of the Convention and of "other treaties" (Article 64 para. 1 of the American Convention), *compare* Buergenthal, in: Mahoney *et al.* (eds.), at 130-133; Héctor Fix-Zamudio, 'The European and the Inter-American Courts of Human Rights: A brief Comparison', in: Paul Mahoney/ Franz Matscher/ Herbert Petzold/ Luzius Wildhaber (eds.), *Protection des droits de l'homme: la perspective européenne – Mélanges à la mémoire de Rolv Ryssdal*, Köln 2000, pp. 507-533, at 514-516.

African Unity.[443] It entered into force on October 21, 1986 three months after the required ratification by "a simple majority of the member states of the Organization of African Unity" was reached.[444] To date, the African Charter is ratified by all 53 States member to the African Union.[445] The Charter guarantees virtually all civil and political "first generation rights"[446] and has two "significant African nuances"[447]: First, it treats individual and collective rights as interlinked and second, it does not only proclaim rights but also duties.[448]

Article 1 of the Charter obliges the State parties to "recognise the rights, duties and freedoms enshrined in this Charter and ... [to] undertake to adopt legislative or other measures to give effect to them." Article 2 provides that "[e]very individual shall be entitled to the enjoyment of the rights and freedoms" of the Charter. These primary obligations include positive and negative duties.[449] The Organization of African Unity's absolute commitment to non-interference in the internal affairs

---

443 African Charter on Human and Peoples' Rights, adopted by the Organization of African Unity Summit at Nairobi, Kenya, on June 27, 1981, OAU Doc. CAB/LEG/67/3/Rev. 5, entry into force on October 21, 1986, reprinted in: 1520 *UNTS* (1988), No. 26363, pp. 217-292 and 21 *ILM* (1982), pp. 59-68, also known as the "Banjul Charter on Human and Peoples' Rights"; Evelyn A. Ankumah, *The African Commission on Human and Peoples' Rights – Practice and Procedures*, The Hague 1996, p. 1; on the origin and history of the Charter *see also* Robertson/ Merrills, *Human Rights*, pp. 242-249.

444 *Compare* Article 63 para. 3 of the African Charter on Human and Peoples' Rights.

445 All 53 African states who composed the Organization of African Unity are now members of the African Union and have ratified the Charter, *see* African Union, *List of Countries which have Signed, Ratified/Acceded to the African Charter on Human and Peoples' Rights*, May 26, 2007.

446 On the controversy concerning the terminology "first generation rights" *see* Roland Rich, 'The Right to Development: A Right of Peoples?', in: James Crawford (ed.), *The Right of Peoples*, Oxford 1988, pp. 39-54, at 40-43.

447 Ankumah, *African Commission*, p. 159.

448 On further particularities *compare* Michael Graf, *Die Afrikanische Menschenrechtscharta und ihre Bedeutung für einschlägiges innerstaatliches Recht am Beispiel Tanzanias*, Hamburg 1997, pp. 29-51.

449 Heyns, in: Evans/ Murray (eds.), at 138.

of States was significantly modified by these explicit promises regarding the African Charter.[450]

The right to life is laid down in Article 4 of the African Charter on Human and Peoples' Rights. This Article reads:

> Human beings are inviolable. Every human being shall be entitled to respect for his life and the integrity of his person. No one may be arbitrarily deprived of this right.

The African Charter, in contrast to the International Covenant and the American Convention, does not provide an explicit exception concerning the death penalty appended to the right to life. Furthermore it is not supplemented by an Additional Protocol aiming at the abolition of the death penalty. However, the African Commission on Human and Peoples' Rights, the "quasi-judicial organ"[451] that is responsible for monitoring the compliance of States within the African Charter and interpreting it,[452] has adopted a resolution urging the State parties to limit the application of the death penalty and reflect on the possibility of abolishing it.[453]

---

[450] Bronwen Manby, 'The African Union, NEPAD, and Human Rights: The Missing Agenda', in: 26 *Hum. Rts. Q.* (2004), pp. 983-1027, at 984.

[451] Anne Pieter van der Mei, 'The New African Court on Human and Peoples' Rights: Towards an Effective Human Rights Protection Mechanism for Africa?', in: 18 *Leiden J. Int'l L.* (2005), pp. 113-129, at p. 114; on the communication procedure *see* Chidi Anselm Odinkalu; Camilla Christensen, 'The African Commission on Human and Peoples' Rights: The Development of its Non-State Communication Procedures', in: 20 *Hum. Rts. Q.* (1998), pp. 235-280; on the African Court of Human Rights *compare also* Makau Mutua, 'The African Human Rights Court: A Two-Legged Stool?', in: 21 *Hum. Rts. Q.* (1999), pp. 342-363, at 353-357.

[452] Article 45 of the African Charter reads: "The functions of the Commission shall be: ... 3. Interpret all the provisions of the present Charter at the request of a State party, an institution of the OAU or an African Organization recognized by the OAU."

[453] Afr. Comm'n H.P.R., *Resolution Urging States to envisage a Moratorium on the Death Penalty*, adopted at the 26th Ordinary Session in Kigali, Rwanda, November 1-15, 1999, DOC/OS (XXVI) INF.19, in: 13th *Activity Report* (1999-2000), Annex IV, pp. 45-46.

I. Article 4 African Charter on Human and Peoples' Rights' Scope of Protection

The right to life as laid down in the African Charter has aspects of a civil right on the one hand, and of an economic and social right on the other hand. While the latter part aims at sufficient standards of life and is of no interest for the present study, the former part entails negative as well as positive obligations.[454]

In the context of humans being "inviolable", this term is understood as "not to be profaned", dishonoured or injured and has been referred to as a "more philosophical" content.[455] The core protection of the right to life results from the provision "no one may be arbitrarily deprived", which is almost identical to the wording of Article 6 para. 1 of the International Covenant and Article 4 para. 1 of the American Convention and can probably be traced back to the formulation of these provisions. As a consequence, the "substantial jurisprudence" by the Human Rights Committee is also referred to in interpreting Article 4 of the African Charter.[456] Nevertheless, this article refers to "this right" whereas the International Covenant and the American Convention state: "No one shall be arbitrarily deprived of his life."[457] Thus, in addition to the concept of "arbitrariness", the scope of protection of the African Charter's Article 4 depends on the concept of "respect for ... life".

1. The Defensive Function (status negativus)

The African Commission has stated in connection with the right to life:

> It would be a narrow interpretation of this right to think it can only be violated when one is deprived of it. It cannot be said that the right to respect for one's life and the dignity of his person, which

---

[454] Ouguergouz, *La Charte africaine*, pp. 91-92.

[455] Emmanuel G. Bello, 'The African Charter on Human and Peoples' Rights – A Legal Analysis', in: 194 *RdC* (1985-V), pp. 9-268, at 152.

[456] Heyns, in: Evans/ Murray (eds.), at 147.

[457] *Compare supra*, Part One, Chapters B) and C).

this article guarantees would be protected in a state of constant fear and/or threats, as experienced by [the complainant].[458]

Thus, the central obligation put on a State by Article 4 is to refrain from all encroachment of the life of a person.[459] Whereas deprivation of life and deprivation of "respect for life" do not differ, the latter may go further than the former.

It has been argued that "the right to life and integrity are subject to law or may be denied in circumstances prescribed by law" due to the term "arbitrarily".[460] This assessment may find support by the use of "arbitrary" in Article 6 of the Charter, which uses "(non-)arbitrarily" as an example to specify general "reasons and conditions previously laid down by law".[461] However, the interpretation of "arbitrary" as "illegal" is insufficient.[462] As described above, in connection with the ICCPR, the term "arbitrarily" comprises more than mere "prescription by law". Such prescription is a necessary but not sufficient condition for the deprivation of a life to be "non-arbitrary": Beside the "prescription by law", the deprivation of a life must additionally adhere to international human rights standards and cannot be exclusively determined by national sources. Thus, the same standards as developed above do apply.[463]

Similarly to the Inter-American Human Rights System, the cases involving the right to life which the African Commission has dealt with up to now have been so blatant and unmistakably arbitrary that the commission did not develop clear principles defining what exactly constitutes a violation of the right to life.[464] Examples given by the Commis-

---

[458] Afr. Comm'n H.P.R., *Kazeem Aminu v. Nigeria*, Communications 205/97, in: 13th *Activity Report* (1999-2000), Annex V, pp. 112-116, at 114 (para. 18).

[459] Ouguergouz, *La Charte africaine*, p. 92; Heyns, in: Evans/ Murray (eds.), at 138.

[460] Umozurike Oji Umozurike, *The African Charter on Human and Peoples' Rights*, The Hague 1997, p. 33.

[461] Article 6 African Charter reads: "Every individual shall have the right to liberty and to the security of his person. No one may be deprived of his freedom except for reasons and conditions previously laid down by law. In particular, no one may be arbitrarily arrested or detained."

[462] Ouguergouz, *La Charte africaine*, p. 93.

[463] *Compare supra*, Part One, Chapter B) I. 1. b).

[464] Ankumah, *African Commission*, p. 115.

sion include "[d]enying people food and medical attention, burning them in sand and subjecting them to torture to the point of death",[465] shooting and killing "peacefully striking workers ... by the police"[466] as well as the "massacre of a large number of ... villagers by ... armed forces ... for reasons of their membership of a particular ethnic group."[467] "Extra judicial executions"[468] are generally regarded as a violation of Article 4 as well as executions without due process.[469] The same holds

---

465 Afr. Comm'n H.P.R., *Malawi African Association, Amnesty International, Ms. Sarr Diop, Union Interafricaine des Droits de l'Homme and RADDHO, Collectif des Veuves et Ayants-droit, Association Mauritanienne des Droits de L'Homme v. Islamic Republic of Mauritania*, Communications 54/91, 61/91, 98/93, 164/97-196/97 and 210/98, in: 13th *Activity Report* (1999-2000), Annex V, pp. 138-162, at 157 (para. 120).

466 Afr. Comm'n H.P.R., *Krischna Achutan (on behalf of Aleke Banda), Amnesty International on behalf of Orton and Vera Chirwa and Amnesty International on behalf of Orton and Vera Chirwa v. Malawi*, Communications 64/92, 68/92 and 78/92, in: 8th *Activity Report* (1994-1995), Annex VI (No. 11), at paras. 5-6; on this case *compare also* Ankumah, *African Commission*, pp. 114-115.

467 Afr. Comm'n H.P.R., *Organisation Mondiale Contre la Torture and Association Internationale des Juristes Democrates, Commission Internationale des Juristes (CIJ), Union Interafricaine des Droit de l'Homme v. Rwanda*, Communications 27/89, 46/91, 49/91 and 99/93, in: 10th*Activity Report* (1996-1997), Annex X, pp. 49 52, at 51 (para. 24).

468 Afr. Comm'n H.P.R., *Free Legal Assistance Group, Lawyers' Committee for human Rights, Union Interafricaine des Droits de l'Homme, Les Témoins de Jehova v. Zaire*, Communications 25/89, 47/90, 56/91 and 100/93, in: 9th Activity Report (1995-1996), Annex VIII, at para. 43; Afr. Comm'n H.P.R., *Organisation Mondiale Contre la Torture and Association Internationale des Juristes Democrates, Commission Internationale des Juristes (CIJ), Union Interafricaine des Droit de l'Homme v. Rwanda*, Communications 27/89, 46/91, 49/91 and 99/93, in: 10th *Activity Report* (1996-1997), Annex X, pp. 49-52, at 51 (para. 24); Afr. Comm'n H.P.R., *Amnesty International, Comité Loosli Bachelard, Lawyers Committee for Human Rights, Association of Members of the Episcopal conference of East Africa v. Sudan*, Communications 48/90, 50/91, 52/91 and 89/93, in: 13th *Activity Report* (1999-2000), Annex V, pp. 124-138, at 132 (para. 48).

469 Afr. Comm'n H.P.R., *Malawi African Association, Amnesty International, Ms. Sarr Diop, Union Interafricaine des Droits de l'Homme and RADDHO, Collectif des Veuves et Ayants-droit, Association Mauritanienne des Droits de L'Homme v. Islamic Republic of Mauritania*, Communications 54/91, 61/91,

true for "wide spread terrorisations and killings" but also for the "pollution and environmental degradation to a level humanly unacceptable" and thus destroying the basis of living of a group.[470] The Commission furthermore extended the protection of Article 4 in cases in which the victim is still alive if he fears for his life and has to go into hiding to escape State suppressions.[471] Many of the respective decisions are however based on "the absence of a substantive response by the Government"[472] and thus did not demand detailed discussion of the prerequisites of Article 4.

2. *The Beneficiary Function* (status positivus)

The African Charter entails a general obligation to protect which comprises different aspects: First, it covers a State's failure to act in cases of its responsibility for an individual. The protection of the right to life thus *inter alia* includes a duty for the State not to purposefully let a person die while in its custody. Thus, the denial of medication to a prisoner to the extent that his life is seriously endangered, even though it does not lead to his death, does violate Article 4.[473] Second, the duty to pro-

---

98/93, 164/97-196/97 and 210/98, in: 13th *Activity Report* (1999-2000), Annex V, pp. 138-162, at 157 (para. 120); Afr. Comm'n H.P.R., *Forum of Conscience v. Sierra Leone*, Communication 223/98, in: 14th *Activity Report* (2000-2001), Annex V, pp. 43-46, at 44 (para. 19).

470 Afr. Comm'n H.P.R., *The Social and Economic Rights Action Center and the Center for Economic and Social Rights v. Nigeria*, Communication 155/96, in: 15th *Activity Report* (2001-2002), Annex V, pp. 31-44, at 43 (para. 67).

471 Afr. Comm'n H.P.R., *Kazeem Aminu v. Nigeria*, Communications 205/97, in: 13th *Activity Report* (1999-2000), Annex V, pp. 112-116, at 114 (paras. 17-18).

472 Afr. Comm'n H.P.R., *Commission Nationale des Droits de l'Homme et des Libertés de la Federation Nationale des Unions de Jeunes Avocats de France v. Chad*, Communication 74/92 (1995), in: 9th *Activity Report* (1995-1996), Annex VIII, at para. 26; Afr. Comm'n H.P.R., *Amnesty International, Comité Loosli Bachelard, Lawyers Committee for Human Rights, Association of Members of the Episcopal conference of East Africa v. Sudan*, Communications 48/90, 50/91, 52/91 and 89/93, in: 13th *Activity Report* (1999-2000), Annex V, pp. 124-138, at 133 (para. 52).

473 Afr. Comm'n H.P.R., *International Pen, Constitutional Rights Project, Interights on behalf of Ken Saro-Wiwa Jr. and Civil Liberties Organisation v.*

tect refers to the State's obligation to ensure that other individuals do not violate a person's rights.[474] This duty also affects the scope of protection of Article 4. For example, in a decision against Chad, the African Commission held the government of Chad accountable for several killings and disappearances as well as an assassination by unknown people, due to the fact that the government had not attempted to prevent these acts: "If a State neglects to ensure the rights in the African Charter, this can constitute a violation, even if the State or its agents are not the immediate cause of the violation."[475] In a decision against Sudan, the Commission stated:

> In addition to the individuals named in the communications, there are thousands of other executions .... Even if these are not all the work of forces of the government, the government has a responsibility to protect all people residing under its jurisdiction.[476]

In consequence, Sudan was held responsible for having violated Article 4 irrespective of whether certain executions in question were committed by State officials.[477]

The positive duty also has effects on the burden of proof in the proceedings before the Commission. This burden – at least concerning the

Nigeria, Communications 137/94, 139/94, 154/96 and 161/97, in: 12th *Activity Report* (1998-1999), Annex V, pp. 62-73, at 71 (para. 104).

[474] *See* Afr. Comm'n H.P.R., *Commission Nationale des Droits de l'Homme et des Libertés de la Federation Nationale des Unions de Jeunes Avocats de France v. Chad*, Communication 74/92 (1995), in: 9th *Activity Report* (1995-1996), Annex VIII, at para. 20; *see also* Heyns, in: Evans/ Murray (eds.), at 138; Ouguergouz, *La Charte africaine*, p. 92.

[475] Afr. Comm'n H.P.R., *Commission Nationale des Droits de l'Homme et des Libertés de la Federation Nationale des Unions de Jeunes Avocats de France v. Chad*, Communication 74/92 (1995), in: 9th *Activity Report* (1995-1996), Annex VIII, at para. 20.

[476] Afr. Comm'n H.P.R., *Amnesty International, Comité Loosli Bachelard, Lawyers Committee for Human Rights, Association of Members of the Episcopal conference of East Africa v. Sudan*, Communications 48/90, 50/91, 52/91 and 89/93, in: 13th *Activity Report* (1999-2000), Annex V, pp. 124-138, at 132 (para. 50).

[477] *Id.*, at 131-133 (paras. 47-52).

submission of the "*prima facie* case" – generally rests on the complainant:[478]

> It is not for the Commission to verify the authenticity of the post-mortem reports or the truth of the government's defence. The burden is on the complainant to furnish the Commission with evidence of his allegations. In the absence of concrete proof, the Commission cannot hold the latter to be in violation ... of the Charter.[479]

However, this allocation is reversed under certain circumstances:

> [W]here allegations of human rights abuse go uncontested by the government concerned, even after repeated notifications, the Commission must decide on the facts provided by the complainant and treat those facts as given .... This principle conforms with the practice of other international human rights adjudicatory bodies and the Commission's duty to protect human rights.[480]

This principle to take the violation "as proven, or at the least probable or plausible"[481] represents a long standing practice of the Commission.[482] Another effect of this positive duty is a duty to investigate: Not

---

[478] *Compare* Rachel Murray, 'Evidence and Fact-Finding by the African Commission', in: Malcolm Evans/ Rachel Murray (eds.), *The African Charter on Human and Peoples' Rights: The System in Practice, 1986-2000*, Cambridge 2002, pp. 100-136, at 111.

[479] Afr. Comm'n H.P.R., *Sir Dawda K Jawara v. Gambia*, Communications 147/95 and 149/96, in: 13th *Activity Report* (1999-2000), Annex V, pp. 96-107, at 104 (para. 53).

[480] Afr. Comm'n H.P.R., *Commission Nationale des Droits de l'Homme et des Libertés de la Federation Nationale des Unions de Jeunes Avocats de France v. Chad*, Communication 74/92 (1995), in: 9th *Activity Report* (1995-1996), Annex VIII, at para. 25.

[481] Afr. Comm'n H.P.R., *Amnesty International, Comité Loosli Bachelard, Lawyers Committee for Human Rights, Association of Members of the Episcopal conference of East Africa v. Sudan*, Communications 48/90, 50/91, 52/91 and 89/93, in: 13th *Activity Report* (1999-2000), Annex V, pp. 124-138, at 133 (para. 52).

[482] *See also* Afr. Comm'n H.P.R., *Free Legal Assistance Group, Lawyers' Committee for human Rights, Union Interafricaine des Droits de l'Homme, Les Témoins de Jehova v. Zaire*, Communications 25/89, 47/90, 56/91 and 100/93, in: 9th *Activity Report* (1995-1996), Annex VIII, at para. 40; Afr. Comm'n H.P.R., *Malawi African Association, Amnesty International, Ms. Sarr Diop, Union Interafricaine des Droits de l'Homme and RADDHO, Collectif des Veuves*

only the failure to prevent killings, but also the failure to investigate killings or disappearances that took place can be a violation of Article 4, even if the deeds are not committed by State agents.[483] The case against Chad illustrates that it is often a combination of failure to act in order to protect a person and the failure to investigate a killing afterwards: "The Minister responsible ... refused to issue protection. Subsequently, the Minister did not initiate investigation[s] into the killing."[484] Even in cases of governments being more cooperative, the quality of investigations has to meet certain standards. In the cases against Sudan,

> [t]he investigations undertaken by the Government are a positive step, but their scope and depth fall short of what is required to prevent and punish extra-judicial executions. Investigations must be carried out by entirely independent individuals, provided with the necessary resources, and their findings should be made public and prosecutions initiated in accordance with the information uncovered.[485]

---

et Ayants-droit, Association Mauritanienne des Droits de L'Homme v. Islamic Republic of Mauritania, Communications 54/91, 61/91, 98/93, 164/97-196/97 and 210/98, in: 13th *Activity Report* (1999-2000), Annex V, pp. 138-162, at 153 (para. 92); Afr. Comm'n H.P.R., *Amnesty International, Comité Loosli Bachelard, Lawyers Committee for Human Rights, Association of Members of the Episcopal conference of East Africa v. Sudan*, Communications 48/90, 50/91, 52/91 and 89/93, in: 13th *Activity Report* (1999-2000), Annex V, pp. 124-138, at 133 (para. 52); Afr. Comm'n H.P.R., *Mouvement Burkinabé des Droits de l'Homme et des Peuples v. Burkina Faso*, Communication 204/97, 14th *Activity Report* (2000-2001), Annex V, pp. 78-86, at 84 (para. 42).

483 Afr. Comm'n H.P.R., *Commission Nationale des Droits de l'Homme et des Libertés de la Federation Nationale des Unions de Jeunes Avocats de France v. Chad*, Communication 74/92 (1995), in: 9th *Activity Report* (1995-1996), Annex VIII, at para. 25; Ankumah, *African Commission*, p. 115.

484 Afr. Comm'n H.P.R., *Commission Nationale des Droits de l'Homme et des Libertés de la Federation Nationale des Unions de Jeunes Avocats de France v. Chad*, Communication 74/92 (1995), in: 9th *Activity Report* (1995-1996), Annex VIII, at para. 5.

485 Afr. Comm'n H.P.R., *Amnesty International, Comité Loosli Bachelard, Lawyers Committee for Human Rights, Association of Members of the Episcopal conference of East Africa v. Sudan*, Communications 48/90, 50/91, 52/91 and 89/93, in: 13th *Activity Report* (1999-2000), Annex V, pp. 124-138, at 132 (para. 51); *see also* Afr. Comm'n H.P.R., *Mouvement Burkinabé des Droits de*

The commission constituted in this case consisted of the District Prosecutor and police and security officials, and thus ran the risk of overlooking "the possibility that police and security forces may be implicated in the very massacres they are charged to investigate."[486] Such a commission of enquiry, in the Commission's view, by its very composition, does not provide the required guarantees of impartiality and independence and eventually leads to a violation of Article 4 of the African Charter, as it does not provide adequate evidence to satisfy the Commission.[487]

II. Exceptions – Non-Arbitrary Deprivation of Life

The rights covered by the African Charter are not guaranteed in an absolute manner.[488] "Clawback clauses" are included in several substantive provisions of the African Charter.[489] The rights in question are only guaranteed e.g. with the possibility of limiting them for "reasons and conditions previously laid down by law",[490] "subject to law and order",[491] "within the law"[492] or to persons that "abide by the law".[493]

---

l'Homme et des Peuples v. Burkina Faso, Communication 204/97, 14th *Activity Report* (2000-2001), Annex V, pp. 78-86, at 82 (para. 42).

486 Afr. Comm'n H.P.R., *Amnesty International, Comité Loosli Bachelard, Lawyers Committee for Human Rights, Association of Members of the Episcopal conference of East Africa v. Sudan*, Communications 48/90, 50/91, 52/91 and 89/93, in: 13th *Activity Report* 1999-2000), Annex V, pp. 124-138, at 132 (para. 51).

487 *Id.*, at 132-133 (paras. 51-52).

488 *See e.g.* Ouguergouz, *La Charte africaine*, p. 257.

489 Ankumah, *African Commission*, p. 176-177; *c.f.* Bello, 194 *RdC* (1985-V), at 179.

490 Article 6 African Charter reads: "Every individual shall have the right to liberty and to the security of his person. No one may be deprived of his freedom except for reasons and conditions previously laid down by law. In particular, no one may be arbitrarily arrested or detained."

491 Article 8 African Charter reads: "Freedom of conscience, the profession and free practice of religion shall be guaranteed. No one may, subject to law and order, be submitted to measures restricting the exercise of these freedoms."

Other rights are guaranteed only "subject to the obligation of solidarity provided for in Article 29",[494] if exercised "in accordance with the provisions of the law"[495] or "in accordance with the provisions of the appropriate law".[496] Article 4 does not include such a "clawback clause".

Thus, even though it has been stressed that Article 4 is not "diluted by qualificatory annexes",[497] the fact that this article does not expressly prohibit the death penalty cannot serve as evidence for the right to life being absolute under the African Charter.[498] Capital punishment under certain conditions, killings which result from self-defence, deaths resulting from the use of reasonable force in law enforcement and killings in war which are not forbidden under international law regulating the conduct of armed conflict, are regarded as non-arbitrary deprivations of life under the African Charter.[499]

---

492 Article 9 para. 2 African Charter reads: "Every individual shall have the right to express and disseminate his opinions within the law."

493 Article 10 para. 2 African Charter reads: "Every individual shall have the right to free association provided that he abides by the law." and Article 12 African Charter reads: "Every individual shall have the right to freedom of movement and residence within the borders of a State provided he abides by the law."

494 Article 10 para. 2 African charter reads: "Subject to the obligation of solidarity provided for in Article 29 no one may be compelled to join an association."

495 Article 13 para. 1 African Charter reads: "Every citizen shall have the right to participate freely in the government of his country, either directly or through freely chosen representatives in accordance with the provisions of the law."

496 Article 14 African charter Reads: "The right to property shall be guaranteed. It may only be encroached upon in the interest of public need or in the general interest of the community and in accordance with the provisions of appropriate law."

497 Graf, *Afrikanische Menschenrechtscharta*, pp. 35-36: "Art. 4 ... [gilt] ... uneingeschränkt und [ist] nicht durch qualifizierende Zusätze verwässert."

498 Ouguergouz, *La Charte africaine*, p. 92.

499 Ankumah, *African Commission*, p. 113.

As a consequence of the word "arbitrary" in Article 4, the death penalty is not prohibited under the Charter,[500] but it is restricted: If it is imposed in a trial violating the fair trial guarantees of Article 7 of the Charter, the subsequent death penalty is arbitrary and thus transgresses Article 4.[501]

Concerning the deprivation of life in the course of administrative police action, the commission has given very little guidance so far. It stated that shooting by police officers to kill peacefully striking workers violates the right to life,[502] but up to now did not give details on situations less obvious. In this respect Article 4 of the African Charter is interpreted parallel to Article 6 ICCPR.[503]

The same holds true in respect to deprivations of life in armed conflicts: The African Commission followed the same assessment that is used in connection with the ICCPR and the American Convention. It stated that even in "a civil war, civilians in areas of strife are especially vulnerable and the State must take all possible measures to ensure that they are treated in accordance with international humanitarian law" in order

---

500 Graf, *Afrikanische Menschenrechtscharta*, p. 36; Ankumah, *African Commission*, p. 113.

501 Afr. Comm'n H.P.R., *International Pen, Constitutional Rights Project, Interights on behalf of Ken Saro-Wiwa Jr. and Civil Liberties Organisation v. Nigeria*, Communications 137/94, 139/94, 154/96 and 161/97, in: 12th *Activity Report* (1998-1999), Annex V, pp. 62-73, at 71 (para. 103); Afr. Comm'n H.P.R., *Malawi African Association, Amnesty International, Ms. Sarr Diop, Union Interafricaine des Droits de l'Homme and RADDHO, Collectif des Veuves et Ayants-droit, Association Mauritanienne des Droits de L'Homme v. Islamic Republic of Mauritania*, Communications 54/91, 61/91, 98/93, 164/97-196/97 and 210/98, in: 13th *Activity Report* (1999-2000), Annex V, pp. 138-162, at 157 (para. 120); Afr. Comm'n H.P.R., *Forum of Conscience v. Sierra Leone*, Communication 223/98, in: 14th *Activity Report* (2000-2001), Annex V, pp. 43-46, at 44 (para. 19).

502 Afr. Comm'n H.P.R., *Krischna Achutan (on behalf of Aleke Banda), Amnesty International on behalf of Orton and Vera Chirwa and Amnesty International on behalf of Orton and Vera Chirwa v. Malawi*, Communications 64/92, 68/92 and 78/92, in: 8th *Activity Report* (1994-1995), Annex VI (No. 11), at paras. 5-6.

503 Ankumah, *African Commission*, pp. 115-116; *compare supra*, Part One, Chapter B) II.

not to violate Article 4.[504] The Commission thus follows the principle that international humanitarian law is the *lex specialis* according to which the arbitrariness of a killing is judged.[505]

III. No Explicit Non-Derogability of Article 4

The African Charter does not mention the right to life as a non-derogable right.[506] Such a rule might seem superfluous, as the African Charter does not contain an explicit derogation clause setting out the procedures to be followed during times of war or national disasters.[507] Thus, the Commission has held that this lack of a derogation clause means that States cannot derogate from the rights of the Charter at any time, be it during war, situations of emergency or peace.[508] However, the African Charter does provide for other possibilities for limiting the rights protected. Article 27 of the African Charter under the heading "Duties" reads:

> (1) Every Individual shall have duties towards his family and society, the State and other legally recognized communities and the international community. (2) The rights and freedoms of each individual shall be exercised with due regard to the rights of others, collective security, morality and common interest.

---

504 Afr. Comm'n H.P.R., *Amnesty International, Comité Loosli Bachelard, Lawyers Committee for Human Rights, Association of Members of the Episcopal conference of East Africa v. Sudan*, Communications 48/90, 50/91, 52/91 and 89/93, in: 13th *Activity Report* (1999-2000), Annex V, pp. 124-138, at 132 (para. 50).

505 *Compare supra*, Part One, Chapter B) II. 6.

506 *C.f.* Ramcharan, 30 *Nether. Int'l L. Rev.* (1983), at 319.

507 *C.f.* Heyns, in: Evans/ Murray (eds.), at 139; Nigel S. Rodley, *The Treatment of Prisoners under International Law*, Oxford 1987, p. 145; on the background *compare* Leon Wessels, 'Derogation from Human Rights. A possible Dispensation for Africa and southern Africa', in: 27 *S. Afr. Yb. Int'l L.* (2002), pp. 120-139, at 133; Oraá, *States of Emergency*, pp. 209-210.

508 Afr. Comm'n H.P.R., *Commission Nationale des Droits de l'Homme et des Libertés de la Federation Nationale des Unions de Jeunes Avocats de France v. Chad*, Communication 74/92 (1995), in: 9th *Activity Report* (1995-1996), Annex VIII, at para. 21.

According to the African Commission "[t]he only legitimate reasons for limitations to the rights and freedoms or the African Charter are to be found in Article 27 (2)."[509] While restrictions concerning "due regard to the rights of others" are unproblematic, "collective security, morality and common interest" are broad and undefined and thus regarded as problematic.[510] Para. 2 is interpreted restrictively.[511] Whereas article 27 para. 2 could play a role as a general limitation clause concerning all rights, these limitations are restricted to those acceptable under international human rights law, that are thus regarded as being applicable to the rights in the African Charter.[512] Such limitations, according to the African Commission, must be strictly proportionate with and absolutely necessary for the respective advantages and may not erode a right such that the right itself becomes illusory.[513] To this extent, these limitations correspond with the standards applicable in connection with the ICCPR and the American Convention.

Notwithstanding the absence of a derogation clause, the right to life is understood to be "supreme" and thus non-derogable.[514] This finds support in the fact that several articles of the African Convention explicitly state that exceptions are permitted under certain circumstances, but no such statement is included in Article 4.[515] The Commission itself refers

---

[509] Afr. Comm'n H.P.R., *Media Rights Agenda, Constitutional Rights Project, Media Rights Agenda and Constitutional Rights Project v. Nigeria*, Communications 105/93, 128/94, 130/94 and 1523/96, in: 12th *Activity Report* (1998-1999), Annex V, pp. 52-61, at 58 (para. 68); *see also* Afr. Comm'n H.P.R., *Constitutional Rights Project, Civil Liberties Organisation and Media Rights Agenda v. Nigeria*, Communications 140/94, 141/94, 145/95, in: 13th *Activity Report* (1999-2000), Annex V, pp. 54-62, at 60 (para. 41).

[510] Ankumah, *African Commission*, p. 170.

[511] Ouguergouz, *La Charte africaine*, p. 260.

[512] Heyns, in: Evans/ Murray (eds.), at 140 (footnote 11).

[513] Afr. Comm'n H.P.R., *Constitutional Rights Project, Civil Liberties Organisation and Media Rights Agenda v. Nigeria*, Communications 140/94, 141/94, 145/95, in: 13th *Activity Report* (1999-2000), Annex V, pp. 54-62, at 61 (para. 42).

[514] Ankumah, *African Commission*, p. 112; *c.f.* Nsereko, in: Ramcharan (ed.), at 273.

[515] Ramcharan, in: Ramcharan (ed.), at 15-16.

to non-derogable rights, even though it confirms that the concept of derogation is alien to the African Charter:

> Whilst the Commission is aware that states may face difficult situations the Charter does not contain a general provision permitting states to derogate from their responsibilities in times of emergency, especially for what is generally referred to as non-derogable rights.[516]

Thus, it is accepted that some, but not all rights are derogable under the African Charter.[517] At least the four non-derogable rights commonly accepted by other human rights treaties are also non-derogable in the African system,[518] i.e. the right to life, the right to be free from torture and other inhumane treatment or punishment, the right to be free from slavery or servitude, and the principle of non-retroactivity of penal law.[519] In consequence, irrespective of whether and to what extent the possibility of derogating under the African Charter is accepted,[520] the right to life is not derogable.

IV. Conclusion: Killings Under the African Charter

The Protection of the right to life under the African Charter on Human and Peoples' Rights is again very similar to the one under the International Covenant on Civil and Political Rights as well as the American Convention on Human Rights. The decisive phrase referring to the right to life is "No one may be arbitrarily deprived of this right." This standard encompasses the same possible exceptions as the other human

---

516 Afr. Comm'n H.P.R., *Amnesty International, Comité Loosli Bachelard, Lawyers Committee for Human Rights, Association of Members of the Episcopal conference of East Africa v. Sudan*, Communications 48/90, 50/91, 52/91 and 89/93, in: 13th *Activity Report* (1999-2000), Annex V, pp. 124-138, at 131 (para. 42).

517 Oraá, *States of Emergency*, pp. 209-210.

518 Oraá, *States of Emergency*, pp. 229.

519 *Compare Id.*, p. 96.

520 *Compare* the comprehensive discussion of this topic in Ouguergouz, *La Charte africaine*, pp. 255-288; *compare also* Oraá, *States of Emergency*, pp. 209-269.

rights treaties referred to above; the death penalty is not prohibited absolutely but its restrictions are lower in the African system. The loss of life in administrative action is not generally prohibited, but subject to the standards of Article 27 para. 2, including a strict standard of proportionality. The African Commission regards the right to life as non-derogable albeit the African Charter does not provide a general derogation clause. But it accepts that the right to life is not absolute and is subject to humanitarian law standards as *leges speciales* in situations where these standards are applicable.

E. The European Convention on Human Rights

The (European) Convention for the Protection of Human Rights and Fundamental Freedoms[521] is the core of the European Human Rights System. The text of the Convention was drafted under the auspices of the Council of Europe and adopted in Rome in 1950.[522] It entered into force on September 3, 1953[523] after the required number of 10 ratifications was reached.[524]

---

[521] European Convention on Human Rights, formally entitled "Convention for the Protection of Human Rights and Fundamental Freedoms", adopted at Rome, Italy, on November 4, 1950, entry into force on September 3, 1953, reprinted in: *European Treaty Series* No. 5 and 213 *UNTS* (1955), No. 2889, pp. 222-261.

[522] On the history of the Convention *see* Robertson/ Merrills, *Human Rights*, pp. 121-124; on the legislative history of Article 2 *see* Bertrand G. Ramcharan, 'The Drafting History of Article 2 of the European Convention on Human Rights', in: Bertrand G. Ramcharan (ed.), *The Right to Life in International Law*, Dordrecht 1985, pp. 57-61.

[523] The text of the Convention was amended according to several additional protocols. All amendments by earlier Protocols have been replaced by Protocol No. 11 to the Convention for the Protection of Human Rights and Fundamental Freedoms, restructuring the control machinery established thereby, adopted at Strasbourg, France on May 11, 1994, entry into force on November 1, 1998, *European Treaty Series* No. 155. It was followed by Protocol No. 12 to the Convention for the Protection of Human Rights and Fundamental Freedoms, Introducing a General Prohibition of Discrimination, adopted at Rome, Italy on November 4, 2000, entry into force on April 1, 2005, *European Treaty Series* No. 177 and Protocol No. 13 to the Convention for the Protection of Human

The importance of the right to life is underlined by the fact that it is the first substantive right set out in the European Convention.[525] However, in contrast to the prohibition of torture,[526] the protection of the right to life is not absolute.[527] Article 2 ECHR reads:

> (1) Everyone's right to life shall be protected by law. No one shall be deprived of his life intentionally save in the execution of a sentence of a court following his conviction of a crime for which this penalty is provided by law. (2) Deprivation of life shall not be regarded as inflicted in contravention of this Article when it results from the use of force which is no more than absolutely necessary: (a) in defense of any person from unlawful violence; (b) in order to effect a lawful arrest or to prevent the escape of a person lawfully detained; (c) in action lawfully taken for the purpose of quelling a riot or insurrection.

The protection is supplemented by two Additional Protocols aiming at the abolition of the death penalty in times of peace[528] and in times of war.[529]

Rights and Fundamental Freedoms Concerning the abolition of the death penalty in all circumstances, adopted at Vilnius, Lithuania on May 3, 2002, entry into force on July 1, 2003, *European Treaty Series* No. 187. Protocol No. 14 to the Convention for the Protection of Human Rights and Fundamental Freedoms, Amending the Control System of the Convention, adopted at Strasbourg, France on May 13, 2004, *Council of Europe Treaty Series* No. 194, is not in force yet.

524 *Compare* Article 66 para. 2 of the Convention.

525 Stefan Trechsel, 'Spotlights on Article 2 ECHR, the Right to Life', in: Wolfgang Benedek/ Hubert Isak/ Renate Kicker (eds.), *Development and Developing International and European Law: Essays in Honour of Konrad Ginther on the Occasion of his 65th Birthday*, Frankfurt am Main 1999, pp. 671-686, p. 671; Jan Michael Bergmann, *Das Menschenbild der Europäischen Menschenrechtskonvention*, Baden-Baden 1995, p. 131.

526 Article 3 of the European Convention.

527 On possible exceptions *see infra* Part One, Chapter E) II.

528 Protocol No. 6 to the Convention for the Protection of Human Rights and Fundamental Freedoms concerning the Abolition of the Death Penalty, adopted at Strasbourg, France on April 28, 1983, entry into force on March 1, 1985, *European Treaty Series* No. 114.

I. Article 2 European Convention on Human Rights' Scope of Protection

The existence of the right to life is not explicitly laid down in Article 2 ECHR. While other substantial guarantees of the Convention read "Everyone has the right to ...",[530] Article 2 ECHR takes the existence of the right to life for granted.[531] Unlike other articles, it additionally formulates a "positive" duty to protect[532] and thus stresses an aspect that is generally laid down in Article 1 of the Convention: "The High Contracting Parties shall secure ... the rights and freedoms defined in Section I of this Convention."[533] Article 2 European Convention's

---

[529] Protocol No. 13 to the Convention for the Protection of Human Rights and Fundamental Freedoms Concerning the abolition of the death penalty in all circumstances, adopted at Vilnius, Lithuania on May 3, 2002, entry into force on July 1, 2003, *European Treaty Series* No. 187.

[530] *Compare* Article 5 ("Everyone has the right to liberty and security of person."), Article 8 ("Everyone has the right to respect for his private and family life, his home and his correspondence."), Article 9 ("Everyone has the right to freedom of thought, conscience and religion;"), Article 10 ("Everyone has the right to freedom of expression."), Article 11 ("Everyone has the right to freedom of peaceful assembly and to freedom of association with others, including the right to form and to join trade unions for the protection of his interests.") and similar Article 12 ("Men and women of marriageable age have the right to marry and to found a family, ...").

[531] Article 2 para. 1: "Everyone's right to life ..."; *c.f.* Torkel Opsahl, 'The Right to Life', in: Ronald St. John Macdonald/ Franz Matscher/ Herbert Petzold (eds.), *The European System for the Protection of Human Rights*, Dordrecht 1993, pp. 207-223, at 207; *critically* Francis G. Jacobs; Robin C.A. White, *The European Convention on Human Rights*, 2nd ed., Oxford 1996, p. 41.

[532] Article 2 para. 1: "Everyone's right to life shall be protected by law.", *compare* Jens Meyer-Ladewig, *Konvention zum Schutz der Menschenrechte und Grundfreiheiten*, Baden-Baden 2003, Art. 2, para. 7 (p. 45); Villiger, *Handbuch EMRK*, para. 277 (p. 171); David J. Harris/ Michael O'Boyle/ Colin Warbrick, *Law of the European Convention on Human Rights*, London 1995, p. 37; Dijk/ Hoof, *European Convention*, p. 297.

[533] It is argued that this addition in Article 2 does not affect the substance of the right to life, as, according to Articles 1 and 13, "the obligations of the authorities under the Convention in any event include the duty to provide legal guarantees against violations by others, as well as the duty to respect the rights themselves.", *see* Jacobs/ White, *European Convention*, p. 41.

scope of protection thus can be divided into two categories: its defensive function and its beneficiary function.[534]

1. The Defensive Function (status negativus)

Like the other human rights conventions, the European Convention grants the individual a right to ward off encroachments on his life by the State.[535] But the wording of Article 2 is not entirely clear as to the question of whether *any* encroachments on a person's life are covered, or only *certain* ones:

Article 2 para. 1 ECHR contains the prohibition "No one shall be deprived of his life *intentionally* ...". This formulation equals the system of other prohibitions in the Convention,[536] apart from the necessary "intention". It is the only instance where the Convention refers to a *mens rea* in connection with the interference with a protected right.[537] The use of the word "intentionally", and "intentionnellement" in the likewise authentic French text,[538] is open to various interpretations:

---

[534] Harris *et al.*, *European Convention*, p. 37.; *compare generally* Georg Ress, 'The Duty to Protect and to Ensure Human Rights under the European Convention on Human Rights', in: Eckart Klein (ed.), *The Duty to Protect and Ensure Human Rights*, Berlin 2000, pp. 165-205, at 165-167.

[535] *See e.g.* Felix Ermacora/ Manfred Nowak/ Hannes Tretter (eds.), *Die Europäische Menschenrechtskonvention in der Rechtsprechung der österreichischen Höchstgerichte*, Wien 1983, Article 2, para. 6.3 (pp. 123-126); on the corresponding duty to protect *compare* Trechsel, in: Benedek *et al.* (eds.), at 673-678.

[536] Compare Article 3 ("No one shall be subjected to torture or to inhuman or degrading treatment or punishment."), Article 4 para. 1 ("No one shall be held in slavery or servitude.") and para. 2 ("No one shall be required to perform forced or compulsory labour."), and Article 7 ("No one shall be held guilty of any criminal offence on account of any act or omission which did not constitute a criminal offence under national or international law at the time when it was committed.").

[537] Trechsel, in: Benedek *et al.* (eds.), at 679.

[538] *See* Article 59, para. 4 ECHR; *compare* Shabtai Rosenne, 'The Meaning of "Authentic Text" in Modern Treaty Law', in: Rudolph Bernhardt/ Wilhelm Karl Geck/ Günther Jaenicke/ Helmut Steinberger (eds.), *Völkerrecht als Rechtsordnung – Internationale Gerichtsbarkeit – Menschenrechte: Festschrift für Hermann Mosler*, Berlin 1983, pp. 759-784, at 772-773.

a) Does "Intentional Deprivation" Require Dolus?

According to the ordinary meaning of the term, consequences are intended if they are "meant", desired or aimed at or if they are the reason, purpose or objective of an action.[539] A closer look at the word "intention" is taken in the criminal law context. As laid out above, the degrees of intention reach from direct intention of the first degree and direct intention of second degree to *dolus eventualis*.[540]

The second sentence of Article 2 itself indicates which degree of intention could be referred to; the death penalty is laid down as one or even the only exception to the prohibition of "intentional deprivation". The death penalty is *per se* executed with *dolus directus* of the first degree, as the death of the person is the aim of an execution.[541] Some scholars are thus of the opinion that the second sentence of Article 2 para. 1 has to be understood as "No one shall be deprived of his life with direct intention of the first degree ...". They argue that capital punishment is the only case in which the intentional killing of a person can be accepted under the Convention.[542]

This has been criticised by other authors who reason that it would for example even prohibit lethal acts in self-defence.[543] At first sight, these exceptions enumerated in Article 2 para. 2 seem to be in conflict with the apparently sole exception laid down in para. 1, i.e. the death penalty. However, the exceptions laid down in para. 2 do not necessarily require direct intention of the first degree.[544] In cases of self-defence, the aim of the action is to stop the attack, not to kill the attacker. The person defending himself would not regard himself as having failed if the attack

---

[539] *Compare* Wilson, *Criminal Theory*, p. 149; Simester/ Sullivan, *Criminal Law*, p. 126-127; Duff, *Intention*, pp. 36-37.

[540] *Compare supra*, Introduction, Chapter C) II. 1.

[541] *Compare supra*, Introduction, Chapter C) II. 1. a).

[542] Bergmann, *Menschenbild*, p. 134; *similarly,* Meyer-Ladewig, *Menschenrechte und Grundfreiheiten*, Art. 2, para. 1 (p. 43).

[543] Trechsel, in: Benedek *et al.* (eds.), at 679-680; Eur. Ct. H.R., *McCann*, Series A, No. 324, p. 46 (para. 138).

[544] Gerd Seidel, *Handbuch der Grund- und Menschenrechte auf staatlicher, europäischer und universeller Ebene*, Baden-Baden 1996, p. 8; Frowein/ Peukert (eds.), *EMRK-Kommentar*, Art. 2, para. 10 (p. 35).

was stopped but the attacker survives.[545] Thus, self-defence at the utmost requires direct intention of second degree.[546] The same holds true for the other exceptions laid down in para. 2; they do include intention, even direct intention, as to the death of a person. But they do not cover direct intention of the first degree; if the killing of a person is the purpose or main aim of an action, this killing is prohibited by the convention.[547] According to Article 2 ECHR, the death of a person may only be the unavoidable result of force employed in order to pursue another aim, e.g. to save a hostage who is threatened with being killed.[548] In such cases, the death of the person in question is accepted as being a virtually certain consequence of achieving the purpose and thus covered by *dolus eventualis*, or even a necessary precondition to achieve another purpose and thus covered by direct intention of second degree.

Therefore, the interpretation that according to Article 2 para. 1 no one shall be deprived of his life exclusively with direct intention of the first degree is too narrow. The exceptions of para. 2 show that deprivation of life with direct intention of second degree or with *dolus eventualis* is also covered by the prohibition stated in para. 1; the explicit exceptions would not be necessary if the scope of para. 1 was so narrow that it only covered direct intention of the first degree.

b) Does Article 2 Cover Negligent Deprivation of Life?

On the other hand, the fact that the second sentence of Article 2 para. 1 refers to "intentional killing" has been interpreted as meaning that unintentional, i.e. negligent killings do not constitute a violation of Article 2.[549]

---

[545] *But see* Nowak, *CCPR Commentary*, Art. 6, para. 12 (footnote 35, p. 110).

[546] *Compare supra*, Part One, Chapter B) II. 2.

[547] Frowein, in: Denninger/ Hinz (eds.), at 117; Ermacora *et al.* (eds.), *Europäische Menschenrechtskonvention*, Art. 2, para. 6.4.1 (p. 127); Frowein/ Peukert (eds.), *EMRK-Kommentar*, Art. 2, para. 12 (p. 36).

[548] *Compare e.g.* Ermacora *et al.* (eds.), *Europäische Menschenrechtskonvention*, Art. 2, para. 6.4.1 (p. 127).

[549] Trechsel, in: Benedek *et al.* (eds.), at 680; Ermacora *et al.* (eds.), *Europäische Menschenrechtskonvention*, Art. 2, para. 6.3.2 (p. 124); *but see* Heinz Guradze, *Die Europäische Menschenrechtskonvention: Konvention zum Schutze*

There is almost no reported discussion of the drafts of Article 2 ECHR,[550] but the decision in *X v. Belgium*[551] by the European Commission on Human Rights[552] has been interpreted as supporting the thesis that Art. 2 ECHR protects exclusively against intentional killings and not against negligent killings.[553] This decision bases its argument on the fact that it could not be proven that the constable who fired a shot intended to kill the victim. At the same time the Commission also stated that "he must be considered to have acted in self-defence."[554] Thus, it is not entirely clear which of these two arguments was the decisive one and the Commission's reasoning has thus been criticised as "unsatisfactory".[555] Later, the Commission made clear that the obligation arising from Article 2 goes beyond a prohibition of intentional deprivation and thus opened the possibility of covering negligent deprivations:[556]

---

der Menschenrechte und Grundfreiheiten nebst Zusatzprotokollen – Kommentar, Berlin 1968, Article 2, para. 4 (p. 48), stating that the word "intentional" emphasises that actions by state agents are covered, but cannot serve as *argumentum e contrario* and thus does not exclude negligent killings.

550 James Edmund Sandford Fawcett, *The Application of the European Convention on Human Rights*, 2nd ed., Oxford 1987, p. 34.

551 Eur. Comm'n H.R., *X v. Belgium*, Appl. No. 2758/66, Decision of May 21, 1969, in: 12 *Yb. Eur. Conv. Hum. Rts.* (1969), pp. 174-193.

552 The Commission held its first session in July 1954 and was abolished pursuant to Protocol No. 11 to the Convention for the Protection of Human Rights and Fundamental Freedoms, restructuring the control machinery established thereby, adopted at Strasbourg, France on May 11, 1994, entry into force on November 1, 1998, *European Treaty Series* No. 155. *C.f.* Erik Fribergh/ Mark E. Villiger, 'The European Commission of Human Rights', in: Ronald St. John Macdonald/ Franz Matscher/ Herbert Petzold (eds.), *The European System for the Protection of Human Rights*, Dordrecht 1993, pp. 605-620; Jens Meyer-Ladewig/ Herbert Petzold, 'Der neue ständige Europäische Gerichtshof für Menschenrechte', in: 52 *NJW* (1999), pp. 1165-1166, at 1165.

553 Frowein/ Peukert (eds.), *EMRK-Kommentar*, Art. 2, para. 5 (p. 31).

554 Eur. Comm'n H.R., *X v. Belgium*, 12 *Yb. Eur. Conv. Hum. Rts.* (1969), at 192.

555 Jacobs/ White, *European Convention*, p. 45.

556 Eur. Comm'n H.R., *Association X v. United Kingdom*, Appl. No. 7154/ 75, Decision of July 12, 1978, 14 *D.R.* (1979), pp. 31-39, at 32; Andrew Clapham, 'The "Drittwirkung" of the Convention', in: Ronald St. John Macdonald/

If the text of the Convention is examined thoroughly, the exceptions in the second paragraph of Article 2 show that the scope of protection must also include negligent killings. The exceptions cover killings that are the result of absolutely necessary force. Thus, unlikely and unforeseeable results are also covered by the exception.[557] This would not be necessary, if such unintended killings would not be prohibited by the respective rule. Then, para. 2 could simply refer to "killings that are necessary" instead of killings that are the result of necessary acts. Thus, Article 2 of the Convention must refer to intentional *and* unintentional killings.[558] It also covers a duty to abstain from acts which needlessly endanger life.[559] This scope of protection is by now also clarified by the European Court of Human Rights,[560] the body who has the task of interpreting the Convention authoritatively according to Article 32 ECHR.[561]

In consequence, the defensive function of Article 2 covers a prohibition on States depriving persons of their lives and acting in a way that may result in the death of a person, subject to the exceptions described *infra*.

2. *The Beneficiary Function* (status positivus)

The prohibition on intentional deprivation of life is understood to be addressed not only to the national authorities of a Party State, but also

---

Franz Matscher/ Herbert Petzold (eds.), *The European System for the Protection of Human Rights*, Dordrecht 1993, pp. 163-206, at 177-178.

557 Anne Peters, *Einführung in die Europäische Menschenrechtskonvention*, München 2003, p. 36.

558 Gollwitzer, *Menschenrechte*, Art. 2 MRK/Art. 6 IPBPR, para. 7 (p. 156).

559 Dijk/ Hoof, *European Convention*, p. 297.

560 Eur. Ct. H.R., *McCann*, Series A, No. 324, p. 46 (para. 148).

561 Formerly Article 45 of the Convention; *compare* Johan Callewaert, 'The Judgments of the Court: Background and Content', in: Ronald St. John Macdonald/ Franz Matscher/ Herbert Petzold (eds.), *The European System for the Protection of Human Rights*, Dordrecht 1993, pp. 713-731, at 725; *compare also* Paul Mahoney/ Søren C. Prebensen, 'The European Court of Human Rights', in: Ronald St. John Macdonald/ Franz Matscher/ Herbert Petzold (eds.), *The European System for the Protection of Human Rights*, Dordrecht 1993, pp. 621-643; Meyer-Ladewig/ Petzold, 52 *NJW* (1999), pp. 1165-1166.

to private persons.[562] As violations of the Convention can only be invoked in relation to State authorities, this assessment encompasses a positive duty of these authorities.[563] 'Protect' thus refers to the State's positive duty to ensure that other individuals do not violate a person's rights,[564] i.e. to secure the right to life by putting in place effective criminal-law provisions to deter the commission of offences against the person.[565] Furthermore, the Commission has stated that the first sentence of Article 2 refers to a general obligation of all authorities to take appropriate measures to protect life, and not merely to the legislator; the State is enjoined "to take appropriate steps to safeguard life".[566] The duty to protect life entails an obligation to reduce life threatening acts by the State to absolutely necessary cases and in compliance with the principle of proportionality. In enforcing such acts, all options for protecting life must be taken.[567]

This positive duty also influences the standards of proof applied by the European Court on Human Rights:

a) Effects on the Standards of Proof Applicable

In *Cyprus v. Turkey*, the Commission still considered itself unable to reach a conclusion as to the liability under Article 2 in the absence of evidence on the deaths of missing persons. This was partly due to the

---

[562] Eur. Comm'n H.R., *Mrs W. v. United Kingdom*, Appl. No. 9348/81, Decision of February 28, 1983, 32 *D.R.* (1983), pp. 190-210, at 199-200; Eur. Comm'n H.R., *Mrs W. v. Ireland*, Appl. No. 9360/81, Decision of February 28, 1983, 32 *D.R.* (1983), pp. 211-219, at 213; Dröge, *Positive Verpflichtungen*, p. 379; Dijk/ Hoof, *European Convention*, p. 297; Clapham, in: Macdonald *et al.*, at 177.

[563] Dijk/ Hoof, *European Convention*, p. 297; it does, however, not go as far as imposing positive duties to protect the right to life of others upon private persons, *see* Clapham, in: Macdonald *et al.*, at 178-179 with further references.

[564] *See also* Heyns, in: Evans/ Murray (eds.), at 138.

[565] Eur. Ct. H.R., *Cemil Kiliç v. Turkey*, Appl. No. 22492/93, Judgment of March 28, 2000, *ECHR* 2000-III, pp. 75-147, at 96 (para. 62).

[566] Eur. Comm'n H.R., *Association X*, 14 *D.R.* (1979), at 32; *see also* Eur. Comm'n H.R., *Mrs W. v. UK*, 32 *D.R.* (1983), at 199-200.

[567] Eur. Ct. H.R., *McCann*, Series A, No. 324, pp. 46-47 (paras. 151-156); Grabenwarter, *Menschenrechtskonvention*, § 20, para. 14 (p. 137).

fact that Turkey refused to give access to the Commission to the places of detention of the persons in question and to respond to the allegations.[568] The European Court generally applied relatively strict rules concerning the level of proof. Unlike the Inter-American Commission on Human Rights and the UN Human Rights Committee,[569] it initially was not willing to base decisions merely on the fact that the respondent State did not provide adequate information.[570]

Hence, the European Court gave little attention to the right to life until the late 1980's.[571] Later it held that where an individual is taken into custody in good health but is found to be injured at the time of release, it is incumbent on the State to provide a plausible explanation of how those injuries were caused. If the State fails to do so, an issue arises under Article 3 of the Convention.[572] Following this assessment, it also held that Article 5 imposes an obligation on the State to account for the whereabouts of any person taken into detention and who has thus been placed under the control of the authorities.[573] Finally, the Court acknowledged that

> [w]hether the failure on the part of the authorities to provide a plausible explanation as to a detainee's fate, in the absence of a body, might also raise issues under Article 2 of the Convention will de-

---

568 Eur. Comm'n H.R., *Cyprus v. Turkey*, Appl. No. 8007/77, Report of October 4, 1983, 72 *D.R.* (1992), pp. 5-117, at 37-39 (paras. 116 123); *but see* Eur. Ct. H.R., *Cyprus v. Turkey*, Appl. No. 25781/94, Judgement (Grand Chamber) of May 10, 2001, *ECHR* 2001-IV, pp 1-477, at 39-41 (paras. 130-136).

569 *Compare supra*, Part One, Chapters B) I. 2. a) and C) I. 2. a) respectively.

570 *Compare* Eur. Ct. H.R., *Ireland v. UK*, Series A, No. 25, at p. 65 (para. 161).

571 Fionnuala D. Ní Aoláin, 'The Evolving Jurisprudence of the European Convention Concerning the Right to Life', in: 19 *Nether. Q. Hum. Rts.* (2001), pp. 21-42, at 21.

572 Eur. Ct. H.R., *Tomasi v. France*, Appl. No. 12850/87, Judgment of August 27, 1992, Series A, No. 241-A, at pp. 40-41 (paras. 108-111); Eur. Ct. H.R., *Ribitsch v. Austria*, Appl. No. 18896/91, Judgment of December 4, 1995, Series A, No. 336, at pp. 25-26 (para. 34); Eur. Ct. H.R., *Selmouni v. France*, Appl. No. 25803/94, Judgment of July 28, 1999 (Grand Chamber), *ECHR* 1999-V, pp. 149-256, at 179 (para. 87); *see also* Eur. Ct. H.R., *Mikheyev v. Russia*, Appl. No. 77617/01, Judgment of January 26, 2006, para. 102.

573 Eur. Ct. H.R., *Koçeri Kurt*, *ECHR* 1998-III, at 1185 (para. 124).

> pend on all the circumstances of the case, and in particular on the existence of sufficient circumstantial evidence, based on concrete elements, from which it may be concluded to the requisite standard of proof that the detainee must be presumed to have died in custody.[574]

In this respect, the period of time which elapsed since the person was placed in detention was referred to as a relevant factor, although not decisive in itself, in determining whether the situation gives rise to issues which go beyond a mere irregular detention, in violation of Article 5.[575]

Even though the Court thus followed the example of the Inter-American Court of Human Rights in dealing with disappearances,[576] it maintained remarkably high standards; the circumstantial evidence in *Kurt v. Turkey* was not presumed sufficient, even though *Üzeyir Kurt* was last seen surrounded by soldiers and subsequently not heard of for four and a half years.[577] Eventually the fact that *Abdulvahap Timurtaş's* detention was proven and that he was not heard of for six and a half years sufficed to convince the Court that the right to life had been violated, due to the fact that the Authorities did not provide any explanation as to what occurred after *Timurtaş's* apprehension.[578] The European Court's jurisprudence concerning disappearances is – by now – also referred to by other tribunals with regard to disappearances of persons

---

574 Eur. Ct. H.R., *Timurtaş v. Turkey*, Appl. No. 23531/94, Judgment of June 13, 2000, *ECHR* 2000-VI, pp. 303-395, at 330 (para. 82); *see also* Eur. Ct. H.R., *Ertak v. Turkey*, Appl. No. 20764/92, Judgment of May 9, 2000, *ECHR* 2000-V, pp. 157-241, at 235 (para. 131), where the Court regarded the evidence as sufficient to come to the conclusion beyond reasonable doubt, and Eur. Ct. H.R., *Çakıcı v. Turkey*, Appl. No. 23657/94, Judgment of July 8, 1999 (Grand Chamber), *ECHR* 1999-IV, pp. 583-730, at 610 (paras. 85-87), where the victim was presumed dead based on circumstantial evidence.

575 Eur. Ct. H.R., *Timurtaş*, *ECHR* 2000-VI, at 330-331 (para. 83).

576 *Compare supra*, Part One, Chapter C) I. 2. a); *see also* Tigroudja/ Panoussis, *La Cour interaméricaine*, para. 144 (pp. 191-192).

577 Eur. Ct. H.R., *Koçeri Kurt*, *ECHR* 1998-III, at 1182 (para. 108).

578 Eur. Ct. H.R., *Timurtaş*, *ECHR* 2000-VI, at 331-332 (paras. 85-86); *compare also* Eur. Ct. H.R., *Avşar v. Turkey*, Appl. No. 25657/94, Judgment of July 10, 2001, *ECHR* 2001-VII, pp. 83-151, at 109-110 (paras. 412-416).

from official custody and the creation of a presumption of responsibility.[579]

However, even in cases in which such circumstantial evidence does not sufficiently support the allegations, the right to life may still be violated due to a lack of efficient investigation on the part of the State party:[580]

b) The Duty to Investigate as Part of the Rights to Life

The Commission formerly acknowledged that "Article 2, paragraph 1 ... may, like other Articles of the Convention ... impose positive obligations on the State" even though it was very reticent concerning the extent of such duties.[581] Later, it went further and accepted that Article 2 does contain a procedural element which is satisfied by effective and independent criminal prosecution concerning the person who violated the life of another person.[582]

This concept was widened by the Court; whereas a killing by a private person does not automatically in itself entail a breach of Article 2,[583] the Court reiterates that the obligation to protect the right to life under Article 2 of the Convention, read in conjunction with the State's general duty under Article 1 of the Convention to secure to everyone the rights

579 Human Rights Chamber for Bosnia and Herzegovina, *Josip, Božana and Tomislav Matanović v. Republika Srpska*, Case No. CH/96/1, Decision (Merits) of July 11, 1997, at para. 35; Human Rights Chamber for Bosnia and Herzegovina, *Ratko Grgić v. Republika Srpska*, Case No. CH/96/15, Decision (Merits) of, August 5, 1997, at para. 6.

580 This was for example the case in Eur. Ct. H.R., *Nesibe Haran v. Turkey*, Appl. No. 28299/95, Judgment of October 6, 2005, paras. 64-78.

581 Eur. Comm'n H.R., *Laurence Dujardin and Others v. France*, Appl. No. 16734/90, Decision of September 2, 1991, in: 72 *D.R.* (1992), pp. 236-244, at 243.

582 *See e.g.* Eur. Comm'n H.R., *The Taylor, Crampton, Gibson and King Families v. United Kingdom*, Appl. No. 23412/94, Decision of August 30, 1994, 79-A *D.R.* (1994), pp. 127-137, at 135-137; *see also* Kara E. Irwin, 'Prospects for Justice: The Procedural Aspect of the Right to Life under the European Convention on Human Rights and its Application to Investigations of Northern Ireland's Bloody Sunday', in: 22 *Fordham Int'l L.J.* (1999), pp. 1822-1859, at 1838-1851.

583 Harris *et al.*, *European Convention*, p. 39.

and freedoms defined in the Convention, also requires by implication that there should be some form of effective official investigation when individuals have been killed.[584] The form of investigation which will satisfy this "positive procedural obligation"[585] may vary with the different circumstances, but whatever mode is employed, the authorities must act of their own volition once the matter has come to their attention. They have to react promptly and may not delay the investigation,[586] and they must take the reasonable steps available to them to secure the evidence.[587] To be effective, the investigation into alleged ill-treatment by State agents has to be independent,[588] including independence in practical terms; the investigation may not rely exclusively on the information provided by the authorities involved in the incident in question.[589] The inquiries must, to a certain degree, be transparent for

---

[584] *See* Eur. Ct. H.R., *McCann*, Series A, No. 324, p. 49 (para. 161); *see also* Eur. Ct. H.R., *Mehmet Kaya*, *ECHR* 1998-I, at 324-326 (paras. 86-92); Eur. Ct. H.R., *Ergi v. Turkey*, Appl. No. 23818/94, Judgment of July 28, 1998, *ECHR* 1998-IV, pp. 1751-1806, at 1778 (para. 82); Eur. Ct. H.R., *Cemil Kiliç*, *ECHR* 2000-III, at 100 (para. 78); Eur. Ct. H.R., *Akdeniz v. Turkey*, Appl. No. 25165/94, Judgment of May 31, 2005, paras. 103-112.

[585] Ress, in: Klein (ed.), at 170.

[586] Eur. Ct. H.R., *Yaşa v. Turkey*, Appl. No. 22495/93, Judgment of September 2, 1998, 1998-VI, pp. 2411-2463, at 2439-2440 (paras. 102-104); Eur. Ct. H.R., *McKerr v. United Kingdom*, Appl. No. 28883/95, Judgment of May 4, 2001, *ECHR* 2001-III, pp. 475-619, at 518 (para. 114); Eur. Ct. H.R., *Hugh Jordan v. United Kingdom*, Appl. No. 24746/94, Judgment of May 4, 2001, *ECHR* 2001-III, pp. 537-540 (Extract), at 539 (para. 138); Eur. Ct. H.R., *Çakıcı*, *ECHR* 1999-IV, at 608, 610-611 and 616 (paras. 80, 87 and 106); Eur. Ct. H.R., *Mahmut Kaya v. Turkey*, Appl. No. 22535/93, Judgment of March 28, 2000, *ECHR* 2000-III, pp. 149-240, at 182-183 (paras. 106-107).

[587] Eur. Ct. H.R., *Paul and Audrey Edwards v. United Kingdom*, Appl. No. 46477/99, Judgment of March 14, 2002, *ECHR* 2002-II, pp. 137-221, at 164-165 (paras. 69-71); *compare also* Eur. Ct. H.R., *İlhan v. Turkey*, Appl. No. 22277/93, Judgment (Grand Chamber) of June 27, 2000, *ECHR* 2000-VII, pp. 267-363, at 288 (para. 63).

[588] Eur. Ct. H.R., *Oğur v. Turkey*, Appl. No. 21594/93, Judgment of May 20, 1999 (Grand Chamber), *ECHR* 1999-III, pp. 519-634, at 552 (paras. 91-92); Eur. Ct. H.R., *Güleç v. Turkey*, Appl. No. 21593/93, Judgment of July 27, 1998, *ECHR* 1998-IV, pp. 1698-1750, at 1733 (paras. 81-82).

[589] Eur. Ct. H.R., *Ergi*, *ECHR* 1998-IV, at 1778-1779 (paras. 83-84).

the public,[590] or at least the facts have to be disclosed to the relatives of the victim.[591] They have to be given adequate access to the decisive documents.[592] This obligation to investigate "is not an obligation of result, but of means"[593] and thus the lack of conclusion of a given investigation does not automatically render it ineffective.[594]

The lack of an effective investigation is thus directly linked to a violation of Article 2 of the European Convention, following an example that had already been given by the Inter-American Court of Human Rights.[595] The duty to enforce the law to protect life requires investigating properly all suspicious deaths, including deaths in custody and the prosecution of both public and private offenders. This also includes the investigation of disappearances in circumstances that may suggest death.[596] This assessment on the one hand ensures the practical effectiveness at the domestic level of Article 2. On the other hand, it appears to be a reaction to the case load and the resulting backlog of cases the Court faced due to time-consuming fact-finding missions when national institutions failed to effectively investigate alleged breaches of the Convention.[597] But still, even in cases when the *ex post facto* investigations meet the demands established above, according to the European Court the right to life can be violated:

---

590 *Compare* Eur. Ct. H.R., *McKerr*, *ECHR* 2001-III, at 517 (para. 112).

591 Eur. Ct. H.R., *Oğur*, *ECHR* 1999-III, at 552 (para. 92).

592 Eur. Ct. H.R., *Hugh Jordan*, *ECHR* 2001-III, at 537 (para. 124).

593 Eur. Ct. H.R., *Paul and Audrey Edwards*, *ECHR* 2002-II, at 165 (para. 71).

594 Eur. Ct. H.R., *Akdeniz v. Turkey*, Appl. No. 25165/94, Judgment of May 31, 2005, para. 04; *compare also* Eur. Ct. H.R., *Mikheyev v. Russia*, Appl. No. 77617/01, Judgment of January 26, 2006, para. 107.

595 Inter-Am. Ct. H.R., *Angel Manfredo Velásquez-Rodríguez*, Series C, No. 4, paras. 174-182. *Compare supra*, Part One, Chapter C) I. 2. b).

596 Harris *et al.*, *European Convention*, p. 39; Opsahl, in: Macdonald *et al.* (eds.), at 211.

597 Alastair R. Mowbray, *The Development of Positive Obligations under the European Convention on Human Rights by the European Court of Human Rights*, Oxford 2004, pp. 29-30.

c) The Duty to Ensure Adequate Planning and Control of Security Forces' Operations

Since the Court's famous judgement in *McCann*, "it is not solely the moment where the lethal discharge of a weapon takes place which is under scrutiny but the broader context in which a fatality occurs."[598] This goes even beyond the duty to effectively investigate the circumstances of any deprivation of life:

In *McCann*, three members of an active unit of the Irish Republican Army (IRA), the Provisional IRA, were shot in Gibraltar by soldiers of the Special Air Service (SAS), the principal special forces organisation of the British Army. The three had been subject to intense surveillance prior to their deaths and were effectively allowed to enter Gibraltar in order to arrest them at a later moment. As they were suspected of carrying the trigger device for a bomb suspected to be installed in a car parked by one of the three, they were shot in course of the attempted arrest. The exact facts concerning that incident remained somewhat unclear,[599] but it was undisputed that there was no bomb in Gibraltar, nor were the three IRA members carrying any arms or any object connected with any possible detonation of a bomb.[600]

Commission and Court did not regard the right to life violated either by the shooting itself, as it was regarded justified from the perspective of the acting officers, or based on the alleged inadequacy of the *ex post facto* inquiries.[601] While the Commission thus considered the right to life not to have been violated at all, the Court went further; it found that the instructions and information relayed to the acting officers "rendered inevitable the use of lethal force".[602] It thus examined the control and organisation of the whole operation leading to the deaths of

[598] Ní Aoláin, 19 *Nether. Q. Hum. Rts.* (2001), at 32.

[599] Eur. Ct. H.R., *McCann*, Series A, No. 324, pp. 11-30 (paras. 13-96).

[600] *Id.*, p. 30 (paras. 93 and 96).

[601] The Commission declared the case admissible to the Court, but concluded by 11 votes to 6 that there had been no violation of Article 2 of the Convention, Eur. Comm'n H.R., *McCann, Farrel and Savage v. United Kingdom*, Appl. No. 18984/91, Opinion of March 4, 1994, Series A, No. 324 (Annex), pp. 74-92, at 79-81 (paras. 193-201); Eur. Ct. H.R., *McCann*, Series A, No. 324, pp. 47-49 (paras. 157-164) and pp. 58-59 (para. 200).

[602] Eur. Ct. H.R., *McCann*, Series A, No. 324, p. 59 (para. 201).

McCann, Farrel and Savage. The Court *inter alia* disapproved of the fact that the three suspects had not been arrested while crossing the border, which in the Court's view would have been possible if a more rigorous border surveillance had been mounted. This failure seemed to strike the court as a paradox, as the aim of the whole operation was to prevent injury and destruction in Gibraltar. The easy access the suspects had to Gibraltar rendered that objective almost meaningless.[603] This failure to arrest the suspects put their lives at greater risk. Additionally, the soldiers that were ordered to effect the arrest were trained in a way incompatible with the degree of caution expected by law-enforcement officials in a democratic society, even when dealing with alleged terrorists.[604] This assessment stresses that the court regards the right to life as applying equally to all transgressors, no matter how heinous their alleged activities may be. Suspecting terrorist activities does not absolve a State from guaranteeing each individual the same due process rights.

The nine dissenting judges in *McCann* issued a joint opinion that fundamentally disagreed with the majority's assessment: They first called upon the Court to "resist the temptations offered by the benefit of hindsight".[605] Second, they strongly criticized the Court in its demand for "the authorities to act within the constraints of the law, while the suspects were operating in a state of mind in which members of the security forces were regarded as legitimate targets and incidental death or injury to civilians as of little consequence, would inevitably give the suspects a tactical advantage which should not be allowed to prevail."[606] This assessment, in addition to its referral to "legitimate targets", contains elements that resemble an international humanitarian law perspective, i.e. a distinction according to a certain status of a person, namely that of an alleged terrorist in the present case.

Contrary to this, the decision of the Court stresses that human rights and particularly the right to life do not depend on a person's assumed status such as "alleged terrorist". It shows an unwillingness to base protection of life on a "worst case scenario" approach as taken by the State. The Court did not even refer to the margin of appreciation doctrine and

---

603 *Id.*, pp. 59-60 (paras. 203-205).

604 *Id.*, pp. 61-62 (para. 212).

605 *Id.*, Joint Dissenting Opinion, pp. 65-73, at 66 (para. 8).

606 *Id.* (para. 9).

thus ensured an equally high standard of protection concerning the right to life that applies to the whole European system.[607]

Interestingly, the minority in its joint dissenting opinion was "satisfied that no failings have been shown in the organisation and control of the operation by the authorities"[608] It thus implicitly accepted the standards developed by the majority, but disagreed on the question of whether these standards were met in the case. Thus, even though the Court was almost equally divided in that case, it laid the foundation for its willingness to scrutinise the care taken by member States' authorities in implementing security forces' operations.[609] This approach was retained by the Court in later cases and extended into violent situations not involving terrorism.[610]

II. Exceptions – Permissible Deprivation of Life

In contrast to the Articles protecting the right to life in the other conventions examined, Article 2 of the European Convention sets out ex-

---

[607] Ní Aoláin, 19 *Nether. Q. Hum. Rts.* (2001), at 30-31; on the doctrine *see* Arai-Takahashi, *Margin of Appreciation*, pp. 2-8; Ronald St. John Macdonald, 'The Margin of Appreciation', in: Ronald St. John Macdonald/ Franz Matscher/ Herbert Petzold (eds.), *The European System for the Protection of Human Rights*, Dordrecht 1993, pp. 83-124.

[608] Eur. Ct. H.R., *McCann*, Series A, No. 324, Joint Dissenting Opinion, pp. 65-73, at 73 (para. 25).

[609] Mowbray, *Positive Obligations*, p. 9.

[610] *See e.g.* Eur. Ct. H.R., *Andronicou and Constantinou v. Cyprus*, Appl. No. 25052/94, Judgment of October 9, 1997, *ECHR* 1997-VI, pp. 2059-2151, at 2102 and 2107 (paras. 181-182 and 192); Eur. Ct. H.R., *Ergi*, *ECHR* 1998-IV, at 1776-1779 (paras. 79-86); Eur. Ct. H.R., *Isayeva v. Russia*, Appl. No. 57950/00, Judgment of February 24, 2005, paras. 182-183; Eur. Ct. H.R., *Isayeva, Yusupova and Bazayeva v. Russia*, Appl. Nos. 57947/00, 57948/00 and 57949/00, Judgment of February 24, 2005, paras. 181-182. Both latter cases considering "whether the *planning and conduct* of the operation were consistent with Article 2 of the Convention." (emphasis added) and coming to a negative result, *see* paras. 200-201 and 199-200 respectively. On the central question in these cases, i.e. the international humanitarian law implications of the cases, *see infra*, Part One, Chapter E) II. 3.

plicit exceptions to this right. Beside the death penalty, this concerns the exceptions enumerated in para. 2 of the Article.

1. *The Death Penalty*

Capital punishment is explicitly legal under Article 2 para. 1, 2nd sentence. It is, however, subject to two additional protocols, which aim at the abolishment of the death penalty. Additional Protocol No. 6, which is in force for all member States of the Convention except for Russia,[611] abolishes the death penalty in times of peace, but in its Article 2 permits exceptions in times of war or the threat of war, with certain restrictions.[612] This assessment was changed by Additional Protocol No. 13, which aimed at the abolishment of capital punishment even in times of war.[613] The abolition of the death penalty is non-derogable according to Article 2 of Protocol No. 13.[614] This far reaching prohibition is not ratified by all States party to the Convention: It only applies to 40 of the 47 member States.[615] Even despite this fact, the European system is further developed in abolishing the death penalty than the other human rights treaty regimes. As seen above, the death penalty is abolished in the Second Optional Protocol to the ICCPR, but reservations permit-

---

611 Council of Europe, *Chart of Signatures and Ratifications of Protocol No. 6 to the Convention for the Protection of Human Rights and Fundamental Freedoms concerning the Abolition of the Death Penalty*, Status as of February 21, 2008.

612 Article 2 of the Additional Protocol No. 6 reads: "A State may make provision in its law for the death penalty in respect of acts committed in time of war or of imminent threat of war; such penalty shall be applied only in the instances laid down in the law and in accordance with its provisions. The State shall communicate to the Secretary General of the Council of Europe the relevant provisions of that law."

613 Article 1 of Protocol No. 13 reads: "The death penalty shall be abolished. No one shall be condemned to such penalty or executed."

614 Article 2 of Protocol No. 13 reads: "No derogation from the provisions of this Protocol shall be made under Article 15 of the Convention."

615 Council of Europe, *Chart of Signatures and Ratifications of Protocol No. 13 to the Convention for the Protection of Human Rights and Fundamental Freedoms Concerning the abolition of the death penalty in all circumstances*, Status as of February 21, 2008.

ting capital punishment are permitted.[616] The American Convention only prohibits the reestablishment of the death penalty in States which have already abolished it,[617] and the African Charter does not address the issue at all and thus only prohibits the capital punishment if it amounts to an "arbitrary execution".[618]

In consequence of the wide acceptance of the death penalty's complete abolition and the almost complete acceptance of its abolition in peace times, the procedural safeguards included in Article 2 are factually obsolete: They include a judicial decision that is preceded by a fair and public hearing in the sense of Article 6, the punishment may not amount to a degrading treatment in the sense of Article 3,[619] and it may not be retroactive or discriminatory.[620] However, killings that are not of a penal but of a preventive character are at the focus of this examination. Such killings could never be justified under Art. 2 para. 1, 2nd sentence, but they can be permitted under Article 2 para. 2 of the European Convention:

2. Exceptions Enumerated in Article 2 Para. 2

It is accepted, that the European Convention lists cases that are also regarded non-arbitrary under the other conventions.[621] According to para. 2 of Article 2,

---

616 *See supra*, Part One, Chapter B) II. 1.

617 *See supra*, Part One, Chapter C) II. 1.

618 *See supra*, Part One, Chapter D) II.

619 *Compare* Eur. Ct. H.R., *Soering*, Series A, No. 161; *compare also* Jacobs/ White, *European Convention*, p. 47; Rosalyn Higgins, 'Extradition, the Right to Life, and the Prohibition against Cruel and Inhuman Punishment and Treatment: Similarities and Differences under the ECHR and the ICCPR', in: Paul Mahoney/ Franz Matscher/ Herbert Petzold/ Luzius Wildhaber (eds.), *Protection des droits de l'homme: la perspective européenne – Mélanges à la mémoire de Rolv Ryssdal*, Köln 2000, pp. 605-615.

620 Dijk/ Hoof, *European Convention*, pp 303-304.

621 *Compare e.g.* Rodley, *Treatment of Prisoners*, p. 149; Nowak, *CCPR Commentary*, Art. 6, para. 14 (p. 111); Kretzmer, 16 *Eur. J. Int'l L.* (2005), at 177.

> Deprivation of life shall not be regarded as inflicted in contravention of this Article when it results from the use of force which is no more than absolutely necessary: (a) in defence of any person from unlawful violence; (b) in order to effect a lawful arrest or to prevent the escape of a person lawfully detained; (c) in action lawfully taken for the purpose of quelling a riot or insurrection.

These exceptions are regarded as "exhaustive and must be narrowly interpreted".[622] According to the *travaux préparatoires*, they exclusively refer to the second sentence of Article 2 para. 1:[623] Originally, the first sentence of Article 2 was an autonomous paragraph and the exceptions enumerated in former para. 3 only referred to "violation du paragraphe précedent", i.e. to former para. 2 that contained the text of the later second sentence of the later para. 1.[624] It was subject to some debate whether these "law-enforcement exceptions"[625] cover intentional as well as unintentional killings[626] or whether they only permit unintentional killings.[627] This might be partly due to different assessments of

---

[622] Eur. Comm'n H.R., *Kathleen Stewart v. United Kingdom*, Appl. No. 10044/82, Decision of July 10, 1984, 39 *D.R.* (1984), pp. 162-185, at 169 (para. 13); *see also* Harris *et al.*, *European Convention*, p. 44; Villiger, *Handbuch EMRK*, para. 279 (p. 172); *see generally* Bernhardt, *Auslegung*, pp. 182-185.

[623] Ermacora *et al.* (eds.), *Europäische Menschenrechtskonvention*, Art. 2, para. 6.1 (p. 105); Partsch, in: Bettermann *et al.* (eds.), at 336 (footnote 319); Benjamin Kneihs, 'Recht auf Leben und Terrorismusbekämpfung – Anmerkungen zur jüngsten Judikatur des EGMR zu Art. 2 EMRK', in: Christoph Grabenwarter/ Rudolf Thienel (eds.), *Kontiunuität und Wandel der EMRK – Studien zur Europäischen Menschenrechtskonvention*, Kehl am Rhein 1998, pp. 21-43, at 22-23.

[624] Council of Europe (ed.), *Collected edition of the "Travaux préparatoires" of the European Convention on Human Rights*, Vol. 3: Committee of Experts, 2 February – 10 March 1950, The Hague 1976, pp. 596 and 621; For an overview over the drafting history *see* Ermacora *et al.* (eds.), *Europäische Menschenrechtskonvention*, Art. 2, para. 6.1 (pp. 103-105).

[625] Sarah Joseph, 'Denouncement of the Death on the Rock: the Right to Life of Terrorists', in 14 *Nether. Q. Hum. Rts.* (1996), pp. 5-22, at 7.

[626] *See e.g.* Frowein/ Peukert (eds.), *EMRK-Kommentar*, Art. 2, para. 1 (p. 29); Dijk/ Hoof, *European Convention*, p. 306.

[627] *See e.g.* Bergmann, *Menschenbild*, p. 134.

the concept of "intention" by the different authors.[628] By now, the court and the Commission have clarified this question: The text of Article 2, read as a whole,

> indicates that paragraph 2 does not primarily define situations where it is permitted intentionally to kill an individual, but defines the situations where it is permissible to 'use force' which may result, as the unintended outcome of the use of force, in the deprivation of life.[629]

If the first part of para. 2 is examined thoroughly, it becomes clear that the European Convention generally does not accept killings with direct intention of the first degree: "Deprivation of life shall not be regarded as inflicted in contravention of this Article when it results from the use of force which is no more than absolutely necessary" to reach one of the three aims enumerated. Thus, the aim that is strived for with *dolus directus* of the first degree may not be the death of the person targeted; if this person survives the force used against him, the action is not regarded as having failed as long as one of the aims enumerated is reached.[630] The only other case would be the death penalty, which is thus accepted as the only exception concerning a killing with direct intention of the first degree.[631] Hence, a targeted killing, i.e. a killing with direct intention of the first degree,[632] is not possible under the Convention, irrespective of the motives for such a killing. However, this does not exclude killings with intention of a lesser degree, e.g. preventive killings. Such cases must adhere to the strict test of "absolute necessity":

---

628 *Compare supra*, Introduction, Chapter C) II. 1. *Compare also* the discussion of this topic by Kneihs, in: Grabenwarter/ Thienel (eds.), at 33-34.

629 Eur. Comm'n H.R., *Kathleen Stewart*, 39 *D.R.* (1984), at 170 (para. 15); quoted in and relied upon by the Eur. Ct. H.R., *McCann*, Series A, No. 324, p. 46 (para. 148); *see also* Eur. Ct. H.R., *Oğur*, *ECHR* 1999-III, at 548 (para. 78).

630 *Compare supra*, Introduction, Chapter C) II. 1. b).

631 *Compare* Ermacora *et al.* (eds.), *Europäische Menschenrechtskonvention*, Art. 2, para. 6.4.1 (pp. 126-134, at 127); Frowein/ Peukert (eds.), *EMRK-Kommentar*, Art. 2, para. 10 (p. 35) referring to "Absicht", i.e. *dolus directus* of first degree.

632 *Compare supra*, Introduction, Chapter C) II. 1. b).

a) The Test of Absolute Necessity

The cases of deprivation of life listed in Article 2 para. 2 do not fall under the prohibition of Article 2 para. 1 subject to the condition that the force used is "no more than absolutely necessary". The force used must thus be "strictly proportionate to the achievement of the aims set up in sub-paragraphs 2(a), (b) and (c) of Article 2."[633]

Contrary to the other human rights conventions examined above, the European Convention already contains the cases that are regarded as legitimate aims and in which the use of force is considered, by the Convention itself, as capable of furthering these aims.[634] The sole standard that has to be applied to these cases is therefore that of "absolute necessity", corresponding to the tests of necessity of the means and of proportionality in the narrow sense as applied above.[635]

It is the force used that has to fulfil the criterion of absolute necessity, not the deprivation of life, as the death of the person is a side effect of the action.[636] In the context of other Articles, the Court has reaffirmed that "necessary" implies a "pressing social need".[637] However, the ad-

---

633 Eur. Ct. H.R., *McCann*, Series A, No. 324, p. 46 (para. 149); Eur. Ct. H.R., *Oğur*, *ECHR* 1999-III, at 548 (para. 78); the death penalty is not subject to "absolute necessity", *see* Jordan J. Paust, 'The Right to Life in Human Rights Law and the Law of War', in: 65 *Sask. L. Rev.* (2002), pp. 411-425, at 417.

634 *Compare* Otto Lagodny, in: Wolfram Karl (ed.), *Internationaler Kommentar zu Europäischen Menschenrechtskonvention*, 5th ed., Köln 2003, Art. 2, para. 66 (p. 25).

635 *Compare supra*, Part One, Chapter B) II.; Dijk/ Hoof, *European Convention*, p. 305; on the Courts usual assessment concerning proportionality *see* John Joseph Cremona, 'The Proportionality Principle in the Jurisprudence of the European Court of Human Rights', in: Ulrich Beyerlin (ed.), *Recht zwischen Umbruch und Bewahrung: Völkerrecht, Europarecht, Staatsrecht – Festschrift für Rudolf Bernhardt*, Berlin 1995, pp. 323-330, at 327.

636 Opsahl, in: Macdonald *et al.* (eds.), at 216; Dijk/ Hoof, *European Convention*, p. 305.

637 Eur. Ct. H.R., *Handyside*, Series A, No. 24, p. 22 (para. 48); Eur. Ct. H.R., *Sunday Times v. United Kingdom*, Appl. No. 6538/74, Judgment of April 26, 1979, Series A, No. 30, pp. 35-37 (para. 59) (both concerning Article 10 para. 2); Eur. Ct. H.R., *Dudgeon v. United Kingdom*, Appl. No. 7525/76, Judgment of October 22, 1981, Series A, No. 45, p. 21 (para. 51) (concerning Article 8 para. 2); *compare also* Kai Hailbronner, 'Die Einschränkung von Grundrechten in einer demokratischen Gesellschaft. Zu den Schrankenvorbehalten der

verb 'absolutely' indicates that a stricter and more compelling test of necessity must be applied than in the context of other provisions of the convention.[638]

> In assessing whether the use of force is strictly proportionate, regard must be had to the nature of the aim pursued, the dangers to life and limb inherent in the situation and the degree of the risk that the force employed might result in loss of life. The Commission's examination must have due regard to all the relevant circumstances surrounding the deprivation of life.[639]

This assessment can be broken down into several sub-questions: First, is the use of force absolutely necessary, or could other measures be employed to reach one of the aims enumerated in para. 2 of the Article? Second, if no other measures are available, is it absolutely necessary to use lethal force, or could some lesser degree of force be employed?[640] Third, is there a proportionate relation between the force used and the interest pursued?[641]

Europäischen Menschenrechtskonvention', in: Rudolph Bernhardt/ Wilhelm Karl Geck/ Günther Jaenicke/ Helmut Steinberger (eds.), *Völkerrecht als Rechtsordnung – Internationale Gerichtsbarkeit – Menschenrechte: Festschrift für Hermann Mosler*, Berlin 1983, pp. 359-385, at 362-368; Marc-André Eissen, 'The Principle of Proportionality in the Case-Law of the European Court of Human Rights', in: Ronald St. John Macdonald/ Franz Matscher/ Herbert Petzold (eds.), *The European System for the Protection of Human Rights*, Dordrecht 1993, pp. 125-146, at 126-131.

[638] Eur. Comm'n H.R., *Kathleen Stewart*, 39 *D.R.* (1984), at 170-171 (para. 18); Eur. Comm'n H.R., *John Kelly v. United Kingdom*, Appl. No. 17579/90, Decision of January 13, 1993, 74 *D.R.* (1984), pp. 139-155, at 145-146; *compare also* John Smith, 'The Right to Life and the Right to kill in Law Enforcement', in: 144 *New L.J.* (1994), No. 6639, pp. 354-356; Villiger, *Handbuch EMRK*, para. 282 (p. 173).

[639] Eur. Comm'n H.R., *Kathleen Stewart*, 39 *D.R.* (1984), at 171 (para. 19); *see also* Mowbray, *Positive Obligations*, p. 15; on the development of the Court's use of the proportionality principle *see* Cremona, in: Beyerlin (ed.), pp. 323-330.

[640] *Compare also* Kretzmer, 16 *Eur. J. Int'l L.* (2005), at 178.

[641] Dijk/ Hoof, *European Convention*, p. 305; Kneihs, in: Grabenwarter/ Thienel (eds.), at 26.

b) The Use of Force in Defence of Any Person from Unlawful Violence

The first exception stated in Article 2 para. 2 of the Convention is that of self-defence or the defence of another person from unlawful violence. The defence of property is not covered[642] and a warning is necessary before firearms are used.[643] It has been argued by *Trechsel* that it should also be possible under the Convention to face "an attack on a power plant, an important bridge or any other subject, threatening not life but enormous damage" by using "possibly lethal force".[644] However, the decision made in the Convention is clear: Only in cases of violence against a person, may the right to life of the offender be at disposition. In cases of other threats as described above, the State may only take recourse to non-lethal means.

Examples which were regarded as satisfying the standard of "absolute necessity" include the following:

For the police to fire shots at a group of heavily armed bank robbers who, at least in part, resist an arrest and detonate a hand grenade, has been interpreted as the force no more than absolutely necessary, both in self-defence and in order to effect an arrest.[645]

The shooting even with intent to kill was regarded as justified from the point of view of the acting officers in *McCann* by both the Commission and the Court; one soldier stated expressly that his intention had been "to kill McCann 'to stop him becoming a threat and detonating that

---

[642] Opsahl, in: Macdonald *et al.* (eds.), at 216; Marion Wössner, *Die Notwehr und ihre Einschränkung in Deutschland und in den USA*, Berlin 2006, pp. 62-66; Frank Bisson, *Die lebensgefährliche Verteidigung von Vermögenswerten*, Frankfurt am Main 2002, pp. 138-148; Tanja Stiller, *Grenzen des Notwehrrechts bei der Verteidigung von Sachwerten*, Frankfurt am Main 1999, pp. 184-190; Olivia Lührmann, *Tötungsrecht zur Eigentumsverteidigung? Eine Untersuchung des Notwehrrechts unter verfassungsrechtlichen, menschenrechtlichen und rechtsvergleichenden Gesichtspunkten*, Frankfurt am Main 1999, p. 226, pp. 280-281; Villiger, *Handbuch EMRK*, para. 279 (p. 172); Harris *et al.*, *European Convention*, p. 48.

[643] Eur. Ct. H.R., *Oğur*, *ECHR* 1999-III, at 549-550 (para. 82).

[644] Trechsel, in: Benedek *et al.* (eds.), at 682; a similar, albeit in his own words "extraordinary theoretical" case is raised by Frowein/ Peukert (eds.), *EMRK-Kommentar*, Art. 2, para. 14 (p. 37).

[645] Eur. Comm'n H.R., *Wolfgram (W.) v. Germany*, Appl. No. 11257/84, Decision of October 6, 1986, 49 *D.R.* (1986), pp. 213-220, at 216.

bomb'"[646] while the attack commander declared that "the intention at the moment of fire was to kill since this was the only way to remove the threat. He added that this was the standard followed by any soldier in the army who opens fire."[647] It was thus accepted that shooting to kill was the only way to be sure that the suspects could not press the button that would cause the alleged bomb to explode.[648] Such "honest belief" which is perceived for good reasons to be valid at the time can still be justified under Article 2 even if it proves wrong. "To hold otherwise would put an unrealistic burden on law enforcement officers."[649] This implies that shooting with direct intention of second degree concerning the death of the targeted person can be necessary under the European Convention in a situation as immediate as described by the acting officers. It amounts to the "paradigmatic case in which use of force would be justifiable" as serious violence against a person to be protected is so imminent "that trying to arrest the perpetrator would allow him time to carry out his threat".[650]

Similarly, the Court accepted in *Andronicou and Constantinou* that the officers honestly and reasonably believed that they as well as the hostage were at risk from the armed hostage taker and were thus entitled to open fire in order to eliminate that risk.[651] On the other hand, the firing of more than 50 shots at the door behind which *Mehmet Gül* stood was

---

[646] Eur. Ct. H.R., *McCann*, Series A, No. 324, p. 24 (para. 63).

[647] *Id.*, p. 27 (para. 80).

[648] Eur. Comm'n H.R., *McCann*, Series A, No. 324 (Annex), at 87 (para. 233); Eur. Ct. H.R., *McCann*, Series A, No. 324, pp. 58-59 (para. 200); *Ex post facto* it became clear that the three people objectively did not pose any immediate threat, as there was no bomb, nor were they carrying any arms or any object connected with any possible detonation of a bomb, *compare supra*, Part One, Chapter E) I. 2. c).

[649] Karen Reid, *A Practitioner's Guide to the European Convention on Human Rights*, 2nd Edition, London 2004, para. IIB-392 (p. 499).

[650] Kretzmer, 16 *Eur. J. Int'l L.* (2005), at 179.

[651] Eur. Ct. H.R., *Andronicou and Constantinou*, *ECHR* 1997-VI, at 2107 (para. 192); *compare also* Eur. Ct. H.R., *Brady v. United Kingdom*, Appl. No. 55151/00, Decision of April 3, 2001 (unreported), declaring the application inadmissible on the basis that the shooting policeman acted in the belief that the robber had a gun.

declared as not justified by any reasonable belief of the officers that their lives were at risk from the occupants of the flat.[652]

Regarding the intention concerning the death as an effect of the use of force, it could again be doubted whether the use of force described in the cases above is necessary: Especially in *McCann*, direct intention concerning the death of the three suspects was accepted by the Court. The aim of the action was to stop the suspect from carrying out his threat. This is most likely also possible if the force is used with *dolus eventualis* or even less intention concerning the actual death of the person targeted, i.e. if the law enforcement agent hopes that the person targeted will survive the use of force. But again, this intention is not visible. Independently of whether the marksman hopes that the offender will survive or knows that he will die, the result of his shot will be the same.[653]

This does not hold true if the aim is to punish the suspect for past acts, or to deter other potential offenders.[654] The Commission thus relativised its statement in *McCann* by stressing that

> a policy of shooting to kill terrorist suspects in preference to the inconvenience of resorting to the procedures of criminal justice would be in flagrant violation of the Conventions rights to life and to a fair trial.[655]

Such a policy was not found in *McCann*, but the shootings were eventually regarded in a wider approach and it was thus made clear that, the very far reaching statements concerning the use of force with direct intention of second degree are only applicable to exceptional cases: As less restrictive means were available at an earlier time, i.e. it would have been possible to arrest the suspects who were later killed at the border, the right to life was violated by the shootings of the suspects in *McCann* nevertheless. This again places the focus on the question of immediacy, but with a wider perspective: Generally, the same considerations as developed in connection with the ICCPR also apply to the Eu-

---

[652] Eur. Ct. H.R., *Gül v. Turkey*, Appl. No. 22676/93, Judgment of December 14, 2000 (unreported), paras. 81-83.

[653] *Compare supra*, Part One, Chapter B) II. 2. b) (2).

[654] Kretzmer, 16 *Eur. J. Int'l L.* (2005), pp. 179.

[655] Eur. Comm'n H.R., *McCann*, Series A, No. 324 (Annex), at 82 (para. 206).

ropean Convention.[656] Beyond that, *McCann* shows that a situation that looks *per se* imminent must not in all circumstances satisfy that requirement. Imminence is not only a question concerning the moment of the use of force, but also concerning the overall approach of the security forces to the situation. If earlier possibilities to eliminate a threat are ignored, the mere imminence in the more acute situation thus provoked does not render the use of force "absolutely necessary".

This does not imply that the security forces may no longer act in such a situation. The duty to protect potential victims does still exist. However, the State has manoeuvred itself into a dilemma; it can only fulfil this duty by violating the right to life of the offender. The offender is still responsible for the threat he poses and thus merits less protection than the innocent victims.[657] Therefore, the use of force to stop the threat is still the better solution. But it does entail responsibility of the State for a violation of the right to life under the Convention. This fact will hopefully have the effect that State authorities avoid such quandaries by adequately planning and organising law enforcement actions. This is the lesson to be learned from *McCann*.

c) The Use of Force in Order to Effect a Lawful Arrest or to Prevent the Escape of a Person Lawfully Detained

According to Article 2 para. 2 *lit.* b, a killing that is the result of the use of force absolutely necessary to effect a lawful arrest or to prevent the escape of a person lawfully detained does not violate the right to life under the Convention. The wording shows that the death of the targeted person may not be directly intended, at least not with direct intention of the first degree.[658] Concerning an arrest, there is serious difficulty in the way of justifying shooting with intent to kill, which has been condensed to the statement: "You cannot arrest a corpse."[659] Thus, the death of the person targeted may only be a side-effect but

---

[656] *Compare supra*, Part One, Chapters B) II. 2. b) (5) and (6).

[657] *See also* Kneihs, in: Grabenwarter/ Thienel (eds.), at 34.

[658] Frowein, in: Denninger/ Hinz (eds.), pp. 112-121, at 117; Frowein/ Peukert (eds.), *EMRK-Kommentar*, Art. 2, para. 12 (p. 26).

[659] Smith, 144 *New L.J.* (1994), No. 6639, at 355; *see also* Joseph, 14 *Nether. Q. Hum. Rts.* (1996), at 9; *but see* Trechsel, in: Benedek *et al.* (eds.), at 683-684.

never the aim of the action.[660] To intent to kill, whether with *dolus directus* of first or second degree, is not consistent with the purpose of arrest under the Convention, which is to bring a person before the appropriate authorities, and ignores the possibility of a later arrest.[661] The death of the person may never be intended. Laws that permit the use of such force are not allowed under Article 2.[662]

Cases in which the Court and the Commission were confronted with the use of force in order to effect an arrest include the following examples:

The Commission regarded it as the force "no more than absolutely necessary" for the police to fire shots at a group of heavily armed bank robbers who, at least in part, resisted an arrest and detonated a hand grenade, both in self-defence as well as in order to effect an arrest.[663] This shows that as soon as an arrest is met with serious resistance, the wider exception of self-defence will also be applicable. It is thus neither sure whether the police officers intended to kill nor what the outcome of the decision would have been if the reason for the shots had been exclusively the arrest of the robbers.

The Commission declared the application inadmissible in *John Kelly* on the basis that the soldiers who were shooting at teenage joyriders fleeing in a stolen car believed that they were confronted by terrorists who had to be prevented from "further terrorist activities."[664] As arrest is used in Article 2 para. 2 without any further specification, recourse is taken to Article 5 of the Convention.[665] An arrest may thus *inter alia* serve to prevent the commission of an offence or fleeing after having done so (Article 5, para. 1, *lit.* c).[666] The decision in *Kelly* has neverthe-

---

660 Gollwitzer, *Menschenrechte*, Art. 2 MRK/Art. 6 IPBPR, para. 20 (pp. 164-165); Villiger, *Handbuch EMRK*, para. 282 (p. 173).

661 Harris *et al.*, *European Convention*, p. 52.

662 *Id.*, p. 38.

663 Eur. Comm'n H.R., *Wolfgram*, 49 *D.R.* (1986), at 216.

664 Eur. Comm'n H.R., *John Kelly*, 74 *D.R.* (1984), at 141.

665 *See e.g.* Ermacora *et al.* (eds.), *Europäische Menschenrechtskonvention*, Art. 2, para. 6.4.3 (p. 136).

666 Article 5 para. 1 reads: "Everyone has the right to liberty and security of person. No one shall be deprived of his liberty save in the following cases and in accordance with a procedure prescribed by law:

less been heavily criticized on the basis that the offence to be prevented by using force was much too vague. It is a very dangerous doctrine that would allow a fleeing person to be shot down because, if he gets away, sooner or later, he is likely to participate in acts of violence.[667] Furthermore, the soldiers did not try to hit the tyres of the speeding car, but aimed at the persons. It may thus be doubted whether their objective really was to arrest the suspects. The European Court, applying its standards of today, may have come to the converse result in that case.

It did so in *Aytekin*, regarding as not justified the shooting of a civilian who passed through a checkpoint without stopping. This decision was, however, based on the fact that the victim's behaviour was not shown to be suspicious.[668] The killing of two unarmed absconding conscripts in

---

a) the lawful detention of a person after conviction by a competent court;

b) the lawful arrest or detention of a person for non-compliance with the lawful order of a court or in order to secure the fulfilment of any obligation prescribed by law;

c) the lawful arrest or detention of a person effected for the purpose of bringing him before the competent legal authority on reasonable suspicion of having committed an offence or when it is reasonably considered necessary to prevent his committing an offence or fleeing after having done so;

d) the detention of a minor by lawful order for the purpose of educational supervision or his lawful detention for the purpose of bringing him before the competent legal authority;

e) the lawful detention of persons for the prevention of the spreading of infectious diseases, of persons of unsound mind, alcoholics or drug addicts or vagrants;

f) the lawful arrest or detention of a person to prevent his effecting an unauthorised entry into the country or of a person against whom action is being taken with a view to deportation or extradition."

667 Smith, 144 *New L.J.* (1994), No. 6639, at 356; *see also* Joseph, 14 *Nether. Q. Hum. Rts.* (1996), at 10; Trechsel, in: Benedek *et al.* (eds.), at 684.

668 Eur. Ct. H.R., *Aytekin v. Turkey*, Appl. No. 22880/93, Judgment of September 3, 1998, *ECHR* 1998-VII, pp. 2807-2843, at 2825-2829 (paras. 77-86); the case was declared inadmissible on the basis that the applicant failed to exhaust local remedies. The responsible soldier was held responsible in a national court.

an attempt to arrest them, by the use of an automatic rifle, was regarded as excessive force especially as other options to arrest them existed.[669]

Concerning the prevention of an escape, it was regarded as proportionate to shoot a person fleeing from custody in the foot without intending to kill him.[670] On the other hand, the lethal shootings at the border between Eastern and Western Germany were not regarded as necessary under Article 2 para. 2, as the Court considered that

> the deaths of the fugitives were in no sense the result of a use of force which was 'absolutely necessary'; the State practice implemented in the GDR by the applicants did not protect anyone against unlawful violence, was not pursued in order to make any arrest that could be described as 'lawful' according to the law of the GDR, and had nothing to do with the quelling of a riot or insurrection, as the fugitives' only aim was to leave the country.[671]

Interestingly, the Convention itself only expressly refers to the relation between the use of force and the aim to effect an arrest. It does not include the reason for the arrest in question in this balance. Such a balance seems to be reasonable and it is regarded as necessary to at least exclude inequitable cases e.g. concerning minor offences or persons that should be granted more protection, like mentally handicapped persons or minors.[672] Due to this consideration, the use of force resulting in death is regarded as not being justified in the case of an arrest when no

---

[669] Eur. Ct. H.R., *Nachova and others v. Bulgaria*, Appl. Nos. 43577/98 and 43579/98, Judgment of February 26, 2004 (unreported), paras. 96-109. This assessment was confirmed by the Grand Chamber: Eur. Ct. H.R., *Nachova and others v. Bulgaria*, Appl. Nos. 43577/98 and 43579/98, Judgment (Grand Chamber) of July 6, 2005, *ECHR* 2005-VII (not yet published), paras. 98-109.

[670] Eur. Comm'n H.R., *M.D. v. Turkey*, Appl. No. 28518/95, Decision of June 30, 1997 (unreported).

[671] Eur. Ct. H.R., *Streletz, Keßler and Krenz v. Germany*, Appl. Nos. 34044 /96, 35532/97, 44801/98, Judgment of March 22, 2001, *ECHR* 2001-II, pp. 351-461, at 448-449 (para. 96); *compare also* Grit Hokema, 'Das Urteil des Europäischen Gerichtshofs für Menschenrechte in der Sache Streletz, Keßler und Krenz – Eine späte Genugtuung für die Opfer des DDR-Grenzregimes', in: 14 *HuV-I* (2001), pp. 107-110, at 108.

[672] Trechsel, in: Benedek *et al.* (eds.), at 685.

serious danger is reasonably to be feared from the person concerned.[673] The same is argued in connection with preventing an escape: The right to life generally overrides the interest of enforcing criminal law. Exceptions are thus not based on the seriousness of the imputed or performed offence but on the danger envisaged from the perpetrator.[674] The use of force resulting in death is regarded as not justified in the case of the escape of a prisoner when no serious danger is reasonably to be feared from the person concerned.[675] Others limit the exception of *lit.* b to "dangerous persons".[676]

This assessment might seem to go beyond the text of the Convention; the test of "absolute necessity" *prima facie* only refers to possible milder means to achieve the aims enumerated in Article 2 para. 2. However, as stated by Commission in *Stewart*, it has to be assessed whether the use of force is "strictly proportionate", including "all the relevant circumstances surrounding the deprivation of life."[677]

Thus, even if no milder means are available, the use of force can be disproportionate, i.e. not meet the requirements of proportionality in the narrow sense. In cases that necessitate the use of force to reach a legitimate aim it may still not be possible to strike a proper balance between the injury caused to the individual by the interfering action and the desired aim.[678] This demands the motive, of an arrest or of the prevention of an escape, to be included into the considerations concerning its proportionality,[679] as done in the examples mentioned above.

---

[673] Dijk/ Hoof, *European Convention*, p. 305; Desch, 36 *ÖZöRV* (1985), at 112.

[674] Kremnitzer, in: Fleck (ed.), *Rechtsfragen*, at 202.

[675] Dijk/ Hoof, *European Convention*, p. 305.

[676] Frowein/ Peukert (eds.), *EMRK-Kommentar*, Art. 2, para. 12 (p. 36).

[677] Eur. Comm'n H.R., *Kathleen Stewart*, 39 *D.R.* (1984), at 171 (para. 19); *see also* Mowbray, *Positive Obligations*, p. 15; on the development of the Court's use of the proportionality principle *see* Cremona, in: Beyerlin (ed.), pp. 323-330.

[678] *Compare supra*, Part One, Chapter B) II. 3. c).

[679] *Compare also* Gollwitzer, *Menschenrechte*, Art. 2 MRK/Art. 6 IPBPR, para. 22 (p. 165); Dijk/ Hoof, *European Convention*, p. 305.

d) The Use of Force in Action Lawfully Taken for the Purpose of Quelling a Riot or Insurrection

According to Article 2 para. 2 lit. c, a killing that is the result of the use of force absolutely necessary in action lawfully taken for the purpose of quelling a riot or insurrection is not arbitrary. A riot is regarded as any illegal rout of a crowd which is committing or threatens to commit considerably violent acts.[680] This, according to the Court, clearly includes an assembly of 150 persons throwing missiles at a patrol of soldiers to the point that they risked serious injury.[681] The meaning of insurrection is rather open, from active armed resistance by a larger number of persons[682] up to an organisation that factually controls a relevant part of the State territory and stands its ground contra the government.[683]

Beside the exigencies of the Convention, the use of firearms must also be "lawful" under the corresponding national law.[684] Again, the test of "absolute necessity" requires resorting to the mildest equally effective means. This means that law enforcement personnel have to use "less lethal weapons" such as truncheons, water cannon, chemical irritant agents, distraction devices, kinetic impact munitions or electrical incapacitation devices.[685] As a consequence of *McCann*, the duty to adequately plan a riot control operation entails a duty to equip the law enforcement personnel with such "less lethal weapons"; if, by adequately planning an operation, a later situation in which the use of lethal force becomes inevitable can be avoided, the right to life encompasses a duty to conduct such planning. Therefore, the State has to ensure that the law enforcement personnel are equipped adequately to be able to react

---

680 Gollwitzer, *Menschenrechte*, Art. 2 MRK/Art. 6 IPBPR, para. 23 (pp. 165-166); Frowein/ Peukert (eds.), *EMRK-Kommentar*, Art. 2, para. 15 (p. 38).

681 Eur. Comm'n H.R., *Kathleen Stewart*, 39 *D.R.* (1984), at 172 (para. 25).

682 Gollwitzer, *Menschenrechte*, Art. 2 MRK/Art. 6 IPBPR, para. 23 (p. 166).

683 Ermacora *et al.* (eds.), *Europäische Menschenrechtskonvention*, Art. 2, para. 6.4.4 (pp. 136-137).

684 Eur. Comm'n H.R., *X v. Belgium*, 12 *Yb. Eur. Conv. Hum. Rts.* (1969), at 186-188.

685 *See* Bozeman/ Winslow, 5 *Internet J. Resc. & Disaster Med.* (2005), No. 1; 42 *Rev. dr. mil.* (2003), at 385.

by adequate means to different threats, including the ability to use milder, less or non lethal means.[686]

Such means have been subject to the Commission's jurisprudence; the use of a plastic baton round can be "absolutely necessary" even though it is dangerous and can cause serious injuries and death, particularly if it strikes the head. This is at least true in the context of Northern Ireland, where disturbances have been "used as a cover for sniper attack" even though in the case in question no such attack took place.[687] The evidence presented to the Commission in *Stewart* indicated that plastic bullets, although dangerous, are less dangerous than alleged.[688] The use of CS gas is considered by the Commission as milder than the maximum amount of force that can be "absolutely necessary" under Article 2 para. 2. It is furthermore not considered to be contrary to Article 3 of the Convention.[689] The Court, like the Commission, accepts that e.g. rubber bullets or tear gas are milder means that have to be used instead of fire arms.[690]

If this wide range of "less lethal weapons" that are especially designed to fend off crowds is taken into consideration, only very limited cases remain in which resort to lethal force is necessary. A large portion of these cases, if not all, will additionally be covered by self-defence or defence of others.[691] Thus, as long as the threshold to an armed conflict is not yet reached, it is very unlikely that lethal force to quell a riot or insurrection can be justified under the Convention at all.

---

[686] Eur. Ct. H.R., *Güleç*, *ECHR* 1998-IV, at 1729-1730 (paras. 71-73).

[687] Eur. Comm'n H.R., *Kathleen Stewart*, 39 *D.R.* (1984), at 172-173 (paras. 27-30); on the injuries caused by such plastic round batons *see* Hughes *et al.*, 22 *Emergency Medicine Journal* (2005), pp. 111-112 (with further references).

[688] Harris *et al.*, *European Convention*, p. 47.

[689] Eur. Comm'n H.R., *X and Y v. United Kingdom*, Appl. Nos. 7126/75 and 7573/76, Decision of March 9, 1977 (unpublished), in: 1 *Digest of Strasbourg Case Law relating to the European Convention on Human Rights*, para. 2.2.3 (p. 87).

[690] Eur. Ct. H.R., *Güleç*, *ECHR* 1998-IV, at 1729-1730 (paras. 71-73).

[691] *See also* Desch, 36 *ÖZöRV* (1985), at 112.

3. Non-Derogability of Article 2 and Deprivation of Life in the Course of Armed Conflict

Article 2 is included in the list of non-derogable rights laid down in Article 15 para. 2 of the Convention.[692] The right to life can thus not be derogated from even in "time of war or other public emergency threatening the life of the nation". The same applies to Protocol No. 6[693] and Protocol No. 13[694] and therefore to the complete abolition of the death penalty.

However, Article 15 para. 2 excludes "deaths resulting from lawful acts of war" from the non-derogable part of Article 2. Thus, the European Convention expressly does what the International Covenant only does implicitly: it refers to international humanitarian law. On the one hand, this stresses that acts of war are first and foremost judged according to international humanitarian law as the *lex specialis* – also to the European Convention. On the other hand, it clarifies that lawful acts or war do not violate Article 2 of the Convention under the precondition that the state of emergency has been declared by the Member State.[695] It is

---

[692] Article 15 paras. 1 and 2 read: "1. In time of war or other public emergency threatening the life of the nation any High Contracting Party may take measures derogating from its obligations under this Convention to the extent strictly required by the exigencies of the situation, provided that such measures are not inconsistent with its other obligations under international law. 2. No derogation from Article 2, except in respect of deaths resulting from lawful acts of war, or from Articles 3, 4 (paragraph 1) and 7 shall be made under this provision."

[693] Article 3 of Protocol No. 6 reads: "No derogation from the provisions of this Protocol shall be made under Article 15 of the Convention." However, it has to be kept in mind that Article 2 of the Protocol permits states to "make provision in its law for the death penalty in respect of acts committed in time of war or of imminent threat of war; such penalty shall be applied only in the instances laid down in the law and in accordance with its provisions." Thus, instead of a derogation, the possibility to curtail the abolition of the death penalty in advance in relation to war or the threat of war exists nevertheless.

[694] Article 2 of Protocol No. 13 reads: "No derogation from the provisions of this Protocol shall be made under Article 15 of the Convention." Furthermore, according to Article 3, "[n]o reservation may be made under Article 57 of the Convention in respect of the provisions of this Protocol."

[695] Heike Krieger, 'Die Verantwortlichkeit Deutschlands nach der EMRK für seine Streitkräfte im Auslandseinsatz', in: 62 *ZaöRV* (2002), pp. 669-702, at

nevertheless not comparable to other derogations, as lawful acts of war can only be executed in relation to the enemy,[696] and not *vis-à-vis* the own population.[697]

While the content of these *leges speciales* rules will be discussed infra,[698] the question arises whether and to which extent the European Court of Human Rights can apply international humanitarian law. As shown above, the Inter-American Commission willingly directly applies international humanitarian law, whereas the Inter-American Court is more reluctant and only interprets the American Convention with reference to humanitarian law.[699]

The European Court has consistently refused to apply international humanitarian law.[700] Recently, Common Article 3 of the 1949 Geneva Conventions was invoked before the Court,[701] but the Court stuck strictly to human rights in assessing the situation.[702] This could, however, be a distraction in order to avoid the question of whether the situation is an armed conflict or not. Intrinsically, the Court seems to apply

---

693-694. No derogation concerning a state of war has yet been issued, *see* Reid, *European Convention*, para. II B-084 (p. 251).

[696] Partsch, in: Bettermann *et al.* (eds.), at 310 (footnote 252).

[697] Frowein/ Peukert (eds.), *EMRK-Kommentar*, Art. 15, para. 12 (p. 484).

[698] *See infra*, Part Two.

[699] Compare supra, Part One, Chapter C) II. 4.

[700] Noëlle Quénivet, 'Isayeva v. the Russian Federation and Isayeva, Yusupova and Bazayeva v. the Russian Federation: Targeting Rules according to Article 2 of the European Convention on Human Rights', 18 *HuV-I* (2005), pp. 219-226, at 220; *but see e.g.* the referral to the 1949 Geneva Convention III in Eur. Ct. H.R., *Engel and others v. Netherlands (Merits)*, Appl. Nos. 5100/71; 5101/71; 5102/71; 5354/72 and 5370/72, Judgment of June 8, 1976, Series A, No. 22, para. 72.

[701] Eur. Ct. H.R., *Isayeva, Yusupova and Bazayeva v. Russia*, Appl. Nos. 57947/00, 57948/00 and 57949/00, Judgment of February 24, 2005, paras. 161-167.

[702] *Id.*, paras. 168-199.

international humanitarian law standards,[703] even though in an admittedly strict and human rights influenced interpretation.[704]

III. Conclusion: Killings Under the European Convention

According to Article 2 ECHR, the death of a person may only be the unavoidable result of force employed in order to pursue another aim. This covers intentional as well as unintentional killings. The European Court follows the Inter-American Commission and Court's example in accepting a shift of the burden of proof in certain cases *inter alia* involving disappearances, even though it seems to be more reluctant in doing so.[705] However, the European Court has elaborated extensive guidelines on the need for effective investigations.[706] It has furthermore stressed that the responsibility of States concerning the death of a person cannot only result from the act of killing *per se*, but also from a poor overall planning of an operation that inevitably leads to a situation where the use of lethal force is necessary, even though alternatives would have been possible earlier. In this respect, it went further than any other human rights organ.

Under the European Convention and its additional protocols, the death penalty is almost completely abolished in peace times as well as in times of war. However, Article 2 of the Convention entails three further exceptions concerning the right to life:

These exceptions do not allow targeted killings as the formulation of Article 2 para. 2 excludes the possibility of killing with direct intention of the first degree. The aim of the action which may result in the death of a person must be one of the three objectives enumerated, subject to the test of "absolute necessity". The force used must thus be "strictly proportionate to the achievement of the aims set up in sub-paragraphs

---

703 *See* Quénivet, 18 *HuV-I* (2005), at 221-222; *but see* William Abresch, 'A Human Rights Law of Internal Armed Conflict: The European Court of Human Rights in Chechnya', in: 16 *Eur. J. Int'l L.* (2005), pp. 741-767.

704 *Compare infra*, Part Four, Chapters C) II. 1. and 3.

705 For additional examples of such cross fertilisation *see* Buergenthal, in: Mahoney *et al.* (eds.), pp. 123-133.

706 *Compare* Mowbray, *Positive Obligations*, pp. 40-41.

2(a), (b) and (c) of Article 2."[707] This includes, beside the duty to resort to the mildest means possible, a test of necessity in the narrow sense.

Concerning self-defence or the defence of another person, this includes force used with direct intention of second degree towards the death of the targeted person; in order to save a life, it is legal under the Convention to use force and know for sure that this force will be lethal for the targeted person who causes an immediate threat to the victim. Immediacy, however, has to be assessed in a broad concept: Since *McCann*, it is clear that earlier opportunities for using milder means have to be included into these considerations. The State may not wait until a threat has become so immediate that only lethal force can stop it.

Concerning an arrest, intentional deprivation of life seems to be contrary to the Convention, even though the Court has not yet been very strict in this regard. However, the purpose of arresting a suspect demands that the suspect survives. If the purpose, on the other hand, is to prevent a deed, the use of lethal force in defence of any person is obviously not excluded. Concerning the prevention of an escape, this standard may be more relaxed. But in both cases the overall balance between the objective of the action and the force used has to be struck.

Finally, the intentional use of lethal force in order to quell a riot is never necessary if the possibilities offered by "less lethal weapons" are considered. If force of such amount is used by the rioters that the use of lethal force on the side of the State seems necessary, this is either the case in self-defence or defence of another person or the conflict has reached the threshold of an armed conflict.[708] Then, international humanitarian law standards do apply, even though the European Court still avoids calling a spade a spade in that regard.

---

[707] Eur. Ct. H.R., *McCann*, Series A, No. 324, para. 149 (p. 46); Eur. Ct. H.R., *Oğur*, *ECHR* 1999-III, at 548 (para. 78); the death penalty is not subject to "absolute necessity", *see* Paust, 65 *Sask. L. Rev.* (2002), at 417.

[708] On this question *compare infra*, Part Four; Fionnuala D. Ní Aoláin, 'The Relationship between Situations of Emergency and Low-Intensity Armed Conflict', in: 28 *Isr. Yb. Hum. Rts.* (1998), pp. 97-106.

F. Other Treaties Protecting the Right to Life

Other treaties that also protect the right to life, such as the Genocide Convention and the United Nations Convention on the Rights of the Child[709] do not entail provisions that are explicitly relevant to the problem at hand. Those treaties that regulate the law of war or international humanitarian law and thus set out the rules for the protection of life in the circumstances of armed conflicts and related situations are examined *infra*.[710] But "treaty law on its own provides an ultimately unsatisfactory patchwork quilt of obligations" still leaving many States largely untouched.[711] This leaves the non-treaty rules of international law concerning the right to life to be considered:

G. General International Law Protection of the Right to Life

The general existence of certain human rights as customary international law and/or general principles of law is widely accepted today.[712] It is

---

[709] Convention on the Rights of the Child, adopted by the UN General Assembly on November 20, 1989, Resolution 44/25, Annex, UN GAOR 44th Sess., Supp. No. 49, pp. 166-173, UN Doc. A/44/49 (1989), entry into force on September 2, 1990, reprinted in: 1577 *UNTS* (1990), No. 27531, pp. 3-177.

[710] *Compare infra*, Part Two.

[711] Bruno Simma/ Philip Alston, 'The Sources of Human Rights Law: Custom, jus cogens, and General Principles', in: 12 *Austl. Yb. Int'l L.* (1992), pp. 82-108, at 82.

[712] *See e.g.* Theodor Meron, *Human Rights and Humanitarian Norms as Customary Law*, Oxford 1989, pp. 79-114; Oscar Schachter, 'International Law in Theory and practice: General Course in Public International Law', in: 178 *RdC* (1982-V), pp. 9-395, at 333-342; American Law Institute, *Restatement of the Law (Third) – The Foreign Relations Law of the United States*, St. Paul, Minnesota 1987, § 701 (Vol. 2, pp. 152-161), at p. 152; Alfred Verdross/ Bruno Simma, *Universelles Völkerrecht: Theorie und Praxis*, 3rd ed., Berlin 1984, pp. 822-823 (para. 1234). *Compare also* Article 61 of the African Charter which refers to "African practices consistent with international norms on human and peoples' rights, customs generally accepted as law, general principles of law recognized by African states as well as legal precedents and doctrine" as subsidiary measures to determine the principles of law to be considered by the Commis-

however less clear, which rights are exactly covered by which of these principles. It is argued that the right to life may be considered as a norm of customary international law or as a general principle of international law.[713]

I. Customary International Law

Customary international law consists of "international custom, as evidence of a general practice accepted as law".[714] It is thus constituted by two elements: the objective element is "a general practice" and the subjective element is *opinio iuris sive necessitatais*, meaning "a belief that this practice is rendered obligatory by the existence of a rule of law requiring it".[715]

Traditionally, the emphasis in this relation was on State practice rather than on *opinio iuris*: The emergence of a general or extensive, uniform, consistent and settled practice[716] was later joined by the appreciation of that practice as legally binding, i.e. *opinio iuris*.[717] Thus it was exclusive-

---

sion, and Article 4 of the International Covenant that requires derogations from the obligations of States party to the Covenant "are not inconsistent with their other obligations under international law".

713 Ramcharan, in: Ramcharan (ed.), at 3.

714 *Compare* Article 38 para. 1 *lit.* b of the ICJ-Statute; Michael Barton Akehurst, 'Custom as a Source of International Law', in: 47 *Brit. Yb. Int'l L.* (1974-75), pp. 1-53, at 1 and 31-32; Mark E. Villiger, *Customary International Law and Treaties*, Dordrecht 1985, pp. 12-32 (paras. 38-80).

715 ICJ, *North Sea Continental Shelf, Federal Republic of Germany v. Denmark; Federal Republic of Germany v. The Netherlands*, Judgment of February 20, 1969, I.C.J. Reports 1969, pp. 3-57, at 44; *c.f.* ICJ, *Military and Paramilitary Activities in and against Nicaragua, Nicaragua v. United States of America*, Judgment (Merits) of June 27, 1986, I.C.J. Reports 1986, pp. 14-150, at 97; *see also* ICJ, *Legality of the Threat or Use of Nuclear Weapons*, Advisory Opinion of July 8, 1996, I.C.J. Reports 1996, pp. 225-593, at 253 (para. 64); ICJ, *Continental Shelf, Libyan Arab Jamahiriya v. Malta*, Judgment of June 3, 1985, I.C.J. Reports 1985, pp. 11-187, at 29-30 (para. 27).

716 Consisting of acts as opposed to claims, *see e.g.* Anthony A. D'Amato, *The Concept of Custom in International Law*, Ithaca, N.Y. 1971, p. 88.

717 *Compare e.g.* PCIJ, *SS "Lotus"*, Judgment of September 7, 1927, Series A, No. 10 (1927), p. 18 and the reasoning on pp. 22-31; *see also* Simma/ Alston, 12

ly the past that was taken into account empirically when assessing the law.[718]

Nevertheless, general practice is not to be confused with universal practice: not every State necessarily needs to participate – expressly or tacitly – in that practice. In certain fields, the practice of some States is of overriding importance, as not every State is a significant actor in that field.[719]

This leads to a second approach, according to which the practice only serves to bring the *opinio iuris* to fore and thus has an evidentiary rather than constitutive function. *Opinio iuris* can thus manifest itself more or less instantly.[720] According to this "progressive, streamlined theory, customary law, more or less stripped of the traditional practice requirement" would consist of "proclamation, exhortation, repetition, incantation, lament."[721]

Whereas the traditional approach is inductive, it is faced with a rather deductive alternative. An intermediary approach still maintains practice

---

Austl. Yb. Int'l L. (1992), at 88; The emphasis on state practice partly is so strong that *opinio iuris* was partly dispensed altogether, *see* Hans Kelsen, 'Théorie du droit international coutumier', in: 1 *Revue internationale de la théorie du droit, Nouvelle Série* (1939), pp. 253-270, at 264-266, who criticises that although the Permanent Court in *Lotus* rejected an alleged customary law rule due to the absence of *opinio iuris*, the Court never actually proved the positive existence of an *opinio iuris* to support a rule of customary law in any of its cases; *see also* Paul Guggenheim, *Lehrbuch des Völkerrechts*, Basel 1948, Vol. 1, pp. 46-47 and Paul Guggenheim, *Traité de Droit international public*, Geneva 1953, Vol. 1, pp. 46-48. *Kelsen* and *Guggenheim* both later abandoned this position, *see* Hans Kelsen, *Principles of International Law*, 2nd ed., New York 1966, p. 440; Paul Guggenheim, *Traité de Droit international public*, 2nd ed., Geneva 1967, pp. 101-103.

718 The "basic norm" stipulated by Hans Kelsen, *Principles of International Law*, New York 1952, pp. 417-418 is thus: "The states ought to behave as they have customarily behaved."

719 Robert Jennings; Arthur Watts (eds.), *Oppenheim's International Law*, Vol. I (Peace), 9th ed., Harlow 1992, p. 29.

720 *See e.g.* Bin Cheng, 'Custom: the Future of General State Practice in a Divided World', in: Ronald St. John Macdonald/ Douglas M. Johnston (eds.), *The Structure and Process of International Law: Essays in Legal Philosophy Doctrine and Theory*, The Hague 1983, pp. 513-554, at 530-548.

721 Simma/ Alston, 12 *Austl. Yb. Int'l L.* (1992), at 107 and 89 respectively.

as an integral part of customary international law, but accepts that practice changed from a retrospective on State behaviour into "paper practice": Rules or principles that have been proclaimed for instance in the UN General Assembly are taken as the starting point for the development of customary law and State practice follows. Such practice may "consist of ... statements that certain conduct is permitted, required or forbidden by international law".[722] This may go as far as regarding the law creation as complete as soon as the rule is formulated.[723] This approach is "progressive" insofar as it does not depend on retrospection concerning practice.[724] It is similar to the concept of "instant" customary law.[725]

The latter two assessments can explain the status of human rights as customary international law by referring to the Universal Declaration of Human Rights[726] that, according to these approaches, has either instantly or due to the subsequent practice become customary law.[727] They thus *inter alia*, regard the right to life, as laid down in the Universal Declaration, as customary international law. According to Article 3

---

[722] Akehurst, 47 *Brit. Yb. Int'l L.* (1974-75), at 53; *compare also* Michael Byers, *Custom, Power and the Power of Rules – International Relations and Customary International Law*, Cambridge 1999, pp. 133-136.

[723] *See* Louis B. Sohn, '"Generally Accepted" International Rules', in: 61 *Wash. L. Rev.* (1986), pp. 1073-1080, at 1077-1078.

[724] Simma/ Alston, 12 *Austl. Yb. Int'l L.* (1992), at 90.

[725] On this concept *compare* Roberto Ago, 'Science juridique et droit international', in: 90 *RdC* (1956-II), pp. 849-955, at 932-933; Bin Cheng, 'United Nations resolutions on Outer Space: "Instant" International Customary Law?', in: 5 *Indian J. Int'l L.* (1965), pp. 23-48, at 23-24.

[726] UN GA Res. 217 (III) A (December 10, 1948), *International Bill of Human Rights – Universal Declaration of Human Rights*, UN GAOR, 3rd Sess., Part 1, UN Doc. A/810 (1948), pp. 71-77.

[727] *See e.g.* UN Comm'n H.R., *Report on the Human Rights Situation in Iran by Special Representative Reynaldo Galindo Pohl*, UN Doc. E/CN.4/ 1987/23 (January 28, 1987), para. 22; Myres Smith MacDougal/ Harold D. Lasswell/ Lung-Chu Chen, *Human Rights and World Public Order: The Basic Policies of an International Law of Human Dignity*, New Haven, Conn. 1980, pp. 274 and 325; *compare also* Louis B. Sohn, 'The New International Law: Protection of the Rights of Individuals Rather than States', in: 32 *Am. U. L. Rev.* (1982), pp. 1-64, at 16-17; *but see* Alfred Verdross, '*Jus Dispositivum* and *Jus Cogens* in International Law', in: 60 *Am. J. Int'l L.* (1966), pp. 55-63, at 59.

of the Declaration, "Everybody has the right to life, liberty and the security of person." To the same effect, the Universal Declaration is regarded as "indirectly constituting international treaty law" as it represents an authoritative interpretation of the term human rights in the UN Charter.[728]

However, the line of argument that is most adequate for this examination is distinguishing between the customary international law status of individual human rights. The four non-derogable rights common to the ICCPR, American Convention and ECHR are thus considered to be customary international law.[729] Regarding the right to life, it is undisputed that genocide is prohibited by custom international law.[730] It is furthermore argued, that the prohibition of "murder or causing of disappearances" is also covered by custom,[731] referring to the killing of individuals

> other than as lawful punishment ... or as necessary under exigent circumstances, for example by police officials in line of duty in defense of themselves or of other innocent persons, or to prevent a serious crime.[732]

---

728 Manfred Nowak, *Introduction to the International Human Rights Regime*, Leiden 2003, p. 76; Sohn, 32 *Am. U. L. Rev.* (1982), at 16-17; *compare also* MacDougal *et al.*, *Human Dignity*, p. 325; *see also* Inter-Am. Ct. H.R., *Interpretation of the American Declaration of the Rights and Duties of Man within the Framework of Article 64 of the American Convention on Human Rights.* Advisory Opinion No. OC-10/89 of July 14, 1989, Series A, No. 10, para. 43, concerning the American Declaration of the Rights and Duties of Man as an authoritative interpretation of the human rights referred to in the OAS Charter; *but see* Schachter, 178 *RdC* (1982-V), at 335.

729 Oraá, *States of Emergency*, p. 96.

730 *See e.g.* ICJ, *Reservations to the Convention on the Prevention and Punishment of the Crime of Genocide*, Advisory Opinion of May 28, 1951, I.C.J. Reports 1951, pp. 14-69, at 23; Schachter, 178 *RdC* (1982-V), at 336; Meron, *Customary Law*, pp. 110-111 with further references.

731 American Law Institute, *Restatement of the Law (Third)*, § 702 (Vol. 2, pp. 161-175), at p. 161; Schachter, 178 *RdC* (1982-V), at 336.

732 American Law Institute, *Restatement of the Law (Third)*, § 702 (Vol. 2, pp. 161-175), Comment f (pp. 163-164).

This entails "a duty to exercise due diligence to deter and prevent ... conduct" by private actors violating the right.[733]

It may be difficult to prove the existence of the right to life as customary international law if reference is made to the traditional understanding of practice and *opinio iuris*, but, as *Meron* puts it, "those rights which are most crucial to the protection of human dignity and of universal accepted values of humanity, and whose violation triggers broad condemnation by the international community, will require a lesser amount of confirmatory evidence."[734] This, at least in part, corresponds *Kirgis'* view that the elements of custom are not fixed and mutually exclusive, but are interchangeable along a sliding scale:

> On the sliding scale, very frequent, consistent State practice establishes a customary rule without much (or any) affirmative showing of an opinio juris, so long as it is not negated by evidence of non-normative intent. As the frequency and consistency of the practice decline in any series of cases, a stronger showing of an opinio juris is required. At the other end of the scale, a clearly demonstrated opinio juris establishes a customary rule without much (or any) affirmative showing that governments are consistently behaving in accordance with the asserted rule.[735]

To this extent, a wide variety of "evidence" can be brought forward in support of the right to life's customary character. The right to life is recognised in Article 3 of the Universal Declaration of Human Rights, in Article I of the American Declaration of the Rights and Duties of Man,[736] in Article I of the Universal Islamic Declaration of Human Rights,[737] in the human rights treaties referred to above,[738] and in addi-

---

733 Schachter, 178 *RdC* (1982-V), at 336-337.

734 Meron, *Customary Law*, p. 94; *similarly,* Schachter, 178 *RdC* (1982-V), at 334; in support but also critically Simma/ Alston, 12 *Austl. Yb. Int'l L.* (1992), at 95-96.

735 Kirgis, 81 *Am. J. Int'l L.* (1987), at 149.

736 American Declaration of the Rights and Duties of Man, by the, O.A.S. Res. XXX (1948), adopted at the O.A.S. General Assembly, 9th Session March 30-May 2, 1948 in Bogotá, Colombia, OEA/Ser.L./V./II.23, doc. 21 rev. 6 (1948).

737 Universal Islamic Declaration of Human Rights, proclaimed by the Islamic Council in Paris, France on September 19, 1981, reprinted in: 4 *European Human Rights Reports* (1982), pp. 433-441.

tional international instruments.[739] It is included in numerous national constitutions[740] and municipal law.[741] The General Assembly frequently urged the member States to "respect as a minimum standard the content of Articles 6 [right to life], 14 [fair trial] and 15 [no retroactive penalty] of the International Covenant on Civil and Political Rights"[742] and referred to the "duty" of all States to observe the Universal Declaration,[743] which has also been referred to by various national courts as a source of standards for judicial decisions.[744] States have been criticising

---

[738] On treaties as a source for customary law *see* D'Amato, *International Law*, pp. 180-187; *but see* Akehurst, 47 *Brit. Yb. Int'l L.* (1974-75), at 42-53.

[739] *See e.g.* Article 8 para. 1 of the UN Comm'n H.R., Sub-Commission on Prevention of Discrimination and Protection of Minorities, *Declaration on Minimum Standards*, adopted by a group of experts at a meeting in Turku/Åbo, Finland, Dezember 1990, UN Doc. E/CN.4/Sub.2/1991/55 (August 12, 1991), reprinted in: 31 *Int'l Rev. Red Cross* (1991), No. 282, pp. 328-336, reading: "Every human being has the inherent right to life. This right shall be protected by law. No one shall be arbitrarily deprived of his or her life."

[740] Stefan Kadelbach, *Zwingendes Völkerrecht*, Berlin 1992, p. 286; Przetacznik, 9 *Rev. dr. hom.-Hum. Rts. J.* (1976), at 600-603; Christoph H. Schreuer, 'The Impact of International Institutions on the Protection of Human Rights in Domestic Courts', in: 4 *Isr. Yb. Hum. Rts.* (1974), pp. 76-87; Egon Schwelb, 'The Influences of the Universal Declaration of Human Rights on International and National Law', in: 53 *ASIL Proc.* (1959), pp. 217-229, at 222-226 with further references. While *Desch* found the right to life in 87 of 168 constitutions analysed by him, he stresses that additionally many states are bound by treaty provisions protecting the right to life, which adds up to 70 percent of states that explicitly recognise the right to life as protected, *see* Desch, 36 *ÖZöRV* (1985), at 82-84. This quota has been rising further since *Desch's* study, *see* Kadelbach, *Zwingendes Völkerrecht*, p. 287.

[741] W. Paul Gormley, 'The Right to Life and the Rule of Non-Derogability: Peremptory Norms of *Jus Cogens*', in: Bertrand G. Ramcharan (ed.), *The Right to Life in International Law*, Dordrecht 1985, pp. 120-159, at 125.

[742] *See e.g.* UN GA Res. 35/172 (December 15, 1980), *Arbitrary or Summary Executions*, UN GAOR, 35th Sess., Supp. No. 48, UN Doc. A/35/48 (1980), p. 195; UN GA Res. 36/22 (November 9, 1981), *Arbitrary or Summary Executions*, UN GAOR, 36th Sess., Supp. No. 51, UN Doc. A/36/51 (1981), pp. 168-169.

[743] Schwelb, 53 *ASIL Proc.* (1959), at 219 with further references.

[744] Schreuer, 4 *Isr. Yb. Hum. Rts.* (1974), pp. 76-87; Schwelb, 53 *ASIL Proc.* (1959), at 222-228 with further references.

other States for human rights violations for a long time.[745] And last but not least, the International Court of Justice has asserted in *Barcelona Traction* that the most basic human rights not only amount to customary international law, but even give rise to obligations *erga omnes*.[746]

While the right to life is widely adhered to in practice,[747] the practice does not necessarily have to be "in absolute rigorous conformity with the rule."[748] Continuous and gross violations of the right to life do not challenge the right as such. In the contrary: The efforts taken by States to conceal these violations show that the rule's existence is very well accepted and that these States feel bound by it.[749] Hence, violations of the accepted basic human rights of the person are regarded as violations, and not as "State practice" that nullifies the legal force of the right.[750] In consequence, the right to life is now regarded as enjoying the status of customary international law[751] and rightly so.

---

745 *See already* Oscar Schachter, 'International Law Implications of U.S. Human Rights Policies', in: 24 *N.Y.L. Sch. L. Rev.* (1977), pp. 63-87, at 66-74.

746 ICJ, *Barcelona Traction Light and Power Company, Limited, Second Phase*, Judgment of February 5, 1970, I.C.J. Reports 1970, pp. 3-357, at 32 (paras. 33-34).

747 *Compare* Ramcharan, in: Ramcharan (ed.), at 14-15.

748 ICJ, *Military and Paramilitary Activities in and against Nicaragua, Nicaragua v. United States of America*, Judgment (Merits) of June 27, 1986, I.C.J. Reports 1986, pp. 14-150, at 98 (para. 186).

749 Simma/ Alston, 12 *Austl. Yb. Int'l L.* (1992), at 91-92 and 97-98; Gormley, in: Ramcharan (ed.), at 144-145.

750 Schachter, 178 *RdC* (1982-V), at 336; *compare also* Kadelbach, *Zwingendes Völkerrecht*, p. 287.

751 *See e.g.* Meron, *Customary Law*, pp. 94-95; Carlson/ Gisvold, *International Covenant*, p. 1; Sohn, 32 *Am. U. L. Rev.* (1982), at 16-17; UN Comm'n H.R., *Report on the Human Rights Situation in Iran by Special Representative Reynaldo Galindo Pohl*, UN Doc. E/CN.4/1987/23 (January 28, 1987), paras. 4-5; American Law Institute, *Restatement of the Law (Third)*, § 702 (Vol. 2, pp. 161-175), at p. 161; Richard B. Lillich, 'Civil Rights', in: Theodor Meron (ed.), *Human Rights in International Law: Legal and Policy Issues*, 2nd repr., Oxford 1984, pp. 115-170, at 121; Dinstein, in: Henkin (ed.), at 115.

II. General Principles of Law and Natural Law Foundations

Another way in which the right to life is regarded as having acquired the standard of general international law is that of a general principle of law.[752] The principles of the Universal Declaration have a considerable influence on many national constitutions, statutes and judicial decisions.[753] Additionally, most of the legal systems of the world are based on such traditional and almost universal norms as the punishment of homicide.[754] The right to life is "a fundamental right in any society, irrespective of its degree of development or the type of culture".[755] Therefore, the right to life is now regarded as part of the corpus of "general principles of law recognized by civilized nations" in the sense of Article 38 of the ICJ-Statute.[756]

As general principles are regarded to have a certain "natural law flavour"[757] others directly assign a natural law or at least related basis to the right to life: The framers of the ICCPR referred to the "inherent" right and thus at least regarded this right as pre-existing, in a moral order or perhaps even in an immaculate *jus naturale*.[758] It has been doubted whether these sources can always be distinguished clearly, as "principles common to legal systems often reflect natural law principles that

---

[752] *See generally* Martti Koskennienmi, 'General Principles: Reflections on Constructivist Thinking in International Law', in: 18 *Oikeustiede – Jurisprudentia* (1985), pp. 121-163.

[753] Przetacznik, 9 *Rev. dr. hom.-Hum. Rts. J.* (1976), at 600-603; Schachter, 24 *N.Y.L. Sch. L. Rev.* (1977-1978), at 67-68.

[754] Desch, 36 *ÖZöRV* (1985), at 82.

[755] UN Comm'n H.R., *Human Rights in Chile*, UN Doc. E/CN.4/1983/9 (February 18, 1983), para. 19.

[756] Ramcharan, 30 *Nether. Int'l L. Rev.* (1983), at 299; Schachter, 24 *N.Y.L. Sch. L. Rev.* (1977-1978), at 75-76; Simma/ Alston, 12 *Austl. Yb. Int'l L.* (1992), at 103-106 giving examples of national courts and the International Court of Justice in support of this thesis; *compare also* Schwelb, 53 *ASIL Proc.* (1959), at 218; *but see* Schachter, 178 *RdC* (1982-V), at 335.

[757] Simma/ Alston, 12 *Austl. Yb. Int'l L.* (1992), at 107.

[758] Dinstein, in: Henkin (ed.), at 114; Henkin, in: Henkin (ed.), at 1 and 12; Ramcharan, in: Ramcharan (ed.), at 19; *compare also* Przetacznik, 9 *Rev. dr. hom.-Hum. Rts. J.* (1976), at 590-591.

underlie international law."[759] The right to life is thus guaranteed under general international law. Hence, it is guaranteed *vis-à-vis* all States, including those which are not party to any of the above mentioned conventions.[760]

III. Content and Exceptions of the Right to Life in General International Law

The scope of the right to life under general international law is at least regarded as "similar" to that laid down in the conventions discussed above.[761] It includes a duty of the State to respect it, to protect it, and to punish offenders guilty of the violation of this right.[762] In the context of the Universal Declaration of Human Rights, which is regarded as one of the main sources for the right to life in general international law,[763] the word "arbitrary" was chosen *inter alia* "to describe action for which the agent was not required to show just cause either before a court of law or before public opinion."[764] Thus, the protection by law and the prohibition of arbitrary deprivation, referring to "illegal" as well as "unjust" acts, is included in the right to life under general international law.[765]

But here, as in the treaties examined above, the protection of the right to life is not absolute; it is widely accepted that capital punishment, at

---

[759] Louis Henkin, 'International Law: Politics, Values and Functions', in: 216 *RdC* (1989-IV), pp. 9-416, at 61.

[760] Dinstein, in: Henkin (ed.), at 115.

[761] Gormley, in: Ramcharan (ed.), at 122.

[762] These principles are laid down in numerous national constitutions, *see* Przetacznik, 9 *Rev. dr. hom.-Hum. Rts. J.* (1976), at 600-603.

[763] *Compare supra*, Part One, Chapter G) I.

[764] Statement by UK delegate Mrs. Corbet, in: UN General Assembly, Third Committee (Social, Humanitarian and Cultural), UN GAOR 3rd Committee, 3rd Sess., Part 1, p. 354; *compare also* Weissbrodt/ Hallendorff, 21 *Hum. Rts. Q.* (1999), at 1093.

[765] Lillich, in: Meron (ed.), at 121-122; *compare also* Hassan, 10 *Harv. Int'l L.J.* (1969), pp. 225-262; Marcoux, 5 *B.C. Int'l & Comp. L. Rev.* (1982), pp. 345-376.

least for "the most serious crimes",[766] cannot be said to be prohibited by customary international law.[767] This and further exceptions have to be interpreted restrictively. The Universal Declaration, for example lays down stringent conditions for limiting the rights and freedoms enshrined in it. To be permissible, the limitation must fulfil the requirements of Article 29 of the Universal Declaration.[768] Especially, limitations must be determined by law and may be imposed solely in order to secure due recognition and respect for the rights and freedoms of others and to meet "the just requirements of morality, public order and the general welfare in a democratic society." Self-defence is a concept that derives from self-preservation of man and is generally accepted as being moral.[769] Thus, self-defence and the defence of others, but also the other exceptions stated in Article 2 of the European Convention are regarded as permitted under general international law.[770]

Additionally, it has to be acknowledged that the exceptions are probably wider than those exceptions laid down in the human rights conventions and restricted in the very far-reaching jurisprudence of the convention organs. Most of all, judicial, quasi-judicial or supervisory bodies such as those established according to the human rights treaties examined above may establish and reflect the agreement of the parties re-

---

766 *Compare* Desch, 36 *ÖZöRV* (1985), at 110.

767 Lillich, in: Meron (ed.), at 122; American Law Institute, *Restatement of the Law (Third)*, § 702 (Vol. 2, pp. 161-175), Comment f (at 163-164); Lauri Hannikainen, *Peremptory Norms (jus cogens) in International Law: Historical Development, Criteria, Present Status*, Helsinki 1988, p. 516.

768 Article 29 of the Universal Declaration of Human Rights reads: "(1) Everyone has duties to the community in which alone the free and full development of his personality is possible. (2) In the exercise of his rights and freedoms, everyone shall be subject only to such limitations as are determined by law solely for the purpose of securing due recognition and respect for the rights and freedoms of others and of meeting the just requirements of morality, public order and the general welfare in a democratic society. (3) These rights and freedoms may in no case be exercised contrary to the purposes and principles of the United Nations."

769 Przetacznik, 9 *Rev. dr. hom.-Hum. Rts. J.* (1976), at 591-592.

770 Kadelbach, *Zwingendes Völkerrecht*, p. 288; Desch, 36 *ÖZöRV* (1985), at 107-108.

garding the interpretation of these treaties.[771] Furthermore, it is true that this has also a significant role in generating customary rules.[772] However, this rule should not be overestimated; it is, for example, regarded as legitimate under general international law to use lethal force in order to prevent a serious crime, irrespective of whether the life of a person is threatened.[773] A prohibition of the use force in defence of property can thus not be considered to be part of general international law.[774] Furthermore, the very strict standards developed concerning the fighting of a riot cannot be directly transferred to all States, as the milder means discussed above are unfortunately not available to all police forces and a duty to provide such means, similar to that under the European Convention, does not exist in general international law.[775] Thus, under general international law a government may have a wider discretion in choosing the means to fight a riot or insurrection.[776]

On the other hand, it has to be acknowledged that the UN Code of Conduct for Law enforcement Officials in part provides for standards as strict as those developed with regard to the European Convention. The Commentary on Article 3 of the UN Code reads:

> In general, firearms should not be used except when a suspected offender offers armed resistance or otherwise jeopardizes the lives of

---

[771] *Compare* Article 31, para. 3, subpara. B of the Vienna Convention on the Law of Treaties.

[772] Meron, *Customary Law*, p. 100; *compare also* the interpretation along the lines of the ICCPR and the ECHR by Lars Adam Rehof, 'Article 3', in: Asbjørn Eide; Gudmundur Alfredsson (eds.), *The Universal Declaration of Human Rights: A Commentary*, Oslo 1992, pp. 73-85.

[773] American Law Institute, *Restatement of the Law (Third)*, § 702 (Vol. 2, pp. 161-175), Comment f (at 163-164).

[774] *But see* Desch, 36 *ÖZöRV* (1985), at 107.

[775] *Compare* Kadelbach, *Zwingendes Völkerrecht*, pp. 290-291, seeing differences between the European and American standards on the one hand, and Africa and Asia on the other hand.

[776] However, the statement that it is "not *necessarily unlawful* if a government virtually annihilates an armed rebel or insurgent movement" by Hannikainen, *Peremptory Norms*, p. 516, can only hold true to the extent which is also legal under international humanitarian law.

others and less extreme measures are not sufficient to restrain or apprehend the suspected offender.[777]

As any exception to a human right is subject to the principle of proportionality, the same considerations concerning necessity and immediacy also apply under general international law.[778] Whereas not all milder means may be available in every nation's context, the decisions concerning the means used and the threshold of immediacy are generally the same.

A further exception is that of killings which result from legal acts in an armed conflict; these are subject to international humanitarian law and, as far as they adhere to these standards, legal under general international human rights law.[779] This is the case for the treaty provisions protecting the right to life, and also under general international law. These standards cannot be derogated from.

IV. The Right to Life as *jus cogens*

"[G]eneral international law contains rules which have the character of *jus cogens*" as "every positive order has its roots in the ethics of a certain community, that cannot be understood apart from its moral basis."[780] The roots of this category of rules are partly seen in antiquity and Roman law and in natural law.[781] Since the famous *obiter dictum* of

---

[777] UN GA Res. 34/169 (December 17, 1979), *UN Code of Conduct for Law Enforcement Officials*, GA Res. 34/169, Annex, UN GAOR, 34th Sess., Supplement. No. 46, UN Doc. A/34/46 (1979), pp. 185-187, at 186 (Article 3, commentary c).

[778] *See also* Desch, 36 *ÖZöRV* (1985), at 107.

[779] Kadelbach, *Zwingendes Völkerrecht*, p. 288; Desch, 36 *ÖZöRV* (1985), at 114-15.

[780] Alfred Verdross, 'Forbidden Treaties in International Law', in 31 *Am. J. Int'l L.* (1937), pp. 571-577, at 571, referring to the general principle forbidding states to conclude treaties *contra bonos mores*, at 572-577; *see also* Andreas L. Paulus, '*Jus Cogens* in a Time of Hegemony and Fragmentation: An Attempt at a Re-appraisal', in: 25 *Nord. J. Int'l L.* (2005), pp. 297-334, at 300-302 on the development that lead to *Verdross*' formulation of a substantive notion of *jus cogens* and a current perspective (at 324 *et seqq.*).

[781] Gormley, in: Ramcharan (ed.), at 122-123, with further references.

the International Court of Justice in *Barcelona Traction*, it is widely accepted that the most basic human rights are not only part of general international law, but give also rise to obligations *erga omnes*.[782] This core category of rights has been interpreted as including those human rights that amount to *jus cogens*,[783] i.e. which are norms of general international law which are peremptory.[784] During the drafting of the Vienna Convention some members of the International Law Commission (ILC) suggested three objective indicia to identify a peremptory norm. First, whether it is incorporated into multilateral agreements and is prohibited from derogation therein. Second, whether a large number of nations perceive the norm to be essential to the international public order, whereby the norm is reflected in general custom and is perceived and acted upon as an obligatory rule of higher international standing. And third, whether the norm has been recognised and applied by international tribunals, such that when violations occur, the norm is treated in practice as a *jus cogens* rule with appropriate consequences ensuing.[785]

---

782 ICJ, *Barcelona Traction Light and Power Company, Limited, Second Phase*, Judgment of February 5, 1970, I.C.J. Reports 1970, pp. 3-357, at 32 (paras. 33-34).

783 Verdross, 60 *Am. J. Int'l L.* (1966), at 59-60; Charles de Visscher, 'Positivisme et jus cogens', in: 75 *R.G.D.I.P.* (1971), pp. 5-11; Gormley, in: Ramcharan (ed.), at 120; David S. Mitchell, 'The Prohibition of Rape in International Humanitarian Law as a Norm of *Jus Cogens*: Clarifying the Doctrine', in: 15 *Duke J. Comp. & Int'l L.* (2005), at 229; Paulus, 25 *Nord. J. Int'l L.* (2005), at 315 ("more or less identical contents"); *but see* Theodor Meron, 'On a Hierarchy of International Human Rights', in: 80 *Am. J. Int'l L.* (1986), pp. 1-23, at 11 ("Despite a certain overlap, the latter is narrower than the former.").

784 *Compare e.g.* Article 53 of the Vienna Convention on the Law of Treaties: "A treaty is void if, at the time of its conclusion, it conflicts with a peremptory norm of general international law. For the purposes of the present Convention, a peremptory norm of general international law is a norm accepted and recognized by the international community of states as a whole as a norm from which no derogation is permitted and which can be modified only by a subsequent norm of general international law having the same character."

785 *See* the discussions on Article 13 of the Vienna Convention on the Law of Treaties in UN General Assembly, ILC, Summary Records of the 683rd Meeting, reprinted in: *UN Yb. ILC* (1963), Vol. I, pp. 60-67, at 63; UN General Assembly, ILC, Summary Records of the 685th Meeting, reprinted in: *UN Yb. ILC* (1963), Vol. I, pp. 73-79, at 74.

The four non-derogable rights common to the ICCPR, American Convention and ECHR are thus considered to be not only customary international law but also norms of *jus cogens*.[786] The right to life is accepted to be *jus cogens* by numerous authors,[787] by international organs[788] and by national courts[789] and is thus non-derogable.[790] Again however, the exact content of the right which is regarded to be part of *jus cogens* is not without controversy:

---

[786] Meron, 80 *Am. J. Int'l L.* (1986), at 11; Oraá, *States of Emergency*, p. 96.

[787] Gormley, in: Ramcharan (ed.), at 146-148; Kretzmer, 16 *Eur. J. Int'l L.* (2005), at 185; Kremnitzer, in: Fleck (ed.), *Rechtsfragen*, at 201; Lillich, in: Meron (ed.), at 121 (footnote 35); Francisco Forrest Martin, 'Using International Human Rights Law for Establishing a Unified Use of Force Rule in the Law of Armed Conflict', in: 64 *Sask. L. Rev.* (2001), pp. 347-396 at 362-363; MacDougal *et al.*, *Human Dignity*, p. 274; Melzer, *Targeted Killing*, pp. 214-221; Meron, 80 *Am. J. Int'l L.* (1986), at 11; Paust, 65 *Sask. L. Rev.* (2002), at 412-413; Ramcharan, in: Ramcharan (ed.), at 14-15; Ramcharan, 30 *Nether. Int'l L. Rev.* (1983), at 308 and 311 *et seqq.*; Rodley, *Treatment of Prisoners*, p. 145; *See also* Simma/ Alston, 12 *Austl. Yb. Int'l L.* (1992), at 103, who regard the source of this right rather to be a general principle of law than customary, but nevertheless interpret it to have *jus cogens* quality.

[788] *See e.g.* UN Comm'n H.R., *Human Rights in Chile*, UN Doc. E/CN.4/1983/9 (February 18, 1983), para. 19; Inter-Am. Comm'n H.R., *Victims of the Tugboat "13 de Marzo" v. Cuba*, Case 11.436, Report No. 47/96 of October 16, 1996, in: *Annual Report* (1996), OEA/Ser.L/V/II.95 Doc. 7 rev. (March 14, 1997), Chapter III, at para. 79. *Compare also* ICJ, *South West Africa, Ethiopia v. South Africa and Liberia v. South Africa, second phase*, Judgment of July 18, 1966, I.C.J. Reports 1966, pp. 6-505, Dissenting Opinion of Judge K. Tanaka, pp. 250-324, at 298: "surely the law concerning the protection of human rights may be considered to belong to the jus cogens". On the Inter-American Court on Human Rights' jurisprudence on the non-derogability of the right to life and its *jus cogens* character *see* Davidson, *Inter-American Court*, pp. 190-192.

[789] Jordan J. Paust, *International Law as Law of the United States*, Durham, N.C. 1996, p. 195 (footnote 121 citing numerous U.S. cases recognizing that the right to life is a basic human right); *see also* American Law Institute, *Restatement of the Law (Third)*, § 702 (Vol. 2, pp. 161-175), Comment n (at 167). *But see* Kremnitzer, in: Fleck (ed.), *Rechtsfragen*, at 201, referring to the "supreme" status of the right to life, "an almost *jus cogens* right" (my translation).

[790] Gormley, in: Ramcharan (ed.), at 135-138; *see generally* Robert Kolb, 'Jus Cogens, Intangibilité, Intransgressibilité, Derogation "positive" et "negative"', in: 105 *R.G.D.I.P.* (2005), pp. 303-330, at 323-324.

The *Restatement* regards violations of the *jus cogens* rights cited as "violations of customary international law only if practiced, encouraged, or condoned by the government of a State as official policy."[791] Others also apply the same standard as developed in connection with the conventions above: "[T]he arbitrary killing of a single individual violates the peremptory nature of *jus cogens*."[792] Similarly, *Meron* regards due process rights as part of the *jus cogens* as they "are fundamental and indispensable for ensuring any other right."[793] This would include the due process aspects of the right to life as developed above[794] and provide for an equally high standard of protection.

This is rather a question of the general content of the right to life in general international law and the possible exceptions. The *jus cogens* character of the right is congruent with the fact that a right is non-derogable. The right cannot have a non-derogable core and a wider scope that is derogable but nevertheless part of *jus cogens*,[795] unless possible derogations are also covered by *jus cogens* and form thus part of the right itself. Thus, if it is generally accepted, that the right to life is part of *jus cogens*, then this applies to its whole scope of protection as shown above.

H. Conclusion: The Human Right to Life

In the treaties examined as well as in general international law, the right to life offers a high, albeit not absolute, standard of protection. The prohibition of arbitrary deprivation of life appears in the International Covenant, in the American Convention and in the African Charter, but

---

[791] American Law Institute, *Restatement of the Law (Third)*, § 702 (Vol. 2, pp. 161-175), Comment b (at 162).

[792] Gormley, in: Ramcharan (ed.), at 148; *see also* Hannikainen, *Peremptory Norms*, p. 517.

[793] Meron, 80 *Am. J. Int'l L.* (1986), at 11.

[794] *Compare supra*, Part One, Chapters B) I. 2. a) and b), Chapters C) I. 2. a) and b) and Chapter D) I. 2.

[795] *But see* A. Redelbach, 'Protection of the Right to Life by Law and by Other Means', in: Bertrand G. Ramcharan (ed.), *The Right to Life in International Law*, Dordrecht 1985, pp. 182-220, at 186 (Figure 2).

is not used in the European Convention. Nevertheless, the content of the right under the different conventions is almost identical. However, the conventions as well as general international law leave room for several exceptions:

The death penalty, which is prohibited to differing degrees under the conventions, is a possible exception but its use must adhere to high procedural standards. An abolition of the death penalty cannot yet be established under general international law, but the treaty regimes show that there is a strong tendency in this general direction. The death penalty is, under all conventions as well as under general international law, the only case in which the death of a person may be the aim or end of an action; in any other context, killings with *dolus directus* of the first degree are not permitted. Thus, targeted killings, as defined above,[796] are "arbitrary" and thus illegal under treaty law as well as general international law.

However, force may be used in order to address immediate threats. In this context, the classical concept of immediacy applies: Force may only be used if the realisation of a threat can immediately be triggered by the alleged offender without any further steps in between. This use of force is subject to proportionality: The force used has to be necessary, i.e. it must be the mildest means capable of addressing the threat.[797] The European Court has shown that this requirement is strongly related to the question of immediacy; at an earlier stage, milder means are probably available. In consequence, the proportionality of the use of force has to be assessed from an overall perspective rather than based solely on the moment force was used.

There are different threats that may be addressed by such force: First, under treaty law and undisputedly general international law self-defence and the defence of other persons are accepted aims. Under treaty law, and explicitly so under the European Convention, it is not legal to use such force in order to defend property. General international law seems not to extend that far. The use of such force is additionally accepted in order to prevent serious crimes, even if this encompasses deeds that do not threaten the life of other humans. The death of the person targeted may only be a side-effect of the use of such force.

---

[796] *Compare supra*, Introduction, Chapter C) II. 1. b).

[797] *Compare also Melzer's* almost identical conclusion: Melzer, *Targeted Killing*, p. 239 and Melzer, in: Gill/ Fleck (eds.), at 281 (para. 17.03).

Whereas a strict theoretical consideration would require this force to be a merely undesired side-effect, it is clear that in practice the death of the targeted person is virtually certain in many situations. This can be accepted if the aim of the operation is to save another person's life.

Second, another accepted aim of the use of force is the arrest of a person. However, in such a situation, the person's death may not be intended, either under the conventions or under general international law.

Third, in order to prevent the escape of a detainee, force may be used but the detainee's death may at the most be intended with *dolus eventualis*. The human rights treaties – and at the forefront the European Convention – seem to be stricter on this point than general international law. They are interpreted as additionally requiring proportionality between the threat the detainee causes if he escapes and the force that is used to prevent his escape. It is unlikely that such a high standard exists in general international law. Here, it is more likely that the escape as such is regarded as a threat legitimising the use of lethal force.

Fourth, quelling a riot or insurrection is a legitimate aim for the use of force but under the conventions, again especially the European convention, lethal force may not be used at all. The standard of protection that requires an overall assessment of the situation requires States to equip their agents with "less lethal weapons" that are fully capable of quelling a riot without killing rioters. Again, the standard in general international law is less strict; whereas resort to milder means is obligatory here as well, a far reaching duty to equip the forces in a certain manner can not be considered as existing under customary international law.

It has to be kept in mind that these reasons may coincide; law enforcement personnel may act in self-defence if necessary in each of these situations, but "collateral damages" are not accepted. Under human rights law, it is exclusively the person that causes a threat that may be targeted. The death of innocent third persons can never be justified.

These principles are explicitly non-derogable under the conventions but also under general-international law; the right to life is part of *jus cogens* and may not be derogated. Nevertheless, in a situation that is not exclusively covered by human rights, additional exceptions do exist. If the killing of a person is legal under international humanitarian law applicable in that situation, it is also legal under human rights law. The standards of international humanitarian law will be examined in part two, *infra*, whereas the question of the existence of further justifications or excuses will be addressed in part three.

Generally, the standard of protection is higher under the treaty regimes than under general international law. The former offer additional procedural aspects of protection, i.e. by shifting the burden of proof in certain cases (e.g. those involving disappearances).[798] The most important aspect is that they offer procedures at all. However, the core questions are treated in the same manner; exceptions to the right to life are subject to proportionality. Penal killings may only be employed in the strictly limited cases of capital punishment. Preventive force may only be used in immediate situations, i.e. to prevent an imminent threat caused by the targeted person itself. In consequence, the right to life does permit preventive killings under strict preconditions, but prohibits all targeted killings.

---

[798] On the burden of proof *vis-à-vis* the public with regard to the U.S. Predator drone attack on a car in Yemen *see* Rosa Ehrenreich Brooks, 'War Everywhere: Rights, National Security Law, and the Law of Armed Conflict in the Age of Terror', in: 153 *U. Pa. L. Rev.* (2004), pp. 675-761, at 751-752.

Part Two – International Humanitarian Law

> War consists largely of acts that would be criminal if performed in time of peace. ... Such conduct is not regarded as criminal if it takes place in the course of war, because the state of war lays a blanket of immunity over the warriors. But the area of immunity is not unlimited, and its boundaries are marked by the laws of war.[1]

International humanitarian law is a relatively new term. It is not used in the 1949 Geneva Conventions but stems from the 1974-1977 conference drafting the Additional Protocols.[2] The term originally comprised the law protecting individuals – wounded military personnel, prisoners of war and civilians – and mitigating the effects of an armed conflict, i.e. the so called Geneva law.[3] Originally, this branch was distinguished from the law of war proper, governing the methods and means of warfare, i.e. the so called "Hague Law".[4]

As both areas apply to control the hostilities and always a certain degree of overlap existed between them, they are no longer juxtaposed.[5] The distinction was finally abandoned by the 1977 Additional Protocols that cover areas of both the traditional Hague and Geneva law. The term "international humanitarian law" thus comprises all rules of international law designed to regulate the treatment of the individual – civil-

---

1 Telford Taylor, *Nuremberg and Vietnam: an American Tragedy*, Chicago 1970, p. 19; for a comprehensive history *see* Stephen C. Neff, *War and the Law of Nations: A General History*, Cambridge 2006.

2 Christopher Greenwood, 'Historical Development and Legal Basis', in: Dieter Fleck (ed.), *The Handbook of Humanitarian Law in Armed Conflicts*, Oxford 1999, pp. 1-38, at 9 (para. 102).

3 Hilaire McCoubrey/ Nigel D. White, *International Law and Armed Conflict*, Aldershot 1992, p. 257; *See infra*, Part Two, Chapter A) II.

4 *See infra*, Part Two, Chapter A) I.

5 UK Ministry of Defence, *The Manual of the Law of Armed Conflict*, Oxford 2004, para. 1.9 (p. 3); Dinstein, *Conduct of Hostilities*, pp. 12-13.

ian or military, wounded or active – in armed conflicts.[6] It is also referred to by the expressions of *jus in bello,*[7] "the law of war",[8] "the law of armed conflict", "international humanitarian law applicable in armed conflict", or more simply "international humanitarian law",[9] or "IHL" for short,[10] which are not absolutely equivalent but often used interchangeably.

In contrast to this, the *jus ad bellum* comprises the rules covering the resort to force, i.e. the general prohibition on the use of force and its exceptions. But regardless of the justification or the legality of any resort to force, the individual members of that conflict are bound by the law of armed conflict.[11] However, "international humanitarian law bestows rights not only on human beings as such, but also (and chiefly) on States. The adjective 'humanitarian' describes the contents of the norms and not the subject bound by them."[12]

---

6 Greenwood, in: Fleck (ed.), *Handbook*, at 1 and 9 (paras. 101 and 102.1); Elizabeth Chadwick, *Self-Determination, Terrorism and the International Humanitarian Law of Armed Conflict*, The Hague 1996, p. 5; Dinstein, *Conduct of Hostilities*, pp. 12-13.

7 Michael Byers, *War Law: International Law and Armed Conflict*, London 2005, p. 115. The Term "*jus in bello*" or "law of warfare" is unsatisfactory insofar as the norms in questions are also in effect in international armed conflicts falling short of full-fledged wars, *see* Dinstein, *Conduct of Hostilities*, pp. 13-14.

8 As opposed to "the law of war proper", referring to the Hague Conventions, *see* Chadwick, *Self-Determination*, p. 5.

9 ICJ, *Legality of the Threat or Use of Nuclear Weapons*, Advisory Opinion of July 8, 1996, I.C.J. Reports 1996, pp. 226-593, at 256 (para. 75). The term "international humanitarian law" should, however, not create the false impression that the rules governing hostilities are – and have to be – truly humanitarian in nature. Not few of them reflect countervailing constraints of military necessity, *see* Dinstein, *Conduct of Hostilities*, pp. 13 and 16-20.

10 UK Ministry of Defence, *Manual*, para. 1.2 (p. 2).

11 *Id.*, para. 1.7 (p. 3).

12 Yoram Dinstein, 'Human Rights in Armed Conflict: International Humanitarian Law', in: Theodor Meron (ed.), *Human Rights in International Law*, Oxford (Clarendon Press) 1984, pp. 345-368, at 347.

A. The Relevant Sources of Law

Beside the two branches of the Hague and the Geneva law, international humanitarian law largely consists of customary international law, which is to a great amount identical with the said treaty provisions.

I. The Hague Law

The Hague Conventions of 1899 and 1907 were adopted by the peace conferences of those years and cover the conduct of hostilities on land, sea and even in the air (by balloons).[13] The six texts of 1899 were revised and amended by the 14 instruments of 1907. While some of these texts have not really stood the test of time and have fallen by the wayside, others have become part of customary international law.[14] The provisions of the two Hague Conventions on land warfare, like most of the substantive provisions of the Hague Conventions of 1899 and 1907, are considered as embodying rules of customary international law. As such they are also binding on States which are not formally parties to them. The latter is especially true for the "Martens Clause"[15] that first

---

[13] Earlier sources dealing with the law regarding the means and methods of warfare are the Lieber Code of 1963 by U.S. President Abraham Lincoln, General Order No. 100 of April 24, 1863, *Instructions for the Government of the Armies of the United States in the Field*, drafted by Francis Lieber ("Lieber Instructions"/"Lieber Code"), reprinted in: Dietrich Schindler; Jiří Toman (eds.), *The Laws of Armed Conflicts: A Collection of Conventions, Resolutions and Other Documents*, 3rd ed., Dordrecht 1988, pp. 3-23 and the Institute of International Law, *The Laws of War on Land*, Oxford, September 9, 1880 ("Oxford Manual"/"Manual d'Oxford"), reprinted in: Schindler/ Toman (eds.), *Collection*, pp. 36-48.

[14] *C.f.* Dinstein, *Conduct of Hostilities*, pp. 10-11.

[15] The clause reads: "Until a more complete code of the laws of war is issued, the High Contracting Parties think it right to declare that in cases not in cluded in the Regulations adopted by them, populations and belligerents remain under the protection and empire of the principles of international law, as they result from the usages established between civilized nations, from the laws of humanity and the requirements of the public conscience." It was developed by the Livonian professor Friedrich von Martens (1845-1909), delegate of Tsar Nicholas II at the Hague Peace Conferences, *see* Greenwood, in: Fleck (ed.), at 28 (para. 129).

appeared in the preamble to the 1899 Hague Convention II[16] with respect to the laws and customs of war on land and set minimum standards for these conflicts.[17] It is also true for the 1907 Hague Convention IV.[18] In 1946 the Nuremberg International Military Tribunal ruled with regard to that convention:

> The rules of land warfare expressed in the Convention undoubtedly represented an advance over existing International Law at the time of their adoption ... but by 1939 these rules ... were recognized by all civilized nations and were regarded as being declaratory of the laws and customs of war.[19]

Similarly, the International Military Tribunal for the Far East expressed in 1948:

> Although the obligation to observe the provisions of the Convention as a binding treaty may be swept away by operation of the 'general participation clause', or otherwise, the Convention remains as good evidence of the customary law of nations,... .[20]

The provisions relevant for the present examination are part of the 1907 Hague Regulations annexed to the 1907 Hague Convention IV.[21] These

---

[16] Convention (II) with Respect to the Laws and Customs of War on Land, adopted at The Hague, Netherlands, 29 July 1899, entry into force on 4 September 1900, reprinted in: Schindler/ Toman (eds.), *Collection*, pp. 69-93.

[17] Greenwood, in: Fleck (ed.), *Handbook*, at 28-29 (para. 129).

[18] Convention (IV) Respecting the Laws and Customs of War on Land, signed October 18, 1907 at The Hague, entry into Force January 26, 1910, reprinted in: James Brown Scott (ed.), *The Hague Conventions and Declarations of 1899 and 1907*, 3rd ed., New York 1918, pp. 100-127 (English translation by US Department of State, with minor corrections by J.B. Scott), reprinted in: 2 *Am. J. Int'l L.* (1908), Suppl., pp. 97-117.

[19] International Military Tribunal (Nuremberg), Judgments and Sentences of October 1, 1946, reprinted in: 41 *Am. J. Int'l L.* (1947), pp. 172-333, at 248-249.

[20] International Military Tribunal for the Far East (Tokyo), *In re Hirota* and others, Judgement of November 12, 1948, reprinted in: 15 *Annual Digest* (1948), Case No. 118, pp. 356-376, at 366.

[21] Regulations Respecting the Laws and Customs of War on Land (1907 Hague Regulations), annexed to the 1907 Hague Convention (IV) Respecting the Laws and Customs of War on Land, signed October 18, 1907 at The Hague, entry into Force January 26, 1910, reprinted in: Scott (ed.), *Conventions*, pp. 100-127 (English translation by US Department of State, with minor correc-

rules also serve the protection of persons affected by war and might contain provisions of relevance to the question at hand. They are regarded as representing customary international law and thus are binding on all States, including non-party-States.[22]

II. The Geneva Law

Being concerned with methods and means of warfare, including controls on weapons types and usage and on tactics and the general conduct of hostilities, the Hague law has long been divided from the Geneva law which is concerned with the protection of the victims of armed conflict, i.e. wounded military personnel, prisoners of war and civilians. Nevertheless, both sectors are based upon the concern for the

---

tions by J.B. Scott). The 1907 Hague Regulations were drafted on the first Hague peace conference in 1899 as a revision of the "Brussels Declaration", the Project of an International Declaration Concerning the Law and Customs of War, adopted by the Conference of Brussels, August 27, 1874 (Brussels Declaration), reprinted in: 1 *Am. J. Int'l L.* (1907), Supplement, pp. 96-103. The authentic language of the 1907 Hague Regulations is French and there are differences between the English translation used by the UK and by the US. This fact will be addressed where appropriate. *C.f.* Adam Roberts/ Richard Guelff (eds.), *Documents on the Laws of War*, 3rd edition, Oxford 2000, p. 73.

[22] *Compare e.g.* International Military Tribunal (Nuremberg), Judgments and Sentences of October 1, 1946, reprinted in: 41 *Am. J. Int'l L.* (1947), pp. 172-333, at 248-249; International Military Tribunal for the Far East (Tokyo), *In re Hirota* and others, Judgement of November 12, 1948, reprinted in: 15 *Annual Digest* (1948), Case No. 118, pp. 356-376, at 365-366; U.S. Military Tribunal (Nuremberg), *U.S. v. von Leeb* et al. (German High Command Trial), Judgment of October 28, 1948, reprinted in: 15 *Annual Digest* (1948), Case No. 119, pp. 376-398, at 384; U.S. Department of Navy, *Commander's Handbook on the Law of Naval Operations*, NWP 1-14M, Washington, D.C. 1995, paras. 11.1-11.3 (p. 11-1); Richard R. Baxter, 'Treaties and Customs', in: 129 *RdC* (1970-I), pp. 27-105, at 58-61; Eyal Benvenisti, *The International Law of Occupation*, Princeton, N.J. 1993, pp. 109 and 112; Gerhard von Glahn, *Law Among Nations*, 6th ed., New York 1992, p. 737; Meron, *Internal Strife*, p. 6; Thomas S. Kuttner, 'Israel and the West Bank: Aspects of the Law of Belligerent Occupation', in: 7 *Isr. Yb. Hum. Rts.* (1977), pp. 162-221, at 171-172; Schmitt, 17 *Yale J. Int'l L.* (1999), at 630.

moderation and mitigation of warfare and its consequences.[23] The original Geneva Convention of 1864[24] related to the wounded in armies in the field, and was revised and replaced in 1906,[25] in 1929[26] and finally in 1949, after the Second World War had had exposed the inadequacies of the existing law.[27] The Geneva law now consists of the four 1949 Geneva Conventions and two 1977 Additional Protocols.

1. The 1949 Geneva Conventions

The four Conventions are: the 1949 Geneva Convention I,[28] dealing with amelioration of the condition of the wounded and sick in armed forces in the field, which replaced the Conventions of 1864, 1906 and 1929; the 1949 Geneva Convention II,[29] dealing with the wounded,

---

23 Hilaire McCoubrey, *International Humanitarian Law: Modern Developments in the Limitation of Warfare*, 2nd ed., Aldershot 1998, p. 2.

24 Convention for the Amelioration of the Condition of the Wounded in Armies in the Field, adopted at Geneva, Switzerland, on August 22, 1864, entry into force on June 22, 1865, reprinted in: Schindler/ Toman (eds.), *Collection*, pp. 280-281.

25 Convention for the Amelioration of the Condition of the Wounded and Sick in Armies in the Field, adopted at Geneva, Switzerland, on July 6, 1906, entry into force on August 9, 1907, reprinted in: Schindler/ Toman (eds.), *Collection*, pp. 301-310.

26 Convention for the Amelioration of the Condition of the Wounded and Sick in Armies in the Field, adopted at Geneva, Switzerland, on July 27, 1929, entry into force on September 24, 1931, reprinted in: Schindler/ Toman (eds.), *Collection*, pp. 326-334. The latter Convention was replaced by the 1949 Geneva Convention I and is no longer in operation following the universal acceptance of the 1949 Geneva Conventions.

27 *C.f.* UK Ministry of Defence, *Manual*, para. 1.28 (p. 12).

28 Geneva Convention (I) for the Amelioration of the Condition of the Wounded and Sick in Armed Forces in the Field of 12 August 1949, adopted at Geneva, Switzerland, on August 12, 1949, entry into force on October 21, 1950, *Final Record of the Diplomatic Conference of Geneva of 1949*, Berne 1949, Vol. I, pp. 205-218, reprinted in: 75 *UNTS* (1950), No. 970, pp. 31-83.

29 Geneva Convention (II) for the Amelioration of the Condition of Wounded, Sick and Shipwrecked Members of Armed Forces at Sea of 12 August 1949, adopted at Geneva, Switzerland, on August 12, 1949, entry into force on October 21, 1950, *Final Record of the Diplomatic Conference of Geneva of*

sick, and shipwrecked at sea, replaced the 1907 Hague Convention X;[30] the 1949 Geneva Convention III,[31] dealing with the treatment of prisoners of war, replaced the Convention of 1929[32] and the 1949 Geneva Convention IV,[33] dealing with the protection of civilian persons in times of war.

The four 1949 Geneva Conventions have gained virtually universal acceptance. With currently 194 State parties, almost every State in the world is a contracting party to them.[34] While the Conventions' binding nature is generally based on their status as treaties, they are generally considered to embody customary international law.[35] This is especially true for those provisions that can be traced back to earlier Geneva Conventions and the 1907 Hague Regulations.[36] Thus, *inter alia*, the 1949 Geneva Convention IV is widely regarded as a codification of customary international law.[37] The ICJ pointed out in its *Nicaragua* decision

---

1949, Berne 1949, Vol. I, pp. 225-236, reprinted in: 75 *UNTS* (1950), No. 971, pp. 85-133.

30 Convention (X) for the Adaptation to Maritime Warfare of the Principles of the Geneva Convention, adopted at The Hague, Netherlands, on October 18, 1907, entry into force on October 26, 1910, reprinted in: Schindler/ Toman (eds.), *Collection*, pp. 314-318.

31 Geneva Convention (III) relative to the Treatment of Prisoners of War of 12 August 1949, adopted at Geneva, Switzerland, on August 12, 1949, entry into force on October 21, 1950, *Final Record of the Diplomatic Conference of Geneva of 1949*, Berne 1949, Vol. I, pp. 242-276, reprinted in: 75 *UNTS* (1950), No. 972, pp. 135-285.

32 Convention relative to the Treatment of Prisoners of War, adopted at Geneva, Switzerland, on July 27, 1929, entry into force on December 19, 1930, reprinted in: Schindler/ Toman (eds.), *Collection*, pp. 341-364.

33 Geneva Convention (IV) relative to the Protection of Civilian Persons in Time of War of 12 August 1949, adopted at Geneva, Switzerland, on August 12, 1949, entry into force on October 21, 1950, *Final Record of the Diplomatic Conference of Geneva of 1949*, Berne 1949, Vol. I, pp. 297-330, reprinted in: 75 *UNTS* (1950), No. 973, pp. 287-417.

34 Including the Republic of Montenegro (since August 2, 2006), Nauru (June 27, 2006), *compare* International Committee of the Red Cross, State Parties to the 1949 Geneva Conventions.

35 UK Ministry of Defence, *Manual*, para. 1.30.3 (p. 14).

36 Meron, *Internal Strife*, p. 6.

37 Imseis, 44 *Harv. Int'l L.J.* (2003), pp. 65-138, at 66.

that "the Geneva conventions are in some respects a development, and in other respects no more than the expression" of fundamental principles of humanitarian law.[38]

Due to their universal acceptance, an inquiry into the customary character of the 1949 Geneva Conventions might appear academic.[39] However, their customary character is still of great importance. The ICJ's *Nicaragua* decision has shown that an international tribunal may sometimes be able to apply customary international law even though it lacks the competence to apply certain treaty provisions:

> Article 3 which is common to all four Geneva Conventions of 12 August 1949 defines certain rules to be applied in the armed conflicts of a non-international character. There is no doubt that, in the event of international armed conflicts, these rules also constitute a minimum yardstick, in addition to the more elaborate rules which are also to apply to international conflicts; and they are rules which, in the Court's opinion, reflect what the Court in 1949 called 'elementary considerations of humanity' ... The Court may therefore find them applicable to the present dispute, and is thus not required to decide what role the United States multilateral treaty Reservation might otherwise play in regard to the treaties in Question.[40]

Furthermore, in some States in which treaties do not form part of the national law, national courts can not apply them, but can and do apply rules of customary international law.[41] Furthermore, due to the wide acceptance of customary rules, the *si omnes* or general participation clause laid down in Article 2 of the 1949 Hague Convention IV looses much of its relevance.[42] The binding character of the single rules exam-

---

[38] ICJ, *Military and Paramilitary Activities in and against Nicaragua, Nicaragua v. United States of America*, Judgment (Merits) of June 27, 1986, I.C.J. Reports 1986, pp. 14-150, at 113 (para. 218).

[39] *Compare* Meron, *Customary Law*, pp. 3-4.

[40] ICJ, *Military and Paramilitary Activities in and against Nicaragua, Nicaragua v. United States of America*, Judgment (Merits) of June 27, 1986, I.C.J. Reports 1986, pp. 14-150, at 114 (para. 218).

[41] *C.f.* Greenwood, in: Fleck (ed.), *Handbook*, at 24 (para. 125.2).

[42] *See e.g.* UN Secretary-General, *Respect for Human Rights in Armed Conflicts*, Report of November 20, 1969, 24th Sess., Agenda Item 61, UN Doc. A/7720 (November 20, 1969), p. 22; *compare also* International Military Tribunal for the Far East (Tokyo), *In re Hirota* and others, Judgement of November

ined for the purpose of this treatise will be dealt with in connection with their content.[43]

2. *The 1977 Additional Protocols*

In 1977, the 1949 Geneva Conventions were complemented by two additional protocols relating to the protection of victims of international (I)[44] and non-international (II)[45] armed conflicts. These Protocols do not supersede the 1949 Geneva Conventions; as it is stressed in the last paragraph of the 1977 Additional Protocol I's preamble, both apply and their texts merely complement the original texts of the 1949 Geneva Conventions.[46] If the rules of one instrument are stricter than the other, the stricter rule applies.[47]

A major difference between the 1949 Geneva conventions and the 1977 Additional Protocol I is that the latter expands the definition of international armed conflicts to certain conflicts fought by peoples "in exer-

---

12, 1948, reprinted in: 15 *Annual Digest* (1948), Case No. 118, pp. 356-376, at 365-366; U.S. Military Tribunal (Nuremberg), *U.S. v. von Leeb* et al. (German High Command Trial), Judgment of October 28, 1948, reprinted in: 15 *Annual Digest* (1948), Case No. 119, pp. 376-398, at 384.

43 *See infra*, Part Two, Chapters B) and C).

44 Protocol Additional to the Geneva Conventions of 12 August 1949, and relating to the Protection of Victims of International Armed Conflicts (Protocol I), adopted at Geneva, Switzerland, on June 8, 1977, entry into force December 7, 1978, International Committee of the Red Cross, Protocols Additional to the Geneva Conventions of 12 August 1949, Geneva 1977, pp. 3-87; reprinted in: 1125 *UNTS* (1979), No. 17512, pp. 3-608.

45 Protocol Additional to the Geneva Conventions of 12 August 1949, and relating to the Protection of Victims of Non-International Armed Conflicts (Protocol II), adopted at Geneva, Switzerland, on June 8, 1977, entry into force on December 7, 1978, International Committee of the Red Cross, Protocols Additional to the Geneva Conventions of 12 August 1949, Geneva 1977, pp. 89-101; reprinted in: 1125 *UNTS* (1979), No. 17513, pp. 609-699.

46 Dinstein, *Conduct of Hostilities*, p. 11.

47 *Compare e.g.* Michael Bothe/ Karl Josef Partsch/ Waldemar A. Solf, *New Rules for Victims of Armed Conflicts: Commentary on the two 1977 Protocols additional to the Geneva Conventions of 1949*, The Hague 1982, Protocol I, Article 1, para. 2.12 (p. 45), Article 37, para. 2.4.1 (p. 204) and Article 96, para. 2.2 (p. 554).

cise of their right to self-determination". Unlike the 1949 Geneva Conventions, the 1977 Additional Protocols I and II are not accepted universally.[48] They are ratified by 167 and 163 States respectively, but – for example – not by the United States or Israel.[49] Thus, while much of the 1977 Additional Protocols are regarded as representing customary international law[50] or at least a consensus,[51] some provisions, including the broad definition of an international armed conflict, are much contested.[52] These provisions will later be criticised in their context as far as they are relevant to the present topic.[53]

The relation of treaty law to customary law is explicitly stressed by the Protocol itself. Article 1 para. 2 of the 1977 Additional Protocol I reads:

---

48 *C.f.* Christopher Greenwood, 'Customary Law Status of the 1977 Geneva Protocols', in: Astrid J.M. Delissen; Gerard J. Tanja (eds.), *Humanitarian Law of Armed Conflict: Challenges ahead – Essays in Honour of Frits Kalshoven*, Dordrecht 1991, pp. 93-114.

49 On the background from the perspective of the then chairman of the US delegation to the negotiations of the Protocols *see* George H. Aldrich, 'Why the United States of America should ratify Additional Protocol I', in: Astrid J.M. Delissen/ Gerard J. Tanja (eds.), *Humanitarian Law of Armed Conflict: Challenges ahead – Essays in Honour of Frits Kalshoven*, Dordrecht 1991, pp. 127-144, at 127-130; *c.f.* Bernard Dougherty/ Noëlle Quénivet, 'Has the Armed Conflict in Iraq Shown once more the Growing Dismission Regarding the Definition of a Legitimate Target? What and Who Can be Lawfully Targeted?', in: 16 *HuV-I* (2003), pp. 188-196, at 189. Interestingly, one of the first states to ratify both Protocols was Yugoslavia, the state with the then fourth largest army in Europe, *see* Detter, *Law of War*, p. 143.

50 *See e.g.* European Commission for Democracy through Law (Venice Commission), *Opinion on the possible Need for further Development of the Geneva Conventions*, Opinion No. 245/2003, adopted by the Venice Commission on December 12-13, 2003, Doc. No. CDL-AD (2003) 18, para. 7; Greenwood, in: Fleck (ed.), *Handbook*, at 25-26 (para. 127.2); Meron, *Customary Law*, p. 62; Dieter Fleck, 'The Protocols Additional to the Geneva Conventions and Customary International Law', in: 29 *Rev. dr. mil.* (1990), pp. 497-517.

51 A consensus also the United States played a major role in creating, *see* Aldrich, in: Delissen/ Tanja (eds.), at 127-130 and 144.

52 Dinstein, *Conduct of Hostilities*, p. 11; Ruth Wedgwood, 'Al Qaeda, Terrorism, and Military Commissions', in: 96 *Am. J. Int'l L.* (2002), pp. 328-337, at 336.

53 *See infra*, Part Four, Chapter C) III.

> In cases not covered by this Protocol or by other international agreements, civilians and combatants remain under the protection and authority of the principles of international law derived from established custom, from the principles of humanity and from the dictates of public conscience.

The 1977 Additional Protocol II develops and supplements the humanitarian protection provided by common Article 3 of the 1949 Geneva Conventions in internal armed conflicts, i.e. the protection of those who take "no active part in the hostilities, including members of armed forces who have laid down their arms and those placed 'hors de combat' by sickness, wounds, detention, or any other cause." It was applied for the first time in the conflict in El Salvador in the 1980s.[54]

III. Other International Humanitarian Instruments

Most other international humanitarian instruments, such as the 1954 Convention for the protection of cultural property[55] and the 1980 Convention on excessively injurious weapons,[56] are of minor importance for the question at hand. Their provisions could – if at all – come into play when it comes to the question of collateral damage.[57]

---

54 Christopher Greenwood, 'Scope of Application of Humanitarian Law', in: Dieter Fleck (ed.), *The Handbook of Humanitarian Law in Armed Conflicts*, Oxford 1999, pp. 39-63, at 48 (para. 211.3); Greenwood, in: Delissen/ Tanja (eds.), at 113.

55 Convention for the Protection of Cultural Property in the Event of Armed Conflict, adopted at The Hague, Netherlands on May 14, 1954, entry into force on August 7, 1956, reprinted in: Schindler/ Toman (eds.), *Collection*, pp. 747-768.

56 Convention on Prohibitions or Restrictions on the Use of Certain Conventional Weapons Which May be Deemed to be Excessively Injurious or to Have Indiscriminate Effects, adopted at Geneva, Switzerland on October 10, 1980, entry into force on December 2, 1983, reprinted in: Schindler/ Toman (eds.), *Collection*, pp. 179-184.

57 *See infra*, Part Two, Chapter D) II. 2.

IV. Customary International Humanitarian Law

As no single treaty – and no cluster of treaties – covers the whole span of international humanitarian law, customary international law remains of immense significance.[58] Even though many of the above mentioned instruments represent – in whole or in part – customary international law, they are still supplemented by further rules of customary international law.[59] These rules are partially restated by certain groups of experts, for example in the Turku Declaration on Minimum Humanitarian Standards[60] or the San Remo Manual on the Protection of Victims of Non-International Armed Conflicts[61] or the International Committee of the Red Cross itself, that in 1978 condensed the principles of the 1949 Geneva Conventions into seven Fundamental Rules of Humanitarian Law Applicable in Armed Conflicts.[62]

Some of the customary rules are regarded to amount to *jus cogens*.[63] The notion of customary international humanitarian law continues to

---

[58] Dinstein, *Conduct of Hostilities*, p. 6.

[59] This concerns especially naval warfare, *see* UK Ministry of Defence, *Manual*, para. 1.12.2 (p. 5).

[60] UN Comm'n H.R., Sub-Commission on Prevention of Discrimination and Protection of Minorities, *Declaration on Minimum Standards*, adopted by a group of experts at a meeting in Turku/Åbo, Finland, Dezember 1990, UN Doc. E/CN.4/Sub.2/1991/55 (August 12, 1991), reprinted in: 31 *Int'l Rev. Red Cross* (1991), No. 282, pp. 328-336; *compare also* Asbjørn Eide/ Allen Rosas/ Theodor Meron, 'Combating Lawlessness in Gray Zone Conflicts Through Minimum Humanitarian Standards', in: 89 *Am. J. Int'l L.* (1995), pp. 215-223, at 219.

[61] International Institute of Humanitarian Law, *The Manual on the Law of Non-International Armed Conflict (San Remo Manual)*, Sanremo 2006.

[62] International Committee of the Red Cross, 'Fundamental Rules of Humanitarian Law Applicable in Armed Conflicts', in: 18 *Int'l Rev. Red Cross* (1978), No. 206, pp. 247-249.

[63] *See e.g.* Mitchell, 15 *Duke J. Comp. & Int'l L.* (2005), pp. 219-257; Rafael Nieto Navia, 'International Peremptory Norms (*jus cogens*) and International Humanitarian Law', in: Lal Chand Vohrah *et al.* (eds.), *Man's Inhumanity to Man – Essays on International Law in Honour of Antonio Cassese*, The Hague 2003, pp. 595-641.

be important,[64] *inter alia* due to the much discussed International Committee of the Red Cross' study on customary international humanitarian law.[65] The customary character of the rules relevant to the present examination will be addressed jointly with their content *infra*.

B. The Basic Principles Underlying International Humanitarian Law

Despite the detailed codification of much customary international law into the above mentioned treaties, four fundamental principles underlie the whole law of armed conflict. In 1966, in continuation of his groundbreaking article of 1937[66], *Verdross* came to the conclusion that the "humanitarian principles underlying these conventions are basic principles of general international law with the character of *jus cogens*."[67] These principles are military necessity, humanity, distinction, and proportionality.[68] The law is intended to minimize the suffering caused by an armed conflict rather than to impede military efficiency.[69] It thus is a

---

64 Theodor Meron, 'The Continuing Role of Custom in the Formation of International Humanitarian Law', 90 *Am. J. Int'l L.* (1996), pp. 238-249.

65 Henckaerts/ Doswald-Beck (eds.), *Humanitarian Law*, Vol. I, Rules; Vol. 2.1, Practice, Part 1; Vol. 2.2, Practice, Part 2, Cambridge 2005; on the studies background *see* Jean-Marie Henckaerts, 'Study on Customary International Humanitarian Law: A Contribution to the Understanding and Respect for the Rule of Law in Armed Conflict', in: 87 *Int'l Rev. Red Cross* (2005), No. 857, pp. 175-212, at 175-186; *compare also* Dieter Fleck, 'International Accountability for Violations of the *Jus in Bello*: The Impact of the ICRC Study on Customary International Humanitarian Law', in: 11 *J. Confl. Sec. L.* (2006), pp. 179-199; Theodor Meron, 'Revival of Customary Humanitarian Law', in: 99 *Am. J. Int'l L.* (2005), pp. 817-834; Malcolm MacLaren/ Felix Schwendimann, 'An Exercise in the Development of International Law: The New ICRC Study on Customary International Humanitarian Law', in: 6 *German L. J.* (2005), pp. 1217-1242; Louise Doswald-Beck, 'Developments in Customary International Humanitarian Law', in: 15 *SZIER* (2005), pp. 471-498.

66 Verdross, 31 *Am. J. Int'l L.* (1937), pp. 571-577.

67 Verdross, 60 *Am. J. Int'l L.* (1966), at 55.

68 UK Ministry of Defence, *Manual*, para. 2.1 (p. 21).

69 *Id.*

compromise between the diametrically opposed impulses of military necessity and humanitarian requirements.[70]

I. Military Necessity

According to the long established principle of military necessity,[71] a belligerent shall only use that degree and kind of force, not otherwise prohibited by the law of armed conflict, that is required in order to achieve the legitimate purpose of the conflict, namely the complete or partial submission of the enemy at the earliest possible moment with the minimum expenditure of life and resources.[72] First, this general principle is the basis of numerous specific rules of international humanitarian law, e.g. the prohibition of the use of weapons causing unnecessary suffering, the prohibition of unnecessary destruction of property[73] and the prohibition of causing excessive collateral damage.[74] Second, the principle of necessity operates as an extra restraint by prohibiting acts which are not otherwise illegal, as long as they are not necessary for the achievement of a legitimate goal.[75] On the other hand, mili-

---

70 Greenwood, in: Fleck (ed.), *Handbook*, at 32 (para. 131); Dinstein, *Conduct of Hostilities*, p. 16.

71 Already laid down in Articles 14-16 of the Lieber Code. For comprehensive overviews *see* Elmar Rauch, 'Le concept de nécessité militaire dans le droit de la guerre', in: 19 *Rev. dr. pén. mil.* (1980), pp. 205-237 and William V. O'Brian, 'The Meaning of "Military Necessity" in International Law', in: 1 *World Polity* (1957), pp. 109-176.

72 UK Ministry of Defence, *Manual*, para. 2.2 (pp. 21-22); Greenwood, in: Fleck (ed.), *Handbook*, at 30 (para. 130).

73 *C.f.* Dinstein, *Conduct of Hostilities*, p. 18.

74 On this principle, *see infra*, Part Two, Chapter D) II. 2.

75 Greenwood, in: Fleck (ed.), *Handbook*, at 33 (para. 132.2); Marco Sassòli, 'Targeting: The Scope and Utility of the Concept of "Military Objectives" for the Protection of Civilians in Contemporary Armed Conflicts', in: David Wippman/ Matthew Evangelista (eds.), *New Wars, New Laws? Applying the Laws of War in 21st Century Conflicts*, Ardsley, N.Y. 2005, pp. 181-210, at 183-184; *Compare also* Dworkin, in: Wippman/ Evangelista (eds.), at 69-73.

tary requirements are incorporated in all rules of humanitarian law, as well as humanitarian requirements:[76]

II. Humanity

The principle of humanity prohibits the infliction of suffering, injury, or destruction not actually necessary for the accomplishment of a legitimate military purpose.[77] It is connected to the principle of necessity insofar, as once a legitimate military purpose is achieved, the infliction of suffering is unnecessary. On the other hand, the principle of humanity confirms the basic immunity of civilians from attack, as they generally make no contribution to the hostilities.[78] Insofar, it is also linked to the principle of distinction.

III. Proportionality

The principle of proportionality links necessity and humanity. Civilian immunity from attack does not make unlawful all unavoidable civilian casualties which result from legitimate attacks upon military objectives. As long as the casualties are not excessive in relation to the concrete and direct military advantage anticipated, they are legal.[79]

IV. Distinction *ratione personae*

King William of Prussia stated in 1870: "I conduct war with the French soldiers, not with the French citizens."[80] This statement refers to the fundamental distinction concerning persons taking part in or affected

---

[76] Dinstein, *Conduct of Hostilities*, p. 17.

[77] UK Ministry of Defence, *Manual*, para. 2.4 (p. 23).

[78] *Id.*, para. 2.4.1 (p. 23).

[79] *Id.*, para. 2.4.2 (p. 23); Delbrück, *EPIL*, Vol. 7, pp. 396-400; *compare also* Cohen/ Shany, 5 *J. Int'l Crim. Just.* (2007), pp. 310-321.

[80] King William of Prussia on August 11, 1870, cited in Benvenisti, *Law of Occupation*, p. 27.

by a conflict which is made by international humanitarian law; it distinguishes civilians and combatants. The principle of distinction between combatants and civilians is "the root of the law of war"[81] applicable in both international and non-international armed conflicts.[82] This primary legal status of a person as a civilian or a combatant has decisive consequences. The primary status is decisive for the protection afforded to a person. A civilian may, in general, not be attacked. A combatant may not be punished for the mere participation in the conflict. This distinction is fundamental in order to reduce as much as possible the adverse consequences of the war for the civilian population. Thus, parties of a conflict must at all times distinguish between the civilian population and combatants in order to spare civilian population and property. Attacks shall be directed solely against military objectives. Neither the civilian population as such nor civilian persons shall be the object of attack.[83]

Additionally, the primary status of a person is also decisive for the legal consequences of a persons' conduct, e.g. if a combatant violates international humanitarian law.[84] Furthermore, the acquisition of a new, secondary status, e.g. as a prisoner of war, is also linked to the primary status of being a combatant (who falls into the power of the enemy forces).

The principle of distinction is also referred to as the principle of discrimination of non-combatant immunity.[85] To enable its realisation, it is on the other hand necessary that combatants distinguish themselves from civilians. Combatants "may try to become invisible in the landscape, but not in the crowd."[86] These rules are recognised in numerous

---

81 Detter, *Law of War*, p. 141.

82 Henckaerts/ Doswald-Beck (eds.), *Humanitarian Law*, Vol. 1, p. 3.

83 Greenwood, in: Fleck (ed.), *Handbook*, at 32 (para. 130.5).

84 Knut Ipsen, 'Combatants and Non-Combatants', in: Dieter Fleck (ed.), *The Handbook of Humanitarian Law in Armed Conflicts*, Oxford 1999, pp. 65-104, at 65 (Intr.); Marco Sassòli/ Antoine Bouvier, *How does Law Protect in War? Cases, Documents and Teaching Materials on Contemporary Practice in International Humanitarian Law*, 2nd ed., Geneva 2006, p. 143.

85 Judith Gail Gardam, *Non-Combatant Immunity as a Norm of International Humanitarian Law*, Dordrecht 1993, p. 2.

86 Denise Bindschedler-Robert, 'A Reconsideration of the Law of Armed Conflicts', in: Joseph E. Johnson (ed.), *Report of the Conference on Contem-*

military manuals and form one of the basic principles of international humanitarian law. But although it is an inherent part of both customary and conventional law governing the conduct of war,[87] it did not receive precise articulation in a treaty document before the adoption of the 1977 Additional Protocol I.

However, distinction is practically impossible without a definition of at least one of the categories. The drafters of the Geneva Conventions and the Additional Protocols opted for the definition of a combatant.[88] This definition and the protection of combatants will be dealt with first. The definition of civilians seems straight forward; civilians are all persons other than combatants.[89] In consequence of the negative definition of civilians, the specifics of that concept and their protection will be dealt with second.[90] This concise system has been challenged by those who claim that a third category of so called "unlawful combatants" exists. This claim will be dealt with third.[91]

C. Combatants

The primary status as a combatant has various consequences. It entails immunity from criminal prosecution for those warlike acts which do not violate the laws and customs of war and the right to be treated as a

---

porary Problems of the Law of Armed Conflicts: Geneva, 15.-20. September 1969, New York 1971, pp. 1-61, at 43.

87 *See e.g.* UN GA Res. 2444 (October 19, 1968), *Respect for Human Rights in Armed Conflicts*, UN GAOR 23rd Sess., Supp. No. 18, pp. 50-51, UN Doc. A/7218 (1969), at operative para. 1 *lit.* c (p. 50); Walter Reed, 'Laws of War: The Developing Law of Armed Conflict – Some Current Problems', in: 9 *Case W. Res. J. Int'l L.* (1977), pp. 17-38, at 23; Sassòli, in: Wippman/ Evangelista (eds.), at 182-183.

88 Dougherty/ Quénivet, 16 *HuV-I* (2003), at 189; Yves Sandoz, *Commentary on the Additional Protocols of 8 June 1977 to the Geneva Conventions of 12 August 1949*, Dordrecht 1987, para. 1665 (p. 509).

89 Hans-Peter Gasser, 'Protection of the Civilian Population', in: Dieter Fleck (ed.), *The Handbook of Humanitarian Law in Armed Conflicts*, Oxford 1999, pp. 209-292, at 210 (para. 501.2); Sassòli/ Bouvier, *Law in War*, p. 144.

90 *See infra*, Part Two, Chapter D).

91 *See infra*, Part Two, Chapter E).

prisoner of war, if captured by the adversary.[92] On the other hand, a combatant is, by status, a legitimate target, even when he does not endanger the lives or interests of the other party to the conflict.[93] These consequences can certainly only apply if the status of the combatants is well defined. And this definition varies in the sphere of an international or a non-international armed conflict. The expression "combatant"[94] can be used in two senses. Originally, it referred to persons factually engaged in combat, whether they had a right to do so or not. Later, the term was used legally – and is used throughout this treatise – to describe persons who have a right to take direct part in hostilities.[95]

---

92 *See e.g.* Françoise Bouchet-Saulnier, *The Practical Guide to Humanitarian Law*, Lanham, Maryland 2002, p. 50; Myres Smith MacDougal/ Florentino P. Feliciano, *Law and minimum World Public Order: The legal Regulation of International Coercion*, 2nd print, New Haven, N.Y. 1967, p. 712; Waldemar A. Solf/ Edward R. Cummings, 'A Survey of Penal Sanctions Under Protocol I to the Geneva Conventions of August 12, 1949', in: 9 *Case W. Res. J. Int'l L.* (1977), pp. 205-251, at 212 and 215. Combatant immunity does not mean that "combatant status prevents the captor from prosecuting them for acts amounting to crimes committed during the course of the fighting", as *Gross* phrased it, *see* Gross, *Struggle of Democracy*, p. 47. Combatants may and must be prosecuted for crimes committed during the course of the fighting, namely those acts which are criminal under international humanitarian law. Combatant immunity only entails that they may not be prosecuted for acts which would be illegal if committed outside a war, but are legal in the context of war, e.g. the killing of an enemy combatant, and that they may not be punished for the mere fact of taking part in the hostilities.

93 *C.f.* Kretzmer, 16 *Eur. J. Int'l L.* (2005), at 190-191.

94 For a short overview of the historical development of the concept *see* Josh Kastenberg, 'The Customary International Law of War and Combatant Status: Does the Current Executive Branch Policy Determination on Unlawful Combatant Status for Terrorists run Afoul of International Law, or is it just Poor Public Relations?', in: 39 *Gonz. L. Rev.* (2003/4), pp. 495-537, at 499-509; Karma Nablusi, 'Evolving Conceptions of Civilians and Belligerents: One Hundred Years After the Hague Peace Conference', in: Simon Chesterman (ed.), *Civilians in War*, Boulder, Colorado 2001, pp. 9-24.

95 Regina Buß, *Der Kombattantenstatus: Die kriegsrechtliche Entstehung eines Rechtsbegriffs und seine Ausgestaltung in Verträgen des 19. und 20. Jahrhunderts*, Bochum 1992, p. 1; *see also* UK Ministry of Defence, *Manual*, para. 4.2.1 (p. 38).

I. Combatant Status in International Armed Conflicts

For the sphere of an international armed conflict, the term "combatant" was codified for the first time in Article 43 para. 2 of the 1977 Additional Protocol I:

> Members of the armed forces of a Party to a conflict (other than medical personnel and chaplains covered by Article 33 of the Third Convention) are combatants, that is to say, they have the right to participate directly in hostilities.

This rule is accepted to represent customary international law[96] and comes – at least if read in context – to the same definition of combatants that is presupposed in earlier documents.[97] It was drafted to solve the problems of defining "armed forces" and "combatants" in the 1949 Geneva Conventions:[98]

These instruments only define prisoners of war and thus allow an inference on combatant status. Article 4 A para. 2 of the 1949 Geneva Convention III lays down criteria which can be traced back to Article 1 of the 1907 Hague Regulations. Beside members of regular armed forces, the 1949 Geneva Convention III also covers members "of other militias and members of other volunteer corps ..." who fulfil the following conditions: (a) that of being commanded by a person responsible for his subordinates; (b) that of having a fixed distinctive sign recognizable at a distance; (c) that of carrying arms openly; (d) that of conducting their operations in accordance with the laws and customs of war.[99] It is not a precondition of combatant status to be armed.[100]

---

[96] *Compare e.g.* Henckaerts/ Doswald-Beck (eds.), *Humanitarian Law*, Vol. 1, p. 11 (Rule 3); Ipsen, in: Fleck (ed.), *Handbook*, at 65 and 70; UK Ministry of Defence, *Manual*, para. 4.2 (p. 38).

[97] Detter, *Law of War*, pp. 137 and 142.

[98] Ray Murphy, 'Prisoners of War and Contemporary Conflicts: The Case of the Taliban and al Qaeda Detainees', in: 41 *Rev. dr. mil.* (2002), pp. 141 167, at 151.

[99] *Compare infra*, Part Two, Chapter C) I. 2.

[100] The function of unarmed combatants can consist of carrying out reconnaissance missions, transmitting information, maintaining communications and transmissions, supplying guerrilla forces with arms and food, hiding guerrilla fighters, *see* Sandoz, *Additional Protocols*, para. 1695 (p. 528, note 35).

1. Members of the Armed Forces

The term "members of the armed forces" refers to all military personnel, whether they belong to the land, sea or air forces and form the core of the category of combatants.[101] The 1949 Geneva Convention III does not entail a definition of armed forces. This is only codified in Article 43 para. 1 of the 1977 Additional Protocol I:

> The armed forces of a Party to a conflict consist of all organized armed forces, groups and units which are under a command responsible to that Party for the conduct of its subordinates, even if that Party is represented by a government or an authority not recognized by an adverse Party. Such armed forces shall be subject to an internal disciplinary system which, *inter alia*, shall enforce compliance with the rules of international law applicable in armed conflict.

This definition resembles those developed earlier by legal scholars, including the same elements, namely an organization legitimated by the State which permanently serves defence and combat purposes and is under a command responsible to that State and wearing an emblem recognizable at a distance.[102] The last element is included in Article 44 para. 3 of the 1977 Additional Protocol I. However, the definition of "armed forces" under the 1977 Additional Protocol I is wider than the traditional understanding referred to in the 1907 Hague Regulations and the 1949 Geneva Conventions. The latter instruments distinguish regular armed forces and irregular armed forces, both being able to acquire prisoner-of-war status.[103] The 1977 Additional Protocol I does not distinguish in that manner any more. It can be understood either as widening the concept of armed forces and including "irregulars",[104] or as eliminating the distinction altogether.[105]

---

[101] Jean S. Pictet (ed.), *The Geneva Conventions of 12 August 1949: Commentary, Vol. 3, Geneva Convention relative to the Treatment of Prisoners of War*, Geneva 1960, p. 51; Detter, *Law of War*, p. 135; MacDougal/ Feliciano, *International Coercion*, p. 544.

[102] *C.f.* Buß, *Kombattantenstatus*, pp. 200-203.

[103] *See infra*, Part Two, Chapter C) I. 2.

[104] "Irregular" is sometimes – including here – used to describe persons who are not members of the regular armed forces but nevertheless qualify as combatants and prisoners of war. Sometimes it is used to refer to those who take part in the hostilities but do not qualify for combatant status, *see* Frits Kalsho-

A recent example for the problems attached to the definition of members of armed forces are the Taliban fighters in the 2001 conflict between Afghanistan and the United States.[106] The argument by the United States that members of the Taliban were not "members of armed forces" in the above mentioned sense was partly based on the assumption that the Taliban was not the *de facto* government of Afghanistan and therefore its armed forces were unprotected.[107]

Article 4 para. 3 of the 1949 Geneva Convention III and Article 43 para. 1 of the 1977 Additional Protocol I explicitly state that the status of combatant is not excluded if the one belligerent does not recognise the government of the other belligerent to which a member of regular armed forces professes allegiance. In consequence of this rule the Taliban fighters did not lose their status as members of the regular armed forces

---

ven, 'The Position of Guerrilla Fighters under the Law of War', in: 11 *Rev. dr. pén. mil.* (1972), pp. 55-91, at 65-66.

[105] Detter, *Law of War*, p. 139; *compare also* Wolfgang Hermann, 'Armed Combatants who Cannot Distinguish Themselves From the Civilian Population', in: 21 *Rev. dr. pén. mil.* (1982), pp. 72-75, at 73. Murphy, 41 *Rev. dr. mil.* (2002), at 151 favours the latter option.

[106] *Compare* Georg Nolte, 'Guantanamo und Genfer Konventionen: eine Frage der *lex lata* oder *de lege ferenda*?', in: Horst Fischer/ Ulrike Froissart/ Wolff Heintschel von Heinegg/ Christian Raap (eds.), *Krisensicherung und Humanitärer Schutz – Crisis Management and Humanitarian Protection: Festschrift für Dieter Fleck*, Berlin 2004, pp. 393-404, at 394-398.

[107] The US regarded Afghanistan as "a failed state because the Taliban did not exercise full control over the territory and people, was not recognized by the international community, and was not capable of fulfilling its international obligations" and that "the Taliban and its forces were, in fact, not a government, but a militant, terrorist-like group.", *see* U.S. Council to the President Alberto R. Gonzales, 'Decision re Application of the Geneva Convention on Prisoners of War to the conflict with al Qaeda and the Taliban', Memorandum to President George W. Bush, January 25, 2002, p. 1; *see also* U.S. Attorney General John Ashcroft, Memorandum to President George W. Bush, February 1, 2002, p. 1; U.S. President George W. Bush, Memorandum of February 7, 2002, to Vice President Dick Cheney, *et al. C.f.* Evan J. Wallach, 'The Logical Nexus Between the Decision to deny Application of the Third Geneva Convention to the Taliban and Al Qaeda and the Mistreatment of Prisoners in Abu Ghraib', in: 36 *Case W. Res. J. Int'l L.* (2004), pp. 541-638, at 542.

due to the fact that the United States did not recognise the Taliban government of Afghanistan.[108]

Another line of argument is based on the finding that the Taliban was the *de facto* government of Afghanistan, but its forces did not meet the requirements of Article 4 A para. 2 of the 1949 Geneva Convention III.[109] It is disputed whether the four criteria for evaluating combatants status laid down in Article 4 A para. 2 of the 1949 Geneva Convention III only apply to "[m]embers of other militias and members of other volunteer corps" or also to regular armed forces according to para. 1 of the article. The textual meaning and structural framework suggests the former; the conditions are included in para. 2 and according to the wording, exclusively apply to those persons referred to in that paragraph.[110] Thus, members of regular armed forces or militias and volunteer groups in the sense of Article 4 para. 1 of the 1949 Geneva Convention III are considered by some authors to be combatants without any consideration whether their overall conduct satisfies the criteria laid down in para. 2.[111]

---

[108] *See also* European Commission for Democracy through Law, Opinion No. 245/2003, para. 18; Yutaka Arai-Takahashi, 'Disentangling Legal Quagmires: The Legal Characterisation of the Armed Conflicts in Afghanistan since 6/7 October 2001 and the Question of Prisoner of War Status', in: 5 *Yb. Int'l Hum. L.* (2002), pp. 61-105, at 95-97; Roberta Arnold, 'Terrorism and IHL: A Common Denominator?', in: Roberta Arnold/ Pierre-Antoine Hildbrand (eds.), *International Humanitarian Law and the 21st Century's Conflicts: Changes and Challenges*, Lausanne 2005, pp. 5-23, at 16; Silvia Borelli, 'The Treatment of Terrorist Suspects Captured Abroad: Human Rights and Humanitarian Law', in: Andrea Bianchi/ Yasmin Naqvi (eds.), *Enforcing International Law Norms Against Terrorism*, Oxford 2004, pp. 39-61, at 43; Jochen Abraham Frowein, 'Der Terrorismus als Herausforderung für das Völkerrecht', in: 62 *ZaöRV* (2002), pp. 879-905, at 894-895; Kretzmer, 16 *Eur. J. Int'l L.* (2005), at 188; Murphy, 41 *Rev. dr. mil.* (2002), at 150-151.

[109] *Compare* Wallach, 36 *Case W. Res. J. Int'l L.* (2004), at 542; John C. Yoo, 'The Status of Soldiers and Terrorists under the Geneva Conventions', in: 3 *Chin. J. Int'l L.* (2004), pp. 135-150, at 139-140.

[110] *See e.g.* Kirby Abbott, '"Terrorists: Criminals, Combatants or ... ?": The Questions of Combatancy', in: Canadian Council on International Law (ed.), *The Measure of International Law: Effectiveness, Fairness and Validity*, The Hague 2004, pp. 366-385, at 376.

[111] *See* George H. Aldrich, 'The Taliban, Al Qaeda, and the Detention of Illegal Combatants', in: 96 *Am. J. Int'l L.* (2002), pp. 891-898, at 894; Michael J.

On the other hand, when the 1907 Hague Regulations – the source of the four conditions included in para. 2 of Article 4 A – were drafted, these conditions were taken for granted concerning traditional armed forces.[112] For example, the drafters of the 1949 Convention, like those of the Hague Convention, discussed whether it was necessary to specify the sign which members of armed forces should have for purposes of recognition,[113] and not whether they should wear such a sign. It is understood that customary international law required regular armed forces to adhere to the criteria prior to 1949[114] and that their application to them is implied in Article 4 A of the 1949 Geneva Convention III.[115] While the stringency of the criteria may vary, it is broadly accepted that the armed forces of a State must generally fulfil these conditions.[116] These four conditions represent the codification of customary interna-

---

Matheson, 'U.S. Military Commissions: One of Several Options', in: 96 *Am. J. Int'l L.* (2002), pp. 354-358, at 355 seems to base his assessment on the same assumption, even though he does not explicitly state so.

[112] Buß, *Kombattantenstatus*, p. 200; *compare also* Abbott, in: Canadian Council on International Law (ed.), at 376-377; Wedgwood, 96 *Am. J. Int'l L.* (2002), at 335.

[113] *Compare* Pictet (ed.), *Geneva Conventions*, Vol. 3, p. 52.

[114] Arai-Takahashi, 5 *Yb. Int'l Hum. L.* (2002), at 79; Abbott, in: Canadian Council on International Law (ed.), at 376-378; Wedgwood, 96 *Am. J. Int'l L.* (2002), at 335-336.

[115] Steven R. Ratner, '*Jus ad Bellum* and *Jus in Bello* after September 11', in: 96 *Am. J. Int'l L.* (2002), pp. 905-921, at 912.

[116] *See e.g.* Israel, Military Court Ramallah, *Military Prosecutor v. Omar Mahmud Kassem* et al., Case No. 4/69, Judgment of April 13, 1969, reprinted in: 42 *Int'l L.R.* (1971), pp. 470-483, at 479; Detter, *Law of War*, p. 136; Yoram Dinstein, 'The Distinction between Unlawful Combatants and War Criminals', in: Yoram Dinstein/ Mala Tabory (eds.), *International Law at a Time of Perplexity: Essays in Honour of Shabtai Rosenne*, Dordrecht 1989, pp. 103-116, at 105; *similarly*, Horst Fischer, 'Protection of Prisoners of War', in: Dieter Fleck (ed.), *The Handbook of Humanitarian Law in Armed Conflicts*, Oxford 1999, pp. 321-367, at 335 (para. 705.1); W. Thomas Mallison/ Sally V. Mallison, 'The Juridical Status of Irregular Combatants under the International Humanitarian Law of Armed Conflict', in: 9 *Case W. Res. J. Int'l L.* (1977), pp. 39-78, at 44-45, 48 and 61-62; Wedgwood, 96 *Am. J. Int'l L.* (2002), at 335; Arai-Takahashi, 5 *Yb. Int'l Hum. L.* (2002), at 75-76.

tional law,[117] and will be addressed in detail *infra*.[118] Concerning the example of the Taliban fighters, who have distinguished themselves by using black turbans[119] and have coordinatedly made efforts to defend their territory, the conditions are regarded as at least generally met.[120]

Even though for the members of the armed forces, combatant status is the rule,[121] there are some exceptions. Members of armed forces who may not engage in combat, i.e. non-combatants; according to Article 3 of the 1907 Hague Regulations "[t]he armed forces of the belligerent parties may consist of combatants and non-combatants." The latter are e.g. medical and religious personnel.[122]

---

[117] *See e.g.* Johannes G.C. van Aggelen, 'A Response to John C. Yoo, "the Status of Soldiers and Terrorists under the Geneva Conventions"', in: 4 *Chin. J. Int'l L.* (2005), pp. 167-181, at 168; Ipsen, in: Fleck (ed.), *Handbook*, at 70 (para. 304); Kastenberg, 39 *Gonz. L. Rev.* (2003/4), at 509; Yoo, 3 *Chin. J. Int'l L.* (2004), at 143-144.

[118] *See infra*, Part Two, Chapter C) I. 2.

[119] A distinctive sign may – inter alia – be a cap, a coat or a shirt, *see* Pictet (ed.), *Geneva Conventions*, Vol. 3, p. 59.

[120] European Commission for Democracy through Law, Opinion No. 245/ 2003, para. 25; Jean-Philippe Lavoyer, 'International Humanitarian Law and Terrorism', in: Liesbeth Lijnzaad/ Johanna von Sambeck/ Bahia Tahzib-Lie (eds.), *Making the Voice of Humanity Heard: Essays on Humanitarian Assistance and International Humanitarian Law in Honour of HRH Princess Margriet of the Netherlands*, Leiden 2004, pp. 255-270, at 258; *compare also* Aggelen, 4 *Chin. J. Int'l L.* (2005), at 168; Borelli, in: Bianchi/ Naqvi (eds.), at 43-44; Brooks, 153 *U. Pa. L. Rev.* (2004), at 734; Murphy, 41 *Rev. dr. mil.* (2002), at 150-151; Jiří Toman, 'The Status of Al Quaeda/Taliban Detainees under the Geneva Conventions', in: 32 *Isr. Yb. Hum. Rts.* (2002), pp. 271-304, at 294 and 304; Luisa Vierucci, 'Is the Geneva Convention on Prisoners of War Obsolete? The Views of the Counsel to the US President on the Application of International Law to the Afghan Conflict', in: 2 *J. Int'l Crim. Just.* (2004), pp. 866-871, at 868; *but see* Abbott, in: Canadian Council on International Law (ed.), at 378.

[121] Ipsen, in: Fleck (ed.), *Handbook*, at 66-67 (para. 301); Arai-Takahashi, 5 *Yb. Int'l Hum. L.* (2002), at 75.

[122] *Compare* UK Ministry of Defence, *Manual*, para. 4.2.2 (p. 38); Ipsen, in: Fleck (ed.), *Handbook*, at 66 (para. 301); on the historical development of the protection of medical personnel *see* Leslie C. Green, 'War Law and the Medical Profession', in: Leslie C. Green, *Essays on the Modern Law of War*, 2nd ed., Ardsley, N.Y. 1999, pp. 489-527.

2. *Members of Militias and Volunteer Corps*

Additionally, combatant status is assigned to members of militias and volunteer corps who are not forming part of the armed forces as defined above, but belong to a party to the conflict, if they cumulatively[123] fulfil the four conditions laid down in Article 4 A para. 2 of the 1949 Geneva Convention III and referred to above. These "irregulars" are understood to be included in the definition of armed forces of the 1977 Additional Protocol I, which is wider as the traditional armed forces concept of the 1907 Hague Regulations and the 1949 Geneva Conventions.[124] The requirements that have to be met by these persons to qualify as combatants are divided in to varying numbers of groups. For example, *Kalshoven* separates the preconditions into five categories,[125] *Mallison/ Mallison* refer to six criteria,[126] whereas *Dinstein* addresses seven conditions.[127] These requirements are the following:

a) Being Organized

The first condition is not expressly referred to in Article 4 A para. 2 of the 1949 Geneva Convention III. The term militia is partly understood to include all non-State actors who resort to violence in order to achieve their objectives, covering partisans,[128] guerrillas, revolutionary armies, insurgents, State agents fighting an behalf (but not at the behest) of the State, ethnic armed formations, and warlord movements.[129] The Nuremberg Tribunal observed:

> Many of the defendants seem to assume that by merely characterizing a person a partisan, he may be shot out of hand. But it is not so

[123] *See* Buß, *Kombattantenstatus*, p. 207.

[124] Detter, *Law of War*, p. 139.

[125] Kalshoven, 11 *Rev. dr. pén. mil.* (1972), at 77-82.

[126] Mallison/ Mallison, 9 *Case W. Res. J. Int'l L.* (1977), at 49 63.

[127] Dinstein, *Conduct of Hostilities*, pp. 37-41; Yoram Dinstein, 'Unlawful Combatancy', in: 32 *Isr. Yb. Hum. Rts.* (2002), pp. 247-270, at 256-260.

[128] Pictet (ed.), *Geneva Conventions*, Vol. 3, p. 52.

[129] A "working definition" by Marie-Joëlle Zahar, 'Protégés, Clients, Cannon Fodder: Civil-Militia Relations in Internal Conflicts', in: Simon Chesterman (ed.), *Civilians in War*, Boulder, Colorado 2001, pp. 43-65, at 44-45.

> simple as that. If the partisans are organized and are engaged in what international law regards as legitimate warfare ..., they are entitled to be protected as combatants.[130]

It is thus required that a person is member in an "organized" group. This is necessary in order to facilitate the compliance with the other conditions of Article 4 para. 2 of the Convention. Combatants must act in a hierarchic framework subject to supervision.[131] The requirement is met by rudimentary elements of military organization. Thus, a corporal's squad on detached duty meets the requirement as well as irregulars who were part of a military unit which has become broken due to the exigencies of combat. It also applies to a single individual who has been separated from his unit.[132]

b) Belonging to a Party to the Conflict

The second condition of belonging to a party to the conflict can be interpreted in two ways. First, it could refer to the facts that persons, to enjoy combatant status, must act on behalf of a State, i.e. have a certain relationship with a belligerent government.[133] Second, it could also cover those persons who are part of a movement that is not a State but party to the conflict itself. The latter interpretation is supported by the use of "party to the conflict" in Common Article 3, referring to all parties in a non-international armed conflict. On the other hand, in Article 4 A para. 1, the term seems to refer to States, as they have regular armed forces. Nevertheless, the rule was invented *inter alia* to cover movements such as Marshal Tito's partisan forces in the Second World War, who were not associated to a State party and took part in allegiance to their own resistance movement which was party to the con-

---

[130] U.S. Military Tribunal (Nuremberg), *U.S. v. Otto Ohlendorf* et al. (Einsatzgruppen Trial), Judgment of April 4, 1948, reprinted in: 15 *Annual Digest* (1948), Case No. 217, pp. 656-668, at 662.

[131] Dinstein, *Conduct of Hostilities*, p. 39; Dinstein, 32 *Isr. Yb. Hum. Rts.* (2002), at 258; Hermann, 21 *Rev. dr. pén. mil.* (1982), at 73.

[132] Mallison/ Mallison, 9 *Case W. Res. J. Int'l L.* (1977), at 49-50.

[133] Dinstein, *Conduct of Hostilities*, pp. 39-40; Dinstein, 32 *Isr. Yb. Hum. Rts.* (2002), at 258.

flict.[134] It must now at least be possible to subsume subjects of international law within the limits drawn by Article 1 para. 4 of the 1977 Additional Protocol I under this precondition.[135]

c) Being Commanded by a Person Responsible for His Subordinates

Similar to the requirement of being organized, the requirement of a responsible military command entails a hierarchical authority which assumes responsibility for the actions of the members.[136] It shall exclude the possibility of activities of individuals on their own, known as *franc-tireurs*. There is not legitimate private war of one person against the enemy.[137] The persons responsible for their subordinates do not have to be regular officers of the armed forces.[138] They may be either civilian or military, but they have to be responsible for the actions taken on their orders as well as for actions which they were unable to prevent. Their competence must be considered in the same way as that of a military commander. The core element of the this condition is to provide for an organisational structure that enforces discipline and ensures that the three other conditions will be met.[139]

d) Having a Fixed Distinctive Sign Recognizable at a Distance

The need to wear a fixed distinctive emblem recognizable at a distance, replaces the uniform normally worn by regular troops. The requirement has two aspects, distinction, i.e. the sign must identify and characterize the forces using it, and fixity.[140] The term "fixed" expresses that it must be worn constantly, in all circumstances. To ensure that the sign is distinctive, all members of any militia or volunteer corps must exclu-

---

[134] Mallison/ Mallison, 9 *Case W. Res. J. Int'l L.* (1977), at 54-55; *compare also* Murphy, 41 *Rev. dr. mil.* (2002), at 151, who refers "allegiance to a government or an authority".

[135] Hermann, 21 *Rev. dr. pén. mil.* (1982), at 73.

[136] Mallison/ Mallison, 9 *Case W. Res. J. Int'l L.* (1977), at 55.

[137] Dinstein, 32 *Isr. Yb. Hum. Rts.* (2002), at 256.

[138] Mallison/ Mallison, 9 *Case W. Res. J. Int'l L.* (1977), at 55.

[139] Pictet (ed.), *Geneva Conventions*, Vol. 3, p. 59.

[140] Dinstein, 32 *Isr. Yb. Hum. Rts.* (2002), at 256.

sively use this sign, but may add additional emblems indicating rank or special functions. To ensure that persons on board a vehicle, aeroplane or boat, are still distinctive, the sign must – similar to a flag flown by a ship – also be shown on the vehicle concerned.[141]

Size and nature of the signs possible and the way they have to be worn are not specified in the 1949 Geneva Convention III. Thus, the term "recognizable at a distance" is open to interpretation. This requirement has been interpreted narrowly in the sense that "the silhouette of an irregular combatant standing against the skyline should be at once distinguishable from that of a peaceful inhabitant by naked eye of ordinary individuals, at a distance at which the form of an individual can be determined."[142] It may be fulfilled by a dress differing from that worn by civilians,[143] by wearing caps, armbands, coats, shirts,[144] or an emblem or coloured sign worn on the chest[145] but e.g. the Soviet star in a cap might not be sufficient.[146]

e) Carrying Arms Openly

The condition to carry arms openly does not require to carry arms visible at all times. The rationale behind this rule is that opposing forces shall be able to recognise members of militias or volunteer groups as combatants in the same way as members of regular armed forces, whatever their weapons may be.[147] It is thus closely interrelated with the re-

---

141 Pictet (ed.), *Geneva Conventions*, Vol. 3, pp. 59-60.

142 Lassa Francis Lawrence Oppenheim/ Hersch Lauterpacht, *International Law: A Treatise*, Vol. II, *Disputes, War and Neutrality*, 7th ed., London 1952, p. 257 (footnote 2).

143 Israel, Military Court Ramallah, *Military Prosecutor v. Omar Mahmud Kassem et al.*, Case No. 4/69, Judgment of April 13, 1969, reprinted in: 42 *Int'l L.R.* (1971), pp. 470-483, at 479, at 478.

144 Mallison/ Mallison, 9 *Case W. Res. J. Int'l L.* (1977), at 56. Although especially hats may frequently be taken off and do thus not seem fully adequate.

145 Pictet (ed.), *Geneva Conventions*, Vol. 3, p. 60.

146 U.S. Military Tribunal (Nuremberg), *U.S. v. Wilhelm List* et al. (Hostage Trial), Judgment of February 19, 1948, reprinted in: 15 *Annual Digest* (1948), Case No. 215, pp. 632-653, at 639.

147 Pictet (ed.), *Geneva Conventions*, Vol. 3, p. 61.

quirement to wear a distinctive sign. It shall e.g. hinder a civilian to enter a military post on a false pretext and then open fire,[148] but does not mean that a hand-grenade or revolver cannot be placed in a pocket or under a coat.[149] The duty to carry arms openly seems to be somewhat weakened according to Article 44 of the 1977 Additional Protocol I. Here, the requirement is reduced to carrying arms openly

> (a) during each military engagement, and (b) during such time as he is visible to the adversary while he is engaged in a military deployment preceding the launching of an attack in which he is to participate.

This only applies to "exceptional situations".[150] Hence, the core of the rule is the same; in short, it states that a person, when visible to the adversary, in order to keep combatant status, has to distinguish himself from unarmed civilians by carrying his arms openly.[151]

f) Conducting Operations in Accordance with the Laws and Customs of War

This condition is essential as it embraces those conditions listed above. It is undisputed that the forces, in order to be covered by the definition of "combatant", must ensure that their members comply with the laws and customs of war. While it is not required that combatants strictly observe all details of humanitarian law to keep their status, this condition requires them to respect the Geneva Conventions to the fullest extent possible.[152] Those who want to rely on international humanitarian law must be willing to respect it themselves.[153]

It is not entirely clear whether the requirement is a group requirement or an individual one. If the great majority of members of an organisa-

---

[148] Dinstein, 32 *Isr. Yb. Hum. Rts.* (2002), at 258; Dinstein, *Conduct of Hostilities*, pp. 38-39; *compare also infra*, Part Two, Chapter C) III. 1.

[149] Pictet (ed.), *Geneva Conventions*, Vol. 3, p. 61.

[150] Hermann, 21 *Rev. dr. pén. mil.* (1982), at 74.

[151] Yves Sandoz/ Christophe Swinarski/ Bruno Zimmermann (eds.), *Commentary on the Additional Protocols of 8 June 1977 to the Geneva Conventions of 12 August 1949*, Dordrecht 1987, paras. 1706-1714 (pp. 533-536).

[152] Pictet (ed.), *Geneva Conventions*, Vol. 3, p. 61.

[153] Dinstein, 32 *Isr. Yb. Hum. Rts.* (2002), at 258.

tion observes the criterion, little reason exists to deny combatant status to single members that are in breach with the laws and customs of war.[154] Their behaviour is rather a question of individual criminal responsibility than of status. If, on the contrary, a large majority of members of an organisation does not fulfil the fourth condition, it is difficult to distinguish single members of that organisation and grant them the combatant status,[155] even though this assessment is supported by some authors.[156] Thus, the condition of conducting operations in accordance with the laws and customs of war at least has a strong collective aspect.[157]

g) Non-Allegiance to the Detaining Power

Concerning prisoner-of-war status, the non-allegiance to the detaining power is partly required as an additional – unwritten – condition. It especially refers to the fact that a national detained by his own State shall not enjoy prisoner-of-war status.[158] If these conditions are applied to the example of the 2001 conflict in Afghanistan, al-Qaeda members cannot be regarded to be entitled to the status of combatants. They are neither members or "form part" of or "belong"[159] to the regular armed

---

[154] *See also* Gerald L. Neuman, 'Humanitarian Law and Counterterrorist Force', in: 14 *Eur. J. Int'l L.* (2003), pp. 283-298, at 294; The US Field Manual phrases: "This condition is fulfilled if most of the members of the body observe the laws and customs of war, notwithstanding the fact that the individual member concerned may have committed a war crime.", *see* U.S. Department of the Army, *The Law of Land Warfare*, Field Manual No. 27-10 (July 18, 1956), Washington, D.C. 1956, para. 64 *lit.* d.

[155] *See also* Allan Rosas, *The Legal Status of Prisoners of War: A Study in International Humanitarian Law applicable in Armed Conflicts*, Helsinki 1976, pp. 361 and 363; Howard Sidney Levie, *Prisoners of War in International Armed Conflict*, Newport 1978, pp. 52-53.

[156] Neuman, 14 *Eur. J. Int'l L.* (2003), at 294; with a different reasoning based on Article 44 para. 2 of the 1977 Additional Protocol I also Arai-Takahashi, 5 *Yb. Int'l Hum. L.* (2002), at 78.

[157] *Compare also* Kalshoven, 11 *Rev. dr. pén. mil.* (1972), at 85-86 and 89-90.

[158] Dinstein, 32 *Isr. Yb. Hum. Rts.* (2002), at 259-260.

[159] The mere act of fighting in concert is not sufficient to meet the test of "belonging to a Party to the conflict" in that context, *see* Rowe, 3 *Melb. J. Int'l L.* (2002), at 315-316.

forces of a State, nor do they fulfil the abovementioned criteria, especially at least general adherence to the laws of war.[160] Additionally to members of militias, some authors are of the opinion that the definition of combatant should also include civilians taking part in hostilities, to avoid the possibility of moving from civilian to combatant status back and forth according to activities conducted.[161] This question will be addressed in the chapter dealing with civilians taking direct part in hostilities *infra*.[162]

3. *"Levée en masse"*

But there are also undisputed cases in which persons can, by participating in the hostilities, acquire combatant status even without cumulatively fulfilling the conditions laid out above. This is the case if the inhabitants of a territory which has not been occupied, on the approach of the enemy, spontaneously take up arms to resist the invading troops without having had time to organize themselves into armed units. Persons taking part in this so-called *levée en masse* are regarded as combatants if they carry their arms openly and if they respect the laws and customs of war.[163] This rule is laid down in Article 2 of the 1907 Hague Regulations, in Article 4 A para. 6 of the 1949 Geneva Convention III and represents customary international law.[164]

---

[160] European Commission for Democracy through Law, Opinion No. 245/ 2003, para. 32; Arai-Takahashi, 5 *Yb. Int'l Hum. L.* (2002), at 99-102; Arnold, in: Arnold/ Hildbrand (eds.), at 15-16; Frowein, 62 *ZaöRV* (2002), at 895; Rowe, 3 *Melb. J. Int'l L.* (2002), at 312 and 315-317; Vierucci, 2 *J. Int'l Crim. Just.* (2004), at 868; Yoo, 3 *Chin. J. Int'l L.* (2004), at 139; *compare also* Daniel C. Prefontaine, 'Under International Law is there a Category of Prisoner in Armed Conflicts Known as an "Unlawful or Unprivileged or Enemy Combatant"?, in: Canadian Council on International Law (ed.), *The Measure of International Law: Effectiveness, Fairness and Validity*, The Hague 2004, pp. 386-395, at 391; *but see* Murphy, 41 *Rev. dr. mil.* (2002), at 150-151 and Borelli, in: Bianchi/ Naqvi (eds.), at 45 who both at least tend to treat both – the Taliban and al-Qaeda – as covered by Article 4 A of the 1949 Geneva Convention III.

[161] *See e.g.* Dinstein, *Conduct of Hostilities*, p. 27.

[162] *See infra*, Part Two, Chapter D) II.1. c).

[163] Yoram Dinstein, *Conduct of Hostilities*, p. 42.

[164] Ipsen, in: Fleck (ed.), *Handbook*, at 79-80 (para. 310).

4. Conclusion: Combatant Status

Those persons who meet the criteria provided in Article 4 A of the 1949 Geneva Convention III and Article 44 of the 1977 Additional Protocol I and laid out above – including a *levée en masse* – qualify as combatants. This means – *inter alia* – that they may take part in hostilities and may not be punished for this participation alone, but will acquire prisoner-of-war status if they are captured by the adversary. It includes further that they may generally be made the object of attack. Persons who do not fulfil the conditions discussed above do not qualify as combatants. Whether they are thus civilians by primary status or can acquire a third primary status such as "unlawful combatant", has no consequences whatsoever for the protection of combatants and will thus will be examined *infra*.[165]

II. Fighters in Non-International Armed Conflicts

Until the adoption of the 1977 Additional Protocol II, common Article 3 of the 1949 Geneva Conventions stood alone in the sphere of non-international armed conflicts. Article 3 does not address the issue of combatants. It provides basic protection to persons not taking part in the hostilities, or who have laid down their arms, or who are *hors de combat*. It does not provide for any protective rule specifically applicable to either combatants or prisoners. There is no immunity from punishment – even capital punishment – for the mere participation in the conflict.[166] This lack of protection can be closed by means of recognizing fighters as belligerents or by means of a special agreement between the parties to the conflict proposed in Article 3 with the aim of applying "all or part of the other provisions" of the 1949 Geneva Conventions. Both means have very rarely been used, as the insurgents would

---

[165] *See infra*, Part Two, Chapters D) and E).

[166] *Compare e.g.* Inter-Am. Comm'n H.R., *Report on Terrorism*, para. 70; Rosemary Abi-Saab, 'Humanitarian Law and Internal Conflicts: The Evolution of Legal Concern', in: Astrid J.M. Delissen; Gerard J. Tanja (eds.), *Humanitarian Law of Armed Conflict: Challenges ahead – Essays in Honour of Frits Kalshoven*, Dordrecht 1991, pp. 209-223, at 217; Knut Dörmann, 'The Legal Situation of "Unlawful/ Unprivileged Combatants"', in: 85 *Int'l Rev. Red Cross* (2003), No 849, pp. 45-74, at 47.

then be immune from criminal liability for fighting and would acquire prisoner-of-war status when captured.[167] However, it is understood

> that the conflicts referred to in Article 3 are armed conflicts, with 'armed forces' on either side engaged in 'hostilities' – conflicts, in short, which are in many respects similar to an international war, but take place within the confines of a single country.[168]

This shows that the insurgents or rebels are understood to at least resemble regular armed forces. Thus, it is not an oxymoron to describe a "combatant engaged in a non-international armed conflict".[169] *Gasser* is of the opinion that "[i]n internal armed conflicts also, it is generally evident who is in fact involved in acts of violence and who is not."[170]

The missing definition of "combatant" was not made up for in the 1977 Additional Protocol II. Situations of internal conflict thus still lack a definition of "combatant" or "armed forces"[171] due to States being unwilling to grant the status of combatants – and most of all prisoner-of-

---

[167] The only examples for a recognition were the American Civil War (1861-1865), the Spanish Civil War (1936-1939) and the Nigerian War on the secession of Biafra (1967-1969), *see* Arne Willy Dahl, 'The Legal Status of the Opposition Fighter in International (*sic!*) Armed Conflict', in: 43 *Rev. dr. mil.* (2004), pp. 137-153, at 139 (The article refers to internal armed conflicts.). Cuba in 1958 and Angola in 1975 are two of the rare examples of a special agreement, *see* Abi-Saab, in: Delissen/ Tanja (eds.), at 217 (footnote 18); *compare also* Charles Zorgbibe, 'Pour une réaffirmation du droit humanitaire des conflicts armés internes', in: 97 *J. dr. int'l* (1970), pp. 658-683, at 666.

[168] Pictet (ed.), *Geneva Conventions*, Vol. 3, p. 37.

[169] *But see* Michael Newton, 'Unlawful Belligerency After September 11: History Revisited and Law Revised', in: David Wippman/ Matthew Evangelista (eds.), *New Wars, New Laws? Applying the Laws of War in 21st Century Conflicts*, Ardsley, N.Y. 2005, pp. 75-110, at 92.

[170] Gasser, in: Fleck (ed.), *Handbook*, at 210 (para. 501.2).

[171] International Committee of the Red Cross; T.M.C. Asser Institute, *Direct Participation in Hostilities under International Humanitarian Law*, Summary Report of expert seminar in the Hague, June 2, 2003, Annex 1 to International Committee of the Red Cross, *International Humanitarian Law and the Challenges of Contemporary Armed Conflicts*, Report prepared in September 2003 for the 28th International Conference of the Red Cross and Red Crescent, Geneva, December 2003, ICRC Doc. 03/IC/09, pp. 27-39, at 33.

war status – to non-State actors.[172] However, the 1977 Additional Protocol II refers to civilians, e.g. in Article 13 para. 3. It is furthermore accepted that the principle of distinction also applies to non-international armed conflicts.[173] Thus, there must be a category of "non-civilians" to be distinguished from civilians. The existence of such a group was also presupposed when the 1977 Additional Protocol II was drafted. Then, civilians were defined as "anyone who is not a member of the armed forces or of an organized armed group."[174] The "non-civilian" category will be referred to here as "fighters".[175] The Protocol adopted some criteria concerning their status – albeit fewer than the 1977 Additional Protocol I. Thus, some argue in favour of applying either the basic conditions of the 1949 Geneva Conventions or, by analogy, the provisions of 1977 Additional Protocol I.[176] But the criteria given by the 1977 Additional Protocol II suffice at least to define fighters:

1. Defining Criteria

According to Article 1 para. 1, the parties to a non-international armed conflict are a State's armed forces

---

[172] Arai-Takahashi, 5 *Yb. Int'l Hum. L.* (2002), at 90; Doswald-Beck, 88 *Int'l Rev. Red Cross* (2006), No. 864, at 889; Kretzmer, 16 *Eur. J. Int'l L.* (2005), at 197; Yves Sandoz/ Christophe Swinarski/ Bruno Zimmermann (eds.), *Commentaire des Protocoles additionnels du 8 juin 1977 aux Conventions de Genève du 12 août 1949*, Genève 1986, para. 4441 (p. 1368).

[173] Henckaerts/ Doswald-Beck (eds.), *Humanitarian Law*, Vol. 1, p. 3 and pp. 5-8.

[174] The text was not included into the Convention as part of a package aimed at the adoption of a simplified text, *compare id.*, p. 19 with further references.

[175] It has to be submitted that the word "fighter" would be translated as "combatant" in a number of languages, *compare id.*, p. 13. The 1998 Rome Statute of the International Criminal Court in the context of non-international armed conflicts refers to "a combatant adversary" in Art. 8 para. 2 *lit.* e (ix), *see* Rome Statute of the International Criminal Court, adopted at Rome, Italy, on 17 July 1998, entry into force on 1 July 2002, U.N. Doc. A/CONF.183/9 (1998), reprinted in: 2187 *UNTS*, No. 38544, pp. 90-158. However, "fighter" at least in this English treatise seems to be adequate to distinguish this concept from that of "combatants", referring to persons who are entitled to prisoner-of-war status when captured.

[176] Detter, *Law of War*, pp. 145-146.

> and dissident armed forces or other organized armed groups which, under responsible command, exercise such control over a part of its territory as to enable them to carry out sustained and concerted military operations and to implement this Protocol.

Thus, there have to be *dissident armed forces* or at least an *organized armed group* party to the conflict,[177] the latter implying a level of organisation similar to that of regular armed forces.[178] A *responsible command* must exist, which means that a more collective character than sporadic acts of individuals is needed.[179] It is not necessary for the responsible command to reach the level of a rigid military hierarchy. Some *de facto* authority is sufficient, if it covers the ability to plan and carry out concerted and sustained military operations as well as the ability to impose discipline required to *implement the protocol*.[180] But it is unclear whether the dissident forces must manifest the ability to apply the 1977 Additional Protocol II by doing so or whether it is sufficient that they have the ability to do so.[181]

The requirement of territorial control by the rebels it is not based on the proportion of the territory or the duration and degree of control. It rather refers to the quality of control which enables the insurgents to exercise their authority and conduct military operations.[182] In view of guerrilla warfare and the highly mobilised warfare of today, territorial control may continuously change. A too strict interpretation of this

---

[177] Lindsay Moir, *The Law of Internal Armed Conflict*, Cambridge 2002, p. 36; *compare also* ICTY, *Prosecutor v. Duško Tadić*, Case No. IT-94-1-AR72, Decision on the Defence Motion for Interlocutory Appeal on Jurisdiction of October 2, 1995, reprinted in: 105 *Int'l L.R.* (1997), pp. 419-648, at 488-489 (para. 70).

[178] Bothe *et al.*, *1977 Protocols*, Art. 1 Prot. II, para. 2.5 (p. 626).

[179] Hilaire McCoubrey/ Nigel D. White, *International Organizations and Civil Wars*, Aldershot 1995, pp. 65-66.

[180] Bothe *et al.*, *1977 Protocols*, Art. 1 Prot. II, para. 2.8 (p. 627); Sylvie-Stoyanka Junod, 'Additional Protocol II: History and Scope', in: 33 *Am. U. L. Rev.* (1983), pp. 29-40, at 37; Moir, *Internal Armed Conflict*, p. 105.

[181] *Compare* UK Ministry of Defence, *Manual*, para. 3.7 (p. 32).

[182] Bothe *et al.*, *1977 Protocols*, Art. 1 Prot. II, para. 2.8 (p. 627); Junod, 33 *Am. U. L. Rev.* (1983), at 37; Moir, *Internal Armed Conflict*, p. 105.

precondition would thus confine the personal application of the 1977 Additional Protocol II to insurgents in classical civil wars.[183]

In the sphere of a non-international armed conflict, the members of the armed forces of a State as well as the members of an organized armed group fulfilling the conditions discussed above are fighters that resemble combatants in the international sphere and may thus be targeted.[184]

2. *Problems Concerning Distinction*

This leaves a problem concerning distinction, as no rule comparable to Article 4 A para. 2 1949 Geneva Convention III exists according to which fighters are required to wear a fixed distinctive sign recognizable at a distance. The emphasis in 1977 Additional Protocol II is rather on the protection of all persons affected by the hostilities. According to Article 2 para. 1 the "Protocol shall be applied … to all persons affected by an armed conflict". It furthermore does not permit an inference from prisoner-of-war status on combatant status as the protection of those persons "whose liberty has been restricted" also does not distinguish between fighters and civilians.[185] However, also fighters in non-international armed conflicts have the duty to distinguish themselves from civilians.[186]

a) Active Participation as the Criterion

To avoid the difficulties of distinction, some authors try to tie the definition of fighters in non-international armed conflicts to parts of Common Article 3 of the 1949 Geneva Conventions: "Persons taking no active part in the hostilities" receive a special protection. Some authors interpret this provision in a way that defines fighters as only those per-

---

183 Abi-Saab, in: Delissen/ Tanja (eds.), at 216.

184 *See e.g.* International Institute of Humanitarian Law, *San Remo Manual*, para. 1.1.2.

185 Compare Articles 4 and 5 of the 1977 Additional Protocol II.

186 Dahl, 43 *Rev. dr. mil.* (2004), at 144.

sons who take active part in hostilities:[187] "In internal armed conflicts also, it is generally evident who is in fact involved in acts of violence and who is not."[188]

This assessment is attractive as it creates no special difficulty in distinguishing fighters from civilians. On the other hand, it would restrict the opposing party – in most cases the government – to fighting against these fighters only when they are actually fighting and create an imbalance between the parties to the conflict.[189] If this were true, there would be no difference between these fighters and civilians, who may – as will be examined thoroughly *infra*[190] – also be opposed while taking direct part in hostilities. This similar – if not same – treatment is understood to be fudging the differences of civilians and fighters and thus to weaken the principles regarding the protection of civilians.[191]

b) Group Membership as the Criterion

This critique can be circumvented to a certain degree by including a – at least more – permanent aspect. Other authors are of the opinion that active participation may be the starting point, but persons should not only be regarded as fighters for such time as they take direct part in hostilities. The participation rather shows that they belong to a group that takes part in the hostilities. Now, as long as an armed conflict continues, members of this group – subject to the conditions developed above – are regarded as fighters and thus may be targeted, even while

---

187 Rodley, *Treatment of Prisoners*, pp. 152-153; *see also* Kenneth W. Watkin, *Combatants, Unprivileged Belligerents and Conflicts in the 21st Century*, Cambridge 2003, pp. 9-10.

188 Gasser, in: Fleck (ed.), *Handbook*, at 210 (para. 501.2).

189 *See also* Henckaerts/ Doswald-Beck (eds.), *Humanitarian Law*, Vol. 1, p. 21.

190 *See infra*, Part Two, Chapter D) II. 1. c).

191 Kretzmer, 16 *Eur. J. Int'l L.* (2005), at 198; Michael N. Schmitt, 'The Principle of Discrimination in 21st Century Warfare', 2 *Yale Hum. Rts. & Dev. L.J.* (1999), pp. 143-182, at 160-161; Dinstein, 32 *Isr. Yb. Hum. Rts.* (2002), at 249.

not directly engaged in hostilities. Other persons are civilians. They may only be targeted while they take direct part in the hostilities.[192]

The UN Human Rights Inquiry Commission seems to support this approach. It found that the combatant status of certain targeted persons was only shown "unconvincing for two related reasons; they were not participating in the hostilities at the time they were killed; and no evidence was provided ... to back up [the] contentions of a combat role despite their civilian appearance."[193] Nevertheless, difficulties may arise in this approach concerning the evidence required to establish that the person in question was in fact a combatant. In many cases this evidence will have to be based on intelligence information.[194] However, it is not necessarily required to provide such evidence in advance. The same problem of evidence arises in the context of self-defence taken by a State; this right is not subordinated to a prior demonstration i.e. to the United Nations Security Council that it is legal under international law.[195] Parallel to the requirement developed by the European Court of Human Rights in *McCann*,[196] the State may react with force, but must be able to prove later, that the force used was justified.

This mode of distinction still runs the risk of not being consistent as it does not include the requirement of a distinctive emblem or sign as required by the 1949 Geneva Convention III. Thus, using this approach, a certain degree of evidence would be needed to support the appraisal that the person in question is a fighter involved in a respective group.[197] Evidence that will in many cases be based on intelligence information

---

[192] Fionnuala D. Ní Aoláin, *The Politics of Force: Conflict Management and State Violence in Northern Ireland*, Belfast 2000, p. 239; Kretzmer, 16 *Eur. J. Int'l L.* (2005), at 199.

[193] UN Comm'n H.R., *Question of the Violation of Human Rights in the Occupied Arab Territories, including Palestine – Report of the Human Rights Inquiry Commission established pursuant to Commission Resolution S-5/1 of 19 October 2000*, UN Doc. E/CN.4/2001/121 (March 16, 2001), p. 19 (para. 62); *compare also* ICRC, *Interpretive Guidance*, Geneva 2009, pp. 71-73 ("continuous combat function").

[194] Kretzmer, 16 *Eur. J. Int'l L.* (2005), at 199.

[195] *Compare e.g.* Thomas M. Franck, 'Terrorism and the Right of Self-Defense', in: 95 *Am. J. Int'l L.* (2001), pp. 839-842, at 842.

[196] *Compare Supra*, Part One, Chapter E) I. 2 b).

[197] Kretzmer, 16 *Eur. J. Int'l L.* (2005), at 199.

and, according to *Kretzmer*, should not be laid open necessarily in advance.[198] Another proposal to substitute the requirement of military insignia is to replace it by the open carrying of weapons.[199]

c) Discussion

As a consequence of the second assessment, i.e. if States are allowed to attack fighters while they are not taking active part in hostilities, this could amount to a license to kill members of a rebel or insurgent group. States could choose the best of both worlds; in non-international armed conflict, they do not have to grant prisoner-of-war status to captured fighters, but can attack them whenever and wherever they wish to.[200]

On the other hand, the consequence of the first assessment would be that there is no difference between civilians and fighters. This does not automatically mean that the protection of civilians is in danger; the principle of distinction shall serve the protection of civilians from attack. This aim does not suffer if the protection of fighters is increased. If both are protected in the same manner and may only be opposed while directly taking part in hostilities, the protection of civilians does not suffer necessarily. Especially in situations in which it is likely that fighters and civilians are confused due to the absence of a distinctive sign, an identical – high – level of protection may be the only possibility to achieve the protection necessary for civilians. It may even serve the principle of distinction if fighters who look like civilians may not be attacked. Additionally, as fighters in a non-international armed conflicts do not enjoy combatant immunity and prisoner-of-war status if captured by the adversary, distinction may be of minor importance. However, as the opposing party to the conflict according to this approach

---

[198] Interestingly, Kretzmer relies on a statement by Thomas Franck in this context: "[T]he right of a state to defend itself against attack is not subordinated in law to *prior* requirement to demonstrate to the satisfaction of the Security Council that it is acting against the party guilty of attack. The law does have an evidentiary requirement, but it arises, not before, the right to self-defence is exercised." *see* Franck, 95 *Am. J. Int'l L.* (2001), at 842. Kretzmer, however, applies this statement "in the course of an armed conflict", *see* Kretzmer, 16 *Eur. J. Int'l L.* (2005), at 199 (footnote 136).

[199] Detter, *Law of War*, p. 146.

[200] Kretzmer, 16 *Eur. J. Int'l L.* (2005), at 200.

would be very restricted in confronting fighters, the general level of protection would very likely suffer. As *Dinstein* phrased it:

> Should nothing be theoretically permissible to a belligerent engaged in war, ultimately everything will be permissible in practice – because the rules will be ignored.[201]

This must not necessarily hold true in an absolute manner, but the danger of a tendency towards a reduced overall level of protection does exist. It is difficult to imagine that government armed forces should not be allowed to attack rebel or insurgent forces if they are organised like regular armed forces, e.g. living in barracks or camps and have a military infrastructure, etc. Active and direct participation cannot be the only criterion in that regard.[202]

The first approach furthermore is contradictory to the fact that common Article 3 of the 1949 Geneva Conventions applies to persons who "have laid down their arms and those placed hors de combat" and thus refers to a definite or at least a longer period of non-participation in hostilities. The general understanding behind this resembles that of the defining criteria in 1977 Additional Protocol II; there is indeed a distinction between civilians and fighters. Such a distinction is usually based on a permanent status, such as the membership to a group, and not on temporary behaviour. It also rather refers to group characteristics than to exclusively individual characteristics.[203]

3. Conclusion

The degree of involvement into an organisation which takes part in the hostilities seems to be an at least practicable criterion in distinguishing civilians and fighters in non-international armed conflicts. To establish this involvement, intelligence information, military insignia or at least the fact that a person carries certain arms may be sufficient. However, if it is possible to attack fighters while not taking direct part in hostilities, the distinguishing criteria must be applied strictly, i.e. in a way to re-

---

201 Dinstein, *Conduct of Hostilities*, pp. 1-2.

202 *See also* Henckaerts/ Doswald-Beck (eds.), *Humanitarian Law*, Vol. 1, p. 21.

203 *Compare* Watkin, *Combatants*, pp. 9-10.

duce the group of fighters to clear cases.[204] This culminates in the maxim *in dubio pro* civilian status. Such an assessment does not restrain the opposing belligerent in a dangerous manner. In cases of doubt, the person in question may still be opposed if it takes direct part in hostilities and thus poses a direct threat.[205] Thus, persons who cannot be identified evidently as members of a belligerent organisation should be treated as civilians.[206] However, as will be developed *infra*, the protection that applies to fighters in internal armed conflicts is not identical with that applicable to combatants in international armed conflicts.

III. Protection of Combatants and Fighters

Even though combatants and fighters may generally be made the object of attack both in international and non-international armed conflicts,[207] they may not be targeted in an unrestricted manner by any means. It is – *inter alia* – prohibited to resort to perfidy, to attack persons who are *hors de combat* and to carry out executions without previous judgment.

1. Prohibition of Perfidy

Killing – as well as injuring or capturing – an adversary by resort to perfidy is prohibited in international as well as in non-international armed conflicts.[208] *Immanuel Kant* expressed the necessity to refrain from acts that make it impossible for the parties to a conflict to trust each other in a future peace. He referred to – *inter alia* – the use of

---

204 *See also* Doswald-Beck, 88 *Int'l Rev. Red Cross* (2006), No. 864, at 891.

205 *See infra*, Part Two, Chapter D) II. 1. c).

206 *Compare* ICRC, *Interpretive Guidance*, Geneva 2009, pp. 74-76.

207 This general rule is disputed by some authors who regard the direct participation of a person in a non-international armed conflict as decisive, and not group membership, *compare* Doswald-Beck, 88 *Int'l Rev. Red Cross* (2006), No. 864, at 889-890.

208 Henckaerts/ Doswald-Beck (eds.), *Humanitarian Law*, Vol. 1, pp. 221-223 (Rule 65); Melzer, in: Gill/ Fleck (eds.), at 295-296 (paras. 17.04.16-17.04.18).

"Meuchelmörder" (assassins) and "Brechen der Kapitulation" (infringement of surrender).[209]

Perfidy can affect the legality of a killing in different manners. First, the killing may be perfidious *per se* due to the fact that an individual person is targeted at all. Second, it can be perfidious due to the status of the targeted person. And third, even in cases in which it is justified to kill a certain person, the means employed may be illegal due to perfidy.

a) General Definition of Perfidy

Hugo Grotius, one of the first authors to address ruses of war and perfidy,[210] identified the intention to betray the adversary's confidence as the core element of perfidy.[211] Such considerations then rather concerned *Staatsraison* and reputable conduct by States as the reason for the prohibition of perfidy as *Kant* understood it.[212] It follows from the generally acknowledged legal maxim that the requirements of *bona fide* must be observed in international practice.[213] Today, perfidy is charac-

---

[209] "Es soll sich kein Staat im Kriege mit einem andern solche Feindseligkeiten erlauben, welche das wechselseitige Zutrauen im künftigen Frieden unmöglich machen müssen: als da sind, Anstellung der *Meuchelmörder* (percussores), *Giftmischer* (venefici), *Brechung* der *Kapitulation*, *Anstiftung* des *Verraths* (perduellio) in dem bekriegten Staat etc.", Immanuel Kant, *Zum ewigen Frieden. Ein philosophischer Entwurf*, Königsberg 1795, p. 12; *see also* Johann Caspar Bluntschli, *Das moderne Völkerrecht der civilisierten Staaten als Rechtsbuch dargestellt*, Nördlingen 1868, p. 313 (para. 561).

[210] Earlier writings by Thomas Aquinus, Francisco Suárez and Alberico Gentili expressed similar thoughts in connection with the moral of stratagems, *compare* George P. Politakis, 'Stratagems and the Prohibition of Perfidy with a Special Reference to the Laws of War at Sea', in: 45 *ÖZöRV* (1993), pp. 253-308, at 261-262.

[211] Hugo Grotius, *De Iure Belli ac Pacis Libri III in quibus ius naturae et gentium, item iuris publici praecipua explicantur*, Parisiis 1625, Chapter IV, paras. XVIII. 1-6; English translation reprinted in: Leon Friederman (ed.), *The law of War: A Documentary History*, Vol. 1, pp. 16-149, at 38-41.

[212] Wolfgang Voit, 'Humanitäre Aspekte der Regeln über Perfidie und Kriegslist', in: 22 *NZWehrR* (1980), pp. 19-25, at 23; on the historical development *see* Politakis, 45 *ÖZöRV* (1993), at 257-265.

[213] Dieter Fleck, 'Ruses of War and Prohibition of Perfidy', in: 13 *Rev. dr. pén. mil.* (1974), pp. 269-314, at 277.

terized by the abuse of the opponents confidence in the protection provided by international law.[214] The element of betrayal is still the central part of the definition as given in Article 37 para. 1 of the 1977 Additional Protocol I:

> It is prohibited to kill, injure or capture an adversary by resort to perfidy. Acts inviting the confidence of an adversary to lead him to believe that he is entitled to, or is obliged to accord, protection under the rules of international law applicable in armed conflict, with intent to betray that confidence, shall constitute perfidy.[215]

But the background has changed due to the humanitarian character of the 1949 Geneva Conventions and the 1977 Additional Protocols. It now rather refers to the application of the rules.[216] It protects the trust in the protection by international humanitarian law and the readiness to respect it.[217] A main danger of a betrayal of this trust is that it will reduce the adversary's willingness to honour the humanitarian rules. Article 37 para. 1, 2nd sentence of the 1977 Additional Protocol I gives a complete definition of perfidy.[218] Cases that do not fall within this definition do not fall within Article 37 para. 1 1st sentence 1977 Additional Protocol I.[219] The second sentence covers two constellations:

First, it covers acts inviting the confidence of an adversary to lead him to believe that "he is entitled to ... protection". Examples for this constellation are difficult to find.[220] It does not refer to a person that actu-

---

214 Friedhelm Krüger-Sprengel, 'Kriegslist und Perfidieverbot – Völkerrechtliche Regeln für das Verhalten zwischen Kombattanten', in: 13 *NZWehrR* (1971), pp. 161-170, at 169.

215 *For earlier definitions compare e.g.* Krüger-Sprengel, 13 *NZWehrR* (1971), at 169; Dieter Fleck, 'Kriegslisten und Perfidieverbot', in: Dieter Fleck/ Michael Bothe (eds.), *Beiträge zur Weiterentwicklung des humanitären Völkerrechts für bewaffnete Konflikte*, Hamburg 1973, pp. 105-148; Oppenheim/ Lauterpacht, *International Law*, p. 430; *compare also* Henry Wager Halleck, *International Law or Rules Regulating the Intercourse of States in Peace and War*, San Francisco 1861, reprint: Amsterdam 1970, p. 400.

216 *Compare* Sandoz *et al.* (eds.), *Additional Protocols*, para. 1483 (p. 430).

217 Voit, 22 *NZWehrR* (1980), at 25.

218 On the drafting history of the articles concerning perfidy *see* Fleck, 13 *Rev. dr. pén. mil.* (1974), at 285-292.

219 Voit, 22 *NZWehrR* (1980), at 25.

220 *Id.*, at 24.

ally enjoys a certain protection but to a person that wrongly believes that he is protected in such a manner, while not being so objectively.

Second, it refers to acts inviting the confidence of an adversary to lead him to believe that his opponent is entitled to protection, whereas this is not true objectively, and the opponent betrays this belief. The examples given in the last part of Article 37 para. 1 of the 1977 Additional Protocol I refer exclusively to this second constellation, such as the feigning of truce or surrender, the feigning of incapacitation due to wounds, the use of the adversaries national flag, military uniforms or military badges[221]. Those examples that are relevant for the present examination will be addressed in detail *infra*.[222]

In both cases, in order to be perfidious, the act must be committed with the intent kill, injure or capture by means of the betrayal of confidence, intentions that are obviously given in the cases of targeted or preventive killings. Acts which are intended merely to save one's life, such as feigning death, are not perfidious, whereas the same act would be perfidious if performed with the intention to kill an enemy once he turned his back.[223]

The prohibition of perfidy can be classified as customary international law applicable in international and non-international armed conflicts.[224] It is contained in numerous military manuals and supported by official statements,[225] dating back to the Lieber Code, the Brussels Declaration[226] and the Oxford Manual.[227] Violations of this prohibition consti-

---

[221] *See already* Article 65 of the Lieber Code; Bluntschli, *Völkerrecht*, p. 315 (para. 565); Henckaerts/ Doswald-Beck (eds.), *Humanitarian Law*, Vol. 1, p. 170.

[222] *See infra*, Part Two, Chapter C) III. 1. c).

[223] *Compare* Politakis, 45 *ÖZöRV* (1993), at 268; for further examples *see* Hans-Peter Furrer, *Perfidie in der Geschichte und im heutigen Kriegsvölkerrecht*, Zürich 1988, pp. 82-83.

[224] Henckaerts/ Doswald-Beck (eds.), *Humanitarian Law*, Vol. 1, p. 221 (Rule 65); Krüger-Sprengel, 13 *NZWehrR* (1971), at 163. *Compare also* Dahl, 43 *Rev. dr. mil.* (2004), at 144.

[225] Henckaerts/ Doswald-Beck (eds.), *Humanitarian Law*, Vol. 1, p. 169. *See e.g.* UK Ministry of Defence, *Manual*, para. 5.9 (p. 59).

[226] Project of an International Declaration Concerning the Law and Customs of War, 1 *Am. J. Int'l L.* (1907), Supplement, pp. 96-103.

tute offences under the national legislation of numerous countries.[228] Article 37 of 1977 Additional Protocol I was designed to incorporate the prohibitions contained in Article 23 *lit.* b of the 1907 Hague Regulations.[229] And as Article 37 para. 2 of the Protocol, Article 24 of the Regulations consider ruses of war or stratagems as permitted.

b) Distinction of Perfidy and Ruses of War

To fully comprehend the prohibition of perfidy it is necessary to distinguish perfidious acts from ruses of war or stratagems. Neither of these acts were defined in the 1907 Hague Regulations. Whereas the former acts, as shown above, are traditionally prohibited, the latter acts are traditionally permitted, as was already declared in Article 14 of the Brussels Declaration.[230] This general admissibility of ruses in principle does not render any ruse of war permissible; ruses of war cease to be permissible if they infringe a recognised rule of international law.[231]

Ruses are acts intended to confuse the enemy.[232] The aim of a ruse of war is "luring the enemy to a wrong assessment".[233] Perfidy is a deliberate betrayal of another person's trust, especially in the protection provided by international law, whereas a ruse or deceit involves the ensnaring of another by guile or trickery.[234] As *Carl von Clausewitz* phrased it: "Der listige läßt denjenigen, welchen er betrügen will, die

---

[227] The Institute of International Law, *The Laws of War on Land*, reprinted in: Schindler/ Toman (eds.), *Collection*, pp. 36-48.

[228] Henckaerts/ Doswald-Beck (eds.), *Humanitarian Law*, Vol. 1, p. 169.

[229] Sandoz *et al.* (eds.), *Additional Protocols*, para. 1491 (p. 432); Bothe *et al.*, *1977 Protocols*, Art. 37 Prot. I, para. 2.3 (p. 203).

[230] On the history of ruses of war *see* Krüger-Sprengel, 13 *NZWehrR* (1971), at 164-168.

[231] Fleck, 13 *Rev. dr. pén. mil.* (1974), at 277; Henckaerts/ Doswald-Beck (eds.), *Humanitarian Law*, Vol. 1, p. 203 (Rule 57); UK Ministry of Defence, *Manual*, para. 5.17 (p. 64).

[232] Henckaerts/ Doswald-Beck (eds.), *Humanitarian Law*, Vol. 1, p. 204.

[233] Politakis, 45 *ÖZöRV* (1993), at 255.

[234] *Compare* Krüger-Sprengel, 13 *NZWehrR* (1971), at 169; *compare also* Reed L. Wadley, 'Treachery and Deceit: Parallels in Tribal and Terrorist Warfare?', in: 26 *Stud. Confl. Terror.* (2003), pp. 331-346, at 332.

Irrtümer des Verstandes selber begehen."[235] This principle has not been changed by the humanitarian character of the 1949 Geneva Conventions and the 1977 Additional Protocols. Still, Article 37 para. 2 of the 1977 Additional Protocol I accepts:

> Ruses of war are not prohibited. Such ruses are acts which are intended to mislead an adversary or to induce him to act recklessly but which infringe no rule of international law applicable in armed conflict and which are not perfidious because they do not invite the confidence of an adversary with respect to protection under that law. The following are examples of such ruses: the use of camouflage, decoys, mock operations and misinformation.

The prohibition of perfidy serves the protection of trust into standards and guarantees provided by international humanitarian law.[236] States were willing to accept such restrictions of their military possibilities that are absolutely necessary to achieve humanitarian aims – and thus mainly the protection of civilians. But, as the permission of ruses of war shows, States do not regard it as necessary to protect combatants from their own foolishness or carelessness.[237]

c) Prohibitions of Individual Perfidious Acts

The 1907 Hague Regulations do not contain a general prohibition of perfidy, but lay down an enumeration of prohibitions of singular perfidious acts in Article 23:

> it is especially forbidden … (b) To kill or wound treacherously individuals belonging to the hostile nation or army; … (f) To make improper use of a flag of truce, of the national flag or of the military insignia and uniform of the enemy, as well as the distinctive badges of the Geneva Convention;

The 1977 Additional Protocol I was drafted to fill this gap and provide for a definition in greater detail. However, it does not explicitly cover all aspects that are part of the Regulations' prohibition. Article 37 para. 1 of the 1977 Additional Protocol I gives the following examples:

---

[235] Furrer, *Perfidie*, p. 26.

[236] Voit, 22 *NZWehrR* (1980), at 22.

[237] *Id.*

> … The following acts are examples of perfidy: (a) the feigning of an intent to negotiate under a flag of truce or of a surrender; (b) the feigning of an incapacitation by wounds or sickness; (c) the feigning of civilian, non-combatant status; and (d) the feigning of protected status by the use of signs, emblems or uniforms of the United Nations or of neutral or other States not Parties to the conflict.[238]

This prohibition is undisputedly accepted as one of those norms on the conduct of hostilities which is a codification of customary international law.[239] The only innovation in relation to the 1907 Hague Regulations is the introduction of a prohibition of improper use of emblems and uniforms of the UN.[240]

(1) Targeted Killings Under a "Perfidious Cover"

A first group of perfidious acts is not perfidious *per se*, but is characterized as such by the means the acting person uses to get into the position of performing the act. This includes the feigning of civilian status, of wounds or sickness or the feigning of intent to negotiate or surrender under a flag of truce. The consequence of such conduct is that targeted killings, performed in the context or enabled by such conduct, violate international humanitarian law. Such action is of minor importance concerning the present examination, as the same standards as to any other act committed under such a "perfidious cover" apply. No special questions concerning targeted killings arise in that context:

---

238 *For earlier definitions compare e.g.* Krüger-Sprengel, 13 *NZWehrR* (1971), at 169; Fleck, in: Fleck/ Bothe (eds.), pp. 105-148; Oppenheim/ Lauterpacht, *International Law*, p. 430; *compare also* Halleck, *Intercourse of States*, p. 400.

239 Henckaerts/ Doswald-Beck (eds.), *Humanitarian Law*, Vol. 1, pp. 205-219 (Rules 58-63) and p. 224; International Committee of the Red Cross, *International Humanitarian Law and the Challenges of Contemporary Armed Conflicts*, Report prepared in September 2003 for the 28th International Conference of the Red Cross and Red Crescent, Geneva, December 2003, ICRC Doc. 03/ IC/09, p. 8.

240 Greenwood, in: Delissen/ Tanja (eds.), at 105.

(i) The Feigning of Civilian Status

In an international armed conflict, the feigning of civilian status is relatively unproblematic to identify; combatants and civilians are well defined and distinguishable.[241] If a combatant feigns civilian status and thus its foe must not expect a hostile act, targeted killings by this combatant are perfidious. The prohibition of feigning non-combatant status gives rise to special problems in the sphere of non international armed conflicts, as the distinction between fighters and civilians is blurred due to the character of the conflict.[242] 1977 Additional Protocol I tries to compensate this problem with regard to fighters in conflicts against colonial domination and alien occupation and against racist regimes in the exercise of their right of self-determination.[243] According to Article 44 para. 3 of that Protocol, weaker standards of distinction apply to such fighters in an internationalised armed conflict:

> Recognizing, however, that there are situations in armed conflicts where, owing to the nature of the hostilities an armed combatant cannot so distinguish himself, he shall retain his status as a combatant, provided that, in such situations, he carries his arms openly: (a) during each military engagement, and (b) during such time as he is visible to the adversary while he is engaged in a military deployment preceding the launching of an attack in which he is to participate.

The last sentence of this paragraph stipulates that such behaviour is not regarded as perfidious. The same holds true for internal conflicts; as shown above, a certain involvement in a belligerent group – be it assessed on the basis of intelligence information, military insignia or at least the fact that the person carries his arms openly – is necessary. If such distinguishing criterion is not visible while the person is engaged in an attack, the person does not distinguish itself from civilians and thus acts perfidious in the same manner.

(ii) The Improper Use of Flags and Symbols

The improper use of certain flags and symbols is prohibited by Article 23 *lit.* f of the 1907 Hague Regulations. This rule corresponds custom-

---

241 *Compare supra*, Part Two, Chapter B) I.

242 *Compare supra*, Part Two, Chapter B) II.

243 *See* Article 1 para. 2 of the 1977 Additional Protocol I.

ary international law.[244] According to Article 23 *lit.* f of the 1907 Hague Regulations and Article 37 *lit.* a of the 1977 Additional Protocol I it is prohibited to make improper use of the flag of truce, i.e. to feign an intent to negotiate or of a surrender under a flag of truce. Using the flag of truce[245] or signs that show the intent to surrender[246] in order to kill the adversary is perfidious in an internal as well as in an international armed conflict. This standard also applies to targeted killings. The same applies – according to Article 23 *lit.* f of the 1907 Hague Regulations – to the red cross and red crescent symbols. These emblems are by now covered in detail in Articles 38 and 39 of the 1949 Geneva Convention I.

The improper use of the national flag or of military insignia and uniforms of the enemy is prohibited by Article 23 *lit.* f of the 1907 Hague Regulations. However, the phrasing "to make improper use" shows that it does not prohibit any use, but only improper use.[247] Thus, the true scope of the prohibition depends on the question under which circumstances the use of the said objects is permissible. This is less clear regarding the national flag of the enemy, as it argued that its use it nor prohibited in an absolute manner. It is undisputed that the use in combat of national flag or of military insignia and uniforms of the enemy is – and always was – perfidious.[248] However, based on the terminology "improper use", some argue that there is a "proper use" outside direct combat, e.g. to improve its position in the field.[249] But the question

---

[244] *See* Valentine Jobst III, 'Is the Wearing of the Enemy's Uniform a Violation of the Laws of War?', in: 35 *Am. J. Int'l L.* (1941), pp. 435-442, at 440.

[245] Michael Gimmerthal, *Kriegslist und Perfidieverbot im Zusatzprotokoll vom 10. Juni 1977 zu den vier Genfer Rotkreuz-Abkommen von 1949 (Zusatzprotokoll I)*, Bochum 1990, p. 92.

[246] Gimmerthal, *Kriegslist*, p. 95.

[247] Fleck, 13 *Rev. dr. pén. mil.* (1974), at 279; *see already* Bluntschli, *Völkerrecht*, p. 315 (para. 565), who regards the use of false flags as permitted until the "real clash" of the enemy forces. "Die List ist im Kriege erlaubt und daher auch die Täuschung des Feindes nicht völkerrechtswidrig, sogar nicht die Täuschung durch Uniformen, Fahnen und Flaggen. Vor dem wirklichen Zusammenstoß muß jeder Heereskörper unter seiner wharen Fahne und Flagge erscheinen und darf nur als offenbarer Feind fechten."

[248] Gimmerthal, *Kriegslist*, p. 134.

[249] *Compare* the references id.

whether such a distinction exists or not does not affect the legality of the hostile act itself. If performed under the national flag or of military insignia and uniforms of the enemy, such hostile acts are perfidious in an international as well as in an internal context. This includes targeted killings.

The same applies to the use of booby traps – in an international and non-international context[250] – as a means to kill a combatant. The United Nations Conference on Prohibitions or Restrictions of Use of Certain Conventional Weapons passed the Protocol on Prohibitions or Restrictions on the Use of Mines, Booby Traps and Other Devices.[251] This protocol in Article 2 para. 4 defines as a booby trap

> any device or material which is designed, constructed or adapted to kill or injure, and which functions unexpectedly when a person disturbs or approaches an apparently harmless object or performs an apparently safe act.

An "apparently safe act" would for example be opening a door – which is booby trapped.[252] The use of booby traps in a prohibited manner is perfidious.[253] This principle is further specified in Article 7 of the Protocol on Prohibitions or Restrictions on the Use of Mines, Booby Traps and Other Devices. Its para. 1 prohibits the perfidious use of booby traps, especially to attaché or associate them with internationally recognised protective emblems, signs or signals, sick, wounded or dead persons, burial or cremation sites or graves or medical facilities, medical

---

[250] *Compare* Theodor Meron, 'Cassese's Tadić and the Law of Non-International Armed Conflicts', in: Lal Chand Vohrah *et al.* (eds.), *Man's Inhumanity to Man – Essays on International Law in Honour of Antonio Cassese*, The Hague 2003, pp. 533-538, at 537.

[251] Protocol on Prohibitions or Restrictions on the Use of Mines, Booby Traps and Other Devices as amended on May 3, 1996 (Protocol II to the 1980 Convention as amended on 3 May 1996), entry into force December 3, 1998, U.N. Doc. CCW/CONF.I/16, Part I, Annex B (pp. 14-32), reprinted in: 35 *ILM* (1996), pp. 1209-1218.

[252] Anthony P.V. Rogers, 'A Commentary on the Protocol on Prohibitions or Restrictions on the Use of Mines, Booby-Traps and Other Devices', in: 26 *Rev. dr. pén. mil.* (1987), pp. 185-206, at 190.

[253] Henckaerts/ Doswald-Beck (eds.), *Humanitarian Law*, Vol. 1, pp. 278-279 (Rule 80); Sandoz *et al.* (eds.), *Protocoles additionnels*, para. 1519 (p. 447); on the use of booby traps against civilians *see infra*, Part Two, Chapter D) II. 1. e).

equipment, medical supplies or medical transportation *et cetera*. However, the use of booby traps against combatants is not prohibited in an absolute manner and are in certain circumstances regarded as legitimate means of warfare.[254] Obviously, the same prohibitions apply to booby traps as to all weapons; they may not be designed to cause superfluous injury or unnecessary suffering[255] and may not be used in an indiscriminate manner.[256]

(2) Killings Rendered Perfidious Due to the Status of the Targeted Person

The status of the targeted person can also render targeted killings perfidious. This generally applies to civilians,[257] as the prohibition of perfidy is strongly interrelated with the prohibition to kill civilians due to their protected status.[258] It also applies to civilian leaders of the adversary. Traditionally, killing civil representatives of the adversary was regarded as perfidious and thus prohibited – even before perfidy was codified in the 1907 Hague Regulations.[259] Even though this kind of killings are not uncommon,[260] they are also covered by the prohibition to kill civilians.[261] An exception must be made if members of the government are concerned that have combatant status, or if the person in

---

[254] *See* Parks, 19 *Army Lawyer* (December 1989), No. 204, at 5; UK Ministry of Defence, *Manual*, para. 6.7 (p. 105); Dinstein, *Conduct of Hostilities*, p. 66.

[255] *Compare* Article 3 para. 3 of the Protocol on Prohibitions or Restrictions on the Use of Mines, Booby Traps and Other Devices.

[256] Rogers, 26 *Rev. dr. pén. mil.* (1987), at 187 and 192.

[257] Fleck, 13 *Rev. dr. pén. mil.* (1974), at 278.

[258] *Compare infra*, Part Two, Chapter C) II 1. a).

[259] Gimmerthal, *Kriegslist*, p. 83.

[260] In Iraq, the U.S. announced a policy to target members of the Baath Party. Mere membership in a political party, whatever its dogma might be, does not render a person a legitimate target. The U.S. policy to target these members is illegal and a grave breach of the Geneva Conventions, *compare* Dougherty/Quénivet, 16 *HuV-I* (2003), at 195.

[261] *Compare* Leslie C. Green, *The Contemporary Law of Armed Conflict*, Manchester 1993, p. 137.

question is not targeted personally, but stays in a military objective.[262] While the latter case does not qualify as a targeted killing, no special rules apply to the former cases. However, the targeted killing of military leaders of the adversary is not perfidious. They are combatants and do not possess special protection due to their military rank. They are thus legitimate targets in any armed conflict.[263] Nevertheless, it is perfidious to kill such leaders if they are under special protection, e.g. during truce and peace negotiations.[264]

(3) Killings by Perfidious Means

It is perfidious to instigate enemy combatants to kill their own superiors, to recruit hired killers, to place a price on the head of an adversary,[265] or to offer a reward for his capture "dead or alive".[266] Already according to Article 148 of the Lieber Code "[c]ivilized nations look with horror upon offers of rewards for the assassination of enemies as relapses into barbarism." This prohibition is covered by Article 23 *lit.* b of the 1907 Hague Regulations,[267] but has not explicitly been included into Article 37 of the 1977 Additional Protocol I.[268] However, as the rules on perfidy were not aimed to replace the 1907 Hague Regulations, but were concerned with developing them, it is clear that the prohibition as formulated in Article 23 *lit.* b of the 1907 Hague Regulations has

---

262 *Compare supra*, Part Two, Chapter C) and *infra*, Part Two, Chapter D) II. 2. respectively.

263 Gimmerthal, *Kriegslist*, p. 84; Sassòli, in: Wippman/ Evangelista (eds.), at 202-203; Examples would be the U.S. President, the Secretary of Defense, and the Secretaries of the various armed forces who are all part of the military chain of command and thus legitimate targets, *see* Dougherty/ Quénivet, 16 *HuV-I* (2003), at 195.

264 Wadley, 26 *Stud. Confl. Terror.* (2003), at 336.

265 *See already* Bluntschli, *Völkerrecht*, pp. 313-314 (paras. 561-563); Gimmerthal, *Kriegslist*, pp. 50 and 80. Examples of this practice are those of the US in relation to Manuel Noriega in 1989 and to Mohamed Farah Aidid in Somalia in 1993, *see* Green, *Law of Armed Conflict*, p. 137.

266 Morris Greenspan, *Modern Law of Warfare*, Berkeley 1959, p. 317; UK Ministry of Defence, *Manual*, para. 5.14 (p. 62).

267 Gimmerthal, *Kriegslist*, pp. 84-85.

268 Bothe *et al.*, *1977 Protocols*, Art. 37 Prot. I, para. 2.4.1 (p. 204).

survived in its entirety.[269] Thus, if a person that can be targeted legally is killed by such means, the killing is perfidious. This does not include the use of snipers; their use is not prohibited as such, but they may only target military objectives.[270] some authors are of the opinion that a killing based on intelligence information which is gathered through collaborators by use of threat, extortion and or fraudulence would render a killing treacherous.[271] However, the possible illegality of the gathering of information does not render the action later based on that information illegal.[272] There is no "Fruit of the Poisoned Tree" doctrine in relation to perfidy. However, it is prohibited to offer rewards for the killing of all enemies or of a class of enemy persons, such as officers. However, the background of such a prohibition is the danger of leading to a "no quarter" policy and not perfidy.[273]

(4) Other Perfidious or Treacherous Killings

The prohibition to kill or wound treacherously as laid down in Article 23 *lit.* b of the 1907 Hague Regulations is an example of a prohibited perfidious act. The term treacherously was debated in the drafting process of the 1907 Hague Regulations. It was discussed, whether this term should be replaced by "perfidiously", but treacherously was kept because it is part of the English equivalent to the German "Meuchelmord", the phrase "murder by treachery".[274]

Even though treachery, as construed by early scholars, may be broader than the concept of perfidy, the same basic criteria that are used to distinguish lawful ruses from unlawful perfidies can be applied to determinations of treachery.[275] A treacherous as well as a perfidious murder is based on the unsuspiciousness and defencelessness of the adversary.

---

269 Sandoz *et al.* (eds.), *Additional Protocols*, para. 1488 (p. 431).

270 UK Ministry of Defence, *Manual*, para. 5.12 (p. 62).

271 *See e.g.* Stein, 17 *Ethics & Int'l Aff.* (2003), at 127.

272 Kremnitzer, in: Fleck (ed.), *Rechtsfragen*, at 205.

273 *Compare* UK Ministry of Defence, *Manual*, para. 5.14.1 and footnote 51 (p. 62).

274 Furrer, *Perfidie*, p. 45.

275 Schmitt, 17 *Yale J. Int'l L.* (1999), at 617.

Such behaviour takes advantage of the good faith, i.e. of the trust and confidence of individuals belonging to the hostile army or nation.[276]

This would e.g. apply to civilians not engaged in the hostilities who are generally protected by humanitarian law. Regarding combatants outside a direct confrontation, "the lack of suspicion would be tantamount to impardonable recklessness."[277] A combatant can only rely on good faith in those exceptional cases in which hostile acts are prohibited due to a special relation between him and his adversary.[278] Examples are those shown above, e.g. hostile acts against wounded soldiers or prisoners of war, which are obviously also covered by special rules, and in the other direction, the prohibition on prisoners of war to engage in belligerent acts.[279]

From the seventeenth century onwards, legal scholars tended to regard assassinations as treacherous and forbidden acts, involving a breach of trust or violations of the basic "rules of the game" incumbent on belligerent parties to times of war. This should enable representatives of States to conduct negotiations without being assassinated and reflects considerations of chivalry.[280] It also reflects the understanding as expressed by *Rousseau*: "La guerre n'est donc point une relation d'homme à homme, mais une relation d'État à État".[281]

It is thus a mere coincidence that single persons are enemies – not as human beings or citizens – but as combatants. War is a-personal since it takes place between anonymous soldiers who harbour no personal animosity towards another. They kill and are killed as the representatives of the belligerent States.[282] According to this understanding, a targeted killing of a specific person *qua person* would be *per se* a treacherous.[283]

---

276 Fleck, 13 *Rev. dr. pén. mil.* (1974), at 278; Furrer, *Perfidie*, p. 46.

277 Fleck, 13 *Rev. dr. pén. mil.* (1974), at 278.

278 *Id.*

279 *Id.*, at 278-279.

280 Kremnitzer, in: Fleck (ed.), *Rechtsfragen*, at 204; Zengel, 134 *Mil. L. Rev.* (1991), at 130.

281 Jean-Jacques Rousseau, *Du contrat social*, Paris 1754, Book I, Chapter 4.

282 Kremnitzer, in: Fleck (ed.), *Rechtsfragen*, at 204-205; Krüger-Sprengel, 13 *NZWehrR* (1971), at 167.

283 *But see* U.S. Department of the Army, Field Manual No. 27-10, Article 31; Parks, 19 *Army Lawyer* (December 1989), No. 204, at 5.

However, the assessment of the prohibition of treacherous killings has changed; it still prohibits putting a price upon an enemy's head, as well as offering a reward for an enemy "dead or alive".[284] But it does not prohibit attacks on individual soldiers or officers of the enemy whether in the zone of hostilities, occupied territory, or elsewhere, as long as they are not *hors de combat*.[285] Thus, the targeting of an individual combatant is not *per se* illegal[286] and does not constitute what some refer to as a "wartime assassination". Such an "assassination" would consist of an additional element, i.e. the targeting of an individual *and* the use of treacherous means,[287] or any other aspect concerning the targeted person or the person executing the assassination to make it illegal.[288]

2. *Prohibition to kill Persons* hors de combat

> [O]ne might argue that the whole secret of the law of war lies in the respect for a disarmed man.[289]

This respect is reflected – as indicated above – in the fact that the possibility to target a combatant lawfully ends as soon as he is *hors de combat*. This rule is codified in Article 41 para. 1 of the 1977 Additional Protocol I and represents customary international law applicable both in international and non-international armed conflicts.[290] It has already been laid down in Article 23 *lit.* c of the 1907 Hague Regulations and is one of the most important rules of international humanitarian law.[291] It is also implied in Article 4 of the 1949 Geneva Convention III, which

---

284 Henckaerts/ Doswald-Beck (eds.), *Humanitarian Law*, Vol. 1, pp. 225-226 with further references.

285 Watkin, 15 *Duke J. Comp. & Int'l L.* (2005), at 310.

286 UK Ministry of Defence, *Manual*, para. 5.13 (p. 62).

287 Schmitt, 17 *Yale J. Int'l L.* (1999), at 632; Elizabeth B. Bazan, 'Assassination Ban and E.O. 12333: A Brief Summary', in: *CRS Report For Congress*, RS21037, Updated January 4, 2002, p. 4.

288 *See* UK Ministry of Defence, *Manual*, para. 5.13 (p. 62).

289 Sandoz *et al.* (eds.), *Additional Protocols*, para. 1601 (p. 480).

290 *See e.g.* Greenwood, in: Delissen/ Tanja (eds.), at 106; Henckaerts/ Doswald-Beck (eds.), *Humanitarian Law*, Vol. 1, p. 164 (Rule 47); *compare also* UK Ministry of Defence, *Manual*, para. 5.6 (p. 57).

291 Sandoz *et al.* (eds.), *Additional Protocols*, para. 1601 (p. 480).

refers to combatants who "have fallen into the power of the enemy." However, it was necessary to define more exactly the moment in which a combatant who may be attacked becomes *hors de combat* and may not be attacked any more. Article 41 prohibits the attack on an enemy from the moment that he is rendered *hors de combat* and with no time-limit. Thus, the provision even protects prisoners of war,[292] whose security is mainly dealt with in the 1949 Geneva Convention III. But a person who is *hors de combat* is protected even before having fallen into the power of his adversary.[293]

The protection applies – without exceptions – to combatants and those combatants who are considered to be irregular.[294] The same holds true for fighters in non-international armed conflicts according to the minimum standards as laid down in common Article 3 of the 1949 Geneva Conventions.[295] It also applies to persons who do not have the right to participate directly in hostilities, such as civilians, medical and religious personnel of the armed forces, persons who accompany the armed forces without actually being members thereof, and military personnel assigned to civil defence. In its para. 2, Article 41 of the 1977 Additional Protocol I gives a definition of *hors de combat*:

> A person is hors de combat if: (a) he is in the power of an adverse Party; (b) he clearly expresses an intention to surrender; or (c) he has been rendered unconscious or is otherwise incapacitated by wounds or sickness, and therefore is incapable of defending himself; provided that in any of these cases he abstains from any hostile act and does not attempt to escape.

Thus, first persons are considered to be *hors de combat* if they are in the power of an adverse party. This does not only cover persons having been apprehended, but also – as a formal surrender is not always realistically possible or even prohibited by the national rules of some armies

---

[292] *See also* UK Ministry of Defence, *Manual*, para.5.6, footnote 27 (p. 57).

[293] Fischer, in: Fleck (ed.), *Handbook*, at 334 (para. 705); Sandoz *et al.* (eds.), *Additional Protocols*, para. 1602 (p. 481).

[294] Sandoz *et al.* (eds.), *Additional Protocols*, para. 1606 (p. 483).

[295] Dinstein, in: Meron (ed.), at 350; UK Ministry of Defence, *Manual*, paras. 15.10-15.10.1 (p. 389).

– persons who have exhausted all means of defence. A defenceless adversary is thus *hors de combat*.[296] This also includes

> any unarmed soldier, whether he is surprised in his sleep by the adversary, on leave or in any other similar situation. Obviously the safeguard only applies as long as the person concerned abstains from any hostile act and does not attempt to escape.[297]

This group of persons is especially relevant in the field of targeted killings, as it does not only include persons who surrender, but also persons who do not pose any immediate threat to their adversaries either any more – due to exhaustion of their means of defence – or at the moment they are targeted – due to being guileless and defenceless at such a time. While the immediacy of a threat posed by a combatant usually is not a criterion in deciding whether this person may be targeted under international humanitarian law, it rises at least in situations in which the threat is so marginal or even non-existing that the person has to be regarded *hors de combat*.

Second, combatants who surrender are *hors de combat* if the surrender is unconditional, which means that the only claim those who are surrendering can make is to be treated as prisoners of war. If the intention to surrender is indicated in an absolutely clear manner, the adversary must cease fire immediately. He may not refuse unconditional surrender.[298] Such a situation is rather unlikely to occur in relation to a targeted killing, as such a killing will in most cases will rely on surprise and does not leave the targeted person with the possibility to surrender. On the other hand, if the targeted person perceives that his situation is desperate and thus surrenders, the attack upon him has to be stopped due to him then being *hors de combat*.

Third, incapacitated persons are *hors de combat*. The mere fact that a combatant is wounded does not *per se* mean that he is incapacitated. He might continue to fight, but is *hors de combat* if he surrenders or if he becomes incapable of fighting due to his wounds.[299] In that regard, a person who is targeted individually does not differ from any other combatant who is wounded.

---

[296] Sandoz *et al.* (eds.), *Additional Protocols*, para. 1612 (p. 484).

[297] *Id.*, para. 1614 (p. 485).

[298] *Id.*, para. 1619 (p. 487).

[299] UK Ministry of Defence, *Manual*, para. 5.6.1 (p. 58).

Once a person is *hors de combat*, it is specifically prohibited to deliberately make that person a target. However, this does not necessarily mean that these persons could not be victims of attacks that are not directed at them, but affect them as collateral damage.[300] Such cases do not constitute targeted killings in relation to that person, but if they are a side-effect to the targeted killing of another person, they can render the latter killing illegal.[301]

3. Prohibition to Carry Out Executions without Previous Judgement

According to Article 3 para. 1 *lit.* d common to the 1949 Geneva Conventions "the carrying out of executions without previous judgment pronounced by a regularly constituted court, affording all the judicial guarantees which are recognized as indispensable by civilized peoples" is prohibited. The imposition of a death sentence has further limits concerning the age of the convicted person, pregnant women and mothers of young children and fair trial guarantees. However, these conditions are not of great relevance as targeted killings already lack a conviction under a fair trial. If these criteria are not met, similar to the situation under human rights law, penal aspects cannot justify targeted killings.[302]

4. Further Limits that Apply to Any Attack

Acts against combatants or fighters that are not prohibited due to the rules laid out above can nevertheless be illegal if they violate other principles of international humanitarian law, i.e. the basic principles mentioned at the beginning of that part.[303] In that regard, the principles of military necessity and proportionality are of special interest:

According to the former principle, a belligerent shall only use that degree and kind of force that is required in order to achieve the legitimate purpose of the conflict, namely the complete or partial submission of the enemy at the earliest possible moment with the minimum expendi-

---

300 Sandoz *et al.* (eds.), *Additional Protocols*, para. 1605 (p. 482).

301 *Compare infra*, Part Two, Chapter D) II. 2. b).

302 *See also* Gross, *Struggle of Democracy*, pp. 221 and 229.

303 *See supra*, Part Two, Chapter B).

ture of life and resources.[304] This principle means that a targeted killing of a specific combatant or fighter must be required to subdue the adversary. If it is not necessary, the principle of humanity prohibits such superfluous action.[305] This principle is part of several prohibitions that have been discussed *supra*. It is e.g. not necessary to kill a person hors de combat as this person does not constitute a hindrance to the submission of the enemy any more. This can be transferred to the whole conflict; it is not necessary to kill any further enemy combatant if the opponent party capitulates or has no further means to defend itself. In such an situation, any further attack on adversaries would run the risk of developing into a "no quarter" policy. Whenever the goal of the conflict is reached, the principle of military necessity demands that the hostilities are halted. The prohibition of weapons that cause unnecessary suffering is also aimed at minimising the loss of life during military operations.[306]

According to the principle of proportionality, the losses resulting from a military action should not be excessive in relation to the expected military advantage.[307] This principle entails parts of what is also covered by the principle of military necessity, namely the contribution of an attack to reaching the goal of subduing the adversary.[308] In the context of armed conflicts, this does not amount to a strict positive duty to choose the mildest still effective means, as in the human rights sphere.[309] But there are tendencies to introduce a further reaching principle of proportionality to the question of targeting. This could amount to a duty of using non-lethal weapons where they are of equal effectiveness.[310] This

---

[304] UK Ministry of Defence, *Manual*, para. 2.2 (pp. 21-22); Greenwood, in: Fleck (ed.), *Handbook*, at 30 (para. 130).

[305] *Compare supra*, Part Two, Chapter B) II.

[306] Vera Gowlland-Debbas, 'The Right to Life and Genocide: The Court and an International Public Policy', in: Laurence Boisson de Chazournes/ Philippe Sands (eds.), *International Law, the International Court of Justice, and Nuclear Weapons*, Cambridge 1999, pp. 315-337, at 322.

[307] UK Ministry of Defence, *Manual*, para. 2.6 (p. 25).

[308] *Compare* O'Brian, 1 *World Polity* (1957), at 138.

[309] *See supra*, Part One, Chapters B) II. 2. a)-c).

[310] This proposition is made by David P. Fidler, 'The International Legal Implications of "Non-Lethal" Weapons', in: 21 *Mich. J. Int'l L.* (1999), pp. 51-100, at 88; *see also* Krüger-Sprengel, 42 *Rev. dr. mil.* (2003), at 370.

assessment is certainly consistent and an eligible position *de lege ferenda*. However, *de lege lata*, the emphasis of proportionality is still on collateral damage and the prohibition of indiscriminate attacks, which will be discussed thoroughly *infra*.[311] Additionally, an attack on a legitimate target can be prohibited due to the means or methods employed in this attack. In that regard, the same restriction that apply in any armed conflict also apply to targeted killings, such as the prohibition to use weapons that cause unnecessary suffering such as dum-dum bullets.[312]

IV. Conclusion: Targeted Killings of Combatants

The targeted killing of combatants or fighters in an armed conflict is generally permissible, but subject to important restrictions. A combatant or fighter constitutes a legitimate military objective in an armed conflict, and it is not illegal to target an individual person just because this person is singled out and not only an anonymous part of the opponent troops.[313]

First, a resort to perfidious means in targeting the person is prohibited. This includes certain covers such as false symbols, emblems or uniforms as well as the feigning of civilian status by the targeting person. It also includes instigating enemy combatants to kill their own superiors, recruiting hired killers, placing a price on the head of a person, and offering a reward for his capture "dead or alive".

Second, the possibility of targeting a combatant lawfully ends as soon as he is *hors de combat*, as long as the person concerned abstains from any hostile act and does not attempt to escape. This not only includes cases of surrender and prisoners of war, but also the factual inability to continue to fight of the person targeted. Examples are obviously persons incapacitated due to wounds, but also persons who have exhausted all means of defence or are unarmed, e.g. due to being surprised in their

---

311 *See infra*, Part Two, Chapter D) II. 2. a).

312 *See* Henckaerts/ Doswald-Beck (eds.), *Humanitarian Law*, Vol. 1, pp. 237-296 (Rules 70-86) and Stefan Oeter, 'Methods and Means of Combat', in: Dieter Fleck (ed.), *The Handbook of Humanitarian Law in Armed Conflicts*, Oxford 1999, pp. 105-207, at 122-124 (paras. 407-408) for further details. *See also* Melzer, *Targeted Killing*, pp. 415-418.

313 *See also* Kremnitzer, in: Fleck (ed.), *Rechtsfragen*, at 205.

sleep or on leave or in any other similar situation. The latter group introduces the principle that is decisive in the human rights sphere to preventively kill a person into international humanitarian law. Persons who do not pose any immediate threat to their adversaries are regarded *hors de combat* and may not be targeted.

In all cases of targeted killings of combatants the general principles of international humanitarian law must additionally be adhered to. This especially includes the questions of whether the killing is militarily necessary, i.e. serves the purpose to overpower the adversary, whether it is proportionate in relation to possible collateral damage, and whether the means employed are legal under other provisions of international humanitarian law.

D. Civilians

Beside the rules aiming at the protection of combatants, international humanitarian law also and foremost lays down standards that aim to spare those who do not participate in hostilities, i.e. civilians and/or non-combatants.

I. Civilian Status

According to the negative definition developed above[314] and as laid down in Article 50 para. 1 of the 1977 Additional Protocol I, a civilian is – in short – a person who is not a member of the armed forces.[315] Article 50 of the Protocol excludes those who are covered by the definition of "prisoners of war" as laid down in Article 4 A of the 1949 Geneva Convention III and those who are members of armed forces as defined in Article 43 of the Protocol itself.[316]

---

[314] *See supra*, Part Two, Chapter B) IV.

[315] Gasser, in: Fleck (ed.), *Handbook*, at 210 (para. 501.2); Henckaerts/ Doswald-Beck (eds.), *Humanitarian Law*, Vol. 1, p. 17 (Rule 5).

[316] *Compare supra*, Part Two, Chapter C) I.

Thus, those persons who are not – or no longer – members of the belligerent armed forces[317] or of associated militias, who are not members of incorporated paramilitary police or volunteer corps, including organised resistance units[318] or take part in a *levée en masse*[319] are civilians by their primary status. In consequence of this negative definition, there is no duty of civilians to identify themselves as such. This corresponds the duty of combatants to distinguish themselves actively from the civilian population.[320] Thus, in case of doubt, a person shall be treated as a civilian.[321]

Such doubts may occur more often as armed forces increasingly rely on the technical and administrative support of civilians. Persons who accompany the armed forces, e.g. war correspondents, members of labour units or services responsible for the soldiers' welfare, are by primary status civilians.[322] They are attached to the armed forces without being members and they are not authorized to fight.[323] Persons, who are members of the armed forces but are not authorized to participate directly in hostilities are also referred to as non-combatants.[324] These persons are covered by Article 4 A paras. 4 and 5 of the 1949 Geneva Convention III and are not excluded from the definition of civilians laid down in Article 50 of the 1977 Additional Protocol I:

> (4) Persons who accompany the armed forces without actually being members thereof, such as civilian members of military aircraft crews, war correspondents, supply contractors, members of labour units or of services responsible for the welfare of the armed forces, provided that they have received authorization from the armed

---

[317] *See e.g.* ICTY, *Prosecutor v. Tihomir Blaškić*, Case No. IT-95-14-T, ("Lasva Valley"), Judgment of March 3, 2000, reprinted in: 122 *Int'l L.R.* (2002), pp. 1-250, at 71-72 (para. 180); Gasser, in: Fleck (ed.), *Handbook*, at 210 (501.2); UK Ministry of Defence, *Manual*, para. 5.3.1 (p. 53).

[318] McCoubrey, *Humanitarian Law*, p. 178.

[319] *See supra*, Part Two, Chapter C) I. 3.

[320] *See supra*, Part Two, Chapter C) I.

[321] Gasser, in: Fleck (ed.), *Handbook*, at 210 (para. 501.3).

[322] *Id.*, at 210-211 (para. 501.4).

[323] Ipsen, in: Fleck (ed.), *Handbook*, at 65.

[324] *Id.*, at 66 (para. 301); UK Ministry of Defence, *Manual*, para. 5.3.2 (p. 53-54).

forces which they accompany, who shall provide them for that purpose with an identity card similar to the annexed model.

(5) Members of crews, including masters, pilots and apprentices, of the merchant marine and the crews of civil aircraft of the Parties to the conflict, who do not benefit by more favourable treatment under any other provisions of international law.

According to the 1949 Geneva Convention III, these persons have a special status: If they are captured, they become prisoners of war by their secondary status. At the same time, they are entitled to the protection of civilians under the 1977 Additional Protocol I. In the context of an non-international armed conflict, the same system applies: Those who are not combatants or fighters have the status of civilians.[325] This might be more complicated than in relation to international armed conflicts. However, this is an effect of the more complicated definition of combatant or fighter in that context.[326]

II. Protection of Civilians

The protection of civilians has different aspects. Concerning targeted killings, the most important part is civilian or non-combatant immunity which generally – but not absolutely – prohibits targeting individual civilians (and the civilian populations as such). This question will be addressed first. A second important aspect is that of the effects attacks on legitimate targets may have on civilians nearby, i.e. collateral damage and its proportion to the gained military advantage.

1. Individually Targeted Civilians

Civilian or non-combatant immunity is one of the cornerstones of international humanitarian law. It is also referred to as the principle of distinction or of discrimination[327] and can be traced back to the 1863

---

[325] Gasser, in: Fleck (ed.), *Handbook*, at 210 (para. 501.2).

[326] *See supra*, Part Two, Chapter C) II.

[327] Gardam, *Non-Combatant Immunity*, p. 2; Cruz Roja Española, *Manual básico de derechos humanos y derecho internacional humanitario*, Madrid 2003, p. 32.

Lieber Code[328] and the 1868 St. Petersburg Declaration.[329] It was neither explicitly addressed in 1899 and 1907 Hague Conventions and Regulations[330] nor in the Geneva Conventions, albeit the 1949 Geneva Convention IV refers to the protection of a strictly defined category of civilians.[331] Any provision designed to protect the civilian population from the dangers of military operations was removed from the draft conventions.[332] Only parts of the principle can be found in Common Article 3. Nevertheless, the norm of non-combatant immunity is a fundamental component of international humanitarian law and despite the practices of the Second World War, it represents a customary norm of international law.[333] This customary rule is codified for the first time in the 1977 Additional Protocol I. Article 48 of the Protocol reads:

> In order to ensure respect for and protection of the civilian population and civilian objects, the Parties to the conflict shall at all times distinguish between the civilian population and combatants and between civilian objects and military objectives and accordingly shall direct their operations only against military objectives.

---

[328] *Compare* Article XV, reading: "Military necessity admits of all direct destruction of life or limb of armed enemies, and of other persons whose destruction is incidentally unavoidable in the armed contests of the war; …" and Article XXII, reading: "… The principle has been more and more acknowledged that the unarmed citizen is to be spared in person, property, and honor as much as the exigencies of war will admit."

[329] *Compare* para. 3, reading: "That the only legitimate object which States should endeavour to accomplish during war is to weaken the military forces of the enemy;"

[330] Although it plays a role in Article 25 of the 1907 Hague Regulations which reads: "The attack or bombardment, by whatever means, of towns, villages, dwellings, or buildings which are undefended is prohibited."

[331] According to Article 4 of the 1949 Geneva Convention IV this covers "those who, at a given moment and in any manner whatsoever, find themselves, in case of a conflict or occupation, in the hands of a Party to the conflict or Occupying Power of which they are not nationals."

[332] Jean S. Pictet (ed.), *The Geneva Conventions of 12 August 1949: Commentary, Vol. 4, Geneva Convention relative to the Protection of Civilian Persons in Time of War*, Geneva 1958, p. 10.

[333] Gardam, *Non-Combatant Immunity*, pp. 27 and 132; Henckaerts/ Doswald-Beck (eds.), *Humanitarian Law*, Vol. 1, p. 19 (Rule 6); Sandoz *et al.* (eds.), *Additional Protocols*, para. 1923 (p. 615).

As this rule is very basic and e.g. does not cover collateral damage, it is supplemented by more specific rules in Article 51 of the 1977 Additional Protocol I.

a) Prohibition to Attack Civilians

Article 51 para. 2 of the 1977 Additional Protocol I and Article 13 para. 2 of the 1977 Additional Protocol II with the identical wording reaffirm the general prohibition to attack civilians and are a codification of a well accepted pre-existing rule of customary international law:[334]

> The civilian population as such, as well as individual civilians, shall not be the object of attack. Acts or threats of violence the primary purpose of which is to spread terror among the civilian population are prohibited.

This rule sets out a general prohibition of targeted killings directed against individual civilians. However, as laid down in para. 3 of the article, the prohibition is not absolute.[335] It can rather be reduced to the formula that "[a]ttacks against persons not taking part in acts of violence shall be prohibited in all circumstances."[336] The effect of this rule is that the targeted killing of a civilian – whether in an international or in an internal armed conflict – is generally prohibited.

b) Prohibition to Target Non-Military Objectives

This prohibition to target individual civilians corresponds the duty to direct attacks only against military objectives: The principle of distinction and civilian immunity is specified in Article 48 of the 1977 Additional Protocol I which states that attacks may only be directed against

---

[334] Gardam, *Non-Combatant Immunity*, p. 115; Green, *Law of Armed Conflict*, p. 151; Greenwood, in: Delissen/ Tanja (eds.), at 108-110; Henckaerts/ Doswald-Beck (eds.), *Humanitarian Law*, Vol. 1, p. 25 (Rule 7); Oeter, in: Fleck (ed.), *Handbook*, at 120 (para. 401.6).

[335] *See infra*, Part Two, Chapter D) II. 1. c).

[336] Article 5 para. 1 of UN Comm'n H.R., Sub-Commission on Prevention of Discrimination and Protection of Minorities, *Declaration on Minimum Standards*, adopted by a group of experts at a meeting in Turku/ Åbo, Finland, December 1990, UN Doc. E/CN.4/Sub.2/1991/55 (August 12, 1991), reprinted in: 31 *Int'l Rev. Red Cross* (1991), No. 282, pp. 328-336.

military objectives. The prohibition was also included in the draft of the 1977 Additional Protocol II but was dropped at the last moment as part of a package aimed at the adoption of a simplified text.[337] This rule is widely regarded as customary international law applicable in international and non-international armed conflicts[338] and is further defined in Article 52 para. 2:

> Attacks shall be limited strictly to military objectives. In so far as objects are concerned, military objectives are limited to those objects which by their nature, location, purpose or use make an effective contribution to military action and whose total or partial destruction, capture or neutralization, in the circumstances ruling at the time, offers a definite military advantage.

Military objectives have to be defined positively, as any object may become an military objective by virtue of its use by the enemy or potential use by the attacker rather than by virtue of its intrinsic Character. For the same reason, it is not possible to form an exhaustive list of military objectives.[339]

The definition given in the 1977 Additional Protocol I is very similar to that given in Paragraph 40 (c) of the U.S. Army Field Manual of 1956 and of 1976.[340] As these Manuals predate the Protocol, this supports the view, that the definition given in the Protocol is declarative of customary international law rather than constitutive.[341] The U.S. itself expressed the view that the definition in that manual corresponds with customary international law. Switzerland also did not change its military

---

[337] Henckaerts/ Doswald-Beck (eds.), *Humanitarian Law*, Vol. 1, pp. 26-27 with further references.

[338] *Id.*, p. 25 (Rule 7) and p. 34 (Rule 10). These rules were for example respected by the protagonists of the 1990-1991 Kuwait conflict: The coalition's annunciation that it would attack only military objectives was phrased very similar to Art. 52 of the 1977 Additional Protocol I. The annunciation that excessive collateral damage civilian casualties would be avoided as far as possible was phrased similar to Art. 51 para. 5 lit. b of the Protocol, *see* Greenwood, in: Fleck (ed.), *Handbook*, at 26 (Para. 127.2).

[339] Sassòli, in: Wippman/ Evangelista (eds.), at 185.

[340] U.S. Department of the Army, Field Manual No. 27-10; U.S. Department of the Army, *The Law of Land Warfare*, Field Manual No. 27-10, Change 1 (July 15, 1976), Washington, D.C. 1976.

[341] Dougherty/ Quénivet, 16 *HuV-I* (2003), at 189.

manual when it became party to the Protocol and thus can be understood as accepting the customary law predating the Protocol now being codified therein.[342] Thus, the definition of a "military objective" can be accepted as representing customary international law,[343] albeit this view is not undisputed: The definition may not include targets previously considered legitimate military objectives,[344] and thus it is argued e.g. by the U.S. that a different definition exists in customary international law.[345] The Commander's Handbook on the Law of Naval Operations states e.g. that "[e]conomic targets of the enemy that indirectly but effectively support and sustain the enemy's war-fighting capability may also be attacked."[346] Other States, e.g. the Netherlands, the United Kingdom and Italy, made reservations regarding the definition of a "military objective",[347] but these reservations only partly clarify which specific areas of land may be military objectives in the understanding of the State and can be subsumed under the definition.[348] "Attack" is defined as any act of violence against the adversary.[349] This includes targeted killings. As targeted killings are initially aimed at a single person, the question of military objective can be relevant in two situations:

First, the person directly targeted has to be a military objective. This is true for combatant members of armed forces and those who take direct

---

342 Sassòli, in: Wippman/ Evangelista (eds.), at 189-190 with further references.

343 *Compare* Henckaerts/ Doswald-Beck (eds.), *Humanitarian Law*, Vol. 1, p. 29 (Rule 8).

344 Jeanne M. Meyer, 'Tearing down the Façade: A critical Look at the current Law on targeting the Will of the Enemy and Air Force Doctrine', in: 51 *A.F. L. Rev.* (2001), pp. 143-182, at 144.

345 *C.f.* Dougherty/ Quénivet, 16 *HuV-I* (2003), at 189; Meyer, 51 *A.F. L. Rev.* (2001), at 144.

346 U.S. Department of Navy, *Commander's Handbook*, para. 8.1.1 (p. 8-1); Michael N. Schmitt, '*Bellum Americanum*: The U.S. View of twenty-first Century War and its possible Implications for the Law of Armed Conflict', in: 19 *Mich. J. Int'l L.* (1998), pp. 1051-1090, at 1076 (footnotes omitted).

347 Dougherty/ Quénivet, 16 *HuV-I* (2003), at 189 (footnote 9).

348 Sassòli, in: Wippman/ Evangelista (eds.), at 186.

349 *See e.g.* Article 49 of the 1977 Additional Protocol I; Sassòli, in: Wippman / Evangelista (eds.), at 184.

part in hostilities without being members of armed forces.[350] The questions arising in relation to the former group are thus the same as discussed above concerning combatant status of the targeted person.[351] The latter group will be discussed *infra*.[352] If it is legal to target that person, possible side effects are dealt with according to the rules of collateral damage:[353] The attack becomes illegal if excessive incidental damage affecting civilians or civilian objects must be expected. Furthermore, precautionary measures must be taken to spare civilians.[354] The same applies to the targeting of larger objects for the reason that the person in question finds itself inside these objects.

Second, even if the person itself is not a legitimate target, the whole targeted object could be a military objective. Then again, the overall legality of the action depends on the question of collateral damage, but with switched roles: The person could be qualified as proportionate collateral damage if it is not excessive in relation to the military advantage gained by the attack on the military objective. Examples for such a situation is the civilian worker in an armament factory or the civilian scientist developing weapons: It is not militarily necessary to target them individually, e.g. by aerial bombardment of their residential area.[355] However, they may be hit as part of an attack on the military objective they are working in.

In the latter situation, if the individual person who is also hit is the motivation for the attack on the whole object, it might be argued that such cases serve to circumvent the prohibition of attacking civilians: The adversary who may not target a certain person directly could just wait until this person enters a legitimate target. However, if the military objective can be targeted legally and the collateral damage is not excessive, this situation is not changed by the mere motivation that is behind the decision to attack a certain legitimate target at a certain time. If consid-

---

[350] UK Ministry of Defence, *Manual*, para. 5.4.1 (p. 54) and para. 5.4.5 (p. 56); Sassòli, in: Wippman/ Evangelista (eds.), at 184 and 200; Watkin, in: Wippman/ Evangelista (eds.), at 139.

[351] *Compare supra*, Part Two, Chapter C).

[352] *Compare infra*, Part Two, Chapter D) II. 1. c).

[353] *Compare infra*, Part Two, Chapter D) II. 2. b).

[354] Sassòli, in: Wippman/ Evangelista (eds.), at 184.

[355] *Id.*, at 202.

ered before the background of the prohibition to use civilians as human shields,[356] it cannot make a difference whether any person or a certain person is inside a military objective: The considerations concerning collateral damage must be the same. The fact that the adversary is satisfied having hit a person he wanted to target anyway may be a reason for an extra careful consideration of the collateral damage issues. However, it has no influence on the standards that have to be applied in such a thorough examination.

The examples given above show that the question of military objectives is of importance, but that the question of collateral damage and proportionality is the more important issue concerning the protection of civilians.[357]

c) Exception: Civilians Taking Direct Part in Hostilities

As shortly addressed above, it is generally but not absolutely prohibited to target individual civilians. The exception is based on the following considerations: Only if belligerents have no reason to fear attacks from the civilian population, they will be prepared to spare civilians from attack. Thus, one of the fundamental rules of international humanitarian law is that civilians generally may not take part in hostilities.[358] Civilians are thus only immune from attack "because, and so long as, civilians do not take up arms."[359] This rule is laid down in Article 3 common to the 1949 Geneva Conventions, Article 51 of the 1977 Additional Protocol I, and in Article 31 of the 1977 Additional Protocol II. It is also part of Article 8 para. 2 *lit.* b (i) of the 1998 Rome Statute of the International Criminal Court and confirmed in Article 5 para. 1 of the Turku Declaration on Minimum Humanitarian Stan-

---

[356] *See* Article 28 of the 1949 Geneva Convention IV; Article 57 para. 7 of the 1977 Additional Protocol I; Gasser, in: Fleck (ed.), *Handbook*, at 218 (paras. 506.1-506.4).

[357] *See infra*, Part Two, Chapter D) II. 2. b).

[358] Gasser, in: Fleck (ed.), *Handbook*, at 210 (paras. 501-501.1); Robert Wayn Gehring, 'Loss of Civilian Protections under the Fourth Geneva Convention and Protocol I', in: 19 *Rev. dr. pén. mil.* (1980), pp. 9-48, at 16. An exception to this rule is the *levée en masse*, *compare supra*, Part Two, Chapter C) I. 3.

[359] Cassese, 'Expert Opinion', para. 6 (p. 4).

dards.[360] Article 51 para. 3 of the 1977 Additional Protocol I and – almost identically – Article 13 para. 3 of the 1977 Additional Protocol II read:

> Civilians shall enjoy the protection afforded by this section, unless and for such time as they take a direct part in hostilities.[361]

This provision is widely regarded as part of customary international law applicable in international and non-international armed conflicts:[362] The corresponding rule is refereed to and applied by courts and tribunals both national and international,[363] it is included either verbatim or by adopting its essence in numerous military manuals, including England, France, Holland, Australia, Italy, Canada, Germany, the United States (Air Force), and New Zealand,[364] and it is accepted to represent customary international law in legal literature.[365]

---

360 Reading: "Attacks against persons not taking part in acts of violence shall be prohibited in all circumstances."

361 Article 13 para. 3 1977 Additional Protocol II only refers to "this part" instead of "this section".

362 Henckaerts/ Doswald-Beck (eds.), *Humanitarian Law*, Vol. 1, pp. 19-21 (Rule 6) with further references on.

363 *See e.g.* Inter-Am. Comm'n H.R., *Juan Carlos Abella ("La Tablada")*, *Annual Report* (1997), at para. 178; Supreme Court of Israel, *"Targeted Killings" (Merits)*, para. 30, 46 *ILM* (2007), at 389; ICTY, *Prosecutor v. Pavle Strugar*, Case No. IT-01-42-T, Judgment of January 31, 2005, para. 277; *compare also* Silva Hinek, 'The Judgment of the International Criminal Tribunal for the Former Yugoslavia in Prosecutor v. Pavle Strugar', in: 19 *Leiden J. l Int'l L.* (2006), pp. 477-490; William J. Fenrick, 'The Prosecution of Unlawful Attack Cases before the ICTY', in: 7 *Yb. Int'l Hum. L.* (2004), pp. 153-189.

364 Supreme Court of Israel, *"Targeted Killings" (Merits)*, para. 30, 46 *ILM* (2007), at 389.

365 Kretzmer, 16 *Eur. J. Int'l L.* (2005), at 192; Dinstein, *Conduct of Hostilities*, p. 11; Cassese, *International Law*, p. 416; Ben-Naftali/ Michaeli, 36 *Cornell Int'l L.J.* (2003), at 269; Marco Roscini, 'Targeting and Contemporary Aerial Bombardment', in: 54 *Int'l & Comp. L.Q.* (2005), pp. 411-444, at 418; Michael N. Schmitt, '"Direct Participation in Hostilities" and 21st Century Armed Conflict', in: Horst Fischer; Ulrike Froissart; Wolff Heintschel von Heinegg; Christian Raap (eds.), *Krisensicherung und Humanitärer Schutz – Crisis Management and Humanitarian Protection: Festschrift für Dieter Fleck*, Berlin 2004, pp. 505-529, at 506-507; Proulx, 56 *Hastings L.J.* (2005), at 879.

The participation of persons not having a claim to lawful combatancy is not a new phenomenon,[366] however, the contemporary "war on terror" and other asymmetrical conflicts have focused attention on the targeting of non-State actors.[367] Before addressing the elements of this exception, it is important to bring to mind the general rule again: The status of "combatant" and "civilian" is connected to a person independently of his or her activities in a period of time: Even civilians taking part in hostilities do not become combatants but remain civilians with less protection.[368] This protection is reduced if the following three elements of "unless and for such time as they take a direct part in hostilities" are fulfilled, namely the terms "hostilities", "taking direct part" and "for such time".

(1) "Hostilities"

The first element of "taking part in hostilities" is the concept of "hostilities" itself. The codified international humanitarian law makes extensive use of the notion of "hostilities" without giving a definition thereof. The word's ordinary meaning can be described as "hostile acts" or "acts of warfare",[369] consisting of "battles, sieges" or "raids".[370] The overall use of the term suggests that it is narrower than the notion of "armed conflict", but wider than the concept of "attack" as used in the 1977 Additional Protocol I.[371] The latter term covers – according to Article 49 para. 1 of the Protocol – "acts of violence against the adversary, whether in offence or in defence". The term "hostilities" is not syn-

---

[366] On historical precedents *see* Lester Nurick; Roger W. Barrett, 'Legality of Guerrilla Forces Under the Laws of War', in: 40 *Am. J. Int'l L.* (1946), pp. 563-583, at 570-580.

[367] Watkin, 15 *Duke J. Comp. & Int'l L.* (2005), at 310. *Compare* Schmitz-Elvenich, *Targeted Killing*, pp. 15-18, who strongly relates the term "asymmetrical warfare" to "international terrorism".

[368] Arnold, in: Arnold/ Hildbrand (eds.), at 14.

[369] Simpson *et al.*, *Oxford Dictionary*, p. 420.

[370] Urdang (ed.), *Synonym Dictionary*, p. 517.

[371] International Committee of the Red Cross; T.M.C. Asser Institute, *Direct Participation in Hostilities under International Humanitarian Law*, Summary Report drafted by Nils Melzer of the third expert meeting in Geneva, October 23-25, 2005, p. 17.

onymous with other concepts that are sometimes used in a similar sense, such as "military operations", "hostile action" or "hostile/ harmful act".[372]

There is a certain hierarchy among the terms referred to above which all can be found in Article 44 para. 3 of the 1977 Additional Protocol I: An "armed conflict" as the broadest term comprises ongoing "hostilities"[373] which consist of "military operations", the latter *inter alia* consisting of single "attacks". This is also supported by the word's ordinary meaning as consisting of several "acts".[374]

However, a second possibility would be to restrict the term "hostilities" to actual engagement in fighting and to understand "military operations" as a wider concept than that. According to the latter assessment, participation in hostilities would then mean taking part in the actual fighting. This narrow understanding would lead to a maximum of protection of civilians and would probably be a criterion that is relatively easy to handle.[375] Such a narrow interpretation finds support in the official commentary to the 1977 Additional Protocols: According to this, hostilities shall be understood to be acts which by their nature and purpose are intended to cause "actual harm" to the personnel and equipment of the adversary.[376]

Such a definition is criticised *inter alia* on the basis that in the drafting process of the 1977 Additional Protocol I, a number of delegations had expressed the view that the term included preparations for combat and return from combat.[377] On the one hand, this statement for the record would have been meaningless if "hostilities" were not understood in a

---

[372] *Id.*, p. 18.

[373] Union Académique Internationale, *Dictionnaire de la terminologie du droit international*, Paris 1960, p. 315, even though "hostilities" has also been used synonymously with "war", *compare e.g.* Preamble of the 1907 Hague Convention III and Article 14 of the 1907 Hague Convention IV.

[374] Simpson *et al.*, *Oxford Dictionary*, p. 420.

[375] *Compare* Gehring, 19 *Rev. dr. pén. mil.* (1980), at 18-19; ICRC/T.M.C. Asser Institute, *Direct Participation*, Summary Report, October 23-25, 2005, pp. 18-19.

[376] Sandoz *et al.* (eds.), *Protocoles additionnels*, para. 1942 (p. 618).

[377] *Compare e.g.* W. Hays Parks, 'Air War and the Laws of War', in: 32 *A.F. L. Rev.* (1990), pp. 1-225, at 133. On the drafting process, *see* Gehring, 19 *Rev. dr. pén. mil.* (1980), at 18-19 (with further references).

narrow manner anyway.[378] It is thus accepted that the term "hostilities" at least is not restricted to actual fighting by using a weapon, but also covers operations preparatory to actual fighting, e.g. a person is carrying the weapon on his way to or from an attack and other conduct posing an immediate threat to the adversary even without using a weapon.[379] This definition would correspond the prevailing intention at the 1974-1977 diplomatic conference to interpret the notion of hostilities very narrowly in order to spare civilians as far as possible. It would – on the other hand – pay regard to the fact that the term "hostilities" was chosen in the drafting process, instead of the notion of direct participation in "military operations" or even "attack". Thus, "hostilities" cannot be restricted exclusively to the actual act of fighting.[380]

The prohibition of directly participating in hostilities is additionally based on another aspect, namely the goal to distinguish civilians from combatants by keeping the civilians away from the traditional battlefield. This purpose could also be reached by means of deterrence, if a broader concept of hostilities is applied and thus civilians must be on guard not to lose their protection.[381]

The content of Articles 48-51 shows that civilians shall be protected from the effects of military operations aimed against specific objects. This implicitly conveys a narrow understanding of the term "hostilities". Hostilities also have to be distinguished from "activities hostile to the security of the State" as referred to in Article 5 of the 1949 Geneva Convention IV.[382] The fact that this article refers to "activities hostile to the security of the State" as a different concept to "hostilities" shows, that there have to be acts that fall under the former concept, but not under the latter. This again supports a narrow interpretation of the concept of "hostilities".

---

378 Gehring, 19 *Rev. dr. pén. mil.* (1980), at 19.

379 Sandoz *et al.* (eds.), *Protocoles additionnels*, para. 1943 (pp. 618-619).

380 *Compare* ICRC/T.M.C. Asser Institute, *Direct Participation*, Summary Report, October 23-25, 2005, p. 19; ICRC, *Interpretive Guidance on the Notion of Direct Participation in Hostilities under International Humanitarian Law*, Geneva 2009, p. 43 ("the (collective) resort by the parties to the conflict to means and methods of injuring the enemy").

381 On this aspect *see* Schmitt, in: Fischer *et al.* (eds.), at 509.

382 *Compare infra*, Part Two, Chapter D) II. 1. d).

Finally, the whole discussion on a narrow or wide concept of hostilities runs the risk of being moot as the overall level of protection additionally depends on the definition of "taking direct part". A narrower definition of "hostilities" could be combined with a broader notion of "direct participation", or a broader concept of "hostilities" could be used in conjunction with "direct participation" being defined more narrowly.[383] Thus, there is not – yet – a definite answer concerning the scope of the term "hostilities".

(2) Taking "Direct" or "Active" Part in Hostilities

"The notion of direct participation in hostilities is complex, emotive, and still inadequately resolved."[384] In opposition to the view of *Gardam*, the issue of direct participation is not "straightforward"[385]: It is rather a "gray area"[386] and thus open to various interpretations.

The first element that has to be examined is the activity of "taking ... part", meaning "to participate", "to take share in some action", "to have a portion or lot in common with others"[387] as well as to "engage in", "play a part in" or "be a party".[388] These terms do not include actions that are merely of support from an external position. They rather refer to a certain involvement in the hostilities, i.e. to be part of them or be somehow "inside". The commentary to 1977 Additional Protocol I considers the two legal formulations "taking ... active part in the hostilities" and "take a direct part in hostilities" synonymous.[389] This was confirmed by the International Criminal Tribunal for Rwanda.[390]

---

[383] *Compare* ICRC/T.M.C. Asser Institute, *Direct Participation*, Summary Report, October 23-25, 2005, p. 20.

[384] Fenrick, 5 *J. Int'l Crim. Just.* (2007), at 337.

[385] *Compare* Gardam, *Non-Combatant Immunity*, pp. 115-116.

[386] Schmitt, in: Fischer *et al.* (eds.), at 509.

[387] Simpson *et al.*, *Oxford Dictionary*, p. 263.

[388] Urdang (ed.), *Synonym Dictionary*, p. 845.

[389] *See e.g.* ICRC/T.M.C. Asser Institute, *Direct Participation*, Summary Report, June 2, 2003, at 28.

[390] ICTR, *Prosecutor v. Jean-Paul Akayesu*, Case No. ICTR-96-4-T, Decision of September 2, 1998, para. 629.

But in connection with the recruitment of children the Preparatory Committee for the Establishment of an International Criminal Court considered these two notions as distinct: The ICC Statute lists among the war crimes "Conscripting or enlisting children under the age of fifteen years (...) or using them to participate actively in hostilities".[391] The delegations eventually adopted the wording "using" and "participate actively"

> in order to cover both direct participation in combat and also active participation in military activities linked to combat such as scouting, spying, sabotage and the use of children as decoys, couriers or at military checkpoints. It would not cover activities clearly unrelated to the hostilities such as food deliveries to an airbase or the use of domestic staff in an officer's married accommodation. However, use of children in a direct support function such as acting as bearers to take supplies to the front line, or activities at the front line itself, would be included within the terminology.[392]

However, such an interpretation finds no support in both words' ordinary meaning: "Active" comprises "effectual, effective, causative, potent, influential"[393] and "having practical results".[394] "Direct" refers to "straight, undeviated" or "immediate"[395] or "proceeding from cause to effect".[396] Thus, both describe that an action has immediate effects.

Furthermore, a distinct understanding of the terms "active" and "direct" is not reflected by their use in Article 3 of the 1949 Geneva Conventions and Article 51 para. 3 of the 1977 Additional Protocol I:[397] Direct participation is covering acts of war which by their nature or purpose are likely to cause actual harm to the personnel and equipment of

---

391 Article 8, para. 2 *lit.* b (xxvi) and *lit.* e (vii) of the 1998 Rome Statute.

392 UN General Assembly, Conference 183, *Report of the Preparatory Committee on the Establishment of an International Criminal Court*, UN Doc. A/Conf.183/2/Add.1 (April 14, 1998), p. 21 (footnote 12).

393 Urdang (ed.), *Synonym Dictionary*, p. 20.

394 Simpson *et al.*, *Oxford Dictionary*, p. 129.

395 Urdang (ed.), *Synonym Dictionary*, p. 294.

396 Simpson *et al.*, *Oxford Dictionary*, p. 702.

397 *Compare* ICRC, *Interpretive Guidance*, Geneva 2009, pp. 43-44.

the enemy armed forces.[398] As shown above, it does not only cover the actual use of a weapon but also certain acts performed without weapons, and thus it is not necessary to define different categories such as proposed by the Preparatory Committee for the Establishment of an International Criminal Court.[399]

Direct participation in hostilities implies a direct or sufficient causal relationship between the activity engaged in and the harm done to the enemy as its immediate consequences at the time and the place where the activity takes place.[400] One element of such a causal relationship is that it is a *conditio sine qua non* or "but for" causation,[401] i.e. the consequences would not have occurred but for the act. This would still hold true for the worker in the armament industry who produces ammunition that is later used in hostilities. Thus, there has to be at least one additional element of proximity that describes a certain immediacy of the consequences caused by the person in question:

Traditionally, it was possible to rely on the geographical proximity of a person to the front line: The closer a person was to the battle zone, the more likely was that person to be involved in the hostilities. Those not engaged in combat often fled the immediate area of hostilities and thus close presence could at least serve as an indication of participation.[402]

However, the battlefield in the traditional sense has largely disappeared as the result of new methods of warfare. This fact renders inoperative definitions of participation in hostilities based on a person's geographic proximity to a combat zone.[403] But geographical proximity is not without importance in assessing whether a person is directly participating: The geographical proximity to belligerent's acts can still serve as an indication. As will be shown *infra*, a certain behaviour may be participa-

---

398 Sandoz *et al.* (eds.), *Protocoles additionnels*, para. 1944 (p. 619) (my emphasis).

399 *See also* Schmitt, in: Fischer *et al.* (eds.), at 507 (in support of the ICTR decision in *Akayesu*).

400 Sandoz *et al.* (eds.), *Protocoles additionnels*, para. 1679 (p. 516) and para. 4787 (p. 1453); ICRC, *Interpretive Guidance*, Geneva 2009, pp. 46-58.

401 Schmitt, in: Fischer *et al.* (eds.), at 508.

402 Schmitt, in: Fischer *et al.* (eds.), at 510-511.

403 ICRC/T.M.C. Asser Institute, *Direct Participation*, Summary Report, June 2, 2003, at 30.

tion if performed geographically close to hostilities, but it may not amount to direct participation if performed at a distance.[404]

The ordinary meaning of "direct" comprises "straight, undeviating in course, not circuitous or croaked" or "straightforward, uninterrupted, immediate" and "effected or existing without intermediation or intervening agency". A "direct action" is an action which takes effect without intermediate instrumentality.[405] Thus, another approach to describe the necessary proximity of a person taking direct part to the consequences of his acts can be described as a "causal proximity".[406] There has to be a "sufficient causal relationship between the act of participants and its immediate consequences."[407] In other words: The consequences – actual harm to the adversary – must be the immediate effect of the act committed by the person in question, without any intermediate instrumentality. The decisive element is thus the immediacy of the impact on the enemy.[408]

Direct participation therefore has to be distinguished from participation in a war effort: The fact that parts of even the whole population contributes to the conduct of hostilities e.g. by working in the armament industry, does not mean that this is participation in hostilities.[409] Thus, such a concept as "quasi-combatants" does not exist. The argument that civilians who contribute to the war effort may be targeted may be based on an misunderstanding concerning military objectives and persons who may be targeted: If a person finds itself inside a military objective, the objective can be targeted irrespective of the status of that person, as long as a civilian casualty would not be excessive in relation to the military advantage gained.[410] This does not make the person a legitimate

[404] *Compare infra*, Part Two, Chapter B)II. 1. c) (2) (iii).

[405] Simpson *et al.*, *Oxford Dictionary*, p. 702; *see also* Urdang (ed.), *Synonym Dictionary*, p. 294.

[406] Schmitt, in: Fischer *et al.* (eds.), at 508.

[407] Sandoz *et al.* (eds.), *Protocoles additionnels*, para. 4787 (p. 1453).

[408] *See e.g.* Sassòli, in: Wippman/ Evangelista (eds.), at 201-202; Inter Am. Comm'n H.R., *Third Report on the Human Rights Situation in Colombia*, OEA/Ser.L/V/II.102, Doc. 9 Rev. 1 (February 26, 1999), Chapter IV, at paras. 54 and 56.

[409] Éric David, *Principes de droit des conflits armés*, 3rd ed., Bruxelles 2002, p. 249 (para. 2.17); Sandoz *et al.* (eds.), *Protocoles additionnels*, para. 1945 (p. 619).

[410] *Compare supra*, Part Two, Chapter D) II. 1. b).

target and does not alter his status as a civilian.[411] The effects of their contributions to the hostilities is not immediate in such a manner. The International Criminal Tribunal for the Former Yugoslavia stated in *Tadić* concerning crimes against persons not taking direct part in hostilities:

> It is unnecessary to define exactly the line dividing those taking an active part in hostilities and those who are not so involved. It is sufficient to examine the relevant facts of each victim and to ascertain whether, in each individual's circumstances, that person was actively involved in hostilities at the relevant time.[412]

Such a case-by-case analysis has certain similarities to the notorious formula "I know it when I see it"[413]: It may be hard to define what direct participation is, but at least many cases can be recognised by intuition.

(i) Clear Cases of Direct Participation

It is clear that civilians are taking part in hostilities when using weapons in an armed conflict, such as civilians manning an anti-aircraft gun or operating other weapons systems.[414] This also covers civilians "trying to capture members of the enemy's armed forces or their weapons, equipment or positions, or laying mines or sabotaging lines of military communication".[415] What applies to laying mines also applies to civilians who carry a bomb to the site of a planned attack.

It is furthermore generally accepted that it is not necessary to carry weapons: Engaging in sabotage of military installations is as well covered[416] as the gathering of intelligence for military purposes.[417] This con-

---

[411] Sassòli, in: Wippman/ Evangelista (eds.), at 201.

[412] ICTY, *Prosecutor v. Duško Tadić*, Case No. IT-94-1-A, Judgment of May 7, 1997, reprinted in: 112 *Int'l L.R.* (1999), pp. 1-285, at 203 (para. 616).

[413] U.S. Supreme Court, *Jacobellis v. Ohio*, Judgment of June 22, 1964, 378 *U.S.* (1964), pp. 184-204, concurring opinion by Justice Potter Stewart, p. 197.

[414] UK Ministry of Defence, *Manual*, para. 5.3.3 (p. 54); Dougherty/ Quénivet, 16 *HuV-I* (2003), at 194; Henckaerts/ Doswald-Beck (eds.), *Humanitarian Law*, Vol. 1, p. 22.

[415] ICRC/T.M.C. Asser Institute, *Direct Participation*, Summary Report, June 2, 2003, at 28.

[416] UK Ministry of Defence, *Manual*, para. 5.3.3 (p. 54).

cept is widened to include civilians who supervise or merely service a weapons system[418] and civilians preparing for a military operation and intending to participate therein, if these actions are directly related to hostilities and thus "represent a direct threat to the enemy".[419]

If a civilian is permanently involved in such activities and an organisational structure up to the degree that he qualifies as a fighter in an non-international armed conflict or a combatant in an international one, participation can ultimately result in a change of status. The person will then, subject to the conditions described above,[420] loose his immunity from attack. This threshold is considerably higher than the one described by some authors who argue for a permanent loss of immunity once a civilian has taken part in hostilities.[421]

(ii) Clear Cases of Non-Direct Participation

On the other hand, "general strategic analysis," or giving "logistical, general support, including monetary aid" is not regarded as direct participation.[422] This holds also true for "civilians working in depots and canteens providing food and clothing for the armed forces or in factories producing weapons platforms" and for civilians who are involved in design or manufacture of weapons and are thus in principle not directly or actively participating in hostilities,[423] even though they perform certain activities normally performed by members of the armed

---

417 Sandoz *et al.* (eds.), *Additional Protocols*, para. 1942 (pp. 618-619); Ruys, *Juristenkrant* (January 17, 2007), at para. 7.

418 Supreme Court of Israel, *"Targeted Killings" (Merits)*, para. 35, 46 *ILM* (2007), at 392.

419 Gasser, in: Fleck (ed.), *Handbook*, at 232 (para. 518).

420 *Compare supra*, Part Two, Chapters C) I. and II.

421 *See infra*, Part Two, Chapter D) II. 1. c) (3) (ii).

422 Dworkin, *Crimes of War Project* (December 15, 2006).

423 UK Ministry of Defence, *Manual*, para. 5.3.3 (p. 54); Dougherty/ Quénivet, 16 *HuV-I* (2003), at 194; ICRC/T.M.C. Asser Institute, *Direct Participation*, Summary Report, June 2, 2003, at 28; However, the U.S. Army has issued a legal opinion that mission essential civilians working at U.S. bases during an armed conflict would be appropriate targets of attack by the enemy, *see* Schmitt, 19 *Mich. J. Int'l L.* (1998), at 1076 with further references.

forces.[424] And – *a fortiori* – a civilian economist who is far away from military operations, involved in the financial planning of the war, cannot be regarded as directly participating.[425] The same holds true in connection with political authorities, as they are generally civilians (unless members of the armed forces) but perform actions that could contribute to the hostilities.[426] Even individual civilians who use proportionate force in individual self-defence, i.e. in response to an unlawful and imminent attack against themselves or their property are not "directly participating" in hostilities, even if they use weapons in such an action.[427]

(iii) Grey Areas

In between these rather clear cases, there is a considerable grey area. What is the common basis of the clear cases? As *Gasser* phrases it, direct participation demands that the actions in question are directly related to hostilities and thus "represent a direct threat to the enemy."[428] Similarly, *Schmitt* regards the "criticality" of the act to the direct application of violence against the enemy as the decisive criterion.[429] Both interpretations correspond to the ordinary meaning of "direct" as developed above.[430]

Such a direct threat is not represented by the worker in the munitions factory, who is distant from the application of force against the enemy. An ammunition factory or a military vehicle maintenance depot itself is

---

[424] Sassòli, in: Wippman/ Evangelista (eds.), at 200-201.

[425] Dougherty/ Quénivet, 16 *HuV-I* (2003), at 195.

[426] ICRC/T.M.C. Asser Institute, *Direct Participation*, Summary Report, June 2, 2003, at 29.

[427] Schmitt, in: Fischer *et al.* (eds.), at 519-520; ICRC/T.M.C. Asser Institute, *Direct Participation*, Summary Report, June 2, 2003, at 32; ICRC, *Interpretive Guidance*, Geneva 2009, p. 61.

[428] Gasser, in: Fleck (ed.), *Handbook*, at 232 (para. 518).

[429] Schmitt, in: Fischer *et al.* (eds.), at 509.

[430] *Compare also* ICRC, *Interpretive Guidance*, Geneva 2009, pp. 46-58, phrasing *inter alia* the requirements of a "threshold of harm" and "direct causation" of this harm.

a legitimate target, but that the workers, when not in the factory, are not. They are not seen as taking direct part in the hostilities.[431]

A person who transports combatants or drives an ammunition truck to the place where the hostilities are taking place is somewhat closer to the hostilities – geographically as well as concerning the threat his acts pose to the adversary. Beside being inside a military objective, this person is regarded as directly participating in hostilities by many.[432] Admittedly, the threat that such an action poses is more immediate than the mere production of weapons. One could thus argue that the driver has forfeited his protection and can be targeted as long as he is participating in hostilities. One might even go as far as declaring the driver a lawful target even at home.

However, the person driving the truck is still far away from "directing a weapon" against the adversary. He is merely supporting combatants who will in a short period of time most likely do so. Is it then really the behaviour of the person driving the truck that is a threat to the enemy? A truck driven by a civilian and transporting combatants can be stopped by either shooting the driver by a sniper, or by destroying the whole truck. The former possibility will prove inefficient as any of the combatants could go on and drive the truck to its destination. It thus becomes clear that not the driver but the truck and the combatants pose a threat to the enemy: The threat the driver poses to the adversary is not immediate. It is not a "direct action" which effects actual harm to the adversary without intermediate instrumentality. The hostile acts still have to be performed by the combatants once they reach their destination.

Nevertheless, the civilian driver is under the risk of being hit by an attack on the military objective he finds himself in, subject to the princi-

---

[431] UK Ministry of Defence, *Manual*, paras. 2.5.2. and 5.3.3 (pp. 24 and 54); Dougherty/ Quénivet, 16 *HuV-I* (2003), at 194; *compare also* Henckaerts/ Doswald-Beck (eds.), *Humanitarian Law*, Vol. 1, pp. 23 and 31-32 with further references.

[432] *See e.g.* Gasser, in: Fleck (ed.), *Handbook*, at 232 (para. 518); Supreme Court of Israel, *"Targeted Killings" (Merits)*, para. 35, 46 *ILM* (2007), at 392.

ple of proportionality. But the fact that he drives that vehicle is not enough to make him an exclusive legitimate target himself.[433]

Admittedly, this interpretation is stricter than accepted by many authors. However, it corresponds with the system that is used by the 1977 Additional Protocol I: It sets out the general rule that civilians may not be attacked. Then it allows for an exception in cases where these civilians take direct part in hostilities. One can argue that this exception, as all "[g]ray areas should be interpreted liberally, i.e., in favour of finding direct participation."[434] *Schmitt* supports this argument in the specific case by referring to aspects of deterrence:

> A liberal approach creates an incentive for civilians to remain as distant from the conflict as possible – in doing so they can better avoid being charged with participation in the conflict and are less liable to being directly targeted.[435]

Schmitt himself admits that it might seem counter-intuitive to broadly interpret the activities that subject civilians to attack, but regards it as likely to enhance the protection of the civil population as a whole by such an interpretation.[436] The deterrence argument cannot be dismissed easily, but it is questionable whether it really corresponds to the system of the 1977 Additional Protocol I:

First, the Protocol Article 51 para. 2 establishes the protection of single civilians and of the population: "The civilian population as such, as well as individual civilians, shall not be the object of attack."[437] It may suggest itself that the protection of many is more important than the protection of a single individual. However, the deterrence argument tries to increase the former one on the cost of the latter, whereas the Protocol demands for both protections.

Second, the Protocol does not impose a prohibition of taking part in hostilities upon civilians. It just states that such civilians will loose their

---

433 *Compare also* UK Ministry of Defence, *Manual*, para. 5.3.3 (p. 54); *compare also* ICRC, *Interpretive Guidance*, Geneva 2009, p. 56 in relation to an ammunition truck.

434 Schmitt, in: Fischer *et al.* (eds.), at 509; Supreme Court of Israel, "*Targeted Killings" (Merits)*, para. 34, 46 *ILM* (2007), at 391.

435 Schmitt, in: Fischer *et al.* (eds.), at 509.

436 *Id.*

437 *Compare also* Article 56 para. 3 of the 1977 Additional Protocol I.

special protection. In Article 45, the 1977 Additional Protocol I even establishes specific rules for persons who have taken part in hostilities, but who are not entitled to prisoner-of-war status, i.e. civilians who have taken part in hostilities. From the individual civilian's point of view there is thus a choice between taking part and loosing protection or maintaining the full protection afforded due to the status as civilian. On the other hand, it is true that a *too* narrow interpretation of direct participation could be counterproductive when it comes to the acceptance of the prohibition of targeting civilians:

> Should nothing be theoretically permissible to a belligerent engaged in war, ultimately everything will be permissible in practice – because the rules will be ignored.[438]

Third, a further possible critique of *Schmitt's* approach is based on the assumption that "[g]ray areas should be interpreted liberally."[439] As shown above, it is the interpretation of an exception to a rule in the focus here. One could counter *Schmitt's* argument by simply relying on the maxim: "Exceptions should be interpreted narrowly."

> Exceptions to rules are, morally speaking, dangerous. We all know that. Once you start opening up for exceptions, you often have no way of stopping since the signal has already been sent that the original rule is not absolute.[440]

It is undisputed that the rule concerned here is not an absolute one. Thus, the exception-argument cannot stand on its own. This argument can furthermore be criticised to represent a *topos*.[441] But the fact that it is an exception we are dealing with should make us cautious not to establish a "slippery slope" and be extra tentative in allowing cases to fall under this exception.

Fourth, it is in the responsibility of the armed forces to distinguish themselves from the civilians. Civilians are not obliged to distinguish themselves from combatants. Respectively, this system requires com-

---

[438] Dinstein, *Conduct of Hostilities*, pp. 1-2.

[439] Schmitt, in: Fischer *et al.* (eds.), at 509; Supreme Court of Israel, *"Targeted Killings" (Merits)*, para. 34, 46 *ILM* (2007), at 391.

[440] Henrik Syse, 'The Importance of Protecting Non-Combatants', in: 8 *Pacem* (2005), pp. 49-55, at 50.

[441] *See* Gerhard Struck, *Topische Jurisprudenz: Argument und Gemeinplatz in der juristischen Arbeit*, Frankfurt am Main 1971, p. 20.

batants to bear the responsibility not to attack civilians and have thus to take certain precautions in attack. To shift parts of this responsibility to the civilians is contrary to this system.

Fifth, another argument for reducing the meaning of "direct participation" to a narrow definition and thus creating more clear cases is the degree of proof that is necessary to convince the adversary that it is legal to attack a certain person:

> When a person is actually taking part in hostilities, the evidence is before us, and we do not face difficult evidentiary issues, such as identification and credibility of intelligence sources.[442]

Which consequences do these considerations have for other "grey cases"? The outsourcing of military activities to private companies, e.g. the maintenance and functioning of weapons systems by employees of the seller, raises similar questions as to the status of such employees.[443] Persons who provide service to weapons systems which combatants use – be the distance from the battlefield as it may – are partly also regarded as taking direct part in hostilities.[444] However, these persons are in the same position as those working in an ammunition factory: They do not pose an immediate threat without any intermediate instrumentality to the adversary, the harm to the adversary is only caused by the combatants using the weapon system later. Nevertheless, the facility the weapon system is serviced in is a military objective and can thus be attacked. This includes the civilian workers, subject to the principle of proportionality.

Furthermore, persons who serve as human shields of their free will are regarded as directly participating in hostilities.[445] The first impulse may be to support this assessment as such an action abuses the opponent's adherence to the prohibition of attacking civilians. On the other hand it will be practically almost impossible to distinguish voluntary human

---

[442] Kretzmer, 16 *Eur. J. Int'l L.* (2005), at 194.

[443] ICRC/T.M.C. Asser Institute, *Direct Participation*, Summary Report, June 2, 2003, at 30.

[444] Supreme Court of Israel, *"Targeted Killings" (Merits)*, para. 35, 46 *ILM* (2007), at 392.

[445] *Id.*; Schmitt, in: Fischer *et al.* (eds.), at 521. *Similarly*, with reference to "guilty civilians" and "innocent civilians", Gross, *Struggle of Democracy*, p. 227.

shields form those who are forced to act as shields.[446] If analysed thoroughly, it becomes clear that also theoretically such voluntary human shields do not take direct part in hostilities: They do not pose any direct harm to the adversary. They seriously endanger the principle of distinction and the prohibition of attacking civilians, but they do not have an immediate impact on the enemy. This does not mean that such an behaviour should be tolerated. It is dangerous for the protection of all civilians and should have harsh – but penal – consequences. This does not include deterrence by attack on the human shields. Additionally, the situation of voluntary human shields is not identical to that of "conventional" forced human shields: The adversary is not in the dilemma in which he has to decide between attacking his equals or refraining from an attack. A human shield normally comes from the side of the adversary and shall thus hinder him from attacking. Voluntary human shields are part of the side under such attack. The decision is thus the same as in any attack on a military objective which will affect civilians: It is legal if the civilian casualties are proportionate. Thus, the argument that voluntary human shields take direct part in hostilities would circumvent this question of proportionality. While voluntary human shields violate international humanitarian law, this does not justify a direct attack on the shields, but the military objective which they are protecting remains a legitimate target.[447]

Finally, it is argued that direct participation also includes the planning or ordering of attacks.[448] Again, an impulse exists to support such a view:

> It would seem odd to say that it is legitimate to attack a group of terrorists-in-training in a camp in Afghanistan, say, but not legitimate to go after the man who is planning the operation for which the others are training. That can't be right.[449]

---

446 Schondorf, 5 *J. Int'l Crim. Just.* (2007), at 308; *compare also* Roland Otto, 'Neighbours as Human Shields? The Israel Defense Forces' "Early Warning Procedure" and International Humanitarian Law', in: 86 *Int'l Rev. Red Cross* (2004), No 856, pp. 771-787, at 780-781.

447 *See also* Schondorf, 5 *J. Int'l Crim. Just.* (2007), at 308; ICRC, *Interpretive Guidance*, Geneva 2009, pp. 56-57.

448 Supreme Court of Israel, *"Targeted Killings" (Merits)*, para. 37, 46 *ILM* (2007), at 392-393; *see also* Ruys, *Juristenkrant* (January 17, 2007), at para. 7.

449 Michael Walzer, *Arguing about War*, New Haven 2004, p. 140.

But such situations have to be examined more differentiated: In the context of an armed conflict, the members of a military group in a training camp would most likely qualify as combatants or fighters and may thus be targeted due to their primary status. If they qualify as fighters or combatants, the same holds true for the head of the group and other members of the chain of command. They may be targeted as well due to their combatant status.

If the group and its members do not qualify as fighters or combatants, the decisive question is whether or not they take direct part in hostilities. This question has to be examined for every person individually subject to the conditions developed above: If a person inflicts actual harm on the adversary and the impact on the enemy is immediate, without any intermediate instrumentality, then this person takes direct part in hostilities. This may be true for persons directly preparing an attack, but it is questionable for persons involved in general training. In the latter case, there is still a considerable margin of time and space between these persons and actual harm. They do thus not – yet – take direct part.

If the same standards are applied to a person planning or ordering an attack, the result also is the same: Such a person inevitably poses a threat to the adversary, but this threat is not direct, as it is still disconnected by the person who will actually perform the attack. Thus, the latter person is most likely taking direct part in the hostilities once involved in the actual attack, whereas the former person is still too remote to be regarded as directly participating.

This result might seem very dissatisfying as thus the "privates" may be hit and the "generals" in the background seem to be spared. In some cases this may be true at least regarding the targeting of these persons – but not in relation to their criminal responsibility. In most cases, however, the importance of the person in the background will correlate with a function in a militant organisation. The more influence the person has on inferiors, the more likely is it that he and the other members of the organisation qualify as fighters or combatants and may thus be targeted anyway.

(3) The Duration of Direct Participation

In contrast to combatants, who can be valid targets without a time limit, i.e. even when they are in retreat or not posing an immediate threat to the attacking armed force,[450] the targeting of civilians taking direct part in hostilities is limited time-wise: They may only be targeted "for such time as they take a direct part in hostilities".

While Article 51 para. 3 of the 1977 Additional Protocol I is widely regarded as part of customary international law,[451] it is argued that the part reading "for such time" as they participate is reaching further than the wording used in Common Article 3 of the 1949 Geneva Conventions. Article 3 para. 1 only refers to persons "taking no active part in the hostilities" without a description of time. The element "for such time" is thus regarded by some authors as not representing customary international law.[452] This argument may find support in Article 8 para. 2 *lit.* b (i) of the 1998 Rome Statute of the International Criminal Court. This article reads in its relevant part:

> (b) Other serious violations of the laws and customs applicable in international armed conflict, within the established framework of international law, namely, any of the following acts: ... (i) Intentionally directing attacks against the civilian population as such or against individual civilians not taking direct part in hostilities;

This definition also omits reference to the words "for such time". However, by others, the full wording of Article 51 para. 3, including "for such time" is held to represent customary international law.[453] This understanding corresponds with the ordinary meaning of "unless": It can refer to "except if" as well as "except when",[454] the latter including an aspect of time. It can be understood as "civilians are protected except

---

450 Watkin, 15 *Duke J. Comp. & Int'l L.* (2005), at 310.

451 *Compare supra*, Part Two, Chapter D) II. 1. c).

452 Israel, Government Brief submitted in the case H.C. 769/02 before the Israeli Supreme Court, cited in Kretzmer, 16 *Eur. J. Int'l L.* (2005), at 193 (footnote 99).

453 Henckaerts/ Doswald-Beck (eds.), *Humanitarian Law*, Vol. 1, pp. 19-20 (Rule 6); Supreme Court of Israel, *"Targeted Killings" (Merits)*, paras. 23 and 29-30, 46 *ILM* (2007), at 384-385 and 388-390.

454 Hornby/ Crowther (eds.), *Oxford Advanced Learner's Dictionary*, p. 1246.

while they 'take direct part' in hostilities" especially if it is taken into account that "take direct part" is in present tense. This also corresponds to the meaning of "active" or "direct", which refer to an immediate threat posed by a person which may be opposed. Once the threat is over, opposition is rendered unnecessary. If understood in this manner, the term "for such time" could give clarification rather than adding new aspects to the pre-existing exception while codifying it.

Thus, according to Article 51 para. 3 of the 1977 Additional Protocol I and customary international law, civilians may only be opposed "for such time" as they are taking direct part in hostilities and if "such time" has passed the protection granted to the civilian returns.[455]

The term "for such time" according to the majority of authors has to be given a narrow meaning.[456] Thus, according to this view, civilians can reclaim the benefit of immunity from attack as soon as they have dropped their arms. They "cannot be killed at any time other than while they are posing an imminent threat to lives."[457] This narrow interpretation has been criticised as reflecting a human rights based approach to the use of force that does not address adequately the group nature of participation in hostilities and the greater level of violence associated

---

[455] Sandoz *et al.* (eds.), *Additional Protocols*, para. 1944 (p. 619); Inter-Am. Comm'n H.R., *Juan Carlos Abella ("La Tablada")*, *Annual Report* (1997), at para. 189 (applying "for such time" also to Common Article 3 of the 1949 Geneva Conventions); Supreme Court of Israel, *"Targeted Killings" (Merits)*, para. 38, 46 *ILM* (2007), at 393; Amnesty International, AI Doc. MDE 15/005/2001 (February 21, 2001), p. 29.

[456] Cassese, 'Expert Opinion', paras 14-15 (pp. 7-9); Sandoz *et al.* (eds.), *Protocoles additionnels*, para. 1944 (p. 633); ICRC, *Interpretive Guidance*, Geneva 2009, pp. 44-45; Eichensehr, 116 *Yale L.J.* (2007), at 1877; Amnesty International, AI Doc. MDE 15/056/2003 (July 4, 2003), p. 2; *similarly,* Frowein, 62 *ZaöRV* (2002), at 892; *but see* Schmitt, in: Fischer *et al.* (eds.), at 510.

[457] Amnesty International, AI Doc. MDE 15/056/2003 (July 4, 2003), p. 2.

with armed conflict.[458] It further has been criticised as opening a "revolving door" of protection for "unlawful combatants".[459]

(i) The "Revolving Door" Theory

"Can an individual be a guerrilla by night and a farmer by day?"[460] Again, it is necessary to draw a more differentiated picture. If a person is a "guerrilla" he is most likely not a civilian by status, but is a fighter or combatant.[461] He keeps this status permanently and may thus be attacked unless he is *hors de combat*. The question has thus to be understood as "Can a person take direct part in hostilities by night and be safe from attack by day?"

If the narrow interpretation especially regarding the duration of direct participation is accepted, the answer is in the affirmative. The consequence is what has been termed as the "revolving door" theory[462] "specific acts approach":[463] A person can remain civilian most of the time and only endanger his protection while actually in the process of carrying out specific acts amounting to direct participation in hostilities.[464]

Does the terrorist thus enjoy "the best of both worlds", as some authors have termed it?[465] Or does his staying with his family while not

---

[458] Watkin, 15 *Duke J. Comp. & Int'l L.* (2005), at 311; however, Watkin relies on criteria used to describe the status of combatants even though they are unarmed in exceptional situations, not direct participation of non-combatants, who are armed in exceptional situations, *compare* Sandoz *et al.* (eds.), *Additional Protocols*, para. 1695 (p. 528, note 35).

[459] *See e.g.* Parks, 32 *A.F. L. Rev.* (1990), at 118-120; Watkin, 15 *Duke J. Comp. & Int'l L.* (2005), at 312-313.

[460] Schmitt, in: Fischer *et al.* (eds.), at 510.

[461] *See e.g.* Ipsen, in: Fleck (ed.), *Handbook*, at 77-78 (para. 309); UK Ministry of Defence, *Manual*, paras. 4.3.2 and 4.5-4.6.2 (pp. 39 and 145); Dinstein, *Conduct of Hostilities*, p. 36.

[462] Watkin, *Combatants*, p. 12.

[463] *Compare* ICRC/T.M.C. Asser Institute, *Direct Participation*, Summary Report, October 23-25, 2005, p. 59; *compare also* ICRC, *Interpretive Guidance*, Geneva 2009, pp. 44-45.

[464] Casey, 32 *Syracuse J. Int'l L. & Com.* (2005), at 337; Doswald-Beck, 88 *Int'l Rev. Red Cross* (2006), No. 864, at 903.

[465] Kretzmer, 16 *Eur. J. Int'l L.* (2005), at 193.

directly taking part in hostilities amount to "human shielding", as others interpret such a behaviour?[466]

> Arguably, a person who leads a double life as a civilian and a militant should not be allowed to benefit from the protections afforded to civilians under the Convention as long as he or she remains in this 'schizophrenic' status.[467]

Thus, it is necessary to take alternatives to this "revolving door" into account.

(ii) The "One Way" Approach

According to a different approach, a civilian who has committed combatant like acts has crossed a line and cannot revert to being a protected civilian:

> A person is not allowed to wear simultaneously two caps: the hat of a civilian and the helmet of a soldier. He who engages in combat at night, while purporting to be a quiet civilian by day is neither a civilian nor a combatant.[468]

A person who took direct part in hostilities thus remains a legitimate target.[469] Such persons should remain at risk of being targeted as long as they act as "combatants", albeit without combatant status. Their status as "unprivileged belligerents" would, according to this approach, be determined by participation in the hostilities by the person until he disengages from such activities in a manner objectively recognizable to the

---

[466] Gross, *Struggle of Democracy*, p. 227; Guiora, 36 *Case W. Res. J. Int'l L.* (2004), at 329.

[467] Shany, in: Schmitt/ Beruto (eds.), at 104.

[468] Dinstein, in: Dinstein/ Tabory (eds.), at 105; *but see* Kremnitzer, in: Fleck (ed.), *Rechtsfragen*, at 211. The conclusion drawn by *Dinstein* that such a person "is an unlawful combatant, who is deprived of the protection of international law (in the form of entitlement to the status of a prisoner of war)" will be dealt with *infra*, Part Two, Chapter E).

[469] Parks, 32 *A.F. L. Rev.* (1990), at 118-120; Israel, Ministry of Foreign Affairs, 'Israel, the Conflict and Peace: Answers to Frequently Asked Questions', November 2007; *compare also* Shany, in: Schmitt/ Beruto (eds.), at 104.

adversary.[470] This approach is thus also referred to as the "affirmative disengagement approach".[471]

The question of direct participation could furthermore be determined by the person's membership and function in a group which takes part in the conflict,[472] i.e. by the so called "membership approach".[473] While mere financial donors or those providing moral support would not be regarded as direct participants to the conflict, those being part of a military like structure would be regarded as "taking direct part". This would include persons belonging to the group, supplying weapons or carrying out intelligence activities.[474] The only possibility for those quasi combatants would then be to become *hors de combat*, i.e. the same possibilities lawful combatants have.[475]

This assessment is very similar to the argument that a contemporary definition of civilians should refer to their "inoffensive character". According to this approach, civilians "can lose their civilian status whenever they become 'offensive' – that is, whenever they take action against military forces or their fellow citizens".[476] Even a statement by the Inter-American Commission on Human Rights has been interpreted in support of such an "one way" approach:[477]

---

470 *See e.g.* Schmitt, in: Arnold/ Quénivet (eds.), at 546: "until he unambiguously opts out through extended nonparticipation or an affirmative act of withdrawal."

471 ICRC/T.M.C. Asser Institute, *Direct Participation*, Summary Report, October 23-25, 2005, p. 59.

472 Watkin, 15 *Duke J. Comp. & Int'l L.* (2005), at 313; *see also* Fenrick, 5 *J. Int'l Crim. Just.* (2007), at 337-338.

473 ICRC/T.M.C. Asser Institute, *Direct Participation*, Summary Report, October 23-25, 2005, p. 59; this also is also the approach taken by the Supreme Court of Israel, *"Targeted Killings" (Merits)*, paras. 39-40, 46 *ILM* (2007), at 393-394.

474 Watkin, 15 *Duke J. Comp. & Int'l L.* (2005), at 313; Watkin, in: Wippman/ Evangelista (eds.), at 153-154.

475 Dinstein, *Conduct of Hostilities*, p. 28; Watkin, 15 *Duke J. Comp. & Int'l L.* (2005), at 313.

476 Slaughter/ Burke-White, 43 *Harv. Int'l L.J.* (2002), at 13.

477 *See* Kretzmer, 16 *Eur. J. Int'l L.* (2005), at 193.

> It is possible in this connection, however, that once a person qualifies as a combatant, whether regular or irregular, privileged or unprivileged, he or she cannot on demand revert back to civilian status or otherwise alternate between combatant and civilian status.[478]

However the Inter-American Commission is referring to a change of status from a civilian to a combatant. Such a change , i.e. in the case of a "a civilian who is incorporated in an armed organization ..., becomes a member of the military and a combatant throughout the duration of the hostilities",[479] has to be distinguished from the case at hand: A civilian who directly takes part in hostilities remains a civilian. He only looses his immunity from attack. As shown above, this is not a general change of status, but a mere reduction of the standard of protection for the time of participation. The further context of the Inter-American Commission's statement shows that the commission was well aware of that fact. They continue:

> If he is wounded, sick or shipwrecked, he is entitled to the protection of the First and Second Conventions (Article 44, paragraph 8), and, if he is captured, he is entitled to the protection of the Third Convention (Article 44, paragraph 1).[480]

Thus, the "one way" approach would not go as far as accepting a change of status from civilian to combatant. What it would do is regarding a person who took part in the hostilities from that time onwards as a legitimate target unless this person is *hors de combat*.

(iii) Critique

Both approaches may lead to inadequate results in extreme cases. A civilian taking direct part in hostilities one single time – according to the "one way" approach – is regarded as a legitimate target from that time onward, even though he might never again be a threat to the adversary. On the other hand, a civilian who has joined a militant group but does not fulfil the conditions of combatant or fighter status could – according to the "revolving door" theory – engage in attacks against the adversary every day and afterwards return home and enjoy protected civilian status with his family.

---

478 Inter-Am. Comm'n H.R., *Report on Terrorism*, para. 69.

479 *Id.*, para. 69 (footnote 211).

480 *Id.*

Especially with the latter case in mind, there are some arguments in support of the "one way" approach: "a civilian who has joined a terrorist organization which has become his 'home', and in the framework of his role in that organization he commits a chain of hostilities, with short periods of rest between them"[481] resembles a combatant and it seems arbitrary to confine possibilities to target such a person. Thus, some authors even argue that the definition of combatant should be expanded to cover any person who takes active part in hostilities.[482] Such a broad definition indeed has the advantage that it avoids the possibility of moving from civilian to "combatant-like" status back and forth according to the activities conducted.

In a larger context, it is argued that due to a limit of targeting civilians to cases where they actually are taking part in hostilities, "the right of self-defence under Article 51 UN charter following an armed attack by a group may become meaningless."[483] This argument is difficult in two regards: First, it runs the risk of mixing *jus ad bellum* and *jus in bello* questions. The overall legality of the participation in an armed conflict by one party to the conflict has no effect on questions of legality of the single persons on either side of the conflict. Even in an war of aggression, the single combatants cannot be punished for the mere fact of fighting. Thus, the question of whether and for which period of time a person is taking direct part in hostilities has to be answered independently of any consideration concerning *jus ad bellum*. In that regard, the same standards apply to self-defence and aggression. Second, the argument is based on the assumption that self-defence is possible by a State against non-State actors. This assumption is highly disputed.[484] Finally, it has to be admitted that even those supporting the "one way" approach accept that a civilian may detach himself from hostilities "entirely, or for a long period" and can thus enjoy protection from attack again.[485]

---

[481] *See e.g.* Supreme Court of Israel, *"Targeted Killings" (Merits)*, para. 39, 46 *ILM* (2007), at 393.

[482] Dinstein, *Conduct of Hostilities*, p. 27.

[483] Kretzmer, 16 *Eur. J. Int'l L.* (2005), at 193.

[484] *Compare infra*, Part Four, Chapter F) I. 2.

[485] *See e.g.* Supreme Court of Israel, *"Targeted Killings" (Merits)*, para. 39, 46 *ILM* (2007), at 393.

There are various arguments against the "one way" approach and it is thus considered as being not consistent with international law:[486] Mainly, this approach would contradict the principle of distinction that is based on clear-cut status of all persons. As a combatant does not lose his combatant status because he infringes a rule of international humanitarian law,[487] a civilian does not lose his status if he takes direct part in hostilities, but loses part of his protection: In armed conflicts, a person has a "status" as civilian or combatant and keeps this "status" even if he performs actions assigned to the other status. This status may be less clear cut in non-international armed conflicts, but the principle that underlies both legal regimes is the same.

Furthermore, if the "one way" approach would be applied consistently, the logical effect of such a step away from civilian status would be that these persons acquire prisoner-of-war status if captured by the adversary in the context of an international armed conflict. It is unlikely that the authors supporting the "one way" approach would regard such a consequence tenable.

The required "detachment" from hostilities to re-establish civilian immunity resembles very much the concept of being *hors de combat*. However, the principle that combatants may be attacked until they are *hors de combat* cannot be transferred to civilians: Unlike combatants, who must generally distinguish themselves from other civilians even while not actually fighting, it is rather difficult to distinguish civilians who took direct part in hostilities form other civilians who did not. If the former group may be attacked, the latter group and in consequence the whole civilian population will be put in jeopardy.[488] This holds true in international as well as in non-international armed conflicts. The protection for the civil population depends on the clear and obvious criteria according to which persons can be targeted legally. The actual involvement in hostile deeds is a very practicable criterion in that regard.

One of the strongest arguments for the "one way" approach is that concerning a person who is a member of a group which takes direct part in hostilities on a regular basis. Such a "combatant-like" approach is proposed by *Watkin*, who argues that the membership in the military

---

486 Casey, 32 *Syracuse J. Int'l L. & Com.* (2005), at 337.

487 *Compare supra*, Part Two, Chapter C) I.

488 Sassòli, in: Wippman/ Evangelista (eds.), at 201.

wing of a group involved in a conflict should be more decisive than individual actions by that person. This argument gains special relevance in the context of non-international armed conflicts, where the status of "combatants" or fighters in not as clear cut from that of civilians. But even this argument cannot convince entirely: The mere fact that a person belongs to a group which promotes or carries out violent and hostile actions does not imply that the person is taking direct part in hostilities. Persons associated with such a group may be killers, superiors who order the acts, colleagues who facilitate them, trainers, colleagues offering general encouragement without actual knowledge of a specific act, persons who disapprove of violent means but who participate in other activities of said organisation and, outside the organisation donors and supporters of different kinds.[489] Different persons may shift from one of those positions to another. Clearly not all of these persons are part of the fighting organisation and therefore not all of them can be targeted.[490] Therefore, any "membership approach" would have to be limited to the fighting members of a group. Then, however, the whole approach is moot: The fighting members are taking direct part in hostilities and may be targeted due to this activity, but subject to individual assessment.[491]

Additionally, the very idea of distinguishing between civilians and combatants is based on the assumption that civilians cannot be attacked due to their status – but exclusively based on their conduct. If an attribute like "membership" to a certain group is equated with direct participation, the difference between status and conduct is blurred. Direct attacks against civilians must thus be based exclusively on the individuals conduct and not on some kind of "status". Thus, it still remains the individual who – under certain circumstances – can be targeted, but not the members of a group. If the drafters of the regulations concerning direct participation had intended to solve this problem based on "membership" or any other similar "status" they would have done so in the Additional Protocols. However, the protocols exclusively refer to individual conduct.

These aspects show that the "revolving door" theory is – at least in principle – the right approach: The very text of Article 51 para. 3 of the

---

[489] Neuman, 14 *Eur. J. Int'l L.* (2003), at 289.

[490] Watkin, 15 *Duke J. Comp. & Int'l L.* (2005), at 311.

[491] *See also* Gehring, 19 *Rev. dr. pén. mil.* (1980), at 19-20.

1977 Additional Protocol I and of Article 13 para. 3 of the 1977 Additional Protocol II – "for such time" – can be interpreted as intending the "revolving door" phenomenon in the drafting process of the Protocols.[492] It pays regard to the important rationale behind the rule that civilians may only be targeted for such time as they participate in hostilities, namely to avoid mistakes in identification.[493] The consequence of direct participation is not a change of status but a decrease of the level of protection due to the threat the person in question poses to the adversary.[494] If this threat disappears, the level of protection increases again. Thus, if a person stops taking direct part in hostilities and returns to his family, he may not be attacked due to the fact that he is no longer a legitimate target. Such an behaviour does not amount to "human shielding", as others interpret it.[495] Only if the direct participation is so closely interrelated to the civil life and family of the person in question, i.e. if he commits hostile acts from his home, he is a legitimate target at home. Then, the question is not that of human shielding but of proportionality in relation to collateral damage.[496]

d) No Exception: Protected Persons Suspected or Engaged in Activities Hostile to the Security of the State

At a first glance, the 1949 Geneva Convention IV might be understood as containing a further exception from the general rule that civilians

---

[492] ICRC/T.M.C. Asser Institute, *Direct Participation*, Summary Report, October 23-25, 2005, p. 50; ICRC, *Interpretive Guidance*, Geneva 2009, p. 70 ("an integral part, not a malfunction").

[493] *See also* Melzer, *Targeted Killing*, pp. 352-353; *compare* Doswald-Beck, 88 *Int'l Rev. Red Cross* (2006), No. 864, at 897; Eichensehr, 116 *Yale L.J.* (2007), at 1877.

[494] Inter-Am. Comm'n H.R., *Juan Carlos Abella ("La Tablada"), Annual Report* (1997), at para. 189.

[495] *See e.g.* Guiora, 36 *Case W. Res. J. Int'l L.* (2004), at 329; *compare also* Gross, *Struggle of Democracy*, p. 227.

[496] *Compare infra*, Part Two, Chapter D) II. 2. b). *Gross* argues similarly, but he draws a distinction between "guilty civilians" who choose to serve as human shields of their own free will and "innocent civilians" who act as human shields involuntarily, *see* Gross, *Struggle of Democracy*, p. 227.

may not be attacked: Article 5 paras. 1 and 2 of the 1949 Geneva Convention IV read:

> Where, in the territory of a Party to the conflict, the latter is satisfied that an individual protected person is definitely suspected of or engaged in activities hostile to the security of the State, such individual person shall not be entitled to claim such rights and privileges under the present Convention as would, if exercised in the favour of such individual person, be prejudicial to the security of such State.
>
> Where in occupied territory an individual protected person is detained as a spy or saboteur, or as a person under definite suspicion of activity hostile to the security of the Occupying Power, such person shall, in those cases where absolute military security so requires, be regarded as having forfeited rights of communication under the present Convention.

This rule only applies to protected persons. According to Article 4 of the Convention, this covers those persons who "find themselves, in case of a conflict or occupation, in the hands of a Party to the conflict or Occupying Power of which they are not nationals." There are thus two main cases of protected persons: First, "enemy nationals" within the national territory of each of the parties to the conflict. Second, "the whole population" of occupied territories – excluding nationals of the occupying power.[497]

The "rights and privileges under the present Convention" include *inter alia* the prohibition to "cause the physical suffering or extermination of protected persons" as laid down in Article 32 of the Convention.[498] This article is part of Part III Section I of the Convention and thus applies to all protected persons. Further rights and privileges only apply to certain groups of protected persons. In that regard, the emphasis of the Convention is on the protected persons in occupied territories, laid

---

497 Pictet (ed.), *Geneva Conventions*, Vol. 4, p. 46.

498 Article 32 of the 1949 Geneva Convention IV reads: "The High Contracting Parties specifically agree that each of them is prohibited from taking any measure of such a character as to cause the physical suffering or extermination of protected persons in their hands. This prohibition applies not only to murder, torture, corporal punishment, mutilation and medical or scientific experiments not necessitated by the medical treatment of a protected person, but also to any other measures of brutality whether applied by civilian or military agents."

down in the 32 paragraphs of Part III Section III of the Convention. In Articles 64-77 it includes inter alia rules on penal law and in its last Article 78 para. 1 states:

> If the Occupying Power considers it necessary, for imperative reasons of security, to take safety measures concerning protected persons, it may, at the most, subject them to assigned residence or to internment.[499]

By using this system the 1949 Geneva Convention IV restricts the choices of measures an occupying power may employ in order to maintain order in an occupied territory: Threats to the security may only be opposed by way of preventive detention or assigned residence under Article 78. These measures are "the most severe and serious measures that an occupying power may adopt against protected residents".[500] The only other possibility according to the Convention is to initiate penal proceedings which have to satisfy the usual procedural standards. Thus, "[t]he Convention does not permit the killing of protected persons under any circumstances."[501]

Nevertheless, it would still be possible to argue that Article 5 para. 1 establishes an exception to this general prohibition of using deadly force against protected persons in order to oppose activities hostile to the occupying State. However, the second paragraph of the Article contradicts such an interpretation: It covers the worst cases of acts hostile to the security of the occupying State and presupposes that even in those cases, persons may only be detained, albeit without the rights of communication under the Convention. By establishing these two categories of threat to the security of the occupying State, the Convention shows that further measures of reaction are not provided for. They are reserv-

---

[499] Paras. 2 and 3 of the Article specify procedural rules concerning this detention.

[500] Supreme Court of Israel, *Ajuri v. IDF Commander in the West Bank ("Assigned Residence")*, H.C.J. 7015/02, Judgment of September 3, 2002, para. 24, English translation reprinted in: Israel Supreme Court, *Judgments of the Israel Supreme Court: Fighting Terrorism within the Law*, Jerusalem 2005, pp. 144-178, at 162 and 125 *Int'l L.R.* (2004), pp. 537-568, at 533. *See also* Pictet (ed.), *Geneva Conventions*, Vol. 4, p. 256.

[501] Shany, in: Schmitt/ Beruto (eds.), at 104.

ed to penal law, including the death penalty subject to due process of law.[502]

> A saboteur, ... is on the one hand, punished in accordance with the Civilians Convention. Granted that he is a "protected person" (Article 4) and that in this capacity he shall be unconditionally 'treated with humanity' (third paragraph of Article 5). A protected person can, however, if 'imperative reasons of security' make this necessary, be subjected to assigned residence or to internment (Article 78). Furthermore, the Occupying Power can under certain circumstances retain a saboteur without judgement (second paragraph of Article 5) and, in the case of prosecution, sentence him to death (second paragraph of Article 68).[503]

Additionally,

> [t]he fundamental guarantees of international humanitarian law may never be questioned. To respect these rights is in no circumstances 'prejudicial to the security of such State'.[504]

Furthermore, it has to be taken into account that the 1949 Geneva Conventions represent the original humanitarian law, i.e. that law referring to the protection of those persons affected by armed conflicts. Opposed to this, the principle of distinction and the prohibition to attack civilians has its source in the "law of war proper",[505] i.e. in the Hague law dealing with means and methods of warfare. It is true that both areas are strongly interrelated. However, the exception laid down in Article 5 para. 1 of the 1949 Geneva Convention IV only refers to "rights and privileges under the present Convention". Thus, this Article cannot refer to rules that exist outside the Convention, namely the prohibition to attack civilians. Article 5 para. 1 of the Convention does not challenge the status of a person as a civilian.[506] It does not even deprive a person of the status of being a protected person. The Article's effect is

---

502 Dinstein, in: Meron (ed.), at 349.

503 Esbjörn Rosenblad, 'Guerrilla Warfare and International Law', in: 12 *Rev. dr. pén. mil.* (1973), pp. 91-134, at 111.

504 Gasser, in: Fleck (ed.), *Handbook*, at 233 (para. 518.7); *see also* Judith Wieczorek, *Unrechtmäßige Kombattanten und humanitäres Völkerrecht*, Berlin 2005, p. 151.

505 Chadwick, *Self-Determination*, p. 5.

506 Wieczorek, *Unrechtmäßige Kombattanten*, p. 110.

only a "somewhat reduced protection for such persons"[507] and relates to the additional privileges which are established by the Convention.[508]

Thus, the prohibition to attack or deliberately kill civilians also applies to protected persons who are suspected of or engaged in activities hostile to the security of the State. As long as the conduct of such persons does not amount to direct participation in the hostilities of an armed conflict, they may only be detained or assigned a new residence – which does not preclude their penal responsibility for their acts.

e) Further Restrictions

In addition to the rules discussed above, which concern the question of whether a person may be targeted as such, an attack on an legitimate target can be illegal due to the means employed. Here, in principle, the same standards apply as in connection with combatants. However, concerning some methods that are arguably legal if directed against combatants, there are further restrictions if the legitimately targeted person is a civilian. This is namely the case if booby traps are used: According to Article 3 para. 7 of the Protocol on Prohibitions or Restrictions on the Use of Mines, Booby Traps and Other Devices

> [i]t is prohibited in all circumstances to direct weapons to which this Article applies, either in offence, defence or by way of reprisals, against the civilian population as such or against individual civilians or civilian objects.

The said article applies according to its first paragraph to mines, booby traps and other devices as defined in Article 2, paras. 1-5 of the Protocol. A booby trap is a

> device or material which is designed, constructed or adapted to kill or injure, and which functions unexpectedly when a person disturbs or approaches an apparently harmless object or performs an apparently safe act.

An example is a hand-grenade if attached to a door and rigged to explode when the door opens.[509] The prohibition of booby traps is of

---

[507] Dörmann, 85 *Int'l Rev. Red Cross* (2003), No 849, at 57-58; *see also* Gehring, 19 *Rev. dr. pén. mil.* (1980), at 25-26.

[508] Wieczorek, *Unrechtmäßige Kombattanten*, p. 110.

special importance regarding targeted killings as such devices have frequently been used to hit individuals, e.g. by booby trapping a cellular phone which then exploded or by booby trapping a phone booth a person regularly uses.[510] Beside the risk of being indiscriminate in their application,[511] booby traps are regarded as illegal if employed against civilians.

Whereas some authors regard this special prohibition as not strictly required, inasmuch as it merely reiterates the general rule of international humanitarian law,[512] it is argued here that this prohibition is absolute.[513] The wording "in all circumstances" clarifies that the prohibition not only restates the general – but not absolute – prohibition to attack civilians, but that it excludes the use of booby traps even against those civilians who may be attacked under the exceptions developed above. According to this system, in relation to civilians, booby traps are prohibited weapons.

f) Conclusion: Targeted Killings of Civilians

As shown above, the exception to the provision of targeting civilians has to be interpreted restrictively. According to conventional and customary international law, civilians may not be targeted, unless and for such time as they take a direct part in hostilities. In that regard, "taking direct part in hostilities" is not restricted to the actual act of firing a weapon, but includes certain preparations thereof. The decisive factor is the threat a civilian poses to the adversary, and this threat may be opposed. This implies that the duration of direct participation also has to be interpreted restrictively: Once the actual threat is over, participation is over and the civilian thus is protected from attack again.

Admittedly, this interpretation is rather restrictive concerning the possibility of targeting such persons. Especially from the adversary's armed

---

509 Marian Nash (Leich), 'Contemporary Practice of the United States Relating to International Law', in: 91 *Am. J. Int'l L.* (1997), pp. 325-348, at 333.

510 Luft, 10 *Mid. E. Q.* (2003), at 5-6 and 13.

511 *Compare infra*, Part Two, Chapter D) II. 2. a).

512 Dinstein, *Conduct of Hostilities*, p. 66; Nash, 91 *Am. J. Int'l L.* (1997), at 335-336.

513 *See also* UK Ministry of Defence, *Manual*, para. 6.7 (p. 105).

forces' the point of view – who are the possible object of attacks by civilians – it is understandable emotionally that they wish to have the extensive possibilities to forcefully react to participating civilians. But in that regard, it is important to exclude aspects of retaliation and ensure that civilians are treated with careful adherence to the rules. Finally, it should not be forgotten that the person, while being a civilian, is still criminally liable for the deeds committed. As they are not authorized to undertake armed acts against the adversary, they can be prosecuted and sentenced as criminals for their direct participation, subject to the rules of Article 45 1977 Additional Protocol I.[514] Albeit direct participation in hostilities by civilians is not a war crime.[515]

Additionally, a relatively high standard concerning the attack on civilians not only serves the protection of the single person who is responsible for hostile acts against the adversary. A high threshold protects foremost those who are not responsible for hostile acts: The lower the preconditions for such attacks are, the more likely is it that the latter persons will be confused with the former. Thus, a higher standard of protection for the non-responsible inevitably entails a higher standard of protection for those responsible. If those responsible are no longer protected, ultimately all non-responsible persons will remain unprotected as well.[516]

These standards apply to international and non-international armed conflicts in the same manner. As shown above, it is more difficult to distinguish civilians and fighters in that context.[517] Thus, direct participation is the safest sign that a person can be subject to attack.

2. *Protection of Civilians not Specifically Targeted*

Attacks against civilians are generally – but with the shown exceptions – banned when they are deliberate. An attack that is legal in relation to the targeted person – and this includes combatants – can nevertheless be

---

[514] Ipsen, in: Fleck (ed.), *Handbook*, at 68 (para. 302).

[515] *Compare* ICRC, *International Humanitarian Law and the Challenges of Contemporary Armed Conflicts*, Report, September 2003, p. 10.

[516] European Commission for Democracy through Law, Opinion No. 245/2003, para. 7.

[517] *Compare supra*, Part Two, Chapter C) II.

illegal due to its effects on other civilians. This is the case when an attack is either indiscriminate or if the collateral damage is disproportionate.

a) Prohibition of Indiscriminate Attacks

The prohibition of indiscriminate attacks is part of the principle of proportionality[518] and can be traced back to the 1923 Hague Rules of Air Warfare.[519] It is expressly laid down in paras. 4 and 5 of Article 51 of the 1977 Additional Protocol I. The former paragraph reads:

> Indiscriminate attacks are prohibited. Indiscriminate attacks are: (a) those which are not directed at a specific military objective; (b) those which employ a method or means of combat which cannot be directed at a specific military objective; or (c) those which employ a method or means of combat the effects of which cannot be limited as required by this Protocol; and consequently, in each such case, are of a nature to strike military objectives and civilians or civilian objects without distinction.

Whereas the fact that indiscriminate attacks are prohibited in international and non-international armed conflicts is undisputed,[520] their definition is less clear. It was argued in the drafting process that the term did not refer to certain means and methods of combat that are indis-

---

518 UK Ministry of Defence, *Manual*, para. 2.6.1 (p. 25).

519 Rules concerning the Control of Wireless Telegraphy in Time of War and Air Warfare, adopted at The Hague, Netherlands on February 19, 1923, reprinted in: Schindler/ Toman (eds.), *Collection*, pp. 207-217. The rules never were never adopted in legally binding form but they are "an authoritative attempt to clarify and formulate rules of law governing the use of aircraft in war", *see* Oppenheim/ Lauterpacht, *International Law*, p. 519. Article 24 para. 3 reads: "Any bombardment of cities, towns, villages, habitations and building which are not situated in the immediate vicinity of the operations of the land forces, is forbidden. Should the objectives specified in paragraph 2 be so situated that they could not be bombed but that an undiscriminating bombardment of the civil population would result therefrom, the aircraft must abstain from bombing".

520 *Compare* Henckaerts/ Doswald-Beck (eds.), *Humanitarian Law*, Vol. 1, p. 37 (Rule 11). The prohibition was included in the draft of the 1977 Additional Protocol II but was dropped at the last moment as part of a package aimed at the adoption of a simplified text, *see ibid.*, p. 38, with further references.

criminate in all circumstances, but rather to the use of legitimate means in situations where they affect civilians in an indiscriminate way.[521] The definition of indiscriminate attacks also has implications of intent: The attacker is not trying to harm the civilian population, i.e. does not act with direct intention, but the injury of civilians is a of no concern to him, i.e. he is acting recklessly or at most with *dolus eventualis*.[522] The indiscriminate character of an attack does not merely depend on the number of civilian casualties, but mainly on the state of mind of the attacker. Thus, the question of whether an attack was indiscriminate depends on the information that was available to the attacker at the time of the attack.[523]

The cases referred to in para. 4 *lit.* a and *lit.* b are straightforward. They are an application of the prohibition on directing attacks against civilian objects and thus depend on the definition of military objectives. This term has been discussed *supra*.[524] Examples of the former case are to fire blindly, i.e. without a clear idea of the nature of the target, into an area controlled by the enemy, to release at random bombs from an aircraft unless it has been established that no civilians of civilian objects are in that area, or to conduct bombings in the absence of adequate equipment or visibility for target identification.[525] The same applies to mines if it is not ensured that the civilian population will not be injured by the mining operation.[526]

The latter problem is especially relevant in regard of targeted killings performed by booby traps: As shown above, it is absolutely prohibited to direct them against individual civilians. Additionally, it is obvious that their indiscriminate use is prohibited, even if they are directed

---

521 Gardam, *Non-Combatant Immunity*, p. 116.

522 *Compare* Heinz Marcus Hanke, 'The 1923 Hague Rules of Air Warfare', in: 33 *Int'l Rev. Red Cross* (1993), No. 292, pp. 12-44, at 26; *see also* Dinstein, *Conduct of Hostilities*, p. 117.

523 Dinstein, *id.*

524 *See supra*, Part Two, Chapter D) II. 1. b).

525 Oeter, in: Fleck (ed.), *Handbook*, at 174-175 (paras. 455.2-455.3); Examples would be "blind weapons" such as the German V-1 and V-2 of the Second World War and the Scud Missiles launched by Iraq against Israel and Saudi Arabia during the 1991 Gulf War, *see* Green, *Law of Armed Conflict*, p. 152.

526 Gerold Würkner-Theis, *Fernverlegte Minen und humanitäres Völkerrecht*, Frankfurt am Main 1990, pp. 102-103 and 141-148.

against combatants. This principle is further specified in Article 7 paras. 2 and 3 of the Protocol on Prohibitions or Restrictions on the Use of Mines, Booby Traps and Other Devices:

> (2) It is prohibited to use booby-traps or other devices in the form of apparently harmless portable objects which are specifically designed and constructed to contain explosive material. (3) Without prejudice to the provisions of Article 3, it is prohibited to use weapons to which this Article applies in any city, town, village or other area containing a similar concentration of civilians in which combat between ground forces is not taking place or does not appear to be imminent, unless either: (a) they are placed on or in the close vicinity of a military objective; or (b) measures are taken to protect civilians from their effects, for example, the posting of warning sentries, the issuing of warnings or the provision of fences.

As a mere embodiment of the general prohibition to use indiscriminate means, these rules concerning booby traps can be regarded as part of that prohibition and thus to represent customary international law. In further relation to indiscriminate means, article 51 para. 4 *lit.* b of the 1977 Additional Protocol I refers to the technical inadequacy of the weapons used: Examples are indiscriminate missile attacks due to the construction of the missile which relies only on a rudimentary guiding system. It also includes bombing raids from extremely high altitudes where the target accuracy becomes unacceptably low.[527]

The cases covered by para. 4 *lit.* c are less clear as it refers to a whole series of limitations on attack: The requirements of the Protocol include *inter alia* rules on the protection of the environment,[528] the prohibition of attacks on works containing dangerous forces[529] and most prominently the principle of proportionality as laid down in Article 51 para. 5 *lit.* b and Article 57 para. 2 *lit.* a (iii) of the 1977 Additional Protocol I. The latter article specifies the precautions which have to be taken in attack in order to comply with the rule of non-combatant immunity.[530]

---

[527] Oeter, in: Fleck (ed.), *Handbook*, at 175 (para. 455.3) with further references.

[528] *See* Article 35 para. 3 and Article 55 para. 1 of the 1977 Additional Protocol I.

[529] *See* Article 56 of the 1977 Additional Protocol I.

[530] *See infra*, Part Two, Chapter D) II. 2. b) (3).

In view of the fact that the principle of proportionality serves to strike a balance between the achievement of military goals and collateral civilian casualties, Article 51 para. 4 *lit.* c can be read as prohibiting attacks which may be expected to cause excessive civilian casualties.[531] This provision reflects customary international law and applies in all armed conflicts.[532] As it is difficult to determine which attacks will fall into this category, it has been criticized as being too vague.[533] The rule allows a considerable degree of latitude for interpretation before an attack will be considered indiscriminate and has thus been criticised as leaving too much room for the military.[534]

After the rather complex and still abstract definition of indiscriminate attacks given in Article 51 para. 4, para. 5 supplements this by two examples.[535] Para. 5 reads:

> Among others, the following types of attacks are to be considered as indiscriminate: (a) an attack by bombardment by any methods or means which treats as a single military objective a number of clearly separated and distinct military objectives located in a city, town, village or other area containing a similar concentration of civilians or civilian objects; and (b) an attack which may be expected to cause incidental loss of civilian life, injury to civilians, damage to civilian objects, or a combination thereof, which would be excessive in relation to the concrete and direct military advantage anticipated.

Para. 5 *lit.* a further specifies indiscriminate attacks and prohibits as examples an area bombing or carpet bombing,[536] which are of no special relevance regarding targeted killings. Para. 5 *lit.* b explicitly clarifies

---

[531] Gardam, *Non-Combatant Immunity*, p. 117.

[532] Kretzmer, 16 *Eur. J. Int'l L.* (2005), at 200; Oeter, in: Fleck (ed.), *Handbook*, at 176-177 (para. 455.4).

[533] Parks, 32 *A.F. L. Rev.* (1990), at 168-170.

[534] Gardam, *Non-Combatant Immunity*, p. 117.

[535] Sandoz *et al.* (eds.), *Additional Protocols*, para. 1967 (p. 623); UK Ministry of Defence, *Manual*, para. 2.6.1 (p. 25); Oeter, in: Fleck (ed.), *Handbook*, at 177 (para. 456).

[536] Gardam, *Non-Combatant Immunity*, p. 117; Henckaerts/ Doswald-Beck (eds.), *Humanitarian Law*, Vol. 1, pp. 43-44 (Rule 13).

what had been accepted as customary international law before:[537] If collateral damage is likely to affect the civilian population, the anticipated damage must not be excessive in relation to the intended military advantage. As the Protocol refers to excessive attacks as a category of indiscriminate attacks, a proportionate attack cannot be regarded as indiscriminate.[538]

b) Proportionality, Collateral Damage and Precautions in Attack

The principle of proportionality is a rule of customary international law derived from the general principle of law.[539] It is – in part – already reflected in Article 15 of the Lieber Code[540] and is codified in Article 51 para. 5 *lit.* b of the 1977 Additional Protocol I,[541] prohibiting attacks which may be expected to cause civilian casualties which would be excessive in relation to the concrete and direct military advantage anticipated. This principle is the inevitable link between the principles of military necessity and humanity, where they lead to contradictory results.[542]

---

[537] Greenwood, in: Delissen/ Tanja (eds.), at 109; Henckaerts/ Doswald-Beck (eds.), *Humanitarian Law*, Vol. 1, p. 46 (Rule 14).

[538] Friedhelm Krüger-Sprengel, 'Le Concept de Proportionalité dans le Droit de la Guerre', in: 19 *Rev. dr. pén. mil.* (1980), pp. 177-204, at 192; Dinstein, *Conduct of Hostilities*, p. 121.

[539] Max Huber, 'Quelques considerations sur une revision éventuelle des Conventions de la Haye relatives à la guerre', in: 37 *Rev. Int'l Croix-Rouge* (1955), pp. 417-482, at 423; Krüger-Sprengel, 19 *Rev. dr. pén. mil.* (1980), at 187.

[540] Article 15 reads: "Military necessity admits of all direct destruction of life or limb of armed enemies, and of other persons whose destruction is incidentally unavoidable in the armed contests of the war; …"; *compare* Eric Jaworski, '"Military Necessity" and "Civilian Immunity": Where is the Balance?', in: 2 *Chin. J. Int'l L.* (2003), pp. 175-206, at 179.

[541] On the drafting history *see* Judith Gail Gardam, *Necessity, Proportionality and the Use of Force by States*, Cambridge 2004, pp. 88-93.

[542] Bothe *et al.*, *1977 Protocols*, Art. 51 Prot. I, para. 2.6.2 (p. 309); Krüger-Sprengel, 19 *Rev. dr. pén. mil.* (1980), at 180-181; Anthony P.V. Rogers, 'Conduct of Combat and Risks run by the Civilian Population', in: 21 *Rev. dr. pén. mil.* (1982), pp. 293-319, at 297; Sassòli, in: Wippman/ Evangelista (eds.), at 204; UK Ministry of Defence, *Manual*, para. 2.6.2 (p. 25) and para. 5.33.2 (p. 86).

In the past, any unavoidable injury or damage caused to civilians or civilian objects was accepted as "collateral damage".[543] Under contemporary international humanitarian law, the principle of proportionality applies to that question. It is part of treaty law and it is part of customary international law applicable in international and non-international armed conflicts:[544]

> The principle of proportionality, even if finding no specific mention, is reflected in many provisions of Additional Protocol I to the Geneva Conventions of 1949. Thus even a legitimate target may not be attacked if the collateral civilian casualties would be disproportionate to the specific military gain from the attack.[545]

The principle is reiterated in Article 57 para. 2 *lit.* a (iii) of the 1977 Additional Protocol I and attacks which violate the principle of proportionality are war crimes according to Article 8 para. 2 *lit.* b (iv) of the 1998 Rome Statute of the International Criminal Court.

A military objective does not cease to be a military objective as such if an attack would lead to disproportionate collateral civilian casualties. The principle of proportionality only restricts the possibility of attacking that object under the given circumstances. If an attack at another time or by different means would not cause excessive civilian damage, the latter attack on the objective is legal.[546] Furthermore, in determining an objective of an attack among several objectives carrying a similar

---

[543] Dinstein, *Conduct of Hostilities*, p. 119.

[544] *See e.g.* Parks, 32 *A.F. L. Rev.* (1990), at 168-175; Dinstein, *Conduct of Hostilities*, pp. 119-120; Greenwood, in: Delissen/ Tanja (eds.), at 109; Henckaerts/ Doswald-Beck (eds.), *Humanitarian Law*, Vol. 1, pp. 46-49 with further references; UK Ministry of Defence, *The Manual of the Law of Armed Conflict*, Oxford 2004, para. 5.33.2 (p. 86); Gardam, *Necessity*, p. 112; Oeter, in: Fleck (ed.), *Handbook*, at 178 (para. 465.2) with further references.

[545] ICJ, *Legality of the Threat or Use of Nuclear Weapons*, Advisory Opinion of July 8, 1996, Dissenting Opinion of Judge Higgins, I.C.J. Reports 1996, pp. 226-593, at 587 (para. 20).

[546] *Compare* Elmar Rauch, 'Conduct of Combat and Risks Run by the Civilian Population', in: 21 *Rev. dr. pén. mil.* (1982), pp. 66-72, at 67.

military advantage, the one causing least danger to the civilian population must be chosen if possible.[547]

Civilian casualties can be the result of civilians working in military objectives[548] or living in the vicinity of such legitimate targets. Additionally, human error or malfunction of weapons systems can also lead to civilian losses.[549] Generally, a certain percentage of any weapon will malfunction and hit the wrong object.[550] If the latter case happens more frequently with the same certain weapons system, the use of this system could eventually amount to indiscriminate attacks.[551] Similarly, single intelligence errors do not raise questions of proportionality. However, if such failures causing erroneous bombing appear in a pattern, proportionality would be an issue and responsibility for excess during the whole operation could be imputed to higher level decision-makers.[552]

Article 51 para. 5 *lit.* b of the 1977 Additional Protocol I refers to the relation of two matters. First, the "concrete and direct military advantage anticipated" by an attack has to be considered as second, the expected civilian casualties may not be excessive in relation to this advantage.

(1) Direct Military Advantage Anticipated by an Attack

The "military advantage anticipated" by a certain attack very much depends on the understanding of the term "attack". According to Article 49 of the Protocol, this means "acts of violence against the adversary, whether in offence or defence". Earlier, it was in part only under-

---

547 Green, *Law of Armed Conflict*, p. 148; Henckaerts/ Doswald-Beck (eds.), *Humanitarian Law*, Vol. 1, p. 67 (Rule 21); Sassòli, in: Wippman/ Evangelista (eds.), at 205.

548 *Compare supra*, Part Two, Chapter D) II. 1. b).

549 Dinstein, *Conduct of Hostilities*, p. 119 with recent examples.

550 William J. Fenrick, 'The Law applicable to Targeting and Proportionality after Operation Allied Force: A View from the Outside', in: 3 *Yb. Int'l Hum. L.* (2000), pp. 53-80, at 76.

551 *Compare supra*, Part Two, Chapter D) II. 2. a).

552 Fenrick, 3 *Yb. Int'l Hum. L.* (2000), at 76.

stood as covering combat in offence, rather than in defence.[553] The scope of the term attack has a strong influence on the issue of proportionality. If "attack" is interpreted very broadly, the principle of proportionality will have less effect:

> A specific attack on a specific building may cause massive unintended civilian casualties that are clearly excessive in relation to the benefit caused by the destruction of that specific military target. However, if those casualties are the only civilian losses for the entire day's bombing, or even the entire campaign, the collateral losses are much more likely to be seen as proportional to the military advantage gained.[554]

For example, in the context of the Second World War in which well over 30 million people died – including more than 20 million civilians – the atomic bombings of Hiroshima und Nagasaki killed approximately 100,000 people. This number hardly stands out purely in terms of casualties caused. Even in the context of examples of other operations where widespread civilian casualties were caused, they still cannot be described as causing unheard of destruction if compared with the bombings of Dresden, Hamburg and Tokyo. However, it is too broad to determine whether or not a military activity complied with the principle of proportionality at the end of a war or when a lengthy campaign is over.[555] If the term "attack" is understood narrowly, i.e. the single bomb that caused the casualties is regarded as an individual attack, it is more likely that the military advantage of that one bomb is disproportionate to the civilian casualties. On the other hand, one cannot *always* assess proportionality "on a bullet by bullet basis".[556]

It is submitted here that a targeted killing is *per se* an individual attack: It aims at a specific individual person due to a specific reason lying in that person. The strike is thus not part of a larger military operation. It might be part of a general policy to target certain persons. However, the persons targeted are singled out and are not only targeted because they belong to the category of combatants of the adversary. It is thus the in-

---

553 *Compare* Rauch, 21 *Rev. dr. pén. mil.* (1982), at 66; Rogers, 21 *Rev. dr. pén. mil.* (1982), at 302-303.

554 Jaworski, 2 *Chin. J. Int'l L.* (2003), at 193.

555 Fenrick, 3 *Yb. Int'l Hum. L.* (2000), at 76; *compare also* Jaworski, 2 *Chin. J. Int'l L.* (2003), at 195.

556 Fenrick, 3 *Yb. Int'l Hum. L.* (2000), at 76.

dividual strike against one person which has to stand the test of proportionality.[557] Therefore, the general question concerning the interpretation of "attack" can remain open for the purpose of this treatise.[558]

Nevertheless, the military advantage of such an attack is difficult to assess. Generally, the main factor is the target's importance for achieving a particular military objective. The more integral the target's role is to the military strategy, the higher the level is of likely civilian casualties that will still be acceptable.[559] In that regard, it is important that it is a "concrete and direct military advantage" that is required. This formulation was chosen to show

> that the advantage concerned should be substantial and relatively close, and that advantages which are hardly perceptible and those which would only appear in the long term should be disregarded.[560]

These considerations can be applied to the targeting of individual persons to a certain degree: If a person acts as a sniper – be he a combatant or a civilian thus taking direct part in hostilities – the targeting of that person has a direct effect for the adversary: The threat posed by the sniper to the adversary's belligerents is deleted. This clearly is a concrete and direct military advantage. The same holds true if a person is targeted on his way to an attack, again irrespective of the question whether he is a combatant or a civilian thus taking direct part in hostilities. Cases in which the targeted person does not pose such an immediate threat to the adversary are less clear. As shown above, such cases can only exist in relation to combatants, as civilians may only be targeted at all due to such an immediate threat.[561]

Concerning combatants or fighters, different scenarios are possible: If a military leader is targeted during an ongoing military operation, the result may be a direct military advantage as the operation of the adversary will most likely weakened or even be given up without the person in charge. If a military leader is targeted, who is rather pulling the stings in

---

557 *But see* Jaworski, 2 *Chin. J. Int'l L.* (2003), at 204, who is of the opinion that the "scope, or breadth of the action in question is *more than one single attack*, but less than the entire war;" (my emphasis).

558 On the discussion *compare* Gardam, *Necessity*, pp. 99-100.

559 *Id.*, p. 100.

560 Sandoz *et al.* (eds.), *Additional Protocols*, para. 2209 (p. 684).

561 *Compare supra*, Part Two, Chapter D) II. 1. c).

the background, the effects may be less direct. Still, it obviously is a military advantage to weaken or even destroy the leadership circles. This will not be the case if a military leader who is not actively involved in the ongoing conflict is targeted, e.g. the leader of a unit which does not take part in the hostilities: The effect that a possible backup is weakened may still be a military advantage, but it is too remote to be concrete and direct.

It can thus be concluded that the targeting of civilians taking direct part in hostilities – based on the narrow interpretation of taking direct part – always causes a direct military advantage for the adversary. Concerning combatants, at least a certain present relation to the ongoing hostilities is necessary to render the military advantage direct.

(2) Excessive Civilian Damages

Article 51 para. 5 *lit.* b of the 1977 Additional Protocol I refers to "excessive" civilian damage whereas other prefer "disproportionate".[562] The level of protection thus very much depends on the meaning of one word. The rule will provide very little protection if it is interpreted as referring to cases in which the "disproportion is unbearably large".[563] It will provide vast protection if "excessive" is indeed interpreted as "extensive".[564]

As often, the truth seems to be somewhere between the extremes: To confuse "excessive" with "extensive" would mean overstretching the wording of Article 51 para. 5.[565] The ordinary meaning of "excessive" comprises "greater than what is necessary".[566] It thus exclusively describes a relation of one thing to another. "Extensive" means "large in

---

[562] *Compare* e.g. ICJ, *Legality of the Threat or Use of Nuclear Weapons*, Advisory Opinion of July 8, 1996, Dissenting Opinion of Judge Higgins, I.C.J. Reports 1996, pp. 226-593, at 587 (para. 20).

[563] Albrecht Randelzhofer, 'Civilian Objects', in: Rudolf Bernhardt (ed.), *EPIL*, Vol. 3, Amsterdam 1982, pp. 93-96, at 96.

[564] *Compare* Sandoz *et al.* (eds.), *Additional Protocols*, para. 1980 (p. 626).

[565] Greenwood, in: Fleck (ed.), *Handbook*, at 11 (footnote 29); Gardam, *Necessity*, p. 107.

[566] Hornby/ Crowther (eds.), *Oxford Advanced Learner's Dictionary*, p. 383.

amount or scale"[567] and rather describes the amount of something in absolute terms. Thus, even extensive civilian casualties can be acceptable if they coincide with an adequate military advantage of the attack concerned. This could for example be the case if large numbers of civilian workers are killed during an attack on an ammunition factory.[568] This interpretation is also supported by the phrasing of Article 8 para. 2 *lit.* b (iv) of the 1998 Rome Statute, which refers to damages "which would be clearly excessive" to the advantage anticipated and thus sets the threshold even higher.

On the other hand, an "unbearably large" disproportion seems to define the scope of protection too narrowly.[569] The term "excessive" is related to "exceeding", i.e. being greater in quantity than something.[570] Thus, where more damage is done than advantage is achieved, the damage is excessive. This corresponds to rather a 51/49 relation than a 90/10 relation, which might be describing an "unbearably large" disproportion. But still there is no objective possibility "of quantifying the factors of the equation".[571] The military may tend to overstate the importance of the military advantage while others may tend to overstate the casualties. Again, it is the desire to provide for the broadest protection possible that might run counter the fact that wars are fought to be won.

Additionally, the whole assessment of proportionality is based on the assumption that the attacker acts in good faith.[572] If a belligerent fully realises in advance that the destruction of a particular military objective can be accomplished only by injuring civilians, he can balance pros and cons. Only then does the question of proportionality come into play. If a belligerent does not know that civilians will be injured while hitting a military objective, but it happens none the less, the damage may as such be excessive to the advantage. However, at the moment of the targeting decision, according to the information available, such damage was not

---

567 *Id.*, p. 392.

568 UK Ministry of Defence, *Manual*, para. 2.6.3 (p. 26); Dinstein, *Conduct of Hostilities*, p. 121 with further examples.

569 Dinstein, *Conduct of Hostilities*, p. 120.

570 *Compare* Hornby/ Crowther (eds.), *Oxford Advanced Learner's Dictionary*, p. 383.

571 Bothe *et al.*, *1977 Protocols*, Art. 51 Prot. I, para. 2.6.2 (p. 310).

572 Dinstein, *Conduct of Hostilities*, p. 122.

foreseeable. The attack thus is not in violation of Article 51 para. 5 of the 1977 Additional Protocol I.

A possible approach to solve at least the problem of "good faith" could be *ex post* monitoring of targeting decisions.[573] Such examinations are well known from the human rights sphere[574] and have recently been introduced to the field of international humanitarian law.[575] It is perhaps unrealistic to expect transparency concerning targeting decisions during the conflict. However, if the parties know that questionable cases could be investigated retrospectively, some preventive effect could be achieved with the result that targeting decisions would be made even more carefully. At the same time, investigations could be based on records that would have to be kept by the belligerents. This would not only facilitate prosecution in case of grave breaches of international humanitarian law, but also be a source of defence in case of war crimes trials. Disclosure would additionally avoid the impression that international humanitarian law is not respected in war and thus strengthen the importance of international humanitarian law.[576] Additionally, such records could enable military experts to compare practical examples and further develop the best practice together with international humanitarian law experts.[577]

Another factor that is considered in relation to proportionality is the risk for the attacking belligerents. Some methods of attack might minimize the risk for civilians but may involve increased risk to the attacking forces. International humanitarian law is not clear as to the degree of risk that the attacker must accept. The principle of proportionality does not *per se* require armed forces to accept increased risks,[578] whereas other rules – such as the prohibition to use human shields – clearly

---

573 Such as proposed by Sassòli, in: Wippman/ Evangelista (eds.), at 204-205.

574 *Compare supra*, Part One, Chapter B) I. 2 b), Chapter C) I. 2 b) and Chapter E) I. 2 b).

575 Supreme Court of Israel, *"Targeted Killings" (Merits)*, para. 40, 46 *ILM* (2007), at 393-394.

576 Sassòli, in: Wippman/ Evangelista (eds.), at 204-205.

577 Fenrick, 3 *Yb. Int'l Hum. L.* (2000), at 80; Sassòli, in: Wippman/ Evangelista (eds.), at 205-206.

578 UK Ministry of Defence, *Manual*, para. 2.7.1 (pp. 25-26).

prohibit the use of civilians in order to reduce the risk for the forces.[579] Nevertheless, if alternative practically possible methods of attack are available that would reduce collateral risks, the attacker may have to accept the increased risk as being the only way of pursuing an attack proportionately.[580]

> Military casualties incurred by the attacking side are not part of the equation. A willingness to accept some own-side casualties in order to limit civilian casualties may indicate a greater desire to ensure compliance with the principle of proportionality. Military commanders do, however, also have a duty to their own forces to limit casualties.[581]

Thus, if a target is sufficiently important, on the one hand more civilian casualties will still be regarded as proportionate. On the other hand, a commander may also be prepared to accept a greater degree of risk for his own forces in order to ensure that the target is accurately attacked and civilian casualties are diminished.[582]

This still leaves unresolved the problem of defining what exactly is still proportionate and what is disproportionate. It is easier to give answers to this question in extreme cases than in those which are at the border of one category to the other. The common characteristics of targeted killings are first, that it is also a single person or a small group of persons which are targeted. Second, on the other side of the equation are mainly also human beings, if civilian casualties are concerned. Collateral damage to civilian objects are of less relevance as the targeted strikes – at least in the vast majority of cases – have impact in a rather limited sphere. It is thus not necessary to compare an ammunition fac-

---

579 *Compare e.g.* Otto, 86 *Int'l Rev. Red Cross* (2004), No 856, pp. 771-787.

580 UK Ministry of Defence, *Manual*, para. 2.7.1 (pp. 25-26); Jaworski, 2 *Chin. J. Int'l L.* (2003), at 205. *But see* Solon Solomon, 'Targeted Killing and the Soldiers' Right to Life', in: 14 *ILSA J. Int'l & Comp. L.* (2007), pp. 99-120, at 116-120 and Benvenisti, 39 *Isr. L. Rev.* (2006), at 108, concluding that there is no general requirement to risk combatants in order to reduce the risk to civilians, although admitting that a number of the specific rules – such as the prohibition of human shields – entail the assumption of such risks.

581 Fenrick, 3 *Yb. Int'l Hum. L.* (2000), at 78.

582 Anthony P.V. Rogers, 'Zero-Casualty Warfare', in: 82 *Int'l Rev. Red Cross* (2000), No. 837, pp. 165-181, at 179.

tory with a certain number of civilians. What has to be balanced here is life versus life.

Some other authors give extreme and very similar examples in that regard: The destruction of a village with hundreds of civilian casualties in order to eliminate a single enemy sniper is regarded as disproportionate.[583] A fighter-jet attack upon an apartment building known to be populated by civilians, which was aimed at killing a single individual, is also regarded as disproportionate to the objectives of stopping that single individual from committing further terrorist attacks.[584]

If an exclusively quantitative approach would be applied, one could argue that the military advantage of killing one person can at the most be of the same weight as one civilian casualty. On the other hand, if a sniper is causing huge casualties, one will agree that larger civilian collateral damage could be proportionate in stopping him, up to the level where it exceeds the number of "saved lives". In such a situation, the immediacy of a threat that is posed by the targeted person has a strong influence on what is still perceived as proportionate: A military decision-maker could expect little understanding if he did not target a sniper while he is active and causing casualties.

These considerations may not be confused with the question of immediacy and proportionality in relation to the targeted person, as discussed in the human rights context.[585] It is not the life of the person who is targeted that is balanced against his possible victims. The fact that the targeted person is a legitimate objective is the basis for assessing the legality of collateral damage at all.[586] These possible victims are on one side of the equation whereas the military advantage gained by the attack is on the other side.

Another factor discussed – albeit one that may not be taken into account – is the overall legality of the conflict: *Bothe* proposes that in the case of an humanitarian intervention, the "good cause" has an influence

---

583 Dinstein, *Conduct of Hostilities*, pp. 122-123.

584 Casey, 32 *Syracuse J. Int'l L. & Com.* (2005), at 339; Shany, in: Schmitt/Beruto (eds.), at 106-107.

585 *Compare supra*, Part One, Chapters B) II. 2 b) (3)-(6).

586 This question has to be decided according to the standards developed above, *see* Part Two, Chapter C) and Chapter D) II 1. c).

on the application of proportionality.[587] However, these considerations belong to the sphere of *jus ad bellum*. The question whether a State will resort to force at all is also connected to proportionality questions. These questions do not influence the principle of proportionality in *jus in bellum*, namely international humanitarian law.[588]

The factors developed above enable it to deduce at least some rules for assessing the question of proportionality: If the targeted person does not pose a direct threat, but his targeting would still amount to a direct military advantage, civilian casualties must be kept on a very low level: The effect of targeting the person is not instantly, the result is rather something like disturbing the chain of command of the adversary or disturbing supplies of others *et cetera*. To achieve such an effect, it is reasonable to wait for a situation in which only minimum or no civilian casualties will be caused. It is not possible to exactly calculate such casualties in numbers, but the general idea is in the field of the one-to-one relation introduced above.[589] This number rises as soon as the person poses a direct and immediate threat to other persons: In such cases, a collateral damage in the dimension of the number of persons who can be saved *directly* by the attack on the targeted person will most likely still be proportionate. However, this does not justify to assess the proportionality according to possible harm the targeted person may do in the future. It only relates to immediate threats that are opposed by targeting the person. If such threats do not exist, it is still legal to target the person, but not to cause more than minimal civilian casualties. Thus, if the attacking forces or other persons are not in immediate danger if the attack is not carried out, "[q]uite simply, the attack should not be carried out."[590]

---

[587] Michael Bothe, 'The Protection of the Civilian Population and NATO Bombing on Yugoslavia: Comments on a Report to the Prosecutor of the ICTY', in: 12 *Eur. J. Int'l L.* (2001), pp. 531-536, at 535.

[588] *See also* Gardam, *Necessity*, p. 112.

[589] *Shany* regards twelve civilian fatal casualties as disproportionate in such a situation, *see* Shany, in: Schmitt/ Beruto (eds.), at 106-107.

[590] Rogers, 82 *Int'l Rev. Red Cross* (2000), No. 837, at 179.

(3) Consequence: Precautions in Attack

The principles of proportionality and distinction demand certain precautions to be taken in attack, which are *inter alia* laid down in Article 57 para. 2 *lit.* a of the 1977 Additional Protocol I and consists of three parts. First, the persons who plan or decide upon an attack have to do everything feasible, i.e. practicable or practicably possible in the light of all the circumstances,[591] to correctly identify their objectives as military objectives in order to distinguish them from civilian objects. Second, they have to choose their means and methods in a way that avoids or at least minimizes injury to civilians. Third, they must refrain from launching attacks that are expected to be in breach of the principle of proportionality.

Whereas it is undisputed that the principle of proportionality is part of customary international law,[592] it is less clear whether the exact shape the principle has in the 1977 Additional Protocol I does also represent customary international law. The whole targeting policy laid down in Articles 48-57 of the 1977 Additional Protocol I is widely regarded as declaratory of customary international law or as representing developments of customary law which are generally acceptable to the international community.[593] These rules were respected – albeit they were not legally binding as treaty law – by the protagonists of the 1990-1991 Kuwait conflict: The coalition's announcement that it would attack only military objectives was phrased very similarly to Article 52 of the 1977 Additional Protocol I. The announcement that excessive collateral damage civilian casualties would be avoided as far as possible was phrased similarly to Article 51 para. 5 *lit.* b of the Protocol.[594] The emphasis on the protection of the civilian population was even more pronounced in the Kosovo campaign by those NATO members, who are – in part – not bound by the Protocol as a treaty.[595] The practice in the

[591] Green, *Law of Armed Conflict*, pp. 147-148.

[592] Gardam, *Necessity*, pp. 112-113; Henckaerts/ Doswald-Beck (eds.), *Humanitarian Law*, Vol. 1, p. 46 (Rule 14).

[593] Greenwood, in: Fleck (ed.), *Handbook*, at 26 (para. 127.2); Greenwood, in: Delissen/ Tanja (eds.), at 108-103; *compare also* Green, *Law of Armed Conflict*, p. 151; Rogers, 21 *Rev. dr. pén. mil.* (1982), at 303.

[594] Greenwood, in: Fleck (ed.), *Handbook*, at 26 (para. 127.2).

[595] *Compare* Gardam, *Necessity*, p. 112.

Persian Gulf and Kosovo conflicts confirm, that proportionality operates in the broad sense as laid down in the 1977 Additional Protocol I.[596] Thus it can be concluded that the duty to take all feasible precautions to avoid incidental loss of civilian life, i.e. by carefully verifying military targets and by choosing means and methods of warfare with view to avoid loss or civilian life does represent customary international law.[597]

(4) Proportionality and Non-International Armed Conflicts

In its first three paragraphs, Article 13 of the 1977 Additional Protocol II restates the rules of Article 51 paras. 1-3 of the 1977 Additional Protocol I.[598] Unlike this, Article 13 does not contain the specific limitations on the means and methods of combat of Article 51. The former Article does not contain an explicit prohibition of indiscriminate attacks and also no rule on proportionality. The 1977 Additional Protocol II is thus only of limited assistance in inhibiting disproportionate civilian casualties.[599] However, according to Common Article 3 of the 1949 Geneva Conventions, the general rules of international humanitarian law are also applicable in non-international armed conflicts. Among those rules is the prohibition of indiscriminate attacks[600] and thus also the principle of proportionality.[601] Thus, parties to a non-international conflict are also – at minimum – obliged by customary international law to respect the principle of proportionality[602] and take the respective

[596] *Id.*, p. 113.

[597] Henckaerts/ Doswald-Beck (eds.), *Humanitarian Law*, Vol. 1, pp. 51-65 (Rules 15-20) with further references.

[598] *Compare supra*, Part Two, Chapter D) II. 1. a).

[599] *Compare* Gardam, *Necessity*, p. 113.

[600] *Compare* ICTY, *Prosecutor v. Duško Tadić*, Case No. IT-94-1-AR72, Decision on the Defence Motion for Interlocutory Appeal on Jurisdiction of October 2, 1995, reprinted in: 105 *Int'l L.R.* (1997), pp. 419-648, at 520 (para. 127).

[601] Gardam, *Necessity*, p. 127.

[602] *See already* James E. Bond, *The Rules of Riot: Internal Conflict and the Law of War*, Princeton/ N.J. 1974, pp. 93, 97 and 110; Fenrick, 3 *Yb. Int'l Hum. L.* (2000), at 75; Gardam, *Necessity*, p. 85.

precautions in attack.[603] In that regard, the standards are at least comparable to those developed above.

c) Conclusion

It is submitted here that a targeted killing is an attack in the meaning of Article 51 of the 1977 Additional Protocol I as well as Article 13 of the 1977 Additional Protocol II and the corresponding prohibitions of indiscriminate attacks under customary international law. Thus, each targeted killing must be evaluated separately regarding its proportionality in regard to collateral damage. Concerning civilian casualties, one criterion is the direct threat the targeted person poses to possible victims. Collateral casualties in the dimension of the number of persons who can be saved *directly* by the attack on the targeted person will most likely still be proportionate. The standard is considerably higher in cases in which the targeted person does not pose such a direct threat: Civilian casualties must be kept minimal; otherwise it is reasonable to wait for a situation in which only minimum or no civilian casualties will be caused.

3. Prohibition to Direct Reprisals Against the Civil Population

According to Article 51 para. 6 of the 1977 Additional Protocol I, "[a]ttacks against the civilian population or civilians by way of reprisals are prohibited." A more specific prohibition of reprisals against protected persons – i.e. civilians in occupied territory – and their property is laid down in Article 33 para. 3 of the 1949 Geneva Convention IV. A reprisal is an unlawful act which is claimed to be justified in response to equally unlawful acts of the adversary.[604] Thus, the prohibition of reprisals strictly speaking only clarifies that a certain justification is not available if prohibited acts are committed against civilians, while the same prohibited acts may be justified if committed against combatants.

---

[603] *See* Henckaerts/ Doswald-Beck (eds.), *Humanitarian Law*, Vol. 1, pp. 51-65 (Rules 15-20) with further references.

[604] Frits Kalshoven, 'Reprisals and the Protection of Civilians – Two recent Decisions of the Yugoslavia Tribunal', in: Lal Chand Vohrah *et al.* (eds.), *Man's Inhumanity to Man – Essays on International Law in Honour of Antonio Cassese*, The Hague 2003, pp. 481-511, at 481.

Independently from the question of the overall legality of a reprisal, the Protocol makes it clear that civilians may never be the object of such sanctions.

This prohibition is not only laid down in the 1977 Additional Protocol I: The UN General Assembly already in 1970 stressed that "[c]ivilian populations, or individual members thereof, could not be the object of reprisals".[605] This principle is regarded as representing customary international law concerning international armed conflicts.[606] However, as a prohibition such as laid down in the 1977 Additional Protocol I was not included in the 1977 Additional Protocol II due to a lack of consensus, it is not absolutely clear whether such a prohibition can be regarded as a rule of customary law concerning internal armed conflicts.[607] It is prohibited to direct reprisals against civilians and thus an otherwise illegal targeted killing of a civilian cannot be justified as a reprisal.

---

[605] UN GA Res. 2675 (XXV) (December 9, 1970), *Basic Principles for the Protection of Civilian Population in Armed Conflicts*, UN GAOR 25th Sess., Supp. No. 28, UN Doc. A/8028 (1970), p. 76.

[606] *See e.g.* ICTY, *Prosecutor v. Duško Tadić*, Case No. IT-94-1-AR72, Decision on the Defence Motion for Interlocutory Appeal on Jurisdiction of October 2, 1995, reprinted in: 105 *Int'l L.R.* (1997), pp. 419-648, at 513 (para. 112); Inter-Am. Comm'n H.R., *Third Report on the Human Rights Situation in Colombia*, OEA/Ser.L/V/II.102, Doc. 9 Rev. 1 (February 26, 1999), at para. 39; ICTY, *Prosecutor v. Zoran Kupreškić* et al., Case No. IT-95-16-T, Judgment of January 14, 2000, paras. 527-536; Henckaerts/ Doswald-Beck (eds.), *Humanitarian Law*, Vol. 1, p. 519 (Rule 146); Rowe, 3 *Melb. J. Int'l L.* (2002), at 312; *critically* Kalshoven, in: Lal Chand Vohrah *et al.* (eds.), at 492 and 500-501.

[607] *Compare* Kalshoven, in: Lal Chand Vohrah *et al.* (eds.), at 508-509, who argues that the prohibition of reprisals against civilians in internal armed conflicts cannot reach as far as that in international armed conflicts; *but see* ICTY, *Prosecutor v. Zoran Kupreškić* et al., Case No. IT-95-16-T, Judgment of January 14, 2000, paras. 527-536; Henckaerts/ Doswald-Beck (eds.), *Humanitarian Law*, Vol. 1, pp. 526-529 (Rule 148), who support such a prohibition, with further references.

III. Conclusion: Targeted Killings of Civilians

The protection of civilians under international humanitarian law has two important aspects concerning targeted killings: First, if the targeted person has civilian status, it may generally not be targeted, unless and for such time as they take a direct part in hostilities. This direct participation has to be interpreted narrowly, with a strong emphasis on the threat a civilian poses to the adversary. This standard applies in international and non-international armed conflicts in the same manner.

The second important aspect – concerning the targeting of civilians and combatants alike – is the protection of non-targeted persons who might nevertheless suffer from the strike. In that regard, a targeted killing represents an attack in the meaning of Article 51 of the 1977 Additional Protocol I and the corresponding customary international law prohibition of indiscriminate attacks. Thus, each targeted killing must stand the test of proportionality concerning collateral damage. Again, the direct threat posed by the targeted person has a strong influence on possible civilian casualties which could still be acceptable. If it is truly imminent, collateral damages in the dimension of those who can directly be saved by the attack might be acceptable. In less imminent cases, this number strongly decreases until proportionality will finally require the attack to be suspended until no civilian casualties will be caused.

E. Is there a Third Category such as "Unlawful Combatants"?

The Discussion on "unlawful combatants" is not new. However, it has recently become the subject of an intensive debate, mainly due to the U.S. practice in Afghanistan and following the 2001 military campaign.[608] The reactions to the September 11, 2001 events reopened a dis-

[608] According to the official U.S. policy, "[e]ven though the detainees are not entitled to POW privileges, they will be provided many POW privileges as a matter of policy", *see* U.S. President George W. Bush, 'Status of Detainees at Guantanamo', White House Fact Sheet of February 7, 2002. *Compare the critique by* Vierucci, 2 *J. Int'l Crim. Just.* (2004), pp. 866-871.

cussion on the division between persons and incidents subject to the law of war and those persons and incidents subject to criminal law.[609]

While the discussion on "unlawful combatants" centres on the status of persons who are detained and who are thus unlikely to become the subject of a targeted killing, the discussion on an additional status can also have consequences for the topic at hand: If there is such an additional category, it has to be examined whether the rules regarding combatants or the rules regarding civilians as developed above apply to this category of persons,[610] or whether a different set of rules – or even no rules at all – apply to them.

The basic principles for this discussion is the distinction between combatants and civilians: As shown above, in international armed conflicts the primary status of being a combatant entails the right to directly take part in hostilities. Combatants are thus also referred to as "legitimate", "lawful", or "privileged" combatants.[611] They cannot be punished for the mere participation in the hostilities, but only for violations of international humanitarian law. If captured by the adversary, combatants acquire prisoner-of-war status as their secondary status and benefit from the Protection of the 1949 Geneva Convention III. On the other hand, these advantages are faced by the fact that combatants are legitimate military targets.[612]

Opposed to this, a civilian is a person who does not fulfil the preconditions of combatant status as laid out *supra*.[613] Civilians are generally entitled to protection from direct attack and from the side-effects of attacks on military targets. In return to this protection, they may not take direct part in hostilities – except for the relatively rare cases of a *levée en masse*. Civilians who nevertheless participate directly in the hostili-

---

[609] Newton, in: Wippman/ Evangelista (eds.), at 78.

[610] *Compare supra*, Part Two, Chapters C) and D) respectively.

[611] *See e.g.* Antonio Cassese, 'Mercenaries: Lawful Combatants or War Criminals?', in: 40 *ZaöRV* (1980), pp. 1-30, at 5; Detter, *Law of War*, pp. 137 and 148; Dinstein, *Conduct of Hostilities*, pp. 29-33; Herbert Schwab, *Irreguläre Kombattanten als Kriegsgefangene*, Würzburg 1976, p. 147; Dörmann, 85 *Int'l Rev. Red Cross* (2003), No 849, at 45.

[612] *Compare supra*, Part Two, Chapter C).

[613] *See supra*, Part Two, Chapter C) I.

ties become – for the time they do so – legitimate targets, but keep their primary status as civilians.[614]

Beside these notions of combatant, civilian and prisoner of war, an additional term is used, namely that of the "unlawful combatant": Combatants are granted prisoner-of-war status in order to prevent them from rejoining the opposite side and re-enforce the enemy. Civilians may generally only detained if there is a specific charge against them. The fact that civilians shall be released unless specific proof is brought against them may be the reason that led the U.S. government to coin the concept of "unlawful combatants": The U.S., unlike Israel or the U.K., does not have emergency laws allowing for the preventive detention of terrorist suspects.[615]

I. Terminology and Its Historical Basis

The treaties of international humanitarian law do not contain the term "unlawful combatant". Nevertheless, the notion of this term is not a new development: Phrases like "unlawful combatant", "illegal combatant" or "unprivileged belligerent"[616] or combinations thereof are and have been used in court decisions[617] as well as treatise on the law of war and military manuals.[618]

The term "unlawful combatant" dates back to a case before the U.S. Supreme Court against German soldiers in World War II: The soldiers had landed on the U.S. Coast and proceeded in civilian dress to New York.

---

[614] *Compare supra*, Part Two, Chapter D).

[615] Arnold, in: Arnold/ Hildbrand (eds.), at 14.

[616] *See e.g.* Julius Stone, *Legal Controls of International Conflict: A Treatise on the Dynamics of Disputes- and War-Law*, New York 1954, p. 549; Newton, in: Wippman/ Evangelista (eds.), pp. 75-110.

[617] *See e.g.* U.S. Supreme Court, *Ex Parte Quirin* et al., Judgment of July 31, 1942, 317 *U.S.* (1942), pp. 1-48, at 30-31; Supreme Court of Israel, *"Targeted Killings" (Merits)*, para. 26, 46 *ILM* (2007), at 387; District Court of Tel Aviv and Jaffa, *State of Israel v. Marwan Barghouti*, Criminal Case No. 92134/02, December 12; Inter-Am. Comm'n H.R., *Report on Terrorism*, para. 69.

[618] *See e.g.* Ipsen, in: Fleck (ed.), *Handbook*, at 68 (para. 302); UK Ministry of Defence, *Manual*, para. 4.2.1 (p. 38); Detter, *Law of War*, p. 148; Dinstein, *Conduct of Hostilities*, p. 29.

In *Ex Parte Quirin et al.*, the Supreme Court held that they could be tried before a military commission for attempting to commit hostile acts against the United States. By passing the U.S. boundaries in order to destroy military targets

> without uniform or other emblem signifying their belligerent status, or by discarding that means of identification after entry, such enemies become unlawful belligerents subject to trial and punishment.[619]

Examples given by the Court for such persons are the following:

> The spy who secretly and without uniform passes the military lines of a belligerent in time of war, seeking to gather military information and communicate it to the enemy, or an enemy combatant who without uniform comes secretly through the lines for the purpose of waging war by destruction of life or property, are familiar examples of belligerents who are generally deemed not to be entitled to the status of prisoners of war, ...[620]

The Court thus ties the term "unlawful combatant" to deeds by a person which are regarded as unlawful and thus subject to prosecution. The decisive aspect is that the persons did not wear uniforms and thus were not recognisable as combatants. They thus had no right to take part in hostilities. In consequence, these persons cannot, according to the Supreme Court, acquire the secondary status of prisoner of war. However, the Court did not entertain the question of which status the persons should have instead, but only states that "in addition they are subject to trial and punishment by military tribunals for acts which render their belligerency unlawful."[621] The definition developed by the Supreme Court thus refers to persons who do not fulfil the preconditions of combatant status as now laid down in the 1949 Geneva Convention III and 1977 Additional Protocol I.[622] It is contended that

---

619 U.S. Supreme Court, *Ex Parte Quirin* et al., Judgment of July 31, 1942, 317 *U.S.* (1942), pp. 1-48, at 37.

620 *Id.*, at 31.

621 *Id.*

622 *Compare supra*, Part Two, Chapter C) I.

"[u]nlawful combatants are combatants who fail to qualify as prisoners of war."[623]

II. New Notions

The question whether or not there is in fact a category of "unlawful combatants", whether it amounts to a primary status like that of civilian and (lawful) combatant and if so, what it implies, is highly disputed.[624] The concept consists of two aspects: "Combatant" expresses that the person in question takes direct part in hostilities, whereas "unlawful", "illegal" or "unprivileged" expresses that the person violates the law – either by taking part in hostilities without being privileged to do so, or by committing other illegal acts. The latter case is referred to by the Supreme Court in *Ex Parte Quirin*, while the former is commonly used today: Mostly the term "unlawful combatant" is understood as describing all persons who take direct part in hostilities without being entitled to do so. According to the 2002 Israeli Incarceration of Unlawful Combatants Law,

> 'unlawful combatant' means a person who has participated either directly or indirectly in hostile acts against the State of Israel or is a member of a force perpetrating hostile acts against the State of Israel, where the conditions prescribed in Article 4 of the Third Geneva Convention of 12th August 1949 with respect to prisoners-of-war and granting prisoner-of-war status in international humanitarian law, do not apply to him;[625]

Unlike "lawful combatants", "unlawful combatants" have no right to engage in hostilities and do not enjoy immunity from prosecution for their taking part in hostilities.[626] The term would thus include civilians

---

[623] Jason Callen, 'Unlawful Combatants and the Geneva Conventions', in: 44 *Va. J. Int'l L.* (2004), pp. 1025-1072, at 1030.

[624] *See e.g.* Kretzmer, 16 *Eur. J. Int'l L.* (2005), at 190; Dörmann, 85 *Int'l Rev. Red Cross* (2003), No 849, at 46.

[625] Article 2 para. 2 of the Israeli Incarceration of Unlawful Combatants Law (5762-2002), English translation reprinted in: 32 *Isr. Yb. Hum. Rts.* (2002), pp. 389-392, at 389.

[626] Aldrich, 96 *Am. J. Int'l L.* (2002), at 892; Richard R. Baxter, 'So called "Unprivileged Belligerency": Spies, Guerrillas, Saboteurs', in: 28 *Brit. Yb. Int'l*

taking direct part in hostilities,[627] members of militias and of other volunteer corps – including those of organized resistance movements – who are not integrated in the regular armed forces but belong to a party of the conflict,[628] if they do not fulfil the preconditions of combatant status as laid out above.[629] "Unlawful combatants" thus do not qualify as combatants in the ordinary meaning.[630] The term "unprivileged belligerents" is thus regarded as being more technically correct in describing

> civilians who forfeit their protection from attack by conducting hostile activities without the privileges accruing to 'combatants' under the established laws of war.[631]

L. (1952), pp. 323-345, at 328; Dinstein, in: Dinstein/ Tabory (eds.), at 103-105; Dinstein, 32 *Isr. Yb. Hum. Rts.* (2002), at 249; Gross, 15 *Fla. J. Int'l L.* (2003), at 416-417; Michael H. Hoffman, 'Terrorists are Unlawful Belligerents, not Unlawful Combatants: A Distinction with Implications for the Future of International Humanitarian Law', in: 34 *Case W. Res. J. Int'l L.* (2002), pp. 227-230, at 229; Michael H. Hoffman, 'Quelling Unlawful Belligerency: The Judicial Status and Treatment of Terrorists under the Laws of War', in: 31 *Isr. Yb. Hum. Rts.* (2001), pp. 161-181, at 166; Kretzmer, 16 *Eur. J. Int'l L.* (2005), at 190; Newton, in: Wippman/ Evangelista (eds.), at 84; Robert A. Peal, 'Combatant Status Review Tribunals and the Unique Nature of the War on Terror', in: 58 *Vand. L. Rev.* (2005), pp. 1629-1670, at 1638; Rosenblad, 12 *Rev. dr. pén. mil.* (1973), at 111 and 120; Michael P. Scharf, 'Defining Terrorism as the Peacetime Equivalent of War Crimes: Problems and Prospects', in: 36 *Case W. Res. J. Int'l L.* (2004), pp. 359-375, at 369; Solf/ Cummings, 9 *Case W. Res. J. Int'l L.* (1977), at 215-216; Yoo, 3 *Chin. J. Int'l L.* (2004), at 143; U.S. Supreme Court, *Ex Parte Quirin* et al., Judgment of July 31, 1942, 317 *U.S.* (1942), pp. 1-48, at 31; Pictet (ed.), *Geneva Conventions*, Vol. 4, p. 53; Rosas, *Prisoners of War*, p. 419; Gregory M. Travalio, 'Terrorism, International Law, and the Use of Military Force', in: 18 *Wis. Int'l L.J.* (2000), pp. 145-191, at 184-185. *Compare also* Inter-Am. Comm'n H.R., *Report on Terrorism*, para. 68.

627 *See supra*, Part Two, Chapter D) II. 1. c).

628 *See* Dörmann, 85 *Int'l Rev. Red Cross* (2003), No 849, at 46-47.

629 *See supra*, Part Two, Chapter C) I.

630 Wieczorek, *Unrechtmäßige Kombattanten*, p. 38.

631 Newton, in: Wippman/ Evangelista (eds.), at 85; *see also* Silvia Borelli, 'Casting Light on the Legal Black Hole: International Law and Detentions Abroad in the War on Terror', in: 87 *Int'l Rev. Red Cross* (2005), No. 857, pp. 39-68, at 51; Jan Klabbers, 'Rebel with a Cause? Terrorists and Humanitarian Law', in: 14 *Eur. J. Int'l L.* (2003), pp. 283-312, at 301.

Similar terms are that of “enemy combatants” and “unlawful belligerents” and “quasi-combatants” and “battlefield unlawful combatants”: First, the terms “enemy combatant” or “unlawful enemy combatant” are also used with regard to those persons detained by the United States in Guantánamo. This term seems to imply that these persons are not treated as prisoners of war, but that international humanitarian law is applied to them nevertheless.[632] The United States government apparently grouped both “lawful” and “unlawful combatants” into this broader category of “enemy combatants”.[633]

Second, the term “unlawful belligerents” is partly distinguished from “unlawful combatants”: While the latter are understood to operate during armed conflicts and usually against legitimate military objectives, the former – according to *Hoffman* – more often act in times of peace and quite often against legally protected sites or persons. Thus, *Hoffman* refers to “terrorists” as being “unlawful belligerents” in a similar way as pirates were in the 18th and 19th centuries: The mere fact that military means are used to address the threat they pose does not mean that the law of war applies to them.[634]

Third, the term “quasi-combatant” is proposed to describe civilians who contribute so fundamentally to the military effort or the war effort – e.g. by working in an ammunition factory – that they should lose their civilian status although the do not directly participate in hostilities.[635]

Fourth, the term “battlefields unlawful combatants” is used to describe “unlawful combatants who are involved directly in the fight on the battlefields, as opposed to those “unlawful combatants” who operate behind the enemy lines, i.e. in the home territory of an enemy country or in occupied territory, as spies or saboteurs.[636]

---

632 Wieczorek, *Unrechtmäßige Kombattanten*, p. 35.

633 Watkin, 15 *Duke J. Comp. & Int’l L.* (2005), at 383.

634 Hoffman, 34 *Case W. Res. J. Int’l L.* (2002), at 229; Hoffman, 31 *Isr. Yb. Hum. Rts.* (2001), at 166-167.

635 Robert Wayn Gehring, ‘Changing Rules for Changing Forms of Warfare’, in: 42 *Law & Contemp. Probs.* (1978), pp. 86-139, at 105-109.

636 Callen, 44 *Va. J. Int’l L.* (2004), at 1028; a similar distinction is made by Baxter, 28 *Brit. Yb. Int’l L.* (1952), at 328-329.

III. The Status of "Unlawful Combatants"

The decisive question is whether the term "unlawful combatant" is only describing a group of persons that falls into one of the traditional categories of international humanitarian law – i.e. combatant, civilian and prisoner-of-war status – or whether it constitutes a particular status.

1. "Unlawful Combatants" in International Armed Conflicts

Concerning international armed conflicts, the term "unlawful combatant" can be used in the common manner: It can refer to persons who took direct part in hostilities without the right to do so. As described above, traditionally a person can either have the primary status of a combatant or of a civilian. If either of those persons has taken direct part in hostilities and is captured on the battlefield, it may not be obvious to which category that person belongs. In these situations Article 5 of the 1949 Geneva Convention III and Article 45 of the 1977 Additional Protocol I provide for a procedure to determine the captive's status by a "competent tribunal".[637]

In consequence, if a person who took direct part in hostilities does not meet the conditions to qualify as a prisoner of war, he will not benefit from the protection laid down in the 1949 Geneva Convention III. These persons could then "enjoy no protection under international law"[638] or fall into the personal scope of application of the 1949 Geneva Convention IV:

a) "Unlawful Combatants" as "Unprotected Persons"

According to one opinion, "unlawful combatants" constitute their own status in international humanitarian law.[639] They are object to direct at-

---

[637] Dörmann, 85 *Int'l Rev. Red Cross* (2003), No 849, at 47.

[638] Detter, *Law of War*, p. 148.

[639] Richard R. Baxter, 'The Duties of Combatants and the Conduct of Hostilities (Law of The Hague)', in: Henry Dunant Institute; United Nations Educational, Scientific and Cultural Organization (eds.), *International Dimensions of Humanitarian Law*, Geneva 1988, pp. 93-133, at 105-106; Dinstein, in: Dinstein/ Tabory (eds.), at 105; Dinstein, 32 *Isr. Yb. Hum. Rts.* (2002), at 249; Kastenberg, 39 *Gonz. L. Rev.* (2003/4), at 498, 517-518 and 537.

tack and may be targeted in hostilities.[640] According to some authors, they fall outside the protection that is granted to prisoners of war under the 1949 Geneva Convention III on the one hand, and also outside the protection that is granted to protected persons under the 1949 Geneva Convention IV on the other hand.[641] They thus "cannot claim the privileges appertaining to lawful combatancy. Nor ... enjoy the benefits of civilian status".[642] Therefore they have been referred to as "extra-conventional persons".[643] However, a minimum standard of protection is granted to them by most authors,[644] i.e. the fundamental guarantees such as due process of law[645] or the minimal guarantees of Common Article 3 of the 1949 Geneva Conventions.[646]

---

640 Yoo, 3 *Chin. J. Int'l L.* (2004), at 143; Detter, *Law of War*, p. 148.

641 *See e.g.* Baxter, in: Henry Dunant Institute *et al.* (eds.), at 105-106; Baxter, 28 *Brit. Yb. Int'l L.* (1952), at 328; Detter, *Law of War*, p. 148; Robert Kogod Goldmann; Brian D. Tittemore, 'Unprivileged Combatants and the Hostilities in Afghanistan: Their Status and Rights under International Humanitarian and Human Rights Law' in: American Society of International Law, Task Force on Terrorism, December 2002, p. 38; Christopher Greenwood, 'International Law and the "War against Terrorism"', in: 78 *Int'l Aff.* (2002), pp. 301-318, at 316; Peter Malanczuk, *Akehurst's Modern Introduction to International Law*, 7th ed., London 1997, p. 354; Newton, in: Wippman/ Evangelista (eds.), at 84. Interestingly, the following authors do not even take into account the possibility that "unlawful combatants" could fall into the scope of application of the 1949 Geneva Convention IV: K. Elizabeth Dahlstrom, 'The Executive Policy toward Detention and Trial of foreign Citizens at Guantanamo Bay', in: 21 *Berkeley J. Int'l L.* (2003), pp. 662-682; Dinstein, 32 *Isr. Yb. Hum. Rts.* (2002), at 249; Peal, 58 *Vand. L. Rev.* (2005), at 1638-1639 and 1669; Yoo, 3 *Chin. J. Int'l L.* (2004), pp. 135-150.

642 Dinstein, *Conduct of Hostilities*, p. 29.

643 Paul E. Kantwill; Sean Watts, 'Hostile Protected Persons or "Extra-Conventional Persons": How Unlawful Combatants in the War on Terrorism posed Extraordinary Challenges for Military Attorneys and Commanders', in: 28 *Fordham Int'l L.J.* (2005), pp. 681-741, at 681 (footnote 1).

644 *See e.g.* Neuman, 14 *Eur. J. Int'l L.* (2003), at 295.

645 Dinstein, in: Dinstein/ Tabory (eds.), at 111-112. *Dinstein* emphasises the fact that "unlawful combatants" do not acquire prisoner-of-war status if captured. He does not explicitly reject the idea that they could qualify as protected persons, but only mentions the fundamental protections under Article 75 of the 1977 Additional Protocol I. Detter, *Law of War*, p. 148, accepts "that even spies may claim certain fundamental guaranties under the Protocol such as due pro-

Some furthermore distinguish the group of "battlefield unlawful combatants" from others: Normal "unlawful combatants" are those who operate behind the enemy lines, i.e. in the home territory of an enemy country or in occupied territory, as spies or saboteurs. "Battlefields unlawful combatants" are "unlawful combatants" who are directly involved in the fight on the battlefields. It is argued that the latter group – if captured – is neither entitled to protection under the Third nor the Fourth Geneva Convention and "remain outside the Geneva Convention framework."[647] The supporters of this assessment *inter alia* argue that unlawful combatants pose unique risks to civilians, as distinction is made difficult and will lead to civilian casualties. Thus, the Geneva Conventions are understood to create incentives for combatants on the battlefield to distinguish themselves from civilians by denying protection to "battlefield unlawful combatants."[648]

The opinion that "unlawful combatants" – whether only those who were in the battlefield or all – are not protected persons under the 1949 Geneva Convention IV is based on the following arguments, the first of them being rather rhetorical than legal: First, the term "unlawful combatant" seems to create the impression that only "combatants" are concerned and that thus no other convention than the 1949 Geneva Convention III could apply to them anyway.[649] Second, it is regarded as to-

---

cess of law"; *see also* Malanczuk, *Akehurst's Introduction*, p. 354; Sven Peterke, 'Die Umgehung rechtsstaatlicher Garantien durch Bestimmung Terrorverdächtiger zu „feindlichen Kombattanten“: Zur Entscheidung des New Yorker Bundesberufungsgerichts in der Sache „Padilla v. Rumsfeld“', in: 17 *HuV-I* (2004), pp. 39-46, at 41.

646 *Compare* U.S. Supreme Court, *Salim Ahmed Hamdan v. Donald H. Rumsfeld, Secretary of Defense,* et al., Case No. 05-184, Decision of June 29, 2006, reprinted in: 45 *ILM* (2006), pp. 1130-1203 at 1155 (paras. VI D iv-v).

647 Callen, 44 *Va. J. Int'l L.* (2004), at 1029; *see also* Baxter, 28 *Brit. Yb. Int'l L.* (1952), at 328; Baxter, in: Henry Dunant Institute *et al.* (eds.), at 105, who limits the scope of application of 1949 Geneva Convention IV to "unlawful combatants" operating in occupied territory. *Compare also* Rosas, *Prisoners of War*, p. 411. According to Kalshoven, 11 *Rev. dr. pén. mil.* (1972), at 70-71, this is an "all too technical" approach which could be solved by way of analogy.

648 Callen, 44 *Va. J. Int'l L.* (2004), at 1029-1030.

649 *Compare* Dinstein, 32 *Isr. Yb. Hum. Rts.* (2002), at 249; Yoo, 3 *Chin. J. Int'l L.* (2004), pp. 135-150 and Dahlstrom, 21 *Berkeley J. Int'l L.* (2003), pp. 662-682 who all are totally silent on the Fourth Geneva Convention.

tally inappropriate to use the term civilian in connection with persons who are "armed with automatic weapons and bombs" as this "contradicts common sense."[650] Third, it is argued that the status of "unlawful combatants" pays regard to the double nature of such a person: It is regarded as not acceptable that a person can be a civilian and a fighter simultaneously.[651] Fourth, the 1949 Geneva Convention IV does not explicitly address civilians who take up arms on the battlefield. This fact is understood as suggesting that unlawful combatants captured on the battlefield are not covered by the Convention.[652] The limitations of Article 5 of the 1949 Geneva Convention IV are interpreted as only relating to occupied territory. Thus, the battlefield is regarded as not being covered by the Convention,[653] with the effect, that "unlawful combatants", who by definition take part in the hostilities, would not be covered. Fifth, it is argued that the drafting process supports such an interpretation, as delegations stressed that the concept of the convention was to protect civilian victims and not illegitimate bearers of arms.[654]

---

[650] David, 17 *Ethics & Int'l Aff.* (2003), at 138-139; *see also* Kretzmer, 16 *Eur. J. Int'l L.* (2005), at 212 ("unrealistic"); Peal, 58 *Vand. L. Rev.* (2005), at 1638 ("illogical"); *but see* Marco Sassòli, '"Unlawful Combatants": the Law and Whether it Needs to be Revised', in: 97 *ASIL Proc.* (2003), pp. 196-200, at 198: "[B]orderline cases never correspond to the ideal type of a category and fall nevertheless under its provisions."

[651] Dinstein, in: Dinstein/ Tabory (eds.), at 105; but compare the discussion on direct participation in hostilities, *supra*, Part Two, Chapter D) II. 1. c).

[652] Callen, 44 *Va. J. Int'l L.* (2004), at 1038; On the other hand *Jinks* stresses that the 1949 Geneva Convention IV "does not, however, expressly limit the application of the Convention to persons taking no part in the hostilities", Derek Jinks, 'The Declining Significance of POW Status', in: 45 *Harv. Int'l L.J.* (2004), pp. 367-442, at 383.

[653] Baxter, 28 *Brit. Yb. Int'l L.* (1952), at 328; Toman, 32 *Isr. Yb. Hum. Rts.* (2002), at 295-296.

[654] Newton, in: Wippman/ Evangelista (eds.), at 101; albeit *Newton* admits that "[a] number of delegations explicitly confirmed that the textual provisions of the Geneva Conventions did not foreclose the traditional category of unlawful combatants", *id.*

b) "Unlawful Combatants" as "Protected Persons"

According to another opinion, "unlawful combatants" may exist as a group of persons who share common characteristics, but does not qualify as a status distinct from civilians and combatants. As it is commonly accepted that "unlawful combatants" do not qualify as combatants proper, they are thus regarded as civilians by primary status.[655] The categories of civilian and combatant are mutually exclusive and complement one another.[656]

"Unlawful Combatants" are furthermore understood to qualify as falling within the scope of the 1949 Geneva Convention IV:[657] Its field of application is defined in Article 4 para. 1 and covers "protected persons", i.e. persons who find themselves in the hands of a party to the conflict or of the occupying power of which they are not nationals. As shown above, this covers "enemy nationals" within the national territory of each of the parties to the conflict and "the whole population" of occupied territories – excluding nationals of the occupying power.[658] According to Article 4 para. 4, this excludes persons who benefit from the protection of the 1949 Geneva Convention I-III. Thus, prisoners of

---

[655] Supreme Court of Israel, *"Targeted Killings" (Merits)*, paras. 26-28, 46 *ILM* (2007), at 387-388; Arnold, in: Arnold/ Hildbrand (eds.), at 14; Dörmann, 85 *Int'l Rev. Red Cross* (2003), No 849, at 50 and 56; Sassòli, 97 *ASIL Proc.* (2003), at 196; *compare also* Cassese, 40 *ZaöRV* (1980), at 5; Prefontaine, in: Canadian Council on International Law (ed.), at 392.

[656] Sandoz *et al.* (eds.), *Protocoles additionnels*, para. 1917 (p. 625); Arnold, in: Arnold/ Hildbrand (eds.), at 14 and 16.

[657] *See e.g.* ICRC, *International Humanitarian Law and the Challenges of Contemporary Armed Conflicts*, Report, September 2003, p. 9; Borelli, in: Bianchi/ Naqvi (eds.), at 45-46; Borelli, 87 *Int'l Rev. Red Cross* (2005), No. 857, at 50-51; Dörmann, 85 *Int'l Rev. Red Cross* (2003), No 849, at 48-58; Jinks, 45 *Harv. Int'l L.J.* (2004), at 380-387; Stein, 17 *Ethics & Int'l Aff.* (2003), at 128-130; Nolte, in: Fischer *et al.* (eds.), at 398; Luisa Vierucci, 'Prisoners of War or Protected Persons *qua* Unlawful Combatants? The Judicial Safeguards to which Guantanamo Bay Detainees are Entitled', in: 1 *J. Int'l Crim. Just.* (2003), pp. 284-314, at 298; Wieczorek, *Unrechtmäßige Kombattanten*, pp. 108-111. Callen, 44 *Va. J. Int'l L.* (2004), at 1031, supports this view for "unlawful combatants operating in occupied territory or in the home territory of a belligerent nation" but disagrees concerning "battlefield unlawful combatants", *but see* Jinks, 45 *Harv. Int'l L.J.* (2004), at 393-397.

[658] *See supra*, Part Two, Chapter D) II. 1. d).

war – who fall under the Third Convention – do not fall under the Fourth Convention. Therefore, even persons who do not qualify as prisoners of war because they did not respect the conditions which would entitle them to this status fall under the 1949 Geneva Convention IV.[659] "Every person in enemy hands must have some status under international law."[660] As the ICTY phrased it:

> It is important, however, to note that this finding is predicated on the view that there is no gap between the Third and the Fourth Geneva Conventions. If an individual is not entitled to the protections of the Third Convention as a prisoner of war (or of the First or Second Conventions) he or she necessarily falls within the ambit of Convention IV, provided that its article 4 requirements are satisfied.[661]

Also, the fact that the person in question has taken direct part in hostilities without being privileged to do so does not exclude his protection under the Fourth Convention: According to Article 5 of the 1949 Geneva Convention IV, limited derogations concerning the rights of "protected persons" are possible. These derogations apply to those "protected persons" who are detained as spies or saboteurs of who are engaged in activities hostile to the security of the State.[662] Some of these activities certainly qualify as direct participation in hostilities, but do not deprive the person of its status as a "protected person".[663] These derogations would not have been necessary if such persons did not fall under the Fourth Conventions.[664] Furthermore, Article 45 para. 3 of the 1977 Additional Protocol I contains an implicit confirmation of the above mentioned interpretation of Article 5 of the 1949 Geneva Convention IV. It reads:

---

659 Dörmann, 85 *Int'l Rev. Red Cross* (2003), No 849, at 49.

660 Pictet (ed.), *Geneva Conventions*, Vol. 4, p. 51.

661 ICTY, *Prosecutor v. Zejnil Delalić* et al., Case No. IT-96-21-T ("Čelebići"), Judgment of November 16, 1998, para. 271.

662 *See supra*, Part Two, Chapter D) II 1. d).

663 *See e.g.* European Commission for Democracy through Law , Opinion No. 245/2003, para. 43 (p. 14); Rosenblad, 12 *Rev. dr. pén. mil.* (1973), at 111; Dörmann, 85 *Int'l Rev. Red Cross* (2003), No 849, at 50; Wieczorek, *Unrechtmäßige Kombattanten*, p. 110.

664 Sassòli, 97 *ASIL Proc.* (2003), at 197.

> Any person who has taken part in hostilities, who is not entitled to prisoner-of-war status and who does not benefit from more favourable treatment in accordance with the Fourth Convention shall have the right at all times to the protection of Article 75 of this Protocol. In occupied territory, any such person, unless he is held as a spy, shall also be entitled, notwithstanding Article 5 of the Fourth Convention, to his rights of communication under that Convention.

First, the paragraph presupposes that the 1949 Geneva Convention IV is applicable to some "unlawful combatants" as it refers to persons who do not benefit "from more favourable treatment in accordance with the Fourth Convention".[665] Second, the referral to the protection afforded by Article 5 of the Fourth Convention – and its restriction concerning spies – shows that "unlawful combatants" are generally covered by the Fourth Convention.[666] This interpretation is also laid down in the U.S. military Manual:

> If a person is determined by a competent tribunal, acting in conformity with Article 5 [of the 1949 Geneva Convention III] not to fall within any of the categories listed in Article 4 [of the 1949 Geneva Convention III], he is not entitled to be treated as a prisoner of war. He is, however, a 'protected person' within the meaning of Article 4 [1949 Geneva Convention IV].[667]
>
> Subject to qualifications set forth in paragraph 248 [of this manual], those protected by [the 1949 Geneva Convention IV] also include all persons who have engaged in hostile or belligerent conduct but who are not entitled to treatment as prisoners of war.[668]

Furthermore, the *travaux préparatoires* of the 1949 Geneva Conventions are interpreted to support such an interpretation: Whereas the term "unlawful combatant" was not used in the drafting process, reference can be found to persons violating the laws of war, saboteurs and

---

[665] European Commission for Democracy through Law, Opinion No. 245/2003, paras. 40-41 (p. 13).

[666] Bothe *et al.*, *1977 Protocols*, Art. 45 Prot. I, para. 2.4 (pp. 261-262); Dörmann, 85 *Int'l Rev. Red Cross* (2003), No 849, at 51; Jinks, 45 *Harv. Int'l L.J.* (2004), at 385-386; *compare also* Watkin, 15 *Duke J. Comp. & Int'l L.* (2005), at 283.

[667] U.S. Department of the Army, Field Manual No. 27-10, para. 73.

[668] *Id.*, para. 247. Para. 248 of the manual refers to the Article 5 of the 1949 Geneva Convention IV.

spies. In the view of the drafters of the Third Convention, these persons should neither be entitled to prisoners of war status, nor to protection identical with that of "peaceful" civilians, but they should be entitled to humane treatment and not summarily executed. The final version was based on the understanding that persons who are not entitled to protection under the Third Convention should be protected under the Fourth Convention with the effect that all persons who took direct part in hostilities are protected, whether they conformed to the laws of war or not.[669]

The interpretation that "battlefield unlawful combatants" are not covered by Articles 4 and 5 of the 1949 Geneva Convention IV[670] may find its source in the fact that the Convention provides for different specific protections to aliens in the territory of an enemy party to the conflict and persons in occupied territory. This interpretation cannot convince if the concept of "occupied territory" is understood in a broader manner than in Article 42 of the 1907 Hague Regulations: According to the ICRC Commentary,

> [s]o far as individuals are concerned, the application of the Fourth Geneva Convention does not depend upon the existence of a state of occupation within the meaning of the Article 42 referred to above. The relations between the civilian population of a territory and troops advancing into that territory, whether fighting or not, are governed by the present Convention. There is no intermediate period between what might be termed the invasion phase and the inauguration of a stable regime of occupation. Even a patrol which penetrates into enemy territory without any intention of staying there must respect the Conventions in its dealings with the civilians it meets. ... The Convention is quite definite on this point: all persons who find themselves in the hands of a Party to the conflict or an

---

669 *See* Dörmann, 85 *Int'l Rev. Red Cross* (2003), No 849, at 52-58; *see also* European Commission for Democracy through Law, Opinion No. 245/2003, para. 41 (p. 13); Jinks, 45 *Harv. Int'l L.J.* (2004), at 383-384; Sassòli, 97 *ASIL Proc.* (2003), at 196; *but see* Newton, in: Wippman/ Evangelista (eds.), at 100-102.

670 *Compare supra*, Part Two, Chapter E) III. 1. a).

Occupying Power of which they are not nationals are protected persons.[671]

Thus, "[n]o loophole is left"[672] between the scope of the Third and the Fourth Geneva Convention.[673] Even *Callen* must therefore admit that "[t]his broad interpretation of what constitutes occupied territory makes some sense."[674] It is difficult to delineate battlefield areas, as the hostilities often occur in territory that later is occupied by an opposing power. Therefore, the drafters of the Convention may have believed that the definition of occupied territory was broad enough to cover all categories of "unlawful combatants".[675]

The further argument that combatants need incentives to distinguish themselves from civilians and should thus be deterred by depriving any protection from "unlawful combatants" is also not convincing: Such an incentive is already fully realised by the fact that such "unlawful combatants" will not acquire prisoner-of-war status and may be tried for their participation in the hostilities. "[T]he only effective sanction against perfidious attacks in civilian dress is deprivation of prisoner-of-war status."[676] Deterrence can thus not be an argument for the denial of the remaining protection.[677]

Finally, the ultimate aim of international humanitarian law is to uphold the basic humanitarian principles in situations of armed conflict.[678] This would not be the case if a person would fall outside any category under international humanitarian law and thus enjoy no protection at all. It is

---

[671] Pictet (ed.), *Geneva Conventions*, Vol. 4, p. 60; *see also* Aggelen, 4 *Chin. J. Int'l L.* (2005), at 173; *but see* Gasser, in: Fleck (ed.), *Handbook*, at 244 (paras. 528 and 528.1).

[672] Pictet (ed.), *Geneva Conventions*, Vol. 4, p. 60.

[673] Aggelen, 4 *Chin. J. Int'l L.* (2005), at 173; Jinks, 45 *Harv. Int'l L.J.* (2004), at 423; Lavoyer, in: Lijnzaad *et al.* (eds.), at 258; Sassòli, 97 *ASIL Proc.* (2003), at 197; Stein, 17 *Ethics & Int'l Aff.* (2003), at 128-130; Vierucci, 1 *J. Int'l Crim. Just.* (2003), at 298.

[674] Callen, 44 *Va. J. Int'l L.* (2004), at 1043.

[675] *Id.*

[676] Rosas, *Prisoners of War*, p. 344; *see also* Yoo, 3 *Chin. J. Int'l L.* (2004), at 137 and 143.

[677] *But see e.g.* Callen, 44 *Va. J. Int'l L.* (2004), at 1029-1030.

[678] *See e.g.* Murphy, 41 *Rev. dr. mil.* (2002), at 151.

important to stress once again that the application of the Fourth Geneva Convention to "unlawful combatants" would not prevent the trial of them even though they qualify as protected persons:[679] The Convention – according to Articles 72 and 73 – only requires that protected persons have free choice of counsel, the right to present evidence and call witnesses and rights of appeal "provided for by the laws applied by the court".

2. *"Unlawful Combatants" in Non-International Armed Conflicts*

In the context of non-international armed conflicts, the term "unlawful combatant" is difficult to apply: International humanitarian law does not foresee a combatant's privilege for such conflicts. Thus, all persons captured in this context come under the identical protection as laid down in Common Article 3 of the 1949 Geneva Conventions and in Articles 4-6 of the 1977 Additional Protocol II, as well as customary international law. These rules apply to all persons who have taken direct part in the hostilities, irrespective of whether a person is a member of the armed forces of a State, of an armed rebel group, or is a civilian who only temporarily took part in the hostilities.[680] It is thus unclear which group is exactly referred to when *Jinks* relates that protection especially to "unlawful combatants".[681] These guarantees apply to all persons in the context of an non-international armed conflict.

IV. Conclusion: No such Third Status Exists

The term "unlawful combatants" describes persons who took direct part in the hostilities without fulfilling the preconditions of combatant status. These persons are thus, by primary status, civilians. This is reflected in the system of the Third and Fourth Geneva Conventions,

---

679 *See e.g.* Aldrich, 96 *Am. J. Int'l L.* (2002), at 893 (footnote 12); Bothe *et al.*, *1977 Protocols*, Art. 45 Prot. I, para. 2.4 (pp. 261-262); David, *Conflits Armés*, pp. 397-398; McCoubrey, *Humanitarian Law*, p. 137; Rosenblad, 12 *Rev. dr. pén. mil.* (1973), at 98; Dörmann, 85 *Int'l Rev. Red Cross* (2003), No 849, at 58-59 with further references; Sassòli, 97 *ASIL Proc.* (2003), at 198.

680 Dörmann, 85 *Int'l Rev. Red Cross* (2003), No 849, at 47-48.

681 Jinks, 45 *Harv. Int'l L.J.* (2004), at 414.

which suffice to deal with "unlawful combatants" and do not have to be adapted to "new challenges". "Indeed, the main problem today is not a lack of rules, but the proper implementation of existing rules."[682] This solution complies with the fundamental principle in international humanitarian law that a person is either a civilian, subject to domestic and international criminal proceedings in case of unlawful participation in warfare, or a combatant to which the prisoner of war regulations apply and who is subject to the war crimes provisions of international humanitarian law.

For the reasons shown above "unlawful combatants" are, in principle, protected by the 1949 Geneva Convention IV as other "protected persons". It is thus a matter of taste whether they are referred to as "unlawful combatants", "unprivileged belligerents" or simply "civilians". However, the latter two terms describe their situation best: By their primary status, these persons are civilians and due to their direct participation in hostilities they can also be called "belligerents", albeit without the privileges of combatant immunity.

The question whether a person is such an "unlawful combatant" must be answered on an individual basis, and not according to group membership: A combatant does not become an "unlawful combatant" merely because other members of the armed forces or unit to which he belongs commit war crimes.[683] This only happens if the group or unit systematically violates the laws of war in course of its operations in such a manner that it can be regarded as not being subject to an effective disciplinary system and therefore not being an armed force under international law any more. Then, members of such groups could loose their combatant status insofar as the group they belong to no longer represent armed forces under international humanitarian law. Their further participation in the hostilities would then be that of non-combatants.[684]

The whole concept of "unlawful combatants" thus only refers to a subcategory of civilians. Article 5 of the 1949 Geneva Convention IV gives the detaining power of such persons certain competences to restrict

---

[682] Lavoyer, in: Lijnzaad *et al.* (eds.), at 268.; *compare also* Sassòli, 97 *ASIL Proc.* (2003), at 199-200 *and already* Rosenblad, 12 *Rev. dr. pén. mil.* (1973), at 122.

[683] Jordan J. Paust, 'War and Enemy Status after 9/11: Attacks on the Laws of War', in: 28 *Yale J. Int'l L.* (2003), pp. 325-336, at 332.

[684] *Compare* UK Ministry of Defence, *Manual*, para. 4.3.4 (pp. 39-40).

their rights in comparison to "peaceful civilians". However, these restriction do not entail any exception of the general immunity from attack. Thus, the fact that a person took direct part in hostilities and is thus referred to as "unlawful combatant" does not deprive him from the protection from attack as shown above: He remains a civilian and is immune from attack unless – and for such time – as he takes direct part in hostilities.[685]

V. Consequence: No Special Status of "Terrorists" Under International Humanitarian Law

This system of the status of combatant or civilian applies to all persons, including those who are referred to as "terrorists": Prior to 2001, the question as to the status of "terrorists" under international humanitarian law would not have arisen. Traditionally, governments vehemently denied that their opponents were anything but criminals. The former feared that the latter gained a psychological and legal advantage if called "combatants" and their struggle "war". Terrorists were thus regarded as civilian criminals and were considered exclusively within the national criminal system of each country affected. Concerning activities that spread out in many countries and included persons of different nationalities, the jurisdiction and competence to prosecute, try and punish was examined according to the principles of territoriality, nationality, universality or the protective principle. The countries which prosecuted "terrorists" applied their national criminal law, but also "terrorists" benefited from the fundamental judicial and procedural guarantees provided by human rights law. Obviously, those countries which tolerated or even supported the activity of "terrorists" would neither extradite nor prosecute those persons.[686]

In the light of this lack of effective prosecution of terrorists, and most of all, under the impression of the devastating September 11 attacks,

---

[685] *See supra*, Part Two, Chapter D); *see also* Wieczorek, *Unrechtmäßige Kombattanten*, pp. 124-125; Silja Vöneky, 'The Fight against Terrorism and the Rules of the Law of Warfare', in: Christian Walter; Silja Vöneky; Volker Röben; Frank Schorkopf (eds.), *Terrorism as a Challenge for National and International Law: Security versus Liberty?*, Berlin 2004, pp. 925-949, at 945-946.

[686] Toman, 32 *Isr. Yb. Hum. Rts.* (2002), at 287.

acts of terrorists were popularly and demonstratively referred to as "war" in order to emphasize the magnitude of the shock that they represent.[687] In consequence, the paradigms started to shift at least according to some authors: It was tried to capture "terrorists" by the terminology of war, and also by the concepts that are provided for by international humanitarian law. In that regard "terrorists" operating on an international level could – for example – be regarded as members of an organisation "belonging to a Party to the conflict".[688] The link of al-Qaeda with the Taliban regime and thus with the State Afghanistan has served as precedent to consider this question.[689] Whereas it might seem attractive to allow combatant status to terrorists, as they would then be legitimate targets under international humanitarian law,[690] this status entails prisoner-of-war status once a person is captured and is thus regarded as less desirable. Others are of the opinion that terrorists who attack civilians are "illegal combatants" not entitled to prisoner-of-war status but legitimate targets.[691] The answer cannot be given in a general manner:

> Terrorism is not a legal notion. This very fact indicates the difficulty, if not the impossibility, of determining how terrorism and responses to it may be identified historically or defined within a legal regime.[692]

"Terrorist" is thus not a term that describes a well defined type of person but is itself a largely disputed concept.[693] It is not a status compara-

---

687 *Id.*, at 273.

688 Article 4A (2) 1949 Geneva Convention III; *compare e.g.* Lavoyer, in: Lijnzaad *et al.* (eds.), at 258. *But see infra*, Part Four, Chapter F) I.

689 Rowe, 3 *Melb. J. Int'l L.* (2002), at 315.

690 This seemed to be the Israeli position, supported by Shany, in: Schmitt/ Beruto (eds.), at 104.

691 Guiora, 36 *Case W. Res. J. Int'l L.* (2004), at 328; Newton, in: Wippman/ Evangelista (eds.), at 106-109.

692 Gabor Rona, 'Interesting Times for International Humanitarian Law: Challenges from the "War on Terror"', in: 27 *Fletcher F. World Aff.* (2003), pp. 55-74, at 60-61; *compare also* Kremnitzer, in: Fleck (ed.), *Rechtsfragen*, at 206.

693 *Compare supra*, Introduction, Chapter F) II.

ble to civilian or combatant.[694] Thus, in the context of an international armed conflict, a person – who may by some be referred to as a "terrorist" – could qualify as a combatant if he fulfils the preconditions of that status as laid down *supra*.[695] It is rather unlikely that a person who comes under any accepted definition of "terrorist" would be part of the armed forces of a given State,[696] or that "terrorists" would form a group "belonging to a Party to the conflict". It is regarded as one main distinguishing criterion that "terrorists" are – as a rule – not fighting in the name of an existing State.[697] However, the label "terrorist" is applied to a range of acts that would not be contrary to international law if they were carried out by the armed forces of a State in an armed conflict, e.g. attacks on military targets with weapons that are not prohibited by international humanitarian law.[698] On the other hand, even acts by armed forces can constitute "terrorist acts".[699] Thus, the test has to be made

---

694 *See e.g.* Frowein, 62 *ZaöRV* (2002), at 893; *but see* Gross, *Struggle of Democracy*, p. 51, who concludes that "[u]nder international law, terrorists are unlawful combatants".

695 *See supra*, Part Two, Chapter C) I.

696 Kretzmer, 16 *Eur. J. Int'l L.* (2005), at 191.

697 Klabbers, 14 *Eur. J. Int'l L.* (2003), at 310.

698 Greenwood, 19 *Isr. Yb. Hum. Rts.* (1989), at 189; Leslie C. Green, 'Terrorism and Armed Conflict: The Plea and the Verdict', in: 19 *Isr. Yb. Hum. Rts.* (1989), pp. 131-166, at 165; Lavoyer, in: Lijnzaad *et al.* (eds.), at 263-264; Torsten Stein, 'How much Humanity do Terrorists deserve?', in: Astrid J.M. Delissen; Gerard J. Tanja (eds.), *Humanitarian Law of Armed Conflict: Challenges ahead – Essays in Honour of Frits Kalshoven*, Dordrecht 1991, pp. 567-581, at 572. On the other hand, *Greenwood* is of the opinion that a common feature of *most* "terrorist acts" is that they would be a violation of the laws of war if committed by armed forces in an armed conflict, *id.*

699 For example, Article 33 of the 1949 Geneva Convention IV explicitly prohibits "[c]ollective penalties and likewise all measures of intimidation or of terrorism". Article 51 para. 2 of the 1977 Additional Protocol I prohibits "acts or threats of violence the primary purpose of which is to spread terror among the civilian population." *Compare further* Müllerson, 32 *Isr. Yb. Hum. Rts.* (2002), at 32-33; Daniel O'Donnell, 'International Treaties against Terrorism and the Use of Terrorism during Armed Conflict and by Armed Forces', in: 88 *Int'l Rev. Red Cross* (2006), No 864, at 863-866; Stein, in: Delissen/ Tanja (eds.), at 573; Arnold, in: Arnold/ Hildbrand (eds.), at 22. *Vöneky* draws the conclusion from the provisions quoted above that there "are no provisions in international law stating that the applicability of the law of armed conflict is expressly

independently from any status for every individual person and a general answer cannot be given. The topic is even more controversial when it comes to the 1977 Additional Protocol I: As the Protocol in its Article 1 para. 4 refers to "armed conflicts which peoples are fighting against colonial domination and alien occupation and against racist regimes in the exercise of their right of self-determination", it is more disputed whether persons fall under the scope of the protocol. The Protocol has even been criticised as an "encouragement to terrorists" by U.S. President Ronald Reagan.[700] Again, while it seems clear that 1977 Additional Protocol I does not afford any protection to "terrorists",[701] an individual that is protected by the convention can at the same time be regarded as a "terrorist" by some observers.

The topic is even less clear when it comes to non-international armed conflicts: As the distinction between civilians and fighters is very much disputed in that regard,[702] it is difficult when it comes to categorizing such a controversial concept as "terrorism". Some try to give general answers: *Kretzmer*, for example, qualifies persons involved in the "terrorist" activities of an international "terrorist" group as combatants in a non-international armed conflict. This approach allows states to enjoy the best of both worlds: These persons would be legitimate targets, but they would not gain prisoner-of-war status if captured, neither would they be immune from prosecution for fighting. It would furthermore invite states to change from the law-enforcement to the non-international armed conflict model as soon as possible, because they could then circumvent due process guarantees and enjoy almost unrestricted discretion in targeting their suspected enemies. Thus, in *Kretzmer's* view, this approach has to be mitigated.[703] Even other authors who support the approach that terrorists are combatants that "die on the 'battlefield'" limit targeted killings to cases "when arrest is not an option".[704]

---

excluded with regard to terrorist acts.", *see* Vöneky, in: Walter *et al.* (eds.), at 927-928. Whether this is a sufficient basis for a general applicability of the law of armed conflict to "terrorism" will be examined *infra*, Part Four, Chapter F).

700 Greenwood, 19 *Isr. Yb. Hum. Rts.* (1989), at 187.

701 Detter, *Law of War*, p. 145; *compare also* Gross, 15 *Fla. J. Int'l L.* (2003), at 419-421.

702 *Compare supra*, Part Two, Chapter C) II.

703 Kretzmer, 16 *Eur. J. Int'l L.* (2005), at 194-200.

704 Guiora, 36 *Case W. Res. J. Int'l L.* (2004), at 329-330.

But again, a general answer is not possible: As there is not the "prototype of a terrorist" who either qualifies as a civilian or combatant or fighter in any context, every person has to be regarded individually: Someone who meets the definition of fighter in a non-international armed conflict may well be regarded as a "terrorist" by some, and as not a "terrorist" by others. Insofar, one cannot but agree with *Higgins'* conclusion:

> 'Terrorism' is a term without legal significance. It is merely a convenient way of alluding to activities, whether of States or individuals, widely disapproved of and in which either the methods used are unlawful, or the targets protected, or both. ... The term is at once a shorthand to allude to a variety of problems with some common elements, and a method of indicating community condemnation for the conduct concerned.[705]

In consequence, "terrorists" do not *per se* meet the conditions to be regarded as combatants or civilians. It is, however, more likely that they do not fulfil the preconditions of combatants status or the status of fighters respectively. Thus, most persons who may be referred to as "terrorists" are most likely civilians.[706] In that case, they are immune

---

[705] Rosalyn Higgins, 'The General International Law of Terrorism', in: Rosalyn Higgins; Maurice Flory (eds.), *Terrorism and International Law*, London 1996, pp. 13-29, at 28. It is true that the International Convention for the Suppression of the Financing of Terrorism, adopted by the General Assembly of the United Nations on December 9, 1999, GA Res. 54/109, UN Doc. A/RES/54/109 (February 25, 2000), entry into force on April 10, 2002, reprinted in: 39 *ILM* (2000), pp. 270-280, ties legal consequences to what may be called "terrorism". However, the Convention according to Article 2, para. 1 *lit.* b refers to any "act intended to cause death or serious bodily injury to a civilian, or to any other person not taking an active part in the hostilities in a situation of armed conflict, when the purpose of such act, by its nature or context, is to intimidate a population, or to compel a Government or an international organization to do or to abstain from doing any act." It does not expressly define such acts a "terrorist" acts, nor – and most importantly – does it define any person as being a "terrorist".

[706] Arnold, in: Arnold/ Hildbrand (eds.), at 22; Davis Brown, 'Use of Force against Terrorism after September 11: State Responsibility, Self Defense, and other Responses', in: 11 *Cardozo J. Int'l & Comp. L.* (2003), pp. 1-53, at 24-25; Joan Fitzpatrick, 'Jurisdiction of Military Commissions and the Ambiguous War on Terrorism', in: 96 *Am. J. Int'l L.* (2002), pp. 345-354, at pp. 353-354;

from attack unless – and for such time – as they take direct part in hostilities.[707]

F. Conclusion: Targeted Killings and International Humanitarian Law

The legality of targeted killings in the context of armed conflicts – international as well as non-international ones – depends first and foremost on the primary status of the targeted person. As *Frowein* put it:

> Die bewaffnete Aktion darf sich nur gegen Personen richten, die den Kombattanten-Status haben oder ihn haben könnten, wenn sie sich völkerrechtsmäßig verhalten würden. Der Waffeneinsatz ist aber grundsätzlich nicht möglich gegen Personen, die nicht selbst an einer bewaffneten Aktion teilnehmen oder dabei sind, sie konkret vorzubereiten.[708]

The targeted killing of combatants (in international armed conflicts) or fighters (in non-international a armed conflicts) is generally permissible, but subject to certain restrictions. The targeted killing of civilians (in both contexts) is generally prohibited, but may be legal by way of a strictly limited exception. This is only the case while a civilian takes direct part in the hostilities.[709] This direct participation has to be inter-

---

Watkin, *Combatants*, p. 10; Vöneky, in: Walter *et al.* (eds.), at 937. *But see e.g.* Gross, 15 *Fla. J. Int'l L.* (2003), at 423-424.

[707] *Compare supra*, Part Two, Chapter D) II. 1 c); *see also* Wieczorek, *Unrechtmäßige Kombattanten*, pp. 124-125; Vöneky, in: Walter *et al.* (eds.), at 945-946; Coracini, in: Manacorde/ Nieto (eds.), *at* 398. *Compare also* Guiora, 36 *Case W. Res. J. Int'l L.* (2004), at 331, who states: "Targeted killing can only be implemented against those terrorists who either directly or indirectly participate in terrorism in a fashion that is equivalent to involvement in armed conflict."

[708] Frowein, 62 *ZaöRV* (2002), at 892: "The armed attack may only be aimed at persons which have combatant status or would have this status if they behaved in accordance to international law. Generally, the use of force is not feasible against persons neither taking part in the hostilities nor being in the process of preparing themselves to do so." (my translation).

[709] *See also* Melzer, in: Gill/ Fleck (eds.), at 288-289 (para. 17.03.3); Schmahl, in: Tomuschat *et al.* (eds.), at 257-263.

preted narrowly, with a strong emphasis on the threat a civilian poses to the adversary. This threat may be opposed by the use of force, again, subject to the same restrictions as concerning the targeting of combatants.

Independently of what is understood by the terms "unlawful combatant" or "terrorist", those concepts do not represent any status under international humanitarian law. Thus, the standards that apply to either combatants or civilians apply to any person, including those who are referred to by different authors using different definitions as "unlawful combatants" or terrorists". Most likely – but not as a rule – these persons are civilians by their primary status. Many of those persons – but again not all of them – may be taking direct part in hostilities. In this case, they may be targeted independently of how they are referred to. However, every person's status and the question of participation have to be evaluated individually. Thus, to "terrorists", the same rules apply as to other civilians and combatants.

Second, in all cases of targeting a person who has been identified as a legitimate objective, the general principles of international humanitarian law have to be observed. Thus, the killing must be militarily necessary, i.e. serve the purpose to overpower the adversary, and it may not be executed by illegal means and methods. It is prohibited to resort to perfidious means, i.e. using certain covers such as false symbols, emblems or uniforms, feigning civilian status as well as instigating enemy combatants to kill their own superiors, recruiting hired killers, placing a price on the head of a person, and offering a reward for his capture "dead or alive". Furthermore, once a person is *hors de combat*, it may no longer be targeted. This includes persons who have exhausted all means of defence or are unarmed. Thus, a person who does not pose any immediate threat to their adversaries any more is regarded *hors de combat* and may not be targeted.

Third, the overall legality of a targeted killing – once it is established that the objective is legitimate and the means are not prohibited – depends on the impact of the attack on other persons and objects. The collateral damage expected must be proportionate in relation to the military advantage which will be achieved. In that regard, a targeted killing has to be evaluated as one attack with the effect, that it alone – and not a larger military operation – must stand the test of proportionality concerning collateral damage. Once again, the threat which is posed by the targeted person is decisive: An imminent threat may be opposed by means and methods that cause collateral damages in the dimension of those who can directly be saved, as long as the mildest possible means are used. This number strongly decreases in less immediate cases and will frequently require that the attack is suspended until no civilian casualties will be caused.

Thus, human rights law and international humanitarian law constitute a complex and interweaved system of standards, according to which certain killings are permissible in different situations. It is to be assumed that this complex system is self-contained. However, as some authors argue with additional justifications or excuses for targeted killings, such as self-defence in the meaning of the UN Charter in response to an international armed attack by non-State actors.[710] It has to be examined whether such an argument can be made at all, if the specifics of human rights law and international humanitarian law are taken into account. This question will be dealt with in part three, *infra*, whereas the question of the applicability of the relevant international law will be addressed in part four.

---

[710] *See e.g.* Guiora, 36 *Case W. Res. J. Int'l L.* (2004), at 323-326; Rowe, 3 *Melb. J. Int'l L.* (2002), at 304-311; Schmitz-Elvenich, *Targeted Killing*, pp. 50-161, in particular pp. 104-121; Solis, 60 *Nav. War C. Rev.* (2007), at 130-131; Wiebe, 11 *Tulsa J. Comp. & Int'l L.* (2003), at 386-401. *Compare also* Maogoto, 31 *Brook. J. Int'l L.* (2006), at 405; Janse, 36 *Isr. Yb. Hum. Rts.* (2006), pp. 149-180.

Part Three – No Additional Justifications or Excuses

A conduct by a state which would otherwise be considered a breach of a primary rule of international law may not be wrongful under certain circumstances. The consequences of a breach of a primary rule are laid down in the secondary rules of international law, i.e. the law of state responsibility.[1] It has to be examined whether this set of rules can provide for justifications or excuses for the infringement of the prohibitions or limitations on targeted killings as developed above.

Generally, "[e]very internationally wrongful act of a state entails the international responsibility of that state."[2] This principle has often been applied or referred to by the Permanent Court of International Justice,[3] by the International Court of Justice[4] and by numerous Arbitral Tribunals.[5]

---

1 Cassese, *International Law*, p. 244; James Crawford, *The ILC's Articles on State Responsibility: Introduction, Text and Commentaries*, Cambridge 2002, pp. 74-75.

2 Article 1 of the ILC Articles on State Responsibility; *see already* Franco-Mexican Claims Commission, *Estate of Jean-Baptiste Caire (France) v. United Mexican States*, June 7, 1929, in: 5 *RIAA*, pp. 516-534, at 530; *compare also* Cassese, *International Law*, p. 246.

3 *See e.g.* PCIJ, *S.S. "Wimbledon"*, Judgment of August 17, 1923, Series A, No. 1 (1923), pp. 15-34, at 30; PCIJ, *Factory at Chorzów, Jurisdiction*, Judgment of July 26, 1927, Series A, No. 9 (1927), pp. 4-34, at 21; PCIJ, *Factory at Chorzów, Merits*, Judgment of September 13, 1928 Series A, No. 17 (1928), pp. 4-74, at 29; PCIJ, *Phosphates in Morocco, Preliminary Objections*, Judgment of June 14, 1938, Series A/B No. 74 (1938), pp. 10-30, at 28.

4 *See e.g.* ICJ, *Corfu Channel, Merits*, Judgment of April 9, 1949, I.C.J. Reports 1949, pp. 4-38, at 23; ICJ, *Reparation for Injuries Suffered in the Service of the United Nations*, Advisory Opinion of April 11, 1949, I.C.J. Reports 1949, pp. 174-219, at p. 184; ICJ, *Military and Paramilitary Activities in and against Nicaragua, Nicaragua v. United States of America*, Judgment (Merits) of June 27, 1986, I.C.J. Reports 1986, pp. 14-150, at p. 142 (para. 283) and p. 149

An internationally wrongful act consists of an action or omission which is attributable to the State and constitutes a breach of an international obligation of that state.[6] This applies irrespective of whether the obligation breached results from a treaty[7] or is "any obligation, of whatever origin".[8] As States "are legal entities and therefore *can only* act through agents",[9] the actual behaviour by a natural person has to be attributable to a state to trigger its responsibility.[10] This is generally the case as far as conduct by state organs is concerned,[11] irrespective of whether that conduct exceeds the authority of the organ or contravenes instruc-

---

(para. 292); ICJ, *Gabčíkovo-Nagymaros Project, Hungary v. Slovakia*, Judgment of September 25, 1997, I.C.J. Reports 1997, pp. 7-84, at p. 38 (para. 47).

5 *See e.g. Claims of Italian Subjects Resident in Peru*, Awards of September 30, 1901, in: 15 *RIAA*, pp. 395-453, at 399 (claim of *Don Luis Chiessa*); p. 401 (claim of *Don Jeronimo Sessarego*); p. 404 (claim of *Don Juan B. Sanguinetti*); p. 407 (claim of *Don Pablo Vercelli*); p. 408 (claim of the *Queirolo* brothers); p. 409 (claim of *Don Lorenzo Roggero*); p. 411 (claim of *Don José Miglia*); *Claim of the "Salvador Commercial Company", El Salvador v. United States of America*, Award of May 8, 1902, in: 15 *RIAA*, pp. 465-479, at 477.

6 *See* Article 2 of the ILC Articles on State Responsibility.

7 *Compare* ICJ, *Interpretation of Peace Treaties with Bulgaria, Hungary and Romania (Second Phase)*, Advisory Opinion of July 18, 1950, I.C.J. Reports 1950, pp. 221-254, at 228.

8 *Rainbow Warrior, New Zealand v. France*, Award of April 30, 1990, in: 20 *Reports of International Arbitral Awards* (1990), pp. 217-284, at 251; *see also* Article 12 of the ILC Articles on State Responsibility.

9 Ian Brownlie, 'State Responsibility and the International Court of Justice', in: Malgosia Fitzmaurice; Dan Sarooshi (eds.), *Issues of State Responsibility before International Judicial Institutions*, Oxford 2004, pp. 11-18, at p. 12 (emphasis in the original).

10 Crawford, *State Responsibility*, p. 91 (para. 1).

11 *See* Article 4 of the ILC Articles on State Responsibility; *see also* Ian Brownlie, *System of the Law of Nations – State Responsibility*, Part I, Oxford 1983, pp. 132-144; Clyde Eagleton, *The Responsibility of States in International Law*, New York 1928, pp. 44-45 (para. 13).

tions.[12] The aspect of attribution thus demands no closer examination in connection with targeted killings by state officials.[13]

Some rules on state responsibility lay out circumstances precluding the wrongfulness of conduct that would otherwise be a breach an international obligation.[14] For a long time, there was no substantial agreement on the true meaning of theses concepts,[15] a condition that has improved since the adoption of the ILC Articles on State Responsibility in 2001. These articles – to a large extent – reflect existing law, but have in some respect progressively developed the law as well.[16]

The effect of the circumstances precluding wrongfulness is, generally speaking, the elimination of an objective element of the wrongful act.[17] They operate like defences or excuses in internal law.[18] While certain special rules possibly capable of precluding the wrongfulness of an act have been examined earlier,[19] the following part shall cover the general rules that apply in absence of such *leges speciales*. In doing so, it must

---

12 *Compare* Article 7 of the ILC Articles on State Responsibility; *see also* Brownlie, *State Responsibility*, pp. 145-150; Eagleton, *Responsibility of States*, pp. 54-58 (para. 18).

13 Some aspects concerning the attributability of non-State actors' behaviour to States play though an important role in the discussion on the international or non-international character of an armed conflict, *compare supra*, Part Four, Chapter F) I. 2. b) (2).

14 *Compare* Articles 20-27 of the ILC Articles on State Responsibility; *see also* Crawford, *State Responsibility*, p. 160 (para. 1).

15 Peter Malanczuk, 'Countermeasures and Self-Defence as Circumstances Precluding Wrongfulness in the ILC's Draft Articles on State Responsibility', in: Marina Spinedi; Bruno Simma (eds.), *United Nations Codification of State Responsibility*, New York 1987, pp. 197-286, at 198.

16 Cassese, *International Law*, p. 244.

17 Denis Alland, 'International Responsibility and Sanctions: Self-Defence and Countermeasures in the ILC Codification of Rules governing International Responsibility', in: Marina Spinedi; Bruno Simma (eds.), *United Nations Codification of State Responsibility*, New York 1987, pp. 143-195, at 144.

18 Crawford, *State Responsibility*, p. 162 (para. 7).

19 Examples are individual self-defence concerning the human right to life, *see supra*, Part One, Chapter B) II. 2. or the prohibition on reprisals against the civilian population, *see supra*, Part Two, Chapter D) II. 3.

be kept in mind that individual criminal responsibility, as opposed to state responsibility, is not the subject of this treatise.

A. Concepts Generally Capable of Precluding Wrongfulness

The ILC Articles on State Responsibility provide for six principal circumstances precluding wrongfulness, which are recognised under international law.[20] These general grounds are consent (Article 20), self-defence (Article 21), countermeasures (Article 22), *force majeure* (Article 23), distress (Article 24) and necessity (Article 25).

The circumstances precluding wrongfulness can be divided into two groups. Roughly speaking, these groups depend on the behaviour of that subject of international law which is potentially injured by the conduct of a State. In the first three cases, the injured subject's conduct – in most cases the conduct of another State – is irrelevant, namely *force majeure*, distress and necessity. In the second three cases, the subject's conduct – i.e. the conduct of the other State – gives rise to a reaction by the State in question. This reaction can then consist of a violation of an international obligation, but its wrongfulness can be precluded due to the other State's behaviour, namely in cases of consent, self-defence and concerning countermeasures.[21]

The concepts mentioned above have to be distinguished from similar concepts which are not capable of precluding the wrongfulness of a breach of an international obligation.

First, retorsion, in contrast to "wrongful acts", is a lawful act which is designed to injure the wrongdoing State.[22] It embraces any unfriendly act not amounting to a violation of international law, either in reaction to an unfriendly act or in reaction to a breach of international law by another State.[23] Examples are the cutting of economic aid as far as there is no legal obligation to provide economic aid under special treaty provisions,[24] or the breaking off of diplomatic relations.[25] Retorsion thus

---

20 Crawford, *State Responsibility*, p. 162 (para. 8).

21 *Compare* Alland, in: Spinedi/ Simma (eds.), at 148-149.

22 Malanczuk, *Akehurst's Introduction*, p. 4.

23 Cassese, *International Law*, p. 310.

24 Malanczuk, *Akehurst's Introduction*, p. 4.

does not necessarily imply any breach of an international obligation by either side.[26] Conduct which is characterized as wrongful under international law thus cannot be excused as retorsion.

Second, the characterization of an act of a State as internationally wrongful according to international law is not affected by internal law.[27] This principle has been referred to and applied in numerous cases by the Permanent Court of International Justice,[28] the International Court of Justice[29] and by many arbitral tribunals.[30] It is also reflected in

---

[25] Cassese, *International Law*, p. 310; *for further examples see also* Charles Rousseau, *Le droit des conflits armés*, Paris 1983, pp. 15-16.

[26] Alland, in: Spinedi/ Simma (eds.), at 150; Malanczuk, *Akehurst's Introduction*, p. 4.

[27] Article 2 of the ILC Articles on State Responsibility.

[28] *Compare e.g.* PCIJ, *S.S. "Wimbledon"*, Judgment of August 17, 1923, Series A, No. 1 (1923), pp. 15-34, at 29-30; PCIJ, *Exchange of Greek and Turkish Populations*, Advisory Opinion of February 21, 1925, Series B No. 10 (1925), pp. 6-26, at 20; PCIJ, *Jurisdiction of the Courts of Danzig*, Advisory Opinion of March 3, 1928, Series B No. 15 (1928), pp. 4-27, at 26-27; PCIJ, *Greco-Bulgarian "Communities"*, Advisory Opinion of, July 31, 1930, Series B No. 17 (1930), pp. 4-36, at 32; PCIJ, *Treatment of Polish Nationals and Other Persons of Polish Origin or Speech in the Danzig Territory*, Advisory Opinion of, February 4, 1932, Series A/B No. 44 (1932), pp. 4-44, at. 24-25; PCIJ, *Free Zones of Upper Savoy and the District of Gex*, Judgment of June 7, 1932, Series A/B No. 46 (1932), pp. 95-185, at 167.

[29] *Compare e.g.* ICJ, *Reparation for Injuries Suffered in the Service of the United Nations*, Advisory Opinion of April 11, 1949, I.C.J. Reports 1949, pp. 174-220, at 180; ICJ, *Fisheries, United Kingdom v. Norway*, Judgment of December 18, 1951, I.C.J. Reports 1951, pp. 116-144, at 132; ICJ, *Nottebohm, Preliminary Objections, Liechtenstein v. Guatemala*, Judgment of November 18, 1953, I.C.J. Reports 1953, pp. 111-125, at 123; ICJ, *Application of the Convention of 1902 Governing the Guardianship of Infants, Netherlands v. Sweden*, Judgment of November 28, 1958, I.C.J. Reports 1953, pp. 55-156, at 67; ICJ, *Applicability of the Obligation to Arbitrate under Section 21 of the United Nations Headquarters Agreement of 26 June 1947*, Advisory Opinion of April 26, 1988, I.C.J. Reports 1988, pp. 12-64, at 34-35 (para. 57); ICJ, *Elettronica Sicula S.p.A. (ELSI), United States of America v. Italy*, Judgment of July 20, 1989, I.C.J. Reports 1989, pp. 15-82, at p. 51 (para. 73) and p. 74 (para. 124).

[30] *Compare e.g. Norwegian Shipowners' Claims, Norway v. United States of America*, Award of October 13, 1922, in: 1 *RIAA*, pp. 307-346, at 331; *Tinoco, United Kingdom v. Costa Rica*, Award of October 18, 1923, in: 1 *RIAA*, pp.

Article 27 of the Vienna Convention on the Law of Treaties: "A party may not invoke the provision of its internal laws as justification for its failure to perform a treaty." The same holds true for any other source of an international obligation. Thus, neither can a State rely on its own legislation to limit its international obligations,[31] nor can it rely upon internal law as justification for the breach of an international obligation.[32] Conduct which is characterized as wrongful under international law thus cannot be excused by reference to the legality of that conduct under internal law.[33]

B. Limits to Circumstances Precluding Wrongfulness

However, the circumstances precluding wrongfulness described above have certain common limitations, which could be decisive here. The core of this problem has already become apparent *supra*, concerning those circumstances precluding wrongfulness which depend on the previous behaviour of that subject of international law which is potentially injured by the conduct of a State. As indicated above, this object will in most cases be a State itself. If a State attacks another State and in doing so violates a set of obligations under international law, the victim State, within certain restrictions, obviously is allowed to violate the same set of rules due to self-defence – as a circumstance precluding the wrongfulness of what would violate the prohibition on the use of force in other circumstances.

371-399, at 386; Italian-United States Conciliation Commission, *Wollemborg*, Decision of September 24, 1956, in: 14 *RIAA*, pp. 283-291, at 289; Italian-United States Conciliation Commission, *Flegenheimer*, Decision of September 20, 1958, in: *United Nations, Reports of International Arbitral Awards*, Vol. XIV, pp. 327-390, at 360 (para. 47).

31 *See already* PCIJ, *Free Zones of Upper Savoy and the District of Gex*, Judgment of June 7, 1932, Series A/B No. 46 (1932), pp. 95-185, at p. 167.

32 *See already* PCIJ, *Jurisdiction of the Courts of Danzig*, Advisory Opinion of March 3, 1928, Series B No. 15 (1928), pp. 4-27, at pp. 26-27.

33 Crawford, *State Responsibility*, Article 3, para. 8 (p. 89).

First, concerning the present topic of targeted killings, the object of the State's behaviour is not another Sate but a human individual.[34] Second, the circumstances precluding the wrongfulness of a certain State behaviour do not apply to the breach of *any* obligation under international law, as absolute obligations are excluded from this possibility.

I. Peremptory Norms of General International Law (*Jus Cogens*)

In accordance with Article 26 of the ILC Articles on State Responsibility,[35] circumstances precluding wrongfulness do not operate when they involve the breach of obligations deriving from a peremptory norm of international law.[36] In an (apparent) conflict between primary obligations, one of which arises for a State directly under a peremptory norm of international law, such an obligation must prevail.[37] Circumstances precluding wrongfulness are thus not applicable to *jus cogens*,[38] which forms an exception to the general maxims of *lex posterior derogat legi priori* (a later law repeals an earlier law) and *lex specialis derogat legi generali* (a special law prevails over a general law).[39] It establishes a hi-

---

[34] On consequences and difficulties regarding such constellations *compare* Bernd Grzeszick, 'Rechte des Einzelnen im Völkerrecht', 43 *AVR* (2005), pp. 312-344.

[35] Article 26 reads: "Nothing in this Chapter precludes the wrongfulness of any act of a State which is not in conformity with an obligation arising under a peremptory norm of general international law", referring to Chapter V of the Articles: "Circumstances Precluding Wrongfulness".

[36] *See also* Hannikainen, *Peremptory Norms*, p. 9 and pp. 248-265. For an extensive account of the history of the concept *see ibid.*, pp. 23-156.

[37] Crawford, *State Responsibility*, Article 26, para. 3 (p. 187).

[38] On the terminology *compare* the statement by Humphrey Waldock, in: UN General Assembly, ILC, Summary Records of the 683rd Meeting, reprinted in: *UN Yb. ILC* (1963), Vol. I, pp. 60-67, at 62 (para. 25). On the nature of the concept of *jus cogens see* Paulus, 25 *Nord. J. Int'l L.* (2005), at 300-304 with further references and Michael Byers, 'Conceptualising the Relationship between Jus Cogens and Erga Omnes Rules', in: 66 *Nord. J. Int'l L.* (1997), pp. 211-239, at 220-229.

[39] *See* Kolb, 105 *R.G.D.I.P.* (2005), at 323; Anthony Aust, *Modern Treaty Law and Practice*, Cambridge 2000, p. 201; on the legal status and content of the maxims mentioned *compare* Erich Vranes, 'Lex superior, lex specialis, lex

erarchy of international obligations to the effect that the law of higher rank prevails over that of a lower rank (*lex superior derogat legi inferiori*), *jus cogens* being the *lex superior*[40] or "l'antimatière de la dérogation".[41] According to Article 53 of the Vienna Convention on the Law of Treaties,[42] a rule of *jus cogens* is

> a peremptory norm accepted and recognized by the international community of States as a whole as a norm from which no derogation is permitted and which can be modified only by a subsequent norm of general international law having the same character.

In connection with the Genocide Convention this means for instance that "in no case could one breach of the Convention serve as an excuse for another".[43] Most obligations accepted to represent *jus cogens* and most of those additional candidates for *jus cogens* status do not protect State interests, but rather human or collective interests, from basic human rights to the protection of the environment.[44] Therefore, the question of the legality of targeted killings – touching obligations of States in relation to individuals rather than States – is strongly related to the question of *jus cogens* status of the respective rights.

The prohibitions of aggression, genocide, slavery, racial discrimination, crimes against humanity and torture, and the right to self determination are clearly accepted and recognised peremptory norms of international law. The same holds true, in principle, for war crimes as well as other basic principles of international humanitarian law and probably also the basic rights of the human person in general.[45] Additionally, basic prin-

---

posterior: Zur Rechtsnatur der "Konfliktlösungsregeln"', in: 65 *ZaöRV* (2005), pp. 391-405.

40 Vranes, 65 *ZaöRV* (2005), at p. 402.

41 Kolb, 105 *R.G.D.I.P.* (2005), at 323.

42 For a short overview of the earlier development *see* Byers, 66 *Nord. J. Int'l L.* (1997), at 213-214.

43 ICJ, *Application of the Convention on the Prevention and Punishment of the Crime of Genocide, Counter Claims, Bosnia-Herzegovina v. Yugoslavia*, Order of December 17, 1997, I.C.J. Reports 1997, pp. 243-261, at 258 (para. 35).

44 Paulus, 25 *Nord. J. Int'l L.* (2005), at 305-306.

45 *See e.g.* ICJ, *East Timor, Portugal v. Australia*, Judgment of June 30, 1995, I.C.J. Reports 1995, pp. 90-106, at 102 (para. 29); ICJ, *Military and Paramilitary Activities in and against Nicaragua, Nicaragua v. United States of America*, Judgment (Merits) of June 27, 1986, I.C.J. Reports 1986, pp. 14-150, at 100 (pa-

ciples of environmental law are sometimes regarded as candidates of *jus cogens*, too.[46] As shown above, the human right to life also falls into this category.[47] Again, this does not mean that the right to life in itself is absolute. However, the exceptions are part of the right itself. There are no additional – external – circumstances precluding wrongfulness in connection to the right to life. Due to the *jus cogens* character of the right to life, the exceptions developed above are exclusive.

These exceptions, again, include those under international humanitarian law. Thus, beside the basic principles of international humanitarian law

---

ra. 190); ICJ, *Legal Consequences for States of the Continued Presence of South Africa in Namibia (South-West Africa) Notwithstanding Security Council Resolution 276 (1970)*, Advisory Opinion of June 21, 1971, I.C.J. Reports 1971, pp. 12-345, at 31-32 (paras. 52-53); ICJ, *Western Sahara*, Advisory Opinion of October 16, 1975, I.C.J. Reports 1975, pp. 12-82; at pp. 31-33 (paras. 54-59); Inter-Am. Comm'n H.R., *Victims of the Tugboat*, *Annual Report* (1996), at para. 79; ILC, *Report of the International Law Commission on the Work of its thirty-first Session (14 May-3 August 1979)*, UN Doc. A/34/10, reprinted in: *UN Yb. ILC* (1979), Vol. II, Part Two, pp. 1-192, at p. 115 (Commentary on Draft Article 29). *C.f.* Roberto Ago, 'Droit des traités à la lumière de la Convention Vienne', in: 134 *RdC* (1979-III), pp. 297-331, at p. 324 (footnote 37); Ian Brownlie, *Principles of International Law*, 6th ed., Oxford 2003, pp. 489-490; Byers, 66 *Nord. J. Int'l L.* (1997), at 219; Crawford, *State Responsibility*, Article 26, para. 5 (p. 188); Hannikainen, *Peremptory Norms*, pp. 317-713; Kadelbach, *Zwingendes Völkerrecht*, pp. 210-323; Fritz Münch, 'Bemerkungen zum *ius cogens*', in: Rudolph Bernhardt; Wilhelm Karl Geck; Günther Jaenicke; Helmut Steinberger (eds.), *Völkerrecht als Rechtsordnung – Internationale Gerichtsbarkeit – Menschenrechte: Festschrift für Hermann Mosler*, Berlin 1983, pp. 617-628, p. 627; Georg Nolte, *Eingreifen auf Einladung: Zur völkerrechtlichen Zulässigkeit des Einsatzes fremder Truppen im internen Konflikt auf Einladung der Regierung*, Berlin 1999, pp. 137-140 (on aggression and the problem of consent); Alexander Orakhelashvili, *Peremptory Norms in International Law*, Oxford 2006, pp. 54-55; Paulus, 25 *Nord. J. Int'l L.* (2005), at 306; A. Gómez Robledo, 'Le ius cogens international: sa genèse, sa nature, ses fonctions', in: 172 *RdC* (1981 III), pp. 9-218, at 167-187; Andrés Rigo Sureda, *The Evolution of the Right of Self-Determination: A Study of United Nations Practice*, Leiden 1973, p. 353; Verdross/ Simma, *Völkerrecht*, p. 332 (para. 527); Verdross, 60 *Am. J. Int'l L.* (1966), at 59.

46 *Compare e.g.* ICJ, *Legality of the Threat or Use of Nuclear Weapons*, Advisory Opinion of July 8, 1996, Dissenting Opinion of Judge Weeramantry, I.C.J. Reports 1996, pp. 226-593, at 517.

47 *Compare supra*, Part One, Chapter G) IV.

– which qualify as *jus cogens* anyway – those rules of international humanitarian law which treat the legality or illegality of a killing at the same time amount to *jus cogens* as they form part of the scheme of protection of the right to life. This fact is consistent with the system of international humanitarian law as a non-reciprocal set of norms. It applies irrespectively of the opponent party's acceptance of the set of rules.

II. Human Rights

Independently of whether one accepts that a certain right is of *jus cogens* character, the system of human rights *per se* excludes the possibility of applying general circumstances precluding wrongfulness to human rights violations. Generally, the failure by a State party to a human rights treaty to comply with the legal standards established thereby leads to international responsibility of that State.[48] But unlike other international treaties, human rights conventions comprise more than mere reciprocal engagements between the contracting States. They create objective obligations that are assumed by each contracting State to persons under its jurisdiction, and not to other contracting States.[49] This fact has consequences concerning the possibility of precluding the wrongfulness of such an obligation's violation.

Human rights can thus in general be compared with *jus cogens*[50] or be regarded as protecting the interests of mankind as such. The effect, however, is the same, though: The protected interests are not at the disposal of States, individually or in concert, nor can they be damaged by reprisals or reciprocal non-compliance.[51] It is thus not a State but the protected individual who can – if at all – preclude the wrongfulness of a deed in violation of a treaty right e.g. by consenting to the deed. Exter-

---

48 *See already* PCIJ, *Factory at Chorzów, Merits*, Judgment of September 13, 1928 Series A, No. 17 (1928), pp. 4-74, at 29.

49 *Compare e.g.* Eur. Ct. H.R., *Ireland v. UK*, Series A, No. 25, p. 90 (para. 239); Inter-Am. Ct. H.R., *Restrictions to the Death Penalty*, Series A, No. 3 (1983), para. 50; Matscher, in: Macdonald *et al.* (eds.), at p. 66; Dijk/ Hoof, *European Convention*, pp. 33-34 and pp. 40-41; Orakhelashvili, 14 *Eur. J. Int'l L.* (2003), at 531-532; Meron, *Customary Law*, pp. 99-100.

50 Byers, 66 *Nord. J. Int'l L.* (1997), at 235.

51 *See e.g.* Orakhelashvili, *Peremptory Norms*, p. 53 with further references.

nal circumstances do not have this ability. As an example, reciprocal countermeasures concerning the protection of human rights are inconceivable because the obligations in question are non-reciprocal and are not only due to other States but to the individuals themselves.[52] In short:

> Human rights abuses by opposition groups or individuals can never justify abandonment of human rights principles by a government.[53]

In consequence, the circumstances precluding wrongfulness cannot be applied in relation to human rights. Concerning the case at hand, the right to life – including the exceptions developed above[54] – must thus serve as the only standard in assessing the legality of a targeted killing under human rights law. A violation of this – or any other – human right cannot be justified according to standards of general "external" international law. Only the "internal" standards of that human right and its system apply.

III. International Humanitarian Law

Like human rights law, international humanitarian law is not intended to protect State interests, but it is primarily designed to protect human individuals as such.[55] The obligation to respect and ensure respect for international humanitarian law thus does not depend on reciprocity – whether in international or in non-international armed conflicts.[56] While the 1907 Hague Regulations in Article 2 still limited the application of the provisions on the relations between the contracting parties,[57]

---

52 *See* Eur. Ct. H.R., *Ireland v. UK*, Series A, No. 25, p. 90 (para. 239); Crawford, *State Responsibility*, previous to Article 49, para. 5 (p. 282).

53 Amnesty International, AI Doc. MDE 15/005/2001 (February 21, 2001), p. 1.

54 *Compare supra*, Part One, Chapters B) II., C) II., D) II. and E) II.

55 *See e.g.* ICTY, *Prosecutor v. Zoran Kupreškić et al.*, Case No. IT-95-16-T, Judgment of January 14, 2000, para. 518; Orakhelashvili, *Peremptory Norms*, p. 61.

56 Henckaerts/ Doswald-Beck (eds.), *Humanitarian Law*, Vol. 1, pp. 498-499 (Rule 140).

according Article 1 common to the 1949 Geneva Conventions these Conventions shall be respected "in all circumstances"[58] even if the opponent in an armed conflict is not party to the conventions.[59] Thus, today international humanitarian law claims absolute validity.[60]

This system can be clarified if the most prominent circumstance precluding wrongfulness in connection with war is taken into account, namely self-defence. Self-defence can preclude the wrongfulness of using force against another State. But once this force is used – i.e. an armed conflict is established – international humanitarian law applies and obviously cannot be derogated from or restricted due to self-defence.[61] This is a necessary consequence of the absolute separation between *jus ad bellum* and *jus in bello*.[62] Even authors who accept self-defence as a

---

[57] Article 2 1907 Hague Regulations reads: "The provisions contained in the Regulations referred to in Article 1, as well as in the present Convention, do not apply except between Contracting powers, and then only if all the belligerents are parties to the Convention."

[58] Article 1 common to the 1949 Geneva Conventions reads: "The High Contracting Parties undertake to respect and to ensure respect for the present Convention in all circumstances." On the Article's implications *see* Birgit Kessler, 'The Duty to "Ensure Respect" Under Common Article 1 of the Geneva Conventions: Its Implications on International and Non-International Armed Conflicts', in: 44 *German Yb. Int'l L.* (2002), pp. 498-516.

[59] Common Article 2 para. 3 of the 1949 Geneva Conventions reads: "Although one of the Powers in conflict may not be a party to the present Convention, the Powers who are parties thereto shall remain bound by it in their mutual relations. They shall furthermore be bound by the Convention in relation to the said Power, if the latter accepts and applies the provisions thereof." The limitation laid down in the last sentence continuously looses its relevance due to the universal acceptance of the Conventions.

[60] *Compare* ICTY, *Prosecutor v. Zoran Kupreškić et al.*, Case No. IT-95-16-T, Judgment of January 14, 2000, para. 519, *referring to* ICJ, *Barcelona Traction Light and Power Company, Limited, Second Phase*, Judgment of February 5, 1970, I.C.J. Reports 1970, pp. 3-357, at 32 (paras. 33-34); Stefan Kadelbach, 'Zwingende Normen des humanitären Völkerrechts', in: 5 *HuV-I* (1992), pp. 118-124, at 121.

[61] *See e.g.* Crawford, *State Responsibility*, Article 21, para. 3 (p. 166); *compare also* ICTY, *Prosecutor v. Dario Kordić and Mario Čerkez*, Case IT-95-14/2 ("Lasva Valley"), Judgment of February 26, 2001, para. 452.

[62] *See also* Marco Sassòli, 'State responsibility for violations of international humanitarian law', in: 84 *Int'l Rev. Red Cross* (2002), No. 846, pp. 401-434, at

"legal basis for fighting terrorism" also acknowledge that "[s]elf-defense action against terrorism is not exempt from the humanitarian rules applicable to armed conflict."[63] The same applies to other circumstances precluding wrongfulness: As international humanitarian law was made for armed conflicts, which are by definition emergency situations,[64] the defence claim of necessity is implicitly excluded except where it is explicitly stated otherwise.[65]

Thus, under international humanitarian law, derogations and limitations of the obligations are exclusively possible in those narrow cases which are laid down in the legal regime itself. This is the case in the context of Article 5 of the 1949 Geneva Convention IV and Article 45 para. 3 of the 1977 Additional Protocol I, which are similar to the derogation clauses of human rights treaties. Beside these "internal" cases, there are no "external" circumstances precluding wrongfulness.

Additionally to this system, most norms of international humanitarian law, in particular those prohibiting war crimes, crimes against humanity and genocide, are also accepted as being *jus cogens*.[66] It is even suggested that all rules of international humanitarian law are peremptory. This view is supported by the fact that according to Article 6 para. 1 common to the 1949 Geneva Conventions I, II and III and according to Article 7 of the 1949 Geneva Convention IV, no special agreements shall adversely affect the situation of protected persons.

414-415; *but see* ICJ, *Legality of the Threat or Use of Nuclear Weapons*, Advisory Opinion of July 8, 1996, I.C.J. Reports 1996, pp. 226-593, at 226 (para. 97), implying that the use of nuclear weapons normally violates international humanitarian law, but then stating that it could not "reach a definitive conclusion as to the legality or illegality of the use of nuclear weapons by a State in an extreme circumstance of self-defence, in which its very survival would be at stake".

[63] Gross, 15 *Fla. J. Int'l L.* (2003), at 426.

[64] *Compare supra*, Part Four, Chapters B) and C).

[65] Sassòli, 84 *Int'l Rev. Red Cross* (2002), No. 846, at 415. Examples are Article 33para. 2 of the 1949 Geneva Convention I, Articles 49 para. 2 and 5, 53, 55 para. 3 and 108 para. 2 of the 1949 Geneva Convention IV, and Article 54 para. 5 of the 1977 Additional Protocol I.

[66] *See e.g.* ICTY, *Prosecutor v. Zoran Kupreškić et al.*, Case No. IT-95-16-T, Judgment of January 14, 2000, para. 520; Orakhelashvili, *Peremptory Norms*, p. 61; each with further references.

> It would be difficult to find rules of international humanitarian law that do not directly or indirectly protect rights of protected persons in international armed conflicts. In both international and non-international armed conflicts, those rules furthermore protect 'basic rights of the human person' which are classic examples for *jus cogens*.[67]

Similarly, Article 47 of the 1949 Geneva Convention IV stipulates that the convention prevails over any conflicting agreement. Like *jus cogens*, these provisions bring about the nullity of conflicting agreements, even though they are – unlike *jus cogens* – part of the conventions themselves.[68] However, the fact that the conventions do not allow conflicting agreements makes them non-derogable in their entirety.[69] It thus becomes clear that the 1949 Geneva Conventions were drafted with the intent to distinguish them from *jus dispositivum* – i.e. to give them a non-bilateral character and at least effects similar to *jus cogens*.[70]

C. Conclusion: No Additional Justifications or Excuses

The relevant and decisive rules concerning the legality of a targeted killing are human rights rules and international humanitarian law rules.[71] As such, they are not based on reciprocal relations between States but directly protect individuals – civilians as well as combatants. Insofar, the general circumstances precluding wrongfulness – as summed up in the ILC Articles on State Responsibility – do not apply to them. This is due to the special non-reciprocal character of the decisive rules and may additionally be due to the fact that some of them are of *jus cogens* char-

---

[67] Sassòli, 84 *Int'l Rev. Red Cross* (2002), No. 846, at 414. *Compare also* Jacob Werksman; Ruth Khalastchi, 'Nuclear Weapons and the concept of *jus cogens*: peremptory norms and justice pre-empted?', in: Laurence Boisson de Chazournes; Philippe Sands (eds.), *International Law, the International Court of Justice, and Nuclear Weapons*, Cambridge 1999, pp. 181-198, at 194-195.

[68] Meron, 94 *Am. J. Int'l L.* (2000), at 252.

[69] Orakhelashvili, *Peremptory Norms*, p. 62; *compare also* Nieto-Navia, in: Lal Chand Vohrah *et al.* (eds.), at 635-636.

[70] *Compare* Münch, in: Bernhardt *et al.* (eds.), at 623.

[71] *See supra*, Part One and Part Two.

acter. The latter question, however, can remain open here. Independently of the characterisation of the relevant rights as *jus cogens* or not, the non-bilateral system of these rights renders them non-derogable in an at least similar manner.

All this does not mean that these rights provide absolute protection. This system entails its own "internal" possibilities of derogations, exceptions and limitations. These standards are inherent to the system and exclusively provide for the decisive criteria. Furthermore, as only "internal" exceptions and derogations are possible within the system of law which is applicable, the question of whether this is human rights law or international humanitarian law gains importance. This question will be addressed next.

Part Four – The Applicability of the Relevant International Law

> In our view, international humanitarian law and human rights law must both be respected in the fight against terrorism: IHL when the violence has reached armed conflict level, in addition to human rights law, and human rights law when it has not. IHL and human rights law are distinct, but complementary bodies of law whose application, along with refugee law where appropriate, provides a framework for the comprehensive protection of persons in situations of violence. It is of some concern, therefore, that IHL and human rights are sometimes claimed to be mutually exclusive.[1]

The first line of defence against international humanitarian law is to deny that it applies at all. The situation is similar regarding human rights law. The discussion on the status and rights of the detainees in Guantánamo are only one recent example in which a State tried to circumvent norms of both branches of law. Certain humanitarian law norms were declared inapplicable due to the status of the persons concerned as "unlawful combatants",[2] while human rights obligations were declared as not being applicable due to the location of the detainees.[3]

---

1 International Committee of the Red Cross, 'The relevance of international humanitarian law in contemporary armed conflicts', Official Statement by ICRC President Jakob Kellenberger, September 14, 2004.

2 *See e.g.* U.S. President George W. Bush, White House Fact Sheet of February 7, 2002. On the topic of "unlawful combatants" *see supra*, Part Two, Chapter F.).

3 *Compare* H.R. Committee, *Third Periodic Report of United States to Human Rights Committee*, U.N. Doc. CCPR/C/USA/3 (November 28, 2005), Annex I ('Territorial Application of the International Covenant on Civil and Political Rights').

Another example is the by now inopportune[4] argument by Israel that the West Bank has a status *sui generis*, i.e. beyond the law, as it neither is regarded as being part of Israeli territory, nor as being formally occupied territory.[5] According to the Israeli "Missing Reversioner Theory", in 1967 the West Bank was not the "territory of a High Contracting Party" in the meaning of Article 2 para. 2 of the 1949 Geneva Convention IV and thus the Convention is regarded as not *de lege* applicable by Israel.[6]

Traditionally, humanitarian law conventions are applicable in armed conflicts and address first and foremost nationals of enemy States. It is true that the classic distinction between international and non-international armed conflicts has become less relevant. This is due to the development of a core of substantive international humanitarian law that is applicable in both situations.[7] However, there are still substantive dif-

---

[4] *See* ICJ, *Legal Consequences of the Construction of a Wall in the Occupied Palestine Territory*, Advisory Opinion of July 9, 2004, I.C.J. Reports 2004, pp. 133-271, at 167 (para. 78) and 173-177 (paras. 90-101); *see also* Supreme Court of Israel, *Physicians for Human Rights v. Commander of the IDF Forces in the Gaza Strip*, H.C.J. 4764/04, Judgment of May 30, 2004, para. 10, English translation reprinted in: Israel Supreme Court, *Judgments of the Israel Supreme Court: Fighting Terrorism within the Law*, Jerusalem 2005, pp. 182-207, at 187.

[5] *C.f.* David Kretzmer, *The Occupation of Justice: The Supreme Court of Israel and the Occupied Territories*, State University of New York Press, New York, 2002, pp. 32-34; Richard A. Falk; Burns H. Weston, 'The Relevance of International Law to Israeli and Palestinian Rights in the West Bank and Gaza', in: Emma Playfair (ed.), *International Law and the Administration of Occupied Territories: Two Decades of Israeli Occupation of the West Bank and Gaza Strip*, Oxford 1992, pp. 125-149, at 131; Adam Roberts, 'What is a Military Occupation?', in: 55 *Brit. Yb. Int'l L.* (1984), pp. 249-305, at 281-283; Adam Roberts, 'Prolonged Military Occupation: The Israeli-Occupied Territories 1967-1988', in: Emma Playfair (ed.), *International Law and the Administration of Occupied Territories: Two Decades of Israeli Occupation of the West Bank and Gaza Strip*, Oxford 1992, pp. 25-85, at 43-53.

[6] Yehuda Zvi Blum, 'The Missing Reversioner: Reflections on the Status of Judea and Samaria', in: 3 *Isr. L. Rev.* (1968), pp. 279-301; Meir Shamgar, 'The Observance of International Law in the Administered Territories', in: 1 *Isr. Yb. Hum. Rts.* (1971), pp. 262-277, at 265-266.

[7] *Compare e.g.* the substantive rules collected in Henckaerts/ Doswald-Beck (eds.), *Humanitarian Law*, Vol. 1. The vast majority of these rules apply in both kinds of conflict; *see also* Bahia Tahzib-Lie; Olivia Swaak-Goldman,

ferences, e.g. concerning the status of a combatant in an international conflict or of a fighter in a non-international conflict and its consequence for prisoner-of-war status. As shown above, there are thus also at least some discrepancies concerning the rules applying to targeted killings.

In contrast to international humanitarian law, human rights conventions – which also apply in armed conflicts – foremost apply during peacetime and thus to the State's own nationals. They protect all persons within the jurisdiction of a State party to them. They include possibilities of derogation for certain exceptional situations such as public emergencies or war,[8] but are "intended to apply always and everywhere."[9]

A. The Territorial and Extraterritorial Applicability of Human Rights Provisions

> The least one may expect from states who intervene abroad in the name of the great ideals of freedom, democracy and the rule of law,

---

'Determining the Threshold for the Application of International Humanitarian Law', in: Liesbeth Lijnzaad; Johanna von Sambeck; Bahia Tahzib-Lie (eds.), *Making the Voice of Humanity Heard: Essays on Humanitarian Assistance and International Humanitarian Law in Honour of HRH Princess Margriet of the Netherlands*, Leiden 2004, pp. 239-25, at 240 with further references.

8 Dietrich Schindler, 'Kriegsrecht und Menschenrechte', in: Ulrich Häfelin; Walter Haller; Dietrich Schindler (eds.), *Menschenrechte, Föderalismus, Demokratie – Festschrift zum 70. Geburtstag von Werner Kägi*, Zürich 1979, pp. 327-349, at 327; Dietrich Schindler, 'Human Rights and Humanitarian Law: Interrelationship of the Laws', in: 31 *Am. U. L. Rev.* (1982), pp. 935-943, at 938.

9 UN Secretary-General, *Respect for Human Rights in Armed Conflicts*, Report of September 18, 1970, 25th Sess., Agenda Item 47, UN Doc. A/8052 (September 18, 1970), p. 13 (para. 25); *see also* Hans-Peter Gasser, 'International Humanitarian Law and Human Rights Law in non-international Armed Conflict: Joint Venture or Mutual Exclusion?', in: 45 *German Yb. Int'l L.* (2002), pp. 149-162, at 150.

is that they continue to abide by the same universal human rights standards – whether they act at home or abroad.[10]

It remains to be seen whether this moral appeal really corresponds the legal situation. Traditionally, human rights treaties aimed at protecting individuals from the arbitrary exercise of power by the authorities of their home State. They were thus declared applicable in the territory or under the jurisdiction of the States party to them. However, an exclusively territorial interpretation of the scope of application is no longer tenable. The notion of "jurisdiction" and with it the scope of application – though regulated in the treaties themselves – has been and still is subject to a vast development by the treaty organs.

Applicability in that regard means that the State party to the treaty is bound by it in relation to a certain situation. This question must not be confused with the question of state responsibility, albeit terminology may be similar. The applicability of a treaty is the precondition for state responsibility, as state responsibility entails an international wrongful act. Such an act could be the violation of a human rights treaty, but only if that treaty is applicable, i.e. if the act took place within the "jurisdiction" of the State party as laid down in the treaty. The question of applicability of a human rights treaty is also not the same as the question of jurisdiction of a given treaty organ. The possibility of bringing a case before such an organ is important when it comes to enforcing human rights obligations. However, a State can be bound by a treaty but not be subject to the jurisdiction of the treaty organs. Otherwise, jurisprudence under a treaty may not cover all persons who have rights under that treaty.[11]

---

[10] Rick Lawson, 'The Concept of Jurisdiction and Extraterritorial Acts of State', in: Gerard Kreijen (ed.), *State, Sovereignty, and International Governance*, Oxford 2002, pp. 281-298, at 297.

[11] Martin Scheinin, 'Extraterritorial Effect of the International Covenant on Civil and Political Rights', in: Fons Coomans; Menno T. Kamminga (eds.), *Extraterritorial Application of Human Rights Treaties*, Antwerp 2004, pp. 73-81, at 42-44.

I. The International Covenant on Civil and Political Rights

The scope of application of the International Covenant on Civil and Political Rights refers to both, "territory" and "jurisdiction" of the States party to it. The Article 2 para. 1 Covenant reads:

> Each State Party to the present Covenant undertakes to respect and to ensure to all individuals *within its territory and subject to its jurisdiction* the rights recognized in the present Covenant, without distinction of any kind, such as race, colour, sex, language, religion, political or other opinion, national or social origin, property, birth or other status.[12]

The Covenant thus combines the two terms to the phrase "within its territory and subject to its jurisdiction". The two conditions could thus be applied cumulatively or alternatively. The use of "within its territory" additional to the term "subject to its jurisdiction" gave rise to a narrow interpretation of the Covenant's scope of application. The wording could be interpreted as to require a person to be subject to the jurisdiction of a contracting state *and* within the territory in order to be protected by the convention. Thus, the applicability of the Covenant to actions taken by State agents outside the territory of a State party has been denied.[13] However, such a narrow interpretation would run counter to the object and purpose of the Covenant, as it contains some rights that presumes that the individual can be outside the territory.[14] An example is the right to enter one's own country laid down in Article 12 para. 4 of the Covenant.[15] This fact supports the alternative applications of the two terms.

---

[12] My emphasis.

[13] *See e.g.* Schindler, in: Häfelin *et al.* (eds.), at 334; Schindler, 31 *Am. U. L. Rev.* (1982), at 939; *see also* Michael Dennis, 'Application of Human Rights Treaties Extraterritorially During Times of Armed Conflict and Military Occupation', in: 100 *ASIL Proc.* (2006), pp. 86-90, at 87-89.

[14] Dominic McGoldrick, 'Extraterritorial Application of the International Covenant on Civil and Political Rights', in: Fons Coomans; Menno T. Kamminga (eds.), *Extraterritorial Application of Human Rights Treaties*, Antwerp 2004, pp. 41-72, at 47-48.

[15] Article 12 para. 4 reads: "No one shall be arbitrarily deprived of the right to enter his own country."

The phrase "within its territory and subject to its jurisdiction" can also be read as referring to persons within the territory of a State *as well as* to persons subject to the State's jurisdiction, either in the territory or outside.[16] The latter interpretation is supported by the fact that it avoids redundancy[17] and by the legislative history of the Covenant. The words "within its jurisdiction" which were proposed by the United States, were added because "a State should not be relieved of its obligations under the covenant to persons who remained within its jurisdiction merely because they were not within its territory."[18]

This widely accepted interpretation[19] is strongly supported by the subsequent practice of the Human Rights Committee's jurisprudence,[20] concluding observations[21] and general comments, referring to "all individuals under their jurisdiction",[22]"within the territory *or* under the ju-

---

16 McGoldrick, in: Coomans/ Kamminga (eds.), at 48 observes that the text would have to be phrased with an "or" instead of an "and". However, the "and" can also be read as "as well as", referring to both groups.

17 Orna Ben-Naftali, 'The Extraterritorial Application of Human Rights to Occupied Territories', in: 100 *ASIL Proc.* (2006), pp. 90-95, at 93.

18 *Compare* the discussions and drafts reprinted in Bossuyt, *Travaux Préparatoires*, pp. 53-55.

19 *See e.g.* Buergenthal, in: Henkin (ed.), at 74; John Cerone, 'Minding the Gap: Outlining KFOR Accountability in Post-Conflict Kosovo', in: 12 *Eur. J. Int'l L.* (2001), pp. 469-488, at 475-476; Frowein, 62 *ZaöRV* (2002), at 903; Theodor Meron, 'Extraterritoriality of Human Rights Treaties', in: 89 *Am. J. Int'l L.* (1995), pp. 78-82, at 79; Meron, *Internal Strife*, p. 40; Gowlland-Debbas, in: Boisson de Chazournes/ Sands (eds.), at 323.

20 *See e.g.* H.R. Committee, *Lilian Celiberti de Casariego v. Uruguay*, Communication No. 56/1979, UN Doc. CCPR/C/13/D/56/1979 (July 29, 1981), paras. 10.2-10.3; H.R. Committee, *Delia Saldías de López, on behalf of her husband, Sergio Rubén López Burgos v. Uruguay*, Communication No. 52/ 1979, U.N. Doc. CCPR/C/13/D/52/1979 (July 29, 1981), paras. 12.1-12.3.

21 *See e.g.* H.R. Committee, *Concluding Observations on Israel*, UN Doc. CCPR/CO/78/ISR (August 21, 2003), para. 11; H.R. Committee, *Concluding Observations on Israel*, UN Doc. CCPR/C/79/Add.93 (August 18, 1998), para. 10.

22 H.R. Committee, CCPR General Comment No. 3, *Implementation at the National Level (Article 2)*, 13th Sess., July 29, 1981, reprinted in: Compilation of General Comments and General Recommendations adopted by Human

risdiction of the State"[23] and "all those under a State party's jurisdiction."[24] This is further supported by the fact that Article 1 of the 1966 Optional Protocol to the International Covenant, which was drafted after the draft of the Covenant had been completed, only refers to "jurisdiction" without any reference to the "territory".[25]

This cumulative approach – on the other hand – entails the possibility that a person is on the territory but not under the jurisdiction of a State, e.g. if the territory is under foreign occupation or under control of an internal opposition force.[26] It is thus decisive how far the "jurisdiction" in the meaning of the Covenant reaches. It at least includes situations where a state exercises "effective control" over areas abroad, e.g. by occupying them.[27] In its General Comment No. 31 the Committee stated that "subject to the jurisdiction of the State party" also includes "to those within the power or effective control of the forces of a State party acting outside its territory".[28] It may thus be doubted whether the "ef-

---

Rights Treaty Bodies, U.N. Doc. HRI/GEN/1/Rev.7 (May 12, 2004), p. 125 (para. 1).

23 H.R. Committee, CCPR General Comment No. 23, *Rights of Minorities (Article 27)*, 50th Sess., April 8, 1994, reprinted in: Compilation of General Comments and General Recommendations adopted by Human Rights Treaty Bodies, U.N. Doc. HRI/GEN/1/Rev.7 (May 12, 2004), pp. 158-161, at 158 (para. 4) (emphasis added).

24 H.R. Committee, CCPR General Comment No. 24, at 163 (para. 12).

25 The first sentence of Article 1 of the 1966 Optional Protocol reads: "A State Party to the Covenant that becomes a Party to the present Protocol recognizes the competence of the Committee to receive and consider communications from individuals subject to its jurisdiction who claim to be victims of a violation by that State Party of any of the rights set forth in the Covenant." *See also* Meron, 89 *Am. J. Int'l L.* (1995), at 79.

26 *Compare e.g.* H.R. Committee, *Concluding Observations on Cyprus*, UN Doc. CCPR/C/79/Add.88 (April 6, 1998), para. 3. A recent example where the problem was discussed in the context of the European Convention is Eur. Ct. H.R., *Ilaşcu and others v. Moldova and the Russian Federation (Merits)*, Appl. No. 48787/99, Judgment of July 8, 2004, *ECHR* 2004-VII, pp. 1-348, at 259-272 (paras. 300-352).

27 H.R. Committee, *Concluding Observations on Israel*, UN Doc. CCPR/C/79/Add.93 (August 18, 1998), para. 10.

28 H.R. Committee, CCPR General Comment No. 31, *The Nature of the General Legal Obligation Imposed on State Parties to the Covenant*, May 26,

fective control" that was described earlier really relates to a territory, or rather to a person.

Several reasons exist to conclude that an exercise of jurisdiction for the purpose of applying the Covenant does not require territorial control to the extent exercised by Israel in the Occupied Palestinian Territory.[29] The Human Rights Committee stated that Article 2 para 1 of the Covenant does not imply that a states party cannot be held responsible for violations of rights committed by its agents on the territory of another state, whether with the acquiescence of that state or in opposition to it:

> In line with this, it would be unconscionable to so interpret the responsibility under article 2 of the Covenant as to permit a State party to perpetrate violations of the Covenant on the territory of another State, which violations it could not perpetrate on its own territory.[30]

Thus, not only armed forces engaged in an occupation abroad are restrained by the Covenant, but also civilian agents and officials exercising power and authority, especially in law enforcement.[31] This interpretation of the term "jurisdiction" does not necessarily mean that a State party to the Covenant must guarantee all aspects of all Covenant rights outside its territory. Especially positive obligations – such as the procedural rights and an effective investigation of the taking of life – may be difficult to enforce. As *Tomuschat* phrased it in his individual opinion to *López Burgos*:

> [A] State party is normally unable to ensure the effective enjoyment of the rights under the Covenant to its citizens abroad, having at its disposal only the tools of diplomatic protection with their limited potential. ... Never was it envisaged, however, to grant States parties unfettered discretionary power to carry out wilful and deliberate at-

---

2004, UN Doc. CCPR/C/21/Rev.1/Add.13, reprinted in: Compilation of General Comments and General Recommendations adopted by Human Rights Treaty Bodies, U.N. Doc. HRI/GEN/1/Rev.7 (May 12, 2004), pp. 192-197, at 194-195 (para. 10).

29 John Cerone, 'The Application of Regional Human Rights Law Beyond Regional Frontiers: The Inter-American Commission on Human Rights and US Activities in Iraq', in: *ASIL Insight* (2005), No. 10 (October 25, 2005).

30 H.R. Committee, *Delia Saldías de López*, para. 12.3.

31 Meron, 89 *Am. J. Int'l L.* (1995), at 80.

tacks against the freedom and personal integrity of their citizens living abroad.[32]

In that regard, *Scheinin* proposes "a contextual assessment of the state's factual control in respect of facts and events that allegedly constitute a *violation* of a human right."[33] It thus becomes clear that there is no reason not to apply at least the negative obligations of the protected rights, i.e. its defensive function, the obligation to refrain from any active violation of the rights by state agents. The State can fully control whether it actively engages in conduct that infringes an individual's right, even abroad. Thus, States are obliged to observe the rights and obligations of the Covenant when acting within their territory but having effect abroad[34] and when acting abroad.[35]

It is worth noting that the Human Rights Committee, in its 2003 concluding observations on Israel and thus after the European Court of Human Rights had argued for a narrow interpretation of "jurisdiction"

---

[32] H.R. Committee, *Delia Saldías de López*, Individual Opinion by Tomuschat, Appendix. *Compare also* McGoldrick, in: Coomans/ Kamminga (eds.), at 46 and 62; Scheinin, in: Coomans/ Kamminga (eds.), at 75-77. As another example, the Government of the Netherlands disagreed with the Committee's suggestion that the Covenant was applicable to the conduct of Dutch blue helmets in Srebrenica. The Commission withdrew that suggestion as the victims in Srebrenica were not subject to the jurisdiction of the Netherlands. The Netherlands did not have the authority necessary to prevent the atrocities committed by Serbian forces. Additionally, the blue helmets were part of an UN mandate and thus their conduct is first attributed to the mandate and not the national State. On this question see generally Krieger, 62 *ZaöRV* (2002), at 677-686; *see also* Heintze, 18 *HuV-I* (2005), at 179. Thus, the Committee clarified that the Netherlands were not obliged under the Covenant to investigate and assess the events of 1995, even though the Netherlands did engage in such investigations. *See* H.R. Committee, *Concluding Observations on the Netherlands*, U.N. Doc. CCPR/CO/72/NET/Add.1 (April 29, 2003), paras. 18-19.

[33] Scheinin, in: Coomans/ Kamminga (eds.), at 76.

[34] Examples include the extradition that (allegedly) involves mistreatment in the receiving State, *compare e.g.* H.R. Committee, *C. v. Australia*, Communication No. 900/1999, UN Doc. CCPR/C/76/D/900/1999 (October 28, 2002).

[35] Carlson/ Gisvold, *International Covenant*, p. 18; Nowak, *CCPR Commentary*, Art. 2, paras. 26-28 (pp. 41-42).

on the basis of "effective control" over territory in its much discussed *Banković* decision,[36] did not refer any more to "effective control".[37]

> The Committee ... reiterates that, in the current circumstances, the provisions of the Covenant apply to the benefit of the population of the Occupied Territories, for all conduct by the State party's authorities or agents in those territories that affect the enjoyment of rights enshrined in the Covenant and fall within the ambit of *State responsibility* of Israel under the principles of public international law.[38]

The referral to "State responsibility" has to be understood in an untechnical sense.[39] However, it makes clear that the Committee accepts that the attribution of an act to the State is a sufficient basis to apply the Covenant in relation to this act.

This position was endorsed by the International Court of Justice in its Advisory Opinion on the *Legal Consequences of the Construction of a Wall in the Occupied Palestinian Territory* in 2004. Here, the ICJ opined that the Covenant as well other human rights conventions Israel is party to applied to Israel's conduct in the Occupied Territories. Particularly, the Court found that the Covenant "is applicable in respect of acts done by a State in the exercise of its jurisdiction outside its own territory."[40] In doing so, the Court cited the Human Rights Committee.[41] Most importantly, assessing the applicability of the Covenant, the

---

36 Eur. Ct. H.R., *Banković and others v. Belgium and others*, Appl. No. 52207/99, Decision of December 12, 2001 (Grand Chamber), *ECHR* 2001-XII, pp. 333-390.

37 It still had done so in the 1998 concluding observations, *see* H.R. Committee, *Concluding Observations on Israel*, UN Doc. CCPR/C/79/Add.93 (August 18, 1998), para. 10.

38 H.R. Committee, *Concluding Observations on Israel*, UN Doc. CCPR/CO/78/ISR (August 21, 2003), para. 11 (my emphasis).

39 Actual state responsibility – beside attribution to a state – would require the violation of a rule of international law.

40 ICJ, *Legal Consequences of the Construction of a Wall in the Occupied Palestine Territory*, Advisory Opinion of July 9, 2004, I.C.J. Reports 2004, pp. 133-271, at 180 (para. 111).

41 The Court referred to H.R. Committee, *Concluding Observations on Israel*, UN Doc. CCPR/C/79/Add.93 (August 18, 1998) and H.R. Committee, *Concluding Observations on Israel*, UN Doc. CCPR/CO/78/ISR (August 21, 2003), para. 11.

Court quoted exactly that paragraph that is also quoted here, including "state responsibility" as a sufficient criterion for such jurisdiction.[42]

Therefore, it must be concluded that anybody who is directly affected by a State's action can be regarded, for the purpose of the Covenant, as being subject to that State's jurisdiction.[43] This is especially true for a person whose right to life is at stake due to an active behaviour of a State. For example, in the context of Iran's report under the Covenant, the Human Rights Committee addressed the *fatwa* pronounced on *Salman Rushdie*. This was done even though it concerned a possible assassination in the United Kingdom or wherever Mr. *Rushdie* might appear. The Committee thus presumed that performing an assassination or inciting non-State actors to perform it would entail "jurisdiction" over the deprivation of Mr. *Rushdie's* life.[44] It can therefore be concluded that

> the assassination of a targeted individual with a cruise missile, an anthrax letter sent form the neighboring country, a sniper's bullet in the head from the distance of 300 meters, or a poisoned umbrella tip on a crowded street all constitute 'effective control' in respect of the targeted individual and his or her enjoyment of human rights when undertaken by agents of a foreign state.[45]

To return to the concept of "exercising effective control", which first was referred to by the Human Rights Committee as proof of "jurisdiction" under the Covenant, one can phrase this phenomenon also as "*ad*

---

[42] ICJ, *Legal Consequences of the Construction of a Wall in the Occupied Palestine Territory*, Advisory Opinion of July 9, 2004, I.C.J. Reports 2004, pp. 133-271, at 180 (para. 110); *compare also* ICJ, *Case Concerning Armed Activities on the Territory of the Congo, Democratic Republic of Congo v. Uganda (new application of 2002)*, Judgment of December 19, 2005, I.C.J. Reports 2005 (not published yet), paras. 216 and 220.

[43] *See also* McGoldrick, in: Coomans/ Kamminga (eds.), at 62; *compare also* H.R. Committee, *Delia Saldías de López*, para. 12.3; H.R. Committee, CCPR General Comment No. 31, at 194-195 (para. 10); Kretzmer, 16 *Eur. J. Int'l L.* (2005), at 184; Joan Fitzpatrick, 'Speaking Law to Power: The War Against Terrorism and Human Rights', in: 14 *Eur. J. Int'l L.* (2003), pp. 241-264, at 241.

[44] *Compare* H.R. Committee, *Concluding Observations on the Islamic Republic of Iran*, UN Doc. CCPR/C/79/Add.25 (August 3, 1995), para. 9; *see also* Scheinin, in: Coomans/ Kamminga (eds.), at 80.

[45] Scheinin, in: Coomans/ Kamminga (eds.), at 77-78.

hoc control over a person" which establishes "jurisdiction" in relation to that person. Thus, every targeted killing by a state agent falls within the jurisdiction of the targeting State under the International Covenant on Civil and Political Rights and is thus subject to the standards laid down therein.

II. The American Convention on Human Rights

The threshold concerning the application of the Inter-American human rights instruments is very similar to that of the International Covenant, if not identical. According to Article 1 para. 1 of the Convention, the

> States Parties to this Convention undertake to respect the rights and freedoms recognized herein and to ensure to all persons *subject to their jurisdiction* the free and full exercise of those rights and freedoms, without any discrimination for reasons of race, color, sex, language, religion, political or other opinion, national or social origin, economic status, birth, or any other social condition.[46]

Again, the term jurisdiction is decisive, and again it is widely accepted that this can include extraterritorial application of the Convention.[47] The Inter-American Court has not yet had the opportunity to judge on the interpretation of that term regarding extraterritoriality. The only case in which it touched the issue is *Fairén-Garbi*. Here, the Court left the question open, as it regarded it not as proven that Honduras was involved in the alleged violations of rights.[48] However, the Inter-American Commission on Human Rights has taken the same wide view as Human Rights Committee.[49] The Commission made clear that control over an individual – and nothing more – is the decisive criterion in or-

[46] My emphasis.

[47] *See e.g.* Inter-Am. Comm'n H.R., *Victor Saldaño v. Argentina*, Report No. 38/99 (March 11, 1999), in: *Annual Report* (1998), OEA/Ser.L/V/II.102, Doc. 6 rev. (April 16, 1999), Chapter III, at paras. 17-20; Schindler, in: Häfelin *et al.* (eds.), at 334.

[48] Inter-Am. Ct. H.R., *Fairén-Garbi*, Series C, No. 6, para. 161; *compare also* Douglass Cassel, 'Extraterritorial Application of Inter-American Human Rights Instruments', in: Fons Coomans; Menno T. Kamminga (eds.), *Extraterritorial Application of Human Rights Treaties*, Antwerp 2004, pp. 175-181, at 175.

[49] *See also* Kretzmer, 16 *Eur. J. Int'l L.* (2005), at 184.

der to apply the instruments. Hints in that direction can already be found in its 1985 Report on the Situation of Human Rights in Chile. Here, the Commission addressed the deaths of two former members of the Chilean Government under the heading "Murders committed outside Chile" without any reference to the question of applicability. It addressed the case of *Orlando Letelier del Solar*, who had been killed in Washington, D.C. by agents of the Chilean Government[50] and that of *Carlos Prats González*, who had been killed by such agents in Buenos Aires.[51]

Concerning the U.S. invasion in Grenada, the Commission declared a case admissible concerning the bombing by U.S. aircraft of a mental health hospital in Grenada before ground troops arrived.[52] Similarly, in ruling that a case involving the U.S. invasion in Panama was admissible, the Commission made no effort to examine whether the alleged violations took place before or after the U.S. gained effective control of the territory. Neither did the Commission examine whether the violations took place inside or outside the territory controlled by the U.S.[53] Identically, concerning the U.S. intervention in Grenada, the Commission did not examine in *Coard*[54] whether the alleged violations took place

---

50 Inter-Am. Comm'n H.R., *Report on the Human Rights Situation in Chile*, OEA/Ser.L/V/II.66, Doc. 17 (September 27, 1985), paras. 81-88.

51 *Id.*, paras. 89-91.

52 Inter-Am. Comm'n H.R., *Disabled Peoples' International v. United States (US military intervention in Grenada, Richmond Hill Insane Asylum)*, Case 9213, Report No. 3/96 (March 1, 1996), in: *Annual Report* (1995), OEA/ Ser.L/V/II.91, Doc. 7 (February 28, 1996), Chapter III, at para. 2 (A friendly settlement was subsequently reached).

53 Inter-Am. Comm'n H.R., *Salas et al. v. United States (US military intervention in Panama)*, Case 10.573, Report No. 31/93 (October 14, 1993), in: *Annual Report* (1993), OEA/Ser.L/V.85 Doc. 9 rev. (February 11, 1994), Chapter III, Analysis, at paras. 2-6. The United States are not a member State to the American Convention on Human Rights, but bound by the American Declaration on Rights and Duties of Man, which is applied by the Commission to all OAS member States, *see* Christina M. Cerna, 'Extraterritorial Application of the Human Rights Instruments of the Inter-American System', in: Fons Coomans; Menno T. Kamminga (eds.), *Extraterritorial Application of Human Rights Treaties*, Antwerp 2004, pp. 141-174, at 143-144.

54 Inter-Am. Comm'n H.R., *Coard et al. v. United States (US military intervention in Grenada)*, Case 10.951, Report No. 109/99 (September 29, 1999), in:

before or after the territory was secured by the U.S. military. The Commission found that the phrase "subject to its jurisdiction"

> may, under given circumstances, refer to conduct with an extraterritorial locus where the person concerned is present in the territory of one state, but subject to the control of another state – usually through the acts of the latter's agents abroad.[55]

It made clear that neither the victim's nationality nor geographic location was decisive, but only the authority or control that was exercised over the victim. The decisive element is thus not control over territory, but over the individual. Such authority existed if a person was taken in custody by State agents abroad.[56]

The clearest case regarding the threshold of authority and control that is required in order to make the Convention applicable can be found in *Alejandre v. Cuba*, also know as the *Brothers to the Rescue* case.[57] Here, two civilian airplanes belonging to the organization "Brothers to the Rescue" were downed by a military aircraft of the Cuban Air Force in international airspace. Reiterating the principle stated in the *Coard* case the Commission again cited the standard of "control." In this case, the victims were clearly neither on Cuban territory nor on any territory over which Cuba had any control, nor were they brought within Cuban territory. It is thus control over the persons killed and not over any territory that is relevant for the Commission, which concluded,

> when agents of a state, whether military or civilian, exercise power and authority over persons outside national territory, the state's obligation to respect human rights continues. ... The Commission finds conclusive evidence that agents of the Cuban State, although outside

---

Annual Report (1999), OEA/Ser.L/V/II.106, Doc. 6 rev. (April 13, 1999), Chapter III.

55 *Id.*, para. 37.

56 Here, the Commission refers to Meron, 89 *Am. J. Int'l L.* (1995), at 81 and quotes "Where agents of the state, whether military or civilian, exercise power and authority (jurisdiction or de facto jurisdiction) over persons outside national territory, the presumption should be that the state's obligation to respect the pertinent human rights continues."

57 Inter-Am. Comm'n H.R., *Armando Alejandre ("Brothers to the Rescue")*, *Annual Report* (1999).

> their territory, placed the civilian pilots of the 'Brothers to the Rescue' organization under their authority.[58]

If this standard is applied, it is hard to imagine a situation where an active human rights violation by a state agent would fail to meet this test.[59] The *Brothers to the Rescue* case of the Inter-American Commission is of special importance in two regards: First, the situation examined by the Commission resembles very much that of a targeted killing by a State agent. The Commission has thus made clear, that every and all cases of targeted killing by State agents of member States – irrespective of both the perpetrator's and victim's location – are subject to the American Convention on Human Rights. Second, the situation in *Brothers to the Rescue* also resembles that of the leading case of the European Court of Human Rights in that regard, namely *Banković*.[60] Here, the Inter-American Commission has set an important and clear precedent that should be taken into account by the other treaty based human rights organs.[61]

III. The European Convention on Human Rights

The European Convention on Human Rights also refers to the term "jurisdiction" of the member states. Article 1 of the Convention reads:

> The High Contracting Parties shall secure to everyone within their jurisdiction the rights and freedoms defined in Section I of this Convention.

Section I starts with the protection of the right to life in Article 2 and encompasses all substantial rights protected under the Convention. Again, it is clear and undisputed that the Convention applies to the territory of the States party to it. It is also accepted, that the Convention applies to certain extraterritorial situations. However, it is disputed, as to how far this extraterritorial application reaches. The question of the

---

58 *Id.*, para. 25.

59 Cerone, *ASIL Insight* (2005), No. 10 (October 25, 2005).

60 *Compare infra*, Part Four, Chapter A) III.

61 Interestingly, the Convention refers to the jurisprudence of the European Court in its decision, *see* Inter-Am. Comm'n H.R., *Armando Alejandre ("Brothers to the Rescue")*, *Annual Report* (1999), at para. 24.

Convention's extraterritorial applicability thus gave rise to several cases before the European Commission and Court of Human Rights.

1. Effective Control Over Territory

The first important case raising this question was Cyprus against Turkey on the issue of the 1974 Turkish intervention in northern Cyprus.[62] Whereas Turkey submitted that the Convention was not applicable since Cyprus did not constitute Turkish territory, the Commission of Human Rights rejected the idea of limiting the obligations under the Convention to the mere territory of a specific state. The Commission argued,

> that authorised agents of a state, including diplomatic or consular agents and armed forces, not only remain under its jurisdiction when abroad but bring any person or property 'within the jurisdiction' of that state, to the extent that they exercise authority over such persons or property. Insofar as, by their acts or omissions, they affect such persons or property, the responsibility of the State is engaged.[63]

Describing the degree of control the Turkish armed forces exercised, the Commission continued:

> In this respect it is not contested by the responsible Government that Turkish armed forces have entered the island of Cyprus, operating solely under the direction of the Turkish government, and under established rules governing the structure and command of these armed forces including the establishment of military courts. It follows that these armed forces are authorised agents of Turkey and that they bring any other persons or property in Cyprus 'within the jurisdiction' of Turkey, in the sense of Article 1 of the Convention, to the extent that they exercise control over such persons or property.[64]

---

62 Eur. Comm'n H.R., *Cyprus v. Turkey*, Appl. Nos. 6780/74 and 6950/75, Decision of May 26, 1975, 2 *D.R.* (1975), pp. 125-151.

63 *Id.*, at 136.

64 *Id.*, at 137.

This Interpretation of Article 1 of the Convention has been upheld in several cases concerning Cyprus.[65] The Commission's interpretation has also been confirmed in the *Loizidou* case by the European Court of Human Rights.[66] Here, the Court stated concerning the term "jurisdiction" in the meaning of Article 1 of the Convention:

> In addition, the responsibility of Contracting Parties can be involved because of acts of their authorities, whether performed within or outside national boundaries, which produce effects outside their own territory.[67]

The Court then relativised its statement by referring to "effective control" of a State over foreign territory:

> [T]he responsibility of a Contracting Party may also arise when as a consequence of military action – whether lawful or unlawful – it exercises effective control of an area outside its national territory. The obligation to secure, in such an area, the rights and freedoms set out in the Convention derives from the fact of such control whether it be exercised directly, through its armed forces, or through a subordinate local administration.[68]

It is important to acknowledge that the Court only referred to the "obligation to secure the rights and freedoms set out in the Convention" in such an area due to the control. This refers to the positive obligation under the Convention, an obligation that clearly can only be fulfilled if a minimum degree of control is established, and corresponds the con-

---

65 *See e.g.* Eur. Comm'n H.R., *Cyprus v. Turkey*, Appl. No. 8007/77, Decision of July 10, 1978, in: 13 *D.R.* (1978), pp. 85-230, at 148.

66 Eur. Ct. H.R., *Loizidou (Prelim. Obj.)*, Series A, No. 310, p. 24 (para. 64). *See also* Eur. Ct. H.R., *Loizidou v. Turkey (Merits)*, Judgment (Grand Chamber) of December 18, 1996, *ECHR* 1996-VI, No. 26, pp. 2216-2259, at 2231 and 2234-2236 (paras. 43, 52 and 56); *compare also* Gérard Cohen-Jonathan, 'L'affaire Loizidou devant la Cour européenne des droits de l'homme. Quelques observations', in: 102 *R.G.D.I.P.* (1998), pp. 123-144, at 126-139.

67 Eur. Ct. H.R., *Loizidou (Prelim. Obj.)*, Series A, No. 310, pp. 23-24 (para. 62); *see also* Eur. Ct. H.R., *Loizidou (Merits)*, *ECHR* 1996-VI, at 2234-2235 (para. 52); Eur. Ct. H.R., *Drozd and Janousek v. France and Spain*, Appl. No. 12747/87, Judgment of June 26, 1992, Series A, No. 240, p. 29 (para. 91) with further references.

68 Eur. Ct. H.R., *Loizidou (Prelim. Obj.)*, Series A, No. 310, pp. 23-24 (para. 62).

cept of "jurisdiction to enforce".[69] The first part of the Court's statement, concerning extraterritorial acts which can cause responsibility of a State party rather refers to the Conventions negative obligations, i.e. the defensive function or the duty to refrain from any activity violating a Convention right. Such activities by State agents do not depend on "effective control" but only on the factual possibility to execute such an act. The duty to refrain from such activities does not require the State to have effective control of any territory, but only of its own behaviour through its agents.

This interpretation finds support in the *Cyprus v. Turkey* judgment[70] which followed *Loizidou*. Here, the Court made clear that since Turkey had "effective overall control", its responsibility could not only be confined to the acts of its own agents therein – i.e. the negative obligations – but was engaged by the acts of the local administration which survived by virtue of Turkish support. Turkey's "jurisdiction" under Article 1 was therefore considered to extend to securing the *entire range* of substantive Convention rights in northern Cyprus, including positive obligations.[71] This does though not necessarily mean that "effective overall control" is required for a state to be held responsible under the Convention. It rather shows that such a high degree of control entails the duty to secure the entire range of substantive rights. Arguably, if the control of Turkey would have been more limited, its responsibility would have been "confined to the acts of its own soldiers or officials in northern Cyprus",[72] i.e. the negative obligation.[73] Similar to *Cyprus v. Turkey*, *de facto* control was accepted by the Court in *Ilaşcu*,[74] due to the "effective authority, or at the very least under the decisive influence,

---

69 *Compare* the example of the Netherlands blue helmets in Srebrenica, *supra*, Part Four, Chapter A) I.; *compare also* Krieger, 62 *ZaöRV* (2002), at 672.

70 Eur. Ct. H.R., *Cyprus v. Turkey*, *ECHR* 2001-IV, pp. 1-477.

71 *Id.*, at 25 (para. 77).

72 *Id.*

73 *Compare also* Rick Lawson, 'Life after *Bankovic*: Extraterritorial Application of the European Convention on Human Rights', in: Fons Coomans; Menno T. Kamminga (eds.), *Extraterritorial Application of Human Rights Treaties*, Antwerp 2004, pp. 83-123, at 98-99.

74 Eur. Ct. H.R., *Ilaşcu*, *ECHR* 2004-VII, pp. 1-348.

of the Russian Federation" in Transdniestria[75] as being enough to establish jurisdiction.

The leading case of the European Court on "jurisdiction" in the meaning of Article 1 is *Banković*.[76] The case concerned deaths resulting from the bombing by the North Atlantic Treaty Organisation (NATO) members of the Radio Televizije Srbije (Radio-Television Serbia) headquarters in Belgrade as part of NATO's campaign of air strikes against the Federal Republic of Yugoslavia during the Kosovo conflict. Here, the Court dealt with the question of the degree of control required to include actions "within the jurisdiction" of a State Party in the meaning of Article 1 of the Convention. Due to the positive attitude of the States party to the European Convention towards human rights protection, it was expected that the Court would attribute actions of armed forces outside the territory of the member states to them and make these actions subject to the Convention.[77] The Court stated:

> In sum, the case-law of the Court demonstrates that its recognition of the exercise of extra-territorial jurisdiction by a Contracting State is exceptional: it has done so when the respondent State, through the effective control of the relevant territory and its inhabitants abroad as a consequence of military occupation or through the consent, invitation or acquiescence of the Government of that territory, exercises all or some of the public powers normally to be exercised by that Government.[78]

In consequence, the Court denied that the victims of the bombardment were within the jurisdiction of the NATO States. According to the Court, such a bombardment – in contrast to a situation of occupation – does not establish sufficient control to establish such jurisdiction.[79] The judgment in *Banković* was accepted by some authors,[80] but also caused

---

75 *Id.*, at 282 (para. 393).

76 Eur. Ct. H.R., *Banković*, *ECHR* 2001-XII, pp. 333-390.

77 Heintze, 18 *HuV-I* (2005), at 179.

78 Eur. Ct. H.R., *Banković*, *ECHR* 2001-XII, at 355 (para. 71).

79 *Id.*, at 359 (para. 82).

80 *See e.g.* Christopher Greenwood, 'Remarks on "Bombing for Peace: Collateral Damage and Human Rights"', in: 95 *ASIL Proc.* (2002), pp. 100-104; Krieger, 62 *ZaöRV* (2002), at 670-672; Georg Ress, 'State Responsibility for Extraterritorial Human Rights Violations: The Case of Banković', in: 6 *ZeuS*

extensive criticism. The Courts assessment of jurisdiction was called "unduly restrictive"[81] and "flawed"[82] and many authors are of the opinion that the Court should have accepted that jurisdiction was given in the case.[83] Now, is this restrictive interpretation really "flawed", or as others out it: Did the Court really get it all wrong?[84] There are several points that do indeed justify critique of the Court's judgment in *Banković*.

First, the Court strongly relies on the drafting history of the European Convention, whereas it has stressed elsewhere that the Convention has to be seen "in the light of present day conditions"[85] and thus has to be interpreted dynamically and evolutively.[86] The mainly historical assessment of the question by the Court contradicts the object and purpose of the Convention and the principle of effective protection.[87] The Court itself has stressed elsewhere that the aim of an interpretation is to achieve effective protection.[88] A teleological emphasis on the object and

---

(2003), pp. 73-90, at 86-89; Schmidt-Radefeldt, in: Fleck (ed.), *Rechtsfragen*, at 108-111.

[81] Michał Gondek, 'Extraterritorial Application of the European Convention on Human Rights: Territorial Focus in the Age of Globalization?', in: 52 *Nether. Int'l L. Rev.* (2005), pp. 349-387, at 385.

[82] Kerem Altiparmak, '*Bankovic*: An Obstacle to the Application of the European Convention on Human Rights in Iraq?', in: 9 *J. Confl. Sec. L.* (2004), pp. 213-251, at 214 and 231.

[83] *See e.g.* Lawson, in: Coomans/ Kamminga (eds.), at 85 and 109-116; Bernhard Schäfer, 'Der Fall Banković oder Wie eine Lücke geschaffen wird', in: 7 *MRM* (2002), pp. 149-163, at 163; Dinah Shelton, 'The Boundaries of Human Rights Jurisdiction in Europe', in: 13 *Duke J. Comp. & Int'l L.* (2003), pp. 95-153, at 128.

[84] *Compare* Lawson, in: Coomans/ Kamminga (eds.), at 85: "The Court got it all wrong."

[85] Eur. Ct. H.R., *Tyrer*, Series A, No. 26, pp. 15-16 (para. 31).

[86] *Compare e.g.* Eur. Ct. H.R., *Marckx*, Series A, No. 31, p. 19 (para. 41); Eur. Ct. H.R., *Soering*, Series A, No. 161, p. 40 (para. 102); Eur. Ct. H.R., *Loizidou (Prelim. Obj.)*, Series A, No. 310, pp. 26-27 (para. 71).

[87] Altiparmak, 9 *J. Confl. Sec. L.* (2004), at 226-228; Schäfer, 7 *MRM* (2002), at 159.

[88] *See e.g.* Eur. Ct. H.R., *Airey*, Series A, No. 32, p. 15 (para. 26); Eur. Ct. H.R., *Artico*, Series A, No. 37, p. 16 (para. 33); Eur. Ct. H.R., *Soering*, Series A,

purpose of a human rights treaty allows a dynamic or evolving interpretation that can move a treaty away from the original intent of its drafters.[89] Additionally, "[i]t is not unlikely that the drafters of the Convention did not give much thought at all to any extraterritorial impact of the Convention."[90]

Second, in assessing the ordinary meaning of the term "jurisdiction", the Court states that jurisdiction is "as a general rule, defined and limited by the sovereign territorial rights of the other relevant States."[91] Thus, "a State's competence to exercise jurisdiction over its own nationals abroad is subordinate to that State's and other States' territorial competence"[92] and hence has an "essentially territorial notion ..., other bases of jurisdiction being exceptional and requiring special justification in the particular circumstances of each case".[93] All this is beyond doubt, but does not necessarily lead to the conclusion the Court draws from it. This conclusion is "that Article 1 of the Convention must be considered to reflect this ordinary and essentially territorial notion of jurisdiction".[94] What the Court is discussing when it refers to the concept of "jurisdiction" under general international law is rather substantive jurisdiction, i.e. the question of whether it is permissible for a State to act and exercise its jurisdiction abroad. Obviously, such an exercise of jurisdiction finds its limits in the jurisdiction of other States. The fact that a state may not be authorized to exercise such jurisdiction does not mean that a state does not factually do so nevertheless. A State may, for example, legally stop a foreign vessel within its territorial sea and thereby act within its territorial jurisdiction. The same state could also stop the same vessel in the high seas – with the effect that the action would most likely be illegal because it was performed outside the State's territorial jurisdiction. Nevertheless, when the State acted, it exercised power or authority and thus jurisdiction of the vessel – be it legal in the

---

No. 161, p. 34 (para. 87); Eur. Ct. H.R., *Lala*, Series A, No. 297-A, p. 14 (para. 34).

89 Shelton, 13 *Duke J. Comp. & Int'l L.* (2003), at 125.

90 Lawson, in: Coomans/ Kamminga (eds.), at 90.

91 Eur. Ct. H.R., *Banković*, *ECHR* 2001-XII, at 351-352 (para. 59).

92 *Id.*, at 352 (para. 60).

93 *Id.*, at 352 (para. 61).

94 *Id.*

first case and illegal in the second case.[95] The question of whether jurisdiction is limited by other States is thus totally independent from the question which was relevant in *Banković*, namely whether the affected persons *de facto* made subject to the NATO State's control – and thus subject to its remedial jurisdiction[96] – in that situation.[97] The latter question rather resembles the question of whether the extraterritorial behaviour of a State organ is attributable to the "sending" state. According to a well-established principle of public international law, it is.[98]

In that regard, it is interesting to note that in *Loizidou*, the Turkish Government had argued that the question of jurisdiction in Article 1 of the Convention was not identical with the question of State responsibility under international law and that Article 1 "was not couched in terms of State responsibility".[99] Then, the Court did not follow the Turkish arguments and held Turkey responsible under the Convention, whereas in *Banković* it did not accept that the concept of "jurisdiction" under the Convention is similar to the concept of "attribution" under the law of state responsibility.

Third, although the Court has acknowledged that cross-reference to other international instruments is a legitimate means of interpretation,[100] it has not taken due regard of the developments of the Inter-American System and the International Covenant concerning the applicability of human rights and their relation to humanitarian law in similar situations. It only referred to the *Coard* case[101] and did not mention

---

[95] Orakhelashvili, 14 *Eur. J. Int'l L.* (2003), at 539-540; *but see* Michael O'Boyle, 'The European Convention on Human Rights and Extraterritorial Jurisdiction: A Comment on "Life after *Bankovic*"', in: Fons Coomans; Menno T. Kamminga (eds.), *Extraterritorial Application of Human Rights Treaties*, Antwerp 2004, pp. 125-139, at 130-131.

[96] Orakhelashvili, 14 *Eur. J. Int'l L.* (2003), at 540-541.

[97] Scheinin, in: Coomans/ Kamminga (eds.), at 79-80.

[98] *Compare also* Lawson, in: Coomans/ Kamminga (eds.), at 86 (footnote 13).

[99] Eur. Ct. H.R., *Loizidou (Merits)*, *ECHR* 1996-VI, at 2233-2234 (para. 51).

[100] *See e.g.* Eur. Ct. H.R., *Soering*, Series A, No. 161, pp. 34-35 (para. 88).

[101] Inter-Am. Comm'n H.R., *Coard*, *Annual Report* (1999); *compare* Eur. Ct. H.R., *Banković*, *ECHR* 2001-XII, at 343-344 (para. 23).

the *Brothers to the Rescue* case.[102] The latter is of special importance, as it is very similar to the situation of *Banković* and the Inter-American Commission accepted that it fell under the jurisdiction of the American Convention.[103]

Fourth, whereas in *Loizidou*, the Court tried to close a gap in the Convention system, it can be criticized for opening one in *Banković*: "Who, if not the State executing the action in question, should be accountable for that action?"[104] Even though the European Convention System is a regional system for the protection of human rights, it has to be acknowledged that its establishment was strongly motivated by the desire to promote the universal protection of human rights. And as *Orakhelashvili* phrased it:

> The European Convention on Human Rights was adopted as an instrument to protect the rights and interests of individual human beings rather than of state parties.[105]

On the other hand, *Banković* is not completely unreasonable. *Klein* e.g. concludes that *Banković* is legally problematic but politically understandable.[106] In that regard, it has to be noticed that *Banković* was argued and decided within weeks after and under the strong impressions of the events of September 11, 2001.[107] In his speech on the occasion of the opening of the judicial year 2002 of the European Court, its President *Wildhaber* stated:

> Our perception of last year is coloured by the tragic events of 11 September and their aftermath. Terrorism raises two fundamental issues which human rights law must address. Firstly, it strikes directly at democracy and the rule of law, the two central pillars of the Euro-

---

[102] Inter-Am. Comm'n H.R., *Armando Alejandre ("Brothers to the Rescue")*, *Annual Report* (1999).

[103] *See supra*, Part Four, Chapter A) II.

[104] Schäfer, 7 *MRM* (2002), at 159 (my translation).

[105] Orakhelashvili, 14 *Eur. J. Int'l L.* (2003), at 529.

[106] Eckart Klein, 'Der Schutz der Menschenrechte in bewaffneten Konflikten', in: 9 *MRM* (2004), pp. 5-17, at 14; *see also* Shelton, 13 *Duke J. Comp. & Int'l L.* (2003), at 128.

[107] Altiparmak, 9 *J. Confl. Sec. L.* (2004), at 250; Hurst Hannum, 'Remarks on "Bombing for Peace: Collateral Damage and Human Rights"', in: 95 *ASIL Proc.* (2002), pp. 96-99, at 99.

> pean Convention on Human Rights. It must be therefore be possible for democratic States governed by the rule of law to protect themselves effectively against terrorism; human rights law must be able to accommodate this need. The European Convention should not be applied in such a way as to prevent States from taking reasonable and proportionate action to defend democracy and the rule of law.[108]

Under the impression of September 11, 2001, the Court was thus very reluctant to examine the legality of the NATO strikes since the traditional international law on the use of force was – at least – challenged at that time. However, it has to be kept in mind that – concerning the question of arbitrary deprivation – it is not the overall legality of the NATO intervention – i.e. the *jus ad bellum* – that is relevant but exclusively the *jus in bello*.[109] And furthermore, the Court is one of the few organs which can, in fact, examine whether States are indeed "governed by the rule of law" while protecting themselves against terrorism.

It is likely that the Court feared "opening the flood gates"[110] in case it accepted jurisdiction over every extraterritorial conduct of a member State's armed force. This fear is unfounded for two reasons: First, it was considered desirable by the drafters of the Convention "to widen as far as possible the categories of persons who are to benefit by the guarantees of the Convention".[111] "As far as possible" entails that no impossible burden should be placed on the member States, but it also includes the obligation not to disregard human rights obligations where it is indeed possible – even abroad.[112] Second, the effect of the derogation clause of Article 15 of the Convention is that – if States use the clause – only the non-derogable rights can be brought before the Court at all.[113]

---

[108] Luzius Wildhaber, President of the Eur. Ct. H.R., Speech given at Strasbourg on January 31, 2002, in: *The Council Of Europe's Contribution to the Enlargement of the European Union – Speeches given by the President of the Court of Justice of the European Communities and by the President of the European Court of Human Rights on the occasion of the opening of the judicial year*, CoE Doc. SdC (2002) 6, pp. 8-12, at 8.

[109] On this discussion *compare supra*, Part One, Chapter B) I. 1. d) (3).

[110] Lawson, in: Kreijen (ed.), at 294.

[111] Council of Europe (ed.), "*Travaux préparatoires*", Vol. 3, p. 200.

[112] Lawson, in: Kreijen (ed.), at 294.

[113] Krieger, 62 *ZaöRV* (2002), at 689-690.

Thus, the "flood gates" will most likely not be opened regarding the number of cases brought before the Court. It will, however, face the Court with a new challenge it has avoided by declaring *Banković* inadmissible. Many cases concerning the extraterritorial application of the Convention will include questions of international humanitarian law. In contrast to the Inter-American Court, the European Court is very reluctant in applying this branch of law.[114]

Additionally, the Court could even be interpreted as having tried to establish a preventive argument for future cases e.g. concerning the conduct of U.K. troops in Iraq.[115] It stressed the regional character of the European Convention and already argued in *Banković* that the Federal Republic of Yugoslavia was not a State party and thus "clearly does not fall within this legal space."[116]

2. *"De facto Control" Over Persons*

Strasbourg locuta, causa finita? Beside the cases referring to the control over a certain territory – be it occupation or for other factual reasons – at least the European Commission had earlier accepted that single acts can fall into the jurisdiction of a State without such control over the territory in question. Already 1975, the Commission stated in relation to *Rudolf Hess* who was detained by the four allied powers of the Second World War in Berlin:

> There is in principle, from a legal point of view, no reason why the acts of the British authorities in Berlin should not entail the liability of the United Kingdom under the Convention.[117]

The application was declared inadmissible due the fact that the four powers were jointly responsible for Mr. *Hess*. The Commission may

---

114 *Compare also* Heintze, 18 *HuV-I* (2005), at 182; Orakhelashvili, 14 *Eur. J. Int'l L.* (2003), at 538.

115 *Compare* Altiparmak, 9 *J. Confl. Sec. L.* (2004), at 214; Cerone, *ASIL Insight* (2005), No. 10 (October 25, 2005).

116 Eur. Ct. H.R., *Banković*, *ECHR* 2001-XII, at 358 (para. 80); *Cerna* supports the "espace juridique" assessment of the Court, *see* Cerna, in: Coomans/Kamminga (eds.), at 169-171.

117 Eur. Comm'n H.R., *Ilse Hess v. United Kingdom*, Appl. No. 6231/73, Decision of May 28, 1975, 2 *D.R.* (1975), pp. 72-76, at 73.

have been swayed by the danger that a finding that the United Kingdom violated the Convention would put it the position where it could not change this situation due to the other allied powers.[118]

In *Stocké*, concerning an alleged unlawful detention of a German citizen lured to Germany from France by a police informer, the Commission stated that

> authorized agents of a State not only remain under its jurisdiction when abroad, but bring any other person 'within the jurisdiction' of that State to the extent that they exercise authority over such persons. Insofar as the State's acts or omissions affect such persons, the responsibility of the State is engaged.[119]

Regrettably, the Court did not find it necessary to address the issue of jurisdiction in that case, but directly turned to the question of whether the conduct abroad did amount to a violation of Article 5 para. 1 of the Convention.[120] Similar to the Commission's assessment, in 2000, the Court declared the case of *Issa* and others admissible without seeing the necessity to address the question of jurisdiction. The case concerned cross-border military operations by Turkish troops "aimed at pursuing and eliminating terrorists who were seeking shelter in northern Iraq." In that operation, the troops allegedly shot several Kurdish persons, i.e. outside Turkish territory and not in a territory which was controlled in a way northern Cyprus was in earlier cases.[121] However, in the merits judgement in 2004 – after *Banković* – the Court declared that the victims did not come under the jurisdiction of Turkey in the meaning of the European Convention.[122] But by now, even the Court admits that also single acts can establish jurisdiction in the meaning of the European Convention and distinguishes such cases from *Banković*. The

---

[118] *See also* Lawson, in: Coomans/ Kamminga (eds.), at 91-92.

[119] Eur. Comm'n H.R., *Stocké v. Germany*, Appl. No. 11755/85, Report of October 12, 1989, Series A, No. 199, Annex, pp. 21-32, at 24 (para. 166).

[120] Eur. Ct. H.R., *Stocké v. Germany*, Appl. No. 11755/85, Judgment of March 19, 1991, Series A, No. 199, pp. 15-19 (paras. 47-55).

[121] Eur. Ct. H.R., *Issa v. Turkey (Admissibility)*, Appl. No. 31821/96, Decision of May 30, 2000 (unreported); see also Cerna, in: Coomans/ Kamminga (eds.), at 171 (footnote 85).

[122] Eur. Ct. H.R., *Issa v. Turkey (Merits)*, Appl. No. 31821/96, Judgment of November 16, 2004, reprinted in: 41 *Eur. Hum. Rts. Rep.* (2005), pp. 567-591, at 587-591 (paras. 65-82).

Court accepted in *Öcalan* that the applicant was under Turkish jurisdiction in Kenya:

> In the instant case, the applicant was arrested by members of the Turkish security forces inside an aircraft in the international zone of Nairobi Airport. Directly after he had been handed over by the Kenyan officials to the Turkish officials the applicant was under effective Turkish authority and was therefore brought within the "jurisdiction" of that State for the purposes of Article 1 of the Convention, even though in this instance Turkey exercised its authority outside its territory.[123]

It has to be stressed that this mode of arrest and the transport to Turkey were *inter alia* subject of *Öcalan's* application which was accepted by the Court. The Court thus – at least in that case – accepted that control over a person is sufficient in a foreign territory that is far form being "within the legal space" of the European Convention. Regrettably, the Court did not develop this assessment further in *Issa*. Similarly to the Court's approach in *Öcalan*, it is acknowledged by authors who accept *Banković* that the "capturing of combatants" establishes jurisdiction due to the capturing State's responsibility for the treatment of the captured person – irrespective of the question of whether they actually qualify as prisoners of war.[124] Such cases would not be covered if one exclusively relied on the standards developed in of *Banković*.[125]

It is difficult to understand that in the same situation, a person who is not captured, but targeted, should not be subject to the State's jurisdiction, while that very State has the power to decide whether the person shall be captured or killed and while the European Convention contains the rules that apply to such a decision.[126] In the worst case, this could lead to a "no quarter" policy in order to avoid the inconveniences of human rights protection. It must thus be concluded that also in the

---

[123] Eur. Ct. H.R., *Öcalan v. Turkey (Merits and Just Satisfaction)*, Appl. No. 46221/99, Judgment of March 12, 2003, reprinted in: 37 *Eur. Hum. Rts. Rep.* (2003), pp. 238-319, at 274-275 (para. 93); Eur. Ct. H.R., *Öcalan v. Turkey (Merits and Just Satisfaction)*, Appl. No. 46221/99, Judgment (Grand Chamber) of May 12, 2005, *ECHR* 2005-IV, pp. 47-211, at 164-165 (para. 91).

[124] Krieger, 62 *ZaöRV* (2002), at 688.

[125] Altiparmak, 9 *J. Confl. Sec. L.* (2004), at 228.

[126] *Compare supra*, Part Two, Chapter E) II. 2.; *see also* Altiparmak, 9 *J. Confl. Sec. L.* (2004), at 230.

framework of the European Convention, "control entails responsibility",[127] or better: "*contrôle oblige*".[128] The latter phrase is more precise as it is control which obliges a State to respect the European Convention. Only if a State fails to do so, is it responsible for a violation under the Convention. Jurisdiction in the meaning of Article 1 of the Convention is thus rather a relationship between the State and the individual, and not exclusively between the State and a territory.

> It is the nexus between the person affected, whatever his nationality, and the perpetrator of the alleged violation which engages the possible responsibility of the State and not the place where the action takes place.[129]

> This reading gives expression to the object and purpose of the HR Conventions which is to protect individuals from the improper exercise of power, whereas a narrower, territorially-based meaning, would exclude certain individuals from protection, but not from power.[130]

Therefore, it can be concluded that the European Convention on Human Rights also applies to the extraterritorial exercise of State authority by State agents.[131] In the context of the present examination, this means that any targeted killing by agents of a State, even if performed extraterritorially, falls within the jurisdiction in the meaning of Article 1 of that State and is thus subject to the European Convention. This is true as any act of targeted killing entails *ad hoc* control over the person. This may not be obvious in a situation such as *Banković*, as the persons that

---

[127] Lawson, in: Kreijen (ed.), at 297; *see* Scheinin, in: Coomans/ Kamminga (eds.), at 80.

[128] Lawson, in: Coomans/ Kamminga (eds.), at 86.

[129] Françoise Hampson, 'Using International Human Rights Machinery to Enforce the International Law of Armed Conflicts', in: 31 *Rev. dr. pén. mil.* (1992), pp. 117-147, at 122; *see also* Ralph Wilde, 'Legal "Black Hole"? Extraterritorial State Action and International Treaty Law on Civil and Political Rights', in: 26 *Mich. J. Int'l L.* (2005), pp. 739-806, at 804-806; *compare also* Meron, 94 *Am. J. Int'l L.* (2000), at 273; Scheinin, in: Coomans/ Kamminga (eds.), at 80.

[130] Ben-Naftali, 100 *ASIL Proc.* (2006), at 92.

[131] Schindler, in: Häfelin *et al.* (eds.), at 334 ("..., soweit die Organe dieser Staaten dort hoheitliche Akte ausführen."); *see also* Wilde, 26 *Mich. J. Int'l L.* (2005), at 804-806.

died were not specifically targeted. But the very possibility of singling out and targeting an individual person is proof of a high standard of control the targeting State has. This control may not encompass the whole area and may not meet the standard of *Banković*. However, it suffices to have ultimate control over the question of life and death of the targeted person. How could a state exercise its jurisdiction over a person more directly than in deciding on life and death and ultimately executing that decision?

IV. The African Charter on Human and Peoples' Rights

The African Charter differs from the other instruments in as much as it does not refer to "jurisdiction" in delimiting the scope of application. Article 1 of the African Charter on Human And Peoples' Rights reads:

> The Member States of the Organisation of African Unity, parties to the present Charter shall recognise the rights, duties and freedoms enshrined in the Charter and shall undertake to adopt legislative or other measures to give effect to them.

Article 2 of the Charter reads:

> Every individual shall be entitled to the enjoyment of the rights and freedoms recognised and guaranteed in the present Charter without distinction of any kind such as race, ethnic group, colour, sex, language, religion, political or any other opinion, national and social origin, fortune, birth or any status.

The primary obligations laid down in these two articles include positive and negative duties.[132] Even though Article 2 was not originally drafted to define the application *ratione personae*, but as a pure non-discrimination clause, it has been interpreted as a clause describing jurisdiction. The African Commission stated in *Rencontre Africaine pour la Defence des Droits de l'Homme v. Zambia* in relation to Article 2:

---

[132] Bello, 194 *RdC* (1985-V), at 148-149; Heyns, in: Evans; Murray (eds.), at 138. However, it has bee criticized that the far reaching obligations are foremost a lip service, *see* Allain/ O'Shea, 24 *Hum. Rts. Q.* (2002), at 124-125.

> This imposes an obligation on the contracting state to secure the rights protected in the Charter to all persons within their jurisdiction, nationals or non-nationals.[133]

Article 62 of the Charter obliges the member States to give a report "on the legislative measures taken with a view to give effect to the rights and freedoms recognised and guaranteed by the present Charter."[134] This reporting mechanism shows that – similar to the other human rights systems – the emphasis of the Charter protection is on the territory of the member states, at least when it comes to positive obligations. This was also underlined by the Commission which stated in *Amnesty International et al. v. Sudan*:

> In addition to the individuals named in the communications, there are thousands of other executions in Sudan. Even if these are not all the work of forces of the government, the government has a responsibility to protect all people residing under its jurisdiction.[135]

On the other hand, the reporting guidelines include as one topic which is expected to be part of the State reports the following question: "How is the State, as an interested party, using the Charter in its international relations, particularly in ensuring respect for it?"[136] Thus, it is at least expected that states promote the Charter rights internationally and use their political influence to ensure that other states respect them. Furthermore, according to Article 1, the rights must be guaranteed by the member States in an unlimited manner. This principle is also not limited in Article 56 of the Charter, which provides admissibility conditions for

---

[133] Afr. Comm'n H.P.R., *Rencontre Africaine pour la Defence des Droits de l'Homme v. Zambia*, Communication 71/92, in 10th Activity Report (1996-1997), Annex V, pp. 60-63, at 62 (para. 22).

[134] On the reporting mechanism *compare* Bello, 194 *RdC* (1985-V), at 121-127.

[135] Afr. Comm'n H.P.R., *Amnesty International, Comité Loosli Bachelard, Lawyers Committee for Human Rights, Association of Members of the Episcopal conference of East Africa v. Sudan*, Communications 48/90, 50/91, 52/91 and 89/93, in: 13th *Activity Report* (1999-2000), Annex V, pp. 124-138, at 132 (para. 50).

[136] Malcom Evans; Tokunbo Ige; Rachel Murray, 'The Reporting Mechanism of the African Charter on Human and Peoples' Rights', in: Malcolm Evans; Rachel Murray (eds.), *The African Charter on Human and Peoples' Rights: The System in Practice, 1986-2000*, Cambridge 2002, pp. 36-60, at 49.

communications to the Commission, but does not address the issue of jurisdiction as an admissibility criterion.[137] Additionally, the Protocol establishing the African Court of Human and Peoples' Rights[138] does not contain any further limitation of jurisdiction. Article 3 para. 1 of this Protocol reads:

> The jurisdiction of the Court shall extend to all cases and disputes submitted to it concerning the interpretation and application of the Charter, this Protocol and any other relevant Human Rights instrument ratified by the States concerned.

Thus, concerning any extraterritorial effect of active state behaviour, the Charter does not exclude or even regulate its applicability. This corresponds to the intent of the drafter to give the Court the widest possible jurisdiction.[139] It can therefore be concluded that the scope of application is at least congruent with that of the International Covenant and the American Conventions and that of European Convention beyond *Banković*. The States are under a negative obligation not to interfere actively with the rights protected under the Charter, i.e. not to kill in a violation of the right to life under the Charter. This obligation applies to all persons who are affected, whether in or outside the territory of the acting member State.

The impact of such a broad interpretation is of course relativised by the fact that not just any case which falls into the scope of the Charter can be brought before the newly established African Court of Human Rights and Peoples' Rights. Due to the insistence of some States, a compromise was reached concerning that question. According to Article 5 para. 3 of the Protocol establishing the Court, individuals can only ac-

---

[137] *Compare* Bello, 194 *RdC* (1985-V), at 101-109; Frans Viljoen 'Admissibility under the African Charter', in: Malcolm Evans; Rachel Murray (eds.), *The African Charter on Human and Peoples' Rights: The System in Practice, 1986-2000*, Cambridge 2002, pp. 61-99, pp. 66-94.

[138] Protocol to the African Charter on Human and Peoples' Rights on the Establishment of an African Court on Human and Peoples' Rights, adopted at Ouagadougou, Burkina Faso on June 9, 1998, entry into force on January 25, 2004, OAU Doc. OAU/LEG/EXP/AFCHPR/PROT (III), reprinted in: 24 *Refugee Surv. Q.* (2005), p. 152 (Extract).

[139] Julia Harrington, 'The African Court on Human and Peoples' Rights', in: Malcolm Evans; Rachel Murray (eds.), *The African Charter on Human and Peoples' Rights: The System in Practice, 1986-2000*, Cambridge 2002, pp. 305-334, at 318.

cess the Court if it has granted them permission to do so. This is done pursuant to Article 34 para. 6 by a declaration "at the time of the ratification or thereafter". Most importantly, the "Court shall not receive any petition under article 5 (3) involving a State Party which has not made such a declaration."[140]

V. Customary International Law

A conclusion of the chapters above is that in connection with the treaty regimes protecting human rights, the question of cases being within the "jurisdiction" of the States party is of greatest importance when it comes to the question of whether those cases are admissible before the treaty organs. The question of "jurisdiction" is thus mainly a question of human rights enforcement. Under customary international law, no such enforcement mechanisms exist. Additionally, customary international law – *per se* – applies to the entire community of States except those who are persistent objectors to a specific rule of customary international law. Thus, an obligation under customary law does not have a scope that is restricted to certain territorial boundaries.

As shown above, at least the defensive function of the right to life – i.e. the negative obligation of States not to violate the right actively – not only represents customary international law, but also amounts to a peremptory norm or *jus cogens*. Thus, all States are obliged to respect the right to life of every human being, irrespective of where that person is located. Again, this only applies to the defensive function. The far reaching positive obligations that exist under the treaty systems cannot be regarded as representing general international law. But concerning the right to life – including its exceptions – every State is obliged not to kill arbitrarily any person in or outside its territory.

---

140 *Compare* Mei, 18 *Leiden J. Int'l L.* (2005), at 121.

VI. Conclusion

The extraterritorial application of human rights treaties is a highly debated issue.[141] One of the reasons for States being rather unwilling to accept the application of these treaties to cases outside their territory is the relatively effective system of enforcement these treaties contain. This system including individual applications to commissions or courts entails the risk that a possible violation of a human right will not only be asserted but investigated and judged upon.

Following the *Banković* decision of the European Court, it has been doubted whether international human rights norms apply to actions of states against transnational terrorists outside their borders.[142] This doubt has been challenged and thus the *Banković* decision has been criticized as being "disappointing in many respects."[143] The examination above has shown that this critique is well founded. One must agree with *Scheinin* when he proposes that any act of killing entails *ad hoc* control over the person. Thus, he is of the opinion that the Human Rights Committee would not have declared a case such as *Banković* inadmissible.[144]

The examination has shown that this assessment is also accepted by the Inter-American System and that it is in line with the African System. The Inter-American Commission "has pushed the jurisdictional envelope" regarding the exercise of extraterritorial jurisdiction of the OAS member states, and has gone further than the European Court.[145] The Inter-American Commission generally accepted that such effective con-

---

[141] The question was e.g. considered as being one of the fundamental questions of international law that were addressed at the 100th annual meeting of the American Society of International Law, *see* Dennis, 100 *ASIL Proc.* (2006), pp. 86-90; Ben-Naftali, 100 *ASIL Proc.* (2006), pp. 90-95; Robert McCorquodale, 'Spreading Weeds beyond their Garden: Extraterritorial Responsibility of States for Violations of Human Rights by Corporate Nationals', in: 100 *ASIL Proc.* (2006), pp. 95-102; *compare also* Cerone, 12 *Eur. J. Int'l L.* (2001), at 475-481.

[142] Neuman, 14 *Eur. J. Int'l L.* (2003), pp. 283-298.

[143] Orna Ben-Naftali; Yuval Shani, 'Living in Denial: The Application of Human Rights in the Occupied Territories', in: 37 *Isr. L. Rev.* (2003), pp. 17-118 at 81.

[144] Scheinin, in: Coomans/ Kamminga (eds.), at 77-78.

[145] Cerna, in: Coomans/ Kamminga (eds.), at 173.

trol over a person was sufficient to regard a person as being subject to the jurisdiction of a State.[146] The African Commission has explicitly stated that jurisdiction is not congruent with territory under the African Charter and a wide interpretation of the Charter is not only possible, but also demanded by the fact that it does not contain any restricting clause as to jurisdiction.

It has also been shown that the notion of "jurisdiction" as control in relation to a person rather then with a territory is in line with the European Convention, albeit the European Court disagreed in *Banković*. The Court put the emphasis on the effective control of territory or the consent by the territorial state, but relativised this assessment when it accepted that effective control over a person can also be sufficient as a basis for the application of the Convention.[147]

A State cannot perpetrate human rights violations on the territory of another State, which it cannot perpetrate on its own territory. It may not be responsible for the positive guarantees of the human rights in the same manner,[148] but concerning the infringements of rights by active deeds of state agents – i.e. the negative, defensive function of the human rights – States have the same responsibility abroad as on their own territory. Jurisdiction in the meaning of the human rights treaties can be established due to "exercising effective control" over a territory. In those cases, the State must fully observe the negative as well as the positive obligations of the rights protected. However, also "*ad hoc* control over a person" establishes "jurisdiction" over that person with the effect, that as an absolute minimum, the State must observe the negative obligations of the human rights treaties and refrain from actively violating these rights.

The example of targeted killings can illustrate this. If a state agent shoots at a targeted person and both are within the territory of one

---

146 Inter-Am. Comm'n H.R., *Armando Alejandre ("Brothers to the Rescue")*, *Annual Report* (1999), at para. 25; *compare also* Cassel, in: Coomans/ Kamminga (eds.), at 178.

147 *Compare* Eur. Ct. H.R., *Banković*, *ECHR* 2001-XII, at 355 (para. 71); Eur. Ct. H.R., *Öcalan*, 37 *Eur. Hum. Rts. Rep.* (2003), at 274-275 (para. 93); Eur. Ct. H.R., *Öcalan (GC)*, *ECHR* 2005-IV, at 164-165 (para. 91).

148 *But see* McCorquodale, 100 *ASIL Proc.* (2006), pp. 95-102, who argue in support of extraterritorial application of positive obligations where factually possible.

State, the action clearly falls within that State's jurisdiction under the human rights treaties. If the agent shoots from inside the territory at a person outside the territory, the same principles are applied almost unanimously, as the action takes place inside the territory and only the effect takes place outside. Lastly, if the State agent himself leaves the territory of his national State and shoots the targeted person who is outside the territory also from outside the territory, he still exercises power and authority over that person – in the same manner as in the two other cases. He thus still exercises jurisdiction over that person, even though this exercise can collide with the territorial jurisdiction of the State in the territory in which the action takes place. This collision of substantive jurisdiction, however, does not exclude the sending state from being responsible for the conduct. The conduct remains within what *Orakhelashvili* refers to as remedial jurisdiction,[149] i.e. the jurisdiction in the meaning of the human rights treaties. This notion of jurisdiction "signifies the ability to rule, to exercise the powers of government vis-à-vis individuals who are affected by these powers."[150]

In consequence, this means that any targeted killing by state agents falls within the jurisdiction under the treaties of the acting State and thus is subject to the standards of the right to life as developed above.[151] It does not mean that all rights apply fully in all situations, as derogations are possible. However, the right to life is non-derogable, and "[s]uch fundamental principles as the prohibition of the arbitrary taking of life ... must always be protected."[152] Thus, any targeted killing by a state agents is subject to the human rights regime the nation state of that state agent is member to. Hence, one can conclude with *Kretzmer*: "A state's duty to respect the right to life (as opposed to its duty to ensure that right) follows its agents, wherever they operate."[153] Any narrower reading of the term jurisdiction in the human rights treaties would exclude certain individuals from protection, but not from power.[154]

---

149 Orakhelashvili, 14 *Eur. J. Int'l L.* (2003), at 540-541.

150 Ben-Naftali, 100 *ASIL Proc.* (2006), at 92.

151 *See also* Schmahl, in: Tomuschat *et al.* (eds.), at 243-244.

152 Meron, 89 *Am. J. Int'l L.* (1995), at 80.

153 Kretzmer, 16 *Eur. J. Int'l L.* (2005), at 185.

154 Ben-Naftali, 100 *ASIL Proc.* (2006), at 92.

B. The Law Applicable in Times of a Public Emergency Falling Short of Being an Armed Conflict

The general principle that human rights apply "always and everywhere" is relativised in situations of public emergency. In such situations, a certain derogation from some human rights is possible. Thus, human rights generally apply even in times of public emergency, but not to their full extent. On the other hand, as long as such public emergencies fall short of being an armed conflict – a non-international armed conflict being the more likely but not exclusive possibility – international humanitarian law is not applicable at all.[155]

I. Human Rights and Public Emergencies

Apart form the African Charter on Human and Peoples' Rights, all human rights treaties shown above contain explicit emergency clauses. These clauses enable States in situations of public emergency the derogate from some – but not from all rights laid down in theses conventions. The International Covenant on Civil and Political Rights contains a derogation clause in its Article 4. Its paras. 1 and 2 read:

> (1) In time of public emergency which threatens the life of the nation and the existence of which is officially proclaimed, the State Parties to the present Covenant may take measures derogating from their obligations under the present Covenant to the extent strictly required by the exigencies of the situation, provided that such measures are not inconsistent with their other obligations under international law and do not involve discrimination solely on the ground of race, colour, sex, language, religion or social origin. (2) No derogation from articles 6, 7, 8 (paragraphs 1 and 2), 11, 15, 16 and 18 may be made under this provision.

The derogation clause does not – unlike those of the European and American Conventions – refer to "war". This is not due to an oversight, but the consequence of the UN General Assembly adopting the Covenant. The General Assembly wanted to avoid the expression in order to avoid any – although indirect – reason for considering war as legitimate

[155] *Compare e.g.* UK Ministry of Defence, *Manual*, para. 1.33.3 (p. 16).

under international law.[156] Nevertheless, it is clear that an armed conflict is a situation that falls within the expression "public emergency that threatens the life of the nation".[157] The fact that "war" is included in "public emergency which threatens the life of the nation" was also reaffirmed by the International Court of Justice in its *Wall* advisory opinion.[158]

The definition of the term "public emergency",[159] although difficult, can remain open concerning the present examination. According to para. 2 of the Covenant, no derogation from Article 6 – protecting the right to life – is permissible. This corresponds to the fact that the right to life is first regarded as being *jus cogens* and thus a peremptory norm that cannot be derogated from.[160] Second, that the right to life, as laid down in the Covenant, also includes itself possible exceptions. These exceptions have been discussed thoroughly *supra*. They apply identically, in times of "peace" and in times of "public emergency".

---

[156] Christina M. Cerna, 'Human Rights in Armed Conflict: Implementation of International Humanitarian Law Norms by Regional Intergovernmental Human Rights Bodies', in: Frits Kalshoven; Yves Sandoz (eds.), *Implementation of International Humanitarian Law*, Dordrecht 1989, pp. 31-67, at 46.

[157] *Compare* Pocar, in: Vohrah *et al.* (eds.), at 729-730.

[158] ICJ, *Legality of the Threat or Use of Nuclear Weapons*, Advisory Opinion of July 8, 1996, I.C.J. Reports 1996, pp. 225-593, at 240 (para. 25).

[159] *See e.g.* H.R. Committee, CCPR General Comment No. 5, *Derogations (Article 4)*, 13th Sess., July 28, 1981, reprinted in: Compilation of General Comments and General Recommendations adopted by Human Rights Treaty Bodies, U.N. Doc. HRI/GEN/1/Rev.7 (May 12, 2004), pp. 127-128; H.R. Committee, CCPR General Comment No. 29, at 185 (para. 3); Subrata Roy Chowdhury, *Rule of Law in a State of Emergency*, London 1989, pp. 11-88; Jost Delbrück, 'Safeguarding Internationally Protected Human Rights in National Emergencies: New Challenges in View of Global Terrorism', in: Jürgen Bröhmer; Christine Langenfeld; Roland Bieber; Stefan Weber; Christian Calliess; Joachim Wolf (eds.), *Internationale Gemeinschaft und Menschenrechte: Festschrift für Georg Ress zum 70. Geburtstag am 21. Januar 2005*, Köln 2005, pp. 47-54, at 39-40; Stefanie Schmahl, 'Derogation von Menschenrechtsverpflichtungen in Notstandslagen', in: Dieter Fleck (ed.), *Rechtsfragen der Terrorismusbekämpfung durch Streitkräfte*, Baden-Baden 2004, pp. 125-146, at 126-131.

[160] ICJ, *Legality of the Threat or Use of Nuclear Weapons*, Advisory Opinion of July 8, 1996; I.C.J. Reports 1996, pp. 225-593, at 240 (para. 25).

The same principle applies to the European Convention on Human Rights. Article 15 paras. 1 and 2 of the Convention read:

> (1) In time of war or other public emergency threatening the life of the nation any High Contracting Party may take measures derogating from its obligations under this Convention to the extent strictly required by the exigencies of the situation, provided that such measures are not inconsistent with its other obligations under international law. (2) No derogation from Article 2, except in respect of deaths resulting from lawful acts of war, or from Articles 3, 4 (paragraph 1) and 7 shall be made under this provision.[161]

The Convention thus refers explicitly to war, but identically to the International Covenant excepts the right to life (Article 2) from the derogation clause. In opposition to the Covenant, the European Convention expressly refers to "lawful acts of war" as an exception from the prohibition to deprive life.

The system of the American Convention on Human Rights is again the same. Article 27 paras. 1 and 2 of the American Convention read:

> (1) In time of war, public danger, or other emergency that threatens the independence or security of a State Party, it may take measures derogating from its obligations under the present Convention to the extent and for the period of time strictly required by the exigencies of the situation, provided that such measures are not inconsistent with its other obligations under international law and do not involve discrimination on the ground of race, color, sex, language, religion, or social origin. (2) The foregoing provision does not authorize any suspension of the following Articles: Article 3 (Right to Judicial Personality, Article 4 (Right to Life), Article 5 (Right to Humane Treatment), Article 6 (Freedom from Slavery), Article 9 (Freedom from Ex Post Facto Laws), Article 12 (Freedom of Conscience and Religion), Article 17 (Rights of the Family), Article 18 (Right to a Name), Article 19 (Rights of the Child), Article 20 (right to Nation-

---

[161] On the drafting history of the article *compare* Cerna, in: Kalshoven/ Sandoz (eds.), at 46-47. *Compare also* Daphna Shraga, 'Human Rights in Emergency Situations under the European Convention on Human Rights', in: 16 *Isr. Yb. Hum. Rts.* (1986), pp. 217-242.

> ality), and Article 23 (Right to Participate in Government) or of the judicial guarantees essential for the protection of such rights.[162]

The African Charter on Human and Peoples' Rights – as the only regional human rights treaty – does not regulate states of emergency nor does it contain an explicit derogation clause.[163] The absence of a derogation clause is most likely due to different opinions on such a clause during the drafting process. It was certainly part of the thinking during the drafting conferences, but ultimately not included into the Charter.[164] Nevertheless, Zimbabwe for example declared a state of emergency in 1987 and took measures derogating from Article 7, i.e. the right to be tried without undue delay.[165] The topic of derogation was also addressed by the African Commission on Human and Peoples' Rights, but it came to a different conclusion:

> The African Charter, unlike other human rights instruments, does not allow for states parties to derogate from their treaty obligations during emergency situations. Thus, even a civil war in Chad cannot be used as an excuse by the State violating or permitting violations of rights in the African Charter.[166]

This position has been criticised as "too rigid" and impossible to accept for States in practice.[167] It has further been criticised on the basis that "derogation from human rights is a regular occurrence" in Africa,[168] and that African States are at least as likely as any other State to face se-

---

[162] For a short overview on the application of the derogation clause in the Inter-American System *see* Cerna, in: Kalshoven/ Sandoz (eds.), at 49-51.

[163] *Compare* Oraá, *States of Emergency*, p. 210; Anna-Lena Svensson-MacCarthy, *The International Law of Human Rights and States of Exception: With Special Reference to the "travaux préparatoires" and the Case-Law of the International Monitoring Organs*, The Hague 1998, p. 4.

[164] Oraá, *States of Emergency*, p. 210; Wessels, 27 *S. Afr. Yb. Int'l L.* (2002), at 131-132.

[165] Oraá, *States of Emergency*, p. 210.

[166] Afr. Comm'n H.P.R., *Commission Nationale des Droits de l'Homme et des Libertés de la Federation Nationale des Unions de Jeunes Avocats de France v. Chad*, Communication 74/92 (1995), in: 9th *Activity Report* (1995-1996), Annex VIII, at para. 21.

[167] Oraá, *States of Emergency*, pp. 209-210.

[168] Wessels, 27 *S. Afr. Yb. Int'l L.* (2002), at 135; *compare also* Bello, 194 *RdC* (1985-V), at 71-72.

rious crises situations.[169] Albeit the protection regime of the African Charter thus seems to be absolute, many of the substantial rights of the Charter contain "clawback" clauses, which restrict the rights in a very broad sense.[170] Concerning the right to life, however, the system of the African Charter has the same effect as the other treaties referred to above. It has been observed – referring to the right to life – that "there is no mention of this as a non-derogable right".[171] This is true, but such an explicit acknowledgment the non-derogability is not necessary in connection with the African Charter. The Charter, like the other treaties,

> contains a relativist limitation on the right to life while affirming that 'no one may be arbitrarily deprived of this right.' Using these standards, nonderogability means that even in times of war or other public emergency, persons cannot be arbitrarily killed.[172]

The African Commission has acknowledged this fact in connection with the right to life when it found that Chad – albeit relying on a state of civil war – had violated that right.[173]

The conclusion is thus – as indicated *supra* – in relation to all human rights treaties, the right to life is not derogable in times of public emergency and the same standards apply as in times of "peace". The only difference to times of peace is the following: According to all the treaties, killings which are lawful under international humanitarian law are accepted exceptions from the right to life. Thus, in situations in which international humanitarian law is applicable, the standards that have been developed above apply additionally to the human rights standards.[174] This does not only hold true for the treaty protection of the right to life, but also for the customary international law protection of

---

[169] Svensson-MacCarthy, *States of Exception*, p. 198.

[170] Ankumah, *African Commission*, p. 8 and pp. 176-177; Bello, 194 *RdC* (1985-V), at 70; Svensson-MacCarthy, *States of Exception*, p. 198.

[171] Ramcharan, 30 *Nether. Int'l L. Rev.* (1983), at 319.

[172] Paust, 65 *Sask. L. Rev.* (2002), at 415-416 (footnotes omitted).

[173] Afr. Comm'n H.P.R., *Commission Nationale des Droits de l'Homme et des Libertés de la Federation Nationale des Unions de Jeunes Avocats de France v. Chad*, Communication 74/92 (1995), in: 9th *Activity Report* (1995-1996), Annex VIII, at paras. 23-26.

[174] *See supra*, Part Two.

that right. Because of the character of the right to life as a *jus cogens*, "when the right to life is applicable, no derogation is permitted merely on the basis of a general claim that a public emergency creates a need to violate the right to life."[175]

II. International Humanitarian Law and Public Emergency

The internal use of force against criminal and terrorist activity is not regulated by the law of armed conflict, unless the activity is of such a nature that it amounts to an armed conflict.[176] As shown above, human rights law applies to "peacetime". This does not necessarily mean peace and tranquillity, but at least an absence of serious violence which severely disrupts normal law and order within a State.[177] Internal disturbances and tensions, disorganized and short-lived internal hostilities such as 'isolated and sporadic acts of violence', although conflicts of a kind, are regarded by Article 1 para. 2 of the 1977 Additional Protocol II as being "not armed conflicts" and thus beyond the ambit of the Protocol and common Article 3 of the 1949 Geneva Conventions. Such disturbances are clearly not governed by international humanitarian law.[178]

Thus, even though the term "public emergency" as used in the human rights treaties includes situations of "war", not every public emergency reaches the level of violence which is the precondition for international

---

[175] Paust, 65 *Sask. L. Rev.* (2002), at 413; *compare also* Gormley, in: Ramcharan (ed.), at 135-140; Kremnitzer, in: Fleck (ed.), *Rechtsfragen*, at 201; H.R. Committee, CCPR General Comment No. 24, at 163 (para. 10).

[176] *See e.g.* UK Ministry of Defence, *Manual*, para. 1.33.3 (p. 16); Stein, in: Delissen/ Tanja (eds.), at 573; *see also* Gasser, 45 *German Yb. Int'l L.* (2002), at 150, who generally regards terrorism as outside the scope of application of international humanitarian law. *Compare also* Roberta Arnold, 'Human Rights in Times of Terrorism', in: 66 *ZaöRV* (2006), pp. 297-319. The question of whether certain acts of "terrorism" demand for the application of international humanitarian law will be examined *infra*, Part Four, Chapter F) II.

[177] Gasser, 45 *German Yb. Int'l L.* (2002), at 157.

[178] Faïza Patel King; Olivia Swaak-Goldman, 'The Applicability of International Humanitarian Law to the "War Against Terrorism"', in: 15 *Hague Yb. Int'l L.* (2003), pp. 39-49, at 48; Moir, *Internal Armed Conflict*, p. 101.

humanitarian law being applicable. The only – albeit indirect – application of international humanitarian law in such a situation is the following: Common Article 3 of the 1949 Geneva Conventions, it is argued, serves as a minimum protection standard in a situation of public emergency. The derogation of human rights in such a situation should not go as far as providing a lower protection than that laid down as a minimum for non-international armed conflicts. Since the crucial human right for the question of targeted killings is the non-derogable right to life, this possible influence of Common Article 3 is of no relevance for the present question.

As will be seen *infra*, it is not easy to find the exact boundary between situations of emergency and armed conflict. It has thus been argued that especially "permanent emergencies ... are the place where both currents of law meet", i.e. human rights and international humanitarian law.[179] However, it is submitted here that this is a question which exclusively depends on the definition of non-international armed conflict.

C. The Law Applicable in Non-International Armed Conflicts

> It is now generally recognized, even by the most sceptical, that international human rights law continues to apply during all armed conflicts alongside international humanitarian law (IHL).[180]

This has not always been the case. In earlier decades – until the 1970s – human rights law was considered as being not applicable in situations of armed conflict.[181] It was regarded as being mutually exclusive from international humanitarian law, as both concepts are based on completely different historical roots. International humanitarian law bestows rights not only on human beings as such, but chiefly on states. It was designed to apply in armed conflicts, i.e. in an extraordinary situation – and for the protection of the respective interests of the (State)

---

[179] Ní Aoláin, 28 *Isr. Yb. Hum. Rts.* (1998), at 97.

[180] Doswald-Beck, 88 *Int'l Rev. Red Cross* (2006), No. 864, at 881; *see also* Henckaerts/ Doswald-Beck (eds.), *Humanitarian Law*, Vol. 1, pp. 299-300.

[181] Yoram Dinstein, 'The International Law of Inter-State Wars and Human Rights', in: 7 *Isr. Yb. Hum. Rts.* (1977), pp. 139-153, at 148.

parties. The adjective 'humanitarian' rather describes the contents of the norms and not the subject bound by them. Human rights law deals with limitations on regular governmental activities *vis-à-vis* the individual in "normal" situations. It confers rights directly on individuals under international law.[182] Today, beside human rights law, international humanitarian law is applicable whenever a situation of violence reaches the level of an armed conflict.[183] This is the case when there is a resort to armed force between states, protracted armed violence between governmental authorities and organized armed groups, or such violence between armed groups within the state.[184]

The situation that is most similar to a "public emergency" is that of an non-international armed conflict. Since 1945, the vast majority of armed conflicts have been internal rather than international in character.[185] There are different situations in which force is used in an internal conflict. Not all of them amount to an armed conflict, and not all of them are regarded as an internal armed conflict. These different situations are internal disturbances, "normal" internal armed conflicts and "special" internal armed conflicts referred to in Article 1 para. 4 of the 1977 Additional Protocol I, which are treated as international armed conflicts.[186]

---

[182] Dinstein, in: Meron (ed.), at 347 and 365; Heike Krieger, 'A Conflict of Norms: The Relationship Between Humanitarian Law and Human Rights Law in the ICRC Customary Law Study', in: 11 *J. Confl. Sec. L.* (2006), pp. 265-291, at 266.

[183] ICRC, *International Humanitarian Law and the Challenges of Contemporary Armed Conflicts,* Report, September 2003, p. 8.

[184] *See e.g.* ICTY, *Prosecutor v. Duško Tadić*, Case No. IT-94-1-AR72, Decision on the Defence Motion for Interlocutory Appeal on Jurisdiction of October 2, 1995, reprinted in: 105 *Int'l L.R.* (1997), pp. 419-648, at 488-489 (para. 70).

[185] Moir, *Internal Armed Conflict*, p. 1.

[186] As will be seen below, the "normal" non-international armed conflicts may additionally be divided in those which exclusively fall under Common Article 3 to the 1949 Geneva Conventions and those which meet the higher threshold of the 1977 Additional Protocol II. *See also* UK Ministry of Defence, *Manual*, para. 3.9 (p. 33). However, this distinction has no consequences for the present examination.

I. Internal Disturbances

Internal disturbances and tensions, such as riots, isolated and sporadic acts of violence or other acts of a similar nature do not amount to non-international armed conflicts. They belong to the situations described above as "public emergencies". In consequence, human rights law applies to them – possibly including derogations thereof – and international humanitarian law does not apply at all to these situations.[187] The decision to exclude these situations from the scope of international humanitarian law was based on the assumption that they were covered by human rights.[188]

In most human rights treaties, the question concerning the threshold between a "peaceful situation" with full human rights protection and a "public emergency" entailing the possibility of derogating from certain rights is one to be answered according to the standards laid down in the individual treaties themselves. However, concerning the right to life, this threshold is not relevant, as this right is non-derogable. Typically, internal disturbances and tensions are

> situations in which there is no non-international armed conflict as such, but there exists a confrontation within a country, which is characterized by a certain seriousness or duration and which involves acts of violence. ... In these situations, which do not necessarily degenerate into open struggle, the authorities in power call upon extensive police forces, or even armed forces, to restore internal order.[189]

Internal disturbances thus may include any, or all, of the following characteristics: mass arrests; a large number of persons detained for security reasons; administrative detention, especially for long periods; probable ill-treatment, torture or material or psychological conditions of detention likely to be seriously prejudicial to the physical, mental or moral integrity of detainees; maintaining detainees incommunicado for

---

187 *See supra*, Part Four, Chapter B); *see also* Sandoz *et al.* (eds.), *Protocoles additionnels*, para. 4378 (p. 1352); UK Ministry of Defence, *Manual*, para. 3.5.1 (p. 31) with further examples (footnote 16).

188 Sandoz *et al.* (eds.), *Protocoles additionnels*, para. 4378 (p. 1352).

189 International Committee of the Red Cross, 'Protection and Assistance Activities in Situations not Covered by International Humanitarian Law', in: 70 *Int'l Rev. Red Cross* (1988), No. 262, pp. 9-37, at 13.

long periods; repressive measures taken against family members of persons having a close relationship with those deprived of their liberty mentioned above; the suspension of fundamental judicial guarantees, either by the proclamation of a state of emergency or by a de facto situation; large-scale measures restricting personal freedom such as relegation, exile, assigned residence, displacements; allegations of forced disappearances; increase in the number of acts of violence (such as sequestration and hostage-taking) which endanger defenceless persons or spread terror among the civilian population.[190]

The opposite delimitation of internal disturbances is that towards a situation of armed conflict. This threshold is not part of the concept of public emergency, as this notion also refers to "war" at least concerning the International Covenant on Civil and Political Rights.[191] This delimitation is dependent on the definition of an armed conflict. As soon as this definition is met, the application of human rights is not exclusive any more, as the threshold for the additional application of international humanitarian law is reached.[192] However,

> [t]he line separating an especially violent situation of internal disturbances from the 'lowest' level ... armed conflict may sometimes be blurred and, thus, not easily determined. When faced with making such a determination, what is required in the final analysis is a good faith and objective analysis of the facts in each particular case.[193]

II. Non-International Armed Conflicts

Non-international armed conflicts are armed confrontations between a State authority and an armed group or between two or more organized

---

[190] *Id.*

[191] The other two conventions containing a derogation clause explicitly refer to "war" beside "public emergencies".

[192] *See e.g.* Peter H. Kooijmans, 'In the Shadowland between Civil War and Civil Strife: Some Reflections on the Standard-Setting Process', in: Astrid J.M. Delissen; Gerard J. Tanja (eds.), *Humanitarian Law of Armed Conflict: Challenges ahead – Essays in Honour of Frits Kalshoven*, Dordrecht 1991, pp. 225-247, at 241.

[193] Inter-Am. Comm'n H.R., *Juan Carlos Abella ("La Tablada"), Annual Report* (1997), at para. 153.

armed groups, within the territory of a state. They involve significant, intense or sustained use of armed force beyond the level of internal disturbances.[194] The relation of human rights and international humanitarian law is more complex when it comes to non-international armed conflicts as opposed to international armed conflicts.[195] While the rules of international humanitarian law always apply to situations in which force is used between states, violence involving non-State actors is primarily regarded as a matter governed by domestic law, subject to the standards of international human rights.

1. Human Rights in Non-International Armed Conflicts

The internal use of force against criminal and terrorist activity is not regulated by the law of armed conflict, unless the activity is of such a nature that it amounts to an armed conflict. Nevertheless, human rights law applies.[196] The fact that the human rights conventions contain derogation clauses for cases of war or public emergency threatening the life of the nation makes it clear that they generally apply to such situations.[197] Some authors have argued that only the non-derogable rights of the human rights conventions applied in case of an armed conflict.[198] However, derogations must be declared and are not an automatic effect of a certain level of violence. Furthermore, limited military activities do not necessarily fulfil the preconditions of derogations. Thus, for exam-

---

[194] International Institute of Humanitarian Law, *San Remo Manual*, para. 1.1.1.

[195] *Cf.* Gasser, 45 *German Yb. Int'l L.* (2002), pp. 149-162; Kretzmer, 16 *Eur. J. Int'l L.* (2005), at 186.

[196] UK Ministry of Defence, *Manual*, para. 1.33.3 (p. 16).

[197] Schindler, in: Häfelin *et al.* (eds.), at 332; *compare also* Jochen Abraham Frowein, 'The Relationship between Human Rights Regimes and Regimes of Belligerent Occupation', in: 28 *Isr. Yb. Hum. Rts.* (1998), pp. 1-16, at 2-3.

[198] *See e.g.* Morris Greenspan, 'The Protection of Human Rights in Time of Warfare', in: 1 *Isr. Yb. Hum. Rts.* (1971), pp. 228-245, at 229-230; *compare also* Athur Henry Robertson, 'Human Rights as the Basis of International Humanitarian Law', in: Etienne Boéri *et al.* (eds.), *I Diritto dell'Uomo come base del Diritto Internazionale Umanitario: Atti del Convegno Internatzionale die Diritto Umanitario, Sanremo – 24/27.IX.1970*, Lugano-Bellinzona 1970, pp. 55-76, at 66-69.

ple, the military activities of Turkey on Cyprus in 1974 are not regarded to represent a "public emergency threatening the life of the nation" in the meaning of Article 15 of the Convention.[199]

In consequence, the human rights rules concerning targeted killings, namely the right to life and its possible exceptions, also apply in non-international armed conflicts. However, these exceptions include – as shown above – killings which are legal under international humanitarian law. Thus, the question concerning the application of the latter set of rules is decisive for the scope of possible exceptions.

2. *International Humanitarian Law in Non-International Armed Conflicts*

Cerna has argued that the level of violence which justifies a derogation under the human rights treaty regimes is equivalent to the threshold required to trigger the applicability of international humanitarian law.[200] This may – if at all – exclusively be true concerning the level of violence, but the application of international humanitarian law does not exclusively depend on that level. It has further preconditions.

The two decisive rules concerning the scope of the additional application of the humanitarian law rules in such situations are Common Article 3 of the 1949 Geneva Conventions and Article 1 of the 1977 Additional Protocol II. Article 3, however, the "mini-convention"[201] for non-international armed conflicts, does not address the definition of such a conflict. It reads in part:

> In the case of armed conflict not of an international character occurring in the territory of one of the High Contracting Parties, each Party to the conflict shall be bound to apply, as a minimum, the following provisions: (1) Persons taking no active part in the hostilities, ... shall in all circumstances be treated humanely, ... To this end, the following acts are and shall remain prohibited ... (a) violence to life and person ... (d) the passing of sentences and the carrying out of executions without previous judgment ... .

---

199 Schindler, in: Häfelin *et al.* (eds.), at 335.

200 Cerna, in: Kalshoven/ Sandoz (eds.), at 56.

201 *Compare e.g.* Kooijmans, in: Delissen/ Tanja (eds.), at 227.

The Article thus contains in part the rules concerning the protection of life which has already been shown above and makes clear that these minimum standards as well as the international humanitarian law rules shown above apply.[202] However, the Article only vaguely defines non-international armed conflicts.[203] The lower threshold seems to be the mutual use of armed force, but no indication is given as to the intensity of this force which is necessary to make the provision applicable.[204]

The second important rule – containing more information for the question at hand – is Article 1 of the 1977 Additional Protocol II. It describes the scope of application of the Protocol with the following words:

> This Protocol, which develops and supplements Article 3 common to the Geneva Conventions of 12 August 1949 without modifying its existing conditions of application, shall apply to all armed conflicts which are not covered by Article 1 of the Protocol Additional to the Geneva Conventions of 12 August 1949, and relating to the Protection of Victims of International Armed Conflicts (Protocol I) and which take place in the territory of a High Contracting Party between its armed forces and dissident armed forces or other organized armed groups which, under responsible command, exercise such control over a part of its territory as to enable them to carry out sustained and concerted military operations and to implement this Protocol. This Protocol shall not apply to situations of internal disturbances and tensions, such as riots, isolated and sporadic acts of violence and other acts of a similar nature, as not being armed conflicts.

Thus, Article 1 is more precise but also considerably more restrictive in defining non-international armed conflicts. As Common Article 3, Article 1 refers to armed conflicts not of an international character (i.e. not covered by Article 1 of the 1977 Additional Protocol I). Insofar it is identical with Common Article 3. But it reduces the scope to conflicts between the armed forces of a State and dissident armed forces or other organized groups, to the effect that conflicts between two such non-state groups are not covered by the 1977 Additional Protocol II. Furthermore, those groups have to be under responsible command – a pre-

---

[202] *See supra*, Part Two, Chapter D).

[203] *Compare* Abi-Saab, in: Delissen/ Tanja (eds.), at 215-216.

[204] Kooijmans, in: Delissen/ Tanja (eds.), at 227.

condition of combat status, as shown above – and must exercise control over part of the State's territory. The last condition is indeed very restrictive especially if one takes guerrilla tactics into account, which *per se* are not based on the establishment and defence of a certain territory but rather strikes at different places in different times. Such tactics alone would thus not be sufficient to open the scope of application of the 1977 Additional Protocol II. The last words of para. 2 of Article 1 were even added in order to impose a restrictive interpretation of the scope of application of Common Article 3.[205] This, however, is excluded due to Article 1 itself, as it applies "without modifying its (Article 3) existing conditions of application".

It can thus be concluded that although Protocol II has expanded and improved the content of protection applicable in non-international armed conflicts, the scope of application of the 1977 Additional Protocol II – as laid down in its Article 1 – is too restrictive.[206] Beyond the Protocol – and the rules relevant to the topic of targeted killings are not exclusively based on the Protocol but at large represent customary international law – the notion of internal armed conflict is wider. Thus, it is the threshold of Article 3 that has to be met to apply those rules which exist beside the 1977 Additional Protocol II. This concerns four criteria: the territorial scope of application, the temporal scope of application, the parties to the conflict, and the intensity of hostilities.[207]

First, according to Common Article 3, the conflict takes place "in the territory" of a State party to the 1949 Geneva Conventions. According to the International Criminal Tribunal for the Former Yugoslavia, this concerns "the whole territory under the control of a party, whether or not actual combat takes place there".[208] International humanitarian law thus applies "outside the narrow theatre of combat operations".[209] This is in line with international humanitarian law as a whole, e.g. concerning the protection of prisoners of war and civilians. This does at the same time mean that international humanitarian law also applies in non-

[205] Abi-Saab, in: Delissen/ Tanja (eds.), at 216-217 with further references.

[206] Meron, *Internal Strife*, at 45-46.

[207] Tahzib-Lie/ Swaak-Goldman, in: Lijnzaad *et al.* (eds.), at 244.

[208] ICTY, *Prosecutor v. Duško Tadić*, Case No. IT-94-1-AR72, Decision on the Defence Motion for Interlocutory Appeal on Jurisdiction of October 2, 1995, reprinted in: 105 *Int'l L.R.* (1997), pp. 419-648, at 488-489 (para. 70).

[209] *Id.*, (para. 69).

international armed conflicts where non-state entities operate across State lines.[210] It is not necessary that the parties to the conflict in fact control any part of the territory the conflict takes place on. Thus, also if a rebel group chooses not to attach themselves to a particular territory as a means of tactical advantage, the conflict can still amount to an armed conflict.[211]

Second, concerning the temporal scope of application, the ICTY has stated in *Tadić* that "protracted" hostilities are necessary to establish a non-international armed conflict.[212] However, the Inter-American Commission on Human Rights in *La Tablada* regarded the situation in question "despite its brief duration" as triggering the application of the provisions of Common Article 3, as well as other rules relevant to the conduct of internal armed conflicts.[213] This view is shared by the International Committee of the Red Cross and several scholars.[214] Once applicable, the international humanitarian law rules then apply until a peaceful settlement of the conflict is reached.[215]

Third, the parties to the conflict are not primarily State parties but also – or even exclusively – non-state entities. These non-state entities must

---

[210] Tahzib-Lie/ Swaak-Goldman, in: Lijnzaad *et al.* (eds.), at 245; *compare also* Articles 1 and 7 of the ICTR Statute, referring inter alia to "Rwandan citizens responsible for such violations committed in the territory of neighbouring States" and "The territorial jurisdiction of the International Tribunal for Rwanda shall extend to the territory of Rwanda including its land surface and airspace as well as to the territory of neighbouring States in respect of serious violations of international humanitarian law committed by Rwandan citizens." *See* UN SC Res. 955 (November 8, 1994, *Establishing the International Tribunal for Rwanda, with Annexed Statute*), U.N. Doc. S/RES/955 (1994).

[211] Tahzib-Lie/ Swaak-Goldman, in: Lijnzaad *et al.* (eds.), at 246 with further references.

[212] ICTY, *Prosecutor v. Duško Tadić*, Case No. IT-94-1-AR72, Decision on the Defence Motion for Interlocutory Appeal on Jurisdiction of October 2, 1995, reprinted in: 105 *Int'l L.R.* (1997), pp. 419-648, at 488-489 (para. 70).

[213] Inter-Am. Comm'n H.R., *Juan Carlos Abella ("La Tablada"), Annual Report* (1997), at para. 156.

[214] Tahzib-Lie/ Swaak-Goldman, in: Lijnzaad *et al.* (eds.), at 247-248 with further references.

[215] ICTY, *Prosecutor v. Duško Tadić*, Case No. IT-94-1-AR72, Decision on the Defence Motion for Interlocutory Appeal on Jurisdiction of October 2, 1995, reprinted in: 105 *Int'l L.R.* (1997), pp. 419-648, at 488-489 (para. 70).

possess a certain degree of military organization.[216] Indications – but not necessary preconditions – for such an "organized armed groups" are: an organized military force under responsible command; possession of a part of the territory of the State and exercise of *de facto* authority over persons within this part of the territory; the group purports to have the characteristics of a state and agrees to be bound by international humanitarian law; recourse to regular military forces of the State is necessary to confront the group; the Government of the State in question either recognises it as belligerents or it claims itself the right of a belligerent.[217] The actions of such groups can be distinguished from "mere acts of banditry or unorganised ... insurrections"[218] and resemble that of "military units or, in case of war or civil strife, armed bands or irregulars or rebels".[219] Then, the obligations under international humanitarian law also bind the non-State party.[220]

Fourth, a certain intensity of the hostilities is required to qualify a situation as a non-international armed conflict.[221] This "magnitude" is regarded as more important than the question of "protracted violence".[222] It entails the presence of military operations on the part of both

---

216 ICTY, *Prosecutor v. Duško Tadić*, Case No. IT-94-1-A, Judgment of May 7, 1997, reprinted in: 112 *Int'l L.R.* (1999), pp. 1-285, at 179 (para. 562); Inter-Am. Comm'n H.R., *Juan Carlos Abella ("La Tablada")*, *Annual Report* (1997), at para. 152; Moir, *Internal Armed Conflict*, p. 36.

217 Jean S. Pictet (ed.), *The Geneva Conventions of 12 August 1949: Commentary, Vol. 1, Geneva Convention for the Amelioration of the Condition of the Wounded and Sick in Armed Forces in the Field*, Geneva 1952, pp. 49-50. *See also supra*, Part Two, Chapter C) II.

218 ICTR, *Prosecutor v. Jean-Paul Akayesu*, Case No. ICTR-96-4-T, Decision of September 2, 1998, para. 620.

219 ICTY, *Prosecutor v. Duško Tadić*, Case No. IT-94-1-A, Judgment (Merits Appeal) of July 15, 1999, reprinted in: 124 *Int'l L.R.* (2003), pp. 63-212, at 109 (para. 120).

220 *Compare* Tahzib-Lie/ Swaak-Goldman, in: Lijnzaad *et al.* (eds.), at 252.

221 *See e.g.* ICTR, *Prosecutor v. Jean-Paul Akayesu*, Case No ICTR-96-4-T, Decision of September 2, 1998, para. 625.

222 *Compare e.g.* Inter-Am. Comm'n H.R., *Juan Carlos Abella ("La Tablada")*, *Annual Report* (1997), at paras. 154-156.

sides.[223] Traditionally, three different levels of internal conflicts were characterised: rebellion, insurgency and belligerency. The lowest level, that of a rebellion, was understood as a modest, sporadic challenge of the state authority and would be an internal disturbance rather than an armed conflict. The second level which is referred to as insurgency refers to a more substantial attack against the order of the State. The insurgents are sufficiently organised to mount a credible threat to the government. Such a situation would thus qualify as an armed conflict. The same is true for the third situation which equals the second, but in which the State party to the conflict recognises the insurgents as belligerents and thus accepts explicitly that the threshold to an armed conflict has been crossed.[224]

It has been argued that those acts which would constituted "grave breaches of international humanitarian law" if judged by that standard would amount to an armed conflict.[225] This criterion tells little about intensity though, as the concept of grave breaches covers severe acts directed against protected persons and can thus be met by an act against a single person.[226] Furthermore, it has been submitted that cases where an organized group systematically carries out planned and coordinated attacks against civilians which cause serious harm amount to an armed conflict.[227] Again, beside the criterion of "serious harm" such a definition does not characterize the level of violence. It would certainly apply to the "troubles" in Northern Ireland as well as the violent activities of the Basque group *Euskadi Ta Askatasuna* (ETA), neither of which have been regarded as armed conflicts. It seems rather to refer to the general phenomenon of "terrorism" than to an armed conflict.

---

[223] René Provost, *International Human Rights and Humanitarian Law*, Cambridge 2002, p. 266. This does not mean that the use of police forces by the State does *per se* preclude the application of international humanitarian law, *compare* Moir, *Internal Armed Conflict*, p. 39.

[224] *Compare* Moir, *Internal Armed Conflict*, pp. 4-5.

[225] Gross, *Struggle of Democracy*, p. 53.

[226] Examples of greave breaches are the wilful killing, mutilation, torture, or inhumane treatment of protected persons, *see* Rüdiger Wolfrum, 'Enforcement of International Humanitarian Law', in: Dieter Fleck (ed.), *The Handbook of Humanitarian Law in Armed Conflicts*, Oxford 1999, pp. 517-550, at 531 (para. 1209) with further references.

[227] Gross, *Struggle of Democracy*, p. 53.

A possible assessment of defining the threshold between disturbance and armed conflict is the following: by resorting to military means in order to quell a rebellion, the government expressly or tacitly has to admit that it is not able to protect the right to life under peacetime standards, and that its actions must be judged according to the law of armed conflict.[228] It is a core feature of the concept of "armed conflict" that the government claims for itself the right to use armed force in cases not covered by individual self-defence or defence of vital public interests against imminent attack. The government departs from a "police doctrine" of apprehension of suspected criminals, minimum use of force, and respect for the life of the criminal and other human beings alike. Instead, it resorts to a "military doctrine": Searching and attacking enemy fighters as a group, using maximum force in encounters in order to overwhelm the adversary and accepting losses among civilians as collateral damage within the limits of proportionality.[229] If this is taken into account, it becomes clear that *Cerna's* assessment to see a national emergency as the equivalent of an armed conflict cannot be right.[230] Derogations under human rights treaties are not only possible in case armed forces are engaged under a "military doctrine" but also under a "law enforcement doctrine".

Thus, as a general rule one can conclude that only hostilities that are similar to an international war, for example, armed forces being engaged on either side, can be defined as an "armed conflict" in a non-international context.[231] However, in the non-international context the threshold may be higher than in the international context. In the latter case, an isolated event can be regarded as an armed conflict. A higher standard was considered as being necessary to distinguish non-international armed conflicts from banditry, terrorist activities, unorganised short-lived insurrections, all of which should be within domestic concern of the states.[232] It corresponds to the State's desire to treat internal con-

---

228 Dahl, 43 *Rev. dr mil.* (2004), at 143.

229 *Id.*

230 *Compare supra*, Part Four, Chapter C) II. 2.

231 Jean S. Pictet (ed.), *The Geneva Conventions of 12 August 1949: Commentary, Vol. 2, Geneva Convention for the Amelioration of the Condition of Wounded, Sick and Shipwrecked Members of Armed Forces at Sea*, Geneva 1960, p. 33; *compare also* Meron, *Internal Strife*, p. 46.

232 Jean S. Pictet (ed.), *Geneva Conventions*, Vol. 1, pp. 49-50.

flicts as far as possible as a situation exclusively subject to their national jurisdiction and without any external control or the application of any external parameters.

On the other Hand, the International Committee of the Red Cross has argued for a lower threshold, assuming that the classification as an armed conflict would extend the legal protection of the persons involved in a conflict.[233] Following the idea to provide the broadest possible protection, the Inter-American Commission on Human Rights also chose a relatively low threshold concerning the applicability international humanitarian law. Regarding Common Article 3 of the 1949 Geneva Conventions, the Commission did not require the existence of large-scale and generalized hostilities or a situation comparable to a civil war in which dissident armed groups exercise control over parts of national territory. It found that Common Article 3 shall be applied as widely as possible, despite the ambiguities in its threshold of application.[234] In *La Tablada*, the Commission stated:

> What happened there was not equivalent to large scale violent demonstrations, students throwing stones at the police, bandits holding persons hostage for ransom, or the assassination of government officials for political reasons – all forms of domestic violence not qualifying as armed conflicts.
>
> What differentiates the events at the La Tablada base from these situations are the concerted nature of the hostile acts undertaken by the attackers, the direct involvement of governmental armed forces, and the nature and level of the violence attending the events in question. More particularly, the attackers involved carefully planned, coordinated and executed an armed attack, i.e., a military operation, against a quintessential military objective – a military base. The officer in charge of the La Tablada base sought, as was his duty, to repulse the attackers, and President Alfonsín, exercising his constitutional authority as Commander-in-Chief of the armed forces, ordered that military action be taken to recapture the base and subdue the attackers.
>
> The Commission concludes therefore that, despite its brief duration, the violent clash between the attackers and members of the Argen-

---

[233] *C.f.* Moir, *Internal Armed Conflict*, p. 33.

[234] Inter-Am. Comm'n H.R., *Juan Carlos Abella ("La Tablada"), Annual Report* (1997), at para. 152.

tine armed forces triggered application of the provisions of Common Article 3, as well as other rules relevant to the conduct of internal hostilities.[235]

3. The Relationship of Human Rights and Humanitarian Law in Non-International Armed Conflicts

The above quote of the Inter-American Commission on Human Rights is representative for large parts of the relationship between the two branches of law. What the Commission did, was referring to international humanitarian law as the *lex specialis* applying to the question of whether the killing of the persons attacking the military base was arbitrary, i.e. it supplemented the human rights protection by applying standards of international humanitarian law.[236] It may be doubted whether the characterisation of a situation as an armed conflict rather than a "public emergency" really raises the level of protection. It has to be taken into account that a situation of armed conflict means that combatants (international) or fighters (non-international) may be attacked even in situations where they do not pose an immediate threat as would be required under human rights law. The same holds true if the narrow interpretation of civilians who "take direct part in hostilities" proposed above is not accepted, and such civilians are made targets while not posing any immediate threat. In most situations comparable to *La Tablada* this would not make much of a difference, as the situation of an ongoing attack upon an army barrack entails the possibility of the state agents to shoot in individual self-defence. However, there may be differences. Thus, to achieve the highest possible level of protection, it is necessary to pay due regard to the first element discussed *supra*, namely the organisational requirement of the insurgents which exists parallel to the threshold of violence. Even a high level of violence does not *per se* amount to an non-international armed conflict, if this organisational requirement is not fulfilled.

---

[235] *Id.*, paras. 154-156.

[236] *Compare also* Frowein, 28 *Isr. Yb. Hum. Rts.* (1998), at 9 and 11; Henckaerts/ Doswald-Beck (eds.), *Humanitarian Law*, Vol. 1, pp. 299-300; Nowak, *CCPR Commentary*, Art. 4, para. 27 (pp. 85-86); Hans-Joachim Heintze, 'The European Court of Human Rights and the Implementation of Human Rights Standards During Armed Conflict', in: 45 *German Yb. Int'l L.* (2002), pp. 60-77, at 64.

The African Commission on Human and Peoples' Rights has also shown a similar assessment, when it stated:

> Even if Sudan is going through a civil war, civilians in areas of strife are especially vulnerable and the state must take all possible measures to ensure that they are treated in accordance with international humanitarian law.[237]

The European Court of Human Rights has been interpreted as having taken a different approach in *Isayeva*, concerning the bombing by Russian military planes of a civilian convoy on October 29, 1999 near Grozny.[238] Being reluctant to resort to international humanitarian law, the Court up to that judgment could have relied on the argument that the cases concerned did not amount to internal armed conflicts.[239] However, in *Isayeva* the situation was regarded as clearly being an internal armed conflict.[240] Nevertheless, the Court did not refer to that concept in its own argument of the situation, but stressed in the very first sentence of its assessment that no derogation from Article 2 of the European Convention is possible "in peacetime".[241] The Court apparently directly applied human rights law rather than turning to humanitarian law. According to *Abresch*, it thus did not address possible excep-

---

[237] Afr. Comm'n H.P.R., *Amnesty International, Comité Loosli Bachelard, Lawyers Committee for Human Rights, Association of Members of the Episcopal conference of East Africa v. Sudan*, Communications 48/90, 50/91, 52/91 and 89/93, in: 13th *Activity Report* (1999-2000), Annex V, pp. 124-138, at 132 (para. 50).

[238] Eur. Ct. H.R., *Isayeva, Yusupova and Bazayeva v. Russia*, Appl. Nos. 57947/00, 57948/00 and 57949/00, Judgment of February 24, 2005; *compare also* Eur. Ct. H.R., *Isayeva v. Russia*, Appl. No. 57950/00, Judgment of February 24, 2005, with the same reasoning.

[239] Examples would be the situation of Turkey and the PKK and of the UK and the IRA, *compare* Abresch, 16 *Eur. J. Int'l L.* (2005), at 755-756.

[240] *See e.g. id.*, at 754; Andreas L. Paulus, 'The Protection of Human Rights in Internal Armed Conflict in Europe – Remarks on the *Isayeva* decision of the European Court of Human Rights', in: *Uppsala Yb. East Eur. L.* (2006), pp. 61-80, at 62-63; *compare also* the submissions by the applicants and the third party submissions, Eur. Ct. H.R., *Isayeva, Yusupova and Bazayeva v. Russia*, Appl. Nos. 57947/00, 57948/00 and 57949/00, Judgment of February 24, 2005, paras. 140, 162-167.

[241] *Id.*, para. 168, leaving "room for criticism of the reasoning" of the Court here, *see* Paulus, *Uppsala Yb. East Eur. L.* (2006), at 78.

tions to the protection of the right to life provided for by international humanitarian law, but exclusively applied the exceptions which are laid down in the European Convention itself.[242] However, the Court argues that no fighters or combatants were present in the convoy which was attacked, that could have justified the use of force.[243] It further considers the question of proportionality regarding collateral damage – albeit without referring to that term – based on the assumption that there had been a legitimate target.[244] Before these considerations, the Court had stated in response to the Russian argument that the killings were justified under that provision that it

> is also prepared to accept that if the planes were attacked by illegal armed groups, that could have justified use of lethal force, thus falling within paragraph 2 of Article 2.[245]

This has been interpreted as stating that there is no rule *per se* that insurgents may be targeted with lethal force and the Court has been praised for having taken a new approach that shows great promise.[246] However, it is not that clear whether the Court really took a new approach or rather – although tacitly – applied standards of international humanitarian law in that case.[247] Taking the Court's reluctance to explicitly refer to humanitarian law standards into account, the latter interpretation seems much more likely.[248] The interpretation by *Abresch*

---

[242] Abresch, 16 *Eur. J. Int'l L.* (2005), at 767; *compare also* Krieger, 11 *J. Confl. Sec. L.* (2006), at 275. *Similarly*, Francisco Forrest Martin, 'The Unified Use of Force Rule Revisited: The Penetration of the Law of Armed Conflict by International Human Rights Law', in: 65 *Sask. L. Rev.* (2002), pp. 405-410, at 410 argues that international human rights law penetrates and fills in lacunae in the law of armed conflict via the Martens Clause, and that thus the human right to life sets the standards in targeting.

[243] Eur. Ct. H.R., *Isayeva, Yusupova and Bazayeva v. Russia*, Appl. Nos. 57947/00, 57948/00 and 57949/00, Judgment of February 24, 2005, paras. 178-180.

[244] *Id.*, paras. 181-200.

[245] *Id.*, para. 178; *compare identically* Eur. Ct. H.R., *Isayeva v. Russia*, Appl. No. 57950/00, Judgment of February 24, 2005, para. 172.

[246] Abresch, 16 *Eur. J. Int'l L.* (2005), at 767.

[247] This is the interpretation of Quénivet, 18 *HuV-I* (2005), at 221-222. *Compare also* Melzer, *Targeted Killing*, pp. 392-393.

[248] *Compare* Paulus, *Uppsala Yb. East Eur. L.* (2006), at 78.

ignores that there is indeed a distinction between civilians and fighters in non-international armed conflicts and that – at least if an admittedly high level of military organization is reached – it is difficult to argue that fighters should not at all be made the object of an attack beyond the mere reaction to them "taking direct part in hostilities".[249] If this is taken into account, and if the concept of fighter is interpreted narrowly, the differences between the two assessment are at the vanishing point. The principle of proportionality is built into the rules of international humanitarian law, e.g. as part of prohibition of excessive death, injury or suffering. This question will thus also be relevant to an inquiry into whether particular deaths are arbitrary, if recourse is taken to international humanitarian law.[250] This law should not generally be interpreted as remaining behind the basic standard established in the corresponding human rights law. On the contrary, when e.g. Protocol II in its more detailed provisions establishes a higher standard than the International Covenant, this higher standard prevails, on the basis of the fact that this rule is *lex specialis* in relation to the corresponding human rights law. On the other hand, human rights rules which have not been reproduced in humanitarian law and which provide for a higher standard of protection should be regarded as applicable. It is a general rule for the application of concurrent instruments of human rights and humanitarian law that they implement and complement each other instead of forming a basis for limitations.[251]

4. Conclusion

These considerations have the following consequences for the question of targeted killings in non-international armed conflicts: First, civilians may only be targeted according to the narrow exceptions provided for by the human right to life. One of those exceptions is that of international humanitarian law concerning the direct participation in hostilities. Second, fighters in non-international armed conflicts – as a very narrowly defined category – may also be targeted beyond their direct participation. However, the difficulties of distinguishing them from civilians and the need to limit targeting to clearly identifiable persons

---

249 *Compare supra*, Part Two, Chapter C) II.

250 Paust, 65 *Sask. L. Rev.* (2002), at 416.

251 Bothe *et al.*, *1977 Protocols*, Introduction Prot. II (p. 636).

demands a very restrictive interpretation of that concept. It has to be reduced to clear-cut cases. Thus, the possibility to attack fighters is restricted to those who live and train in a situation identically to that of regular armed forces and those who at the moment of attack take direct part in hostilities. The effect of these considerations is thus that – beside those persons who are clearly and actively involved in military groups that meet the high requirements shown above – the targeting of any person in a non-international armed conflict is narrowly related to the immediacy of a threat that person poses.

At the same time, the existence of a non-international armed conflict does not exclude the possibility of an international armed conflict at the same time. For example, in the *Nicaragua* case, the International Court of Justice held that there was a non-international armed conflict between Nicaraguan forces and the contras, while at the same time the conflict between Nicaragua and the United States was an international conflict.[252] The possibility of such a co-existence was confirmed by the International Criminal Tribunal for the Former Yugoslavia in *Tadić*.[253] Insofar, the vague formulation of Common Article 3 of the 1949 Geneva Conventions concerning the scope of application, which was considered at the time as one major defect of this Article, is now considered as one of its main advantages.[254]

III. The Treatment of Certain Non-International Armed Conflicts as International Armed Conflicts

In two situations, conflicts that are factually non-international are treated – at least in part – as if they were international. The first case is that

---

[252] ICJ, *Military and Paramilitary Activities in and against Nicaragua, Nicaragua v. United States of America*, Judgment (Merits) of June 27, 1986, I.C.J. Reports 1986, pp. 14-150, at 114 (para. 219).

[253] ICTY, *Prosecutor v. Duško Tadić*, Case No. IT-94-1-AR72, Decision on the Defence Motion for Interlocutory Appeal on Jurisdiction of October 2, 1995, reprinted in: 105 *Int'l L.R.* (1997), pp. 419-648, at 492-494 (paras. 74-77); ICTY, *Prosecutor v. Duško Tadić*, Case No. IT-94-1-A, Judgment (Merits Appeal) of July 15, 1999, reprinted in: 124 *Int'l L.R.* (2003), pp. 63-212, at 96 (para. 84). *See also infra*, Part Four, Chapter D).

[254] *See also* Abi-Saab, in: Delissen/ Tanja (eds.), at 261.

of an agreement pursuant to Common Article 3 of the 1949 Geneva Conventions. According to para. 2, the parties to the conflict

> should further endeavour to bring into force, by means of special agreements, all or part of the other provisions of the present Convention.

The International Criminal Tribunal for the Former Yugoslavia in *Tadić* in part relied on such agreements, albeit as proof for the parties' perception of the conflict as non-international.[255] The second case is that of Article 1 para. 4 of the 1977 Additional Protocol I. Under traditional international law, wars of national liberation were regarded as civil wars that were essentially within the domestic jurisdiction of the State concerned. However, this assessment was changed due to Article 1 para. 4 of the 1977 Additional Protocol I:

> The situations referred to in the preceding paragraph include armed conflicts in which peoples are fighting against colonial domination and alien occupation and against racist régimes in the exercise of their right of self-determination, as enshrined in the Charter of the United Nations and the Declaration on Principles of International Law concerning Friendly Relations and Co-operation among States in accordance with the Charter of the United Nations.

The preceding para. 3 refers to international armed conflicts as laid down in Common Article 2 of the 1949 Geneva Conventions and declares the Protocol applicable to those armed conflicts. Thus, Article 1 para. 4 declares that "wars of national liberation" have to be treated in the same manner as international armed conflicts, even though they may take place exclusively on the territory of one State – being opposed by armed groups – and thus *per se* meet the definition of non-international armed conflicts as shown above. In consequence, even concerning States which have not ratified the 1977 Additional Protocol I, a conflict between a State and a people fighting against colonial domination

---

[255] ICTY, *Prosecutor v. Duško Tadić*, Case No. IT-94-1-AR72, Decision on the Defence Motion for Interlocutory Appeal on Jurisdiction of October 2, 1995, reprinted in: 105 *Int'l L.R.* (1997), pp. 419-648, at 491-492 (para. 73); *compare further* Yves Sandoz, 'Réflexions sur la mise en oeuvre du droit international humanitaire et sur le rôle du Comité international de la Croix-Rouge en ex-Yougoslavie', in: 3 *Rev. Suisse dr. int'l & eur.* (1993), pp. 461-490, at 466 and 471; Theodor Meron, 'Classification of Armed Conflict in the Former Yugoslavia: Nicaragua's Fallout', in: 92 *Am. J. Int'l L.* (1998), pp. 236-242, at 237 (footnote 11).

or alien occupation might constitute an armed conflict, albeit not an international one.[256]

Article 1 para. 4 applies to "wars of national liberation". The concept of a "national liberation movement" has been used by any group – and also by States in support of such groups – of people seeking to overthrow a government that it is difficult to define.[257] An important indication is the recognition by the international community[258] or by the regional arrangement in the area in which the movement is waging its conflict[259] of such an armed resistance group as being the representative of a people seeking self-determination. In that regard, the question of whether the group serves a social interest is an indication.[260] Examples have been the SWAPO in Namibia's independence, the ANC in South Africa as well as the PLO in connection with the Palestine People.

Furthermore, the aim of the "war of national liberation" must be to overthrow "colonial domination", "alien occupation" or a "racist regime". These concepts may be open to considerable interpretation, but they were chosen with certain situations in mind. "Colonial domination" and "racist regime" were directed essentially at South Africa, Namibia, Rhodesia and at the Portuguese colonies at the time of the drafting,[261] whereas those fighting against "alien occupation" were the Palestinians.[262]

---

256 Kretzmer, 16 *Eur. J. Int'l L.* (2005), at 210.

257 Edward Kwakwa, *The International Law of Armed Conflict: Personal and Material Fields of Application*, Dordrecht 1992, pp. 50-51.

258 UK Ministry of Defence, *Manual*, para. 2.4.2 *lit.* b (p. 30).

259 Such as the Organization of American States, the Council of Europe or the North Atlantic Treaty Organization, *see* Leslie C. Green, 'Enforcement of the Law in Non-International Conflicts', in: Volkmar Götz (ed.), *Liber amicorum Günther Jaenicke – zum 85. Geburtstag*, Berlin 1998, pp. 113-147, at 124-125.

260 Kwakwa, *Law of Armed Conflict*, p. 51.

261 Richard R. Baxter, 'Humanitarian Law or Humanitarian Politics? The 1974 Diplomatic Conference on Humanitarian Law', in 16 *Harv. Int'l L.J.* (1975), pp. 1-26, at 12.

262 Frits Kalshoven, 'Reaffirmation and Development of International Humanitarian Law Applicable in Armed Conflicts: The Diplomatic Conference, Geneva, 1974-1977, Part II', in: 9 *Nether. Yb. Int'l L.* (1978), pp. 107-171, at 122.

As a third element, Article 1 para. 4 refers to "self-determination" as laid down in the UN Friendly Relations Declaration.[263] The declaration in its eight paragraphs dealing with self-determination, states the following rights and duties: The right of all peoples to freely determine their political status; the duty of States to respect this right and to promote its realization; the duty of States to refrain from any forcible action which deprives peoples of this right; the right of peoples to seek and receive support in accordance with the purposes and principles of the Charter in their actions against, and resistance to, such forcible action by States; and the declaration that under the Charter, the territory of a colony or other non-self-governing territory has a status separate and distinct from that of the State administering it.

Additionally, the principle of self-determination is recognised as customary international law, is enshrined in the UN-Charter[264] and has been recognised by a number of declarative General Assembly resolutions.[265] It was initially framed as a right of peoples under "alien subjugation, domination and exploitation",[266] whose struggle was asserted as legitimate by the General Assembly.[267] But the terminology changed to "peoples under colonial rule, foreign domination and alien subjuga-

---

[263] UN GA Res. 2625 (October 24, 1970), *Declaration on Principles of International Law concerning Friendly Relations and Cooperation among States in accordance with the Charter of the United Nations*, UN Doc. A/8082 (1970).

[264] *See generally* ICJ, *Western Sahara*, Advisory Opinion of October 16, 1975, I.C.J. Reports 1975, pp. 12-82.

[265] *See e.g.* UN GA Res. 1514 (December 14, 1960), Declaration on the Granting of Independence to Colonial Countries and Peoples, UN GAOR 15th Sess., Supp. No. 16, U.N. Doc. A/4684 (1960), pp. 66-67; UN GA Res. 2625 (October 24, 1970), Annex, *Declaration on Principles of International Law concerning Friendly Relations and Cooperation among States in accordance with the Charter of the United Nations*, UN GAOR 25th Session, Supp. No. 28, U.N. Doc. A/8028 (1971), pp. 121-124.

[266] UN GA Res. 1514 (December 14, 1960), Declaration on the Granting of Independence to Colonial Countries and Peoples, UN GAOR 15th Sess., Supp. No. 16, U.N. Doc. A/4684 (1960), pp. 66-67, at 67 (operative paragraph 1).

[267] UN GA Res. 2105 (December 20, 1965), *Implementation of the Declaration on the Granting of Independence to Colonial Countries and Peoples*, UN GAOR, 20th Session, Supp. No. 14, UN Doc. A/6014 (1966), pp. 3-4.

tion"[268] and, even further, not only recognised the legitimacy of the struggle, but also its character as an international armed conflict:

> The armed conflicts involving the struggle of peoples against colonial and alien domination and racist régimes are to be regarded as international armed conflicts in the sense of the 1949 Geneva Conventions, and the legal status envisaged to apply to the combatants in the 1949 Geneva Conventions and other international instruments is to apply to the persons engaged in armed struggle against colonial and alien domination and racist régimes.[269]

Thus, self-determination has been defined by the International Court of Justice as the "need to pay regard to the freely expressed will of peoples."[270] According to Article 1 para. 1 of the International Covenant on Civil and Political Rights it entails the right to "freely determine their political status and freely pursue their economic, social and cultural development". There are good reasons to interpret this concept narrowly. The search for self-determination is regarded as being legitimate for a people under colonial rule, but not for a people forming a minority in national territory. A broader definition would endanger the present State system and promote secession with catastrophic consequences e.g. in multi-ethnic regions such as Africa.[271] This danger is already paid regard to in the penultimate paragraph dealing with self-determination in the Friendly Relations Declaration:

> Nothing in the foregoing paragraphs shall be construed as authorizing or encouraging any action which would dismember or impair, totally or in part, the territorial integrity or political unity of sovereign and independent States conducting themselves in compliance

---

[268] UN GA Res. 3246 (November 29, 1974), *Importance of the Universal Realization of the Right of Peoples to Self-Determination and of the Speedy Granting of Independence to Colonial Countries and Peoples for the Effective Guarantee and Observance of Human Rights*, UN GAOR 29th Session, Supp. No. 31, UN Doc. A/9631 (1975), p. 87.

[269] UN GA Res. 3103 (December 12, 1973), Basic Principles of the Legal Status of the Combatants Struggling against Colonial and Alien Domination and Racist Regimes, UN GAOR 28th Session, Supp. No. 30, UN Doc. A/9030 (1974), pp. 142-143.

[270] ICJ, *Western Sahara*, *Western Sahara*, Advisory Opinion of October 16, 1975, I.C.J. Reports 1975, pp. 12-82, at 25.

[271] Kwakwa, *Law of Armed Conflict*, pp. 53-54.

> with the principle of equal rights and self-determination of peoples as described above and thus possessed of a government representing the whole people belonging to the territory without distinction as to race, creed or colour.

On the other hand, the object and purpose of the 1977 Additional Protocol I to provide the broadest possible protection is a strong argument for a broader interpretation at least concerning Article 1 para. 4. Such rights as the prisoner-of-war status only exist in international armed conflicts. Finally, according to Article 96 para. 3 of the Protocol, the authority representing the people must undertake to apply the 1977 Additional Protocol I and the 1949 Geneva Conventions itself and give a corresponding unilateral declaration to the Swiss government.

Article 1 para. 4 has been criticised as being political and for making the motive behind an armed conflict a criterion for the application of humanitarian law.[272] It has to be taken into account though that in those cases where the people in question obtain observer status with the United Nations, their fight for self-determination had already been "internationalised".[273] In the drafting process, the paragraph was supported by a majority of states – mostly Eastern bloc and Third World – at the diplomatic conference.[274] Today, the 1977 Additional Protocol I – including Article 1 para. 4 – has been ratified by no less than 167 State parties – including almost all NATO members but excluding *inter alia* the United States – and thus is almost universally accepted.

This broad level of acceptance may nevertheless not be interpreted as proof of recognition of the Article as customary international law. Whether this is the case or not is not totally clear. Article 1 para. 4 of the 1977 Additional Protocol I engendered so much debate and controversy that in consequence it hindered several States form ratifying the Protocol. Among those are Israel and the United States.[275] The Article went well beyond customary law as it stood in when the Article was drafted and arguably has not met the criteria for being absorbed into

---

[272] Kwakwa, *Law of Armed Conflict*, pp. 56-58 with further references.

[273] Kooijmans, in: Delissen/ Tanja (eds.), at 230.

[274] Kwakwa, *Law of Armed Conflict*, p. 50.

[275] Theodor Meron, 'The Time has come for the United States to Ratify Geneva Protocol I', in: 88 *Am. J. Int'l L.* (1994), pp. 678-686, at 683.

customary law since it's inclusion in the 1977 Additional Protocol I.[276] Even if the article could be regarded as representing customary international law, these States would not be bound by it as they would be persistent objectors to that rule. Thus, it can be concluded that States have either explicitly accepted the Protocol and are thus bound by Article 1 para. 4, or have explicitly rejected the rule and are thus neither bound by the Protocol nor by any parallel rule of customary international law.

The conclusion as to targeted killings in internationalised armed conflicts is the following: Once it is accepted that a conflict is covered by Article 1 para. 4 of the 1977 Additional Protocol I, the rules applicable in international armed conflicts apply.[277] In case the Article does not apply due to the characterization of the conflict as a "war of national liberation", the rules applicable to non-international armed conflicts apply.[278] Finally, if the level of an armed conflict is not reached at all, the rules applicable to public emergencies apply.[279]

D. The Law Applicable in International Armed Conflicts

> There should be no doubt that human rights law applies during times of armed conflict, that human rights are relevant aids for interpretation of the laws of war and vice versa.[280]

Insofar, the situation concerning international armed conflicts is very similar to that of non-international armed conflicts as described above: Generally, human rights law continues to apply, but may be restricted to a certain degree.[281] Additionally, international humanitarian law is applicable as soon as the threshold of an international armed conflict is reached.[282]

---

276 Greenwood, in: Delissen/ Tanja (eds.), at 112.

277 *Compare infra*, Part Four, Chapter D).

278 *Compare supra*, Part Four, Chapter C).

279 *Compare supra*, Part Four, Chapter B).

280 Paust, 65 *Sask. L. Rev.* (2002), at 411.

281 *See e.g. id.*

282 Greenwood, in: Fleck (ed.), *Handbook*, at 39 (para. 201).

Before the adoption of the UN Charter, war *de jure* existed as soon as it was declared by a sovereign state. Following the adoption of the UN Charter and its prohibition of the use of force the term "war" fell out of use and was succeeded by the term "armed conflict",[283] also referred to as "war in the factual sense" as opposed to the earlier concept of declared war.[284] The question of application of international humanitarian law now depends on Common Article 2 para. 1 of the 1949 Geneva Conventions. This Article not only lays down the scope of application of the Conventions themselves, but according to Article 1 para. 3 of the 1977 Additional Protocol I also triggers the application of the Protocol, which shall apply in the same circumstances as the Conventions. Furthermore, other international humanitarian law rules such as the 1907 Hague Regulations – which still refer to times of war as their scope of application – are treated as applicable in international armed conflicts as laid down in the Geneva Conventions.[285] According to Common Article 2 para. 1, the Conventions and thus all these rules shall apply

> to all cases of declared war or of any other armed conflict which may arise between two or more of the High Contracting Parties, even if the state of war is not recognized by one of them.

The last part of this paragraph must be read as "even if the state of war is not recognised by one or *both* of them." This reading corresponds the practice of applying the Geneva Conventions in most armed conflicts since 1945, without admitting that a state of war exists.[286] On the other hand, the conventions are also applicable where a declaration of

---

[283] *Compare* e.g. the text of the four 1949 Geneva Conventions.

[284] Yoram Dinstein, *War, Aggression and Self-Defence*, 4th ed., Cambridge 2005, p. 8; Greenwood, in: Fleck (ed.), *Handbook*, at 41 (para. 202.1).

[285] Greenwood, in: Fleck (ed.), *Handbook*, at 41 (para. 202.2); UK Ministry of Defence, *Manual*, para. 3.2.3 (p. 29).

[286] Pictet (ed.), *Geneva Conventions*, Vol. 4, p. 21; Oppenheim/ Lauterpacht, *International Law*, p. 369; UK Ministry of Defence, *Manual*, para. 3.2.3 (pp. 28-29); *but see* Jean S. Pictet, *Le droit humanitaire et la Protection des Victimes de la Guerre*, Leiden 1973, pp. 49-51. Examples for those exceptional cases, in which State have expressed that they regarded themselves as being at war are a number of Arab States both in 1948 and 1967 with regard to Israel and by Iran and Iraq during their 1980-1988 war, as well as Pakistan in relation to India in 1965, *see* Greenwood, in: Fleck (ed.), *Handbook*, at 43 (para. 203.1).

war is not followed by actual hostilities.[287] Additionally, according to para. 2 of that Article, the Conventions shall also apply

> to all cases of partial or total occupation of the territory of a High Contracting Party, even if the said occupation meets with no armed resistance.

This provision is not intended to affect situations of occupation following the outbreak of actual hostilities. In these cases, Article 2 para. 1 applies.[288] Unfortunately, neither the 1949 Geneva Conventions nor the Protocol give a definition of the term "armed conflict". War has been defined as "a contention between two or more states through their armed forces, for the purpose of overpowering each other and imposing such conditions of peace as the victor pleases."[289] The ICRC Commentary refers to an armed conflict as "[a]ny difference arising between two States and leading to the intervention of members of the armed forces" as an armed conflict within the meaning of Common Article 2.[290] According to the International Criminal Tribunal for the Former Yugoslavia, "an armed conflict exists whenever there is a resort to armed force between States".[291] The second part of this quote, i.e. the part referring to "protracted armed violence" as a precondition of a non-international armed conflict, has already been discussed above. But also in the international sphere, not every resort to armed force establishes an armed conflict.

---

[287] Examples are the declarations of some Latin American States in relation to Germany in the Second World War, *see* Greenwood, in: Fleck (ed.), *Handbook*, at 41 (para. 202.1).

[288] *Id.*; Pictet (ed.), *Geneva Conventions*, Vol. 4, p. 21.

[289] Oppenheim/ Lauterpacht, *International Law*, p. 202.

[290] Pictet (ed.), *Geneva Conventions*, Vol. 3, p. 23.

[291] ICTY, *Prosecutor v. Duško Tadić*, Case No. IT-94-1-AR72, Decision on the Defence Motion for Interlocutory Appeal on Jurisdiction of October 2, 1995, reprinted in: 105 *Int'l L.R.* (1997), pp. 419-648, at 488-489 (para. 70).

I. The Intensity Necessary to Fulfil the Preconditions of an Armed Conflict

To amount to an armed conflict, a certain threshold of intensity has to be met. The replacing of the border police with soldiers or an accidental border incursion by members of the armed forces will not suffice.[292] Neither will the use of force by individual persons or groups of persons. Even the accidental bombing of another country does not *per se* amount to an armed conflict. At the other extreme, a full-scale invasion of another country would clearly amount to an armed conflict.[293]

The use of armed force generally has to go beyond one ore more isolated incidents.[294] Minimal-armed force between states is often referred to as an incident, as in "border incident" or "frontier incident".[295] However, according to *Dinstein*, the law of international armed conflict "is brought to bear upon the conduct of hostilities between sovereign states, even if these hostilities fall short of war, namely, constitute a mere incident."[296] This corresponds the view of *Gill*, who asserts:

> It would be an illogical and inconsistent law of armed conflict which would apply to the temporary occupation of a small portion of a State's territory which offered no resistance; but did not apply to a series of air strikes or special forces operations carried out by a State ... on another State's territory, simply because the target State's armed forces remained outside the fighting.[297]

---

292 UK Ministry of Defence, *Manual*, para. 3.3.1 (p. 29).

293 Greenwood, in: Fleck (ed.), *Handbook*, at 41 (para. 202); UK Ministry of Defence, *Manual*, para. 3.3.1 (p. 29).

294 Greenwood, in: Fleck (ed.), *Handbook*, at 42 (para. 202.3); this conclusion can also be drawn from Art. 1 para. 2 1977 Additional Protocol II *a maiore ad minus*, Vöneky, in: Walter *et al.* (eds.), at 930.

295 ICJ, *Military and Paramilitary Activities in and against Nicaragua, Nicaragua v. United States of America*, Judgment (Merits) of June 27, 1986, I.C.J. Reports 1986, pp. 14-150, at 102-103 (para. 192).

296 Dinstein, *Conduct of Hostilities*, pp. 15-16; *see also* Vöneky, in: Walter *et al.* (eds.), at 930-931.

297 Terry D. Gill, *The 11th of September and the International Law of Military Operations*, Amsterdam 2002, p. 25.

If compared with a non-international armed conflict, it becomes clear that the threshold of violence is not of the same importance when it comes to an international armed conflict. The international character and the fact that regular armed forces of States are involved clearly distinguishes an armed conflict from "internal disturbances and tensions, such as riots, isolated and sporadic acts of violence and other acts of a similar nature". Thus, one can conclude with *Pictet*: "It makes no difference how long the conflict lasts, or how much slaughter takes place."[298]

II. The International Character of an Armed Conflict

Concerning the parties to an international armed conflict, the prevailing view is that it is, by definition, a conflict between States.[299] However, the applicability of the law of international armed conflict is not conditioned on the formal recognition of the statehood of the opposing side.[300] The parties to the conflict only have to satisfy the objective criteria of statehood under international law in order to characterize an armed conflict as international.[301] It is not conditioned on the recognition of the enemy or as a government.[302] This is why, for example, the Taliban regime, which was not recognised by the international community at large, but was in control of most of the territory of Afghanistan was bound – as a *de facto* government – by the law of international armed conflict.[303] Concerning the parties to an international armed conflict, the International Criminal Tribunal for the Former Yugoslavia stated in *Tadić*:

> It is indisputable that an armed conflict is international if it takes place between two or more States. In addition, in case of an internal armed conflict breaking out on the territory of a State, it may be-

---

[298] Pictet (ed.), *Geneva Conventions*, Vol. 1, p. 32.

[299] Derek Jinks, 'September 11 and the Laws of War', in: 28 *The Yale J. Int'l L.* (2003), pp. 1-50, at 20.

[300] Greenwood, in: Fleck (ed.), *Handbook*, at 45 (para. 206).

[301] Dinstein, *Conduct of Hostilities*, p. 16.

[302] *Id.*

[303] Greenwood, 78 *Int'l Aff.* (2002), at 312-313.

> come international (or, depending upon the circumstances, be international in character alongside an internal armed conflict) if (i) another State intervenes in that conflict through its troops, or alternatively if (ii) some of the participants in the internal armed conflict act on behalf of that other State.[304]

While the first alternative precondition, an intervention by another state, can easily be proven on a factual basis, the second precondition is more complex to analyse.[305] Since the International Criminal Tribunal for the Former Yugoslavia's appeal on jurisdiction decision, it is clear that armed conflicts can be of a mixed nature and thus be in part international and in part non-international.[306] On the other hand, the complicated decision of whether a conflict is internal or international due to "internationalisation" has lead to a general critique on the different definition of international and non-international armed conflicts.[307] This has, however, not led yet to a single definition of armed conflict and the differentiations still prevail.

1. Horizontally Mixed Armed Conflicts

Armed conflicts may be mixed horizontally in the sense that they incorporate elements of inter-state hostilities, i.e. between two or more belligerent states, and intra-state hostilities, i.e. between two or more clashing groups within the territory of one of the belligerent states. Such dual conflicts can either take place simultaneously or commence consecutively. In the latter case, either conflict can precede the other. An important feature of such horizontally mixed conflicts is that the in-

---

[304] ICTY, *Prosecutor v. Duško Tadić*, Case No. IT-94-1-A, Judgment (Merits Appeal) of July 15, 1999, reprinted in: 124 *Int'l L.R.* (2003), pp. 63-212, at 96 (para. 84).

[305] *Compare id.*, at 98-121 (paras. 88-145).

[306] ICTY, *Prosecutor v. Duško Tadić*, Case No. IT-94-1-AR72, Decision on the Defence Motion for Interlocutory Appeal on Jurisdiction of October 2, 1995, reprinted in: 105 *Int'l L.R.* (1997), pp. 419-648, at 492-494 (paras. 74-77); *see also* Meron, in: Lal Chand Vohrah *et al.* (eds.), at 533-534.

[307] *See e.g.* James G. Stewart, 'Towards a single Definition of Armed Conflict in International Humanitarian Law: A Critique of Internationalized Armed Conflict' in: 85 *Int'l Rev. Red Cross* (2003), No. 850, pp. 313-350 with further references.

ternal and the international parts have disparate strands. If these strands are not merging, the two conflicts will co-exist and be covered by the respective law applicable to international and non-international armed conflicts respectively.[308]

Examples for such a situation are the (non-international) conflict between the *Contras* and the government of Nicaragua and the (international) actions of the United States against Nicaragua[309] or the (non-international) conflict of the Taliban Regime with the Northern Alliance in Afghanistan and the (international) hostilities between the Taliban and the United States. The law of international armed conflict will then only control the international operations.[310]

2. *Vertically Mixed Armed Conflicts*

A different scenario is referred to as "vertically mixed". An armed conflict may start as an intra-state armed conflict and evolve into an inter-state armed conflict, and thus become vertically mixed or internationalised. This may happen in two situations. First, a foreign State might intervene on the side of one of the parties to the conflict which was – up to that point – a purely internal conflict.[311] This intervention could either take place on behalf of the government fighting against rebels.[312] Such an intervention does not necessarily render the internal conflict

---

[308] Dinstein, *Conduct of Hostilities*, p. 14; Christopher Greenwood, 'The Development of International Humanitarian Law by the International Criminal Tribunal for the former Yugoslavia', in: 2 *Max Planck Yb. U.N. L.* (1998), pp. 97-140, at 117.

[309] ICJ, *Military and Paramilitary Activities in and against Nicaragua, Nicaragua v. United States of America*, Judgment (Merits) of June 27, 1986, I.C.J. Reports 1986, pp. 14-150, at 114 (para. 219).

[310] Dinstein, *Conduct of Hostilities*, pp. 14-15.

[311] UK Ministry of Defence, *Manual*, para. 1.33.6 (p. 16); Greenwood, in: Fleck (ed.), *Handbook*, at 49 (para. 211.4); Meron, 92 *Am. J. Int'l L.* (1998), pp. 236-242; Dinstein, *War, Aggression*, p. 6-7; Arai-Takahashi, 5 *Yb. Int'l Hum. L.* (2002), at 64.

[312] Concerning the question of legality of such an intervention upon invitation comprehensively *see* Nolte, *Eingreifen auf Einladung*. On this question concerning the November 2002 US strike by a Predator Unmanned Aerial Vehicle in Yemen *see* Downes, 9 *J. Confl. Sec. L.* (2004), at 280-281.

international.[313] On the other hand, a foreign State could intervene in aid of rebels. In the latter case, the conflict is from then onwards regarded as an international armed conflict.[314] A second possibility to establish a vertically mixed armed conflict is implosion of a state which has fragmented into two or more states due to a civil war.[315]

An example for the first constellation is the participation of the Federal Republic of Yugoslavia (Serbia-Montenegro) in hostilities in Bosnia-Herzegovina after the latter seceded from Yugoslavia and became an independent State in 1992.[316] The same applies to the armed conflict fought between the Northern Alliance and the Taliban government, that was "internationalised" by virtue of the close link between the Northern Alliance and the U.S.-lead coalition from October 2001 onwards.[317] In consequence, in different phases of an armed conflict, different parts of the law of armed conflict may apply.[318]

3. Several Conflicts or One Situation that Must Be Regarded as a Whole?

There are views that tend to see a conflict as a whole rather than a combination of several conflicts of different quality. Some authors thus came to the conclusion that the fighting in the former Yugoslavia from 1991 onwards must be considered to be one international armed conflict, arguing that to divide it into isolated segments to exclude the application of the rules of international armed conflict would be artifi-

---

313 An example that was regarded as remaining internal by the ICRC is the intervention of the Soviet Union on behalf of the Afghan Government against the *Mujahideen*. Moir, *Internal Armed Conflict*, pp. 50-51; Arai-Takahashi, 5 *Yb. Int'l Hum. L.* (2002), at 67.

314 Arai-Takahashi, *id.*

315 Dinstein, *Conduct of Hostilities*, p. 15.

316 ICTY, *Prosecutor v. Duško Tadić*, Case No. IT-94-1-A, Judgment (Merits Appeal) of July 15, 1999, reprinted in: 124 *Int'l L.R.* (2003), pp. 63-212, at 130 (paras. 160-162).

317 Arai-Takahashi, 5 *Yb. Int'l Hum. L.* (2002), at 64.

318 UK Ministry of Defence, *Manual*, para. 1.33.6 (pp. 16-17).

cial.[319] This is certainly true for situations where – as part of an international armed conflict – nationals of a State fight against their nation State together with armed forces of the enemy State.[320] However, it cannot be the general consequence concerning any conflict situation which has internal and international aspects. The critique concerning the co-existence of several conflicts seems to be very much coined on situations which are vertically mixed. As shown above, in most of these cases – except the intervention of a foreign State on behalf of the State which is the theatre of the conflict – is regarded as one international armed conflict. The situations referred to as horizontally mixed armed conflicts rather resemble different armed conflicts which take place at the same time, but not necessarily at the same place. It is possible that one State is involved in an international armed conflict with another State and at the same time in a totally independent internal armed conflict with a rebel group. At least in the latter case it is difficult to argue that the purely internal conflict should be covered by a different set of rules than any other internal armed conflict, with all the consequences such as combatant immunity and prisoner-of-war status of the insurgents who would otherwise be subject to criminal prosecution. Admittedly, it may factually be difficult to differentiate the internal from the international conflict. There are – as always – grey areas between these extremes and from a certain point of interrelation it will be difficult to distinguish the conflicts from each other. But the International Criminal Tribunal for the Former Yugoslavia has shown that it is possible to a certain degree and has received appraisal for not

> choosing the easy route of considering the entire situation an international armed conflict. ... But that route would have deprived the

---

[319] *See e.g.* James C. O'Brien, 'The International Tribunal for Violations of International Humanitarian Law in the Former Yugoslavia', in: 87 *Am. J. Int'l L.* (1993), pp. 639-659, at 647-648; *compare also* Theodor Meron, 'International Criminalization of Internal Atrocities', in: 89 *Am. J. Int'l L.* (1995), pp. 554-577, at 556; George H. Aldrich, 'Jurisdiction of the International Criminal Tribunal for the Former Yugoslavia', in: 90 *Am. J. Int'l L.* (1996), pp. 64-69, at 66-67; *but see* Green, in: Götz (ed.), at 131-132; Christopher Greenwood, 'International Humanitarian Law and the *Tadić* Case', in: 7 *Eur. J. Int'l L.* (1996), pp. 265-283, at 269-275.

[320] Such an example would be Ukrainians fighting for the German army against the Soviet Union in the Second World War, *see* O'Brien, 87 *Am. J. Int'l L.* (1993), at 647-648.

Tribunal of the opportunity to affirm that serious violations of international law committed in internal wars are crimes under international customary law and to develop and consolidate humanitarian law for the most frequent and the most cruel of conflicts: non-international armed conflicts.[321]

III. Conclusion

The convergence of the two bodies of law with respect to international and internal armed conflict will eventually reach a stage where the focus of examination should turn to the threshold question relating to whether or not there exists an armed conflict.[322] However, concerning the rules relevant to the question of targeted killings, in both situations – internal or international – different standards still apply. With regard to the status of the targeted person as a civilian, a combatant or a fighter in a non-international armed conflict, the distinction is thus necessary. As shown above, the threshold of violence is not as important as it is with regard to non-international armed conflicts. Furthermore, complex situations such as vertically or horizontally mixed armed conflicts are not *per se* but in most cases treated as international armed conflicts, at least if the different components are strongly interrelated. In international armed conflicts – but also in those non-international armed conflicts which are treated in part or as a whole as international armed conflicts – the human right to life applies. However, it is to a large degree influenced by the likewise applicable rules of international humanitarian law. Thus, concerning the killing of combatants as well as civilians, the latter set of rules is the more relevant one. A targeted killing taking place in the context of an armed conflict has to be judged by international humanitarian law standards. If such a killing is legal under international humanitarian law, it cannot be regarded as violating the right to life under human rights law.[323]

---

321 Meron, in: Lal Chand Vohrah *et al.* (eds.), at 534.

322 Moir, *Internal Armed Conflict*, at 50-51.

323 *Compare also* Kretzmer, 16 *Eur. J. Int'l L.* (2005), at 186.

E. Military Occupation

The International Court of Justice and human rights treaty bodies have insisted that human rights law applies alongside international humanitarian law to military occupations.[324] The question as to whether the law is applicable to situations of occupation is thus less disputed than the question of whether a certain situation amounts to an occupation. Examples of states that failed to recognise the applicability of the law of belligerent occupation to their actions in foreign countries under their control are the Indonesian occupation of East Timor, the Soviet occupation of Afghanistan and the Iraqi occupation of Kuwait.[325] Similarly, the Israelis have argued that the West Bank has a status *sui generis*, and according to the "Missing Reversioner Theory" is not occupied in the sense of the 1949 Geneva Conventions.[326]

Article 42 of the Hague Regulations links occupation to war. Accordingly, territory is considered occupied "when it is actually placed under the authority of the hostile army". The 1949 Geneva Convention IV widens the concept in its Article 2, including cases in which it "meets with no armed resistance". This pays regard to the fact that "at the heart of all occupations exists a potential – if not inherent – conflict of interest between occupant and occupied."[327]

---

[324] *See e.g.* ICJ, *Legal Consequences of the Construction of a Wall in the Occupied Palestine Territory*, Advisory Opinion of July 9, 2004, I.C.J. Reports 2004, pp. 133-271, at 177-181 (paras. 102-114); ICJ, *Case Concerning Armed Activities on the Territory of the Congo, Democratic Republic of Congo v. Uganda (new application of 2002)*, Judgment of December 19, 2005, I.C.J. Reports 2005 (not published yet), para. 216; H.R. Committee, CCPR General Comment No. 31, at 195 (para. 11); H.R. Committee, *Concluding Observations on Israel*, UN Doc. CCPR/CO/78/ISR (August 21, 2003), para. 10; UN Comm'n H.R., *Report on the Situation of Human Rights in Kuwait under Iraqi Occupation*, UN Doc. E/CN.4/1992/26 (January 16, 1992), p. 17 (paras. 58-59); Eur. Ct. H.R., *Loizidou (Prelim. Obj.)*, Series A, No. 310, p. 24 (paras. 63-64).

[325] Benvenisti, *Law of Occupation*, pp. 150-151; Imseis, 44 *Harv. Int'l L.J.* (2003), pp. 65-138, at 93.

[326] *C.f.* Kretzmer, *Occupation of Justice*, pp. 32-34; Falk/ Weston, in: Playfair (ed.), at 131; Blum, 3 *Isr. L. Rev.* (1968), pp. 279-301; Shamgar, 1 *Isr. Yb. Hum. Rts.* (1971), at 265-266.

[327] Benvenisti, *Law of Occupation*, p. 4.

Thus, territory is occupied whenever a hostile armed force establishes "effective control" over it.[328] Occupation relates to an international armed conflict, albeit with its own specific rules. The law of occupation, like the law of war, equally applies to lawful and unlawful armies and thus disregards prior acts of aggression.[329] These rules – the 1907 Hague Regulations and the 1949 Geneva Convention IV – do not, as shown above, contain specific standards concerning targeted killings. Thus, generally the rules of human rights law apply. However, the situation in an occupied territory can vary considerably. It can be "calm" in one part or at one time and in other parts or at other times, hostilities can break out.

I. "Calm" Occupations

In situations of "calm" occupation, the occupying power exercises "effective control". Thus, human rights law – including the possibility of derogations – applies and the use of force against any person is generally covered by the "law enforcement model".[330] The essential protection afforded to persons in occupied territories is designed to ensure respect for their lives.[331] As *Nolte* put it:

> Non-derogable human rights are increasingly seen as a source for making more specific the general rules of the law of occupation concerning the power of the occupying force to uphold public order and its limits. In such situations, the requirement of immediacy of the danger, which is a core element of human rights law, apply.[332]

---

[328] David Alonzo-Maizlish, 'When does it end? Problems in the Law of Occupation', in: Roberta Arnold, Pierre-Antoine Hildbrand (eds.), *International Humanitarian Law and the 21st Century's Conflicts: Changes and Challenges*, Lausanne 2005, pp. 97-116, at 98.

[329] Benvenisti, *Law of Occupation*, p. 69.

[330] *See e.g.* Doswald-Beck, 88 *Int'l Rev. Red Cross* (2006), No. 864, at 892; Kretzmer, 16 *Eur. J. Int'l L.* (2005), at 206; Marco Sassòli, 'Legislation and Maintenance of Public Order and Civil Life by Occupying Powers', in: 16 *Eur. J. Int'l L.* (2005), pp. 661-694, at 665-667.

[331] Detter, *Law of War*, p. 182.

[332] Nolte, 5 *Theo. Inq. L.* (2004), at 125 (with further references).

In consequence, the occupying power may only resort to lethal force or force presumably lethal in situations such as self-defence and defence of another person etc., i.e. in those situations which are accepted exceptions form the prohibition to kill under human rights law. As shown above, international humanitarian law can also provide for such exceptions.[333] However, it has to be stressed again that even persons "suspected of or engaged in activities hostile to the security of the State" may not be simply targeted. They are subject to criminal legislation and detention. Article 5 para. 1 of the 1949 Geneva Convention IV does not provide for an exception to the right to life.[334] Thus – at least concerning the right to life – a situation of "calm" occupation does not differ from times of "peace". Certain rights of protected persons under the 1949 Geneva Convention IV can be restricted under certain circumstances.[335] But this does not include the right to life. One can thus only support the Human Rights Committee's statement in connection to targeted killings in occupied territories:

> Before resorting to the use of deadly force, all measures to arrest a person suspected of being in the process of committing acts of terror must be exhausted.[336]

What the Committee referred to is the principle of proportionality as part of the protection of the right to life under the International Covenant on Civil and Political Rights. As shown above, the same applies to the other human rights treaties and the protection of the right to life under customary international law.

On the other hand, the occupying force is also responsible for the security inside the occupied territory. According to article 43 of the 1907 Hague Regulations and articles 29 and 47 *et seqq.* of the 1949 Geneva Convention IV the occupying power assumes responsibility for the occupied territory and its inhabitants and is responsible for "l'ordre et la vie publics".[337] Thus, the occupant has not only the right, but even the

---

333 *See supra*, Part One, Chapter B) II. 6.

334 *See supra*, Part Two, Chapter D) II. 1. d).

335 *Compare* the discussion on "unlawful combatants" and "protected persons", *supra*, Part Two, Chapter E).

336 H.R. Committee, *Concluding Observations on Israel*, UN Doc. CCPR/CO/78/ISR (August 21, 2003), para. 15.

337 The common English translation differs from the authentic French version at this point, reading "public order and safety" compare e.g. Roberts/

responsibility of taking security measures.[338] An occupying power is thus not defenceless if it comes to riots or violent demonstrations in the occupied territory. However, as long as the level of an armed conflict is not reached, these threatening situations must be faced by means which are governed by human rights law, and not through military operations governed international humanitarian law on the conduct of hostilities.[339] This includes the human right to life and thus the necessity to carefully plan the operations in order to limit possible damage, to choose those means which are least dangerous and only resort to the use of deadly force as an absolute last resort. In that regard, the use of non-lethal weapons has to be taken into account.[340] All these actions are subject to the principle of proportionality. Additionally, as long as riots do not amount to an armed conflict, the persons taking part therein may not be treated as civilians who "take direct part in hostilities".[341] In a "calm" occupation, there are no such hostilities – i.e. as part of an armed conflict – in which civilians could take direct part. Thus, civilians who oppose the occupying powers – even by resorting to armed force – generally have to be treated as protected persons "engaged in activities

---

Guelff (eds.), *Documents*, p. 81. This seems to be founded on the semi-official English translation by the US Department of State as given in Scott (ed.), *Conventions*, pp. 100-127. A more adequate translation is already contained in: 2 *Am. J. Int'l L.* (1908), Supp., pp. 97-117, at 112-113, which refers to "public order and life". The correct translation is most likely the one proposed by Edmund H. Schwenk, 'Legislative Power of the Military Occupant under Article 43, Hague Regulations', in: 54 *Yale L.J.* (1945), pp. 393-416, at 393 (footnote 1) and 398: as the French term "la vie publique" encompasses "social functions [and] ordinary transactions which constitute daily life" the term "public order and civil life" seems to come closest to the meaning of "l'ordre et la vie publics", whereas the term "l'ordre" means "security or general safety". *See also* Benvenisti, *Law of Occupation*, p. 7; Sassòli, 16 *Eur. J. Int'l L.* (2005), at 663-664.

[338] It has to be taken in account though that this responsibility laid originally laid down in Article 43 of the 1907 Hague Regulations aims primarily at the interest of the population, *see* Schwenk, 54 *Yale L.J.* (1945), at 400; Christian Meurer, *Die Völkerrechtliche Stellung der vom Feind besetzten Gebiete*, Tübingen 1915, p. 23.

[339] Sassòli, 16 *Eur. J. Int'l L.* (2005), at 665.

[340] Krüger-Sprengel, 42 *Rev. dr. mil.* (2003), at 368.

[341] *Compare supra*, Part Two, Chapter D) II. 1. c).

hostile to the security of the State" with the consequences shown above.

Finally, in the context of an overall "calm" occupation, the occupying power may be faced by armed forces of the occupied State who continue combat operations. If this is the case and such operations reach the level of an armed conflict, they must be treated according to the rules concerning armed conflicts. Such an situation thus amounts to an resumption or outbreak of hostilities in an occupied territory. The precise moment when the level of hostilities might trigger the application of conduct of hostilities rules in a situation of occupation is unclear. At least according to the spirit of the 1949 Geneva Convention IV, occupying powers are generally supposed to ensure security by means of law enforcement measures such as arrest, internment and trial for criminal offences.[342]

II. Special Exception to the Right to Life in Situations of "Calm" Occupation?

It has been argued by authors – who generally accept the human rights and humanitarian law standards regarding targeted killings that were developed above – that targeted killings beyond those standards can be lawful in certain circumstances where there are no other means available.[343] If there has not been a resumption of hostilities, the targeted persons are neither combatants and nor civilians taking direct part in hostilities. Thus, the law enforcement model applies[344] and deadly force could only be used to oppose imminent threats.[345] On the other hand, it is possible that in such a situation the state has in fact not sufficient physical control over the occupied territory e.g. to enforce an arrest. This might be due to factual circumstances or to an agreement accord-

---

342 ICRC/T.M.C. Asser Institute, *Direct Participation*, Summary Report, June 2, 2003, at 33.

343 Doswald-Beck, 88 *Int'l Rev. Red Cross* (2006), No. 864, at 896-897.

344 *See supra*, Part Four, Chapter E) I.

345 *See supra*, Part One.

ing to which the occupying State has given up its jurisdiction in whole or in part.[346]

Now, some authors are of the opinion that the duty of a State to protect its own citizens in such a situation entails the possibility of targeting persons who plan potential lethal actions under the following circumstances:

> (1) It is carried out in an area where the state does not exercise effective control so that it cannot reasonably effect an arrest; and (2) the state authorities have sought to transfer the individual from whatever authority is in control of the area, assuming that there is such an authority; and (3) the individual has engaged in serious, life-threatening, hostile acts and the state has reliable intelligence that the individual will continue to commit such acts against the lives of persons the state is under an obligation to protect; and (4) other measures would be insufficient to address this threat.[347]

Doswald-Beck goes as far as expanding this exception to non-international armed conflicts, concerning fighting members of rebel groups who are at the moment of the targeting not involved in violent acts. She admits that such actions are strongly dependent on the quality of intelligence and procedural requirements and allow considerable potential for abuse.

The doubts of *Doswald-Beck* are well founded, but the main argument against such an exception has another basis. The exception formulated above might be understandable and even regarded as reasonable and necessary from a factual point of view, but it simply does not have a legal basis. It expands the concept of immediacy to a degree which is not compatible to the standards developed above. According to these standards, there is no room for additional exceptions that go beyond those which are provided for by the human rights instruments and the right to life under customary international law itself. And these exceptions are either tied to the imminence of a threat or to the standards of international humanitarian law. As shown above, non of the latter possible

---

[346] The "Areas A" under the Oslo accords in the territories occupied by Israel would be examples for the latter case.

[347] Doswald-Beck, 88 *Int'l Rev. Red Cross* (2006), No. 864, at 897. *Doswald-Beck* refers to a discussion which took place in the University Centre for International Humanitarian Law, Report of the Geneva Expert Meeting, September 1 and 2, 2005, pp. 5-6.

exceptions cover a situation as described by *Doswald-Beck*. They are either tied to the status of the targeted person as a combatant or to his direct participation in hostilities. These standards would be moot if – after accepting that they apply – one would conclude that out of factual needs, they must be set aside in "exceptional situations".

III. Resumption or Outbreak of Hostilities in a Territory Under Occupation

If occupying forces do not succeed in establishing or exercising authority over a certain territory, humanitarian law does not consider this territory as occupied. Thus, the general rules of armed conflict apply to this territory. The same applies as soon as hostilities break out (again) in an occupied territory and the occupying power looses "effective control".[348] The decisive question in that regard is thus that concerning the threshold that has to be crossed to change the situation of a "calm" occupation to that of an armed conflict and trigger the application of the different set of rules.

The mere fact that force is used by the occupying power cannot be decisive. Otherwise, this would render meaningless the rule shown above, i.e. that human rights and the "law enforcement model" apply to "calm" occupations. Even the use of considerable force has to be treated cautious. Otherwise, the occupying power could – by the level of force it uses itself – decide which legal regime applies.[349] Thus, any resumption or outbreak of hostilities must result from those challenging the occupation. Their activities – and not the reaction by the occupying power – must go beyond the level of riots or violent demonstrations as referred to above. An example for this would be the use of military force by the armed forces of the occupied state. Such an resumption of hostilities would allow the occupying power to oppose it by force in accordance with international humanitarian law. It would, however, not mean that the whole occupied territory would be part of an armed con-

---

[348] Alonzo-Maizlish, in: Arnold/ Hildbrand (eds.), at 99-100. *Compare also* Andreas L. Paulus; Mindia Vashakmadze, 'Asymmetrical war and the notion of armed conflict – An attempt at a conceptualization', in: 91 *Int'l Rev. Red Cross* (2009), No. 873, pp. 93-125, at 115.

[349] Doswald-Beck, 88 *Int'l Rev. Red Cross* (2006), No. 864, at 893.

flict again. Those areas not affected by the new hostilities which remain "calm" at the same time remain occupied territory subject to the law of occupation and the rules concerning deadly force as shown above.[350]

A less clear but more common example is that of military resistance activity in an area under occupation by groups who are not officially part of the armed forces of the occupied state. In case these groups come under the international humanitarian law definition of armed forces as shown above,[351] the same rules as to the resumption of hostilities by regular armed forces apply. According to *Cassese*,

> [a]n armed conflict which takes place between an Occupying Power and rebel or insurgent groups – whether or not they are terrorist in character – in occupied territory, amounts to an international armed conflict. There are three reasons for this proposition: (1) internal armed conflicts are those between a central government and a group of insurgents belonging to the *same* State (or between two or more insurrectional groups belonging to that State); (2) the object and purpose of international humanitarian law impose that in case of doubt the protection deriving from this body of law be *as extensive as possible*, and it is indisputable that the protection accorded by the rules on international conflicts is much broader than that relating to internal conflicts; (3) as belligerent occupation is governed by the Fourth Geneva Convention and customary international law, it would be *contradictory* to subject occupation to norms relating to international conflict while regulating the conduct of armed hostilities between insurgents and the Occupant on the strength of norms governing internal conflict. It follows that the rules on international armed conflict also apply to the armed clashes between insurgents in occupied territories and the belligerent Occupant.[352]

This quotation of Cassese is the only source the Israeli Supreme Court relied on when it found that the situation in the Occupied Territory is not only an armed conflict, but also international in character.[353]

---

[350] *Compare also id.*, at 894.

[351] *See supra*, Part Two, Chapter C) I. 2.

[352] Cassese, *International Law*, p. 420.

[353] Supreme Court of Israel, *"Targeted Killings" (Merits)*, para. 21, 46 *ILM* (2007), at 383. *Compare the discussions on its reasoning at* Milanovic, 89 *Int'l Rev. Red Cross* (2007), No. 866, at 382-386; Schondorf, 5 *J. Int'l Crim. Just.* (2007), at 303-305.

Others argue that the test used to establish the existence of a non-international armed conflict should be applied in such a situation. It is acknowledged that the application of this test is an invention, but it is argued that it fits the situation, which is comparable to that of an non-international armed conflict.[354] The test would thus include the elements of intensity and duration of violence that requires the State to resort to military measures.[355] This would mean that – in application of Article 1 para. 2 of the 1977 Additional Protocol I – isolated sporadic attacks by resistance movements would not meet the required threshold.

There are sound arguments in support of this latter assessment. As soon as a situation of occupation has been a "calm" occupation, i.e. the hostilities vanish and the territory is under the effective control of the occupying power, the situation *legally* very much resembles that of a "peaceful" State. The occupying power is the only State – possibly for decades – to exercise exclusive effective control over the territory and possibly no other State is laying claim to that territory.[356] Therefore, as shown above, any disturbances, tensions or riots are treated first and foremost according to those rules applicable "in peace", namely human rights, only accompanied by some additional possibilities of derogation concerning those persons "hostile to the security of the State" as laid down in the law of occupation. If the intensity of violence is higher, the next level such disturbances in a national territory could reach is that of a non-international armed conflict. The latter situation is almost identical to that in a "calm" occupied territory.

Another argument for such a treatment as a non-international armed conflict is the following: in certain occupations, the primary interna-

---

[354] *Compare* Doswald-Beck, 88 *Int'l Rev. Red Cross* (2006), No. 864, at 894; *compare also Ben-Naftali and Michaeli*, who accept that the Palestinian Territories are occupied by Israel and at the same time regard the situation as a non-international armed conflict, *see* Orna Ben-Naftali; Aeyal M. Gross; Keren R. Michaeli, 'Illegal Occupation: Framing the Occupied Palestinian Territory', in: 23 *Berkeley J. Int'l L.* (2005), pp. 551-614; Ben-Naftali/ Michaeli, 36 *Cornell Int'l L.J.* (2003), at 258-262.

[355] *Compare* ICTY, *Prosecutor v. Duško Tadić*, Case No. IT-94-1-AR72, Decision on the Defence Motion for Interlocutory Appeal on Jurisdiction of October 2, 1995, reprinted in: 105 *Int'l L.R.* (1997), pp. 419-648, at 488-489 (para. 70).

[356] Milanovic, 89 *Int'l Rev. Red Cross* (2007), No. 866, at 385.

tional armed conflict finally ceased.[357] An uprising by a resistance movement in such a territory is difficult to regard as an international armed conflict. The insurgents themselves possibly are not purporting to fight on behalf of any State, nor is their struggle directly related to the initial international armed conflict.[358] Even if such a movement would meet the organizational requirements of being an "armed force", it will thus most likely not "belong to a Party to the conflict" within the meaning of Article 4 of the 1949 Geneva Convention III or Article 43 of the 1977 Additional Protocol I.

On the other hand, to treat an uprising in an occupied territory as a non-international armed conflict is also not compatible with the definition of non-international armed conflicts, as this definition comprises conflicts "occurring in the territory of one of the High Contracting Parties".[359] To subsume an uprising in an occupied territory – i.e. a territory outside the accepted international frontiers of the occupying State[360] – under that definition would either expand that concept beyond the wording of Common Article 3 of the 1949 Geneva Conventions or implicitly accept that occupation turned into something rather comparable to an annexation. Both possibilities are outside existing law.

Initially, the law of occupation was not drafted with long term occupations in mind, but also does not limit the duration of occupation.[361] As

---

[357] The most prominent example fur such a situation is that of the Palestinian territories. The international armed conflict that lead to the occupation was between Israel, Jordan and Egypt. None of these States are at war any more. A similar example could be that of Northern Cyprus, if Greek Cypriots not acting on behalf of Cyprus would be involved in an (non-international armed) conflict with Turkey *compare* University Centre for International Humanitarian Law, Report of the Geneva Expert Meeting, September 1 and 2, 2005, p. 27.

[358] Milanovic, 89 *Int'l Rev. Red Cross* (2007), No. 866, at 385-386.

[359] *Compare supra*, Part Four, Chapter C).

[360] Roberts, 55 *Brit. Yb. Int'l L.* (1984), at 300.

[361] Benvenisti, *Law of Occupation*, pp. 144-145. Article 6 para. 3 of the 1949 Geneva Convention IV provides that certain rules cease to apply if the military operations are closed for one year, but most articles dealing with occupation are enumerated as the exceptions that are retained as long as the occupation lasts. This article may even have been replaced by Article 3 *lit.* b of the 1977 Additional Protocol I, which explicitly states that "the application of the Conventions and of this Protocol shall cease ... in the case of occupied territories, on

a strict matter of law, the full range of rights and duties placed upon an occupying power continues to remain in force for the duration of the prolonged period.[362] On the other hand it has to be kept in mind that an occupation is generally part of an international armed conflict. The law of occupation is part of the international humanitarian law applicable to international armed conflicts.[363] Thus, if there is a necessity to apply rules of international humanitarian law, these are those rule applicable in international armed conflicts. The application of the law of occupation actually is an exception to the general rules applicable in international armed conflict, namely for those cases and only to the extent that the armed forces of the occupying power are exercising the authority required for an occupation to exist.[364]

According to this system, there can only be two different status: either an occupation or an ongoing international armed conflict. Thus, any considerable resumption of force which reaches the threshold of an armed conflict – be it by regular troops or irregulars who fulfil the preconditions to qualify as combatants – will re-establish the international armed conflict and thus render the corresponding set of rules applicable.[365]

This not only corresponds the system of the law of occupation, it also leads to logical results: If an occupying power leaves – due to profound violent resistance – the law enforcement sphere and utilizes the more comprehensive possibilities of using force according to the armed conflict paradigm, then also its opponents should enjoy the advantages of the armed conflict paradigm. These advantages are – for those who qualify as combatants – most of all combatant immunity and prisoner-of-war status, two concepts which only exist in international armed conflicts, but not in non-international armed conflicts.

Those who do not qualify as combatants are treated in the same manner in both kinds of conflicts. They are civilians and may only be attacked

---

the termination of the occupation.", *compare* Alonzo-Maizlish, in: Arnold/ Hildbrand (eds.), at 104-107.

[362] Alonzo-Maizlish, in: Arnold/ Hildbrand (eds.), at 104-111.

[363] *Compare e.g.* Roberts, 55 *Brit. Yb. Int'l L.* (1984), at 255-256.

[364] *Compare* University Centre for International Humanitarian Law, Report of the Geneva Expert Meeting, September 1 and 2, 2005, p. 20.

[365] *But see* Milanovic, 89 *Int'l Rev. Red Cross* (2007), No. 866, at 385-386.

while they take direct part in hostilities. They do not enjoy immunity from criminal prosecution for such participation. But they may not be targeted due to their membership in a certain group, unless this group qualifies as irregular armed forces.

If such a situation was treated as a non-international armed conflict, the occupying power would have the possibility to choose the best of both worlds. It could leave the law enforcement model and attack those who qualify as fighters. The inhabitants of the occupied territory – civilians and fighters – would thus only lose major parts of human rights protection but get no additional protection under international humanitarian law in return. Additionally, the somehow diffuse concept of "fighter" would enable the occupying power to expand the group of those who it regards as persons who may be targeted. In a non-international armed conflict, the application of the principle of distinction is more complicated than in an international armed conflict, a fact which might even be welcome to the occupying power.

IV. Conclusion

In situations of "calm" occupation, generally human rights standards apply. In consequence, up to the level of an armed conflict, riots or insurrections have to be dealt with resorting to law enforcement measures. This includes the use of force subject to the human right to life. This standard is not extended by the law of occupation, as this branch of law does not provide for any legal basis to use lethal force that goes beyond that of the human right to life.

If a violent situation in an occupied territory reaches the level of an armed conflict, it cannot be treated according to the standards applicable in non-international armed conflicts. Admittedly, the situation is often similar to such a conflict, as resistance movements which do not meet the definition of regular armed forces are often involved. On the other hand, any occupation is the result of an international armed conflict which is disrupted by a period of "calm" occupation. If this period is not followed by a settlement of the armed conflict – e.g. by a peace treaty – and the hostilities resume, the international armed conflict continues and thus the law applicable in international armed conflicts applies.

In consequence, the human rights law is supplemented by international humanitarian law rules concerning targeted killings. This means that combatants may be targeted, but civilians may generally not – unless and for such time as they take direct part in hostilities.[366]

F. International Humanitarian Law and the "War on Terror"

The term "war on terror" suggests that the efforts to fight international terrorism – at least since September 11, 2001 – fall into the category of an armed conflict. On September 20, 2001, U.S. President *George W. Bush* declared:

> Our war on terror begins with al Qaeda, but it does not end there. It will not end until every terrorist group of global reach has been found, stopped and defeated.[367]

Also earlier U.S. Presidents have declared "wars" on phenomena, such as the "war on poverty"[368] and the "war on drugs".[369] However, these "wars" largely consisted of national legislation addressing the respective problems. The younger term "war on terror" was not coined in reaction to September 11, 2001. Military force had been used previously

366 On the narrow interpretation of this concept *see supra*, Part Two, Chapter D) II. 1. c).

367 U.S. President George W. Bush, 'Address Before a Joint Session of the Congress on the United States Response to the Terrorist Attacks of September 11', September 20, 2001, in: 37 *Weekly Comp. Pres. Doc.* (2001), No. 38, pp. 1347-1351, at 1348.

368 U.S. President Lyndon B. Johnson, 'Proposal for A Nationwide War On The Sources of Poverty', Special Message to Congress, March 16, 1964, in: *Public Papers of U.S. Presidents, Lyndon B. Johnson, 1963-1964*, Washington, D.C. 1965, No. 1, pp. 375-380.

369 On June 17, 1971, U.S. President Nixon declared a "war on drugs", and called drug abuse "public enemy number one in the United States" in a press conference. In practice, his programs and legislation put an emphasis on the treatment for drug addicts, particularly rehabilitating heroin addicts with methadone. However, Nixon's harsh rhetoric expanded a climate of hostility toward those with drug problems, *see* Eric Sterling, 'US Drug Policy', in: 4 *FPIF* (1999), No. 31.

against "terrorist-supporting states"[370] and the term itself had already been used by U.S. President *Ronald Reagan*, who declared a "war against international terrorism", and sent American bombers against Libya in reaction to the involvement of the Libyan Government into the April 5, 1986 bombing of the West Berlin nightclub *La Belle*.[371] Calls for a "war on terror" also accompanied the strike on Iraq following the failed assassination attempt on former U.S. President *George Bush* and the attack on Afghan camps linked to *Osama bin Laden* in 1998.[372] In the trial of Sheikh *Omar Abdel-Rahman* and his nine accomplices for the 1993 World Trade Center bombing, the U.S. Attorney General opened by stating that "this is a case involving a war."[373]

The term can be traced back to a 1977 title of the *Time* magazine. The October 31 cover shows a picture of the Lufthansa flight 181 ("Landshut"), which had been hijacked to Mogadishu by four members of the *Popular Front for the Liberation of Palestine*.[374] There, on October 17./ 18., 1977, a special unit of the German Federal Police (then *Bundesgrenzschutz*) freed all 86 hostages and killed three of the hijackers.[375]

Beside the "war on terror", neither of the above "wars" declared by former U.S. Presidents referred to anything similar to an armed conflict. However, the U.S. President *George W. Bush* seems to take the

---

[370] *See e.g.* Jack M. Beard, 'Military Action against Terrorists under International Law – America's new War on Terror: The Case for Self-Defense under International Law', in: 25 *Harv. J.L. & Pub. Pol'y* (2002), pp. 559-590, at 561-562 with further references.

[371] *See e.g.* Canestaro, 26 *B.C. Int'l & Comp. L. Rev.* (2003), at 24; *compare* German Federal Court of Justice (Bundesgerichtshof), Case No. 5 StR 306/03 (La Belle-Anschlag), Judgment of June 24, 2004, in: 57 *NJW* (2004), pp. 3051-3057; Gross, *Struggle of Democracy*, p. 241.

[372] *See* Gross, 15 *Fla. J. Int'l L.* (2003), at 391.

[373] Richard Bernstein, 'Biggest U.S. Terrorist Trial Begins as Arguments Clash', in: *New York Times*, January 31, 1995, p. A1.

[374] Time Magazine, 'War on Terrorism', Vol. 110, No. 18 (October 31, 1977), front page.

[375] *See generally* Germany, *Dokumentation zu den Ereignissen und Entscheidungen im Zusammenhang mit der Entführung von Hanns Martin Schleyer und der Lufthansa-Maschine "Landshut"*, Presse- und Informationsamt der Bundesregierung, Bonn 1977.

term "war on terror" quite literally, as a real war.[376] Attempts by the U.S. Department of Defense to change the term to "global struggle against violent extremists" have failed.[377] Thus, it has to be carefully examined whether the term "war on terror" has any legal implications, especially regarding the application of international humanitarian law, or whether it only is "stirring rhetoric to rally the nation"[378] and equals such earlier rhetoric.

As shown above, there is no special status under international humanitarian law of a "terrorist".[379] Similarly, the relationship between "terrorism" and international humanitarian law does not depend on the existence of a definition of "terrorism". The threshold of applicability of international humanitarian law is not linked to the question of whether certain acts a regarded as amounting to "terrorism".[380] The question of applicability is solely based on the standards shown above, and not in the hands of a possible party to such a conflict. The same holds true for the application of human rights law and its possible derogations. Different authors argue that international humanitarian law applies to the "war on terror" as it is either a non-international or an international armed conflict.[381] It is clear that the United States and the countries al-

---

[376] *Compare e.g.* Kenneth Roth, 'The Law of War in the War on Terror', in: 83 *Foreign Aff.* (2004), pp. 2-7, at 2.

[377] Richard W. Stevenson, 'President Makes it Clear: Phrase is "War on Terror"', in: *New York Times*, August 4, 2005; George Packer, 'Name Calling', in: *New Yorker*, August 8, 2005.

[378] *Compare* Mary Ellen O'Connell, 'The Legal Case Against the Global War on Terror', in: 36 *Case W. Res. J. Int'l L.* (2004), pp. 349-357, at 349; *compare also* Tawia Ansah, 'War: Rhetoric & Norm Creation in Response to Terror', in: 43 *Va. J. Int'l L.* (2003), pp. 797-860, at 800-818; Upendra Baxi, 'The "War on Terror" and the "War of Terror": Nomadic Multitudes, Aggressive Incumbents, and the "New" International Law', in: 43 *Osgoode Hall L.J.* (2005), pp. 7-43, at 8-10; Markus Kotzur, '"Krieg gegen den Terrorismus" – politische Rhetorik oder neue Konturen des "Kriegsbegriffes" im Völkerrecht?', in: 40 *AVR* (2002), pp. 454-479.

[379] *Compare supra*, Part Two, Chapter E) V.

[380] *See also* Quénivet, in: Arnold/ Hildbrand (eds.), at 26-27.

[381] *See e.g.* Gross, 15 *Fla. J. Int'l L.* (2003), at 456; William K. Lietzau, 'Combating Terrorism: The Consequences of Moving from Law Enforcement to War', in: David Wippman; Matthew Evangelista (eds.), *New Wars, New Laws? Applying the Laws of War in 21st Century Conflicts*, Ardsley, N.Y. 2005, pp. 31-

lied with it constitute one side of the equation.[382] The other side, however is undefined and thus situations referred to as the "war on terror" have to be assessed on a case-by-case basis in order to establish whether those situations fall into the categories of international humanitarian law.

I. Is the "War on Terror" an International Armed Conflict?

The regular framework of traditional humanitarian law does not foresee a scenario of hostilities between a State and a transnational terrorist group.[383] However, the underlying purposes of the laws of war could also apply to conflicts with "terrorist organisations".[384] But does this mean that they apply *de lege lata*? Common Article 2 of the 1949 Geneva Conventions refers to an armed conflict as taking place "between two or more of the High Contracting Parties" and thus means States. On the other hand, it has been argued that it would be

> an illogical and inconsistent law of armed conflict which would apply to the temporary occupation of a small portion of a State's territory which offered no resistance; but did not apply to a series of air strikes or special forces operations carried out by a State against terrorist bases on another State's territory, simply because the target State's armed forces remained outside the fighting and its government was not responsible for the acts of the terrorists.[385]

On the other hand, if the "war on terror" was regarded as an international armed conflict, and even as a single global one, deliberate attacks upon members of the "enemy armed forces" would be lawful worldwide:

51, at 41-47; Neuman, 14 *Eur. J. Int'l L.* (2003), at 291-296. *Compare also* Vöneky, in: Walter *et al.* (eds.), pp. 925-949.

[382] Patel King/ Swaak-Goldman, 15 *Hague Yb. Int'l L.* (2003), at 43.

[383] Arai-Takahashi, 5 *Yb. Int'l Hum. L.* (2002), at 65; Fitzpatrick, 96 *Am. J. Int'l L.* (2002), at 348.

[384] *See e.g.* Eric A. Posner, 'Terrorism and the Laws of War', in: 5 *Chi. J. Int'l L.* (2004), pp. 423-434, at 431-434.

[385] Gill, *The 11th of September*, p. 25.

> If fully applied, this theory would have justified, subject to the principle of proportionality, an ambush attack on José Padilla when he left his plane at a Chicago airport.[386]

Accordingly, "an al-Qaeda member on the streets of a European city like Hamburg could lawfully be targeted."[387]

1. Level of Violence

To meet the threshold of an armed conflict and thus trigger the application of international humanitarian law, as shown above, a certain level of violence is necessary. This level is considerably lower in relation to international armed conflicts as opposed to non-international armed conflicts. Nevertheless, not each situation of a "terrorist nature" including a foreign element qualifies as an armed conflict.[388]

The question of intensity should not be confused with the question whether a certain act amounts to an armed attack triggering the right to self-defence under the *jus ad bellum*. However, those acts which are accepted to qualify as such an armed attack and are the starting point of an armed conflict and thus also trigger the application of the *jus in bellum*. According to *Rowles*, this is the case for such "terrorist attacks" which are "on a scale equivalent to what would be an armed attack if conducted by government forces."[389]

Thus, it has been argued that the level of violence reached by the September 11, 2001 attacks on the World Trade Center – even as an isolated act – is sufficient to establish an armed conflict.[390] It may be doubted

---

386 Marco Sassòli, 'Use and Abuse of the Laws of War in the "War on Terrorism"', in: 22 *L. & Ineq. J.* (2004), pp. 195-221, at 213.

387 Anthony Dworkin, 'Law and the Campaign Against Terrorism: The View from the Pentagon', in: *Crimes of War Project* (December 16, 2002).

388 Quénivet, in: Arnold/ Hildbrand (eds.), at 44.

389 James P. Rowles, 'Responses to Terrorism: Substantive and Procedural Constraints in International Law', 81 *ASIL Proc.* (1987), pp. 307-317, at 314.

390 *See e.g.* Silja Vöneky, 'Die Anwendbarkeit des humanitären Völkerrechts auf terroristische Akte und ihre Bekämpfung', in: Dieter Fleck (ed.), *Rechtsfragen der Terrorismusbekämpfung durch Streitkräfte*, Baden-Baden 2004, pp. 147-166, at 149-150; *compare also* Gross, 15 *Fla. J. Int'l L.* (2003), at 433-443 (with further references).

whether the threat really is of a new quality if past terrorist attacks like the 1993 bombing of the World Trade Center, and the 1995 bombing in Oklahoma City as well as Northern Irish and Basque terrorism is taken into account. Thus, already before September 11, 2001 it had been argued that danger from terrorist organisations entitled states to respond with the use of its armed forces.[391] However, it has to be admitted that concerning quantity, the attacks on the World Trade Center clearly reach the level of attacks that take place in or start an armed conflict. The death toll is higher than that of the World War Two Japanese attack on Pearl Harbour.[392] Especially if the international reaction to the September 11 attacks is taken into account, it can be understood that the level of violence was generally regarded as being comparable to that of an international armed conflict.[393] Beside that, it has also been argued –

---

[391] *See e.g.* Travalio, 18 *Wis. Int'l L.J.* (2000), at 160-161 with further references.

[392] The Pearl Harbor attack left 2,403 Americans dead, while the September 11 attacks killed 2,823 persons in Manhattan and 189 in Washington, D.C., *see* Fred L. Borch, 'Comparing Pearl Harbor and "9/11": Intelligence Failure? American Unpreparedness? Military Responsibility?', in: 67 *J. Mil. Hist.* (2003), pp. 845-860, at 846-847.

[393] *Compare e.g.* UN SC Res. 1368 (September 12, 2001), *Threats to International Peace and Security caused by Terrorist Acts*, U.N. Doc. S/RES/1368 (2001) and UN SC Res. 1373 (September 28, 2001), *Threats to International Peace and Security caused by Terrorist Acts*, U.N. Doc. S/RES/1373 (2000), both referring to "the inherent right of individual or collective self-defence in accordance with the Charter". The North Atlantic Treaty Organization, Statement by the North Atlantic Council of September 12, 2001 (Invocation Article V-attacks on US), Press Release (2001) 124 "agreed that if it is determined that this attack was directed from abroad against the United States, it shall be regarded as an action covered by Article 5 of the Washington Treaty, which states that an armed attack against one or more of the Allies in Europe or North America shall be considered an attack against them all." The statement refers to Article V of the North Atlantic Treaty, signed at Washington, D.C., on April 4, 1949, entry into force on August 24, 1949, reprinted in: 34 *UNTS* (1949), No. 541, pp. 243-255. The Organization of American States invoked the Inter-American Treaty of Reciprocal Assistance, also referred to as the "Rio Treaty", adopted by the Inter-American Conference for the Maintenance of Continental Peace and Security at Rio de Janeiro, Brazil on February 9, 1947, entry into force on March 12, 1948, OAS Treaty Series, Nos. 8 and 61, providing in Article 3 para. 1 that an armed attack against one or more of the parties shall be considered an attack against them all, *see* OAS, Convocation of the Twenty-

directly referring to international humanitarian (and criminal) law terminology – that such acts amount to crimes against humanity.[394] However, it has to be kept in mind that the level of violence is not the only

---

Fourth Meeting of Consultation of Ministers of Foreign Affairs to Serve as Organ of Consultation in Application of the Inter-American Treaty of Reciprocal Assistance, OEA/Ser G, CP/RES. 797 (1293/01), September 19, 2001; *see also* OAS, Twenty-Fourth Meeting of Consultation of Ministers of Foreign Affairs, *Resolution on Terrorist Threat to the Americas*, OEA/Ser.F/II.24, RC.24/RES.1 /01 (September 21, 2001).

See also Beard, 25 *Harv. J.L. & Pub. Pol'y* (2002), at 574-575 and 589-590; Yoram Dinstein, 'Comments on the Presentations by Nico Krisch and Carsten Stahn', in: Christian Walter; Silja Vöneky; Volker Röben; Frank Schorkopf (eds.), *Terrorism as a Challenge for National and International Law: Security versus Liberty?*, Berlin 2004, pp. 915-924, at 921-922; Franck, 95 *Am. J. Int'l L.* (2001), pp. 839-842; for the proceedings of the conference *Franck* refers to in the first footnote of his article *see* Michael Byers; Georg Nolte (eds.), *United States Hegemony and the Foundations of International Law*, Cambridge 2003; Jochen Frowein, 62 *ZaöRV* (2002), at 885-889; Gross, *Struggle of Democracy*, pp. 29-45; Paust, 28 *Yale J. Int'l L.* (2003), at 326; Vöneky, in: Walter *et al.* (eds.), at 931; Watkin, 98 *Am. J. Int'l L.* (2004), at 5. *Compare also* Christian Walter, 'Zwischen Selbstverteidigung und Völkerstrafrecht: Bausteine für ein internationales Recht der "präventiven Terrorismus-Bekämpfung"', in: Dieter Fleck (ed.), *Rechtsfragen der Terrorismusbekämpfung durch Streitkräfte*, Baden-Baden 2004, pp. 23-42, at 26-27; Stahn, in: Walter *et al.* (eds.), at 859-862.

But see Alain Pellet, 'No, This is not War!', in: *Eur. J. Int'l L. Discussion Forum: The Attack on the World Trade Center: Legal Responses* (October 3, 2001). *Compare also* Anderson, in: Wittes (ed.), at 358-359. However, even *Pellet* accepts that "it is not excessive to compare the attack on the Twin Towers to that of Pearl Harbor.", *see* Alain Pellet; Vladimir Tzankov, 'Can a State Victim of a Terror Act have Recourse to Armed Force?', in: 17 *HuV-I* (2004), pp. 68-72, at 71.

394 Antonio Cassese, 'Terrorism is also Disrupting Some Crucial Legal Categories of International Law', in: 12 *Eur. J. Int'l L.* (2001), pp. 993-1002, at 994-995 with further references; Michael Byers, 'Terrorism, the Use of Force and International Law after September 11', in: 51 *The Int'l & Comp. L.Q.* (2002), pp. 401-414, at 413 (footnote 66); Jost Delbrück, 'The Fight Against Global Terrorism: Self-Defense or Collective Security as International Police Action? Some Comments on the International Legal Implications of the "War on Terrorism"', in: 44 *German Yb. Int'l L.* (2001), pp. 9-24, at 22; Greenwood, 78 *Int'l Aff.* (2002), at 305 (footnote 17); Nico J. Schrijver, 'Responding to International Terrorism: Moving the Frontiers of International Law for "Enduring Freedom"?', in: 48 *Nether. Int'l L. Rev.* (2001), pp. 271-292, at 287.

criterion. The U.K. for example explicitly excludes high level violence by terrorists ("concerted acts of terrorism") from its understanding of an armed confect and states that,

> it is the understanding of the United Kingdom that the term 'armed conflict' of itself and in its context denotes a situation of a kind which is not constituted by the commission of ordinary crimes including acts of terrorism whether concerted or in isolation.[395]

Not only *Rowles* himself is of the opinion that a single, one-time attack by a "terrorist group" would not amount to an armed attack which would justify the use of force and thus establish an armed conflict.[396] At the same time, a single forcible reaction to a "terrorist attack" – such as an attack against an operational basis or against a leader of a "terrorist group" – would in itself not be sufficient to meet the threshold of intensity.[397]

2. *Parties to a Possible International Armed Conflict*

Even if it is accepted that the level of violence which is necessary to establish an armed conflict can be reached by a terrorist attack, the further aspects of an armed conflict must also be given. Such a conflict is – as shown above – classically defined by the participation of at least two states. It thus generally does not comprise what has been referred to as "a new form of armed conflict"[398] or "unconventional war"[399] in relation to a terrorist group. However, a possibility to cover such "new conflicts" would be that a non-State actor could be a party to an international armed conflict according to Common Article 2 of the 1949 Geneva Conventions. This possibility is examined first. According to the second possible approach, an armed conflict exists between the victim State of the terrorist attack and the host State of the terrorist group.

---

395 United Kingdom, The Geneva Conventions Act (First Protocol) Order 1998, *Statutory Instruments* (1998), No. 1754, made July 21, 1998, entry into force on July 28, 1998.

396 Rowles, 81 *ASIL Proc.* (1987), at 314.

397 *See e.g.* Vöneky, in: Walter *et al.* (eds.), at 943 with further references.

398 *Compare* Guiora, 36 *Case W. Res. J. Int'l L.* (2004), at 330.

399 Statman, 5 *Theo. Inq. L.* (2004), at 197.

In this constellation the members of the terrorist group could be legitimate targets.

a) An International Armed Conflict between a State and "Terrorist" Non-State Actors?

Not only the U.S. administration under president *George W. Bush* argues that the "war on terror" is an international armed conflict taking place between a State and a non-State actor, i.e. the U.S. and al-Qaeda.[400] This assessment corresponds to the fact that al-Qaeda is said to have "declared a jihad, or holy war, against the United States" in 1996.[401] Thus, the "war" paradigm seems to be used by both sides.[402]

---

[400] *See e.g.* Frank A. Biggio, 'Neutralising the Threat: Reconsidering Existing Doctrines in the Emerging War on Terrorism', in: 34 *Case W. Res. J. Int'l L.* (2002), pp. 1-43, at 4; Jane Gililand Dalton, 'What is War? Terrorism as War After 9/11', in: 12 *ILSA J. Int'l & Comp. L.* (2006), pp. 523-533; Dinstein, in: Walter *et al.* (eds.), at 921-923, albeit *Dinstein* refers to "extra-territorial law enforcement", but based on the right of self-defence against terrorists located in a foreign territory; Robert Kogod Goldman, 'Certain Legal Questions and Issues Raised by the September 11th Attacks', in: 9 *Hum. Rts. Brief* (2001), No. 1, pp. 2-4; Posner, 5 *Chi. J. Int'l L.* (2004), at 424 (subject to some reservations); Ruth Wedgwood, 'Combatants or Criminals? How Washington Should Handle Terrorists: Fighting a War Under its Rules', in: 83 *Foreign Aff.* (2004), pp. 126-129.

But see e.g. Roth, 83 *Foreign Aff.* (2004), pp. 2-7; *compare also* U.S. Supreme Court, *Salim Ahmed Hamdan v. Donald H. Rumsfeld, Secretary of Defense,* et al., Case No. 05-184, Decision of June 29, 2006, reprinted in: 45 *ILM* (2006), pp. 1130-1203, at 1153 (para. VI D ii); Fionnuala D. Ní Aoláin, '"Hamdan" and Common Article 3: Did the Supreme Court Get it Right?', in: 91 *Minn. L. Rev.* (2007), pp. 1525-1563, at 1537-1538.

[401] U.S. District Court for the Eastern District of Virginia, Alexandria Division, *United States v. Zacarias Moussaoui* (Superseding Indictment, June 2002), para. 2.

[402] It has even been taken into account that "a state of hostilities existed between the United States and al Qaeda as early as 1992, when al Qaeda leadership issued a 'fatwa' for jihad against United States forces located in Islamic territory", Dalton, 12 *ILSA J. Int'l & Comp. L.* (2006), at 523; *compare* U.S. National Commission on Terrorist Attacks on the United States, *The 9/11 Commission Report*, Final Report, 2005, p. 59.

One of the arguments that the "war" paradigm must be preferred in comparison to law enforcement and criminal law is that due process rules in criminal proceedings would demand States to share their knowledge and intelligence with the defendants who are – according to some authors – not "ordinary defendants" but "enemies" of the State. This information could then prove to be very useful for terrorist groups and "educate the enemy".[403] It is undisputed that non-State actors like al-Qaeda are not "High Contracting Parties" to the international humanitarian law conventions.[404] However, to support the "war" assessment legally, it has been argued that also a non-State actor such as the organisation al-Qaeda could be a party to an international armed conflict as a "power" under Article 2 para. 3 of the 1949 Geneva Conventions.[405] This paragraph reads:

> Although one of the Powers in conflict may not be a party to the present Convention, the Powers who are parties thereto shall remain bound by it in their mutual relations. They shall furthermore be bound by the Convention in relation to the said Power, if the latter accepts and applies the provisions thereof.

Already the paragraph itself strongly supports the view that "power" only refers to those who can be party to the Conventions, namely States. National liberation movements tried to become party to the Conventions, but could not due to a lack of statehood. The same holds true for governments in exile.[406] If the use of the term "power" is ana-

---

[403] McCarthy, 36 *Case W. Res. J. Int'l L.* (2004), at 518-520.

[404] *See e.g.* Brooks, 153 *U. Pa. L. Rev.* (2004), at 714.

[405] *See e.g.* Dalton, 12 *ILSA J. Int'l & Comp. L.* (2006), at 528-529; *compare also the discussion in* European Commission for Democracy through Law, Opinion No. 245/2003, para. 11.

[406] For example, the provisional government of Algeria, situated in Cairo, made a declaration of accession to the Geneva Conventions in 1960 to depositary Switzerland. In return, Switzerland declined to accept that declaration as the provisional government had not been formally recognised. *See* Detter, *Law of War*, p. 185. In reaction to this situation, the practice evolved to declare the Conventions applicable. Such declarations are directed at the International Committee of the Red Cross, and not at the depositary. Examples are the declarations by the Eritrean People's Liberation Front (EPLF) of February 25, 1977, by the Union National pour l'Indépence d'Angola (UNITA) of July 25, 1980, by the African National Congress (ANC) of November 29, 1980, by the Philippine Moro National Liberation Front (MNLF) of May 18, 1981, by the South-

lysed throughout the 1949 Geneva Convention IV several hints can be found that it refers to a State. Article 4 refers to "nationals" of such a power, Article 9 para. 1 refers to "nationals" and "protecting powers" as well as "neutral powers". Article 11 para. 5 refers to "the territory of the said power", and Articles 36, 39 as well as Article 48 refer to "nationals" and the "territory" of a power. Finally, Article 23 in the English version several times refers to "power" and in para. 4 to "the power which permits their free passage". The likewise authentic French text[407] as usual refers to "puissance" but in para. 4 explicitly refer to "l'Etat qui autorise leur libre passage". Thus, it becomes clear that the terms "power" and "puissance" are used interchangeably with "State" and "l'Etat".

This assessment is also supported by the drafting history. In the discussions on "Powers" which may not be a party to the Convention, it was referred to as "non-Contracting State" or "l'Etat non contractant" respectively.[408] Thus, one cannot but conclude that the Geneva Conventions imply that a "Power" must be a State and cannot merely be a powerful organisation of some kind.[409] Hence, international humanitarian law does *per definitionem* not apply to an international conflict between a State and a non-State actor and such a conflict does not qualify as an international armed conflict.

> In the language of international law there is no basis for speaking of a war on Al-Qaeda or any other terrorist group, for such group cannot be a belligerent, it is merely a band of criminals, and to treat it as anything else risks distorting the law while giving that group a status which to some implies a degree of legitimacy.[410]

West Africa People's Organisation (SWAPO) of August 25, 1981, by the Afghan National Liberation Front (ANLF) of December 24, 1981, by the Palestine Liberation Organization (PLO) of July 7, 1982, etc.

[407] *See* Article 150 of the 1949 Geneva Convention IV.

[408] *See* Pictet (ed.), *Geneva Conventions*, Vol. 4, pp. 24-25.

[409] *See also* European Commission for Democracy through Law, Opinion No. 245/2003, paras. 11-12.

[410] Christoper Greenwood, 'War, Terrorism, and International Law', in: 56 *Current Legal Probs.* (2004), pp. 505-530, at 529; *see also* Paust, 28 *Yale J. Int'l L.* (2003), at 326.

Thus, violence between a state and a transnational terrorist group is not an international armed conflict.[411] Al-Qaeda – as most likely all "terrorist organisations" – also cannot be regarded as oppressed "peoples" entitled to exercise the principle of self-determination against occupying or colonial forces within the meaning of Article 1 para. 4 of 1977 Additional Protocol I.[412] However, this does not automatically mean that acts by such groups can never fall into the ambit of international humanitarian law. This could still be the case if such deeds could be attributed to a State.[413]

b) Armed Conflict between the Victim State of the Attack and a Foreign State Related to the "Terrorist" Group?

Rowe argues that

> from the moment the first plane hit one of the twin towers in New York, the Geneva Conventions (and all other laws of war treaties to which the US and Afghanistan were parties, as well as relevant Customary international law) became applicable.[414]

It is incontrovertible that the armed conflict between the U.S.-led coalition and the State of Afghanistan governed by the Taliban was an international armed conflict from October 7, 2001, i.e. the military intervention by the coalition forces in Afghanistan.[415] However, it is less clear when exactly the whole conflict started. It has been comprehensively

---

[411] *Compare also* Kretzmer, 16 *Eur. J. Int'l L.* (2005), at 202; Paust, 28 *Yale J. Int'l L.* (2003), at 326; Quénivet, in: Arnold/ Hildbrand (eds.), at 47; Rona, 27 *Fletcher F. World Aff.* (2003), at 57; Vöneky, in: Walter *et al.* (eds.), at 931. *But see* Paulus/ Vashakmadze, 91 *Int'l Rev. Red Cross* (2009), No. 873, at 115-119, who see the general possibility of such an international armed conflict under certain circumstances. The question whether such a conflict might qualify as a non-international armed conflict will be examined *infra*, Part Four, Chapter F) II.

[412] *See also* Arai-Takahashi, 5 *Yb. Int'l Hum. L.* (2002), at 66; Vöneky, in: Walter *et al.* (eds.), at 931-932.

[413] *Compare also* Vöneky, in: Fleck (ed.), *Rechtsfragen*, at 150-151.

[414] Rowe, 3 *Melb. J. Int'l L.* (2002), at 312.

[415] *See e.g.* Arai-Takahashi, 5 *Yb. Int'l Hum. L.* (2002), at 65; Patel King/ Swaak-Goldman, 15 *Hague Yb. Int'l L.* (2003), at 44; Vöneky, in: Fleck (ed.), *Rechtsfragen*, at 157.

discussed whether an attack by a non-State actor can amount to an "armed attack" triggering the right to self-defence. It is not necessary to answer this question of *jus ad bellum* here, as international humanitarian law applies to all armed conflicts irrespective to the legality of the State's resort to force in the first place. However, the question has a strong influence concerning the establishment of an armed conflict. If an attack by a non-State actor amounts to an "act of war" and can be attributed to a foreign State, then an armed conflict between the latter State and the victim State of the attack could exist.[416] This is not only the case when a foreign State intervenes in an ongoing non-international armed conflict on the side of the non-State actors. A conflict could also be regarded as international from the moment the non-State actors strike at the victim State in a way attributable to the foreign State.[417] The question of whether an armed conflict can be considered to be international is thus closely related to the problem of State responsibility.[418] Whereas the direct intervention by a foreign State can be proven

---

[416] Dalton, 12 *ILSA J. Int'l & Comp. L.* (2006), at 523; Dinstein, in: Walter *et al.* (eds.), at 919-920; Quénivet, in: Arnold/ Hildbrand (eds.), at 45; Rowe, 3 *Melb. J. Int'l L.* (2002), at 312; Tom Ruys; Sten Verhoeven, 'Attacks by Private Actors and the Right of Self-Defence', in: 10 *J. Confl. Sec. L.* (2005), pp. 289-320, at 314-317. *But see* Mary Ellen O'Connell, 'When is a War not a War? The Myth of the Global War on Terror', in: 12 *ILSA J. Int'l & Comp. L.* (2006), pp. 535-539, at 538, arguing that war "do not begin with an attack. They begin with a counter-attack. States may have the right to engage in a war of self-defense following an attack. If they chose not to do so, there is no war. War, as discussed above requires exchange, intensity and duration."

[417] *See e.g.* ICTY, *Prosecutor v. Duško Tadić*, Case No. IT-94-1-A, Judgment (Merits Appeal) of July 15, 1999, reprinted in: 124 *Int'l L.R.* (2003), pp. 63-212, at 96 (para. 84); ICTY, *Prosecutor v. Tihomir Blaškić*, Case No. IT-95-14-T, ("Lasva Valley"), Judgment of March 3, 2000, reprinted in: 122 *Int'l L.R.* (2002), pp. 1-250, at 43 (paras. 75-76); ICTY, *Prosecutor v. Dario Kordić and Mario Čerkez*, Case No. IT-95-14/2 ("Lasva Valley"), Judgment of February 26, 2001, para. 66.

[418] *See also* Leo van den Hole, 'Towards a Test of the International Character of an Armed Conflict: Nicaragua and Tadic', in: 32 *Syracuse J. Int'l L. & Com.* (2005), pp. 269-289, at 270.

comparatively easily, it is more complex to develop an attribution of a non-State actor's acts to a foreign State.[419]

(1) Non-State Actors as "Other Militias and Members of Volunteer Corps Belonging to a Party to a Conflict"

Concerning the current "war on terror", it might be argued that the hostilities between the U.S.-led forces and the al-Qaeda can be subsumed into the conflict between the U.S. and the Afghan Taliban government. This could be the case if al-Qaeda would qualify as "other militias and members of volunteer corps ... belonging to a Party to a conflict" in the meaning of Article 4A para. 2 of the 1949 Geneva Convention III.[420] However, the mere act of fighting in concert does not meet the test of "belonging".[421] Furthermore, it is unlikely that the al-Qaeda met the four additional conditions of (a) that of being commanded by a person responsible for his subordinates; (b) that of having a fixed distinctive sign recognizable at a distance; (c) that of carrying arms openly; (d) that of conducting their operations in accordance with the laws and customs of war.[422] But most of all, this argument is met by fundamental doubts. Article 4 of the 1949 Geneva Convention III concerns the status of a person as a combatant. It thus refers to "irregulars" who fight along with regular armed forces in an ongoing international armed conflict between States. The international armed conflict is thus presupposed and cannot be established by the "irregulars". The question of whether the 1949 Geneva Conventions apply must be decided according to Article 2 and before the Status of a person in that conflict can be assessed according to the then applicable rules.

---

[419] ICTY, *Prosecutor v. Tihomir Blaškić*, Case No. IT-95-14-T, ("Lasva Valley"), Judgment of March 3, 2000, reprinted in: 122 *Int'l L.R.* (2002), pp. 1-250, at 43 (para. 76).

[420] Arai-Takahashi, 5 *Yb. Int'l Hum. L.* (2002), at 66.

[421] *Id.*

[422] *Compare supra*, Part Two, Chapter C) I.

(2) Attribution According to "*Nicaragua*" or "*Tadić*"?

If the actions by non-State actors are attributable to a foreign State, these actions could be considered as behaviour by that State itself and the formerly internal conflict would amount to an inter-State conflict.[423] In principle, States are generally responsible for their organs' actions, but they are not responsible for the acts of private individuals or groups emanating from their territory or organised therein.[424] Actions by such groups could nevertheless be attributed to a State under certain circumstances, i.e. if they amount to *de facto* State organs. *De facto* State organs are individuals who in fact act on behalf of a state although they do not have the formal status and rank of a state official. This is the case for persons who are under instructions of a State, who are under a certain control of a State or in fact behave as state officials. An example is the Secretary-General of a political party in a one-party State.[425]

(i) "*Nicaragua*" and the International Law Commission: Effective Control

The International Court of Justice in *Nicaragua*[426] had to decide a case of pure State responsibility. The Court ruled that first and obviously, those individuals who are State officials act on behalf of the State. Thus, in *Nicaragua*, high-altitude reconnaissance flights by U.S. airplanes with U.S. crews are clearly attributable to the Untied States.[427]

Second, on the basis of the "effective control test", the Court found that acts committed by persons of unidentified Latin-American nationalities referred to by the Central Intelligence Agency (CIA) as "Unilaterally Controlled Latino Assets" (UCLA) were attributed to the Unit-

---

[423] *Compare e.g.* Dinstein, in: Walter *et al.* (eds.), at 919-920.

[424] *See e.g.* ICJ, *Corfu Channel, Merits*, Judgment of April 9, 1949, I.C.J. Reports 1949, pp.4-38, at 18; Jennings/ Watts (eds.), *Oppenheim's International Law*, Vol. I, pp. 449-551.

[425] Cassese, *International Law*, pp 247-248.

[426] ICJ, *Military and Paramilitary Activities in and against Nicaragua, Nicaragua v. the United States of America*, Judgment (Merits) of June 27, 1986, I.C.J. Rep. 1986, pp. 14-150.

[427] *Id.*, at 52-53 (para. 91).

ed States. The UCLA carried out tasks such as mining Nicaraguan ports and waters and attacks on ports and oil installations.[428] Such acts were attributed to the United States based on two alternative grounds: First, certain acts were attributed as the UCLA had been paid by the U.S. Government and had been given instructions by U.S. agents under whose supervision they acted.[429] Second, certain acts were attributed because U.S. agents had "participated in the planning, direction, support and execution" of operations by the UCLA.[430] Thus, the UCLA had acted under the "effective control" of the United States and their acts were attributed to it.

Third, in connection with the *Contras*, who directed paramilitary activities against Nicaragua from bases in Honduras and Costa Rica, the Court made a significant distinction: Based on the partial dependency of the *Contras* upon the United States, the Court recognised a degree of control exercised by the latter. However, according to the Court, this control did not suffice to make all acts committed by the *Contras* attributable to the United States.[431] Assistance by the United States to the *Contras* constituted a breach of the international law principle of non-intervention,[432] and infringed the territorial sovereignty of Nicaragua.[433] But the Court held that the relationship between the United States and the *Contras* was not close enough as to establish responsibility of the former for breaches of international humanitarian law by members of the latter.[434]

The rule of "effective control" is partly reflected in Article 8 of the ILC Articles on State Responsibility,[435] which reads:

---

[428] *Id.*, at 45 (para. 75).

[429] *Id.*, at 48 (para. 80).

[430] *Id.*, at 50-51 (para. 86).

[431] *Id.*, at 62-65 (paras. 109-116).

[432] *Id.*, at 123-125 (paras. 239-242).

[433] *Id.*, at 127-128 (paras. 250-252).

[434] *Id.*, at 65 (para. 116).

[435] *Compare* Helmut Philipp Aust, 'The Normative Environment for Peace – On the Contribution of the ILC's Articles on State Responsibility', in: Georg Nolte (ed.), *Peace through International Law: The Role of the International Law Commission*, Heidelberg 2009, pp. 13-46, at 41.

> The conduct of a person or group of persons shall be considered an act of a State under international law if the person or group of persons is in fact acting on the instructions of, or under the direction or control of, that State in carrying out the conduct.

The principle of "effective control" was applied by the International Tribunal for the Former Yugoslavia's Trial Chamber in *Tadić*[436] but already contested in a dissenting opinion by Judge *McDonald*, who favoured a test of "dependency and control"[437] and sewed the seeds of the "overall control test".[438]

(ii) "*Tadić*": Overall Control

In *Tadić*, the ICTY dealt directly with the question of whether the conflict in the former Yugoslavia was an international armed conflict. This question was relevant for the jurisdiction of the Tribunal over grave breaches of the 1949 Geneva Conventions.[439] In assessing that question, the Tribunal had to establish whether some individuals (Bosnian Serb forces) had acted on behalf of a foreign country, namely the Federal Republic of Yugoslavia. The Trial Chamber had implicitly found that the Bosnian Serb forces in question were not under the effective control of Federal Republic of Yugoslavia after the Yugoslavian army formally withdrew from Bosnia-Herzegovina. Thus, the conflict was regarded as being non-international and *Duško Tadić's* victims only enjoyed the rel-

---

436 ICTY, *Prosecutor v. Duško Tadić*, Case No. IT-94-1-A, Judgment of May 7, 1997, reprinted in: 112 *Int'l L.R.* (1999), pp. 1-285, at 188-192 (paras. 584-588).

437 *Id.*, Separate and Dissenting Opinion of Judge McDonald regarding the Applicability of Article 2 of the Statute, reprinted in: 112 *Int'l L.R.* (1999), pp. 261-276, at 274-276 (paras. 32-34).

438 *Compare* Hole, 32 *Syracuse J. Int'l L. & Com.* (2005), at 276 (note 31).

439 The ICTY argued that the grave breaches enumerated in the Conventions are covered by universal jurisdiction if committed in an international armed conflict, but that the States party to the Conventions did not want to give other States jurisdiction over serious violations of international humanitarian law committed in their domestic armed conflicts. Thus, to establish the jurisdiction of the Tribunal under Article 2 of its Statute, the conflict had to be international, *see* ICTY, *Prosecutor v. Duško Tadić*, Case No. IT-94-1-AR72, Decision on the Defence Motion for Interlocutory Appeal on Jurisdiction of October 2, 1995, reprinted in: 105 *Int'l L.R.* (1997), pp. 419-648, at 495-497 (paras. 79-80).

atively lower level of protection of Common Article 3 of the 1949 Geneva Conventions.[440]

However, the Appeals Chamber departed from this outcome and – relying on cases of the Iran-United States Claims Tribunal, the European Court of Human Rights and national courts[441] – held that international law provides for different tests that had been applied by State and judicial practice. These tests – according to the Chamber – "do not always require the same degree of control over armed groups or private individuals".[442] First, the Appeals Chamber accepted that the "effective control test" applies to the second group in *Nicaragua*, namely the UCLA:

> Where the question at issue is whether a *single* private individual or a *group that is not militarily organised* has acted as a *de facto* State organ when performing a specific act, it is necessary to ascertain whether specific instructions concerning the commission of that particular act had been issued by that State to the individual or group in question; alternatively, it must be established whether the unlawful act had been publicly endorsed or approved *ex post facto* by the State at issue.[443]

Thus, the actions of such individuals or groups are, in the view of the ICTY, attributable according either to the rules as laid down by the ICJ in *Nicaragua*[444] or to those laid down in the *Tehran Hostages*.[445] Sec-

---

[440] ICTY, *Prosecutor v. Duško Tadić*, Case No. IT-94-1-A, Judgment of May 7, 1997, reprinted in: 112 *Int'l L.R.* (1999), pp. 1-285, at 200 (paras. 607-608).

[441] *Compare* ICTY, *Prosecutor v. Duško Tadić*, Case No. IT-94-1-A, Judgment (Merits Appeal) of July 15, 1999, reprinted in: 124 *Int'l L.R.* (2003), pp. 63-212, at 111-116 (paras. 124-130), with further references, *inter alia* to the Eur. Ct. H.R., *Loizidou (Merits)*, *ECHR* 1996-VI, pp. 2216-2259.

[442] ICTY, *Prosecutor v. Duško Tadić*, Case No. IT-94-1-A, Judgment (Merits Appeal) of July 15, 1999, reprinted in: 124 *Int'l L.R.* (2003), pp. 63-212, at 118-119 (para. 137).

[443] *Id.*

[444] ICJ, *Military and Paramilitary Activities in and against Nicaragua, Nicaragua v. United States of America*, Judgment (Merits) of June 27, 1986, I.C.J. Reports 1986, pp. 14-150, at 50-51 (para. 86).

[445] ICJ, *United States Diplomatic and Consular Staff in Tehran, United States of America v. Iran, Merits*, Judgment of May 24, 1980, I.C.J. Reports 1980, pp. 3-46, at 34-35 (paras. 73-74).

ond, the majority opinion of the Appeals Chamber developed a different standard for "armed forces or militias or paramilitary units". It rejected the "effective control test" and applied an "overall control test" to these groups:

> By contrast, control by a State over subordinate *armed forces or militias or paramilitary units* may be of an overall character (and must comprise more than the mere provision of financial assistance or military equipment or training). This requirement, however, does not go so far as to include the issuing of specific orders by the State, or its direction of each individual operation. Under international law it is by no means necessary that the controlling authorities should plan all the operations of the units dependent on them, choose their targets, or give specific instructions concerning the conduct of military operations and any alleged violations of international humanitarian law. The control required by international law may be deemed to exist when a State (or, in the context of an armed conflict, the Party to the conflict) *has a role in organising, coordinating or planning the military actions* of the military group, in addition to financing, training and equipping or providing operational support to that group. Acts performed by the group or members thereof may be regarded as acts of *de facto* State organs regardless of any specific instruction by the controlling State concerning the commission of each of those acts.[446]

Third, the Appeals Chamber holds that international law also embraces an additional test concerning the assimilation of individuals to State organs.[447] This test is, however, not relevant to the present question, as it concerns the individual responsibility of persons assimilated to ongoing State conduct and thus presupposes such direct conduct by a State.

---

[446] ICTY, *Prosecutor v. Duško Tadić*, Case No. IT-94-1-A, Judgment (Merits Appeal) of July 15, 1999, reprinted in: 124 *Int'l L.R.* (2003), pp. 63-212, at 118-119 (para. 137) (emphasis in the original).

[447] *Id.*, at 119-121 (paras. 141-144). This test is based on World War II cases concerning concentration camp inmates of foreign who were "elevated by the camp administrators to positions of authority over the other internees", *compare* U.K. Military Court (Luneberg), *Trial of Joseph Kramer and 44 Others (The Belsen Trial)*, Judgment of November 17, 1945, in: 2 *Law Reports of Trials of War Criminals* (1947), pp. 1-138, at 1.

(iii) Conclusion: "*Nicaragua*" v. "*Tadić*"?

Obviously, the background of *Nicaragua* and *Tadić* differs: The ICJ had to establish whether a foreign State was internationally responsible for specific acts executed by non-State actors. The ICTY did not have to relate such specific acts to a foreign State, but had to consider whether the general involvement of that State into an ongoing internal conflict rendered that conflict international. It is thus open to discussion whether the basic legal question at issue really was the same.[448] *Meron* states:

> Obviously, the Nicaragua test addresses only the question of state responsibility. Conceptually, it cannot determine whether a conflict is international or internal. In practice, applying the Nicaragua test to the question in *Tadić* produces artificial and incongruous conclusions.[449]

If the different context is taken into account, it suggests itself that the ICJ referred to a more specific test and the ICTY to a more general one, even though it has been argued that the conflict between the two tests "is exaggerated or even does not exist".[450] The ICJ addressed this conflict itself in its recent Judgment on the *Application of the Genocide Convention* and stressed that,

> logic does not require the same test to be adopted in resolving the two issues, which are very different in nature: the degree and nature of a State's involvement in an armed conflict on another State's territory which is required for the conflict to be characterized as international, can very well, and without logical inconsistency, differ from the degree and nature of involvement required to give rise to that State's responsibility for a specific act committed in the course of the conflict.[451]

The Court furthermore not only distinguished its present case concerning State responsibility from the question that arose in *Tadić*. It at least did not reject the "overall control test" where appropriate and could even be read to accept it for such cases:

---

[448] *See* Cassese, *International Law*, p. 249.

[449] Meron, 92 *Am. J. Int'l L.* (1998), at 237.

[450] Hole, 32 *Syracuse J. Int'l L. & Com.* (2005), at 279.

[451] ICJ, *Application of the Convention on the Prevention and Punishment of the Crime of Genocide, Bosnia and Herzegovina v. Serbia and Montenegro*, Judgment of February 26, 2007, para. 405.

> Insofar as the "overall control" test is employed to determine whether or not an armed conflict is international, which was the sole question which the Appeals Chamber was called upon to decide, it may well be that the test is applicable and suitable;[452]

As the ICJ again dealt with a question of State responsibility in its present case, obviously it went on to apply the standards concerning State responsibility, namely Article 8 of the ILC Articles on State Responsibility and "effective control".[453]

Thus, it can be concluded that "overall control" by a State over non-State armed forces, militias or paramilitary units suffices to establish an involvement of that State into a non-international armed conflict to the effect that this conflict becomes international. This principle can be transferred to cases in which it is not an ongoing internal armed conflict which is changed in character, but in which the whole conflict is started by such non-State actors. In the latter case, if the threshold of an armed conflict is met, this conflict is an international armed conflict and triggers the full application of international humanitarian law. However, if a single private individual or groups that are not militarily organised are concerned, even according to the ICTY, a more specific "effective control" is necessary to attribute the actions to a State.

(3) Attribution According to "*Tehran Hostages*"?

It has already been discussed *supra* as part of the ICTY Appeals Chamber's *Tadić* Judgment that acts committed by non-State actors can be attributable to the State on whose territory the act was committed if the latter does not act with due diligence. This is the case, for example, if the acts are publicly endorsed or approved *ex post facto* by the State at issue.[454] To avoid this attribution, the state has to take the necessary measures to prevent such acts, or, after such acts have been performed,

---

[452] *Id.*, para. 404.

[453] *Id.*, paras. 406-407 and 410-420.

[454] ICJ, *United States Diplomatic and Consular Staff in Tehran, United States of America v. Iran, Merits*, Judgment of May 24, 1980, I.C.J. Reports 1980, pp. 3-46, at 34-35 (paras. 73-74); *see also* ICTY, *Prosecutor v. Duško Tadić*, Case No. IT-94-1-A, Judgment (Merits Appeal) of July 15, 1999, reprinted in: 124 *Int'l L.R.* (2003), pp. 63-212, at 118-119 (para. 137).

it has to search for and punish the authors of those acts, as well as pay compensation to the victims.[455]

This standard was applied by the ICJ in *Tehran Hostages*, again concerning State responsibility:[456] In that case, the attack by private individuals on the U.S. Embassy and consular premises could not be directly imputed to the State.[457] Nevertheless Iran was held responsible not only in that it failed to protect the U.S. premises as required by international law, but also as it approved the "occupation" of the premises.[458] Such approval of the conduct by individuals can have retroactive effect.[459]

In relation to the "war on terror", the failure not to hand over named individuals that had been requested by the U.S. may be taken as evidence of a degree of responsibility on the part of Afghanistan itself for the acts of others operating within its territory.[460] However, this is exclusively a question of State responsibility. Even if Afghanistan committed an international wrongful act by not handing over persons involved in the September 11 attacks, this conduct would not automatically establish an armed conflict between Afghanistan and the United

---

[455] Cassese, *International Law*, p. 250.

[456] ICJ, *United States Diplomatic and Consular Staff in Tehran, United States of America v. Iran, Merits*, Judgment of May 24, 1980, I.C.J. Reports 1980, pp. 3-46.

[457] *Id.*, at 29 (para. 58).

[458] *Id.*, at 29-30 (paras. 59-68); *compare also* UN General Assembly, International Law Commission, *Commentaries to the Draft Articles on Responsibility of States for Internationally Wrongful Acts adopted by the ILC at its fifty-third session (2001)*, UN GAOR, 56th Session, Supp. No. 10, UN Doc. A/56/10 (2001), pp. 59-365, at 121. The Articles on State Responsibility seek to formulate, by way of codification but also progressive development, the basic (secondary) rules of international law governing state responsibility, *see* Crawford, *State Responsibility*, p. 74.

[459] *Compare* Article 11 of the UN General Assembly, International Law Commission, *Draft Articles on Responsibility of States*, pp. 43-58; *see also* UN General Assembly, ILC, *First Report on State Responsibility – Addendum 5 (by Special Rapporteur James Crawford)*, UN Doc. A/CN.4/490/Add.5 (July 22, 1998), pp. 42-44 (paras. 283-284).

[460] Dinstein, in: Walter *et al.* (eds.), at 920; Rowe, 3 *Melb. J. Int'l L.* (2002), at 308; *compare also* Walter, in: Fleck (ed.), *Rechtsfragen*, at 40-41.

States.[461] According to the ICJ, such omission can give rise to State responsibility if the omission itself is a violation of a duty under international law.[462] This does not automatically mean that the acts themselves by the non-State actors can be attributed to the State. The ICJ clearly distinguished the former and the latter case when it referred to the "second phase of events" in *Tehran Hostages*.[463] Here, the former mere inactivity on the part of the Iranian government was followed by official approval of the acts in question. The Court in consequence establishes that the

> approval given to these facts by the Ayatollah Khomeini and other organs of the Iranian State, and the decision to perpetuate them, translated continuing occupation of the Embassy and detention of the hostages into acts of that State.[464]

According to the Court, this behaviour constitutes additional breaches of international law and is clearly distinguished form the responsibility established due to inaction on the side of the State.[465] Thus, *Tehran Hostages* shows that mere inaction by a host state may give rise to State responsibility but not make attacks by non-State actors attributable to it in a way that establishes an international armed conflict.

3. Conclusion

What is referred to as the "war on terror" cannot *per se* be considered as an international armed conflict, even though it certainly entailed an international armed conflict between Afghanistan and the U.S.-led coalition.[466] However, an international armed conflict cannot exist between a State and a non-State group. It still can only exist between at least two States. In such a case, it obviously can also involve non-State actors.

---

[461] *But see* Beard, 25 *Harv. J.L. & Pub. Pol'y* (2002), at 578-582.

[462] ICJ, *United States Diplomatic and Consular Staff in Tehran, United States of America v. Iran, Merits*, Judgment of May 24, 1980, I.C.J. Reports 1980, pp. 3-46, at 32 (para. 67).

[463] *Id.*, at 33 (para. 69).

[464] *Id.*, at 35 (para. 74).

[465] *Id.*, at 36 (para. 77).

[466] *See also* Patel King/ Swaak-Goldman, 15 *Hague Yb. Int'l L.* (2003), at 45; *compare also* Fitzpatrick, 96 *Am. J. Int'l L.* (2002), at 347.

> The 'black hole' therefore does not exist: the war against the terrorist organisation is 'swallowed' by the war against the supporting State.[467]

It is also possible to attribute the actions of non-State actors to a State and thus render an ongoing non-international armed conflict international. The basis for such an attribution is similar – but not identical – to that of the attribution in the sphere of State responsibility. *Tadić* and the ICJ in its recent Judgment on the *Application of the Genocide Convention* have shown that the level of "effective control" may be necessary when it comes to State responsibility, but that a considerably lower level of "overall control" is sufficient to render an ongoing non-international armed conflict international.

It is also theoretically possible to attribute an attack by non-State actors to a State and thus establish an international armed conflict between the latter State and the victim State of the attack. However, it is less likely that the preconditions of such an attribution will be met, as the attack by the non-State actors alone must be of such a gravity that it is comparable to an armed attack by a State. The September 11 attacks are the only case in which this argument was presented and gained at least considerable international support. But in the same case it is unlikely that an attribution of these attacks to the State of Afghanistan is possible on the basis of the standards shown above. However, attribution is not the sole point of doubt. This can be illustrated by the *Lockerbie* case, where allegedly agents of the Libyan State blew up an American plane which crashed near the city of Lockerbie in the United Kingdom. Although the case was scrutinized by many international lawyers and even the ICJ, and even though it involved two states, its relevance in terms of international humanitarian law was never discussed.[468]

---

[467] Peter Kooijmans, 'Is there a Change in the Ius ad Bellum and if so, What Does it mean for the Ius in Bello?', in: Liesbeth Lijnzaad; Johanna von Sambeck; Bahia Tahzib-Lie (eds.), *Making the Voice of Humanity Heard: Essays on Humanitarian Assistance and International Humanitarian Law in Honour of HRH Princess Margriet of the Netherlands*, Leiden 2004, pp. 225-237, at 234.

[468] Quénivet, in: Arnold/ Hildbrand (eds.), at 50 with further references.

Since there are thus many and different arguments *not* to treat the "war on terror" *per se* as an *international* armed conflict[469] – and thus not to apply the corresponding international humanitarian law standards to the protagonists of that conflict – it is also argued by some authors that it could qualify – in whole or in part – as a *non-international* armed conflict.

II. Is the "War on Terror" a Non-International Armed Conflict?

According to some authors, the "war on terror" constitutes a non-international armed conflict[470] or at least the international humanitarian law applicable to non-international armed conflicts is regarded as the suitable regime for the "war on terror".[471] It shall apply even though

> international law does not provide expressly for the application of humanitarian law in cases where the state realizes its right to self-defense against a terrorist organization. ... it is essential to apply international humanitarian law, which, since it attracts broad support form the nations of the world, provides a stable normative framework for handling disputes.[472]

1. Level of Violence

Again, one aspect of the perception of a situation as an armed conflict is the level of violence. As shown above, in the context of non-international armed conflicts, the threshold is considerably higher than in the

---

469 This does not exclude the possibility that international armed conflicts are part of what is referred to as the "war on terror" as a whole, *compare supra*, Part Four, Chapter F), 2. b).

470 *See e.g.* Derek Jinks, 'The Applicability of the Geneva Conventions to the "Global War on Terrorism"', in: 46 *Va. J. Int'l L.* (2005), pp. 165-196, at 182; Sassòli, 97 *ASIL Proc.* (2003), at 196-197.

471 *Interestingly*, Peal, 58 *Vand. L. Rev.* (2005), at 1632-1634 concludes that neither the definition of an international nor of an non-international armed conflict are met by the "war on terror". However, because of a "lack of clarity" and as the U.S. characterized the situation as "war", he argues that the "war on terror" should be considered as a non-international armed conflict.

472 Gross, *Struggle of Democracy*, pp. 53-54.

international sphere.[473] This threshold is most likely reached by the September 11 attacks and also by the ongoing hostilities between Afghan Government and U.S. coalition in Afghanistan and the remaining non-State actors, be it Taliban forces or al-Qaeda.[474] But already this statement shows, that there is again probably not a general answer in relation to the whole "war on terror", but an individual assessment for different aspects of that concept. Therefore, single scenarios are possible which could support the conclusion that parts of the "war on terror" are a non-international armed conflict:

First, a State could "harbour" a terrorist organisation without supporting it, but also without taking action to prevent the organisation's activities due to reasons beyond the State's control. Thus, a foreign State could intervene and take action against the organisation – i.e. in support of the government that against these insurgents. Such a situation has been regarded as not being an international armed conflict but rather a non-international armed conflict.[475]

Second, a State might be faced by single or even a series of terrorist acts on its territory. A prominent example is the 23 to 26 October 2002 hostage crisis in Moscow. But also acts of terrorism and series thereof by the IRA in Northern Ireland in the 1970s and 1980s, by the ETA in France and Spain from the 1970s on, and by the Red Army Fraction in Germany in the 1970s could fall into such a category. These examples have been and still are considered sporadic internal disturbances that fall below the threshold of applicability of international humanitarian law.[476] They are generally opposed by police forces and do not force the national government to take recourse to the armed forces. Neither are the groups who engage in such acts organised militarily, nor do they carry out sustained and concerted actions, even though they may be formed according to a certain hierarchy. They are not regarded as belligerents, nor are they in possession of any part of the State territory.[477]

---

[473] *See supra*, Part Four, Chapter C).

[474] Patel King/ Swaak-Goldman, 15 *Hague Yb. Int'l L.* (2003), at 48; *compare also* Vöneky, in: Fleck (ed.), *Rechtsfragen*, at 157.

[475] Kooijmans, in: Lijnzaad *et al.* (eds.), at 234-235.

[476] *See e.g.* Quénivet, in: Arnold/ Hildbrand (eds.), at 31.

[477] On these and other characteristics of non-international armed conflicts *compare supra*, Part Four, Chapter C).

Thus, such acts generally do not amount to an armed conflict[478] and fall within the domestic jurisdiction of States, subject to human rights law.

Third, this assessment might possibly change if acts such as hostage taking occur as part of a larger framework of violence which amounts to a non-international armed conflict. This may be illustrated by the October 2002 Moscow hostage crisis, which in itself does not represent a non-international armed conflict. However, this assessment could be altered if the single action is regarded as part of a general policy by Chechen forces. If the conflict in Chechnya amounts to a non-international armed conflict and the hostage crises in Moscow is linked to that conflict, it could become part of that conflict to the effect that it would also be covered by international humanitarian law applicable to non-international armed conflicts. Concerning the former question, the Russian Federation always claimed that it was only engaged in a police operation when its troops entered Chechnya to prevent Chechens from infiltrating into Dagastan in 1999.[479] However, a majority of authors postulate that the threshold of a non-international armed conflict is met.[480] Concerning the second question, a link could consist of a clear line of hierarchy between the hostage takers and the Chechen government. This link is difficult to establish factually.[481] But even if such a factual link existed, it would still be difficult legally to subsume the Moscow hostage crisis under the ongoing non-international armed conflict. It cannot be regarded as an armed reprisal by which the opposition group was taking the conflict to the capital, as it was directed against civilians. It thus rather fits the understanding of a "terrorist act" than that of an act of war and one must conclude that it thus cannot be regarded as being part of a non-international armed conflict.[482]

---

[478] *See also* Noëlle Quénivet, 'The Moscow Hostage Crisis in the Light of the Armed Conflict in Chechnya', in: 4 *Yb. Int'l Hum. L.* (2001), pp. 348-372, at 367-369.

[479] *Compare* Quénivet, in: Arnold/ Hildbrand (eds.), at 39.

[480] *See e.g.* Abresch, 16 *Eur. J. Int'l L.* (2005), pp. 741-767; Alexander Cherkasov; Tanya Lokshina, 'Chechnya: 10 Years of Armed Conflict', in: 16 *Helsinki Monitor* (2005), pp. 143-149; Quénivet, 4 *Yb. Int'l Hum. L.* (2001), at 355-358.

[481] Quénivet, in: Arnold/ Hildbrand (eds.), at 40.

[482] *See also* Quénivet, 4 *Yb. Int'l Hum. L.* (2001), at 358-372. However, one must pay regard to the fact that the decisive question cannot be the illegality of

One can thus conclude that acts which are traditionally regarded as "terrorist acts" do not reach the level of a non-international armed conflict, most likely even if they are committed in connection to such a conflict.

2. *Non-International Character*

The decisive criterion between an international and a non-international armed conflict is the number of States that are involved in that conflict. International armed conflicts involve at least two States.[483] Thus, as soon as less than two states are involved, and thus an armed conflict is not covered by Article 2 of the 1949 Geneva Conventions, it must be regarded as non-international.[484] Nevertheless, *Jinks* has argued that Common Article 3 could be broadly construed to also extend to conflicts in which one or more States are arrayed against a foreign-based or transnational armed group and that thus the U.S. "war on terror" against al-Qaeda is a non-international armed conflict.[485] *Jinks* admits that this interpretation is not consistent with the drafting history of Common Article 3, but bases his argument on the assumption that

> the Conventions would cover international armed conflicts proper and wholly internal civil wars, but would not cover armed conflicts between a state and a foreign-based (or transnational) armed group or an internal armed conflict that spills over an international border

---

the hostage taking under international humanitarian law. Obviously, also violations of international humanitarian law can be part of an armed conflict and are then prosecuted in accordance with international humanitarian law.

483 *See supra*, Part Four, Chapter D) II.

484 *See supra*, Part Four, Chapter C).

485 Jinks, 46 *Va. J. Int'l L.* (2005), at 188-189; Jinks, 28 *Yale J. Int'l L.* (2003), at 20 and 38. This also seems to be the assumption on which the US Supreme Court based its judgment in Hamdan, *see* U.S. Supreme Court, *Salim Ahmed Hamdan v. Donald H. Rumsfeld, Secretary of Defense,* et al., Case No. 05-184, Decision of June 29, 2006, reprinted in: 45 *ILM* (2006), pp. 1130-1203, at 1153-1154 (paras. D VI. ii-iii). However, the Court is contradictory to its own reasoning when it discusses Hamdan's possible status as a prisoner of war – a status that only exists in connection with an international armed conflict, *see ibid.*, p. 1154 (footnote 61); *compare also* Milanovic, 89 *Int'l Rev. Red Cross* (2007), No. 866, at 378-379; Ní Aoláin, 91 *Minn. L. Rev.* (2007), at 1541-1542.

> into the territory of another state. There is no apparent rationale for such a regulatory gap.[486]

Jinks is right in arguing that any armed conflict should be – and factually is – covered by international humanitarian law either applicable to international or to non-international armed conflicts. But as shown above, an international armed conflict can also exist if a State is only indirectly involved in that conflict or if a foreign State intervenes into a former internal armed conflict.[487] Such a cross border intervention generally renders an internal armed conflict international.[488] Thus, if *Jinks* were consistent, he would have come to the conclusion that the cross border conflict between the U.S. and its allies on the one side, and al-Qaeda on the other side is rather international. The definitions of non-international armed conflicts given in Article 3 common to the 1949 Geneva Conventions and in 1977 Additional Protocol II refer to conflicts "within the territory" of a state party. However, we have seen that the conflict between al-Qaeda and the U.S. does not qualify as an international armed conflict, and this outcome is not only logical but also desired by most States for policy reasons such as combatant and prisoner-of-war status of the non-State actors.

3. Kretzmer's "Mixed Model"

Similar to *Jinks*, *Kretzmer* argues that a conflict between a "transnational terror group" and a State should be treated as a non-international armed conflict, even though he admits that the rules on non-international armed conflicts do not formally apply. He argues that the conflict with al-Qaeda was not "swallowed up by the conflict with Afghanistan". Thus the persons who had mounted the armed attack on the United States were not merely civilians taking a direct part in hostilities between the two states. In the view of *Kretzmer*, the conflict "became one that had both international and non-international aspects."[489] Thus,

---

[486] Jinks, 46 *Va. J. Int'l L.* (2005), at 189.

[487] *Compare supra*, Part Four, Chapter D) II. 2.

[488] The only exception can be the intervention of a foreign State on behalf of the State fighting in an internal armed conflict purely on its own territory, such as the intervention of the Soviet Union on behalf of the Afghan Government against the *mujahidin*, *see* Moir, *Internal Armed Conflict*, pp. 50-51.

[489] Kretzmer, 16 *Eur. J. Int'l L.* (2005), at 195-196.

he is of the opinion that neither the pure law-enforcement approach nor the armed conflict model provide an adequate framework to deal with "transnational terrorism". As such a conflict transcends the borders of the state involved it does not fully fit the model of non-international armed conflict. Therefore he sees the necessity to introduce elements of the law-enforcement model, i.e. human rights standards, into his non-international armed conflict approach, and argues in favour of a "mixed model".[490]

The main problem *Kretzmer* sees regarding conflicts between transnational terrorist groups and a state as non-international armed conflicts is the "almost unlimited power to target persons [the state] claims to be active members of that group, even when they pose no immediate danger and it might be feasible to apprehend them and place them on trial."[491] To limit these powers, he refers to human rights standards: "The only acceptable justification for targeting suspected terrorists is protection of potential victims of terrorist acts."[492]

In using these human rights standards to shape his non-international armed conflict approach, *Kretzmer* then refers to the right to self-defence under Article 51 UN Charter: Parallel to this right, the requirements of necessity and proportionality should apply to the targeting of a suspected terrorist. In consequence, according to *Kretzmer*, a State may not target a suspected terrorist if this is not *necessary*, i.e. if there is a reasonable possibility of apprehending him and putting him on trial. Furthermore, there must be credible evidence that the targeted person is actively involved in planning or preparing further terrorist attacks, even though *Kretzmer* seems to support the "last window of opportunity" approach in this question.[493]

Concerning proportionality, *Kretzmer* balances three factors: First, the danger to the lives of possible victims by the continued activities of the terrorist. Second, the chance of the danger to human life being realized if the activities of the suspected terrorist are not halted immediately.

---

[490] *Id.*, at 186 and 201-204; *similarly,* Supreme Court of Israel, *"Targeted Killings" (Merits)*, para. 40, 46 *ILM* (2007), at 394.

[491] Kretzmer, 16 *Eur. J. Int'l L.* (2005), at 202.

[492] *Id.*

[493] *Id.*, at 203; *compare supra*, Part One, Chapter B) II. 2. b) (3); *see also* Schmitt, 32 *Isr. Yb. Hum. Rts.* (2002), at 110.

And third, the danger that civilians will be killed or wounded in the attack on the suspected terrorist, under the presumption that suspected terrorists should not be targeted when there is a real danger that civilians will be killed or wounded.[494]

As *Kretzmer* sees the danger of a too liberal interpretation of these standards by targeting states, he proposes an institutional mechanism to mitigate that danger: Similar to the "duty to investigate" that has been developed by the European Court of Human Rights as part of the right to life,[495] *Kretzmer* is of the opinion that states are obliged to carry "a thorough and credible legal investigation" in order to determine whether the targeting of a person complies with the standards shown above. Otherwise, legal action must be taken against those responsible.[496]

A very similar approach is taken by *Guiora*, who regards terrorists as "illegal combatants" who may be targeted and die on the "battlefield". On the other hand, he also limits targeted killings to cases in which "arrest is not an option" and excludes persons whose actions do not endanger public safety.[497]

4. Critique

Kretzmer bases his approach on the assumption that

> [a]pplying human rights standards to such a conflict ... faces a serious impediment. As the suspected terrorists are not within the jurisdiction of the victim state, one of the fundamental assumptions of the regimes contemplated in human rights treaties is lacking.[498]

Here, *Kretzmer* is most likely not referring to a narrow and outdated understanding of the applicability of human rights treaties. But even the critique that the human rights regime is less appropriate due to the fact that the persons in question often act from abroad cannot convince. In fact, the situation is the same if the legal regime of non-international armed conflicts is applied to these persons. Furthermore, *Kretzmer*

---

494 Kretzmer, 16 *Eur. J. Int'l L.* (2005), at 203-204.

495 *See supra*, Part One, Chapter E) I. 2 b).

496 Kretzmer, 16 *Eur. J. Int'l L.* (2005), at 204.

497 Guiora, 36 *Case W. Res. J. Int'l L.* (2004), at 329-331.

498 Kretzmer, 16 *Eur. J. Int'l L.* (2005), at 202.

himself resorts to the human rights regime in his second step. While arguing for the treatment of the "war on terror" as a non-international armed conflict, he himself sees the necessity to mitigate this regime by using human rights standards, i.e. the same standards that would be applied in the first place.

It is laudable that *Kretzmer* wants to avoid a "license to kill" for states. But the way he chooses to reach this aim cannot convince entirely: If he is convinced that the human rights rules should apply, why use the detour *via* international humanitarian law and introduce the human rights standards in a way that again is a new approach?

But maybe *Kretzmer's* approach is just smart: In referring to the "duty to investigate" as part of the right to life,[499] *Kretzmer* uses one of the most extensive parts of human rights law, which was developed by the European Court of Human Rights.[500] In contrast to that, police and armed forces traditionally prefer approaches that give them a wider margin of appreciation. In this scope, they choose to decide themselves which means they apply to which case. To label the fight against transnational terrorism as mere law-enforcement, governed by rules of human rights, might deter those forces from accepting a legal regime. If the same content is labelled as an armed conflict, be it a non-international one, subject to certain human rights restraints, the acceptance of the legal regime might be much easier.

Nevertheless this approach bears a high risk in it: It is based on the assumption the legal regime applicable is that of an armed conflict. While *Kretzmer* is ready to accept some restrictions to that regime, others – like *Jinks* – want to apply the armed conflict model exclusively. This model will most likely be very welcome by those who see it as a possibility to expand their acting possibilities in the "war on terror". Once this is accepted, the additional restrictions, however, might easily be forgotten about.

Additionally – and independently of the pros and cons of *Kretzmer's* argument concerning the suitability of the law of internal armed conflict – his assessment is not compatible with the situation *de lege lata*. It is important here to draw a distinction between legal arguments and policy arguments:

---

499 *Id.*, at 204.

500 *See supra*, Part One, Chapter E) I. 2 b).

> [I]t makes no sense to conceptualize a conflict with al Qaeda as an 'internal' armed conflict either: al Qaeda has some presence in the U.S., to be sure, but its permanent U.S. presence appears to be minimal, and it also has some presence in dozens of other states around the globe. It attacks U.S. interests around the globe, and the U.S. accordingly wishes to attack its interests around the globe.[501]

The same applies to the whole "war on terror": It might be true that it shows similarities with a non-international armed conflict – i.e. one party to the conflict being a non-State actor. The international humanitarian law applicable to non-international armed conflicts might thus even be the *lex ferenda* that is regarded suitable to address this situation. But still, the preconditions for its application are not met. According to the law as it is, the "war on terror" cannot be regarded as a non-international armed conflict and thus the respective legal regime does not apply to it. This does not exclude the possibility that parts of the "war on terror" could qualify as non-international armed conflicts. But again, this has to be assessed on a case by case basis. Even then, it is rather unlikely that the preconditions of a non-international armed conflict are met. It rather seems likely that the well known dilemma will gain new relevance: One man's terrorist most likely would be another man's (freedom) fighter in that non-international armed conflict.

III. Conclusion

The concept of "war against terrorism" may be appropriate in a political and journalistic context, but it is incorrect in a legal point of view.[502] It is only a metaphor not different form expressions like "war on poverty" or "war on drugs".[503] As the International Committee of the Red Cross stated:

> The phrase 'war on terror' is a rhetorical device having no legal significance. There is no more logic to automatic application of the

---

[501] Brooks, 153 *U. Pa. L. Rev.* (2004), at 714.

[502] *See also* Arnold, in: Arnold/ Hildbrand (eds.), at 21; Frowein, 62 *ZaöRV* (2002), at 889; Melzer, *Targeted Killing*, pp. 262-269; Allain Pellet; Sarah Pellet, 'The Aftermath of September 11', in: 10 *Tilburg Foreign L. Rev.* (2002), pp. 64-75, at 64-66.

[503] *See also* Dinstein, in: Walter *et al.* (eds.), at 919.

laws of armed conflict to the 'war on terror' than there is to the 'war on drugs,' 'war on poverty' or 'war on cancer'.[504]

However, it has to be admitted that at least the (rhetorical) linkage of "terrorism", (pre-emptive) self-defence and "war" has been developed to a degree which was not accepted before the September 11, 2001 attacks.[505] But this linkage is not a general or legal one.

1. No General Applicability of International Humanitarian Law to the "War on Terror" de lege lata

The "war on terror" is not *per se* an armed conflict,[506] neither international nor non-international. However, the analysis of various aspects of the rhetoric "war on terror" show, that international humanitarian law applies to significant portions thereof.[507] But most importantly, it

---

[504] International Committee of the Red Cross, 'When is a war not a war? – The proper role of the law of armed conflict in the "global war on terror"', Official Statement by the Legal Adviser at the ICRC's Legal Division Gabor Rona (March 16, 2004).

[505] Ansah, 43 *Va. J. Int'l L.* (2003), at 851-860; *compare also* Baxi, 43 *Osgoode Hall L.J.* (2005), at 34-41.

[506] *See also e.g.* Borelli, 87 *Int'l Rev. Red Cross* (2005), No. 857, at 45-46; Fitzpatrick, 96 *Am. J. Int'l L.* (2002), at 346-350; Neuman, 14 *Eur. J. Int'l L.* (2003), at 291-296; O'Connell, 12 *ILSA J. Int'l & Comp. L.* (2006), pp. 535-539; Vöneky, in: Fleck (ed.), *Rechtsfragen*, at 157. *Compare also* Justice *O'Connor*, who wrote in the plurality opinion in *Hamdi* that it is "a clearly established principle of the law of war that detention may last no longer than active hostilities." These hostilities are then described as existing in Afghanistan, hostilities that will eventually end. The opinion does not refer to the "war on terror", *see* U.S. Supreme Court, *Yaser Esam Hamdi* and *Esam Fouad Hamdi* as next friend of *Yaser Esam Hamdi, Petitioners v. Donald H. Rumsfeld, Secretary of Defense,* et al., Judgment of June 28, 2004, 542 *U.S.* (2004), pp. 507-539, at 520-522. *Similarly*, in *Rasul* Justice *Kennedy* distinguishes the case form cases where the detainees are taken from "a zone of hostilities". He indicates that the does not regard the "zone of hostilities" as being worldwide, *see* U.S. Supreme Court, *Shafiq Rasul*, et al., *Petitioners v. George W. Bush, President of the United States*, et al.; *Fawzi Khalid Abdullah Fahad Al Odah*, et al., *Petitioners v. United States* et al., Judgment of June 28, 2004, 542 *United States Reports* (2004), pp. 466-506, at 488 (concurring opinion Justice Kennedy).

[507] *See also* Patel King/ Swaak-Goldman, 15 *Hague Yb. Int'l L.* (2003), at 48.

shows that the question of applicability of international humanitarian law must be and still can be answered according to the well developed traditional standards. Insofar, the "war on terror" in fact does not exist as a legal phenomenon, but as mere rhetoric. It may very well refer to single or several ongoing international and non-international armed conflicts, but it does not capture and put them under one legal umbrella.

Thus, many aspects referred to as being part of the "war on terror" are far from being covered by international humanitarian law, but some certainly are. Those aspects which are not covered by it – and this most likely concerns the majority of cases – are covered by human rights law and the law enforcement paradigm rather than the war paradigm.

Acts of "terrorism" in peacetime, like the Lockerbie incident in 1988, or the Madrid bombings in 2004, should be and have largely been prosecuted according to criminal law. The perpetrators should not be and have not been searched for by means of military occupation of the persons' alleged country of origin. This means, however, that the success of international co-operation in criminal law matters lies in the political willingness of the international community.[508]

On the other hand, this does not mean that international humanitarian law does not apply at all to "terrorist acts". For example, even if the attacks against the Twin Towers would be regarded as a exclusive matter of criminal law, the rules of international humanitarian law were clearly applicable when the U.S. invaded Afghanistan.[509] Thus, once a situation is covered by the framework of international humanitarian law, the acts committed therein and their perpetrators – "terrorists" or not – are judged according to these rules as any other act in an armed conflict.

> [S]tates cannot use indiscriminate weapons because they fight terrorists, they cannot attack inoffensive civilians, they cannot cause unnecessary suffering or excessive damage to civilian objects, etc. States are bound by the same humanitarian rules as they are always bound when they use force in an armed conflict.[510]

This does not mean, that the "terrorist act" itself establishes the applicability of the law of war. This conclusion is shared by many authors, but

[508] Arnold, in: Arnold/ Hildbrand (eds.), at 23.

[509] *Id.*, at 13.

[510] Vöneky, in: Walter *et al.* (eds.), at 947.

nevertheless some of them argue in support of an application of international humanitarian law to the "war on terror" – at the same time admitting that it is not an armed conflict *de lege lata*:

2. *Applicability of International Humanitarian Law to the "War on Terror"* de lege ferenda?

While it is broadly accepted that the "war on terror" does not qualify as an armed conflict *per definitionem*, some still regard the law of war as the suitable legal regime.[511] Irrespectively, these authors are not willing to grant combatant status to the opponent non-State actors. They often are regarded – in sum – as "unlawful combatants" or even "outlaws". In that regard, *Kretzmer* resumes: "An armed conflict model of law ... cannot be applicable if only one party to the conflict has combatants."[512] This possibly touches the core of the problem. One argument often used to show the inadequacy of international humanitarian law in connection with "terrorist organisations" such as al-Qaeda is that of reciprocity: While States would be obliged to follow the rules of international humanitarian law, "terrorist organisations" would not do so. States would thus provide the benefits of international humanitarian law "to those who violate every tenet of the law of armed conflict".[513] Interestingly, the consequence some authors draw from this fact is not that international humanitarian law is not the eligible set of rules, but rather that states should also not be bound by the limitations of international humanitarian law:

> The al Qaeda-US conflict is not symmetrical in the way that an ordinary war is: the US cannot expect to gain any benefits from al Qaeda by treating al Qaeda prisoners in a humane manner given al Qaeda's demonstrated ferocity in its treatment of enemy civilians.[514]

It is certainly significant if the question of applicability of international humanitarian law is merely based on the expectation of gaining benefits for one party to the conflict. Additionally, such an argumentation ignores that international humanitarian law is not based on reciprocity.

---

511 *See e.g. id.*, pp. 925-949.

512 Kretzmer, 16 *Eur. J. Int'l L.* (2005), at 194.

513 *See e.g.* Dalton, 12 *ILSA J. Int'l & Comp. L.* (2006), at 528-529.

514 Posner, 5 *Chi. J. Int'l L.* (2004), at 433.

The Geneva Conventions itself make clear that no breach of the law by the opponent can serve as justification for a breach of the law by the other side. The mistreatment of prisoners of war by one side does not justify the mistreatment of prisoners of war by the other side. Attacks on civilians by one side do not justify reprisals against civilians of the other side in response.[515]

The same holds true for the problems arising concerning the principle of distinction. As "terrorists" will often not distinguish themselves from civilians or have their bases hidden in civilian objects, States would often be prevented from attacking them due to international humanitarian law. This does, however, not lead to the conclusion that States should then not be bound by the prohibition of indiscriminate attacks and of attacks upon the civilian population. It rather shows that the "war" paradigm is not suitable to treat such situations.

These problems show that the law of armed conflict is not a suitable legal regime to generally apply to the "war on terror".[516] The *ratio* behind international humanitarian law is to constrain armed activities to combatants and spare civilians. If a State is opposed by persons or even an organisations which do not submit themselves under international humanitarian law – and more importantly – who do not fit into the categories of that legal regime, there is little reason to "forcefully" submit the situation under this legal regime. Even *Vöneky*, who generally regards the law of war as suitable to face terrorism, has to admit that there is little to gain:[517] First, she argues that the law of war is more detailed than other standards – which may be doubted with regard to human rights. Second, she argues that international humanitarian law provides for a protection against war crimes. The latter is true, but this argument is not decisive. Individual criminal responsibility does not depend on the existence of a situation of armed conflict or "peace". Admittedly, the development of international criminal tribunals has strongly developed the international prosecution of crimes committed in the context of an armed conflict in a way not accepted concerning other crimes. But on the other hand, international humanitarian law renders legal many behaviours which would be illegal if committed outside an armed conflict. Examples are the concept of collateral damage or

515 *Compare supra*, Part Two, Chapter D) II. 3.

516 *But see* Vöneky, in: Walter *et al.* (eds.), at 948-949.

517 Vöneky, in: Walter *et al.* (eds.), at 947-948.

the fact that international humanitarian law does not know a general rule of "arrest rather than kill". It thus may at least be doubted whether international humanitarian law really provides for an overall better protection for potential victims.

Therefore, even if the question of applicability *de lege lata* is left aside, it is still far from clear whether international humanitarian law is the "better law" or even suitable to meet the requirements of opposing "terrorist" threats. Additionally, even if one should support the view that international humanitarian law is suitable to generally apply to the "war on terror", one must at least be ready to apply it consistently. One cannot eat one's cake and have it too. Once the legal regime of international humanitarian law is applicable, a State cannot chose and only apply those rules which suit it's own needs. Once the legal regime applies, all its rules apply. With regard to international humanitarian law, the question of applicability must be – and still can be sufficiently – answered according to the traditional standards shown above. This also holds true for all facets of what is referred to as the "war on terror":

> Just as in the past, the legal framework must adapt to address evolving threats. Therefore, to the extent the events of September 11 were merely a new manifestation of a previously addressed legal problem, the 'novel' issues presented by the global war on terror can be resolved within the existing regime of international humanitarian law.[518]

[518] Newton, in: Wippman/ Evangelista (eds.), at 79.

Part Five – Consequences of the Aforementioned for the Situation in Israel

> Israel has for Years pursued a policy of assassinating its political opponents. Because extrajudicial executions are universally condemned, most governments who practice assassinations surround such actions in secrecy and deny carrying out the killings they may have ordered. Although the Israeli government prefers to talk about 'targeted killings' and 'preventive actions' (or 'pinpointed preventive actions') rather than 'extrajudicial executions,' members of the Israeli government have confirmed that such killings are a deliberate government policy carried out under government orders.[1]

In that regard, it is necessary to distinguish between those secret operations which took place in the past[2] and the recent practice of targeted

---

[1] Amnesty International, *Broken Lives*, pp. 32-33.

[2] For prominent examples *see* Dan Fischer; John M. Brodie, 'Value of Israel's Assassination Policy Debated', in: *Los Angeles Times*, April 22, 1988, p. 1; Schmitt, 17 *Yale J. Int'l L.* (1999), at 626; Luft, 10 *Mid. E. Q.* (2003), at 3-7; Stein, *B'Tselem Position Paper* (January 2001), p. 9. These examples include the April 1973 killings of senior members of the Fatah movement including Yasir Arafat's deputy Yusuf Najjor and the Fatah spokesman Kamal Nasir in Beirut by Israeli commandos and the July 21, 1973 killing of Ahmad Bushiki, a waiter in a restaurant in Lillehammer, Norway by two Mossad agents who intended to kill Ali Hassan Salameh, a leader of the Black September organization who presumably was one of the organizers of the murder of Israeli athletes at the Munich Olympics in September 1972. On April 16, 1988 an Israeli commando landed in Tunis, and killed the head of the Palestinian Liberation Organisation's military branch Khalil al-Wazir (Abu Jihad), the second in seniority in the organization. At that time, Abu Jihad was a top PLO military strategist and had been implicated in several terrorist attacks against Israel. The matter was brought before the Security Council by Tunisia, claiming a violation of its sovereignty and territorial integrity, *see* UN SC, *Letter dated 19 April 1988 from the Permanent Representative of Tunisia to the United Nations addressed to the President of the Security Council*, UN Doc. S/19798 (April 19, 1988). This incident led to UN SC Res. 611 (April 25, 1988, *Israel-Tunisia*), U.N. Doc. S/RES/611 (1988).

killings, which takes place publicly and is discussed openly and justified by the government of Israel.[3]

Between September 2000 and March 2007, according to the local human rights group *B'Tselem*, 210 Palestinian suspected militants and 130 civilians have been killed in targeted strikes carried out by the Israel Defense Forces.[4]

Still in January 2002, the Israeli Supreme Court, sitting as High Court of Justice, declared that it was barred from examining the practice of targeted killings as it would not judge on an ongoing conflict.[5] But already in April 2002, the Court accepted to look into the merits of a case on targeted killings[6] and in December 2006, the Court gave the long-awaited judgment concerning the Israeli practice.[7]

---

3 Prominent examples for the latter practice are those of July 22, 2002, when an Israeli F-16 fighter jet dropped a one ton bomb and killed Salah Shihada, the leader and founder of Hamas' military wing of 'Iss ad-Din al-Qassam' in Gaza. Shihada and his organization was responsible for fifty-two attacks on Israeli targets, killing 220 Israeli non-combatants and sixteen soldiers. The bomb killed fifteen civilians including nine children, and was heavily criticised by the international community, *see* Luft, 10 *Mid. E. Q.* (2003), at 6-7. On March 22, 2004, Hamas spiritual leader *Sheikh Ahmed Yassin* was killed in an Israeli missile attack shortly before dawn as he left a Gaza mosque after morning prayers, *see* Dudkevitch, *Jerusalem Post*, Online Edition, March 22, 2004.

4 According to B'Tselem, the Israeli Information Center for Human Rights in the Occupied Territories, between September 29, 2000 and March 31, 2007, 4039 Palestinians were killed by Israeli security forces, 41 Palestinians were killed by Israeli civilians, 507 Israeli civilians were killed by Palestinians and 316 Israeli security forces personnel were killed by Palestinians. These numbers do not include Palestinians who were killed by an explosive device that they set or was on their person. The numbers above include the Palestinians killed by targeted strikes. For the names and background of these persons *see* B'Tselem, 'Statistics: Fatalities 29.9.2000-31.12.2007'. According to Keller/ Forowicz, 21 *Leiden J. Int'l L.* (2008), at 186, some 38 per cent of those killed in total were bystanders, and only 62 per cent of them were accurately targeted.

5 Supreme Court of Israel, *"Targeted Killings" Admissibility I*. The Court ruled that "the choice of means of war employed by respondents in order to prevent murderous terrorist attacks before they happen, is not among the subjects in which this Court will see fit to intervene." *But see* Ben-Naftali/ Michaeli, 1 *J. Int'l Crim. Just.* (2003), at 372-383.

6 Supreme Court of Israel, *The Public Committee Against Torture in Israel and LAW (Palestine Society for the Protection of Human Rights and the Envi-*

It ruled, that targeted killings are not *per se* illegal and thus much of the immediate press coverage emphasized that the Court had authorized the Israeli policy.[8] Yet, the Court developed numerous criteria that have to be fulfilled to render a targeted killing legal on a case by case basis. The Court bases its decision on the presumption that the killings take place in the context of an international armed conflict and that thus the law of armed conflict is applicable. However, it introduces different aspects that originate from human rights law to the question. The case thus gives rise to questions of the law of armed conflict, the law of occupation and human rights law – and to the relationship of these legal fields.[9]

Due to the December 2006 Judgment by the Israel Supreme Court,[10] the legal case of targeted killings – at least for the time being – seems to have come to an halt. However, the judgment by the Israeli Supreme Court does not answer all relevant questions and it does not provide for satisfactory answers concerning some questions it does address. This concerns the most basic question of the law applicable as well as the question which standards have to be met according to this law to render a killing legal.

---

ronment) v. The State of Israel et al. (*"Targeted Killings" Admissibility II)*, H.C.J. 769/02, Decision of April 18, 2002.

7 Supreme Court of Israel, *"Targeted Killings" (Merits)*, para. 16, 46 *ILM* (2007), at 381.

8 More specific analyses are those of Dworkin, *Crimes of War Project* (December 15, 2006); Mariner, *FindLaw's Writ* (December 22, 2006); Ruys, *Juristenkrant* (January 17, 2007).

9 *See also* Ben-Naftali/ Michaeli, 1 *J. Int'l Crim. Just.* (2003), at 402.

10 Supreme Court of Israel, *"Targeted Killings" (Merits)*, 46 *ILM* (2007), pp. 375-408.

A. The International Law Applicable

> Indeed, every Israeli soldier carries in his pack both the rules of international law and also the basic principles of Israeli administrative law that are relevant to the issue.[11]

This statement by the Israeli Supreme Court describes the national situation in Israel, namely the fact that according to the Israeli constitution, customary international law is part of Israeli law[12] and that Israel's State agents are thus bound by it. However, the decisive question for the present topic is: Which international law is exactly "inside the soldier's pack"? This question is relatively easy to answer regarding human rights obligations, but rather complex in relation to international humanitarian law.

I. The Applicability of Human Rights Law

Israel is party to the International Covenant on Civil and Political Rights[13] and is bound by those human rights which represent customary international law. This includes the right to life, as protected in Article 6 of the Covenant, and by customary international law.[14] While the

---

[11] Supreme Court of Israel, *Ajuri v. IDF Commander in the West Bank ("Assigned Residence")*, H.C.J. 7015/02, Judgment of September 3, 2002, para. 13, English translation reprinted in: Israel Supreme Court, *Judgments of the Israel Supreme Court: Fighting Terrorism within the Law*, Jerusalem 2005, pp. 144-178, at 156 and 125 *Int'l L.R.* (2004), pp. 537-568, at 546-547.

[12] *See e.g.* Supreme Court of Israel, *"Targeted Killings" (Merits)*, para. 19, 46 *ILM* (2007), at 382-383 (with further references); Benvenisti, *Law of Occupation*, pp. 109 and 112; Kuttner, 7 *Isr. Yb. Hum. Rts.* (1977), at 171.

[13] The Covenant entered into force for Israel on January 3, 1992. The only reservation Israel made concerns matters of personal status which are to be governed in Israel by religious law (Art. 23 of the Covenant), *see Bundesgesetzblatt, Teil II*, 1992, No. 19, pp. 429-430.

[14] *See supra*, Part One, Chapter G); *compare also* American Law Institute, *Restatement of the Law (Third)*, § 702 (Vol. 2, pp. 161-175), at 161; Carlson/Gisvold, *International Covenant*, p. 1; Dinstein, in: Henkin (ed.), at 115; Lillich, in: Meron (ed.), at 121; Meron, *Customary Law*, pp. 94-95; Sohn, 32 *Am. U. L. Rev.* (1982), at 16-17.

applicability of the International Covenant to Israeli territory is undisputed,[15] Israel still took the position in 1998 that "the Covenant and similar instruments did not apply directly to the current situation in the occupied territories"[16] due to a lack of jurisdiction over the individuals resident in these areas.[17] This view was strongly opposed to by the Human Rights Committee, which stated that,

> in the current circumstances, the provisions of the Covenant apply to the benefit of the population of the Occupied Territories, for all conduct by the State party's authorities or agents in those territories that affect the enjoyment of rights enshrined in the Covenant and fall within the ambit of State responsibility of Israel under the principles of public international law.[18]

The contrary Israeli Position can be regarded as disproved *at least* since the International Court of Justice confirmed the Covenant's applicability in its advisory opinion concerning the *Legal Consequences of the Construction of a Wall in the Occupied Palestinian Territory* and concluded that,

> the International Covenant on Civil and Political Rights is applicable in respect of acts done by a State in the exercise of its jurisdiction outside its own territory.[19]

This result reflects the reasoning that has been made *supra*, in relation to the territorial and extraterritorial applicability of the Covenant.[20] Thus, the human rights as laid down in the International Covenant – beside those of customary international law character – are generally applicable to targeted killings performed by Israeli officials irrespective

---

15 *Compare e.g.* Seidel, 44 *AVR* (2006), at 126-127.

16 H.R. Committee, Summary Record of the 1675th Meeting (Israel), UN Doc. CCPR/C/SR.1675 (July 21, 1998), para. 27.

17 *Compare* Ben-Naftali/ Shani, 37 *Isr. L. Rev.* (2003), at 18-20.

18 H.R. Committee, *Concluding Observations on Israel*, UN Doc. CCPR/CO/78/ISR (August 21, 2003), para. 11.

19 ICJ, *Legal Consequences of the Construction of a Wall in the Occupied Palestinian Territory*, Advisory Opinion of 9 July 2004, I.C.J. Reports 2004, pp. 131-203, at 179-180 (paras. 110-111).

20 *See supra*, Part Four, Chapter A) I.; *see also* Frowein, 28 *Isr. Yb. Hum. Rts.* (1998), at 6 and 11; Nowak, *CCPR Commentary*, Art. 2, para. 28.

of whether they take place on Israeli territory, in the occupied territories or on foreign territory.

II. The Applicability of International Humanitarian Law

The situation is more complex in relation to international humanitarian law. In order to evaluate the situation correctly form a legal point of view, it is necessary to take into account a certain portion of the historical development.

1. Historical Background

In the late nineteenth century; Palestine was administered as a portion of the Ottoman (Turkish) Empire. In the 1917 Balfour Declaration, the United Kingdom committed itself to "the establishment in Palestine of a national home for the Jewish people.[21] In consequence, after the defeat of the Ottoman Empire in World War I, the authority over Palestine was transferred to the United Kingdom by way of a League of Nations Mandate which incorporated the Balfour Declaration.[22] Ultimately, the Palestine Mandate was referred to the United Nations on April 2, 1947 and on November 29, 1947 the United Nations General Assembly in its Resolution 181 (II) adopted a plan for the partition of the territory into two States: One Jewish and one Arab State with an econo-

---

[21] The full text of the declaration reads: "His Majesty's Government view with favour the establishment in Palestine of a national home for the Jewish people and will use their best endeavours to facilitate the achievement of this object, it being clearly understood that nothing shall be done which may prejudice the civil and religious rights of existing non-Jewish communities in Palestine or the rights and political status enjoyed by Jews in any other country." The Balfour Declaration was issued on November 2, 1917, by Lord Arthur Balfour, British Foreign Secretary, to Lord Rothschild on behalf of the World Zionist Organization, *c.f.* Imseis, 44 *Harv. Int'l L.J.* (2003), pp. 65-138, at 73.

[22] W. Thomas Mallison; Sally V. Mallison, *The Palestine Problem in International Law and World Order*, Harlow 1986, p. 47; *compare also* German Federal Administrative Court (Bundesverwaltungsgericht), Case 1 C 25/92 (Ausländische Staatsangehörigkeit i. S. des § 25 RuStAG), Judgment of September 28, 1993, in: 13 *NVwZ* (1994), pp. 387-389, at 388-389.

mic union and an international administration for the Jerusalem area.[23] The Jewish State should consist of 56.5% of the Palestine territory, including at that time a population of half a million Jews and Arabs respectively. The Arab State should consist of 42.8% of the Palestine territory with an approximate population of 750,000 Arabs and 9,500 Jews at that time.[24]

After a provisional Israeli Government was formed in Tel-Aviv on May 13, 1948, the United Nations Mandate ended and the State of Israel was officially declared on May 14, 1948.[25] It was immediately recognised by the USA and the USSR but also attacked by its Arab neighbours. On April 3, 1949 Israel and Jordan signed an armistice. As an effect of the war, Israel gained 21% of territory in relation to the territory assigned to the State according to the UN partition plan.[26] Contrary to Resolution 181 (II), Jerusalem was divided between Israel and Jordan. Israel annexed western Jerusalem while eastern Jerusalem was incorporated under Jordanian rule.[27] The eastern part of mandatory Palestine, the West Bank of the River Jordan, was conquered by Jordan in the 1948-49 war, but Jordan renounced all of its claims in 1988.[28] The Israeli borders of today are a result of the 1967 Arab-Israeli war. Expecting an immediate attack by Arab Forces, Israel within six days occupied the Sinai Peninsula, the Golan Heights, the Gaza Strip and the West Bank. The United Nations Security Council and also the General Assembly repeatedly demanded the re-establishment of the pre-war situation, demanding the "withdrawal of Israeli armed forces from territories oc-

---

[23] UN GA Res. 181 (II) (November 29, 1947), *Future Government of Palestine ("Palestine Partition Plan")*, UN GAOR, 2nd Session, Supp. No. 1, UN Doc. A/519 (1947), pp. 131-150.

[24] Seidel, 44 *AVR* (2006), at 122.

[25] Declaration of the Establishment of the State of Israel (May 14, 1948), in: 1 *Laws of the State of Israel* (1948), p. 3 (Authorized Translation).

[26] Seidel, 44 *AVR* (2006), at 123.

[27] General Armistice Agreement, Israel and Jordan, signed at Rhodes, on April 3, 1949, reprinted in: 42 *UNTS* (1949), No. 656, pp. 303-325.

[28] King Hussein of Jordan, 'Address to the Nation' concerning the Disengagement from the West Bank and Palestinian Self-Determination, Amman, July 31, 1988, reprinted in: 28 *ILM* (1988), p. 1637.

cupied in the recent conflict".[29] However, Israel did not comply but established a military government in the West Bank and Gaza, which was followed by a Civil Administration in late 1981.[30] It retreated from the Sinai Peninsula in 1982 in accordance to the 1979 peace treaty with Egypt.[31]

On November 22, 1974 the General Assembly passed two resolutions which recognised the cause of Palestinian self-determination and the status of the PLO as the representative of the Palestinian people, and gave the PLO observer status at the United Nations.[32] In the 1990, the peace process started with the Oslo Accords (Oslo I).[33] The Treaty of

---

29 UN SC Res. 242 (November 22, 1967, *The Situation in the Middle East*), UN Doc. S/RES/242 (1967).

30 *See* Joel Singer, 'The Establishment of a Civil Administration in the Areas Administered by Israel', in: 12 *Isr. Yb. Hum. Rts.* (1982), pp. 259-289, including a translation of the Israel Defence Forces Order Concerning the Establishment of a Civil Administration, Order No. 947, November 8, 1981, at 288-289. A similar order was issued on December 1, 1981 (Order No. 725), concerning the Gaza Strip.

31 Israel-Egypt Peace Treaty, signed in Washington, D.C. on March 26, 1979, reprinted in: 18 *ILM* (1979), p. 362.

32 UN GA Res. 3236 (XXIX) (November 22, 1974), *Question of Palestine*, UN Doc. A/RES/3236 (1974); UN GA Res. 3237 (XXIX) (November 22, 1974), *Observer Status for the Palestine Liberation Organization*, UN Doc. A/RES/3237 (1974). See also the prior UN GA Res. 3210 (XXIX) (October 14 1974), *Invitation to the Palestine Liberation Organization*, UN Doc. A/RES/3210 (1974).

33 Israel-PLO Declaration of Principles on Interim Self-Government Arrangements (Oslo I), finalized in Oslo, Norway on August 20, 1993 and signed at Washington, D.C., September 13, 1993, in: 32 *ILM* (1993), p. 1525. *Compare also* the Preamble of the Israel-Jordan Treaty of Peace, singed at the Arava/Araba Crossing Point, on October 26, 1994, in: 34 *ILM* (1994), p. 46, reading in the relevant part: "Aiming at the achievement of a just, lasting and comprehensive peace in the Middle East based an Security Council resolutions 242 and 338 in all their aspects". The Oslo Accords entailed four phases: Israel-PLO Agreement on the Gaza Strip and the Jericho Areas (Cairo Agreement/Gaza-Jericho Agreement), signed at Cairo, Egypt on May 4, 1994, in: 33 *ILM* (1994), p. 626 (phase one); Israel-PLO Agreement on the Preparatory Transfer of Powers and Responsibilities (Treaty of Erez), signed at Erez, Israel, on August 29, 1994, in: 34 *ILM* (1994), p. 455; Israel-PLO Protocol on Further Transfer of Powers and Responsibilities, signed at Cairo, Egypt, on August 27, 1995 (phase two); Israel-

Taba/"Oslo II"[34] constitutes the main peace agreement between Israelis and Palestinians because other subsequent agreements merely built upon the obligations formulated therein.[35]

2. *The Legal Status of the Occupied Palestinian Territories*

> This Opinion is premised on the legal assumption that the applicable law in the discussion of the relevant issues is the body of international customary and treaty rules relating to international armed conflicts, in particular to *occupatio bellica* of foreign territory.[36]

It has to be examined whether the above quoted assumption by *Cassese* bears scrutiny. At the outset, most legal observers accept that at least until the Oslo and subsequent accords between Israel and the PLO, the status of the West Bank and Gaza was that of occupied territories to which the law of belligerent occupation applied.[37] From 1967 on, Israel exercised its power of control throughout the West Bank and the Gaza Strip via military commanders.[38] Thus, also according to the Israeli Supreme Court,

---

PLO Interim Agreement on the West Bank and Gaza Strip (Treaty of Taba/ "Oslo II"), signed at Taba, Egypt on September 24, 1995 and countersigned at Washington, D.C., September 28, 1995, in: 36 *ILM* (1997), p. 557 (phase three); Israel-PLO Wye River Memorandum ("Wye I"), signed at Washington, D.C., on August 23, 1998, in: 37 *ILM* (1998), p. 1251; Israel-PLO Sharm el-Sheikh Memorandum on Implementation Timeline of Outstanding Commitments of Agreements Signed and the Resumption of Permanent Status Negotiations (Sharm el-Sheikh Memorandum/"Wye II"), signed at Sharm el-Sheikh, Egypt on September 4, 1999, in: 38 *ILM* (1999), p. 1465 (delayed phase four).

34 Israel-PLO Interim Agreement on the West Bank and Gaza Strip (Treaty of Taba/"Oslo II"), signed at Taba, Egypt on September 24, 1995 and countersigned at Washington, D.C., September 28, 1995, in: 36 *ILM* (1997), p. 557.

35 *See also* Birgit Schlütter, 'Water Rights in the West Bank and in Gaza', in: 18 *Leiden J. Int'l L.* (2005), pp. 621-644, at 623.

36 Cassese, 'Expert Opinion', before para. 1 (p. 2).

37 *See e.g.* Dov Shefi, 'The Protection of Human Rights in Areas Administered by Israel: United Nations Findings and Reality', in: 3 *Isr. Yb. Hum. Rts.* (1973), pp. 337-361, at 345; Kretzmer, 16 *Eur. J. Int'l L.* (2005), at 205 with further references.

38 Shany, in: Schmitt/ Beruto (eds.), at 97.

> In view of this purpose, the area of Judaea and Samaria and the area of the Gaza Strip should not be regarded as territories foreign to one another, but they should be regarded as one territory. In this territory there are two military commanders who act on behalf of a single occupying power.[39]
>
> [I]rrespective of the fact that a peace treaty has been signed, so along as the Military Government has not left the Gaza Strip and The relevant parties have not agreed otherwise, the respondent continues to retain the territory by force of belligerent occupation and is subject to the laws of customary international law that apply in war-time.[40]

In consequence, albeit the Israeli government has taken no clear position as to the application of the 1907 Hague Regulations, the rules were generally applied, but never accepted as being binding.[41] However, in the view of Israel, the territories were not occupied in a legal sense but "retaken". Thus the 1949 Geneva Convention IV was not applicable.[42] According to the Israeli "Missing Reversioner Theory", in 1967 the

---

[39] Supreme Court of Israel, *Ajuri v. IDF Commander in the West Bank ("Assigned Residence")*, H.C.J. 7015/02, Judgment of September 3, 2002, para. 22, English translation reprinted in: Israel Supreme Court, *Judgments of the Israel Supreme Court: Fighting Terrorism within the Law*, Jerusalem 2005, pp. 144-178, at 161 and 125 *Int'l L.R.* (2004), pp. 537-568, at 551-552.

[40] Supreme Court of Israel, *Affu v. Commander of the IDF Forces in the West Bank*, Israel High Court of Justice, judgment of April 10, 1988 (HCJ 785/87, "Deportation Orders"), reprinted in: 29 ILM (1990), pp. 139-181, at 164 (p. 49 of the judgment).

[41] Benvenisti, *Law of Occupation*, p. 109; Adam Roberts, 'Prolonged Military Occupation: The Israeli-Occupied Territories Since 1967', in: 84 *Am. J. Int'l L.* (1990), pp. 44-103, at 63.

[42] Shamgar, 1 *Isr. Y.B. Hum. Rts.* (1971), at 263; *but see* Shefi, 3 *Isr. Yb. Hum. Rts.* (1973), at 345; The "missing reversioner" argument has been summarized and repeated in many places: *See* Esther Rosalind Cohen, *Human Rights in the Israeli-Occupied Territories, 1967-1982*, Manchester 1985, pp. 43-51; Mallison/ Mallison, *The Palestine Problem*, pp. 252-262; Falk/ Weston, in: Playfair (ed.), at 130-136; Carol Bisharat, 'Palestine and Humanitarian Law: Israeli Practice in the West Bank and Gaza', in: 12 *Hastings Int'l & Comp. L. Rev.* (1988-1989), pp. 337-340; Kathleen A. Cavanaugh, 'Selective Justice: The Case of Israel and the Occupied Territories', in: 26 *Fordham Int'l L.J.* (2002-2003), pp. 934-960, at 944-945; Imseis, 44 *Harv. Int'l L.J.* (2003), pp. 65-138, at 93-95; *compare also* Detter, *Law of War*, pp. 181-182.

West Bank was not the "territory of a High Contracting Party" in the meaning of Article 2 para. 2 of the Fourth Geneva Convention,[43] as it had been occupied by Jordan since the 1948 War.[44] The question has been clarified by now by the International Court of Justice:

> In view of the foregoing, the Court considers that the Fourth Geneva Convention is applicable in any occupied territory in the event of an armed conflict arising between two or more High Contracting Parties. Israel and Jordan were parties to that Convention when the 1967 armed conflict broke out. The Court accordingly finds that that Convention is applicable in the Palestinian territories which before the conflict lay to the east of the Green Line and which, during that conflict, were occupied by Israel, there being no need for any enquiry into the precise prior status of those territories.[45]

Thus, "the whole of the international community – except Israel"[46] accepts that the Fourth Geneva Convention is applicable *de jure*. The vast majority of States Party to the 1949 Geneva Conventions is of the opinion that the Conventions are not only *de facto*, but *de jure* applicable. This view is shared by various UN bodies, i.e. the General Assembly,[47]

---

43 Israel signed the Fourth Geneva Convention on 8 December 1949 and ratified it on 6 July 1951. The only reservation Israel made refers to the use of the Red Shield of David as a distinctive sign of medical services, *c.f.* Reservations and Declarations Concerning the Four Geneva Conventions of 12 August 1949, reprinted in: Dietrich Schindler; Jiří Toman (eds.), *The Laws of Armed Conflicts: A Collection of Conventions, Resolutions and Other Documents*, 2nd ed., Alphen aan den Rijn 1981, p. 506.

44 *Compare* Blum, 3 *Isr. L. Rev.* (1968), pp. 279-301; Shamgar, 1 *Isr. Yb. Hum. Rts.* (1971), at 265-266.

45 ICJ, *Legal Consequences of the Construction of a Wall in the Occupied Palestine Territory*, Advisory Opinion of July 9, 2004, I.C.J. Reports 2004, pp. 133-271, at 177 (para. 101); compare *ibid.*, pp 172-177 (paras. 89-101).

46 Imseis, 44 *Harv. Int'l L.J.* (2003), pp. 65-138, at 97. *Imseis'* statement remains true in relation to the Israeli Government, whereas the Israeli Supreme Court accepts the *de jure* applicability of the Fourth Geneva Convention.

47 *See e.g.* UN GA Res. 36/15(October 28, 1981), *Recent developments in connexion with excavations in eastern Jerusalem*, UN GAOR, 36th Session, Supp. No. 51, UN Doc. A/36/51 (1981), p. 82; UN GA Res. 57/269 (March 5, 2003), *Permanent sovereignty of the Palestinian people in the Occupied Palestinian Territory, including East Jerusalem, and of the Arab population in the occupied Syrian Golan over their natural resources*, UN Doc. A/RES/57/269 (2003).

the Security Council,[48] the Economic and Social Council[49] and the Commission on Human Rights.[50] It is further shared by the vast majority of States.[51] Additionally, the PLO has notified the ICRC that it will 'apply' the Geneva Conventions on numerous occasions.[52] Even the State of Israel agrees at least that the "humanitarian provisions" laid down in the Convention are *de facto* applicable.[53]

a) Changes Due to the Oslo Accords?

However, in the view of many authors, the Oslo Accords and subsequent agreements effected a change in the status of some parts of the Occupied Territories. They are regarded as the territory of the Palestinian Authority, "an entity that is not a State but is a sovereign authority" or even "a State in the making".[54] Also Israel has sometimes claimed

---

[48] *See e.g.* UN SC Res. 452 (July 20, 1979, *Territories occupied by Israel*), UN Doc. S/RES/425 (1979); UN SC Res. 904 (March 18, 1994, *on measures to guarantee the safety and protection of the Palestinian civilians in territories occupied by Israel*), UN Doc. S/RES/904 (1994).

[49] See e.g. UN ECOSOC Res. 2001/2 (July 24, 2001, *Situation of and assistance to Palestinian women*), UN Doc. E/RES/2001/2.

[50] See e.g. UN Comm'n H.R., Res. 2002/8, *Question of the Violation of Human Rights in the Occupied Arab Territories, including Palestine*, UN Doc. E/CN.4/RES/2002/8 (April 15, 2002).

[51] *See e.g.* High Contracting Parties to the Fourth Geneva Convention, 'Declaration on the Convention's Applicability to the Occupied Palestinian Territories', Geneva, 5 December 2001, in: 31 *Journal of Palestine Studies* (2002), 3, pp. 148-150.

[52] Detter, *Law of War*, p. 186, giving as an example the Declaration to the ICRC, 7 June 1982.

[53] *See e.g.* Supreme Court of Israel, *Ajuri v. IDF Commander in the West Bank ("Assigned Residence")*, H.C.J. 7015/02, Judgment of September 3, 2002, English translation reprinted in: Israel Supreme Court, *Judgments of the Israel Supreme Court: Fighting Terrorism within the Law*, Jerusalem 2005, pp. 144-178, at 155-156 and 125 *Int'l L.R.* (2004), pp. 537-568 (para. 13).

[54] Gross, 15 *Temp. Int'l & Comp. L.J.* (2001), at 196 and 199; *compare* Stephan Sina, *Der völkerrechtliche Status des Westjordanlandes und des Gaza-Streifens nach den Osloer Verträgen – The status of the Westbank and the Gaza Strip under public international law after the Oslo Accords*, Berlin 2004, pp. 330-332.

that it is no longer occupying power in relation to the areas administered by the Palestinian Authority.[55] But at the same time, it has treated these territories as occupied, e.g. for assigning residence of certain individuals within the territories.[56] The latter assessment is supported by the view, that the Oslo Accords did not effect a change of status.[57] As often before, the situation has to be examined in detail.

The current status of the territories is substantially determined by the interim provisions of the Oslo Accords, which constitute binding agreements under public international law. Remaining doubts concerning the capacity of a national liberation movement to conclude international agreements have at least been removed with regard to the Palestinian Liberation Organisation.[58] The agreements stay in force until a permanent status agreement is concluded, even though the different pe-

---

[55] *See e.g.* H.R. Committee, *Second Periodic Report of the State of Israel under the International Covenant on Civil and Political Rights*, UN Doc. CCPR/ C/ISR/2001/2 (December 4, 2001), para. 8.

[56] *See e.g.* Supreme Court of Israel, *Ajuri v. IDF Commander in the West Bank ("Assigned Residence")*, H.C.J. 7015/02, Judgment of September 3, 2002, para. 22, English translation reprinted in: Israel Supreme Court, *Judgments of the Israel Supreme Court: Fighting Terrorism within the Law*, Jerusalem 2005, pp. 144-178, at 161 and 125 *Int'l L.R.* (2004), pp. 537-568, at 551-552.

[57] *Compare e.g.* Seidel, 44 *AVR* (2006), at 145; Shany, in: Schmitt/ Beruto (eds.), at 96; Andrew R. Malone, 'Water now: The Impact of Israel's Security Fence on Palestinian Water Rights and Agriculture in the West Bank', in: 36 *Case W. Res. J. Int'l L.* (2004), pp. 639-671, at 649; Michael J. Kelly, 'Critical Analysis of the International Court of Justice Ruling on Israel's Security Barrier', in: 28 *Fordham Int'l L.J.* (2005), pp. 181-228.

[58] *See only* Sina, *Der völkerrechtliche Status*, pp. 16-28 with numerous further references especially on pp. 27-28.

riods provided for in Oslo I[59] and the Sharm el-Sheikh Memorandum/ "Wye II"[60] have long expired.

The territorial jurisdiction of the Palestinian Authority according to the Oslo Accords comprises generally those areas of the West Bank and the Gaza Strip from which the Israeli forces have been withdrawn or redeployed. It is laid down in Article XVII, para. 2, subpara. a of the Treaty of Taba/"Oslo II":

> The territorial jurisdiction of the Council shall encompass Gaza Strip territory, except for the Settlements and the Military Installation Area shown on map No. 2, and West Bank territory, except for Area C which, except for the issues that will be negotiated in the permanent status negotiations, will be gradually transferred to Palestinian jurisdiction in three phases, each to take place after an interval of six months, to be completed 18 months after the inauguration of the Council. At this time, the jurisdiction of the Council will cover West Bank and Gaza Strip territory, except for the issues that will be negotiated in the permanent status negotiations. Territorial jurisdiction includes land, subsoil and territorial waters, in accordance with the provisions of this Agreement.

This included about 40% of the West Bank and 70% of the Gaza Strip in 2002[61] and the whole of the Gaza Strip since the 2005 withdrawal of the Israeli troops. However, Article XI of the Treaty of Taba/"Oslo II" subdivides these territories into areas of three different qualities, referred to as "Areas A", "Areas B" and "Areas C", with different degrees

---

[59] The first sentence of Article I of the Israel-PLO Declaration of Principles on Interim Self-Government Arrangements (Oslo I) reads: "The aim of the Israeli-Palestinian negotiations within the current Middle East peace process is, among other things, to establish a Palestinian Interim Self-Government Authority, the elected Council (the "Council"), for the Palestinian people in the West Bank and the Gaza Strip, for a transitional period *not exceeding five years*, leading to a permanent settlement based on Security Council Resolutions 242 and 338." (emphasis added).

[60] Para. 1, subpara. 4 of the Israel-PLO Sharm el-Sheikh Memorandum on Implementation Timeline of Outstanding Commitments of Agreements Signed and the Resumption of Permanent Status Negotiations (Sharm el-Sheikh Memorandum/"Wye II") reads: "The two Sides will conclude a comprehensive agreement on all Permanent Status issues *within one year* from the resumption of the Permanent Status negotiations;" (emphasis added).

[61] Sina, *Der völkerrechtliche Status*, pp. 66-67.

of control by the Palestinian Authority (A = full, B = shared, C = no control by the Palestinian Authority).

According to Article XI, para. 3, subpara. a of the Treaty of Taba/ "Oslo II", "'Area A' means the populated areas delineated by a red line and shaded in brown on attached map No. 1". The areas marked in such a manner on map No. 1 attached to the treaty includes the Jericho area and the most important Palestinian towns, namely Bethlehem, Jenin, Kalkiya, Nablus, Ramallah und Tulkarem.[62]

According to Article XI, para. 3, subparas. b and c of the Treaty of Taba /"Oslo II",

> 'Area B' means the populated areas delineated by a red line and shaded in yellow on attached map No. 1, and the built-up area of the hamlets listed in Appendix 6 to Annex I, and ... 'Area C' means areas of the West Bank outside Areas A and B, which, except for the issues that will be negotiated in the permanent status negotiations, will be gradually transferred to Palestinian jurisdiction in accordance with this Agreement.

The "Areas A" includes approximately 3-4% of the West Bank, the "Areas B" consist of approximately 23-24% of the West Bank and the remaining 73% constitute "Areas C".[63]

(1) The Status of "Areas A"

According to Article XI, para. 2, subpara. a of the Treaty of Taba/ "Oslo II", the land in these "Areas A" came under the jurisdiction of the Palestinian Council first, with the consequence that in these areas

---

62 *See* Israel-PLO Interim Agreement on the West Bank and Gaza Strip (Treaty of Taba/"Oslo II"), Map No. 1. The map also includes the special case of Hebron, which is divided into an 80% "H-1" area with Palestinian inhabitants and a 20% "H-2" area of Jewish settlements, *see also* Article 2 of the Israel-PLO Protocol Concerning the Redeployment in Hebron, signed at Jerusalem, on January 17, 1997, in: 36 *ILM* (1997), pp. 650-655 and the attached "Hebron Redeployment Map".

63 Sina, *Der völkerrechtliche Status*, pp. 67-68 with further references; *Shehadeh* assumes "Areas A" 1%, "Areas B" 27% and "Areas C" 72%, *see* Raja Shehadeh, *From Occupation to Interim Accords: Israel and the Palestinian Territories*, London 1997, p. 37; *Shany* assumes "Areas A" 10%, "Areas B" 20% and "Areas C" 70%, *see* Shany, in: Schmitt/ Beruto (eds.), at 99.

the functional jurisdiction of the Palestinian Authority includes most importantly the responsibility for internal security and public order in the "Areas A". According to Article XIII, para. 1 of the Treaty of Taba/ "Oslo II",

> The Council will, upon completion of the redeployment of Israeli military forces in each district, ..., assume the powers and responsibilities for internal security and public order in Area A in that district.

This transfer of responsibilities to the Palestinian Authority was endorsed by the military commander through military Proclamation No. 7 which rendered the interim agreement binding in the occupied territories.[64] Due to this far reaching jurisdiction over the "Areas A", their status became controversial. On the one hand it is argued that having relinquished effective control over these areas, Israel can no longer be regarded as an occupying power.[65] Under the Oslo Agreements, Israeli forces are not permitted to enter "Areas A", unless they were responding to an ongoing incident, and then only until they had handed the matter over to the Palestinian police. The reluctance from entering "Areas A" was thus not a political decision, but was necessary to abide by Israel's commitments under an international agreement.[66] According to Art. 42 of the 1907 Hague Regulations,

> Territory is considered occupied when it is actually placed under the authority of the hostile army. The occupation extends only to the territory where such authority has been established and can be exercised.

The fact that the Israeli forces are absent in many areas and are barred from entering these areas by an international agreement with the PLO thus supports the view, that the phase of occupation has ended.[67] At

---

[64] Israel, Military Proclamation No. 7 Concerning the Application of the Interim Agreement (West Bank), issued by the Military Commander on November 23, 1995.

[65] Yoram Dinstein, 'The International Legal Status of the West Bank and the Gaza Strip – 1998', in: 28 *Isr. Yb. Hum. Rts.* (1998), pp. 37-49, at 45; Benvenisti, 9 *Eur. Pub. L.* (2003), at 481, 483-484.

[66] Kretzmer, 16 *Eur. J. Int'l L.* (2005), at 207.

[67] *Compare* the corresponding Israeli position Statement/Supplementary Statement by Israeli State Attorney's Office, submitted on February 3, 2003 to the Israeli Supreme Court, paras. 46-48, cited in: Supreme Court of Israel, *The*

least following the second *Intifada* Israel has not reimposed military control over all sections of Gaza, and attempts to enter the areas under control of the Palestinian Authority are met with force.[68]

On the other hand, the possibility of entering the areas in response to certain incidents and practice have shown, that Israeli Forces can and in fact do exercise jurisdiction in these areas. They are still controlling the whole of the Palestinian Territories despite their withdrawals and redeployments from parts thereof.[69]

According to the law of occupation, the decisive question is whether the occupying power has the ability to exercise effective control over territory.[70] This holds true even though the occupant might at some times fail to actually exercise this control[71] or only exercise it by its air force.[72] The International Military Tribunal at Nuremberg ruled on that question:

> While it is true that the partisans were able to control sections of these countries at various times, it is established that the Germans could at any time they desired assume physical control of any part of the country. The control of the resistance force was temporary

Public Committee Against Torture in Israel and LAW (Palestine Society for the Protection of Human Rights and the Environment) v. The State of Israel et al., H.C.J. 769/02, Petition for a Conditional Order (Order Nisi) and for an Interim Order of January 24, 2002, at para. 40.

68 Kretzmer, 16 *Eur. J. Int'l L.* (2005), at 211.

69 *See e.g.* Sina, *Der völkerrechtliche Status*, p. 343.

70 *See also* Supreme Court of Israel, *Affu v. Commander of the IDF Forces in the West Bank*, Israel High Court of Justice, judgment of April 10, 1988 (HCJ 785/87, "Deportation Orders"), reprinted in: 29 *ILM* (1990), pp. 139-181; Eyal Benvenisti, 'Israel and the Palestinians: What Laws Were Broken?' in: *Crimes of War Project* (May 8, 2002).

71 *See e.g.* UN Comm'n H.R., *Question of the Violation of Human Rights in the Occupied Arab Territories, including Palestine – Report of the Human Rights Inquiry Commission established pursuant to Commission Resolution S-5/1 of 19 October 2000*, UN Doc. E/CN.4/2001/121 (March 16, 2001), p. 13 (para. 41); *see also* Benvenisti, *Crimes of War Project* (May 8, 2002).

72 Gerhard von Glahn, *The Occupation of Enemy Territory: a Commentary on the Law and Practice of Belligerent Occupation*, London 1957, p. 28.

> only and not such as would deprive the German forces of its status of an occupant.[73]

These principles do also apply when this remote control does not serve a future invasion but only serves the protection of the occupying power from attacks out of the occupied territory.[74]

The Oslo Accords leave Israel with the ultimate legal control over the Occupied Territories. Israel still retains total control over who could enter or leave the areas, over their supply of goods and over their access to natural resources. The Military Proclamation No. 7, even though rendering the interim agreement binding in the occupied territories, refers to the same word "region" as the 1967 Military Proclamation No. 2.[75] Under domestic Israeli military law the term "region" therefore remains to refer to the entire West Bank, as prior to the Oslo peace process. This has the legal consequence that every provision that uses the term "region" is still in force over the whole Region, including "Areas A".[76] Additionally, still two military courts of first instance and a military court of appeals are functioning concerning the occupied territory. The Salem court is situated in "Area B" near Jenin and the military court and the court of appeals are situated in Ofer camp in "Area B" near Ramallah. They still exercise jurisdiction over all areas, including "Areas A".[77]

Israeli forces can enter and affect the territories in a manner which is typical for occupation forces. This is especially true for the time after the hostilities between Israel and the Palestinians started in September 2000 and especially after Israel's "Defensive Shield" campaign of April 2002. By April 2002, Israel had rendered the Palestinian Authority largely incapacitated.[78] The Israel Defense Forces (IDF) took control of

---

[73] U.S. Military Tribunal (Nuremberg), *U.S. v. Wilhelm List* et al. (Hostage Trial), Judgment of February 19, 1948, reprinted in: 15 *Annual Digest* (1948), Case No. 215, pp. 632-653, at 638-639.

[74] Gasser, in: Fleck (ed.), *Handbook*, at 243-244.

[75] Article 1 of the Military Proclamation No. 2 defines the "region" as the West Bank region.

[76] *See* Sharon Weill, 'The judicial arm of the occupation: the Israeli military courts in the occupied territories', in: 89 *Int'l Rev. Red Cross* (2007), No. 866, pp. 395-419, at 403.

[77] *Id.*, at 403-419 with further references.

[78] Shany, in: Schmitt/ Beruto (eds.), at 100.

many "Areas A", mostly in the West Bank, while in Gaza most "Areas A" remained under control of the Palestinian Authority. Thus, even if the "Areas A" should have ceased to be occupied territory, after the Oslo Agreements, they would have become occupied territory again, once the IDF effectively controlled those areas.[79] Even in the absence of ground forces, Israel exercises sovereignty over the airspace over the territories and exercises sovereignty by performing undercover activities, snatch operations and last but not least targeted killings.

Israel has retained the final responsibility for security throughout the occupied territories.[80] The fact that for political reasons it has chosen not to exercise this control, when Israel has the capacity to do so, cannot relieve it or its responsibilities as an occupying power. It thus remained an occupying power in all parts of the West Bank and Gaza even after the Oslo Accords came into force.[81]

---

79 Kretzmer, 16 *Eur. J. Int'l L.* (2005), at 207.

80 *Compare* Ariel Meyerstein, 'Case Study: The Israeli Strike Against Hamas Leader Salah Shehadeh', in: *Crimes of War Project* (September 19, 2002).

81 *See also* UN Comm'n H.R., *Question of the Violation of Human Rights in the Occupied Arab Territories, including Palestine – Report of the Human Rights Inquiry Commission established pursuant to Commission Resolution S-5/1 of 19 October 2000*, UN Doc. E/CN.4/2001/121 (March 16, 2001), p. 13 (para. 41); Supreme Court of Israel, *Ajuri v. IDF Commander in the West Bank ("Assigned Residence")*, H.C.J. 7015/02, Judgment of September 3, 2002, para. 22, English translation reprinted in: Israel Supreme Court, *Judgments of the Israel Supreme Court: Fighting Terrorism within the Law*, Jerusalem 2005, pp. 144-178, at 161 and 125 *Int'l L.R.* (2004), pp. 537-568, at 551-552; Benvenisti, *Crimes of War Project* (May 8, 2002); Emanuel Gross, 'Democracy's Struggle Against Terrorism: the Powers of Military Commanders to Decide Upon the Demolition of Houses, the Imposition of Curfews, Blockades, Encirclements and the Declaration of an Area as a Closed Military Area', in: 30 *Ga. J. Int'l & Comp. L.* (2002), pp. 165-231, at 194, 217 and 225; Frits Kalshoven, 'Israel and the Palestinians: What Laws Were Broken?' in: *Crimes of War Project* (May 8, 2002); Milanovic, 89 *Int'l Rev. Red Cross* (2007), No. 866, at 392; Marco Sassòli, 'Israel and the Palestinians: What Laws Were Broken?' in: *Crimes of War Project* (May 8, 2002); Michel Veuthey, 'Israel and the Palestinians: What Laws Were Broken?' in: *Crimes of War Project* (May 8, 2002); UN Commission on Human Rights, *Question of the Violation of Human Rights in the Occupied Arab Territories, including Palestine – Report of the Human Rights Inquiry Commission established pursuant to Commission Resolution S-5/1 of 19 October 2000*, UN Doc. E/CN.4/2001/121 (March 16, 2001); High

What makes this ongoing occupation peculiar is the fact that first, the occupation was effected in an international armed conflict that ended long ago, namely the 1967 Six Day War. Second, the occupation lasts for such a long time – more than 40 years by now. And third, no other States claim sovereignty over the occupied territory. Egypt never claimed sovereignty over the Gaza Strip[82] and Jordan renounced any claims in favour of the Palestinian people's right to self-determination.[83]

(2) The Status of "Areas B" and "Areas C"

This obviously is also true for the "Areas B" and "Areas C", which never were subject to the jurisdiction of the Palestinian Authority to the same degree as the "Areas A".[84] According to Article XI para. 2 *lit.* b of the Taba/Oslo II agreement,

> All civil powers and responsibilities, including planning and zoning, in Areas A and B, set out in Annex III, will be transferred to and assumed by the Council during the first phase of redeployment.

Thus, the influence of the Palestinian Authority in "Areas B" is similar to that in "Areas A", but without jurisdiction concerning internal security. It only includes public order. According to Article XIII, para. 2 of the Treaty of Taba/"Oslo II",

> In Area B the Palestinian Police shall assume the responsibility for public order for Palestinians and shall be deployed in order to accommodate the Palestinian needs and requirements in the following manner: ... The Palestinian Police shall be responsible for handling public order incidents in which only Palestinians are involved. ... .

According to Article XI para. 2 *lit.* c of the Taba/Oslo II agreement,

---

Contracting Parties to the Fourth Geneva Convention, 'Declaration on the Convention's Applicability to the Occupied Palestinian Territories', Geneva, 5 December 2001, in: 31 *Journal of Palestine Studies* (2002), 3, pp. 148-150; Al-Haq, *A Human Rights Assessment of the Declaration of Principles on Interim Self-Government Arrangements for Palestinians*, Ramallah 1993, p. 9.

[82] Benvenisti, *Law of Occupation*, p. 110.

[83] On July 31, 1988, King Hussein declared that Jordan accepted the wishes of the Palestinian people to secede and renounced any claim for sovereignty over the West Bank, *see* King Hussein of Jordan, 28 *ILM* (1988), p. 1637.

[84] *See e.g.* Kretzmer, 16 *Eur. J. Int'l L.* (2005), at 206.

> In Area C, during the first phase of redeployment Israel will transfer to the Council civil powers and responsibilities not relating to territory, as set out in Annex III.

This makes the status of "Areas C" least controversial. The main powers and responsibility rest with the Israeli occupying forces and only a small share of civil powers is transferred to the Palestinian Authority. This fact clearly supports the thesis that "Areas C" still have to be regarded as occupied territory and fall under the Law of occupation.[85] In "Areas C" military administration, headed by the military commander, continues to apply.

3. The Legal Nature of the Conflict

Apart from the question of whether the law of occupation applies to the Occupied Territories, it is also of utmost interest whether the law applicable to armed conflict – internal or international – does also apply. In its December 2006 long-awaited judgment concerning the Israeli practice of targeted killings, the Israeli Supreme Court based its decision on the underlying assumption that its context is that of an international armed conflict:

> The general, principled starting point is that between Israel and the various terrorist organizations active in Judea, Samaria, and the Gaza Strip (hereinafter "the area") a continuous situation of armed conflict has existed since the first *intifada*.[86]

Regrettably, the Court is quick to adopt the war paradigm and gives little attention to other possibilities.[87] The answer is not as straightforward as the Court seems to believe. The corresponding Israeli Government's position[88] was thus directly challenged by the petitioners in the targeted killings case, as it provided the basis for the targeted killings policy as the legitimate targeting of combatants in an armed conflict.

---

85 *Id.*

86 Supreme Court of Israel, *"Targeted Killings" (Merits)*, para. 16, 46 *ILM* (2007), at 381.

87 *Similarly,* Mariner, *FindLaw's Writ* (December 22, 2006).

88 "Currently, Israel is engaged in a situation best defined as an armed conflict." *See* Israel, Ministry of Foreign Affairs, 'Targeting Terrorists', Background Paper (August 1, 2001).

a) Is the Present Situation an Armed Conflict?

According to the Court's assessment, an armed conflict has been continuing since the first *Intifada* – that is since December 1987 – at least until the Court rendered its judgment in December 2006. This period of time includes the time after the signing of the Oslo Accords in 1993 which ended the first *Intifada*, and before the beginning of the second *Intifada* in September 2000. Can this whole period be qualified as an ongoing armed conflict and if so, with as little reasoning as the Court gave in its judgment?

The Court's view is supported by several facts. First, Israeli authorities declared shortly after violence erupted in September 2000, that the level and scope of violence justified it to regard the situation as an "armed conflict short of war"[89] and adopted the position that the conflict between the State of Israel and Palestinian terror organisations is defined as an armed conflict as there was "protracted armed violence between the IDF and organized Palestinian groups".[90] Second, the means employed by the Palestinians, such as guns or missiles, and intelligence reports that support the interpretation that the present conflict was carefully planned in advance are used as evidence to support the view that the present conflict is an "armed conflict".[91] Third, suicide bombers have been described as "foot soldiers" in a sophisticated and organized infrastructure. A successful suicide bombing has been regarded as the "working of a well-orchestrated, difficult to penetrate, highly disciplined, financially solvent terror organization and not an act of a lone individual."[92] And finally, at least according to some authors at some stages of the second *Intifada* the violence reached the threshold required for a situation to be regarded as an armed conflict.[93] According to the statistics published by the Israel Ministry of Defence, between September 29, 2000 and August 29, 2005, 5,198 civilians were injured,

---

[89] Statement by the Government of Israel, cited in U.S., Sharm el-Sheikh Fact Finding Committee, Final Report (2001).

[90] Israel, Government Brief submitted in the case H.C. 769/02 before the Israeli Supreme Court, cited in Kretzmer, 16 *Eur. J. Int'l L.* (2005), at 193 (footnote 99).

[91] Guiora, 36 *Case W. Res. J. Int'l L.* (2004), at 320-321.

[92] *Id.*, at 321.

[93] Kretzmer, 16 *Eur. J. Int'l L.* (2005), at 208.

and 745 civilians were killed. In the same period, 2,236 members of security forces were injured and 319 were killed.[94]

Thus, it is certainly possible to argue that the situation cannot be regarded as one of "riots, isolated and sporadic acts of violence and other acts of a similar nature", which under the 1977 Additional Protocol II do not constitute an armed conflict. Even though the Protocol is not applicable, it is used by some authors to provide guidelines in assessing the existence of an armed conflict.[95] The situation is thus rather regarded by some authors as an armed conflict between Palestinian terrorist groups and Israel.[96]

On the other hand, there are many reasons not to regard the present situation as an ongoing armed conflict.[97] According to the ICTY,

> an armed conflict exists whenever there is a resort to armed force between States or protracted armed violence between governmental authorities and *organised* armed groups or between such groups within a State.[98]

If the assessment of the Israeli Supreme Court was correct, an armed conflict also continued during the relatively calm period of time between the first and the second *Intifada*. There certainly were terrorist attacks during that period, but these attacks can hardly amount to protracted armed violence.[99] Even concerning the second *Intifada*, the United Nations Human Rights Inquiry Commission had doubts regarding the protracted nature of the violence. The Commission

> inclines to the view that sporadic demonstrations/confrontations often provoked by the killing of demonstrators and not resulting in loss of life on the part of Israeli soldiers, undisciplined lynchings (as in the tragic killing of Israeli reservists on 12 October 2000 in Ra-

---

94 Israel Defence Forces, Casualties Since 29.09.2000, Updated 29.08.05.

95 *See* Kretzmer, 16 *Eur. J. Int'l L.* (2005), at 208.

96 *See e.g.* Kremnitzer, in: Fleck (ed.), *Rechtsfragen*, at 207; *c.f.* Jinks, 28 *Yale J. Int'l L.* (2003), at 1; Shany, in: Schmitt/ Beruto (eds.), at 100-101.

97 *See e.g.* Tomuschat, 52 *VN* (2004), at 138.

98 ICTY, *Prosecutor v. Duško Tadić*, Case No. IT-94-1-AR72, Decision on the Defence Motion for Interlocutory Appeal on Jurisdiction of October 2, 1995, reprinted in: 105 *Int'l L.R.* (1997), pp. 419-648, at 488-489 (para. 70); *see also* UK Ministry of Defence, *Manual*, para. 3.3 (p. 29).

99 *See also* Milanovic, 89 *Int'l Rev. Red Cross* (2007), No. 866, at 383.

> mallah), acts of terrorism in Israel itself and the shooting of soldiers and settlers on roads leading to settlements by largely unorganized gunmen cannot amount to protracted armed violence on the part of an organized armed group.[100]

This view is supported by other authors:

> The present level of violence in the Occupied Territories does not cross the threshold of gravity necessary for a state of hostilities to exist. Violence is low-level, isolated and sporadic and does not amount to widespread, organized, military resistance against the Israeli occupation.[101]

For example, the suicide-bombing of Eilat in February 2007 with three victims was the first attack of that kind since the suicide bombing in Tel Aviv in April 2006, which killed ten persons. Thus, between two attacks of the kind Israel responds to with targeted killings, there was some three quarters of a year time without such an attack. As shown above, in the non-international sphere, the threshold of an armed conflict is substantially higher. Only hostilities that are similar to an international war, i.e. when armed forces on either side are engaged, can then be defined as an armed conflict.[102] Sporadic outbreaks of violence and acts of terrorism do not amount to an armed conflict.[103] A non-international armed conflict involves a certain intensity and certain standards pertaining to the military organization of the parties to the conflict.[104] But if the threshold is not reached at all, the situation is still that of an occupation, with the consequence that not the law of armed conflict at large but the special part concerning occupation is applicable.

---

[100] UN Comm'n H.R., *Question of the Violation of Human Rights in the Occupied Arab Territories, including Palestine – Report of the Human Rights Inquiry Commission established pursuant to Commission Resolution S-5/1 of 19 October 2000*, UN Doc. E/CN.4/2001/121 (March 16, 2001), p. 13 (para. 40).

[101] Oxford Public Interest Lawyers (OXPIL), 'Legal Consequences of Israel's Construction of a Separation Barrier in the Occupied Territories', International Law Opinion for the Association for Civil Rights in Israel (ACRI), February 2004, para. 115.

[102] Pictet (ed.), *Geneva Conventions*, Vol. 2, p. 33.

[103] UK Ministry of Defence, *Manual*, para. 3.5.1 (p. 31) with further examples (footnote 16).

[104] ICTY, *Prosecutor v. Duško Tadić*, Case No. IT-94-1-A, Judgment of May 7, 1997, reprinted in: 112 *Int'l L.R.* (1999), pp. 1-285, at 179 (para. 562).

b) If at all, Is It an International, Internationalised or Non-International Armed Conflict?

A conflict between a state and a people is not regarded as an international armed conflict under customary international law.

> Clearly, there is no international armed conflict in the region, as Palestine, despite widespread recognition, still falls short of the accepted criteria of statehood.[105]

Nevertheless, the Israeli Supreme Court found that the situation in the Occupied Territory is not only an armed conflict, but also international in character and refers as sole authority to *Cassese* in support of that view.[106] *Cassese* also in his Opinion written on behalf of the petitioners assumed that the law applicable to the case at hand

> is the body of international customary and treaty rules relating to international armed conflicts, in particular to *occupatio bellica* of foreign territory.[107]

This has been interpreted as indication for the situation *today* being an international armed conflict, and has been criticised on that basis.[108] It is true that naturally, a condition of international armed conflict is indispensable for the imposition of a belligerent occupation as a State can never occupy its own territory.[109] This international armed conflict *Cassese* is referring to in his *Expert Opinion* is the conflict that resulted in the occupation of the West Bank and Gaza in 1967. But this international armed conflict was ended at least by the peace agreements be-

---

105 UN Comm'n H.R., *Question of the Violation of Human Rights in the Occupied Arab Territories, including Palestine – Report of the Human Rights Inquiry Commission established pursuant to Commission Resolution S-5/1 of 19 October 2000*, UN Doc. E/CN.4/2001/121 (March 16, 2001), p. 12 (para. 39).

106 Supreme Court of Israel, *"Targeted Killings" (Merits)*, para. 21, 46 *ILM* (2007), at 383; *see also* Keller/ Forowicz, 21 *Leiden J. Int'l L.* (2008), at 190-193. As its single authority, the Court refers to Cassese, *International Law*, p. 420; *compare also* Milanovic, 89 *Int'l Rev. Red Cross* (2007), No. 866, at 383.

107 Cassese, 'Expert Opinion', before para. 1 (p. 2).

108 Kretzmer, 16 *Eur. J. Int'l L.* (2005), at 208-209.

109 *See e.g.* Leslie C. Green, *The Contemporary Law of Armed Conflict*, 2nd ed., Manchester 2000, p. 257.

tween Israel and both Egypt and Jordan.[110] Nevertheless, when the occupation was established, an international armed conflict existed. Thus, not only in *Cassese's* view, the international law governing occupation is applicable to the West Bank and Gaza Strip, but the applicability of this law alone does not serve as evidence for the existence of a present international armed conflict between Israel and the Palestinians.[111]

Nevertheless, it is argued by some authors that the situation very much resembles that of an international armed conflict.[112] Their argument is based on the assumption that Israel ceased to be an occupying power at least in the "Areas A" and effective authority is in the hands of the Palestinian Authority, those areas take on many characteristics of a foreign state from an Israeli perspective. Israel, however, is bound by treaty not to enter the area to arrest persons suspected of being terrorists, even if the Palestinian Authority refuses to arrest or extradite them.[113] Thus the argument has been raised that the situation is similar to that between the United States and Afghanistan. One could argue that the Palestinian Authority is responsible for attacks carried out from its territory. If it fails to act, Israel would be entitled to do so.[114]

> [I]f the official Palestinian leadership were to pursue an armed conflict with Israel just as one of Israel's neighboring states might or if a group that is not under the control of the Palestinian leadership were to engage in more than sporadic armed conflict with Israel by committing terrorist acts from an area outside Israeli control, the use of preventive force by Israel could be justified even if there is no immediate danger of (terrorist) attacks.[115]

---

[110] Israel-Egypt Peace Treaty, signed in Washington, D.C. on March 26, 1979, reprinted in: 18 *ILM* (1979), p. 362; Israel-Jordan Treaty of Peace, singed at the Arava/ Araba Crossing Point, on October 26, 1994, in: 34 *ILM* (1994), p. 46.

[111] *See also* Milanovic, 89 *Int'l Rev. Red Cross* (2007), No. 866, at 384.

[112] *See e.g.* Shany, in: Schmitt/ Beruto (eds.), at 98.

[113] Article VIII para. 9(b) of Gaza-Jericho Agreement, Annex I – Protocol Concerning Withdrawal of Israeli Forces and Security Arrangements.

[114] Kretzmer, 16 *Eur. J. Int'l L.* (2005), at 207.

[115] Nolte, 5 *Theo. Inq. L.* (2004), at 125; *compare also* Kalshoven, *Crimes of War Project* (May 8, 2002).

The decisive difference to such a Lebanon-type of situation is the degree of control Israel currently has over the Occupied Territory. As shown above, the degree of control by Israel still exceeds that of the Palestinian Authority and thus is not responsible for all attacks carried out from the Occupied Territory. Furthermore, the Palestinian Authority is not a State such attacks could be attributed to. Thus, even if the Palestinian Authority had such control, the attribution *alone* would not render an existing armed conflict international.

Due to this fact, the situation has been interpreted as representing a non-international armed conflict.[116] Even if this assessment were true, such a non-international armed conflict could be internationalised according to Article 1 para. 4 of the 1977 Additional Protocol I. According to this Article, "conflicts which peoples are fighting against colonial domination and alien occupation and against racist regimes in the exercise of their right of self-determination" are international armed conflicts. But due to this provision, which was instituted with the Palestinian Liberation Organization in mind, Israel and the United States refused to join the 1977 Additional Protocol I.[117] Article 1 para. 4 generated much controversy and can thus not be regarded as a customary rule,[118] at least not as one binding Israel, which would be a persistent objector in that regard,[119] as would the United States. Thus, Article 1 para. 4 of the 1977 Additional Protocol I is not applicable between Israel and the Palestinian Authority.

But the fact that the parties to a possible present armed conflict are not States alone cannot serve as evidence for the conflict being non-international. Even though the situation very much resembles that of a non-international armed conflict, the legal preconditions of such a conflict under international humanitarian law – e.g. a conflict "occurring in the territory of one of the High Contracting Parties"[120] – would not be met. As shown above, the resumption or outbreak of hostilities in a ter-

---

[116] Ben-Naftali/ Michaeli, 36 *Cornell Int'l L.J.* (2003), at 256.

[117] Meron, 88 *Am. J. Int'l L.* (1994), at 678 and 683.

[118] *Compare supra*, Part Four, Chapter C) III. *See also* UN Comm'n H.R., Res. 2002/8, *Question of the Violation of Human Rights in the Occupied Arab Territories, including Palestine*, UN Doc. E/CN.4/RES/2002/8 (April 15, 2002); *c.f.* Ben-Naftali/ Michaeli, 36 *Cornell Int'l L.J.* (2003), at 256.

[119] Shany, in: Schmitt/ Beruto (eds.), at 101.

[120] *Compare supra*, Part Four, Chapter C) II.

ritory under occupation rather leads to the resurrection of the underlying original international armed conflict – admittedly with a different party to the conflict on one side.[121]

In consequence, if the situation would amount to an armed conflict, it could only be an international armed conflict.[122] This outcome is also consistent with the object and purpose of international humanitarian law to provide the widest possible protection. In an international armed conflict, there would be combatants with all privileges on either side and not only on one side. Thus, if one side is of the opinion that it finds itself in an armed conflict, at the same time it would have to grant the other side's participants combatant immunity and prisoner-of-war status if captured.

This is not done at the present time but it should not be justified with the existence of a non-international armed conflict where the non-State actors cannot enjoy combatant immunity. It can only be explained by the fact that the threshold of an armed conflict is not met at all – even though the considerable intensity of existing violence and the high numbers of victims on either side must not be misconceived.

III. Conclusion: The Law Applicable to the Situation in the Occupied Territories

The consequence of the considerations above is the following: As shown, the degree of generalized control the Israeli Forces still exercise in the Occupied Territories – either by being present or in most cases by controlling access and keeping the possibility to enter the area at any time – is still of such a high level, that the situation still has to be regarded as an occupation. On the other hand, the level and of violent incidents does not reach the threshold of an ongoing armed conflict. If this level of violence would be reached, the conflict would have to be treated as the resurrection of the underlying international armed conflict.

---

[121] *Compare supra*, Part Four, Chapter E) III.

[122] *See also* Paulus/ Vashakmadze, 91 *Int'l Rev. Red Cross* (2009), No. 873, at 115.

As the degree of generalized control determines the applicability of humanitarian law and human rights law and Israel has such a high level of control, the peace paradigm is rather applicable than the war paradigm.[123] In consequence, as shown above, the decisive standards that apply are the human rights standards, i.e. those of the International Covenant on Civil and Political Rights and customary international law concerning the right to life. As an armed conflict does not exist at the same time, these standards are not supplemented by general international humanitarian law. Thus, there is no different status of persons which would entail a different standard of protection as would be the case for combatants or fighters and civilians if an armed conflict existed. As shown above, also the law of occupation – which at the same time applies – does not include additional possibilities to use lethal force which would go beyond the exceptions accepted with regard to the human right to life.[124]

B. The Standards Applicable to the Targeted Killings by Israeli Forces

Thus, the human rights standards are decisive. These standards will be addressed first. Additionally – due to the fact that many authors are of the opinion that the law of armed conflict is or should be applicable to the question at hand, the standards of international humanitarian law will be applied for the sake of argument.

I. Human Rights Standards

Any targeted killing by Israeli forces has to stand the test of whether it is in accordance with the right to life under human rights law. As shown above, neither the International Covenant – which is binding on Israel and applicable to the occupied territories – nor other human rights instruments or customary international law guarantee the right to life in an absolute manner. Article 6 para. 1 of the International Cove-

---

123 Nolte, 5 *Theo. Inq. L.* (2004), at 125-126.

124 *See supra*, Part Four, Chapter E).

nant prohibits "arbitrary deprivations" of life and thus leaves room for exceptions.

1. Targeted Killings as a Deterrent or Punishment Are Illegal

The death penalty is, under all conventions as well as under general international law, the only case in which the death of a person may be the aim or end of an action; in any other context, killings with *dolus directus* of the first degree are not permitted. Thus, targeted killings, as defined above,[125] are "arbitrary" and thus illegal under treaty law as well as general international law. This especially concerns killings which are is exercised for reasons of restitution or as a penal sanction.[126] As shown above, targeted killings by Israeli Forces have often been justified as penal measures or retribution.[127] These killings obviously never took place after court proceedings which would fulfil the procedural requirements laid down by human rights law for the death penalty. Thus, these killings must be regarded as arbitrary deprivations of life under the International Covenant and at the same time under customary international law.

2. Preventive Killings Are Possible within Narrow Limitations

Other killings have been justified by Israel as being preventive in nature. Such killings can generally be in accordance with the right to life, but only under narrow limitations. Force may be used in order to address immediate threats and in this context, the classical concept of immediacy applies. A preventive killing may only be used if the realisation of a threat can immediately be triggered by the targeted person without any further steps in between. As shown above, this is true for the case of a person who is just about to commit an attack.

However, the use of force – even in such circumstances – is subject to proportionality assessed from an overall perspective. The use of force

---

[125] *Compare supra*, Introduction, Chapter C) II. 1. b).

[126] *See supra*, Part One, Chapters B) II. 1 and III.; *see also* H.R. Committee, *Concluding Observations on Israel*, UN Doc. CCPR/CO/78/ISR (August 21, 2003), para. 15.

[127] *See supra*, Introduction, Chapter A).

has to be necessary, i.e. it must be the mildest means capable of addressing the threat. The further the distance of the targeted person to its potential victim is, the less likely the preventive killing of that person is proportionate. Before resorting to the use of a preventive killing, all measures to arrest a person suspected of being in the process of committing an attack must be exhausted.

It is the distance – concerning time and place of the preventive action – between the targeted person and his potential victims that renders most cases of preventively motivated killings by Israeli forces illegal.[128] A man leaving a mosque in a wheelchair after morning prayers may be highly dangerous as the spiritual leader of a "terror group". However, in that very situation, he does not pose an immediate and direct threat to anybody's life and thus may not be killed preventively.[129]

According to some sources, "an individual will only be targeted if he presents a serious threat to public order and safety based on criminal evidence and/or reliable, corroborated intelligence information clearly implicating him" and "the IDF resorts to targeted killing only when arrest is not an option."[130] Nevertheless, it may be doubted that these considerations were taken account of in many of the reported cases of target killings.[131] This is especially true as Israel officially argued, that another standard of immediacy – the last window of opportunity – ap-

---

[128] *Compare e.g.* Tomuschat, 52 *VN* (2004), at 137.

[129] On March 22, 2004, Hamas spiritual leader Sheikh *Ahmed Yassin* was killed in an Israeli missile attack shortly before dawn as he left a Gaza mosque after morning prayers, *see* Dudkevitch, Jerusalem Post, Online Edition, March 22, 2004.

[130] *Compare* Guiora, 36 *Case W. Res. J. Int'l L.* (2004), at 322 and 329.

[131] *Compare* H.R. Committee, *Concluding Observations on Israel*, UN Doc. CCPR/CO/78/ISR (August 21, 2003), para. 15. In some of the cases investigated by Amnesty International, the targets were killed in circumstances where they might easily have been arrested. It is reported that e.g. Jamal 'Abd al-Razeq and Hani Abu Bakra, both killed in the Gaza Strip, could have been arrested by the soldiers who controlled the road and who reportedly stood just two metres away from Hani Abu Bakra. Instead the soldiers opened fire on the suspects and the uninvolved individuals around them. Dr Thabet Thabet, killed on December 31, 2000 as he was backing out his car from his drive-way, is reported to have often passed through an "Area C" and thus Israeli security services could probably have arrested him there, *see* Amnesty International, AI Doc. MDE 15/005/2001 (February 21, 2001), p. 2 and 8.

plied[132] and has expanded its policy to include the targeting of persons training for an attack.[133]

Another problem that arises with some targeted killings by Israeli forces is that of "collateral damage".[134] Intentional collateral damage is never justified under human rights law. Such an institute only exists in the framework of an armed conflict which is not taking place at present. Thus, whenever a person could be preventively targeted in a legal manner under the human rights standards, the intentional injury or even death of bystanders renders the whole operation illegal. This especially applies to those cases which would not even be considered proportional collateral damage under the standards of international humanitarian law, e.g. the use of a one ton bomb to hit a single person in a crowded neighbourhood, killing fifteen persons including nine children.[135]

---

[132] *Kretzmer* "share[s] the view of other commentators that even if the persons targeted by the IDF in some of the reported cases were legitimate targets, the results tend to show that the attacks did not meet the proportionality test", *see* Kretzmer, 16 *Eur. J. Int'l L.* (2005), at 211; *compare also* Meyerstein, *Crimes of War Project* (September 19, 2002); Ben-Naftali/ Michaeli, 36 *Cornell Int'l L.J.* (2003), at 280.

[133] *Compare* Arieh O'Sullivan , 'The Army Redefines the "Ticking Bomb"', in: *The Jerusalem Post*, September 13, 2004, p. 2.

[134] Innocent people are reported to make up at least 30-35% of the persons killed in Israeli targeted killings, *see* Casey, 32 *Syracuse J. Int'l L. & Com.* (2005), at 316.

[135] On July 22, 2002, a F-16 fighter jet dropped a one ton bomb and killed Salah Shihada (Shehadeh/Shehade), the leader and founder of Hamas' military wing of 'Iss ad-Din al-Qassam in Gaza. Shihada and his organization was allegedly responsible for fifty-two attacks on Israeli targets, killing 220 Israeli noncombatants and sixteen soldiers. At the time of his killing, Shihada was reported of being in the process of organizing a "mega attack" of six terror operations that were to take place simultaneously. The bomb allegedly killed fifteen Persons including nine children, and was heavily criticised by the international community. This action is regarded as being disproportionate due to the collateral damage. Following the killing of Shihada, a hit list of twenty prominent Israeli officials with Prime Minister Ariel Sharon on the top was released by the Popular Army Front-Return Battalions, a Palestinian militant group. *Compare* Meyerstein, *Crimes of War Project* (September 19, 2002); Ruys, *Juristenkrant* (January 17, 2007), at para. 10; Luft, 10 *Mid. E. Q.* (2003), at 6-7; *see also* Casey, 32 *Syracuse J. Int'l L. & Com.* (2005), at 312.

II. International Humanitarian Law

This situation under human rights law could be changed due to international humanitarian law, in case this branch of law was applicable additionally. The latter is true for the law of occupation, but as shown above, the law of occupation alone does not change the legal situation concerning targeted killings.[136] However, the situation would be very different if the law of armed conflict was generally applicable.

1. The Israeli Supreme Court's Assessment: The Law of Armed Conflict

As shown above, the Israeli Supreme Court bases its judgment concerning targeted killings on the assumption that the "general, principle starting point is that between Israel and the various terrorist organizations active in Judea, Samaria, and the Gaza Strip ... a continuous situation of armed conflict has existed since the first *intifada*",[137] i.e. since 1987.

In so far, the Court follows the state attorney, arguing that the terrorist attacks against Israel can be defined as an "'armed conflict' justifying the use of counterforce."[138] This is based on the assessment that the casualties caused – in proportion to the population of Israel – is "a number of times greater than the percentage of casualties in the US in the events of September 11 in proportion to the US population" and that recourse is taken to military means.[139]

In consequence, the Court bases its judgment on the 1907 Hague Convention IV and the 1907 Hague Regulations as the primary source for the present case and on the 1949 Geneva Convention IV as an additional source. This assessment could be supported if the threshold of an

---

[136] *See supra*, Part Four, Chapter E).

[137] Supreme Court of Israel, *"Targeted Killings" (Merits)*, para. 16, 46 *ILM* (2007), at 381.

[138] "In the framework of the current campaign of terrorism, more than 900 Israelis have been killed, and thousands of other Israelis have been wounded to date, since late September 2000.", supplement to the summary on behalf of the State Attorney (on January 26, 2004), p. 30, quoted in Supreme Court of Israel, *"Targeted Killings" (Merits)*, para. 16, 46 *ILM* (2007), at 381.

[139] "Among those means are shooting attacks, suicide bombings, mortar fire, rocket fire, car bombs, *et cetera*", supplement to the summary on behalf of the State Attorney (on January 26, 2004), p. 30, quoted *id.*

armed conflict was met in the present situation – which is actually not the case.[140]

Just for the purpose of examining the Israeli Supreme Court's further reasoning, in the following it will be assumed that in fact the situation represented an international armed conflict. Using the legal framework applicable to an international armed conflict, the Court turns to the question of status concerning the targeted persons. It accepts that the principle of distinction includes two categories of persons: Combatants and non-combatants.[141] This is worth being stressed as by doing so, the Court rejects the present U.S. administration's argument that a third category of so called "unlawful combatants" exists.[142] Thus, the Court considers whether terrorists are combatants or civilians under international humanitarian law.

2. *"Terrorists" Are neither Combatants, nor "Unlawful Combatants" but Civilians*

As shown above, "terrorists" are not combatants according to Article 1 of the 1907 Hague Regulations, Article 13 of the 1949 Geneva Conventions I and II, and Article 4 para. 2 of the 1949 Geneva Convention III. The Israeli Supreme Court, referring to its past jurisprudence, is of the same opinion. It observes that the persons in question do not have a fixed emblem recognizable at a distance and do not conduct their operations in accordance with the laws and customs of war.[143] Additionally, the Court explicitly rejects the idea put forward by the U.S. administration that terrorists are "unlawful combatants" who cannot be

---

140 *Compare supra*, Part Four, Chapters C) and D).

141 Supreme Court of Israel, *"Targeted Killings" (Merits)*, para. 23, 46 *ILM* (2007), at 384-385, referring to ICJ, *Legality of the Threat or Use of Nuclear Weapons*, Advisory Opinion of July 8, 1996, I.C.J. Reports 1996, pp. 225-593, at 257 (para. 78) and Article 48 of the 1977 Additional Protocol I.

142 The Court explicitly rejects such a third category in two paragraphs of its judgment, *see* Supreme Court of Israel, *"Targeted Killings" (Merits)*, paras. 27-28, 46 *ILM* (2007), at 388.

143 Supreme Court of Israel, *"Targeted Killings" (Merits)*, para. 24, 46 *ILM* (2007), at 386.

treated according to the established rules for combatants or civilians in international law.[144]

Therefore, the Court does not regard members of "terrorist groups" as combatants under the laws of war. Instead, it regards them as civilians by status: Civilians are defined negatively, i.e. as those who are not – or no longer – combatants.[145] Thus, in consistent application of the law as laid down in the said conventions[146] and reflected by customary international law[147], the Court acknowledges that

> [m]ilitary attack directed at them is forbidden. Their lives and bodies are protected from the dangers of combat, provided that they themselves do not take a direct part in the combat.[148]

Even a civilian who commits acts of combat

> does not lose his status as a civilian, but as long as he is taking a direct part in hostilities he does not enjoy – during that time – the protection granted to a civilian. He is subject to the risks of attack like those to which a combatant is subject, without enjoying the rights of a combatant, e.g. those granted to a prisoner of war.[149]

---

[144] *Id.*, paras. 27-28, 46 *ILM* (2007), at 388.

[145] *Compare* Article 50 para. 1 of the 1977 Additional Protocol I. *See also* ICTY, *Prosecutor v. Tihomir Blaškić*, Case No. IT-95-14-T, ("Lasva Valley"), Judgment of March 3, 2000, reprinted in: 122 *Int'l L.R.* (2002), pp. 1-250, at 71-72 (para. 180).

[146] *See* Article 27 para. 1 of the fourth Geneva Convention , Article 46 para. 1 of the 1907 Hague Regulations, Article 51 paras. 1-3 of the 1977 Additional Protocol I and Article 13 paras. 1 and 3 of the 1977 Additional Protocol II.

[147] The Court itself refers to Henckaerts/ Doswald-Beck (eds.), *Humanitarian Law*, Vol. 1, Rules 1, 6 and 7 (pp. 3, 19 and 25 respectively). *Compare also* Gasser, in: Fleck (ed.), *Handbook*, at 211 *et seqq.* (para. 502) and at 232 (paras. 517 *et seq.*).

[148] Supreme Court of Israel, "*Targeted Killings*" *(Merits)*, para. 23, 46 *ILM* (2007), at 384-385.

[149] Supreme Court of Israel, "*Targeted Killings*" *(Merits)*, para. 31, 46 *ILM* (2007), at 389-390.

3. Direct Participation by Civilians in Hostilities

At this point, the Court reaches the core of the question, if examined under the law of armed conflict. As the persons in question are civilians, they could be targeted "unless and for such time as they take a direct part in hostilities".[150] The Court thus examines the elements "taking ... part in hostilities", "taking direct part" and "for such time". As shown above, "taking ... part in hostilities" covers acts which by their nature and purpose are intended to cause actual harm to the personnel and equipment of the armed forces or civilian population. It is clear that civilians are taking part in hostilities when using weapons in an armed conflict. The same holds true for an individual who is carrying a bomb to the site of a planned attack. It is furthermore generally accepted that it is not necessary to carry weapons, but that the gathering of intelligence or the preparation for combat, delivering ammunition as well as the planning or ordering of attacks is also covered. On the other hand, "general strategic analysis," or giving "logistical, general support, including monetary aid" is not regarded as direct participation by the Court.[151]

In seeking an interpretation of "direct" in that context, the Court refers to *Michael N. Schmitt* who proposes that such "gray areas should be interpreted liberally, i.e., in favor of finding direct participation."[152] According to this, the Court regards the following cases as direct participation: a person who transports combatants or drives an ammunition truck to or from the place where the hostilities are taking place; a person who operates weapons which combatants use, or supervises their operation, or provides service to them, be the distance from the battlefield as it may;[153] as well as persons who serve as human shields of their own free will.[154] Direct participation – according to the Court – also in-

---

[150] The Court bases its assessment on the wording of Article 51 para. 3 of the 1977 Additional Protocol I; *compare also* Cassese, 'Expert Opinion', paras. 30-35 (pp. 16-18).

[151] *Compare supra*, Part Two, Chapter D), II. 1. c).

[152] Schmitt, in: Fischer *et al.* (eds.), at 509.

[153] Supreme Court of Israel, *"Targeted Killings" (Merits)*, para. 35, 46 *ILM* (2007), at 392.

[154] *Id.*, para. 36, 46 *ILM* (2007), at 392. *But see* Otto, 86 *Int'l Rev. Red Cross* (2004), No 856, at 780-781.

cludes "those who have sent [these persons and] ..., the person who decided upon the act, and the person who planned it."[155]

The Court accepts that according to Article 51 para. 3 of the 1977 Additional Protocol I and customary international law, civilians may only be opposed "for such time" as they are taking direct part in hostilities and that – if "such time" has passed – the protection granted to the civilian returns.[156] It then distinguishes between two opposed cases: First, "a civilian taking a direct part in hostilities one single time, or sporadically, who later detaches himself from that activity" is regarded – if having detached himself from hostilities "entirely, or for a long period" – as protected from attack.[157] Second, "a civilian who has joined a terrorist organization which has become his 'home', and in the framework of his role in that organization he commits a chain of hostilities, with short periods of rest between them" may – according to the Court – be attacked.[158]

With the standards developed above in mind,[159] this assessment by the Israeli Supreme Court cannot convince entirely. The Court has received appraisal for having chosen the "happy medium" concerning the question of direct participation.[160] But first, the Court bases it's approach on the idea of interpreting an exception to a rule broadly. The general rule is that civilians must not be attacked. The concept of direct participation is thus an exception and should rather be interpreted narrowly.

Second, while the Court acknowledges that the status of the person in question remains that of a civilian, nevertheless it's approach is based on the understanding that "[a]ll those persons are performing the function of combatants." However, the exception to the general rule that civilians may not be attacked is not based on the idea that they forfeit their status or their protection an can thus generally be treated like combatants. They will, if captured, not acquire prisoner-of-war status, they

---

155 Supreme Court of Israel, *"Targeted Killings" (Merits)*, para. 37, 46 *ILM* (2007), at 392-393.

156 *Id.*, para. 38, 46 *ILM* (2007), at 393.

157 *Id.*, para. 39, 46 *ILM* (2007), at 393.

158 *Id.*

159 *Compare supra*, Part Two, Chapter D), II. 1. c).

160 Ruys, *Juristenkrant* (January 17, 2007), at para. 8.

may be punished for participating in the hostilities.[161] The background for this exception is that "all these activities ... must be proved to be directly related to hostilities, or, in other words, to *represent a direct threat to the enemy*".[162] This threat "may be *resisted* by force".[163] "[A]nyone performing hostile acts may also be *opposed*".[164] Even the authorities referred to by the Court stress that a direct relationship between a threat (by a civilian) and its opposition is necessary.[165]

Third, as shown above, this suggests that the duration of the participation has to be interpreted rather narrowly.[166] In only accepting the end of such participation if a person has detached himself from hostilities "entirely, or for a long period" the Court covers too many cases. A more narrow assessment has been described and criticised as the so called "revolving door" phenomenon.[167] Some are of the opinion that a civilian may not be attacked *between* two assaults he commits.[168] This picture – in principle – corresponds with the idea behind the direct participation exception. The status of the civilian does not change, but while behaving in a certain way, a civilian may be attacked.

Thus, according to the standards developed in this treatise, the Israeli Supreme Court overstretches the exception concerning the direct participation of civilians in hostilities. Many cases in which, according to the Court, a person could be targeted, his killing would not be justified as resistance or opposition against a person taking direct part in hostilities.

---

161 *Compare supra*, Part Two, Chapter D), II. 1. c).

162 Gasser, in: Fleck (ed.), *Handbook*, at 233 (para. 518.2 *lit.* b). Emphasis added.

163 *Id.*, at 233 (para. 518.2 *lit.* a). Emphasis added.

164 *Id.*, at 233 (para. 501.5). Emphasis added.

165 *Id.*, at 233 (para. 518.2 *lit.* b).

166 *Compare supra*, Part Two, Chapter D), II. 1. c).

167 Parks, 32 *A.F. L. Rev.* (1990), at 118-120; Watkin, *Combatants*, p. 12.

168 *See e.g.* Casey, 32 *Syracuse J. Int'l L. & Com.* (2005), at 337.

III. The Israeli Supreme Court's Further Preconditions for Targeted Killings

The Israeli Supreme Court saw the necessity to developed additional criteria which have to be fulfilled to render a targeted killing legal under its assessment of direct participation. First, it requires well-based information before categorizing a civilian as falling into one of the discussed categories.[169] Second, according to the Court, a civilian taking a direct part in hostilities cannot be attacked if less harmful means can be employed:[170] Thus, if the person taking a direct part in hostilities can be arrested, interrogated, and tried, those are the means which should be employed, albeit not at any cost.[171] Third, according to the Court, after an attack on a civilian suspected of taking a direct part, at such time, in hostilities, a thorough investigation has to be performed retroactively regarding the precision of the identification of the target and the circumstances of the attack upon him.[172] And fourth, if the harm is not only to a civilian directly participating in the hostilities, but also to innocent civilians nearby, the harm to them is collateral damage. That damage must withstand the proportionality test.

While only the last precondition is a classical consideration of the law of armed conflict, the proportionality test concerning the question of performing a targeted killing or an arrest as well as the consideration concerning a retroactive investigation stems from the human rights sphere.[173] In that context, the Court expressly relies on the *McCann* judgment by the European Court of Human Rights.[174]

---

[169] *Compare supra*, Part Two, Chapter D), II. 1. c).

[170] On this requirement, *compare* Melzer, 9 *Yb. Int'l Hum. L.* (2009), at 91-100.

[171] For example, if it involves a unreasonable risk for the lives of the acting soldiers or its harm to nearby innocent civilians is greater than that caused by refraining from it, it is not required, *see ibid.*

[172] Supreme Court of Israel, "*Targeted Killings*" *(Merits)*, para. 40, 46 *ILM* (2007), at 393-394.

[173] *Compare supra*, Part One, Chapter E), I. 2. b); *see also* Milanovic, 89 *Int'l Rev. Red Cross* (2007), No. 866, at 390.

[174] Eur. Ct. H.R., *McCann*, Series A, No. 324, p. 49 (paras. 161-163). *But see* Melzer, 9 *Yb. Int'l Hum. L.* (2009), at 91, who sees Israeli constitutional law as the source.

It is not generally required under the laws of armed conflict to arrest a hostile fighter wherever possible instead of killing him, nor is there any generally recognised provision or customary law calling for an independent investigation of disputed attacks.[175] Nevertheless, the Court introduces these criteria which stem from human rights law, and rightly so.[176] As shown above, human rights law is fully applicable to the question of targeted killings in the occupied territory.[177] Following the International Court of Justice's Advisory Opinion on the *Legal Consequences of the Construction of a Wall in the Occupied Palestinian Territory*,[178] it can be regarded as generally accepted that the situation in the Gaza Strip and the West Bank is still that of an occupation.[179] Thus, targeted killings in this context have to be considered according to human rights standards and especially are subject to the rule of proportionality. And this is exactly what the Court does when considering milder means than a targeted killing – albeit in the wrong legal context.[180]

---

[175] *See also* Dworkin, *Crimes of War Project* (December 15, 2006); *but see* Melzer, 9 *Yb. Int'l Hum. L.* (2009), at 100-112, who sees a certain tendency to develop the former principle from the principle of military necessity.

[176] *But see* Cohen/ Shany, 5 *J. Int'l Crim. Just.* (2007), at 314-315; Schondorf, 5 *J. Int'l Crim. Just.* (2007), at 308-309.

[177] *See supra*, Part Five, Chapter A).

[178] ICJ, *Legal Consequences for States of the Continued Presence of South Africa in Namibia (South-West Africa) Notwithstanding Security Council Resolution 276 (1970)*, Advisory Opinion of June 21, 1971, I.C.J. Reports 1971, pp. 12-345.

[179] *See e.g.* Supreme Court of Israel, "*Targeted Killings*" *(Merits)*, para. 18, 46 *ILM* (2007), at 382; Supreme Court of Israel, *Beit Sourik Village Council v. The Government of Israel* et al. *("Security Fence")*, H.C.J. 2056/04 (Petition for an Order Nisi), Judgment of June 30, 2004, para. 23, English translation reprinted in: 43 *ILM* (2004), pp. 1099-1128, at 1107; Supreme Court of Israel, *Ajuri v. IDF Commander in the West Bank ("Assigned Residence")*, H.C.J. 7015/02, Judgment of September 3, 2002, para. 22, English translation reprinted in: Israel Supreme Court, *Judgments of the Israel Supreme Court: Fighting Terrorism within the Law*, Jerusalem 2005, pp. 144-178, at 161 and 125 *Int'l L.R.* (2004), pp. 537-568, at 551-552; and recently: Yaakov Katz; Rebecca Anna Stoil, 'Peretz orders IDF to prepare for operations in Gaza', in: *Jerusalem Post*, January 29, 2007.

[180] Dworkin sees another reason behind the Court's decision to apply human rights standards: There seems to lie a not explicitly stated principle that in low-

C. Conclusion: The Situation in Israel

Contrary to the Israeli Supreme Court, the result of this treatise is that the targeted killings by Israeli Forces in the Occupied Territory must be judged according to human rights standards. However, this fundamental difference does not mean that the judgment by the Court can be dismissed in total. The judgment contains many achievements and as it "is very well reasoned, one might assume its persuasive impact will be substantial."[181] The Court shows that targeted killings are covered by a legal framework and open to legal control. It imposes significant constraints on the power to kill suspected militants. Based on solid information which indicates that the target is taking a direct part in hostilities, the possibility of an arrest and collateral damages have to be considered. The judgment also requires and independent retroactive investigation of every such attack. It thus factually introduces human rights considerations such as proportionality and a procedural safeguard to the question, even though it approaches it under the law of war. Additionally, the Court also points to the fact that any targeted killing which does not fulfil these conditions may also lead to individual criminal responsibility of the acting persons,[182] even though international criminal responsibility is not addressed explicitly by the Court. But if read carefully, parts of the judgment can be interpreted as stating that certain targeted killings amount to war crimes.[183]

---

intensity armed conflict against terrorist groups, where some fighters may be found in non-battlefield conditions and even in places where law enforcement is still effective, and where it may be difficult to know with any certainty whether suspected enemy fighters are taking part in hostilities or not, there is a place for rules derived from the human rights norm against arbitrary deprivation of life. *See* Dworkin, *Crimes of War Project* (December 15, 2006).

[181] Fenrick, 5 *J. Int'l Crim. Just.* (2007), at 333.

[182] Supreme Court of Israel, *"Targeted Killings" (Merits)*, para. 19, 46 *ILM* (2007), at 382-383. This is regarded as one of the most important achievements of the judgment by Ben-Naftali, 5 *J. Int'l Crim. Just.* (2007), at 328-331; *see also* Cassese, 5 *J. Int'l Crim. Just.* (2007), at 341-342.

[183] In assessing the international humanitarian law applicable according to the Court, it also refers to Article 8 para. 2 of the 1998 Rome Statute of the ICC, enshrining the duty to refrain from harming civilians, unless it represents proportionate collateral damage. Later the Court refers to a hypothetical example which very much resembles the case of Salah Shehada and 15 other persons,

Importantly, in two paragraphs of its judgment,[184] the Court explicitly rejects the idea put forward by the U.S. administration that terrorists are "unlawful combatants" who cannot be treated according to the established rules for combatants or civilians in international law. Furthermore, the Court does not base its argument on Article 51 UN-Charter. This fact has been interpreted as an implicit rejection of the idea to base the fight against terrorism on self-defence[185] and could be another critical address to the United States.[186]

The Court merits praise for going into depth concerning the question of direct participation, as this is one of the most problematic questions of humanitarian law,[187] albeit the Court's finding is not immune to criticism. At the same time, the Court failed to fully lay out its legal reasoning concerning the legal regime applicable. It merits credit for introducing human rights standards, but this introduction is contradictory if the Court's presumption of an international armed conflict is followed consistently. In other areas, the judgment leaves ample room for interpretation, and there is little reason to believe that the Israeli military will interpret it in a restrictive way.[188] This is the case concerning the Court's fairly expansive definition of direct participation in hostilities.

In consequence, the Court's Judgment could, if implemented in good faith, limit Israel's reliance on targeted killings. But it is not only significant in its own right. It is also likely to become an important precedent for other countries engaging in military action against terrorist groups.[189]

---

nine of them children. Thus, *Ben-Naftali* interprets the judgment as implicitly declaring that the case of Shehada was a war crime, *see* Ben-Naftali, 5 *J. Int'l Crim. Just.* (2007), at 330.

[184] Supreme Court of Israel, *"Targeted Killings" (Merits)*, paras. 27-28, 46 *ILM* (2007), at 388.

[185] Ruys, *Juristenkrant* (January 17, 2007), at para. 2.

[186] *C.f.* Dworkin, *Crimes of War Project* (December 15, 2006).

[187] Ruys, *Juristenkrant* (January 17, 2007), at para. 6; *see also* Melzer, *Targeted Killing*, p. 33-34.

[188] An indicator that the government does not believe that the ruling will require any change in IDF practices came just after it was issued, when a government spokesman announced that the IDF was already complying with the Court's stated rules, *see* Mariner, *FindLaw's Writ* (December 22, 2006).

[189] Dworkin, *Crimes of War Project* (December 15, 2006).

Nevertheless, in distinction to the Israeli Supreme Court, it has to be stressed that the decisive law applicable is human rights law and the decisive question is thus: Is a threat of such immediacy that it justifies a preventive killing as the last and mildest of equally effective means?

Conclusion: Targeted Killings and International Law

"It would be monstrous indeed if the attacks on the World Trade Center were to lead to something even more monstrous."[1] Thus, even the reaction to the worst and most treacherous attacks or any action aiming to prevent such incidents must adhere to the rule of law. Any different approach will lead to a Pyrrhic victory[2] and will run the risk of destroying what is meant to be defended. It has to be ensured that what we are fighting for is not lost in the process.[3] As *Nietzsche* phrased it:

> He who battles with monsters has to take care that he does not thereby become a monster. Always remember that when you gaze into the abyss, the abyss gazes back into you.[4]

Kretzmer, in his article on targeted killings concludes that

> unless realistic standards of conduct for states involved in armed conflicts with terrorist groups exist, they will act in an environment infected by the lawlessness that characterizes terrorism. The danger of this lawlessness is such that however imperfect these standards may be, they are preferable to no standards at all.[5]

---

1 Frédéric Megrét, 'War? Legal Semantics and the Move to Violence', in: 13 *Eur. J. Int'l L.* (2002), pp. 361-400, at 400.

2 "The armies separated; and, it is said, Pyrrhus replied to one that gave him joy of his victory that one other such would utterly undo him." The phrase is more often reported as "Another such victory over the Romans and we are undone."

3 Drumbl, 36 *Case W. Res. J. Int'l L.* (2004), at 344.

4 "Wer mit Ungeheuern kämpft, mag zusehn, daß er nicht dabei zum Ungeheuer wird. Und wenn du lange in einen Abgrund blickst, blickt der Abgrund auch in dich hinein.", Friedrich Nietzsche, *Jenseits von Gut und Böse*, Leipzig 1886, Part IV, para. 146 (my translation).

5 Kretzmer, 16 *Eur. J. Int'l L.* (2005), at 212. *See also* Fisher, 45 *Colum. J. Transnat'l L.* (2007), at 757, who states "that international law is not currently in a position to guide State behavior with respect to targeted killing."

While it is true that imperfect rules may be better than no rules, I cannot fully support *Kretzmer's* conclusion. According to the outcome of the present examination, legal standards that are applicable to what is referred to as "armed conflict with terrorist groups" do already exist under international law. These standards are part of human rights law and international humanitarian law:

A. Generally, Human Rights Law Applies to Targeted Killings

The standard generally applicable to targeted killings is that of human rights law. In the human rights treaties examined, as well as in general international law, the right to life offers a high, albeit not absolute, standard of protection which is almost identical under the different conventions. However, the conventions as well as general international law leave room for several exceptions:

The death penalty still is a possible exception but its use must adhere to high procedural standards. It is the only case in which the death of a person may be the aim or end of an action; in any other context, killings with *dolus directus* of the first degree are not permitted. Thus, targeted killings, as defined above,[6] are "arbitrary" and thus illegal under human rights law.

Nevertheless, force may be used in order to address immediate threats, i.e. if the realisation of a threat can immediately be triggered by the alleged offender without any further steps in between. This use of force is subject to proportionality. It must be necessary, i.e. it must be the mildest means capable of addressing the threat. The European Court has shown that this requirement is strongly related to the question of immediacy; at an earlier stage, milder means are probably available. In consequence, the proportionality of the use of force has to be assessed from an overall perspective rather than based solely on the moment force was used.

First, for such force, self-defence and the defence of other persons are accepted aims. The use of such force is additionally accepted in order to

---

6 Namely killings with direct intention of the first degree, *compare supra*, Introduction, Chapter C) II. 1. b).

prevent serious crimes, even if this encompasses deeds that do not threaten the life of other humans. The death of the person targeted may only be a side-effect of the use of such force. Whereas a strict theoretical consideration would require this force to be a merely undesired side-effect, it is clear that in practice, the death of the targeted person is virtually certain in many situations. This can be accepted if the aim of the operation is to save another person's life.

Second, it is accepted that force may be used in order of arresting a person. However, in such a situation, the person's death may not be intended, either under the conventions or under general international law.

Third, in order to prevent the escape of a detainee, force may be used but the detainee's death may at the most be intended with *dolus eventualis*. The human rights treaties seem to be stricter on this point than general international law. They are interpreted as additionally requiring proportionality between the threat the detainee causes if he escapes and the force that is used to prevent his escape.

Fourth, quelling a riot or insurrection is a legitimate of use force but under the conventions lethal force may not be used at all, but the equipment of the state agents with "less lethal weapons" that are fully capable of quelling a riot without killing rioters is necessary. Again, the standard in general international law is less strict; whereas resort to milder means is obligatory here as well.

These reasons for the use of force against a person may coincide. Law enforcement personnel could act in self-defence if necessary in each of these situations, but "collateral damages" are not accepted. Under human rights law, it is exclusively the person that causes a threat that may be targeted. The death of innocent third persons can never be justified.

These principles are explicitly non-derogable under the conventions but also under general-international law; the right to life is part of *jus cogens* and may not be derogated. However, additional exceptions to these standards do exist if international humanitarian law is applicable.

Under human rights law, penal killings may only be employed in the strictly limited cases of capital punishment. Preventive force may only be used in immediate situations, i.e. to prevent an imminent threat caused by the targeted person itself. In consequence, the right to life does permit preventive killings under strict preconditions, but prohibits all targeted killings.

This standard applies to peaceful inner-State situations as well as to situations of "calm" occupation. It still applies in situations of violence and riots which fall short of an armed conflict. Only if an armed conflict exists, are these standards complemented by international humanitarian law. Then, the law of armed conflict is the *lex specialis* in defining what is an "arbitrary" deprivation of life.

B. These Standards Are in Some Situations Amended by International Humanitarian Law

> [E]even when the cannons speak, the military commander must uphold the law. The power of society to stand against its enemies is based on its recognition that it is fighting for values that deserve protection. The rule of law is one of these values.[7]

The legality of targeted killings in the context of armed conflicts – international as well as non-international ones – depends first and foremost on the primary status of the targeted person. In international and non-international armed conflicts combatants and fighters respectively may generally be targeted, but subject to certain restrictions. In both contexts, the targeted killing of civilians is generally prohibited, but may be legal by way of a strictly limited exception. This is only the case while a civilian is directly taking part in the hostilities. This direct participation has to be interpreted narrowly, with a strong emphasis on the threat a civilian poses to the adversary. This threat may be opposed by use of force, again, subject to the same restrictions as concerning the targeting of combatants.

Such concepts as "unlawful combatant" or "terrorist" do not represent any status under international humanitarian law. Thus, the standards that apply to either combatants or civilians apply to any person, including those who are referred to by different authors using different definitions as "unlawful combatants" or terrorists". In most cases these persons actually – but not generally – are civilians by their primary status. Many of them are actually taking direct part in hostilities and thus may be targeted. But every person's status and the question of partici-

---

[7] Justice Aharon Barak, President of the Supreme Court of Israel, *Ajuri v. IDF Commander in the West Bank*, H.C.J. 7015/02, Judgment of September 3, 2002, English translation reprinted in: Israel Supreme Court, *Judgments of the Israel Supreme Court: Fighting Terrorism within the Law*, Jerusalem 2005, pp. 144-178, at 176 and 125 *Int'l L.R.* (2004), pp. 537-568 (para. 41).

pation have to be evaluated individually. Subject to that status, the same rules as to other civilians or combatants apply to them.

In all cases of legitimately targeting a person the general principles of international humanitarian law have to be observed. These standards include militarily necessity and the prohibition of certain means and methods which are e.g. perfidious, i.e. the use of certain false symbols, emblems or uniforms, feigning civilian status as well as instigating enemy combatants to kill their own superiors, recruiting hired killers, placing a price on the head of a person, and offering a reward for his capture "dead or alive". Furthermore, persons who are *hors de combat* may no longer be targeted.

The overall legality of a targeted killing also depends on the legality of any collateral damage. A targeted killing is one attack which must stand the test of proportionality concerning collateral damage. In that regard, also the threat posed by the targeted person is decisive. In less immediate cases it will frequently be required to suspend the attack until no civilian casualties will be caused.

These standards also apply to killings which may be qualified as "assassinations". However, the fact that a certain killing can be referred to as an "assassination" does not have any effect regarding its legality. There is thus no special "prohibition on assassination" relevant to the present topic.

C. No Justifications for Targeted Killings Exist Outside the Human Rights and International Humanitarian Law Systems

The relevant and decisive rules concerning the legality of targeted killings are human rights rules and international humanitarian law rules. As such, they are not subject to reciprocity. Thus, the general circumstances precluding wrongfulness under international law do not apply to them. This does not mean that these rights provide for absolute protection. This system entails its own "internal" possibilities of derogations, exceptions and limitations. These standards are inherent to the system and exclusively provide for the decisive criteria. Thus, neither (non-individual) self-defence nor necessity nor any other of the general circumstances precluding wrongfulness discussed above can render legal a killing which is in violation of the inbuilt standards of human rights law and international humanitarian law.

D. The Most Prominent Cases Do Not Meet these Standards

Also in Israel and the Occupied Territory, contrary to the Israeli Supreme Court's view, human rights standards are decisive. The Israeli Supreme Court felt the necessity to introduce human rights standards to international humanitarian law and thus did not reach a diametrically different result as the present examination. However, if the human rights standards were applied properly, many killings which would be legal according to the Israeli Supreme Court would be illegal according to the present standards.

This result would also be the same under international humanitarian law. Direct participation cannot be interpreted in such an extensive manner as the Israeli Supreme Court did and thus many persons which could be targeted according to the Court, cannot be targeted according to the present standards.

This treaties was never meant to be a case study, especially as little exact and objective information is available concerning specific targeted killings. However, the outcome of this examination is that the most prominent cases of targeted killings, such as those of Sheikh *Yassin* or the U.S.-led Yemen incident do not stand up to the standards developed here. In the absence of an armed conflict, human rights law is applicable to those cases. Even in the framework of an armed conflict, these persons would most likely have been civilians, possibly at some time taking direct part in hostilities. However, in the specific situation these persons were hit, they did not pose an immediate threat to any potential victim. Human rights law would have required the State authorities to capture and try these persons instead of killing them by a targeted strike. Additionally, according to human rights standards, the additional victims beside the targeted person itself cannot be justified.

A major difference between "judicial" responses to terrorism and military ones is the risk of killing or injuring innocent civilians where the military option is chosen. A state may lawfully kill innocent civilians during international armed conflict if their death is not excessive in relation to the direct military advantage anticipated. Such a principle does not apply to the arrest of individuals in order to bring them before a court of law. If these standards are applied consistently, a democratic state might thereby be fighting "with one hand tied behind its back", as the Israeli Supreme Court phrased it.[8] However, the ends do not justify the means, and as *Guillaume-Henri Dufour* phrased it: "il faut sortir de cette lutte non seulement victorieux mais encore sans reproche."[9]

---

8 Supreme Court of Israel, *Public Committee against Torture in Israel v. Government of Israel*, H.C.J. 5100/94, Judgment of September 6, 1999, English translation reprinted in: Israel Supreme Court, *Judgments of the Israel Supreme Court: Fighting Terrorism within the Law*, Jerusalem 2005, pp. 25-58, at 54-55 (para. 39).

9 Quoted in: Sandoz *et al.* (eds.), *Protocoles additionnels*, para. 3346 (p. 974) (footnote 11).

Bibliography/ Index of Authorities

A. Books, Treatises and Articles

Abbott, Kirby, "Terrorists: Criminals, Combatants or ... ?": The Questions of Combatancy', in: Canadian Council on International Law (ed.), *The Measure of International Law: Effectiveness, Fairness and Validity*, The Hague 2004, pp. 366-385 [Kluwer]

Abi-Saab, Rosemary, 'Humanitarian Law and Internal Conflicts: The Evolution of Legal Concern', in: Astrid J.M. Delissen/ Gerard J. Tanja (eds.); *Humanitarian Law of Armed Conflict: Challenges ahead – Essays in Honour of Frits Kalshoven*, Dordrecht 1991, pp. 209-223

Abresch, William, 'A Human Rights Law of Internal Armed Conflict: The European Court of Human Rights in Chechnya', in: 16 *European Journal of International Law* (2005), pp. 741-767 [*Eur. J. Int'l L.*]

Addicott, Jefrey F., 'Proposal for a new Executive Order on Assassination', in: 37 *University of Richmond Law Review* (2003), pp. 751-785 [*U. Rich. L. Rev.*]

Aggelen, Johannes G.C. van, 'A Response to John C. Yoo, "the Status of Soldiers and Terrorists under the Geneva Conventions"', in: 4 *Chinese Journal of International Law* (2005), pp. 167-181 [*Chin. J. Int'l L.*]

Ago, Roberto, 'Droit des traités à la lumière de la Convention Vienne', in: 134 *Recueil des Cours de l'Academie de Droit International de la Haye* (1979-III), pp. 297-331 [*RdC*]

Ago, Roberto, 'Science juridique et droit international', in: 90 *Recueil des Cours de l'Academie de Droit International de la Haye* (1956-II), pp. 849-955 [*RdC*]

Akehurst, Michael Barton, 'Custom as a Source of International Law', in: 47 *British Yearbook of International Law* (1974-75), pp. 1-53 [*Brit. Yb. Int'l L.*]

Al-Haq, *A Human Rights Assessment of the Declaration of Principles on Interim Self-Government Arrangements for Palestinians*, Ramallah 1993 [Al-Haq]

Aldrich, George H., 'The Taliban, Al Qaeda, and the Detention of Illegal Combatants', in: 96 *American Journal of International Law* (2002), pp. 891-898 [*Am. J. Int'l L.*]

Aldrich, George H., 'Why the United States of America should ratify Additional Protocol I', in: Astrid J.M. Delissen/Gerard J. Tanja (eds.); *Humanitarian Law of Armed Conflict: Challenges ahead – Essays in Honour of Frits Kalshoven*, Dordrecht 1991, pp. 127-144 [Nijhoff]

Allain, Jean/ O'Shea, Andreas, 'African Disunity: Comparing Human Rights Law and Practice of North and South African States', in: 24 *Human Rights Quarterly* (2002), pp. 86-125 [*Hum. Rts. Q.*]

Alland, Denis, 'International Responsibility and Sanctions: Self-Defence and Countermeasures in the ILC Codification of Rules governing International Responsibility', in: Marina Spinedi/ Bruno Simma (eds.), *United Nations Codification of State Responsibility*, New York 1987, pp. 143-195 [Oceana Publ.]

Alonzo-Maizlish, David, 'When does it end? Problems in the Law of Occupation', in: Roberta Arnold/ Pierre-Antoine Hildbrand (eds.), *International Humanitarian Law and the 21st Century's Conflicts: Changes and Challenges*, Lausanne 2005, pp. 97-116 [Interuniversitaires Suisses]

Altiparmak, Kerem, '*Banković*: An Obstacle to the Application of the European Convention on Human Rights in Iraq?', in: 9 *Journal of Conflict & Security Law* (2004), pp. 213-251 [*J. Confl. Sec. L.*]

American Law Institute, *Restatement of the Law (Third) – The Foreign Relations Law of the United States*, St. Paul, Minnesota 1987 [American Law Institute Publishers]

Amnesty International, *Broken Lives: A Year of Intifada – Israel, Occupied Territories, Palestinian Authority*, London 2001 [Amnesty International Publications]

Amnesty International, *Israel and the Occupied Territories, State Assassinations and Other Unlawful Killings*, AI Doc. MDE 15/005/2001 (February 21, 2001)

Amnesty International, *Israel and the Occupied Territories: Israel must end its Policy of Assassinations*, AI Doc. MDE 15/056/2003 (July 4, 2003)

Anderson, Kenneth, 'Targeted Killing in U.S. Counterterrorism Strategy and Law', in: Benjamin Wittes (ed.), *Legislating the War on Terror: An Agenda for Reform*, Washington, D.C. 2009, pp. 346-400 [Brookings Institution Press]

Ankumah, Evelyn A., *The African Commission on Human and Peoples' Rights – Practice and Procedures*, The Hague 1996 [Nijhoff]

Ansah, Tawia, 'War: Rhetoric & Norm Creation in Response to Terror', in: 43 *Virginia Journal of International Law* (2003), pp. 797-860 [*Va. J. Int'l L.*]

Anscombe, G.E.M., 'War and Murder', in: Larry May/ Eric Rovie/ Steve Viner (eds.), *The Morality of War: Classical and Contemporary Readings*, Upper Saddle River, N.J 2005, pp. 203-212 [Pearson]

Arai-Takahashi, Yutaka, 'Disentangling Legal Quagmires: The Legal Characterisation of the Armed Conflicts in Afghanistan since 6/7 October 2001 and the Question of Prisoner of War Status', in: 5 *Yearbook of International Humanitarian Law* (2002), pp. 61-105 [*Yb. Int'l Hum. L.*]

Arai-Takahashi, Yutaka, 'So-called Targeted Killings in Volatile Occupied Territories – Critical Appraisal through the Concept of Direct Participation in Hostilities and the Principle of Proportionality', in: 108 *Journal of International Law and Diplomacy* (2009), pp. 1-47 [*J. Int'l L. & Dipl.*]

Arai-Takahashi, Yutaka, *The Margin of Appreciation Doctrine and the Principle of Proportionality in the Jurisprudence of the ECHR*, Antwerp 2002 [Intersentia]

Arnold, Roberta, 'Human Rights in Times of Terrorism', in: 66 *Zeitschrift für ausländisches öffentliches Recht und Völkerrecht* (2006), pp. 297-319 [*ZaöRV*]

Arnold, Roberta, 'Terrorism and IHL: A Common Denominator?', in: Roberta Arnold/ Pierre-Antoine Hildbrand (eds.), *International Humanitarian Law and the 21st Century's Conflicts: Changes and Challenges*, Lausanne 2005, pp. 5-23 [Interuniversitaires Suisses]

Ashkouri, Michael, 'Has United States Foreign Policy towards Libya, Iraq & Serbia violated Executive Order 12333: Prohibition on Assassination?', in: 7 *New England International and Comparative Law Annual* (2001), pp. 155-175 [*New Eng. Int'l & Comp. L. Ann.*]

Aust, Anthony, *Modern Treaty Law and Practice*, Cambridge 2000 [Cambridge Univ. Press]

Aust, Helmut Philipp, 'German Constitutional Law Cases 2004-2006', in: 13 *European Public Law* (2007), pp. 205-222 [*Eur. Pub. L.*]

Aust, Helmut Philipp, 'The Normative Environment for Peace – On the Contribution of the ILC's Articles on State Responsibility', in: Georg Nolte (ed.), *Peace through International Law: The Role of the International Law Commission*, Berlin 2009, pp. 13-46 [Springer]

Banks, William C./ Raven-Hansen, Peter, 'Targeted Killing and Assassination: The U.S. Legal Framework', in: 37 *University of Richmond Law Review* (2003), pp. 667-749 [*U. Rich. L. Rev.*]

Bassiouni, M. Cherif, 'Terrorism: The Persistent Dilemma of Legitimacy', in: 36 *Case Western Reserve Journal of International Law* (2004), pp. 299-306 [*Case W. Res. J. Int'l L.*]

Baumann, Karsten, 'Das Grundrecht auf Leben unter Quantifizierungsvorbehalt: Zur Terrorismusbekämpfung durch "finalen Rettungsabschuß"', in: 57 *Die öffentliche Verwaltung* (2004), pp. 853-861 [*DÖV*]

Bausback, Winfried, 'Terrorismusabwehr durch gezielte Tötungen? Assassination als Mittel des (deutschen) demokratischen Rechtsstaates?', in: 24 *Neue Zeitschrift für Verwaltungsrecht* (2005), pp. 418-420 [*NVwZ*]

Baxi, Upendra, 'The "War on Terror" and the "War of Terror": Nomadic Multitudes, Aggressive Incumbents, and the "New" International Law', in: 43 *Osgoode Hall Law Journal* (2005), pp. 7-43 [*Osgoode Hall L.J.*]

Baxter, Richard R., 'Humanitarian Law or Humanitarian Politics? The 1974 Diplomatic Conference on Humanitarian Law', in 16 *Harvard International Law Journal* (1975), pp. 1-26 [*Harv. Int'l L.J.*]

Baxter, Richard R., 'So called "Unprivileged Belligerency": Spies, Guerrillas, Saboteurs', in: 28 *British Yearbook of International Law* (1952), pp. 323-345 [*Brit. Y.B. Int'l L.*]

Baxter, Richard R., 'Some Existing Problems of Humanitarian Law', in: 14 *Revue de droit pénal militaire et de droit de la guerre* (1975), pp. 297-303 [*Rev. dr. pén. mil.*]

Baxter, Richard R., 'The Duties of Combatants and the Conduct of Hostilities (Law of The Hague)', in: Henry Dunant Institute/

United Nations Educational, Scientific and Cultural Organization (eds.), *International Dimensions of Humanitarian Law*, Geneva 1988, pp. 93-133 [Nijhoff]

Baxter, Richard R., 'Treaties and Customs', in: 129 *Recueil des Cours de l'Academie de Droit International de la Haye* (1970-I), pp. 27-105 [*RdC*]

Bazan, Elizabeth B., 'Assassination Ban and E.O. 12333: A Brief Summary', in: *CRS Report For Congress*, RS21037, updated January 4, 2002, URL: <http://www.fas.org/irp/crs/RS21037.pdf> (last visited February 25, 2008)

Beard, Jack M., 'Military Action against Terrorists under International Law – America's new War on Terror: The Case for Self-Defense under International Law', in: 25 *Harvard Journal of Law and Public Policy* (2002), pp. 559-590 [*Harv. J.L. & Pub. Pol'y*]

Bello, Emmanuel G., 'The African Charter on Human and Peoples' Rights – A Legal Analysis', in: 194 *Recueil des Cours de l'Academie de Droit International de la Haye* (1985-V), pp. 9-268 [*RdC*]

Bénac, Henri, *Dictionnaire des synonymes: Conforme au dictionnaire de l'Académie Française*, Paris 1956 [Hachette]

Ben-Naftali, Orna, 'A Judgment in the Shadow of International Criminal Law', in: 5 *Journal of International Criminal Justice* (2007), pp. 322-331 [*J. Int'l Crim. Just.*]

Ben-Naftali, Orna, 'The Extraterritorial Application of Human Rights to Occupied Territories', in: 100 *American Society of International Law – Proceedings* (2006), pp. 90-95 [*ASIL Proc.*]

Ben-Naftali, Orna/ Michaeli, Keren R., 'Justice-Ability: A Critique of the alleged Non-Justiciability of Israel's policy of Targeted Killings', in: 1 *Journal of International Criminal Justice* (2003), pp. 368-405 [*J. Int'l Crim. Just.*]

Ben-Naftali, Orna/ Michaeli, Keren R., 'We Must Not Make a Scarecrow of the Law': A Legal Analysis of The Israeli Policy of Targeted Killings', 36 *Cornell International Law Journal* (2003), pp. 233-292 [*Cornell Int'l L.J.*]

Ben-Naftali, Orna/ Shani, Yuval, 'Living in Denial: The Application of Human Rights in the Occupied Territories', in: 37 *Israel Law Review* (2003), pp.17-118 [*Isr. L. Rev.*]

Bennoune, Karima, 'Toward a Human Rights Approach to Armed Conflict: Iraq 2003', 11 *University of California Davis Journal of*

International Law & Policy (2004), pp. 171-228 [*U.C. Davis J. Int'l L. & Pol'y*]

Benvenisti, Eyal, 'Ajuri et. al. – Israeli High Court of Justice, 3 September 2002', in: 9 *European Public Law* (2003), pp. 481-491 [*Eur. Pub. L.*]

Benvenisti, Eyal, 'Human Dignity in Combat: The Duty to Spare Enemy Civilians', in: 39 *Israel Law Review* (2006), pp. 81-109 [*Isr. L. Rev.*]

Benvenisti, Eyal, 'Israel and the Palestinians: What Laws Were Broken?' in: *Crimes of War Project* (May 8, 2002), URL: <http://www.crimesofwar.org/expert/me-benvenisti.html> (last visited February 28, 2008)

Benvenisti, Eyal, *The International Law of Occupation*, Princeton, N.J. 1993 [Princeton Univ. Press]

Beres, Louis René, 'Assassinating Saddam Hussein: The View from International Law', in: 19 *Indiana International & Comparative Law Review* (2003), pp. 847-869 [*Ind. Int'l & Comp. L. Rev.*]

Beres, Louis René, 'Assassinating Saddam: A Post-War View from International Law', in: 19 *Denver Journal of International Law and Policy* (1991), pp. 613-623 [*Denv. J. Int'l L. & Pol'y*]

Beres, Louis René, 'Assassination and the Law: A Policy Memorandum', in: 18 *Studies in Conflict and Terrorism* (1995), pp. 299-315 [*Stud. Confl. Terror.*]

Beres, Louis René, 'On *Assassination* as Anticipatory Self-Defense: The Case of Israel', in: 20 *Hofstra Law Review* (1991), pp. 321-340 [*Hofstra L. Rev.*]

Beres, Louis René, 'On *International* Law and Nuclear Terrorism', 24 *Georgia Journal of International and Comparative Law* (1994), pp. 1-36 [*Ga. J. Int'l & Comp. L.*]

Beres, Louis René, 'The Meaning of Terrorism: Jurisprudential and Definitional Clarifications', in: 28 *Vanderbilt Journal of Transnational Law* (1995), pp. 239-250 [*Vand. J. Transnat'l L.*]

Beres, Louis René, 'The Newly Expanded American Doctrine of Preemption: Can it include Assassination?' in: 31 *Denver Journal of International Law and Policy* (2002), pp. 157-178 [*Denv. J. Int'l L. & Pol'y*]

Beres, Louis René, 'The Permissibility of Statesponsored Assassination During Peace and War', in: 5 *Temple International and Compa-*

rative Law Journal (1992), pp. 231-249 [*Temp. Int'l & Comp. L.J.*]

Bergmann, Jan Michael, *Das Menschenbild der Europäischen Menschenrechtskonvention*, Baden-Baden 1995 [Nomos]

Bernhardt, Rudolf, 'Evolutive Treaty Interpretation, Especially of the European Convention of Human Rights', in: 42 *German Yearbook of International Law* (1999), pp. 11-25 [*German Yb. Int'l L.*]

Bernhardt, Rudolf, 'Thoughts on the Interpretation of Human Rights Treaties', in: Franz Matscher/ Herbert Petzold (eds.), *Protecting Human Rights: The European Dimension – Studies in Honour of Gérard J. Wiarda*, Köln 1988, pp. 65-71 [Heymanns]

Bernhardt, Rudolf, *Die Auslegung völkerrechtlicher Verträge*, Köln 1963 [Heymanns]

Bertaud du Chazaud, Henri, *Dictionnaire des synonymes*, Paris 1983 [Le Robert]

Biggio, Frank A., 'Neutralising the Threat: Reconsidering Existing doctrines in the Emerging War on Terrorism', in: 34 *Case Western Reserve Journal of International Law* (2002), pp. 1-43 [*Case W. Res. J. Int'l L.*]

Bindschedler-Robert, Denise, 'A Reconsideration of the Law of Armed Conflicts', in: Joseph E. Johnson (ed.), *Report of the Conference on Contemporary Problems of the Law of Armed Conflicts: Geneva, 15.-20. September 1969*, New York 1971, pp. 1-61 [Carnegie Endowment for International Peace]

Bisharat, George E., 'Facts, Rights, and Remedies: Implementing International Law in the Israel/ Palestine Conflict', in: 28 *Hastings International and Comparative Law Review* (2005), pp. 319-330 [*Hastings Int'l & Comp. L. Rev.*]

Bisson, Frank, *Die lebensgefährliche Verteidigung von Vermögenswerten*, Frankfurt am Main 2002 [Peter Lang]

Blum, Yehuda Zvi, 'The Missing Reversioner: Reflections on the Status of Judea and Samaria', in: 3 *Israel Law Review* (1968), pp. 279-301 [*Isr. L. Rev.*]

Bluntschli, Johann Caspar, *Das moderne Völkerrecht der civilisierten Staaten als Rechtsbuch dargestellt*, Nördlingen 1868 [C.H. Beck]

Bond, James E., *The Rules of Riot: Internal Conflict and the Law of War*, Princeton/ N.J. 1974

Borch, Fred L., 'Comparing Pearl Harbor and "9/11": Intelligence Failure? American Unpreparedness? Military Responsibility?', in: 67 *Journal of Military History* (2003), pp. 845-860 [*J. Mil. Hist.*]

Borelli, Silvia, 'Casting Light on the Legal Black Hole: International Law and Detentions Abroad in the War on Terror', in: 87 *International Review of the Red Cross* (2005), No. 857, pp. 39-68 [*Int'l Rev. Red Cross*]

Borelli, Silvia, 'The Treatment of Terrorist Suspects Captured Abroad: Human Rights and Humanitarian Law', in: Andrea Bianchi/ Yasmin Naqvi (eds.), *Enforcing International Law Norms Against Terrorism*, Oxford 2004, pp. 39-61 [Hart Publishing]

Bossuyt, Marc J., *Guide to the "Travaux Préparatoires" of the International Covenant on Civil and Political Rights*, Dordrecht 1987 [Nijhoff]

Bothe, Michael, 'The Protection of the Civilian Population and NATO Bombing on Yugoslavia: Comments on a Report to the Prosecutor of the ICTY', in: 12 *European Journal of International Law* (2001), pp. 531-536 [*Eur. J. Int'l L.*]

Bothe, Michael/ Partsch, Karl Josef/ Solf, Waldemar A., *New Rules for Victims of Armed Conflicts: Commentary on the two 1977 Protocols additional to the Geneva Conventions of 1949*, The Hague 1982 [Nijhoff]

Bouchet-Saulnier, Françoise, *The Practical Guide to Humanitarian Law*, Lanham, Maryland 2002 [Rowman & Littlefield]

Boyle, C. K., 'The Concept of Arbitrary Deprivation of Life', in: Bertrand G. Ramcharan (ed.), *The Right to Life in International Law*, Dordrecht 1985, pp. 221-244 [Nijhoff]

Boyle, Kevin, 'Terrorism, States of Emergency and Human Rights', in: Wolfgang Benedek/ Alice Yotopoulos-Marangopoulos (eds.), *Anti-Terrorist Measures and Human Rights*, Leiden 2004, pp. 95-116 [Nijhoff]

Bozeman, William P./ Winslow, James E., 'Medical Aspects of Less Lethal Weapons', in: 5 *Internet Journal of Rescue and Disaster Medicine* (2005), No. 1 [*Internet J. Resc. & Disaster Med.*]

Brooks, Rosa Ehrenreich, 'War Everywhere: Rights, National Security Law, and the Law of Armed Conflict in the Age of Terror', in: 153 *University of Pennsylvania Law Review* (2004), pp. 675-761 [*U. Pa. L. Rev.*]

Brown Scott, James (ed.), *The Hague Conventions and Declarations of 1899 and 1907*, 3rd ed., New York 1918, pp. 100-127

Brown, Davis, 'Use of Force against Terrorism after September 11: State Responsibility, Self-Defense, and other Responses', in: 11 *Cardozo Journal of International and Comparative Law* (2003), pp. 1-53 [*Cardozo J. Int'l & Comp. L.*]

Brownlie, Ian, 'State Responsibility and the International Court of Justice', in: Malgosia Fitzmaurice/ Dan Sarooshi (eds.), *Issues of State Responsibility before International Judicial Institutions*, Oxford 2004, pp. 11-18

Brownlie, Ian, *System of the Law of Nations – State Responsibility*, Part I, Oxford 1983 [Clarendon]

Buergenthal, Thomas, 'The European and Inter-American Human Rights Courts: Beneficial Interaction', in: Paul Mahoney/ Franz Matscher/ Herbert Petzold/ Luzius Wildhaber (eds.), *Protection des droits de l'homme: la perspective européenne – Mélanges à la mémoire de Rolv Ryssdal*, Köln 2000, pp. 123-133 [Heymann]

Buergenthal, Thomas, 'The Inter-American System for the Protection of Human Rights', in: *Anuario Jurídico Interamericano* (1981), pp. 80-120, partly reprinted in: Thomas Buergenthal/ Robert Norris/ Dinah Shelton, *Protecting Human Rights in the Americas – Selected Problems*, 2nd ed., Kehl 1986, pp. 3 *et seqq.*

Buergenthal, Thomas, 'To Respect and to Ensure: Stateobligations and Permissible Derogations', in: Louis Henkin (ed.), *The International Bill of Rights: The Covenant on Civil and Political Rights*, New York 1981, pp. 72-91 [Columbia Univ. Press]

Buß, Regina, *Der Kombattantenstatus: Die kriegsrechtliche Entstehung eines Rechtsbegriffs und seine Ausgestaltung in Verträgen des 19. und 20. Jahrhunderts*, Bochum 1992 [UVB Universitätsverlag Dr. N. Brockmeyer]

Byers, Michael, 'Conceptualising the Relationship between *Jus Cogens* and *Erga Omnes* Rules', in: 66 *Nordic Journal of International Law* (1997), pp. 211-239 [*Nord. J. Int'l L.*]

Byers, Michael, 'Terrorism, the Use of Force and International Law after September 11', in: 51 *International and Comparative Law Quarterly* (2002), pp. 401-414 [*Int'l & Comp. L.Q.*]

Byers, Michael, *Custom, Power and the Power of Rules – International Relations and Customary International Law*, Cambridge 1999 [Cambridge Univ. Press]

Byers, Michael, *War Law: International Law and Armed Conflict*, London 2005 [Atlantic Books]

Byers, Michael/ Nolte, Georg (eds.), *United States Hegemony and the Foundations of International Law*, Cambridge 2003 [Cambridge Univ. Press]

Byman, Daniel, 'Do Targeted Killings Work?', in: 85 *Foreign Affairs* (2006), pp. 95-112 [*Foreign Aff.*]

Callen, Jason, 'Unlawful Combatants and the Geneva Conventions', in: 44 *Virginia Journal of International Law* (2004), pp. 1025-1072 [*Va. J. Int'l L.*]

Callewaert, Johan, 'The Judgments of the Court: Background and Content', in: Ronald St. John Macdonald/ Franz Matscher/ Herbert Petzold (eds.), *The European System for the Protection of Human Rights*, Dordrecht 1993, pp. 713-731

Canestaro, Nathan, 'American Law and Policy on Assassinations of Foreign Leaders: The Practicality of Maintaining the Status Quo', in: 26 *Boston College International & Comparative Law Review* (2003), pp. 1-34 [*B.C. Int'l & Comp. L. Rev.*]

Cantor, Norman L., 'On Clear and Present Danger, Clear Probability, and Free Speech Standards in Israel', in: 16 *Israel Yearbook on Human Rights* (1986), pp. 260-290 [*Isr. Yb. Hum. Rts.*]

Carlson, Scott N./ Gisvold, Gregory, *Practical Guide to the International Covenant on Civil and Political Rights*, Ardsley, NY 2003 [Transnational Publishers]

Casey, Demian, 'Breaking the Chain of Violence in Israel and Palestine: Suicide Bombings and Targeted Killings under International Humanitarian Law', in: 32 *Syracuse Journal of International Law and Commerce* (2005), pp. 311-344 [*Syracuse J. Int'l L. & Com.*]

Cassel, Douglass, 'Extraterritorial Application of Inter-American Human Rights Instruments', in: Fons Coomans/ Menno T. Kamminga (eds.), *Extraterritorial Application of Human Rights Treaties*, Antwerp 2004, pp. 175-181 [Intersentia]

Cassese, Antonio, 'Expert Opinion on Whether Israel's Targeted Killings of Palestinian Terrorists is Consonant with International Humanitarian Law', written at the request of the Petitioners in: Supreme Court of Israel, *The Public Committee Against Torture* et al. *v. The Government of Israel* et al. H.C.J. 769/02, URL: <http://www.stoptorture.org.il//eng/images/uploaded/publications/64.pdf> (last visited February 16, 2008)

Cassese, Antonio, 'Mercenaries: Lawful Combatants or War Criminals?', in: 40 *Zeitschrift für ausländisches öffentliches Recht und Völkerrecht* (1980), pp. 1-30 [*ZaöRV*]

Cassese, Antonio, 'On Some Merits of the Israeli Judgment on Targeted Killings', in: 5 *Journal of International Criminal Justice* (2007), pp. 339-345 [*J. Int'l Crim. Just.*]

Cassese, Antonio, 'Terrorism is also Disrupting Some Crucial Legal Categories of International Law', in: 12 *European Journal of International Law* (2001), pp. 993-1002 [*Eur. J. Int'l L.*]

Cassese, Antonio, *International Law*, 2nd ed., Oxford 2005 [Oxford Univ. Press]

Cavanaugh, Kathleen A., 'Rewriting Law: The Case of Israel and the Occupied Territories', in: David Wippman/ Matthew Evangelista (eds.), *New Wars, New Laws? Applying the Laws of War in 21st Century Conflicts*, Ardsley, N.Y. 2005, pp. 227-258 [Transnational Pub.]

Cavanaugh, Kathleen A., 'Selective Justice: The Case of Israel and the Occupied Territories', in: 26 *Fordham International Law Journal* (2003), pp. 934-960 [*Fordham Int'l L.J.*]

Cerna, Christina M., 'Extraterritorial Application of the Human Rights Instruments of the Inter-American System', in: Fons Coomans/ Menno T. Kamminga (eds.), *Extraterritorial Application of Human Rights Treaties*, Antwerp 2004, pp. 141-174 [Intersentia]

Cerna, Christina M., 'Human Rights in Armed Conflict: Implementation of International Humanitarian Law Norms by Regional Intergovernmental Human Rights Bodies', in: Frits Kalshoven/ Yves Sandoz (eds.), *Implementation of International Humanitarian Law*, Dordrecht 1989, pp. 31-67 [Nijhoff]

Cerna, Christina M., 'The Inter-American System for the Protection of Human Rights', in: 16 *Florida Journal of International Law* (2004), pp. 195-212 [*Fla. J. Int'l L.*]

Cerone, John, 'Minding the Gap: Outlining KFOR Accountability in Post-Conflict Kosovo', in: 12 *European Journal of International Law* (2001), pp. 469-488 [*Eur. J. Int'l L.*]

Cerone, John, 'The Application of Regional Human Rights Law Beyond Regional Frontiers: The Inter-American Commission on Human Rights and US Activities in Iraq', in: *American Society of International Law – Insight* (2005), No. 10 (October 25, 2005),

URL: <http://www.asil.org/insights/2005/10/insights051025.html> (last visited February 27, 2008) [*ASIL Insight*]

Chadwick, Elizabeth, *Self-Determination, Terrorism and the International Humanitarian Law of Armed Conflict*, The Hague 1996

Cheng, Bin, 'Custom: the Future of General State Practice in a Divided World', in: Ronald St. John Macdonald/ Douglas M. Johnston (eds.), *The Structure and Process of International Law: Essays in Legal Philosophy Doctrine and Theory*, The Hague 1983, pp. 513-554

Cheng, Bin, 'United Nations resolutions on Outer Space: "Instant" International Customary Law?', in: 5 *Indian Journal of International Law* (1965), pp. 23-48 [*Indian J. Int'l L.*]

Cherkasov, Alexander/ Lokshina, Tanya, 'Chechnya: 10 Years of Armed Conflict', in: 16 *Helsinki Monitor* (2005), pp. 143-149

Chowdhury, Subrata Roy, *Rule of Law in a State of Emergency*, London 1989

Christenson, Gordon A., 'Attributing Acts of Omission to the State', in: 12 *Michigan Journal of International Law* (1991), pp. 312-370 [*Mich. J. Int'l L.*]

Clapham, Andrew, 'The "Drittwirkung" of the Convention', in: Ronald St. John Macdonald/ Franz Matscher/ Herbert Petzold (eds.), *The European System for the Protection of Human Rights*, Dordrecht 1993, pp. 163-206

Cohen, Amichai/ Shany, Yuval, 'A Development of Modest Proportions: The Application of the Principle of Proportionality in the Targeted Killings Case', in: 5 *Journal of International Criminal Justice* (2007), pp. 310-321 [*J. Int'l Crim. Just.*]

Cohen-Jonathan, Gérard, 'L'affaire Loizidou devant la Cour européenne des droits de l'homme. Quelques observations', in: 102 *Revue générale de droit international public* (1998), pp. 123-144 [*R.G.D.I.P.*]

Colón-Collazo, J., 'A Legislative History of the Right to Life in the Inter-American Legal System', in: Bertrand G. Ramcharan (ed.), *The Right to Life in International Law*, Dordrecht 1985, pp. 33-41 [Nijhoff]

Coracini, Celso Eduardo Faria, 'Targeted Killing of Suspected Terrorists during Armed Conflicts: Compatibility with the Rights to Life and to a Due Process?', in: Stefano Manacorde/ Adán Nieto (eds.), *Criminal Law between War and Peace: Justice and Coop-*

eration in Criminal Matters in International Military Interventions, Cuenca 2009, pp. 387-402 [Ed. de la Universidad de Castilla-La Mancha]

Council of Europe (ed.), *Collected edition of the "Travaux préparatoires" of the European Convention on Human Rights*, Vol. 3: Committee of Experts, 2 February-10 March 1950, The Hague 1976 [Nijhoff]

Crawford, James, *The International Law Commission's Articles on State Responsibility: Introduction, Text and Commentaries*, Cambridge 2002 [Cambridge Univ. Press]

Cremona, John Joseph, 'The Proportionality Principle in the Jurisprudence of the European Court of Human Rights', in: Ulrich Beyerlin (ed.), *Recht zwischen Umbruch und Bewahrung: Völkerrecht, Europarecht, Staatsrecht – Festschrift für Rudolf Bernhardt*, Berlin 1995, pp. 323-330 [Springer]

Cruz Roja Española, *Manual básico de derechos humanos y derecho internacional humanitario*, Madrid 2003 [Cruz Roja Española]

D'Amato, Anthony A., *The Concept of Custom in International Law*, Ithaca, N.Y. 1971 [Cornell Univ. Press]

Dahl, Arne Willy, 'The Legal Status of the Opposition Fighter in International (*sic!*) Armed Conflict', in: 43 *Revue de droit militaire et de droit de la guerre* (2004), pp. 137-153 (The Article refers to internal armed conflicts.) [*Rev. dr. mil.*]

Dahlstrom, K. Elizabeth, 'The Executive Policy toward Detention and Trial of foreign Citizens at Guantanamo Bay', in: 21 *Berkeley Journal of International Law* (2003), pp. 662-682 [*Berkeley J. Int'l L.*]

Dalton, Jane Gililand, 'What is War? Terrorism as War After 9/11', in: 12 *ILSA Journal of International and Comparative Law* (2006), pp. 523-533 [*ILSA J. Int'l & Comp. L.*]

David, Éric, *Principes de Droit des Conflits Armés*, 3rd ed., Bruxelles 2002 [Bruylant]

David, Steven R., 'If Not Combatants, Certainly Not Civilians: Response to Yael Stein', in: 17 *Ethics & International Affairs* (2003), No. 1, pp. 138-140 [*Ethics & Int'l Aff.*]

David, Steven R., 'Israel's Policy of Targeted Killing', in: 17 *Ethics & International Affairs* (2003), No. 1, pp. 111-126 [*Ethics & Int'l Aff.*]

David, Steven R., *Fatal Choices: Israel's Policy of Targeted Killing*, Ramat Gan 2002 [Begin-Sadat Center for Strategic Studies]

Davidson, Scott J., *The Inter-American Court of Human Rights*, Aldershot 1992 [Dartmouth]

Davidson, Scott J., *The Inter-American Human Rights System*, Aldershot 1997 [Dartmouth]

Delbrück, Jost, 'Proportionality', in: Rudolf Bernhardt (ed.), *Encyclopedia of Public International Law*, Vol. 7, Amsterdam 1984, pp. 396-400 [North-Holland] [*EPIL*]

Delbrück, Jost, 'Safeguarding Internationally Protected Human Rights in National Emergencies: New Challenges in View of Global Terrorism', in: Jürgen Bröhmer/ Christine Langenfeld/ Roland Bieber/ Stefan Weber/ Christian Calliess/ Joachim Wolf (eds.), *Internationale Gemeinschaft und Menschenrechte: Festschrift für Georg Ress zum 70. Geburtstag am 21. Januar 2005*, Köln 2005, pp. 47-54 [Heymanns]

Delbrück, Jost, 'The Fight Against Global Terrorism: Self-Defense or Collective Security as International Police Action? Some Comments on the International Legal Implications of the "War on Terrorism"', in: 44 *German Yearbook of International Law* (2001), pp. 9-24 [*German Yb. Int'l L.*]

Dennis, Michael, 'Application of Human Rights Treaties Extraterritorially During Times of Armed Conflict and Military Occupation', in: 100 *American Society of International Law – Proceedings* (2006), pp. 86-90 [*ASIL Proc.*]

Desch, Thomas, 'The Concept and Dimensions of the Right to Life (as defined in International Standards and in International Comparative Jurisprudence)', in: 36 *Österreichische Zeitschrift für öffentliches Recht und Völkerrecht* (1985), pp. 77-118 [*ÖZöRV*]

Detter de Lupis Frankopan, Ingrid, *The Law of War*, 2nd ed., Cambridge 2000

Dijk, Pieter van/ Hoof, Godefridus J. H. van, *Theory and Practice of the European Convention on Human Rights*, 3rd ed., The Hague 1998 [Kluwer]

Dinstein, Yoram, 'Comments on the Presentations by Nico Krisch and Carsten Stahn', in: Christian Walter/ Silja Vöneky/ Volker Röben/ Frank Schorkopf (eds.), *Terrorism as a Challenge for National and International Law: Security versus Liberty?*, Berlin 2004, pp. 915-924 [Springer]

Dinstein, Yoram, 'Human Rights in Armed Conflict: International Humanitarian Law', in: Theodor Meron (ed.), *Human Rights in International Law*, Oxford 1984, pp. 345-368 [Clarendon]

Dinstein, Yoram, 'The Distinction between Unlawful Combatants and War Criminals', in: Yoram Dinstein/ Mala Tabory (eds.), *International Law at a Time of Perplexity: Essays in Honour of Shabtai Rosenne*, Dordrecht 1989, pp. 103-116 [Nijhoff]

Dinstein, Yoram, 'The International Law of Inter-State Wars and Human Rights', in: 7 *Israel Yearbook on Human Rights* (1977), pp. 139-153 [*Isr. Yb. Hum. Rts.*]

Dinstein, Yoram, 'The International Legal Status of the West Bank and the Gaza Strip – 1998', in: 28 *Israel Yearbook on Human Rights* (1998), pp. 37-49 [*Isr. Yb. Hum. Rts.*]

Dinstein, Yoram, 'The Right to Life, Physical Integrity, and Liberty', in: Louis Henkin (ed.), *The International Bill of Rights: The Covenant on Civil and Political Rights*, New York 1981, pp. 114-137

Dinstein, Yoram, 'Unlawful Combatancy', in: 32 *Israel Yearbook on Human Rights* (2002), pp. 247-270 [*Isr. Yb. Hum. Rts.*]

Dinstein, Yoram, *The Conduct of Hostilities under the Law of International Armed Conflict*, Cambridge 2004 [Cambridge Univ. Press]

Dinstein, Yoram, *War, Aggression, and Self-Defense*, 4th ed., Cambridge 2005 [Cambridge Univ. Press]

Doehring, Karl, 'Zum "Recht auf Leben" aus nationaler und internationaler Sicht', in: Rudolph Bernhardt/ Wilhelm Karl Geck/ Günther Jaenicke/ Helmut Steinberger (eds.), *Völkerrecht als Rechtsordnung – Internationale Gerichtsbarkeit – Menschenrechte: Festschrift für Hermann Mosler*, Berlin 1983, pp. 145-157 [Springer]

Donohue, John/ Wolfers, Justin J., 'The Death Penalty: No Evidence for Deterrence', in: 3 *Economists' Voice* (2006), No. 5, Article 3, URL: <http://www.bepress.com/ev/vol3/iss5/art3> (last visited May 5, 2006)

Dörmann, Knut, 'The Legal Situation of "Unlawful/ Unprivileged Combatants"', in: 85 *International Review of the Red Cross* (2003), No. 849, pp. 45-74 [*Int'l Rev. Red Cross*]

Doswald-Beck, Louise, 'Developments in Customary International Humanitarian Law', in: 15 *Schweizerische Zeitschrift für internationales und europäisches Recht* (2005), pp. 471-498 [*SZIER*]

Doswald-Beck, Louise, 'The Right to Life in Armed Conflict: Does International Humanitarian Law provide all the Answers?', in: 88 *International Review of the Red Cross* (2006), No. 864, pp. 881-904 [*Int'l Rev. Red Cross*]

Dougherty, Bernard/ Quénivet, Noëlle, 'Has the Armed Conflict in Iraq Shown once more the Growing Dissension Regarding the Definition of a Legitimate Target? What and Who Can be Lawfully Targeted?', in: 16 *Humanitäres Völkerrecht – Informationsschriften* (2003), pp. 188-196 [*HuV-I*]

Downes, Chris, '"Targeted Killings" in an Age of Terror: The Legality of the Yemen Strike', in: 9 *Journal of Conflict & Security Law* (2004), pp. 277-294 [*J. Confl. Sec. L.*]

Dröge, Cordula, *Positive Verpflichtungen der Staaten in der Europäischen Menschenrechtskonvention*, Berlin 2003 [Springer]

Drumbl, Mark A., '"Lesser Evils" in the War on Terrorism', in: 36 *Case Western Reserve Journal of International Law* (2004), pp. 335-348 [*Case W. Res. J. Int'l L.*]

Duff, R. Antony, *Intention, Agency and Criminal Liability: Philosophy of Action and the Criminal Law*, Oxford 1990 [Blackwell]

Dworkin, Anthony, 'Israel's High Court on Targeted Killing: A Model for the War on Terror?', in: *Crimes of War Project* (December 15, 2006), URL: <http://www.crimesofwar.org/onnews/news-highcourt.html> (last visited February 28, 2008)

Dworkin, Anthony, 'Law and the Campaign Against Terrorism: The View from the Pentagon', in: *Crimes of War Project* (December 16, 2002), URL: <http://www.crimesofwar.org/onnews/news-pentagon.html> (last visited February 28, 2008)

Dworkin, Anthony, 'Military Necessity and Due Process: The Place of Human Rights in the War on Terror', in: David Wippman/ Matthew Evangelista (eds.), *New Wars, New Laws? Applying the Laws of War in 21st Century Conflicts*, Ardsley, N.Y. 2005, pp. 53-73 [Transnational Pub.]

Dyke, Vernon Van, *Human Rights, the United States, and World Community*, New York 1970 [Oxford Univ. Press]

Eagleton, Clyde, *The Responsibility of States in International Law*, New York 1928 [New York Univ. Press]

Eichensehr, Kristen F., 'On Target? The Israeli Supreme Court and the Expansion of Targeted Killings', in: 116 *Yale Law Journal* (2007), pp. 1873-1881 [*Yale L.J.*]

Eide, Asbjørn/ Rosas, Allen/ Meron, Theodor, 'Combating Lawlessness in Gray Zone Conflicts Through Minimum Humanitarian Standards', in: 89 *American Journal of International Law* (1995), pp. 215-223 [*Am. J. Int'l L.*]

Eisenstadt, Michael, '"Pre-emptive Targeted Killings" as a Terror Tool: An Assessment of Israel's Approach', in: *Peacewatch*, No. 342 (August 28, 2001), URL: <http://www.washingtoninstitute.org/templateC05.php?CID=2033> (last visited January 23, 2008)

Eissen, Marc-André, 'The Principle of Proportionality in the Case-Law of the European Court of Human Rights', in: Ronald St. John Macdonald/ Franz Matscher/ Herbert Petzold (eds.), *The European System for the Protection of Human Rights*, Dordrecht 1993, pp. 125-146

Ermacora, Felix/ Nowak, Manfred/ Tretter, Hannes (eds.), *Die Europäische Menschenrechtskonvention in der Rechtsprechung der österreichischen Höchstgerichte*, Wien 1983 [Braumüller]

Evans, Malcom/ Ige, Tokunbo/ Murray, Rachel, 'The Reporting Mechanism of the African Charter on Human and Peoples' Rights', in: Malcolm Evans/ Rachel Murray (eds.), *The African Charter on Human and Peoples' Rights: The System in Practice, 1986-2000*, Cambridge 2002, pp. 36-60 [Cambridge Univ. Press]

Falk, Richard A./ Weston, Burns H., 'The Relevance of International Law to Israeli and Palestinian Rights in the West Bank and Gaza', in: Emma Playfair (ed.), *International Law and the Administration of Occupied Territories: Two Decades of Israeli Occupation of the West Bank and Gaza Strip*, Oxford 1992, pp. 125-149 [Clarendon Press]

Fawcett, James Edmund Sandford, *The Application of the European Convention on Human Rights*, 2nd ed., Oxford 1987 [Clarendon Press]

Fenrick, William J., 'The Law applicable to Targeting and Proportionality after Operation Allied Force: A View from the Outside', in: 3 *Yearbook of International Humanitarian Law* (2000), pp. 53-80 [*Yb. Int'l Hum. L.*]

Fenrick, William J., 'The Prosecution of Unlawful Attack Cases before the ICTY', in: 7 *Yearbook of International Humanitarian Law* (2004), pp. 153-189 [*Yb. Int'l Hum. L.*]

Fenrick, William J., 'The Targeted Killings Judgment and the Scope of Direct Participation in Hostilities', in: 5 *Journal of International Criminal Justice* (2007), pp. 332-338 [*J. Int'l Crim. Just.*]

Fidler, David P., 'The International Legal Implications of "Non-Lethal" Weapons', in: 21 *Michigan Journal of International Law* (1999), pp. 51-100 [*Mich. J. Int'l L.*]

Fischer, Horst, 'Protection of Prisoners of War', in: Dieter Fleck (ed.), *The Handbook of Humanitarian Law in Armed Conflicts*, Oxford 1999, pp. 321-367

Fisher, W. Jason, 'Targeted Killing, Norms, and International Law', in: 45 *Columbia Journal of Transnational Law* (2007), pp. 711-758 [*Colum. J. Transnat'l L.*]

Fitzpatrick, Joan, 'Jurisdiction of Military Commissions and the Ambiguous War on Terrorism', in: 96 *American Journal of International Law* (2002), pp. 345-354 [*Am. J. Int'l L.*]

Fitzpatrick, Joan, 'Speaking Law to Power: The War Against Terrorism and Human Rights', in: 14 *European Journal of International Law* (2003), pp. 241-264 [*Eur. J. Int'l L.*]

Fix-Zamudio, Héctor, 'The European and the Inter-American Courts of Human Rights: A brief Comparison', in: Paul Mahoney/ Franz Matscher/ Herbert Petzold/ Luzius Wildhaber (eds.), *Protection des droits de l'homme: la perspective européenne – Mélanges à la mémoire de Rolv Ryssdal*, Köln 2000, pp. 507-533

Fleck, Dieter, 'Kriegslisten und Perfidieverbot', in: Dieter Fleck/ Michael Bothe (eds.), *Beiträge zur Weiterentwicklung des humanitären Völkerrechts für bewaffnete Konflikte*, Hamburg 1973, pp. 105-148 [Heitmann]

Fleck, Dieter, 'Ruses of War and Prohibition of Perfidy', in: 13 *Revue de droit pénal militaire et de droit de la guerre* (1974), pp. 269-314 [*Rev. dr. pén. mil.*]

Fleck, Dieter, 'The Protocols Additional to the Geneva Conventions and Customary International Law', in: 29 *Revue de droit militaire et de droit de la guerre* (1990), pp. 497-517 [*Rev. dr. mil.*]

Franck, Thomas M., 'Terrorism and the Right of Self-Defense', in: 95 *American Journal of International Law* (2001), pp. 839-842 [*Am. J. Int'l L.*]

Fribergh, Erik/ Villiger, Mark E., 'The European Commission of Human Rights', in: Ronald St. John Macdonald/ Franz Matscher/

Herbert Petzold (eds.), *The European System for the Protection of Human Rights*, Dordrecht 1993, pp. 605-620

Friederman, Leon (ed.), *The law of War: A Documentary History*, New York 1972 [Random House]

Frowein, Jochen Abraham, 'Der Terrorismus als Herausforderung für das Völkerrecht', in: 62 *Zeitschrift für ausländisches öffentliches Recht und Völkerrecht* (2002), pp. 879-905 [*ZaöRV*]

Frowein, Jochen Abraham, 'Im Zweifel für den vielleicht tödlichen Schuß?' in: Erhard Denninger/ Manfred O. Hinz (eds.), *Kritik und Vertrauen: Festschrift für Peter Schneider zum 70. Geburtstag*, Frankfurt am Main 1990, pp. 112-121

Frowein, Jochen Abraham, 'The Relationship between Human Rights Regimes and Regimes of Belligerent Occupation', in: 28 *Israel Yearbook on Human Rights* (1998), pp. 1-16 [*Isr. Yb. Hum. Rts.*]

Frowein, Jochen Abraham/ Peukert, Wolfgang (eds.), *Europäische Menschenrechtskonvention – EMRK-Kommentar*, 2nd ed., Kehl am Rhein 1996 [N.P. Engel]

Furrer, Hans-Peter, *Perfidie in der Geschichte und im heutigen Kriegsvölkerrecht*, Zürich 1988 [Juris]

Ganor, Boaz, 'Terrorism: No Prohibition Without Definition', in: The International Policy Institute for Counter-Terrorism, *Articles by ICT-Staff* (October 7, 2001), URL: <http://212.150.54.123/articles/articledet.cfm?articleid=393> (last visited February 17, 2008)

Ganshof van der Meersch, Walter Jean, 'La caractère "autonome" des termes et la "marge d'appréciation" des gouvernements dans l'interprétation de la Convention européenne des Droits de l'Homme', in: Franz Matscher/ Herbert Petzold (eds.), *Protecting Human Rights: The European Dimension – Studies in Honour of Gérard J. Wiarda*, Köln 1988, pp. 201-220 [Heymann]

Gardam, Judith Gail, *Non-Combatant Immunity as a Norm of International Humanitarian Law*, Dordrecht 1993 [Nijhoff]

Garland, Ross, 'The international Court of Justice and Human Rights in the 1990s – linking Peace and Justice through the Right to Life', in: Sienho Yee/ Wang Tieya (eds.), *International Law in the Post-Cold War World: Essays in Memory of Li Haopei*, London 2001, pp. 398-408 [Routledge]

Gasser, Hans-Peter, 'International Humanitarian Law and Human Rights Law in non-international Armed Conflict: Joint Venture or Mutual Exclusion?', in: 45 *German Yearbook of International Law* (2002), pp. 149-162 [*German Yb. Int'l L.*]

Gasser, Hans-Peter, 'Protection of the Civilian Population', in: Dieter Fleck (ed.), *The Handbook of Humanitarian Law in Armed Conflicts*, Oxford 1999, pp. 209-292

Gehring, Robert Wayn, 'Changing Rules for Changing Forms of Warfare', in: 42 *Law and Contemporary Problems* (1978), pp. 86-139 [*Law & Contemp. Probs.*]

Gehring, Robert Wayn, 'Loss of Civilian Protections under the Fourth Geneva Convention and Protocol I', in: 19 *Revue de droit pénal militaire et de droit de la guerre* (1980), pp. 9-48 [*Rev. dr. pén. mil.*]

Gerritzen, Christian, *Synonyms: Sinnverwandte Ausdrücke der englischen Sprache*, Eltville am Rhein 1988 [Bechtermünz]

Gill, Terry D., *The 11th of September and the International Law of Military Operations*, Amsterdam 2002 [Vossiuspers UvA]

Gimmerthal, Michael, *Kriegslist und Perfidieverbot im Zusatzprotokoll vom 10. Juni 1977 zu den vier Genfer Rotkreuz-Abkommen von 1949 (Zusatzprotokoll I)*, Bochum 1990 [Brockmeyer]

Glahn, Gerhard von, *The Occupation of Enemy Territory: a Commentary on the Law and Practice of Belligerent Occupation*, Minneapolis 1957 [Univ. of Minnesota Press]

Godfrey, Brenda L., 'Authorization to Kill Terrorist Leaders and Those who Harbour Them: An international Analysis of Defensive Assassination', in: 4 *San Diego International Law Journal* (2003), pp. 491-512 [*San Diego Int'l L.J.*]

Goldman, Robert Kogod, 'Certain Legal Questions and Issues Raised by the September 11th Attacks', in: 9 *Human Rights Brief* (2001), No. 1, pp. 2-4

Goldmann, Robert Kogod/ Tittemore, Brian D., 'Unprivileged Combatants and the Hostilities in Afghanistan: Their Status and Rights under International Humanitarian and Human Rights Law' in: American Society of International Law, Task Force on Terrorism, December 2002, URL: <http://asil.org/taskforce/goldman.pdf> (last visited February 29, 2008)

Gollwitzer, Walter, *Menschenrechte im Strafverfahren – MRK und IPBPR*, Berlin 2005 [De Gruyter]

Gondek, Michał, 'Extraterritorial Application of the European Convention on Human Rights: Territorial Focus in the Age of Globalization?', in: 52 *Netherlands International Law Review* (2005), pp. 349-387 [*Nether. Int'l L. Rev.*]

Gorelick, Benjamin A., 'The Israeli Response to Palestinian Breach of the Oslo Agreements', in: 9 *New England Journal of International and Comparative Law* (2003), pp. 651-677 [*New Eng. J. Int'l & Comp. L.*]

Gormley, W. Paul, 'The Right to Life and the Rule of Non-Derogability: Peremptory Norms of *Jus Cogens*', in: Bertrand G. Ramcharan (ed.), *The Right to Life in International Law*, Dordrecht 1985, pp. 120-159 [Nijhoff]

Gowlland-Debbas, Vera, 'The Right to Life and Genocide: The Court and an International Public Policy', in: Laurence Boisson de Chazournes/ Philippe Sands (eds.), *International Law, the International Court of Justice, and Nuclear Weapons*, Cambridge 1999, pp. 315-337 [Cambridge Univ. Press]

Grabenwarter, Christoph, *Europäische Menschenrechtskonvention*, 3rd ed., München 2008 [C.H. Beck]

Graf, Michael, *Die Afrikanische Menschenrechtscharta und ihre Bedeutung für einschlägiges innerstaatliches Recht am Beispiel Tanzanias*, Hamburg 1997 [Institut für Afrika-Kunde]

Green, Leslie C., 'Enforcement of the Law in Non-International Conflicts', in: Volkmar Götz (ed.), *Liber amicorum Günther Jaenicke – zum 85. Geburtstag*, Berlin 1998, pp. 113-147

Green, Leslie C., 'Terrorism and Armed Conflict: The Plea and the Verdict', in: 19 *Israel Yearbook on Human Rights* (1989), pp. 131-166 [*Isr. Yb. Hum. Rts.*]

Green, Leslie C., 'War Law and the Medical Profession', in: Leslie C. Green, *Essays on the Modern Law of War*, 2nd ed., Ardsley, New York 1999, pp. 489-527 [Transnational Publishers]

Green, Leslie C., *The Contemporary Law of Armed Conflict*, Manchester 1993 [Manchester Univ. Press]

Greenspan, Morris, 'The Protection of Human Rights in Time of Warfare', in: 1 *Israel Yearbook on Human Rights* (1971), pp. 228-245

Greenwood, Christoper, 'War, Terrorism, and International Law', in: 56 *Current Legal Problems* (2004), pp. 505-530 [*Current Legal Probs.*]

Greenwood, Christopher, 'Customary Law Status of the 1977 Geneva Protocols', in: Astrid J.M. Delissen/ Gerard J. Tanja (eds.); *Humanitarian Law of Armed Conflict: Challenges ahead – Essays in Honour of Frits Kalshoven*, Dordrecht 1991, pp. 93-114 [Nijhoff]

Greenwood, Christopher, 'Historical Development and Legal Basis', in: Dieter Fleck (ed.), *The Handbook of Humanitarian Law in Armed Conflicts*, Oxford 1999, pp. 1-38

Greenwood, Christopher, 'International Humanitarian Law and the *Tadić* Case', in: 7 *European Journal of International Law* (1996), pp. 265-283 [*Eur. J. Int'l L.*]

Greenwood, Christopher, 'International Law and the "War against Terrorism"', in: 78 *International Affairs* (2002), pp. 301-318 [*Int'l Aff.*]

Greenwood, Christopher, 'Remarks on "Bombing for Peace: Collateral Damage and Human Rights"', in: 95 *American Society of International Law – Proceedings* (2002), pp. 100-104 [*ASIL Proc.*]

Greenwood, Christopher, 'Scope of Application of Humanitarian Law', in: Dieter Fleck (ed.), *The Handbook of Humanitarian Law in Armed Conflicts*, Oxford 1999, pp. 39-63

Greenwood, Christopher, 'Terrorism and Humanitarian Law – The Debate over Additional Protocol I', in: 19 *Israel Yearbook on Human Rights* (1989), pp. 187-207 [*Isr. Yb. Hum. Rts.*]

Greenwood, Christopher, 'The Development of International Humanitarian Law by the International Criminal Tribunal for the former Yugoslavia', in: 2 *Max Planck Yearbook of United Nations Law* (1998), pp. 97-140 [*Max Planck Yb. U.N. L.*]

Gross, Emanuel, 'Democracy's Struggle Against Terrorism: the Powers of Military Commanders to Decide Upon the Demolition of Houses, the Imposition of Curfews, Blockades, Encirclements and the Declaration of an Area as a Closed Military Area', in: 30 *Georgia Journal of International and Comparative Law* (2002), pp. 165-231 [*Ga. J. Int'l & Comp. L.*]

Gross, Emanuel, 'The Laws of War waged between Democratic States and Terrorist Organizations: Real or Illusive', in: 15 *Florida Journal of International Law* (2003), pp. 389-480 [*Fla. J. Int'l L.*]

Gross, Emanuel, 'Thwarting Terrorist Acts by attacking the Perpetrators or their Commanders as an Act of Self-Defense: Human Rights versus the State's Duty to protect its Citizens', in: 15

Temple International and Comparative Law Journal (2001), pp. 195-246 [*Temp. Int'l & Comp. L.J.*]

Gross, Emanuel, *The Struggle of Democracy Against Terrorism: Lessons from the United States, the United Kingdom, and Israel*, Charlottesville 2006 [Univ. of Virginia Press]

Gross, Michael L., 'Assassination and Targeted Killing: Law Enforcement, Execution or Self-Defence?', in: 23 *Journal of Applied Philosophy* (2006), pp. 323-335 [*J. Applied Phil.*]

Gross, Michael L., 'Fighting by Other Means in the Mideast: A Critical Analysis of Israel's Assassination Policy', in: 51 *Political Studies* (2003), pp. 1-19 [*Pol. Stud.*]

Grotius, Hugo, *De Iure Belli ac Pacis Libri III in quibus ius naturae et gentium, item iuris publici praecipua explicantur*, Parisiis 1625 [Buon]

Grzeszick, Bernd, 'Rechte des Einzelnen im Völkerrecht', 43 *Archiv des Völkerrechts* (2005), pp. 312-344 [*AVR*]

Guggenheim, Paul, *Lehrbuch des Völkerrechts*, Basel 1948 [Verlag für Recht und Gesellschaft]

Guggenheim, Paul, *Traité de Droit international public*, 2nd ed., Geneva 1967 [Georg]

Guggenheim, Paul, *Traité de Droit international public*, Geneva 1953 [Libraire de l'Université]

Guiora, Amos, 'Targeted Killing as Active Self-Defense', in: 36 *Case Western Reserve Journal of International Law* (2004), pp. 319-334 [*Case W. Res. J. Int'l L.*]

Guradze, Heinz, 'Die Menschenrechtskonventionen der Vereinten Nationen vom 16. Dezember 1966', in: 15 *Jahrbuch für internationales Recht* (1971), pp. 242-273 [*Jb. Int. R.*]

Guradze, Heinz, *Die Europäische Menschenrechtskonvention: Konvention zum Schutze der Menschenrechte und Grundfreiheiten nebst Zusatzprotokollen – Kommentar*, Berlin 1968 [Vahlen]

Hailbronner, Kai, 'Die Einschränkung von Grundrechten in einer demokratischen Gesellschaft. Zu den Schrankenvorbehalten der Europäischen Menschenrechtskonvention', in: Rudolph Bernhardt/ Wilhelm Karl Geck/ Günther Jaenicke/ Helmut Steinberger (eds.), *Völkerrecht als Rechtsordnung – Internationale Gerichtsbarkeit – Menschenrechte: Festschrift für Hermann Mosler*, Berlin 1983, pp. 359-385 [Springer]

Halleck, Henry Wager, *International Law or Rules Regulating the Intercourse of States in Peace and War*, San Francisco 1861, reprint: Amsterdam 1970 [Rodopi]

Hanke, Heinz Marcus, 'The 1923 Hague Rules of Air Warfare', in: 33 *International Review of the Red Cross* (1993), No. 292, pp. 12-44 [*Int'l Rev. Red Cross*]

Hannikainen, Lauri, *Peremptory Norms (jus cogens) in International Law: Historical Development, Criteria, Present Status*, Helsinki 1988 [Lakimiesliiton Kustannus]

Hannum, Hurst, 'Remarks on "Bombing for Peace: Collateral Damage and Human Rights"', in: 95 *American Society of International Law – Proceedings* (2002), pp. 96-99 [*ASIL Proc.*]

Harrington, Julia, 'The African Court on Human and Peoples' Rights', in: Malcolm Evans/ Rachel Murray (eds.), *The African Charter on Human and Peoples' Rights: The System in Practice, 1986-2000*, Cambridge 2002, pp. 305-334 [Cambridge Univ. Press]

Harris, David J., *Cases and Materials on International Law*, 5th ed., London 1998 [Sweet & Maxwell]

Harris, David J./ O'Boyle, Michael/ Warbrick, Colin, *Law of the European Convention on Human Rights*, London 1995 [Butterworths]

Hassan, Parvez, 'The Word "Arbitrary" As Used in the Universal Declaration of Human Rights: "Illegal" or "Unjust"?', in: 10 *Harvard International Law Journal* (1969), pp. 225-262 [*Harv. Int'l L. J.*]

Heffernan, Liz, 'A Comparative View of Individual Petition Procedures under the European Convention on Human Rights and the International Covenant on Civil and Political Rights', in: 19 *Human Rights Quarterly* (1997), pp. 78-112 [*Hum. Rts. Q.*]

Heintze, Hans-Joachim, 'Las Palmeras v. Bamaca-Velasquez und Bakovic v. Loizidou? Widersprüchliche Entscheidungen zum Menschenrechtsschutz in bewaffneten Konflikten', in: 18 *Humanitäres Völkerrecht – Informationsschriften* (2005), pp. 177-182 [*HuV-I*]

Heintze, Hans-Joachim, 'On the Relationship between Human Rights Law Protection and International Humanitarian Law', in: 86 *International Review of the Red Cross* (2004), No 856, pp. 789-814 [*Int'l Rev. Red Cross*]

Heintze, Hans-Joachim, 'The European Court of Human Rights and the Implementation of Human Rights Standards During Armed Conflict', in: 45 *German Yearbook of International Law* (2002), pp. 60-77 [*German Yb. Int'l L.*]

Heinz, Wolfgang S., 'Zu Auslandseinsätzen der Bundeswehr in der Terrorismusbekämpfung: Analysen und Empfehlungen aus der Sicht des internationalen Menschenrechtsschutzes', in: Dieter Fleck (ed.), *Rechtsfragen der Terrorismusbekämpfung durch Streitkräfte*, Baden-Baden 2004, pp. 67-99 [Nomos]

Henckaerts, Jean-Marie, 'Study on Customary International Humanitarian Law: A Contribution to the Understanding and Respect for the Rule of Law in Armed Conflict', in: 87 *International Review of the Red Cross* (2005), No. 857, pp. 175-212 [*Int'l Rev. Red Cross*]

Henckaerts, Jean-Marie/ Doswald-Beck, Louise (eds.), *Customary International Humanitarian Law*, Volume 2.1, Practice, Part 1, Cambridge 2005 [Cambridge Univ. Press]

Henckaerts, Jean-Marie/ Doswald-Beck, Louise (eds.), *Customary International Humanitarian Law*, Volume 2.2, Practice, Part 2, Cambridge 2005 [Cambridge Univ. Press]

Henckaerts, Jean-Marie/ Doswald-Beck, Louise (eds.), *Customary International Humanitarian Law*, Volume 1, Rules, Cambridge 2005 [Cambridge Univ. Press]

Henkin, Louis, 'International Law: Politics, Values and Functions', in: 216 *Recueil des Cours de l'Academie de Droit International de la Haye* (1989-IV), pp. 9-416 [*RdC*]

Henkin, Louis, 'Introduction', in: Louis Henkin (ed.), *The International Bill of Rights: The Covenant on Civil and Political Rights*, New York 1981, pp. 1-31

Hermann, Wolfgang, 'Armed Combatants who Cannot Distinguish Themselves From the Civilian Population', in: 21 *Revue de droit pénal militaire et de droit de la guerre* (1982), pp. 72-75 [*Rev. dr. pén. mil.*]

Heymann, Philip B./ Kayyem, Juliette N., *Preserving Security and Democratic Freedoms in the War on Terrorism – Final Report of the Long-Term Legal Strategy Project*, Cambridge, Mass. 2004 [Belfer Center for Science and International Affairs], URL: <http://www.terrorisminfo.mipt.org/Long-Term-Legal-Strategy.asp> (last visited March 22, 2009)

Heyns, Christof, 'Civil and Political Rights in the African Charter', in: Malcolm Evans/ Rachel Murray (eds.), *The African Charter on Human and Peoples' Rights: The System in Practice, 1986-2000*, Cambridge 2002, pp. 137-177 [Cambridge Univ. Press]

Higgins, Rosalyn, 'Extradition, the Right to Life, and the Prohibition against Cruel and Inhuman Punishment and Treatment: Similarities and Differences under the ECHR and the ICCPR', in: Paul Mahoney/ Franz Matscher/ Herbert Petzold/ Luzius Wildhaber (eds.), *Protection des droits de l'homme: la perspective européenne – Mélanges à la mémoire de Rolv Ryssdal*, Köln 2000, pp. 605-615

Higgins, Rosalyn, 'The General International Law of Terrorism', in: Rosalind Higgins/ Maurice Flory (eds.), *Terrorism and International Law*, London 1996, pp. 13-29 [Routledge]

Hinek, Silva, 'The Judgment of the International Criminal Tribunal for the Former Yugoslavia in Prosecutor v. Pavle Strugar', in: 19 *Leiden Journal of International Law* (2006), pp. 477-490 [*Leiden J. l Int'l L.*]

Hoffman, Michael H., 'Quelling Unlawful Belligerency: The Judicial Status and Treatment of Terrorists under the Laws of War', in: 31 *Israel Yearbook on Human Rights* (2001), pp. 161-181 [*Isr. Yb. Hum. Rts.*]

Hoffman, Michael H., 'Terrorists are Unlawful Belligerents, not Unlawful Combatants: A Distinction with Implications for the Future of International Humanitarian Law', in: 34 *Case Western Reserve Journal of International Law* (2002), pp. 227-230 [*Case W. Res. J. Int'l L.*]

Hokema, Grit, 'Das Urteil des Europäischen Gerichtshofs für Menschenrechte in der Sache Streletz, Keßler und Krenz – Eine späte Genugtuung für die Opfer des DDR-Grenzregimes', in: 14 *Humanitäres Völkerrecht – Informationsschriften* (2001), pp. 107-110 [*HuV-I*]

Holznagel, Bernd, 'Function and Interpretation of Fundamental Rights', in: Albrecht Weber (ed.), *Fundamental Rights in Europe and North America*, The Hague 2002, pp. GER 81-94 [Kluwer]

Hornby, Albert Sydney/ Crowther, Jonathan (eds.), *Oxford Advanced Learner's Dictionary of Current English*, 5th ed., 3rd impression, Oxford 1995 [Oxford Univ. Press]

Huber, Max, 'Quelques considerations sur une revision éventuelle des Conventions de la Haye relatives à la guerre', in: 37 *Revue international de la Croix-Rouge* (1955), pp. 417-482 [*Rev. Int'l Croix-Rouge*]

Hughes, D./ Maguire, K./ Dunn, F./ Fitzpatrick, S./ Rocke, L. G., 'Plastic Baton Round Injuries', in: 22 *Emergency Medicine Journal* (2005), pp. 111-112

Ignatieff, Michael, *The Lesser Evil: Political Ethics in an Age of Terror*, Edinburgh 2004 [Edinburgh Univ. Press]

Imseis, Ardi, 'On the Fourth Geneva Convention and the Occupied Palestinian Territory', in 44 *Harvard International Law Journal* (2003), pp. 65-138 [*Harv. Int'l L.J.*]

Inter-American Commission on Human Rights, *Ten Years of Activities, 1971-1981*, Washington, D.C. 1982 [OAS]

International Committee of the Red Cross, 'International Humanitarian Law and the Challenges of contemporary armed Conflicts: Excerpt of the Report prepared by the International Committee of the Red Cross for the 28th International Conference of the Red Cross and the Red Crescent Geneva, December 2003', in: 86 *International Review of the Red Cross* (2004), No. 853, pp. 213-244 [*Int'l Rev. Red Cross*]

International Committee of the Red Cross, 'Protection and Assistance Activities in Situations not Covered by International Humanitarian Law', in: 70 *International Review of the Red Cross* (1988), No. 262, pp. 9-37 [*Int'l Rev. Red Cross*]

International Committee of the Red Cross, *International Humanitarian Law and the Challenges of Contemporary Armed Conflicts,* Report prepared in September 2003 for the 28th International Conference of the Red Cross and Red Crescent, Geneva, December 2003, ICRC Doc. 03/IC/09

International Committee of the Red Cross, *Interpretive Guidance on the Notion of Direct Participation in Hostilities under International Humanitarian Law*, Geneva 2009 [International Committee of the Red Cross]

International Committee of the Red Cross/ T.M.C. Asser Institute, *Direct Participation in Hostilities under International Humanitarian Law*, Summary Report of expert seminar in the Hague, June 2, 2003, Annex 1 to International Committee of the Red Cross, *International Humanitarian Law and the Challenges of Con-*

temporary Armed Conflicts, Report prepared in September 2003 for the 28th International Conference of the Red Cross and Red Crescent, Geneva, December 2003, ICRC Doc. 03/IC/09, pp. 27-39

International Committee of the Red Cross/ T.M.C. Asser Institute, *Direct Participation in Hostilities under International Humanitarian Law*, Summary Report drafted by Nils Melzer of the third expert meeting in Geneva, October 23-25, 2005

International Institute of Humanitarian Law, *The Manual on the Law of Non-International Armed Conflict (San Remo Manual)*, Sanremo 2006, URL: <http://www.michaelschmitt.org/images/Manual%5B1%5D.Final.Brill.pdf> (last visited February 23, 2008), reprinted in: 36 *Israel Yearbook on Human Rights* (2006), Special Supplement [*Isr. Yb. Hum. Rts.*]

Ipsen, Knut, 'Combatants and Non-Combatants', in: Dieter Fleck (ed.), *The Handbook of Humanitarian Law in Armed Conflicts*, Oxford 1999, pp. 65-104

Irwin, Kara E., 'Prospects for Justice: The Procedural Aspect of the Right to Life under the European Convention on Human Rights and its Application to Investigations of Northern Ireland's Bloody Sunday', in: 22 *Fordham International Law Journal* (1999), pp. 1822-1859 [*Fordham Int'l L.J.*]

Israel Supreme Court, *Judgments of the Israel Supreme Court: Fighting Terrorism within the Law*, Jerusalem 2005 [Israel Supreme Court]

Jackson, Jami Melissa, 'The Legality of Assassination of Independent Terrorist Leaders: An Examination of National and International Implications', in: 24 *North Carolina Journal of International Law and Commercial Regulation* (1999), pp. 669-697 [*N.C. J. Int'l L. & Com. Reg.*]

Jacobs, Francis G./ White, Robin C.A., *The European Convention on Human Rights*, 2nd ed., Oxford 1996

Janse, Daniel, 'International Terrorism and Self-Defence', in: 36 *Israel Yearbook on Human Rights* (2006), pp. 149-180 [*Isr. Yb. Hum. Rts.*]

Jaworski, Eric, '"Military Necessity" and "Civilian Immunity": Where is the Balance?', in: 2 *Chinese Journal of International Law* (2003), pp. 175-206 [*Chin. J. Int'l L.*]

Jellinek, Georg, *System der subjektiven öffentlichen Rechte*, 2nd ed., Tübingen 1905 [Mohr]

Jennings, Robert/ Watts, Arthur (eds.), *Oppenheim's International Law*, Vol. I (Peace), 9th ed., Harlow 1992 [Longman]

Jinks, Derek, 'September 11 and the Laws of War', in: 28 *Yale Journal of International Law* (2003), pp. 1-50 [*Yale J. Int'l L.*]

Jinks, Derek, 'The Applicability of the Geneva Conventions to the "Global War on Terrorism"', in: 46 *Virginia Journal of International Law* (2005), pp. 165-196 [*Va. J. Int'l L.*]

Jinks, Derek, 'The Declining Significance of POW Status', in: 45 *Harvard International Law Journal* (2004), pp. 367-442 [*Harv. Int'l L.J.*]

Jobst, Valentine, III, 'Is the Wearing of the Enemy's Uniform a Violation of the Laws of War?', in: 35 *American Journal of International Law* (1941), pp. 435-442 [*Am. J. Int'l L.*]

Joseph, Sarah, 'Denouncement of the Death on the Rock: The Right to Life of Terrorists', in 14 *Netherlands Quarterly of Human Rights* (1996), pp. 5-22 [*Nether. Q. Hum. Rts.*]

Joseph, Sarah/ Schultz, Jenny/ Castan, Melissa, *The International Covenant on Civil and Political Rights: Cases, Materials, and Commentary*, 2nd ed., Oxford 2004 [Oxford Univ. Press]

Junod, Sylvie-Stoyanka, 'Additional Protocol II: History and Scope', in: 33 *American University Law Review* (1983), pp. 29-40 [*Am. U. L. Rev.*]

Kabaalioğlu, Halûk A., 'The Obligation to 'respect' and to 'ensure' the Right to Life', in: Bertrand G. Ramcharan (ed.), *The Right to Life in International Law*, Dordrecht 1985, pp. 160-181 [Nijhoff]

Kadelbach, Stefan, *Zwingendes Völkerrecht*, Berlin 1992 [Duncker & Humblot]

Kälin, Walter, 'Die Europäische Menschenrechtskonvention als Faktor der europäischen Integration', in: Walter Haller/ Alfred Kölz/ Georg Müller/ Daniel Thürer (eds.), *Im Dienst an der Gemeinschaft: Festschrift für Dietrich Schindler zum 65. Geburtstag* Basel 1989, pp. 529-538

Kalshoven, Frits, 'Israel and the Palestinians: What Laws Were Broken?', in: *Crimes of War Project* (May 8, 2002), URL: <http://

www.crimesofwar.org/expert/me-kalsh.html> (last visited April 1, 2003)

Kalshoven, Frits, 'Reaffirmation and Development of International Humanitarian Law Applicable in Armed Conflicts: The Diplomatic Conference, Geneva, 1974-1977, Part II', in: 9 *Netherlands Yearbook of International Law* (1978), pp. 107-171 [*Nether. Yb. Int'l L.*]

Kalshoven, Frits, 'Reprisals and the Protection of Civilians – Two recent Decisions of the Yugoslavia Tribunal', in: Lal Chand Vohrah *et al.* (eds.), *Man's Inhumanity to Man – Essays on International Law in Honour of Antonio Cassese*, The Hague 2003, pp. 481-511 [Kluwer]

Kalshoven, Frits, 'The Position of Guerrilla Fighters under the Law of War', in: 11 *Revue de droit pénal militaire et de droit de la guerre* (1972), pp. 55-91 [*Rev. dr. pén. mil.*]

Kant, Immanuel, *Zum ewigen Frieden. Ein philosophischer Entwurf*, Königsberg 1795 [Nicolovius]

Kantwill, Paul E./ Watts, Sean, 'Hostile Protected Persons or "Extra-Conventional Persons": How Unlawful Combatants in the War on Terrorism posed Extraordinary Challenges for Military Attorneys and Commanders', in: 28 *Fordham International Law Journal* (2005), pp. 681-741 [*Fordham Int'l L.J.*]

Kaplan, Edward H./ Mintz, Alex/ Mishal, Shaul/ Samban, Claudio, 'What Happened to Suicide Bombings in Israel? Insights from a Terror Stock Model', in: 28 *Studies in Conflict and Terrorism* (2005), pp. 225-236 [*Stud. Confl. Terror.*]

Karl, Wolfram (ed.), *Internationaler Kommentar zu Europäischen Menschenrechtskonvention*, 5th ed. Köln 2003 [Heymanns]

Kasher, Asa/ Yadlin, Amos, 'Assassination and Preventive Killing', in: 25 *SAIS Review of International Affairs* (2005), pp. 41-57 [*SAIS Rev. Int'l Aff.*]

Kasher, Asa/ Yadlin, Amos, 'Fighting Terror: A View from Israel', in: 8 *Pacem – militært tidsskrift for etisk og teologisk refleksjon* (2005), pp. 41-48 [*Pacem*]

Kastenberg, Josh, 'The Customary International Law of War and Combatant Status: Does the Current Executive Branch Policy Determination on Unlawful Combatant Status for Terrorists run Afoul of International Law, or is It Just Poor Public Relations?', in: 39 *Gonzaga Law Review* (2003/4), pp. 495-537 [*Gonz. L. Rev.*]

Keller, Helen/ Forowicz, Magdalena, 'A Tightrope Walk between Legality and Legitimacy: An Analysis of the Israeli Supreme Court's Judgment on Targeted Killing', in 21 *Leiden Journal of International Law* (2008), pp. 185-221 [*Leiden J. Int'l L.*]

Kelly, Michael J., 'Critical Analysis of the International Court of Justice Ruling on Israel's Security Barrier', in: 28 *Fordham International Law Journal* (2005), pp. 181-228 [*Fordham Int'l L.J.*]

Kelsen, Hans, 'Théorie du droit international coutumier', in: 1 *Revue internationale de la théorie du droit, Nouvelle Série* (1939), pp. 253-270

Kelsen, Hans, *Principles of International Law*, 2nd ed., New York 1966 [Holt, Rinhart and Winston]

Kelsen, Hans, *Principles of International Law*, New York 1952 [Rinhart]

Kendall, Nicholas J., 'Israeli Counter-Terrorism: "Targeted Killings" under International Law', in: 80 *North Carolina Law Review* (2002), pp. 1069-1088 [*N.C. L. Rev.*]

Kessler, Birgit, 'The Duty to "Ensure Respect" Under Common Article 1 of the Geneva Conventions: Its Implications on International and Non-International Armed Conflicts', in: 44 *German Yearbook of International Law* (2002), pp. 498-516 [*German Yb. Int'l L.*]

Kipfer, Barbara Ann/ Chapman, Robert L., *Roget's International Thesaurus*, 6th ed., New York, NY 2001 [HarperResource]

Kirgis, Frederic L., 'Custom on a sliding Scale', in: 81 *American Journal of International Law* (1987), pp. 146-151 [*Am. J. Int'l L.*]

Kirkpatrick, Elizabeth MacLaren, *Roget's Thesaurus*, London 1998 [Penguin Books]

Kiss, Alexandre Charles, 'Permissible Limitations on Rights', in: Louis Henkin (ed.), *The International Bill of Rights: The Covenant on Civil and Political Rights*, New York 1981, pp. 290-310

Klabbers, Jan, 'Rebel with a Cause? Terrorists and Humanitarian Law', in: 14 *European Journal of International Law* (2003), pp. 283-312 [*Eur. J. Int'l L.*]

Klein, Eckart, 'Der Schutz der Menschenrechte in bewaffneten Konflikten', in: 9 *MenschenRechtsMagazin* (2004), pp. 5-17 [*MRM*]

Klein, Eckart, 'General Comments – Zu einem eher unbekannten Instrument des Menschenrechtsschutzes', in: Jörn Ipsen/ Edzard Schmidt-Jorzig, *Recht – Staat – Gemeinwohl: Festschrift für Dietrich Rauschning*, Köln 2001, pp. 301-311 [Heymanns]

Klein, Eckart, 'The Duty to Protect and to Ensure Human Rights Under the International Covenant on Civil and Political Rights', in: Eckart Klein (ed.), *The Duty to Protect and Ensure Human Rights*, Berlin 2000, pp. 295-318 [Berlin Verlag]

Kneihs, Benjamin, 'Recht auf Leben und Terrorismusbekämpfung – Anmerkungen zur jüngsten Judikatur des EGMR zu Art. 2 EMRK', in: Christoph Grabenwarter/ Rudolf Thienel (eds.), *Kontiunuität und Wandel der EMRK – Studien zur Europäischen Menschenrechtskonvention*, Kehl am Rhein 1998, pp. 21-43 [N.P. Engel]

Koh, Harold Hongju, 'September 11, 2001 – Legal Response to Terror: The Spirit of the Laws', in: 43 *Harvard International Law Journal* (2002), pp. 23-40 [*Harv. Int'l L.J.*]

Kokott, Juliane, 'The Duty to Protect and to Ensure Human Rights Under the Inter-American System of Human Rights', in: Eckart Klein (ed.), *The Duty to Protect and Ensure Human Rights*, Berlin 2000, pp. 235-276 [Berlin Verlag]

Kokott, Juliane, *Beweislastverteilung und Prognoseentscheidungen bei der Inanspruchnahme von Grund- und Menschenrechten*, Berlin 1993 [Springer]

Kolb, Robert, 'Jus Cogens, Intangibilité, Intransgressibilité, Derogation "positive" et "negative"', in: 105 *Revue générale de droit international public* (2005), pp. 303-330 [*R.G.D.I.P.*]

Kooijmans, Peter H., 'In the Shadowland between Civil War and Civil Strife: Some Reflections on the Standard-Setting Process', in: Astrid J.M. Delissen/ Gerard J. Tanja (eds.); *Humanitarian Law of Armed Conflict: Challenges ahead – Essays in Honour of Frits Kalshoven*, Dordrecht 1991, pp. 225-247

Kooijmans, Peter, 'Is there a Change in the Ius ad Bellum and if so, What Does it mean for the Ius in Bello?', in: Liesbeth Lijnzaad/ Johanna von Sambeck/ Bahia Tahzib-Lie (eds.), *Making the Voice of Humanity Heard: Essays on Humanitarian Assistance and International Humanitarian Law in Honour of HRH Princess Margriet of the Netherlands*, Leiden 2004, pp. 225-237 [Nijhoff]

Koskennienmi, Martti, 'General Principles: Reflections on Constructivist Thinking in International Law', in: 18 *Oikeustiede – Jurisprudentia* (1985), pp. 121-163

Kotzur, Markus, '"Krieg gegen den Terrorismus" – politische Rhetorik oder neue Konturen des "Kriegsbegriffes" im Völkerrecht?', in: 40 *Archiv des Völkerrechts* (2002), pp. 454-479 [*AVR*]

Kremnitzer, Mordechai, 'Präventives Töten', in: Dieter Fleck (ed.), *Rechtsfragen der Terrorismusbekämpfung durch Streitkräfte*, Baden-Baden 2004, pp. 201-222 [Nomos]

Kretzmer, David, 'Targeted Killing of Suspected Terrorists: Extra-Judicial Executions or Legitimate Means of Defence?', in: 16 *European Journal of International Law* (2005), pp. 171-212 [*Eur. J. Int'l L.*]

Kretzmer, David, *The Occupation of Justice: The Supreme Court of Israel and the Occupied Territories*, New York 2002

Krieger, Heike, 'A Conflict of Norms: The Relationship Between Humanitarian Law and Human Rights Law in the ICRC Customary Law Study', in: 11 *Journal of Conflict & Security Law* (2006), pp. 265-291 [*J. Confl. Sec. L.*]

Krieger, Heike, 'Die Verantwortlichkeit Deutschlands nach der EMRK für seine Streitkräfte im Auslandseinsatz', in: 62 *Zeitschrift für ausländisches öffentliches Recht und Völkerrecht* (2002), pp. 669-702 [*ZaöRV*]

Krüger, Hans Christian, *Probleme der Beweiserhebung durch die Europäische Kommission für Menschenrechte*, Saarbrücken 1996 [Europa-Institut]

Krüger-Sprengel, Friedhelm, 'Kriegslist und Perfidieverbot – Völkerrechtliche Regeln für das Verhalten zwischen Kombattanten', in: 13 *Neue Zeitschrift für Wehrrecht* (1971), pp. 161-170 [*NZWehrR*]

Krüger-Sprengel, Friedhelm, 'Le Concept de Proportionalité dans le Droit de la Guerre', in: 19 *Revue de droit pénal militaire et de droit de la guerre* (1980), pp. 177-204 [*Rev. dr. pén. mil.*]

Krüger-Sprengel, Friedhelm, 'Non-Lethal Weapons – a Humanitarian Perspective in Modern Conflict', in: 42 *Revue de droit militaire et de droit de la guerre* (2003), pp. 357-377 [*Rev. dr. mil.*]

Kuper, Leo, 'Genocide and Mass Killings: Illusions and Reality', in: Bertrand G. Ramcharan (ed.), *The Right to Life in International Law*, Dordrecht 1985, pp. 114-119 [Nijhoff]

Kuttner, Thomas S., 'Israel and the West Bank: Aspects of the Law of Belligerent Occupation', in: 7 *Israel Yearbook on Human Rights* (1977), pp. 162-221 [*Isr. Yb. Hum. Rts.*]

Kwakwa, Edward, *The International Law of Armed Conflict: Personal and Material Fields of Application*, Dordrecht 1992 [Kluwer]

Laird, Charlton Grant/ Agnes, Michael, *Webster's New World Roget's A-Z Thesaurus*, 4th ed., New York 1999 [Macmillan]

Lavoyer, Jean-Philippe, 'International Humanitarian Law and Terrorism', in: Liesbeth Lijnzaad/ Johanna von Sambeck/ Bahia Tahzib-Lie (eds.), *Making the Voice of Humanity Heard: Essays on Humanitarian Assistance and International Humanitarian Law in Honour of HRH Princess Margriet of the Netherlands*, Leiden 2004, pp. 255-270 [Nijhoff]

Lawson, Rick, 'Life after *Bankovic*: Extraterritorial Application of the European Convention on Human Rights', in: Fons Coomans/ Menno T. Kamminga (eds.), *Extraterritorial Application of Human Rights Treaties*, Antwerp 2004, pp. 83-123

Lawson, Rick, 'The Concept of Jurisdiction and Extraterritorial Acts of State', in: Gerard Kreijen (ed.), *State, Sovereignty, and International Governance*, Oxford 2002, pp. 281-298 [Oxford Univ. Press]

Lepsius, Oliver, 'Human Dignity and the Downing of Aircraft: The German Federal Constitutional Court Strikes Down a Prominent Anti-terrorism Provision in the New Air-Transport Security Act', in: 7 *German Law Journal* (2006), pp. 761-776 [*German L. J.*]

Levie, Howard Sidney, *Prisoners of War in International Armed Conflict*, Newport 1978 [Naval War College Press]

Lietzau, William K., 'Combating Terrorism: The Consequences of Moving from Law Enforcement to War', in: David Wippman/ Matthew Evangelista (eds.), *New Wars, New Laws? Applying the Laws of War in 21st Century Conflicts*, Ardsley, N.Y. 2005, pp. 31-51 [Transnational Pub.]

Lillich, Richard B., 'Civil Rights', in: Theodor Meron (ed.), *Human Rights in International Law: Legal and Policy Issues*, 2nd repr., Oxford 1984, pp. 115-170

Locke, John, *Two Treatise of Government*, London 1698 [Black Swan]

Lorz, Ralph Alexander, 'Sind gezielte Tötungen mit dem internationalen Recht vereinbar?', Commentary, April 7, 2004, URL: <http:

//www.dias-online.org/86.0.html> (last visited February 17, 2008)

Luft, Gal, 'The Logic of Israel's Targeted Killing: It's Worked – Most of the Time', in: 10 *Middle East Quarterly* (2003), pp. 3-14 [*Mid. E. Q.*]

Lührmann, Olivia, *Tötungsrecht zur Eigentumsverteidigung? Eine Untersuchung des Notwehrrechts unter verfassungsrechtlichen, menschenrechtlichen und rechtsvergleichenden Gesichtspunkten*, Frankfurt am Main 1999 [Peter Lang]

Macdonald, Ronald St. John, 'The Margin of Appreciation', in: Ronald St. John Macdonald/ Franz Matscher/ Herbert Petzold (eds.), *The European System for the Protection of Human Rights*, Dordrecht 1993, pp. 83-124

MacDougal, Myres Smith/ Feliciano, Florentino P., *Law and minimum World Public Order: The legal Regulation of International Coercion*, 2nd print, New Haven, NY 1967 [Yale Univ. Press]

MacDougal, Myres Smith/ Lasswell, Harold D./ Chen, Lung-Chu, *Human Rights and World Public Order: The Basic Policies of an International Law of Human Dignity*, New Haven, Conn. 1980 [Yale Univ. Press]

Machon, Matthew J., *Targeted Killing as an Element of U.S. Foreign Policy in the War on Terror*, Fort Leavenworth 2006 [School of Advanced Military Studies, United States Army Command and General Staff College]

MacLaren, Malcolm/ Schwendimann, Felix, 'An Exercise in the Development of International Law: The New ICRC Study on Customary International Humanitarian Law', in: 6 *German Law Journal* (2005), pp. 1217-1242 [*German L. J.*]

Mahoney, Paul/ Prebensen, Søren C., 'The European Court of Human Rights', in: Ronald St. John Macdonald/ Franz Matscher/ Herbert Petzold (eds.), *The European System for the Protection of Human Rights*, Dordrecht 1993, pp. 621-643

Malanczuk, Peter, 'Countermeasures and Self-Defence as Circumstances Precluding Wrongfulness in the International Law Commission's Draft Articles on State Responsibility', in: Marina Spinedi/ Bruno Simma (eds.), *United Nations Codification of State Responsibility*, New York 1987, pp. 197-286 [Oceana Publ.]

Malanczuk, Peter, *Akehurst's Modern Introduction to International Law*, 7th ed., London 1997 [Routledge]

Mallison, W. Thomas/ Mallison, Sally V., 'The Juridical Status of Irregular Combatants under the International Humanitarian Law of Armed Conflict', 9 *Case Western Reserve Journal of International Law* (1977), pp. 39-78 [*Case W. Res. J. Int'l L.*]

Mallison, W. Thomas/ Mallison, Sally V., *The Palestine Problem in International Law and World Order*, Harlow 1986 [Longman]

Malone, Andrew R., 'Water now: The Impact of Israel's Security Fence on Palestinian Water Rights and Agriculture in the West Bank', in: 36 *Case Western Reserve Journal of International Law* (2004), pp. 639-671 [*Case W. Res. J. Int'l L.*]

Manby, Bronwen, 'The African Union, NEPAD, and Human Rights: The Missing Agenda', in: 26 *Human Rights Quarterly* (2004), pp. 983-1027 [*Hum. Rts. Q.*]

Maogoto, Jackson Nyamuya, 'Walking an International Law Tightrope: Use of Military Force to Counter Terrorism – Willing the Ends', in: 31 *Brooklyn Journal of International Law* (2006), pp. 405-462 [*Brook. J. Int'l L.*]

Marcoux, Laurent Jr., 'Protection From Arbitrary Arrest and Detention Under International Law', in: 5 *Boston College International and Comparative Law Review* (1982), pp. 345-376 [*B.C. Int'l & Comp. L. Rev.*]

Mariner, Joanne, 'The Israeli Supreme Court Rules on "Targeted Killings"', in: *FindLaw's Writ* (December 22, 2006), URL: <http://writ.news.findlaw.com/mariner/20061222.html> (last visited on April 15, 2007)

Martin, Francisco Forrest, 'The Unified Use of Force Rule Revisited: The Penetration of the Law of Armed Conflict by International Human Rights Law', in: 65 *Saskatchewan Law Review* (2002), pp. 405-410 [*Sask. L. Rev.*]

Martin, Francisco Forrest, 'Using International Human Rights Law for Establishing a Unified Use of Force Rule in the Law of Armed Conflict', in: 64 *Saskatchewan Law Review* (2001), pp. 347-396 [*Sask. L. Rev.*]

Maslaton, Matthias, *Notstandsklauseln im regionalen Menschenrechtsschutz – Eine vergleichende Untersuchung der Art. 15 EMRK und Art. 27 AMRK*, Frankfurt am Main 2002 [Lang]

Matheson, Michael J., 'U.S. Military Commissions: One of Several Options', in: 96 *American Journal of International Law* (2002), pp. 354-358 [*Am. J. Int'l L.*]

Matscher, Franz, 'Methods of Interpretation of the Convention', in: Ronald St. John Macdonald/ Franz Matscher/ Herbert Petzold (eds.), *The European System for the Protection of Human Rights*, Dordrecht 1993, pp. 63-81 [Nijhoff]

McAlea, Dominic D., 'Post-Westphalian Crime', in: David Wippman/ Matthew Evangelista (eds.), *New Wars, New Laws? Applying the Laws of War in 21st Century Conflicts*, Ardsley, N.Y. 2005, pp. 111-134 [Transnational Pub.]

McCarthy, Andrew C., 'Terrorism on Trial: The Trials of al Qaeda', in: 36 *Case Western Reserve Journal of International Law* (2004), pp. 513-522 [*Case W. Res. J. Int'l L.*]

McCorquodale, Robert, 'Spreading Weeds beyond their Garden: Extraterritorial Responsibility of States for Violations of Human Rights by Corporate Nationals', in: 100 *American Society of International Law – Proceedings* (2006), pp. 95-102 [*ASIL Proc.*]

McCoubrey, Hilaire, *International Humanitarian Law: Modern Developments in the Limitation of Warfare*, 2nd ed., Aldershot 1998 [Ashgate]

McCoubrey, Hilaire/ White, Nigel D., *International Law and Armed Conflict*, Aldershot 1992 [Dartmouth]

McCoubrey, Hilaire/ White, Nigel D., *International Organizations and Civil Wars*, Aldershot 1995 [Dartmouth]

McCutcheon, Marc, *Roget's Superthesaurus*, 3rd ed., Cincinnati, Ohio 2003 [Writer's Digest Books]

McGoldrick, Dominic, 'Extraterritorial Application of the International Covenant on Civil and Political Rights', in: Fons Coomans/ Menno T. Kamminga (eds.), *Extraterritorial Application of Human Rights Treaties*, Antwerp 2004, pp. 41-72 [Intersentia]

McGoldrick, Dominic, *The Human Rights Committee: Its Role in the Development of the International Covenant on Civil and Political Rights*, Oxford 1991 [Claredon]

McIntyre, T. J./ McMullan, Sinéad, *Criminal Law*, Dublin 2001 [Round Hall]

McNair, Arnold Duncan, *The Law of Treaties*, Oxford 1961 [Clarendon]

Medina Quiroga, Cecilia, *The Battle of Human Rights: Gross, Systematic Violations and the Inter-American System*, Dordrecht 1988 [Nijhoff]

Megrét, Frédéric, 'War? Legal Semantics and the Move to Violence', in: 13 *European Journal of International Law* (2002), pp. 361-400 [*Eur. J. Int'l L.*]

Mei, Anne Pieter van der, 'The New African Court on Human and Peoples' Rights: Towards an Effective Human Rights Protection Mechanism for Africa?', in: 18 *Leiden Journal of International Law* (2005), pp. 113-129 [*Leiden J. Int'l L.*]

Melzer, Nils, 'Targeted Killing or Less Harmful Means? – Israel's High Court Judgment on Targeted Killing and the Restrictive Function of Military Necessity', in: 9 *Yearbook of International Humanitarian Law* (2009), pp. 87-113 [*Yb. Int'l Hum. L.*]

Melzer, Nils, 'Targeted Killings in Operational Law Perspective', in: Terry D. Gill/ Dieter Fleck (eds.), *Handbook of the International Law of Military Operations*, Oxford 2010, pp. 277-301 [Oxford University Press]

Melzer, Nils, *Targeted Killing in International Law*, Oxford 2008 [Oxford University Press]

Melzer, Nils, *Targeted Killing under the International Normative Paradigms of Law Enforcement and Hostilities*, Zürich 2007 [Schulthess Juristische Medien]

Meron, Theodor, 'Cassese's Tadić and the Law of Non-International Armed Conflicts', in: Lal Chand Vohrah *et al.* (eds.), *Man's Inhumanity to Man – Essays on International Law in Honour of Antonio Cassese*, The Hague 2003, pp. 533-538 [Kluwer]

Meron, Theodor, 'Classification of Armed Conflict in the Former Yugoslavia: Nicaragua's Fallout', in: 92 *American Journal of International Law* (1998), pp. 236-242 [*Am. J. Int'l L.*]

Meron, Theodor, 'Extraterritoriality of Human Rights Treaties', in: 89 *American Journal of International Law* (1995), pp. 78-82 [*Am. J. Int'l L.*]

Meron, Theodor, 'On a Hierarchy of International Human Rights', in: 80 *American Journal of International Law* (1986), pp. 1-23 [*Am. J. Int'l L.*]

Meron, Theodor, 'Revival of Customary Humanitarian Law', in: 99 *American Journal of International Law* (2005), pp. 817-834 [*Am. J. Int'l L.*]

Meron, Theodor, 'The Continuing Role of Custom in the Formation of International Humanitarian Law', 90 *American Journal of International Law* (1996), pp. 238-249 [*Am. J. Int'l L.*]

Meron, Theodor, 'The Humanization of Humanitarian Law', in: 94 *American Journal of International Law* (2000), pp. 239-278 [*Am. J. Int'l L.*]

Meron, Theodor, 'The Time has come for the United States to Ratify Geneva Protocol I', in: 88 *American Journal of International Law* (1994), pp. 678-686 [*Am. J. Int'l L.*]

Meron, Theodor, *Human Rights and Humanitarian Norms as Customary Law*, Oxford 1989 [Clarendon]

Meron, Theodor, *Human Rights in Internal Strife: Their International Protection*, Cambridge 1987 [Clarendon]

Meurer, Christian, *Die Völkerrechtliche Stellung der vom Feind besetzten Gebiete*, Tübingen 1915 [Mohr]

Meyer, Jeanne M., 'Tearing down the Façade: A critical Look at the current Law on Targeting the Will of the Enemy and Air Force Doctrine', in: 51 *Air Force Law Review* (2001), pp. 143-182 [*A.F. L. Rev.*]

Meyer-Ladewig, Jens, *Konvention zum Schutz der Menschenrechte und Grundfreiheiten,* Baden-Baden 2003 [Nomos]

Meyer-Ladewig, Jens/ Petzold, Herbert, 'Der neue ständige Europäische Gerichtshof für Menschenrechte', in: 52 *Neue Juristische Wochenschrift* (1999), pp. 1165-1166 [*NJW*]

Meyerstein, Ariel, 'Case Study: The Israeli Strike Against Hamas Leader Salah Shehadeh', in: *Crimes of War Project* (September 19, 2002), URL: <http://www.crimesofwar.org/onnews/news-shehadeh.html> (last visited September 2, 2005)

Miguel, Carlos Ruiz, 'The States of Emergency in the American Convention on Human Rights', in: 33 *Israel Yearbook on Human Rights* (2003), pp. 105-122 [*Isr. Yb. Hum. Rts.*]

Milanovic, Marko, 'Lessons for human rights and humanitarian law in the war on terror: comparing Hamdan and the Israeli Targeted Killings case', in: 89 *International Review of the Red Cross* (2007), No. 866, pp. 373-393 [*Int'l Rev. Red Cross*]

Mitchell, David S., 'The Prohibition of Rape in International Humanitarian Law as a Norm of *Jus Cogens*: Clarifying the Doctrine', in: 15 *Duke Journal of Comparative & International Law* (2005), pp. 219-257

Moir, Lindsay, 'Decommissioned? International Humanitarian Law and the Inter-American Human Rights System', in: 25 *Human Rights Quarterly* (2003), pp. 182-212 [*Hum. Rts. Q.*]

Moir, Lindsay, *The Law of Internal Armed Conflict*, Cambridge 2002 [Cambridge Univ. Press]

Mowbray, Alastair R., *The Development of Positive Obligations under the European Convention on Human Rights by the European Court of Human Rights*, Oxford 2004 [Hart]

Müllerson, Rein, '*Jus ad Bellum* and International Terrorism', in: 32 *Israel Yearbook on Human Rights* (2002), pp. 1-51 [*Isr. Yb. Hum. Rts.*]

Münch, Fritz, 'Bemerkungen zum *ius cogens*', in: Rudolph Bernhardt/ Wilhelm Karl Geck/ Günther Jaenicke/ Helmut Steinberger (eds.), *Völkerrecht als Rechtsordnung – Internationale Gerichtsbarkeit – Menschenrechte: Festschrift für Hermann Mosler*, Berlin 1983, pp. 617-628 [Springer]

Murphy, Ray, 'Prisoners of War and Contemporary Conflicts: The Case of the Taliban and al Qaeda Detainees', in: 41 *Revue de droit militaire et de droit de la guerre* (2002), pp. 141-167 [*Rev. dr. mil.*]

Murray, Rachel, 'Evidence and Fact-Finding by the African Commission', in: Malcolm Evans/ Rachel Murray (eds.), *The African Charter on Human and Peoples' Rights: The System in Practice, 1986-2000*, Cambridge 2002, pp. 100-136 [Cambridge Univ. Press]

Mutua, Makau, 'The African Human Rights Court: A Two-Legged Stool?', in: 21 *Human Rights Quarterly* (1999), pp. 342-363 [*Hum. Rts. Q.*]

Nablusi, Karma, 'Evolving Conceptions of Civilians and Belligerents: One Hundred Years After the Hague Peace Conference', in: Simon Chesterman (ed.), *Civilians in War*, Boulder, Colorado 2001, pp. 9-24

Nash (Leich), Marian, 'Contemporary Practice of the United States Relating to International Law', in: 91 *American Journal of International Law* (1997), pp. 325-348 [*Am. J. Int'l L.*]

Naske, Nina/ Nolte, Georg, 'International Decisions – "Aerial Security Law"', in: 101 *American Journal of International Law* (2007), pp. 466-470 [*Am. J. Int'l L.*]

Neff, Stephen C., *War and the Law of Nations: A General History*, Cambridge 2006 [Cambridge Univ. Press]

Neuman, Gerald L., 'Humanitarian Law and Counterterrorist Force', in: 14 *European Journal of International Law* (2003), pp. 283-298 [*Eur. J. Int'l L.*]

Newton, Michael, 'Unlawful Belligerency After September 11: History Revisited and Law Revised', in: David Wippman/ Matthew Evangelista (eds.), *New Wars, New Laws? Applying the Laws of War in 21st Century Conflicts*, Ardsley, N.Y. 2005, pp. 75-110 [Transnational Pub.]

Ní Aoláin, Fionnuala D., '"Hamdan" and Common Article 3: Did the Supreme Court Get it Right?', in: 91 *Minnesota Law Review* (2007), pp. 1525-1563 [*Minn. L. Rev.*]

Ní Aoláin, Fionnuala D., 'The Evolving Jurisprudence of the European Convention Concerning the Right to Life', in: 19 *Netherlands Quarterly of Human Rights* (2001), pp. 21-42 [*Nether. Q. Hum. Rts.*]

Ní Aoláin, Fionnuala D., 'The Relationship between Situations of Emergency and Low-Intensity Armed Conflict', in: 28 *Israel Yearbook on Human Rights* (1998), pp. 97-106 [*Isr. Yb. Hum. Rts.*]

Ní Aoláin, Fionnuala D., *The Politics of Force: Conflict Management and State Violence in Northern Ireland*, Belfast 2000 [Blackstaff]

Nieto-Navia, Rafael, 'International Peremptory Norms (*jus cogens*) and International Humanitarian Law', in: Lal Chand Vohrah *et al.* (eds.), *Man's Inhumanity to Man – Essays on International Law in Honour of Antonio Cassese*, The Hague 2003, pp. 595-641 [Kluwer]

Nietzsche, Friedrich, *Jenseits von Gut und Böse*, Leipzig 1886

Nolte, Georg, 'General Principles of German and European Administrative Law – A Comparison in Historical Perspective', in: 57 *Modern Law Review* (1994), pp. 191-212 [*Mod. L. Rev.*]

Nolte, Georg, 'Guantanamo und Genfer Konventionen: eine Frage der *lex lata* oder *de lege ferenda*?', in: Horst Fischer/ Ulrike Froissart/ Wolff Heintschel von Heinegg/ Christian Raap (eds.), *Krisensicherung und Humanitärer Schutz – Crisis Management and Humanitarian Protection: Festschrift für Dieter Fleck*, Berlin 2004, pp. 393-404 [Berliner Wiss.-Verl.]

Nolte, Georg, 'Kosovo und Konstitutionalisierung: Zur humanitären Intervention der NATO-Staaten', in: 56 *Zeitschrift für ausländisches öffentliches Recht und Völkerrecht* (1999), pp. 941-960 [*ZaöRV*]

Nolte, Georg, 'Preventive Use of Force and Preventive Killings: Moves into a Different Legal Order', in: 5 *Theoretical Inquiries in Law* (2004), pp. 111-129 [*Theo. Inq. L.*]

Nolte, Georg, 'The *Bundesverfassungsgericht* on the German Aerial Security Law: A *Sonderweg* from the perspective of international law?', in: Christian Tomuschat/ Evelyne Lagrange/ Stefan Oeter (eds.), *The Right to Life*, Leiden 2010, pp. 83-94 [Nijhoff]

Nolte, Georg, 'Weg in eine andere Rechtsordnung – Vorbeugende Gewaltanwendung und gezielte Tötungen', in: *Frankfurter Allgemeine Zeitung*, January 10, 2003, p. 8 [*FAZ*]

Nolte, Georg, *Eingreifen auf Einladung: Zur völkerrechtlichen Zulässigkeit des Einsatzes fremder Truppen im internen Konflikt auf Einladung der Regierung*, Berlin 1999 [Springer]

Nowak, Manfred, *Introduction to the International Human Rights Regime*, Leiden 2003 [Nijhoff]

Nowak, Manfred, *U.N. Covenant on Civil and Political Rights – CCPR Commentary*, Kehl am Rhein 1993 [N.P. Engel]

Nsereko, Daniel D., 'Arbitrary Deprivation of Life: Controls on Permissible Deprivations', in: Bertrand G. Ramcharan (ed.), *The Right to Life in International Law*, Dordrecht 1985, pp. 245 283 [Nijhoff]

Nurick, Lester/ Barrett, Roger W., 'Legality of Guerrilla Forces Under the Laws of War', in: 40 *American Journal of International Law* (1946), pp. 563-583 [*Am. J. Int'l L.*]

O'Brian, William V., 'The Meaning of "Military Necessity" in International Law', in: 1 *World Polity* (1957), pp. 109-176

O'Brien, James C., 'The International Tribunal for Violations of International Humanitarian Law in the Former Yugoslavia', in: 87 *American Journal of International Law* (1993), pp. 639-659 [*Am. J. Int'l L.*]

O'Connell, Mary Ellen, 'The Legal Case Against the Global War on Terror', in: 36 *Case Western Reserve Journal of International Law* (2004), pp. 349-357 [*Case W. Res. J. Int'l L.*]

O'Connell, Mary Ellen, 'When is a War not a War? The Myth of the Global War on Terror', in: 12 *ILSA Journal of International and Comparative Law* (2006), pp. 535-539 [*ILSA J. Int'l & Comp. L.*]

O'Donnell, Daniel, 'International Treaties against Terrorism and the Use of Terrorism during Armed Conflict and by Armed Forces', in: 88 *International Review of the Red Cross* (2006), No 864, pp. 853-880 [*Int'l Rev. Red Cross*]

Odinkalu, Chidi Anselm/ Christensen, Camilla, 'The African Commission on Human and Peoples' Rights: The Development of its Non-State Communication Procedures', in: 20 *Human Rights Quarterly* (1998), pp. 235-280 [*Hum. Rts. Q.*]

Oeter, Stefan, 'Methods and Means of Combat', in: Dieter Fleck (ed.), *The Handbook of Humanitarian Law in Armed Conflicts*, Oxford 1999, pp. 105-207

Onions, Charles Talbut/ Friedrichsen, G. W. S., *The Oxford Dictionary of English Etymology*, Oxford 1966 [Clarendon]

Oppenheim, Lassa Francis Lawrence/ Lauterpacht, Hersch, *International Law: A Treatise*, Vol. II, *Disputes, War and Neutrality*, 7th ed., London 1952 [Longmans]

Opsahl, Torkel, 'The Right to Life', in: Ronald St. John Macdonald/ Franz Matscher/ Herbert Petzold (eds.), *The European System for the Protection of Human Rights*, Dordrecht 1993, pp. 207-223 [Nijhoff]

Oraá, Jaime, *Human Rights in States of Emergency in International Law*, Oxford 1996 [Clarendon]

Orakhelashvili, Alexander, 'Restrictive Interpretation of Human Rights Treaties in the Recent Jurisprudence of the European Court of Human Rights', in: 14 *European Journal of International Law* (2003), pp. 529-568 [*Eur. J. Int'l L.*]

Orakhelashvili, Alexander, *Peremptory Norms in International Law*, Oxford 2006 [Oxford Univ. Press]

Otto, Roland, 'Neighbours as Human Shields? The Israel Defense Forces "Early Warning Procedure" and International Humanitarian Law', in: 86 *International Review of the Red Cross* (2004), No. 856, pp. 771-787 [*Int'l Rev. Red Cross*]

Ouguergouz, Fatsah, *La Charte africaine des droits de l'homme et des peoples – Une approche juridique de droits de l'homme entre tradition et modernité*, Paris 1993 [Presses Universitaires de France]

Oxford Public Interest Lawyers (OXPIL), 'Legal Consequences of Israel's Construction of a Separation Barrier in the Occupied Territories', International Law Opinion for the Association for Civil Rights in Israel (ACRI), February 2004, URL: <http://users.ox.ac.uk/~magd1538/OXPIL%20Israel%20Barrier%20Opinion.pdf> (last visited September 1, 2005)

Parks, W. Hays, 'Air War and the Laws of War', in: 32 *Air Force Law Review* (1990), pp. 1-225 [*A.F. L. Rev.*]

Parks, W. Hays, 'Memorandum of Law: Executive Order 12,333 and Assassination', in: 19 *Army Lawyer* (December 1989), No. 204, pp. 4-9

Partsch, Karl Josef, 'Die Rechte und Freiheiten der europäischen Menschenrechtskonvention', in: Karl August Bettermann/ Franz L. Neumann/ Hans Carl Nipperdey (eds.), *Die Grundrechte – Handbuch der Theorie und Praxis der Grundrechte*, Berlin 1966, Vol. 1.1, pp. 235-492

Patel King, Faïza/ Swaak-Goldman, Olivia, 'The Applicability of International Humanitarian Law to the "War Against Terrorism"', in: 15 *Hague Yearbook of International Law* (2003), pp. 39-49 [*Hague Yb. Int'l L.*]

Patterson, Eric/ Casale, Teresa, 'Targeting Terror: The Ethical and Practical Implications of Targeted Killing', in: 18 *International Journal of Intelligence and Counterintelligence* (2005), pp. 638-652 [*Int'l J. Intell. & Counterintell.*]

Paulus, Andreas L./ Vashakmadze, Mindia, 'Asymmetrical war and the notion of armed conflict – An attempt at a conceptualization', in: 91 *International Review of the Red Cross* (2009), No. 873, pp. 93-125 [*Int'l Rev. Red Cross*]

Paulus, Andreas L., '*Jus Cogens* in a Time of Hegemony and Fragmentation: An Attempt at a Re-appraisal', in: 25 *Nordic Journal of International Law* (2005), pp. 297-334 [*Nord. J. Int'l L.*]

Paulus, Andreas L., 'The Protection of Human Rights in Internal Armed Conflict in Europe – Remarks on the *Isayeva* decision of the European Court of Human Rights', in: *Uppsala Yearbook of East European Law* (2006), pp. 61-80 [*Uppsala Yb. East Eur. L.*]

Paust, Jordan J., 'The Right to Life in Human Rights Law and the Law of War', in: 65 *Saskatchewan Law Review* (2002), pp. 411-425 [*Sask. L. Rev.*]

Paust, Jordan J., 'War and Enemy Status after 9/11: Attacks on the Laws of War', in: 28 *Yale Journal of International Law* (2003), pp. 325-336 [*Yale J. Int'l L.*]

Paust, Jordan J., *International Law as Law of the United States*, Durham, N.C. 1996 [Carolina Academic Press]

Peal, Robert A., 'Combatant Status Review Tribunals and the Unique Nature of the War on Terror', in: 58 *Vanderbilt Law Review* (2005), pp. 1629-1670 [*Vand. L. Rev.*]

Pellet, Alain, 'No, This is not War!', in: *European Journal of International Law Discussion Forum: The Attack on the World Trade Center: Legal Responses* (October 3, 2001), URL: <http://www.ejil.org/forum_WTC/ny-pellet.html> (last visited February 28, 2008)

Pellet, Alain/ Tzankov, Vladimir, 'Can a State Victim of a Terror Act have Recourse to Armed Force?', in: 17 *Humanitäres Völkerrecht – Informationsschriften* (2004), pp. 68-72 [*HuV-I*]

Pellet, Allain/ Pellet, Sarah, 'The Aftermath of September 11', in: 10 *Tilburg Foreign Law Review* (2002), pp. 64-75 [*Tilburg Foreign L. Rev.*]

Peterke, Sven, 'Die Umgehung rechtsstaatlicher Garantien durch Bestimmung Terrorverdächtiger zu „feindlichen Kombattanten": Zur Entscheidung des New Yorker Bundesberufungsgerichts in der Sache „Padilla v. Rumsfeld"', in: 17 *Humanitäres Völkerrecht – Informationsschriften* (2004), pp. 39-46 [*HuV-I*]

Peters, Anne, *Einführung in die Europäische Menschenrechtskonvention*, München 2003 [C.H. Beck]

Pickard, Daniel B., 'Legalizing Assassination? Terrorism, the Central Intelligence Agency, and International Law', in: 30 *Georgia Journal of International and Comparative Law* (2001), pp. 3-35 [*Ga. J. Int'l & Comp. L.*]

Pictet, Jean S. (ed.), *The Geneva Conventions of 12 August 1949: Commentary, Vol. 1, Geneva Convention for the Amelioration of the Condition of the Wounded and Sick in Armed Forces in the Field*, Geneva 1952

Pictet, Jean S. (ed.), *The Geneva Conventions of 12 August 1949: Commentary, Vol. 2, Geneva Convention for the Amelioration of the Condition of Wounded, Sick and Shipwrecked Members of Armed Forces at Sea*, Geneva 1960

Pictet, Jean S. (ed.), *The Geneva Conventions of 12 August 1949: Commentary, Vol. 3, Geneva Convention relative to the Treatment of Prisoners of War*, Geneva 1960

Pictet, Jean S. (ed.), *The Geneva Conventions of 12 August 1949: Commentary, Vol. 4, Geneva Convention relative to the Protection of Civilian Persons in Time of War*, Geneva 1958

Pictet, Jean S., *Le droit humanitaire et la Protection des Victimes de la Guerre*, Leiden 1973 [A.W. Sijthoff]

Pin, Xavier, *Droit pénal général*, Paris 2005 [Dalloz]

Plaw, Avery, 'Fighting Terror Ethically and Legally: The Case of Targeting Terrorists', working paper prepared for the CPSA Conference, June 2006, URL: <http://www.cpsa-acsp.ca/papers-2006/Plaw.pdf> (last visited February 16, 2008)

Pocar, Fausto, 'Human Rights under the International Covenant on Civil and Political Rights and Armed Conflicts', in: Lal Chand Vohrah *et al.* (eds.), *Man's Inhumanity to Man – Essays on International Law in Honour of Antonio Cassese*, The Hague 2003, pp. 729-740 [Kluwer]

Politakis, George P., 'Stratagems and the Prohibition of Perfidy with a Special Reference to the Laws of War at Sea', in: 45 *Österreichische Zeitschrift für öffentliches Recht und Völkerrecht* (1993), pp. 253-308 [*ÖZöRV*]

Posner, Eric A., 'Terrorism and the Laws of War', in: 5 *Chicago Journal of International Law* (2004), pp. 423-434 [*Chi. J. Int'l L.*]

Prebensen, Søren C., 'Evolutive Interpretation of the European Convention on Human Rights', in: Paul Mahoney/ Franz Matscher/ Herbert Petzold/ Luzius Wildhaber (eds.), *Protection des droits de l'homme: la perspective européenne – Mélanges à la mémoire de Rolv Ryssdal*, Köln 2000, pp. 1123-1137 [Heymann]

Prefontaine, Daniel C., 'Under International Law is there a Category of Prisoner in Armed Conflicts Known as an "Unlawful or Unprivileged or Enemy Combatant"?', in: Canadian Council on International Law (ed.), *The Measure of International Law: Effectiveness, Fairness and Validity*, The Hague 2004, pp. 386-395 [Kluwer]

Proulx, Vincent-Jöel, 'If the Hat Fits Wear It, If the Turban Fits Run for Your Life: Reflection on the Indefinite Detention and Targeted Killings of Suspected Terrorists', in: 56 *Hastings Law Journal* (2005), pp. 801-900 [*Hastings L.J.*]

Provost, René, *International Human Rights and Humanitarian Law*, Cambridge 2002 [Cambridge Univ. Press]

Przetacznik, Franciszek, 'The Right to Life as a Basic Human Right', in: 9 *Revue des droits de l'homme – Human Rights Journal* (1976), pp. 585-609 [*Rev. dr. hom.-Hum. Rts. J.*]

Quénivet, Noëlle, 'Isayeva v. the Russian Federation and Isayeva, Yusupova and Bazayeva v. the Russian Federation: Targeting Rules according to Article 2 of the European Convention on Human Rights', 18 *Humanitäres Völkerrecht – Informationsschriften* (2005), pp. 219-226 [*HuV-I*]

Quénivet, Noëlle, 'The Applicability of International Humanitarian Law to Situations of a (Counter-)Terrorist Nature', in: Roberta Arnold/ Pierre-Antoine Hildbrand (eds.), *International Humanitarian Law and the 21st Century's Conflicts: Changes and Challenges*, Lausanne 2005, pp. 25-59 [Interuniversitaires Suisses]

Quénivet, Noëlle, 'The Moscow Hostage Crisis in the Light of the Armed Conflict in Chechnya', in: 4 *Yearbook of International Humanitarian Law* (2001), pp. 348-372 [*Yb. Int'l Hum. L.*]

Quigley, John, *Palestine and Israel: A Challenge to Justice*, Durham 1990 [Duke Univ. Press]

Raines, Joshua, 'Osama, Augustine, and Assassination: The Just War Doctrine and Targeted Killings', in: 12 *Transnational Law & Contemporary Problems* (2002), pp. 217-243 [*Transnat'l L. & Contemp. Probs.*]

Ramcharan, Bertrand G., 'The Concept and Dimensions of the Right to Life', in: Bertrand G. Ramcharan (ed.), *The Right to Life in International Law*, Dordrecht 1985, pp. 1-32 [Nijhoff]

Ramcharan, Bertrand G., 'The Drafting History of Article 2 of the European Convention on Human Rights', in: Bertrand G. Ramcharan (ed.), *The Right to Life in International Law*, Dordrecht 1985, pp. 57 61 [Nijhoff]

Ramcharan, Bertrand G., 'The Drafting History of Article 6 of the International Covenant on Civil and Political Rights', in: Bertrand G. Ramcharan (ed.), *The Right to Life in International Law*, Dordrecht 1985, pp. 42-56 [Nijhoff]

Ramcharan, Bertrand G., 'The Right to Life', in: 30 *Netherlands International Law Review* (1983), pp. 297-329 [*Nether. Int'l L. Rev.*]

Randelzhofer, Albrecht, 'Civilian Objects', in: Rudolf Bernhardt (ed.), *Encyclopedia of Public International Law*, Vol. 3, Amsterdam 1982, pp. 93-96 [North-Holland Publ.]

Ratner, Steven R., '*Jus ad Bellum* and *Jus in Bello* after September 11', in: 96 *American Journal of International Law* (2002), pp. 905-921 [*Am. J. Int'l L.*]

Rauch, Elmar, 'Conduct of Combat and Risks Run by the Civilian Population', in: 21 *Revue de droit pénal militaire et de droit de la guerre* (1982), pp. 66-72 [*Rev. dr. pén. mil.*]

Rauch, Elmar, 'Le concept de nécessité militaire dans le droit de la guerre', in: 19 *Revue de droit pénal militaire et de droit de la guerre* (1980), pp. 205-237 [*Rev. dr. pén. mil.*]

Redelbach, A., 'Protection of the Right to Life by Law and by Other Means', in: Bertrand G. Ramcharan (ed.), *The Right to Life in International Law*, Dordrecht 1985, pp. 182-220 [Nijhoff]

Reed, Walter, 'Laws of War: The Developing Law of Armed Conflict – Some Current Problems', in: 9 *Case Western Reserve Journal of International Law* (1977), pp. 17-38 [*Case W. Res. J. Int'l L.*]

Rehof, Lars Adam, 'Article 3', in: Asbjørn Eide; Gudmundur Alfredsson (eds.), *The Universal Declaration of Human Rights: A Commentary*, Oslo 1992, pp. 73-85

Reid, Karen, *A Practitioner's Guide to the European Convention on Human Rights*, 2nd Edition, London 2004 [Thomson, Seet and Maxwell]

Reindel, Florian, *Auslegung menschenrechtlicher Verträge am Beispiel der Spruchpraxis des UN-Menschenrechtsausschusses, des Europäischen und des Interamerikanischen Gerichtshofs für Menschenrechte*, München 1995 [VVF]

Ress, Georg, 'State Responsibility for Extraterritorial Human Rights Violations: The Case of Banković', in: 6 *Zeitschrift für Europarechtliche Studien* (2003), pp. 73-90 [*ZEuS*]

Ress, Georg, 'The Duty to Protect and to Ensure Human Rights under the European Convention on Human Rights', in: Eckart Klein (ed.), *The Duty to Protect and Ensure Human Rights*, Berlin 2000, pp. 165-205 [Berlin Verlag]

Rich, Roland, 'The Right to Development: A Right of Peoples?', in: James Crawford (ed.), *The Right of Peoples*, Oxford 1988, pp. 39-54 [Clarendon]

Rigo Sureda, Andrés, *The Evolution of the Right of Self-Determination: A Study of United Nations Practice*, Leiden 1973 [Sijthoff]

Robert, Paul, *Dictionnaire alphabétique et analogique de la langue française: les mots et les associations d'idées*, Casablanca 1951 [Soc. du noveau littré]

Roberts, Adam, 'Prolonged Military Occupation: The Israeli-Occupied Territories 1967-1988', in: Emma Playfair (ed.), *International Law and the Administration of Occupied Territories: Two Decades of Israeli Occupation of the West Bank and Gaza Strip*, Oxford 1992, pp. 25-85 [Clarendon Press]

Roberts, Adam, 'Prolonged Military Occupation: The Israeli-Occupied Territories Since 1967', in: 84 *American Journal of International Law* (1990), pp. 44-103 [*Am. J. Int'l L.*]

Roberts, Adam, 'What is a Military Occupation?', in: 55 *British Yearbook of International Law* (1984), pp. 249-305 [*Brit. Y.B. Int'l L.*]

Roberts, Adam/ Guelff, Richard, *Documents on the Laws of War*, 3rd ed., Oxford 2000 [Oxford Univ. Press]

Robertson, Arthur Henry, 'The United Nations Covenant on Civil and Political Rights and the European Convention on Human Rights', in: 43 *British Yearbook of International Law* (1968-69), pp. 21-48

Robertson, Arthur Henry/ Merrills, John G., *Human Rights in the World: An Introduction to the Study of the International Protection of Human Rights*, 4th ed., Manchester 1996

Robertson, Athur Henry, 'Human Rights as the Basis of International Humanitarian Law', in: Etienne Boéri *et al.* (eds.), *I Diritto dell' Uomo come base del Diritto Internazionale Umanitario: Atti del Convegno Internatzionale die Diritto Umanitario, Sanremo – 24/27.IX.1970*, Lugano-Bellinzona 1970, pp. 55-76 [Grassi]

Robledo, A. Gómez, 'Le ius cogens international: sa genèse, sa nature, ses fonctions', in: 172 *Recueil des Cours de l'Academie de Droit International de la Haye* (1981-III), pp. 9-218 [*RdC*]

Rodley, Nigel S., *The Treatment of Prisoners under International Law*, Oxford 1987 [Clarendon]

Rogers, Anthony P.V., 'A Commentary on the Protocol on Prohibitions or Restrictions on the Use of Mines, Booby-Traps and Other Devices', in: 26 *Revue de droit pénal militaire et de droit de la guerre* (1987), pp. 185-206 [*Rev. dr. pén. mil.*]

Rogers, Anthony P.V., 'Conduct of Combat and Risks run by the Civilian Population', in: 21 *Revue de droit pénal militaire et de droit de la guerre* (1982), pp. 293-319 [*Rev. dr. pén. mil.*]

Rogers, Anthony P.V., 'Zero-Casualty Warfare', in: 82 *International Review of the Red Cross* (2000), No. 837, pp. 165-181 [*Int'l Rev. Red Cross*]

Rona, Gabor, 'Interesting Times for International Humanitarian Law: Challenges from the "War on Terror"', in: 27 *Fletcher Forum of World Affairs* (2003), pp. 55-74 [*Fletcher F. World Aff.*]

Rosas, Allan, *The Legal Status of Prisoners of War: A Study in International Humanitarian Law applicable in Armed Conflicts*, Helsinki 1976 [Suomalainen Tiedeakat]

Roscini, Marco, 'Targeting and Contemporary Aerial Bombardment', in: 54 *International and Comparative Law Quarterly* (2005), pp. 411-444 [*Int'l & Comp. L.Q.*]

Rosenblad, Esbjörn, 'Guerrilla Warfare and International Law', in: 12 *Revue de droit pénal militaire et de droit de la guerre* (1973), pp. 91-134 [*Rev. dr. pén. mil.*]

Rosenne, Shabtai, 'The Meaning of "Authentic Text" in Modern Treaty Law', in: Rudolph Bernhardt/ Wilhelm Karl Geck/ Günther Jaenicke/ Helmut Steinberger (eds.), *Völkerrecht als Rechtsordnung – Internationale Gerichtsbarkeit – Menschenrechte: Festschrift für Hermann Mosler*, Berlin 1983, pp. 759-784 [Springer]

Roth, Kenneth, 'The Law of War in the War on Terror', in: 83 *Foreign Affairs* (2004), pp. 2-7 [*Foreign Aff.*]

Rousseau, Charles, *Le droit des conflits armés*, Paris 1983 [Pedone]

Rousseau, Jean-Jacques, *Du contrat social*, Paris 1754

Rowe, Peter, 'Responses to Terror: The New "War"', in: 3 *Melbourne Journal of International Law* (2002), pp. 301-321 [*Melbourne J. Int'l L.*]

Rowles, James P., 'Responses to Terrorism: Substantive and Procedural Constraints in International Law', 81 *American Society of International Law – Proceedings* (1987), pp. 313-317 [*ASIL Proc.*]

Rubin, Paul H., 'Reply to Donohue and Wolfers on the Death Penalty and Deterrence', in: 3 *Economists' Voice* (2006), No. 5, Article 4, URL: <http://www.bepress.com/ev/vol3/iss5/art4> (last visited May 5, 2006)

Rudolf, Beate, 'Beweislastprobleme in Verfahren wegen Verletzung von Art. 3 EMRK', in: 23 *Europäische Grundrechte-Zeitschrift* (1996), pp. 497-503 [*EuGRZ*]

Ruys, Tom, '*Inter arma non silent leges*: Israëlisch Hooggerechtshof spreekt zich uit over "targeted killings"', in: *Juristenkrant*, January 17, 2007, URL: <http://law.kuleuven.be/iir/nl/opinies/Juristenkrant20070117.pdf> (last visited March 24, 2007)

Ruys, Tom, 'Licence to Kill?: State-sponsored Assassination under International Law', in: 44 *Revue de droit militaire et de droit de la guerre* (2005), pp. 13-49 [*Rev. dr. mil.*]

Ruys, Tom/ Verhoeven, Sten, 'Attacks by Private Actors and the Right of Self-Defence', in: 10 *Journal of Conflict & Security Law* (2005), pp. 289-320 [*J. Confl. Sec. L.*]

Sandoz, Yves, 'Réflexions sur la mise en oeuvre du droit international humanitaire et sur le rôle du Comité international de la Croix-Rouge en ex-Yougoslavie', in: 3 *Revue Suisse de droit international et de droit européen* (1993), pp. 461-490 [*Rev. Suisse dr. int'l & eur.*]

Sandoz, Yves/ Swinarski, Christophe/ Zimmermann, Bruno (eds.), *Commentary on the Additional Protocols of 8 June 1977 to the Geneva Conventions of 12 August 1949*, Dordrecht 1987 [Nijhoff]

Sandoz, Yves/ Swinarski, Christophe/ Zimmermann, Bruno (eds.), *Commentaire des Protocoles additionnels du 8 juin 1977 aux Conventions de Genève du 12 août 1949*, Genève 1986 [Nijhoff]

Sapienza, R., 'International Legal Standards on Capital Punishment', in: Bertrand G. Ramcharan (ed.), *The Right to Life in International Law*, Dordrecht 1985, pp. 284-296 [Nijhoff]

Sassòli, Marco, '"Unlawful Combatants": the Law and Whether it Needs to be Revised', in: 97 *American Society of International Law – Proceedings* (2003), pp. 196-203 [*ASIL Proc.*]

Sassòli, Marco, 'Israel and the Palestinians: What Laws Were Broken?', in: *Crimes of War Project* (May 8, 2002), URL: <http://www.crimesofwar.org/expert/me-sassoli.html> (last visited February 18, 2008)

Sassòli, Marco, 'Legislation and Maintenance of Public Order and Civil Life by Occupying Powers', in: 16 *European Journal of International Law* (2005), pp. 661-694 [*Eur. J. Int'l L.*]

Sassòli, Marco, 'State responsibility for violations of international humanitarian law', in: 84 *International Review of the Red Cross* (2002), No. 846, pp. 401-434 [*Int'l Rev. Red Cross*]

Sassòli, Marco, 'Targeting: The Scope and Utility of the Concept of "Military Objectives" for the Protection of Civilians in Contemporary Armed Conflicts', in: David Wippman/ Matthew Evangelista (eds.), *New Wars, New Laws? Applying the Laws of War in 21st Century Conflicts*, Ardsley, N.Y. 2005, pp. 181-201 [Transnational Pub.]

Sassòli, Marco, 'Use and Abuse of the Laws of War in the "War on Terrorism"', in: 22 *Law and Inequality: A Journal of Theory and Practice* (2004), pp. 195-221 [*L. & Ineq. J.*]

Sassòli, Marco/ Bouvier, Antoine, *How does Law Protect in War? Cases, Documents and Teaching Materials on Contemporary Practice in International Humanitarian Law*, 2nd ed., Geneva 2006 [ICRC]

Schabas, William A., 'Developments in the Law of Genocide', in: 5 *Yearbook of International Humanitarian Law* (2002), pp. 131-165 [*Yb. Int'l Hum. L.*]

Schabas, William A., *The Abolition of the Death Penalty in International Law*, 2nd ed., Cambridge 1997 [Cambridge Univ. Press]

Schachter, Oscar, 'International Law Implications of U.S. Human Rights Policies', in: 24 *New York Law School Law Review* (1977-1978), pp. 63-87 [*N.Y.L. Sch. L. Rev.*]

Schachter, Oscar, 'International Law in Theory and Practice: General Course in Public International Law', in 178 *Recueil des Cours de l'Academie de Droit International de la Haye* (1982-V), pp. 9-395 [*RdC*]

Schäfer, Bernhard, 'Der Fall Banković oder Wie eine Lücke geschaffen wird', in: 7 *MenschenRechtsMagazin* (2002), pp. 149-163 [*MRM*]

Scharf, Michael P., 'Defining Terrorism as the Peacetime Equivalent of War Crimes: Problems and Prospects', in: 36 *Case Western Reserve Journal of International Law* (2004), pp. 359-374 [*Case W. Res. J. Int'l L.*]

Scheinin, Martin, 'Extraterritorial Effect of the International Covenant on Civil and Political Rights', in: Fons Coomans/ Menno T. Kamminga (eds.), *Extraterritorial Application of Human Rights Treaties*, Antwerp 2004, pp. 73-81 [Intersentia]

Schindler, Dietrich, 'Human Rights and Humanitarian Law: Interrelationship of the Laws', in: 31 *American University Law Review* (1982), pp. 935-943 [*Am. U. L. Rev.*]

Schindler, Dietrich, 'Kriegsrecht und Menschenrechte', in: Ulrich Häfelin/ Walter Haller/ Dietrich Schindler (eds.), *Menschenrechte, Föderalismus, Demokratie – Festschrift zum 70. Geburtstag von Werner Kägi*, Zürich 1979, pp. 327-349 [Schulthess]

Schindler, Dietrich/ Toman, Jiří (eds.), *The Laws of Armed Conflicts: A Collection of Conventions, Resolutions and Other Documents*, 2nd ed., Alphen aan den Rijn 1981 [Sijthoff & Noordhoff]

Schindler, Dietrich/ Toman, Jiří (eds.), *The Laws of Armed Conflicts: A Collection of Conventions, Resolutions and Other Documents*, 3rd ed., Dordrecht 1988 [Nijhoff]

Schlütter, Birgit, 'Water Rights in the West Bank and in Gaza', in: 18 *Leiden Journal of International Law* (2005), pp. 621-644 [*Leiden J. Int'l L.*]

Schmahl, Stefanie, 'Derogation von Menschenrechtsverpflichtungen in Notstandslagen', in: Dieter Fleck (ed.), *Rechtsfragen der Terrorismusbekämpfung durch Streitkräfte*, Baden-Baden 2004, pp. 125-146 [Nomos]

Schmahl, Stefanie, 'Targeted Killings – A Challenge for International Law?', in: Christian Tomuschat/ Evelyne Lagrange/ Stefan Oeter (eds.), *The Right to Life*, Leiden 2010, pp. 233-266 [Nijhoff]

Schmid, Alex Peter, *Political Terrorism: A Research Guide to Concepts, Theories, Data Bases and Literature*, Amsterdam 1984 [North-Holland Publ.]

Schmidt-Radefeldt, Roman, 'Die Menschenrechtsverpflichtungen von Streitkräften bei antiterroristischen Maßnahmen im Ausland', in: Dieter Fleck (ed.), *Rechtsfragen der Terrorismusbekämpfung durch Streitkräfte*, Baden-Baden 2004, pp. 101-123 [Nomos]

Schmitt, Michael N., '"Direct Participation in Hostilities" and 21st Century Armed Conflict', in: Horst Fischer/ Ulrike Froissart/ Wolff Heintschel von Heinegg/ Christian Raap (eds.), *Krisensicherung und Humanitärer Schutz – Crisis Management and Humanitarian Protection: Festschrift für Dieter Fleck*, Berlin 2004, pp. 505-529 [Berliner Wiss.-Verl.]

Schmitt, Michael N., '*Bellum Americanum*: The U.S. View of twenty-first Century War and its possible Implications for the Law of

Armed Conflict', in: 19 *Michigan Journal of International Law* (1998), pp. 1051-1090 [*Mich. J. Int'l L.*]

Schmitt, Michael N., 'Counter-Terrorism and the Use of Force in International Law', in: 32 *Israel Yearbook on Human Rights* (2002), pp. 53-116 [*Isr. Yb. Hum. Rts.*]

Schmitt, Michael N., 'State Sponsored Assassination in International and Domestic Law', in: 17 *Yale Journal of International Law* (1999), pp. 609-690 [*Yale J. Int'l L.*]

Schmitt, Michael N., 'Targeted Killings in International Law: Law Enforcement, Self-Defense and Armed Conflict', in: Roberta Arnold/ Noëlle Quénivet (eds.), *International Humanitarian Law and Human Rights Law: Towards a New Merger in International Law*, Leiden 2008, pp. 525-553 [Nijhoff]

Schmitt, Michael N., 'The Principle of Discrimination in 21st Century Warfare', 2 *Yale Human Rights and Development Law Journal* (1999), pp. 143-182 [*Yale Hum. Rts. & Dev. L.J.*]

Schmitz-Elvenich, Heiko F., *Targeted Killing: Die völkerrechtliche Zulässigkeit der gezielten Tötung von Terroristen im Ausland*, Frankfurt am Main 2008 [Peter Lang]

Schondorf, Roy S., 'The Targeted Killings Judgment: A Preliminary Assessment', in: 5 *Journal of International Criminal Justice* (2007), pp. 301-309 [*J. Int'l Crim. Just.*]

Schönke, Adolf/ Schröder, Horst/ Lenckner, Theodor (eds.), *Strafgesetzbuch: Kommentar*, 27th ed., München 2006 [C.H. Beck]

Schreuer, Christoph H., 'The Impact of International Institutions on the Protection of Human Rights in Domestic Courts', in: 4 *Israel Yearbook on Human Rights* (1974), pp. 76-87 [*Isr. Yb. Hum. Rts.*]

Schrijver, Nico J., 'Responding to International Terrorism: Moving the Frontiers of International Law for "Enduring Freedom"?', in: 48 *Netherlands International Law Review* (2001), pp. 271-292 [*Nether. Int'l L. Rev.*]

Schwab, Herbert, *Irreguläre Kombattanten als Kriegsgefangene*, Würzburg 1976

Schwelb, Egon, 'The Influences of the Universal Declaration of Human Rights on International and National Law', in: 53 *American Society of International Law – Proceedings* (1959), pp. 217-229 [*ASIL Proc.*]

Schwenk, Edmund H., 'Legislative Power of the Military Occupant under Article 43, Hague Regulations', in: 54 *Yale Law Journal* (1945), pp. 393-416 [*Yale L.J.*]

Seidel, Gerd, 'Die Palästinafrage und das Völkerrecht', in: 44 *Archiv des Völkerrechts* (2006), pp. 121-158 [*AVR*]

Seidel, Gerd, *Handbuch der Grund- und Menschenrechte auf staatlicher, europäischer und universeller Ebene,* Baden-Baden 1996 [Nomos]

Shamgar, Meir, 'The Observance of International Law in the Administered Territories', in: 1 *Israel Yearbook on Human Rights* (1971), pp. 262-277 [*Isr. Y.B. Hum. Rts.*]

Shany, Yuval, 'Israeli Counter-Terrorism Measures: Are they "kosher" under International Law?', in: Michael N. Schmitt/ Gian Luca Beruto (eds.), *Terrorism and International Law: Challenges and Responses*, San Remo 2003, pp. 96-118 [International Institute of Humanitarian Law]

Shefi, Dov, 'The Protection of Human Rights in Areas Administered by Israel: United Nations Findings and Reality', in: 3 *Israel Yearbook on Human Rights* (1973), pp. 337-361 [*Isr. Yb. Hum. Rts.*]

Shehadeh, Raja, *From Occupation to Interim Accords: Israel and the Palestinian Territories*, London 1997 [Kluwer]

Shehadeh, Raja, *Occupier's Law: Israel and the West Bank*, Washington, D.C. 1988 [Institute for Palestine Studies]

Shelton, Dinah, 'The Boundaries of Human Rights Jurisdiction in Europe', in: 13 *Duke Journal of Comparative & International Law* (2003), pp. 95-153 [*Duke J. Comp. & Int'l L.*]

Shraga, Daphna, 'Human Rights in Emergency Situations under the European Convention on Human Rights', in: 16 *Israel Yearbook on Human Rights* (1986), pp. 217-242 [*Isr. Yb. Hum. Rts.*]

Sieghart, Paul, *The International Law of Human Rights*, Oxford 1983 [Clarendon Press]

Simester, Andrew P./ Sullivan, G. Robert, *Criminal Law: Theory and Doctrine*, 2nd ed., Oxford 2003 [Hart Publishing]

Simma, Bruno/ Alston, Philip, 'The Sources of Human Rights Law: Custom, jus cogens, and General Principles', in: 12 *Australian Yearbook of International Law* (1992), pp. 82-108 [*Austl. Yb. Int'l L.*]

Simpson, John Andrew/ Weiner, Edmund S. C./ Murry, James Augustus Henry, *The Oxford English Dictionary*, 2nd ed., Oxford 1989 [Clarendon]

Sina, Stephan, *Der völkerrechtliche Status des Westjordanlandes und des Gaza-Streifens nach den Osloer Verträgen – The status of the Westbank and the Gaza Strip under public international law after the Oslo Accords*, Berlin 2004 [Springer]

Singer, Joel, 'The Establishment of a Civil Administration in the Areas Administered by Israel', in: 12 *Israel Yearbook on Human Rights* (1982), pp. 259-289 [*Isr. Yb. Hum. Rts.*]

Slaughter, Anne-Marie/ Burke-White, William, 'September 11, 2001 – Legal Response to Terror: An International Constitutional Moment', in: 43 *Harvard International Law Journal* (2002), pp. 1-22 [*Harv. Int'l L.J.*]

Smith, John, 'The Right to Life and the Right to kill in Law Enforcement', in: 144 *New Law Journal* (1994), No. 6639, pp. 354-356 [*New L.J.*]

Sohn, Louis B., '"Generally Accepted" International Rules', in: 61 *Washington Law Review* (1986), pp. 1073-1080 [*Wash. L. Rev.*]

Sohn, Louis B., 'The New International Law: Protection of the Rights of Individuals Rather than States', in: 32 *American University Law Review* (1982), pp. 1-64 [*Am. U. L. Rev.*]

Solf, Waldemar A./ Cummings, Edward R., 'A Survey of Penal Sanctions Under Protocol I to the Geneva Conventions of August 12, 1949', in: 9 *Case Western Reserve Journal of International Law* (1977), pp. 205-251 [*Case W. Res. J. Int'l L.*]

Solis, Gary, 'Targeted Killing and the Law of Armed Conflict', in: 60 *Naval War College Review* (2007), pp. 127-146 [*Nav. War C. Rev.*]

Solomon, Solon, 'Targeted Killing and the Soldiers' Right to Life', in: 14 *ILSA Journal of International & Comparative Law* (2007), pp. 99-120 [*ILSA J. Int'l & Comp. L.*]

Stahn, Carsten, '"Nicaragua is dead, long live Nicaragua" – The Right to Self-Defence under Art. 51 UN Charter and International Terrorism', in: Christian Walter/ Silja Vöneky/ Volker Röben/ Frank Schorkopf (eds.), *Terrorism as a Challenge for National and International Law: Security versus Liberty?*, Berlin 2004, pp. 827-877 [Springer]

Statman, Daniel, 'Targeted Killing', in: 5 *Theoretical Inquiries in Law* (2004), pp. 179-198 [*Theo. Inq. L.*]

Stefani, Gaston/ Levasseur, Georges/ Bouloc, Bernard, *Droit pénal général*, 18th ed., Paris 2003 [Dalloz]

Stein, Torsten, 'How much Humanity do Terrorists deserve?', in: Astrid J.M. Delissen/ Gerard J. Tanja (eds.); *Humanitarian Law of Armed Conflict: Challenges ahead – Essays in Honour of Frits Kalshoven*, Dordrecht 1991, pp. 567-581

Stein, Yael, 'By Any Name Illegal and Immoral: Response to "Israel's Policy of Targeted Killing"', in: 17 *Ethics & International Affairs* (2003), No. 1, pp. 127-137 [*Ethics & Int'l Aff.*]

Stein, Yael, 'Israel's Assassination Policy: Extra-Judicial Executions', *B'Tselem Position Paper* (January 2001), URL: <http://www.btselem.org/Download/200101_Extrajudicial_Killings_Eng.doc> (last visited January 23, 2008)

Sterling, Eric, 'US Drug Policy', in: 4 *Foreign Policy in Focus* (1999), No. 31, URL: <http://www.fpif.org/pdf/vol4/31ifdrug.pdf> (last visited July 31, 2007) [*FPIF*]

Stewart, James G., 'Towards a single Definition of Armed Conflict in International Humanitarian Law: A Critique of Internationalized Armed Conflict' in: 85 *International Review of the Red Cross* (2003), No. 850, pp. 313-350 [*Int'l Rev. Red Cross*]

Stiller, Tanja, *Grenzen des Notwehrrechts bei der Verteidigung von Sachwerten*, Frankfurt am Main 1999 [Lang]

Stone, Julius, *Legal Controls of International Conflict: A Treatise on the Dynamics of Disputes- and War-Law*, New York 1954 [Rinehart]

Struck, Gerhard, *Topische Jurisprudenz: Argument und Gemeinplatz in der juristischen Arbeit*, Frankfurt am Main 1971 [Athenäum]

Strüwer, Elisabeth, *Zum Zusammenspiel von humanitärem Völkerrecht und den Menschenrechten am Beispiel des Targeted Killing*, Frankfurt am Main 2010 [Lang]

Svensson-MacCarthy, Anna-Lena, *The International Law of Human Rights and States of Exception: With Special Reference to the "travaux préparatoires" and the Case-Law of the International Monitoring Organs*, The Hague 1998 [Nijhoff]

Syse, Henrik, 'The Importance of Protecting Non-Combatants', in: 8 *Pacem – militært tidsskrift for etisk og teologisk refleksjon* (2005), pp. 49-55 [*Pacem*]

Tahzib-Lie, Bahia/ Swaak-Goldman, Olivia, 'Determining the Threshold for the Application of International Humanitarian Law', in: Liesbeth Lijnzaad/ Johanna von Sambeck/ Bahia Tahzib-Lie (eds.), *Making the Voice of Humanity Heard: Essays on Humanitarian Assistance and International Humanitarian Law in Honour of HRH Princess Margriet of the Netherlands*, Leiden 2004, pp. 239-253 [Nijhoff]

Taylor, Telford, *Nuremberg and Vietnam: an American Tragedy*, Chicago 1970 [Quadrangle]

Thiel, Klaus-Dieter, 'Non-Lethal Weapons: An alternative Option facing unconventional Threats', in: 42 *Revue de droit militaire et de droit de la guerre* (2003), pp. 379-393 [*Rev. dr. mil.*]

Tigroudja, Hélène/ Panoussis, Ioannis K., *La Cour interaméricaine des droits de l'homme: Analyse de la jurisprudence consultative et contentieuse*, Bruxelles 2003 [Nemessis]

Toman, Jiří, 'The Status of Al Quaeda/ Taliban Detainees under the Geneva Conventions', in: 32 *Israel Yearbook on Human Rights* (2002), pp. 271-304 [*Isr. Yb. Hum. Rts.*]

Tomuschat, Christian, 'Gezielte Tötungen (Targeted Killings) – Zugleich ein Kommentar zum Gutachten des Internationalen Gerichtshofs vom 9. Juli 2004', in: 52 *Vereinte Nationen* (2004), pp. 136-140 [*Vereinte Nationen*]

Travalio, Gregory M., 'Terrorism, International Law, and the Use of Military Force', in: 18 *Wisconsin International Law Journal* (2000), pp. 145-191 [*Wis. Int'l L.J.*]

Trechsel, Stefan, 'Spotlights on Article 2 ECHR, the Right to Life', in: Wolfgang Benedek/ Hubert Isak/ Renate Kicker (eds.), *Development and Developing International and European Law: Essays in Honour of Konrad Ginther on the Occasion of his 65th Birthday*, Frankfurt am Main 1999, pp. 671-686

Turner, Robert F., 'It's not really "Assassination": Legal and Moral Implications of intentionally targeting Terrorists and Aggressor-State Regime Elites', in: 37 *University of Richmond Law Review* (2003), pp. 787-810 [*U. Rich. L. Rev.*]

Umozurike, U. Oji, *The African Charter on Human and Peoples' Rights*, The Hague 1997 [Nijhoff]

Union Académique Internationale, *Dictionnaire de la terminologie du droit international*, Paris 1960 [Sirey]

University Centre for International Humanitarian Law, 'The Right to Life in Armed Conflict and Situations of Occupation', Report of the Geneva Expert Meeting, September 1 and 2, 2005, URL: <http://www.adhgeneve.ch/evenements/pdf/colloques/2005/3rapport_droit_vie.pdf> (last visited February 10, 2008)

Urdang, Laurence (ed.), *Longman Synonym Dictionary*, Harlow 1986 [Longman]

Valek, Petr, 'Is Unilateral Humanitarian Intervention Compatible with the U.N. Charter?', in: 26 *Michigan Journal of International Law* (2005), pp. 1223-1256 [*Mich. J. Int'l L.*]

Van den Hole, Leo, 'Towards a Test of the International Character of an Armed Conflict: Nicaragua and Tadic', in: 32 *Syracuse Journal of International Law and Commerce* (2005), pp. 269-289 [*Syracuse J. Int'l L. & Com.*]

Verdross, Alfred, 'Forbidden Treaties in International Law: Comments on Professor Garner's Report on "The Law of Treaties"', in 31 *American Journal of International Law* (1937), pp. 571-577 [*Am. J. Int'l L.*]

Verdross, Alfred, '*Jus Dispositivum* and *Jus Cogens* in International Law', in: 60 *American Journal of International Law* (1966), pp. 55-63 [*Am. J. Int'l L.*]

Verdross, Alfred/ Simma, Bruno, *Universelles Völkerrecht: Theorie und Praxis*, 3rd ed., Berlin 1984 [Duncker & Humblot]

Veuthey, Michel, 'Israel and the Palestinians: What Laws Were Broken?', in: *Crimes of War Project* (May 8, 2002), URL: <http://www.crimesofwar.org/expert/me-veuthey.html>(last visited February 28, 2008)

Vierucci, Luisa, 'Is the Geneva Convention on Prisoners of War Obsolete? The Views of the Counsel to the US President on the Application of International Law to the Afghan Conflict', in: 2 *Journal of International Criminal Justice* (2004), pp. 866-871 [*J. Int'l Crim. Just.*]

Vierucci, Luisa, 'Prisoners of War or Protected Persons *qua* Unlawful Combatants? The Judicial Safeguards to which Guantanamo Bay Detainees are Entitled', in: 1 *Journal of International Criminal Justice* (2003), pp. 284-314 [*J. Int'l Crim. Just.*]

Viljoen, Frans, 'Admissibility under the African Charter', in: Malcolm Evans/ Rachel Murray (eds.), *The African Charter on Human and Peoples' Rights: The System in Practice, 1986-2000*, Cambridge 2002, pp. 61-99 [Cambridge Univ. Press]

Villiger, Mark E., *Handbuch der Europäischen Menschenrechtskonvention (EMRK) unter besonderer Berücksichtigung der schweizerischen Rechtslage*, Zürich 1993 [Schulthess]

Visscher, Charles de, 'Positivisme et jus cogens', in: 75 *Revue générale de droit international public* (1971), pp. 5-11 [*R.G.D.I.P.*]

Voit, Wolfgang, 'Humanitäre Aspekte der Regeln über Perfidie und Kriegslist', in: 22 *Neue Zeitschrift für Wehrrecht* (1980), pp. 19-25 [*NZWehrR*]

Vöneky, Silja, 'The Fight against Terrorism and the Rules of the Law of Warfare', in: Christian Walter/ Silja Vöneky/ Volker Röben/ Frank Schorkopf (eds.), *Terrorism as a Challenge for National and International Law: Security versus Liberty?*, Berlin 2004, pp. 925-949 [Springer]

Vranes, Erich, 'Lex superior, lex specialis, lex posterior: Zur Rechtsnatur der "Konfliktlösungsregeln"', in: 65 *Zeitschrift für ausländisches öffentliches Recht und Völkerrecht* (2005), pp. 391-405 [*ZaöRV*]

Vugt, Gerard A.J.M. van, 'Juridische aspecten van niet-letale wapens', in: 44 *Revue de droit militaire et de droit de la guerre* (2005), pp. 39-64 [*Rev. dr. mil.*]

Wadley, Reed L., 'Treachery and Deceit: Parallels in Tribal and Terrorist Warfare?', in: 26 *Studies in Conflict and Terrorism* (2003), pp. 331-346 [*Stud. Confl. Terror.*]

Waisberg, Tatiana, 'The Colombia-Ecuador Armed Crisis of March 2008: The Practice of Targeted Killing and Incursions against Non-State Actors Harbored at Terrorist Safe Havens in a Third Party State', in: 32 *Studies in Conflict and Terrorism* (2009), pp. 476-488 [*Stud. Confl. Terror.*]

Wallach, Evan J., 'The Logical Nexus Between the Decision to deny Application of the Third Geneva Convention to the Taliban and Al Qaeda and the Mistreatment of Prisoners in Abu Ghraib', in: 36 *Case Western Reserve Journal of International Law* (2004), pp. 541-638 [*Case W. Res. J. Int'l L.*]

Walter, Christian, 'Zwischen Selbstverteidigung und Völkerstrafrecht: Bausteine für ein internationals Recht der "präventiven Terrorismus-Bekämpfung"', in: Dieter Fleck (ed.), *Rechtsfragen der Ter-*

rorismusbekämpfung durch Streitkräfte, Baden-Baden 2004, pp. 23-42 [Nomos]

Walzer, Michael, *Arguing about War*, New Haven 2004 [Yale Univ. Press]

Watkin, Kenneth W., 'Canada/ United States Military Interoperability and Humanitarian Law Issues: Land Mines, Terrorism, Military Objectives and Targeted Killing', in: 15 *Duke Journal of Comparative & International Law* (2005), pp. 281-314 [*Duke J. Comp. & Int'l L.*]

Watkin, Kenneth W., 'Controlling the Use of Force: A Role for Human Rights Norms in Contemporary Armed Conflict', in: 98 *American Journal of International Law* (2004), pp. 1-34 [*Am. J. Int'l L.*]

Watkin, Kenneth W., 'Humans in the Cross-Hairs: Targeting and Assassination in Contemporary Armed Conflict', in: David Wippman/ Matthew Evangelista (eds.), *New Wars, New Laws? Applying the Laws of War in 21st Century Conflicts*, Ardsley, N.Y. 2005, pp. 137-179 [Transnational Pub.]

Watkin, Kenneth W., *Combatants, Unprivileged Belligerents and Conflicts in the 21st Century*, Harvard Program on Humanitarian Policy and Conflict Research, Background Paper prepared for the Informal High-Level Expert Meeting on the Reaffirmation and Development of International Humanitarian Law, Cambridge, June 27-29, 2003, URL: <http://www.ihlresearch.org/ihl/pdfs/Session2.pdf> (last visited February 24, 2008)

Wedgwood, Ruth, 'Al Qaeda, Terrorism, and Military Commissions', in: 96 *American Journal of International Law* (2002), pp. 328-337 [*Am. J. Int'l L.*]

Wedgwood, Ruth, 'Combatants or Criminals? How Washington Should Handle Terrorists: Fighting a War Under its Rules', in: 83 *Foreign Affairs* (2004), pp. 126-129 [*Foreign Aff.*]

Weill, Sharon, 'The judicial arm of the occupation: the Israeli military courts in the occupied territories', in: 89 *International Review of the Red Cross* (2007), No. 866, pp. 395-419 [*Int'l Rev. Red Cross*]

Weill, Sharon, 'The Targeted Killing of Salah Shehadeh: From Gaza to Madrid', in: 7 *Journal of International Criminal Justice* (2009), pp. 617-631 [*J. Int'l Crim. Just.*]

Weissbrodt, David, 'Protecting the Right to Life: International Measures Against Arbitrary or Summary Killings by Governments', in: Bertrand G. Ramcharan (ed.), *The Right to Life in International Law*, Dordrecht 1985, pp. 297-314 [Nijhoff]

Weissbrodt, David/ Hallendorff, Mattias, 'Travaux Préparatoires of the Fair Trial Provisions: Articles 8 to 11of the Universal Declaration of Human Rights', in: 21 *Human Rights Quarterly* (1999), pp. 1061-1096 [*Hum. Rts. Q.*]

Werksman, Jacob/ Khalastchi, Ruth, 'Nuclear Weapons and the concept of *jus cogens*: peremptory norms and justice pre-empted?', in: Laurence Boisson de Chazournes/ Philippe Sands (eds.), *International Law, the International Court of Justice, and Nuclear Weapons*, Cambridge 1999, pp. 181-198 [Cambridge Univ. Press]

Wessels, Johannes/ Beulke, Werner, *Strafrecht Allgemeiner Teil: Die Straftat und ihr Aufbau*, 37th ed., Heidelberg 2007 [Müller]

Wessels, Leon, 'Derogation from Human Rights: A possible Dispensation for Africa and southern Africa', in: 27 *South African Yearbook of International Law* (2002), pp. 120-139 [*S. Afr. Yb. Int'l L.*]

Whitman, Jim, 'Humanitarian Intervention in an Era of Pre-emptive Self-Defence', in: 36 *Security Dialogue* (2005), pp. 259-274

Wiebe, Matthew C., 'Assassination in Domestic and International Law: The Central Intelligence Agency, State-Sponsored Terrorism, and the Right of Self-Defense', in: 11 *Tulsa Journal of Comparative & International Law* (2003), pp. 363-406 [*Tulsa J. Comp. & Int'l L.*]

Wieczorek, Judith, *Unrechtmäßige Kombattanten und humanitäres Völkerrecht*, Berlin 2005 [Duncker & Humblot]

Wiesbrock, Katja, *Internationaler Schutz der Menschenrechte vor Verletzungen durch Private*, Berlin 1990 [Berlin-Verl. Spitz]

Wilde, Ralph, 'Legal "Black Hole"? Extraterritorial State Action and International Treaty Law on Civil and Political Rights', in: 26 *Michigan Journal of International Law* (2005), pp. 739-806 [*Mich. J. Int'l L.*]

Wildhaber, Luzius, President of the European Court of Human Rights, Speech given at Strasbourg on January 31, 2002, in: *The Council of Europe's Contribution to the Enlargement of the European Union – Speeches given by the President of the Court of Justice of the European Communities and by the President of the European*

Court of Human Rights on the occasion of the opening of the judicial year, CoE Doc. SdC (2002) 6, pp. 8-12

Wilner, Alexandre S., 'Targeted Killings in Afghanistan: Measuring Coercion and Deterrence in Counterterrorism and Counterinsurgency', in: 33 *Studies in Conflict and Terrorism* (2010), pp. 307-329 [*Stud. Confl. Terror.*]

Wilson, William, *Central Issues in Criminal Theory*, Oxford 2002 [Hart]

Wingfield, Thomas C., 'Taking Aim at Regime Estates: Assassination, Tyrannicide, and the Clancy Doctrine', in: 22 *Maryland Journal of International Law and Trade* (1998), pp. 287-317 [*Md. J. Int'l L. & Trade*]

Wippman, David, 'Do New Wars call for New Laws? Introduction', in: David Wippman/ Matthew Evangelista (eds.), *New Wars, New Laws? Applying the Laws of War in 21st Century Conflicts*, Ardsley, N.Y. 2005, pp. 1-28 [Transnational Pub.]

Witenberg, Joseph-Charles, 'La théorie des preuves devant les juridictions internationales', in: 56 *Recueil des Cours de l'Academie de Droit International de la Haye* (1936-III), pp. 1-105 [*RdC*]

Witzstrock, Heike, *Der polizeiliche Todesschuß*, Frankfurt am Main 2001 [Lang]

Wolf, Joachim, 'Zurechnungsfragen bei Handlungen von Privatpersonen', in: 45 *Zeitschrift für ausländisches öffentliches Recht und Völkerrecht* (1985), pp. 232-264 [*ZaöRV*]

Wolf, Joachim, *Die Haftung der Staaten für Privatpersonen nach Völkerrecht*, Berlin 1997 [Duncker & Humblot]

Wolfrum, Rüdiger, 'Enforcement of International Humanitarian Law', in: Dieter Fleck (ed.), *The Handbook of Humanitarian Law in Armed Conflicts*, Oxford 1999, pp. 517-550

Wössner, Marion, *Die Notwehr und ihre Einschränkung in Deutschland und in den USA*, Berlin 2006 [Duncker & Humblot]

Würkner-Theis, Gerold, *Fernverlegte Minen und humanitäres Völkerrecht*, Frankfurt am Main 1990 [Lang]

Yoo, John C., 'The Status of Soldiers and Terrorists under the Geneva Conventions', in: 3 *Chinese Journal of International Law* (2004), pp. 135-150 [*Chin. J. Int'l L.*]

Zacklin, Ralph, 'Beyond Kosovo: The United Nations and Humanitarian Intervention', in: Lal Chand Vohrah *et al.* (eds.), *Man's Inhu-*

manity to Man – Essays on International Law in Honour of Antonio Cassese, The Hague 2003, pp. 935-951 [Kluwer]

Zahar, Marie-Joëlle, 'Protégés, Clients, Cannon Fodder: Civil-Militia Relations in Internal Conflicts', in: Simon Chesterman (ed.), *Civilians in War*, Boulder, Colorado 2001, pp. 43-65

Zengel, Patricia, 'Assassination and the Law of Armed Conflict', in: 134 *Military Law Review* (1991), pp. 123-155 [*Mil. L. Rev.*]

Zorgbibe, Charles, 'Pour une réaffirmation du droit humanitaire des conflicts armés internes', in: 97 *Journal du droit international* (1970), pp. 658-683 [*J. dr. int'l*]

Zussman, Asaf/ Zussman, Noam, *Targeted Killings: Evaluating the Effectiveness of a Counterterrorism Policy*, Jerusalem 2005 [Bank of Israel, Research Department]

B. Cases

I. International Tribunals and Human Rights Bodies

African Commission on Human and Peoples' Rights, *Amnesty International, Comité Loosli Bachelard, Lawyers Committee for Human Rights, Association of Members of the Episcopal conference of East Africa v. Sudan*, Communications 48/90, 50/91, 52/91 and 89/93, in: 13th *Activity Report* (1999-2000), Annex V, pp. 124-138

African Commission on Human and Peoples' Rights, *Commission Nationale des Droits de l'Homme et des Libertés de la Federation Nationale des Unions de Jeunes Avocats de France v. Chad*, Communication 74/92 (1995), in: 9th *Activity Report* (1995-1996), Annex VIII

African Commission on Human and Peoples' Rights, *Constitutional Rights Project, Civil Liberties Organisation and Media Rights Agenda v. Nigeria*, Communications 140/94, 141/94, 145/95, in: 13th *Activity Report* (1999-2000), Annex V, pp. 54-62

African Commission on Human and Peoples' Rights, *Forum of Conscience v. Sierra Leone*, Communication 223/98, in: 14th *Activity Report* (2000-2001), Annex V, pp. 43-46

African Commission on Human and Peoples' Rights, *Free Legal Assistance Group, Lawyers' Committee for human Rights, Union Interafricaine des Droits de l'Homme, Les Témoins de Jehova v.*

Zaire, Communications 25/89, 47/90, 56/91 and 100/93, in: 9th Activity Report (1995-1996), Annex VIII

African Commission on Human and Peoples' Rights, *International Pen, Constitutional Rights Project, Interights on behalf of Ken Saro-Wiwa Jr. and Civil Liberties Organisation v. Nigeria*, Communications 137/94, 139/94, 154/96 and 161/97, in: 12th *Activity Report* (1998-1999), Annex V, pp. 62-73

African Commission on Human and Peoples' Rights, *Kazeem Aminu v. Nigeria*, Communications 205/97, in: 13th *Activity Report* (1999-2000), Annex V, pp. 112-116

African Commission on Human and Peoples' Rights, *Krischna Achutan (on behalf of Aleke Banda), Amnesty International on behalf of Orton and Vera Chirwa and Amnesty International on behalf of Orton and Vera Chirwa v. Malawi*, Communications 64/92, 68/ 92 and 78/92, in: 8th *Activity Report* (1994-1995), Annex VI (No. 11)

African Commission on Human and Peoples' Rights, *Malawi African Association, Amnesty International, Ms. Sarr Diop, Union Interafricaine des Droits de l'Homme and RADDHO, Collectif des Veuves et Ayants-droit, Association Mauritanienne des Droits de L'Homme v. Islamic Republic of Mauritania*, Communications 54/91, 61/91, 98/93, 164/97-196/97 and 210/98, in: 13th *Activity Report* (1999-2000), Annex V, pp. 138-162

African Commission on Human and Peoples' Rights, *Media Rights Agenda, Constitutional Rights Project, Media Rights Agenda and Constitutional Rights Project v. Nigeria*, Communications 105/ 93, 128/94, 130/94 and 1523/96, in: 12th *Activity Report* (1998-1999), Annex V, pp. 52-61

African Commission on Human and Peoples' Rights, *Mouvement Burkinabé des Droits de l'Homme et des Peuples v. Burkina Faso*, Communication 204/97, in: 14th *Activity Report* (2000-2001), Annex V, pp. 78-86

African Commission on Human and Peoples' Rights, *Organisation Mondiale Contre la Torture and Association Internationale des Juristes Democrates, Commission Internationale des Juristes (CIJ), Union Interafricaine des Droit de l'Homme v. Rwanda*, Communications 27/89, 46/91, 49/91 and 99/93, in: 10th *Activity Report* (1996-1997), Annex X, pp. 49-52

African Commission on Human and Peoples' Rights, *Rencontre Africaine pour la Defence des Droits de l'Homme v. Zambia*, Communication 71/92, in 10th Activity Report (1996-1997), Annex V, pp. 60-63

African Commission on Human and Peoples' Rights, *Resolution Urging States to envisage a Moratorium on the Death Penalty*, adopted at the 26th Ordinary Session in Kigali, Rwanda, November 1-15, 1999, DOC/OS (XXVI) INF.19, in: 13th *Activity Report* (1999-2000), Annex IV, pp. 45-46

African Commission on Human and Peoples' Rights, *Sir Dawda K Jawara v. Gambia*, Communications 147/95 and 149/96, in: 13th *Activity Report* (1999-2000), Annex V, pp. 96-107

African Commission on Human and Peoples' Rights, *The Social and Economic Rights Action Center and the Center for Economic and Social Rights v. Nigeria*, Communication 155/96, in: 15th *Activity Report* (2001-2002), Annex V, pp. 31-44

European Commission of Human Rights, *Association X v. United Kingdom*, Appl. No. 7154/75, Decision of July 12, 1978, in: 14 *Decisions and Reports* (1979), pp. 31-39 [*D.R.*]

European Commission of Human Rights, *Cyprus v. Turkey*, Appl. No. 8007/77, Decision of July 10, 1978, in: 13 *Decisions and Reports* (1978), pp. 85-230 [*D.R.*]

European Commission of Human Rights, *Cyprus v. Turkey*, Appl. No. 8007/77, Report of October 4, 1983, in: 72 *Decisions and Reports* (1992), pp. 5-117 [*D.R.*]

European Commission of Human Rights, *Cyprus v. Turkey*, Appl. Nos. 6780/74 and 6950/75, Decision of May 26, 1975, in: 2 *Decisions and Reports* (1975), pp. 125-151 [*D.R.*]

European Commission of Human Rights, *Ilse Hess v. United Kingdom*, Appl. No. 6231/73, Decision of May 28, 1975, in: 2 *Decisions and Reports* (1975), pp. 72-76 [*D.R.*]

European Commission of Human Rights, *John Kelly v. United Kingdom*, Appl. No. 17579/90, Decision of January 13, 1993, in: 74 *Decisions and Reports* (1984), pp. 139-155 [*D.R.*]

European Commission of Human Rights, *Kathleen Stewart v. United Kingdom*, Appl. No. 10044/82, Decision of July 10, 1984, in: 39 *Decisions and Reports* (1984), pp. 162-185 [*D.R.*]

European Commission of Human Rights, *Koçeri Kurt v. Turkey*, Appl. No. 24276/94, Report of December 5, 1996, *ECHR* 1998-III, pp. 1203-1232

European Commission of Human Rights, *Laurence Dujardin and Others v. France*, Appl. No. 16734/90, Decision of September 2, 1991, in: 72 *Decisions and Reports* (1992), pp. 236-244 [*D.R.*]

European Commission of Human Rights, *M.D. v. Turkey*, Appl. No. 28518/95, Decision of June 30, 1997 (unreported, accessible via the HUDOC database on <http://www.echr.coe.int/echr>, last visited February 22, 2008)

European Commission of Human Rights, *McCann, Farrel and Savage v. United Kingdom*, Appl. No. 18984/91, Opinion of March 4, 1994, Series A, No. 324 (Annex), pp. 74-92

European Commission of Human Rights, *Mrs W. v. Ireland*, Appl. No. 9360/81, Decision of February 28, 1983, in: 32 *Decisions and Reports* (1983), pp. 211-219 [*D.R.*]

European Commission of Human Rights, *Mrs W. v. United Kingdom*, Appl. No. 9348/81, Decision of February 28, 1983, in: 32 *Decisions and Reports* (1983), pp. 190-210 [*D.R.*]

European Commission of Human Rights, *Stocké v. Germany*, Case No. 11755/85, Report of October 12, 1989, Series A, No. 199, Annex, pp 21-32

European Commission of Human Rights, *The Taylor, Crampton, Gibson and King Families v. United Kingdom*, Appl. No. 23412/94, Decision of August 30, 1994, in: 79-A *Decisions and Reports* (1994), pp. 127-137 [*D.R.*]

European Commission of Human Rights, *Wolfgram (W.) v. Germany*, Appl. No. 11257/84, Decision of October 6, 1986, in: 49 *Decisions and Reports* (1986), pp. 213-220 [*D.R.*]

European Commission of Human Rights, *X and Y v. United Kingdom* Appl. Nos. 7126/75 and 7573/76, Decision of March 9, 1977 (unpublished), in: 1 *Digest of Strasbourg Case Law relating to the European Convention on Human Rights*, para. 2.2.3 (p. 87)

European Commission of Human Rights, *X v. Belgium*, Appl. No. 2758/66, Decision of May 21, 1969, in: 12 *Yearbook of the European Convention on Human Rights* (1969), pp. 174-193 [*Yb. Eur. Conv. Hum. Rts.*]

European Court of Human Rights, *Airey v. Ireland*, Appl. No. 6289/73, Judgment of October 9, 1979, Series A, No. 32

European Court of Human Rights, *Akdeniz v. Turkey*, Appl. No. 25165/94, Judgment of May 31, 2005, *ECHR* 2005 (not yet published, accessible via the HUDOC database on <http://www.echr.coe.int/echr>, last visited February 21, 2008)

European Court of Human Rights, *Andronicou and Constantinou v. Cyprus*, Appl. No. 25052/94, Judgment of October 9, 1997, *ECHR* 1997-VI, pp. 2059-2151

European Court of Human Rights, *Artico v. Italy*, Appl. No. 6694/74, Judgment of May 13, 1980, Series A, No. 37

European Court of Human Rights, *Avşar v. Turkey*, Appl. No. 25657/94, Judgment of July 10, 2001, *ECHR* 2001-VII, pp. 83-151

European Court of Human Rights, *Aytekin v. Turkey*, Appl. No. 22880/93, Judgment of September 3, 1998, *ECHR* 1998-VII, pp. 2807-2843

European Court of Human Rights, *Banković and others v. Belgium and others*, Appl. No. 52207/99, Decision 2001 (Grand Chamber) of December 12, 2001, *ECHR* 2001-XII, pp. 333-390

European Court of Human Rights, *Brady v. United Kingdom*, Appl. No. 55151/00, Decision of April 3, 2001 (unreported, accessible via the HUDOC database on <http://www.echr.coe.int/echr>, last visited February 22, 2008)

European Court of Human Rights, *Çakıcı v. Turkey*, Appl. No. 23657/94, Judgment (Grand Chamber) of July 8, 1999, *ECHR* 1999-IV, pp. 583-730

European Court of Human Rights, *Case "relating to certain aspects of the laws on the use of languages in education in Belgium"*, Appl. Nos. 1474/62; 1677/62; 1691/62; 1769/63; 1994/63 and 2126/64, Judgment of July 23, 1968, Series A, No. 6

European Court of Human Rights, *Cemil Kiliç v. Turkey*, Appl. No. 22492/93, Judgment of March 28, 2000, *ECHR* 2000-III, pp. 75-147

European Court of Human Rights, *Cyprus v. Turkey*, Appl. No. 25781/94, Judgement (Grand Chamber) of May 10, 2001, *ECHR* 2001-IV, pp. 1-477

European Court of Human Rights, *Drozd and Janousek v. France and Spain*, Appl. No. 12747/87, Judgment of June 26, 1992, Series A, No. 240

European Court of Human Rights, *Dudgeon v. United Kingdom*, Appl. No. 7525/76, Judgment of October 22, 1981, Series A, No. 45

European Court of Human Rights, *Engel and others v. Netherlands (Just Satisfaction)*, Appl. Nos. 5100/71; 5101/71; 5102/71; 5354/72 and 5370/72, Judgment of November 23, 1976, Series A, No. 22

European Court of Human Rights, *Engel and others v. Netherlands (Merits)*, Appl. Nos. 5100/71; 5101/71; 5102/71; 5354/72 and 5370/72, Judgment of June 8, 1976, Series A, No. 22

European Court of Human Rights, *Ergi v. Turkey*, Appl. No. 23818/94, Judgment of July 28, 1998, *ECHR* 1998-IV, pp. 1751-1806

European Court of Human Rights, *Ertak v. Turkey*, Appl. No. 20764/92, Judgment of May 9, 2000, *ECHR* 2000-V, pp. 157-241

European Court of Human Rights, *Golder v. United Kingdom*, Appl. No. 4451/70, Judgment of February 21, 1975, Series A, No. 18

European Court of Human Rights, *Gül v. Turkey (Merits)*, Appl. No. 22676/93, Judgment of December 14, 2000 (unreported, accessible via the HUDOC database on <http://www.echr.coe.int/echr >, last visited February 22, 2008)

European Court of Human Rights, *Güleç v. Turkey*, Appl. No. 21593/93, Judgment of July 27, 1998, *ECHR* 1998-IV, pp. 1698-1750

European Court of Human Rights, *Handyside v. United Kingdom*, Appl. No. 5493/72, Judgment of December 7, 1976, Series A, No. 24

European Court of Human Rights, *Hugh Jordan v. United Kingdom*, Appl. No. 24746/94, Judgment of May 4, 2001, *ECHR* 2001-III, pp. 537-540 (Extracts)

European Court of Human Rights, *Ilaşcu and others v. Moldova and the Russian Federation (Merits)*, Appl. No. 48787/99, Judgment of July 8, 2004, *ECHR* 2004-VII, pp. 1-348

European Court of Human Rights, *İlhan v. Turkey*, Appl. No. 22277/93, Judgment (Grand Chamber) of June 27, 2000, *ECHR* 2000-VII, pp. 267-363

European Court of Human Rights, *Ireland v. United Kingdom*, Appl. No. 5310/71, Judgment of January 18, 1978, Series A, No. 25

European Court of Human Rights, *Isayeva v. Russia*, Appl. No. 57950/00, Judgment of February 24, 2005, *ECHR* 2005 (not yet published, accessible via the HUDOC database on <http://www.echr.coe.int/echr>, last visited February 21, 2008)

European Court of Human Rights, *Isayeva, Yusupova and Bazayeva v. Russia*, Appl. Nos. 57947/00, 57948/00 and 57949/00, Judgment of February 24, 2005, *ECHR* 2005 (not yet published, accessible via the HUDOC database on <http://www.echr.coe.int/echr>, last visited February 21, 2008)

European Court of Human Rights, *Issa v. Turkey (Admissibility)*, Appl. No. 31821/96, Decision of May 30, 2000 (unreported, accessible via the HUDOC database on <http://www.echr.coe.int/echr>, last visited February 28, 2008)

European Court of Human Rights, *Issa v. Turkey (Merits)*, Appl. No. 31821/96, Judgment of November 16, 2004, reprinted in: 41 *European Human Rights Reports* (2005), pp. 567-591 [*Eur. Hum. Rts. Rep.*]

European Court of Human Rights, *Koçeri Kurt v. Turkey*, Appl. No. 24276/94, Judgment of May 25, 1998, *ECHR* 1998-III, pp. 1152-1202

European Court of Human Rights, *König v. Germany*, Appl. No. 6232/ 73, Judgment of June 28, 1978, Series A, No. 27

European Court of Human Rights, *Lala v. Netherlands*, Appl. No. 14861/89, Judgment of September 22, 1994, Series A, No. 297-A

European Court of Human Rights, *Loizidou v. Turkey (Merits)*, Appl. No. 15318/89, Judgment (Grand Chamber) of December 18, 1996, *ECHR* 1996-VI, No. 26, pp. 2216-2259

European Court of Human Rights, *Loizidou v. Turkey (Preliminary Objections)*, Appl. No. 15318/89, Judgment of March 23, 1995, Series A, No. 310

European Court of Human Rights, *Mahmut Kaya v. Turkey*, Appl. No. 22535/93, Judgment of March 28, 2000, *ECHR* 2000-III, pp. 149-240

European Court of Human Rights, *Marckx v. Belgium*, Appl. No. 6833 /74, Judgment of June 13, 1979, Series A, No. 31

European Court of Human Rights, *McCann, Farrell and Savage v. United Kingdom*, Appl. No. 18984/91, Judgment (Grand Chamber) of September 27, 1995, Series A, No. 324

European Court of Human Rights, *McKerr v. United Kingdom*, Appl. No. 28883/95, Judgment of May 4, 2001, *ECHR* 2001-III, pp. 475-619

European Court of Human Rights, *Mehmet Kaya v. Turkey*, Appl. No. 22729/93, Judgment of February 19, 1998, *ECHR* 1998-I, pp. 297-361

European Court of Human Rights, *Mikheyev v. Russia*, Appl. No. 77617/01, Judgment of January 26, 2006, *ECHR* 2006 (not yet published, accessible via the HUDOC database on <http://www.echr.coe.int/echr>, last visited February 21, 2008)

European Court of Human Rights, *Nachova and others v. Bulgaria*, Appl. Nos. 43577/98 and 43579/98, Judgment of February 26, 2004 (unreported, accessible via the HUDOC database on <http://www.echr.coe.int/echr>, last visited February 22, 2008)

European Court of Human Rights, *Nachova and others v. Bulgaria*, Appl. Nos. 43577/98 and 43579/98, Judgment (Grand Chamber) of July 6, 2005, *ECHR* 2005-VII (not yet published, accessible via the HUDOC database on <http://www.echr.coe.int/echr>, last visited February 21, 2008)

European Court of Human Rights, *Nesibe Haran v. Turkey*, Appl. No. 28299/95, Judgment of October 6, 2005, *ECHR* 2005 (not yet published, accessible via the HUDOC database on <http://www.echr.coe.int/echr>, last visited February 21, 2008)

European Court of Human Rights, *Öcalan v. Turkey (Merits and Just Satisfaction)*, Appl. No. 46221/99, Judgment of March 12, 2003, reprinted in: 37 *European Human Rights Reports* (2003), pp. 238-319 [*Eur. Hum. Rts. Rep.*]

European Court of Human Rights, *Öcalan v. Turkey (Merits and Just Satisfaction)*, Appl. No. 46221/99, Judgment (Grand Chamber) of May 12, 2005, *ECHR* 2005-IV, pp. 47-211

European Court of Human Rights, *Oğur v. Turkey*, Appl. No. 21594/93, Judgment (Grand Chamber) of May 20, 1999, *ECHR* 1999-III, pp. 519-634

European Court of Human Rights, *Paul and Audrey Edwards v. United Kingdom*, Appl. No. 46477/99, Judgment of March 14, 2002, *ECHR* 2002-II, pp. 137-221

European Court of Human Rights, *Ribitsch v. Austria*, Appl. No. 18896/91, Judgment of December 4, 1995, Series A, No. 336

European Court of Human Rights, *Selmouni v. France*, Appl. No. 25803/94, Judgment (Grand Chamber) of July 28, 1999, *ECHR* 1999-V, pp. 149-256

European Court of Human Rights, *Soering v. United Kingdom*, Appl. No. 14038/88, Judgment of July 7, 1989, Series A, No. 161

European Court of Human Rights, *Stocké v. Germany*, Appl. No. 11755/85, Judgment of March 19, 1991, Series A, No. 199

European Court of Human Rights, *Streletz, Keßler and Krenz v. Germany*, Appl. Nos. 34044/96, 35532/97, 44801/98, Judgment of March 22, 2001, *ECHR* 2001-II, pp. 351-461

European Court of Human Rights, *Sunday Times v. United Kingdom*, Appl. No. 6538/74, Judgment of April 26, 1979, Series A, No. 30

European Court of Human Rights, *Timurtaş v. Turkey*, Appl. No. 23531/94, Judgment of June 13, 2000, *ECHR* 2000-VI, pp. 303-395

European Court of Human Rights, *Tomasi v. France*, Appl. No. 12850/87, Judgment of August 27, 1992, Series A, No. 241-A

European Court of Human Rights, *Tyrer v. United Kingdom*, Appl. No. 5856/72, Judgment of April 25, 1978, Series A, No. 26

European Court of Human Rights, *Yaşa v. Turkey*, Appl. No. 22495/93, Judgment of September 2, 1998, 1998-VI, pp. 2411-2463

Human Rights Committee, CCPR General Comment No. 03, *Implementation at the National Level (Article 2)*, 13th Session, July 29, 1981, reprinted in: Compilation of General Comments and General Recommendations adopted by Human Rights Treaty Bodies, U.N. Doc. HRI\GEN\1\Rev.7 (May 12, 2004), p. 125

Human Rights Committee, CCPR General Comment No. 05, *Derogations (Article 4)*, 13th Session, July 28, 1981, reprinted in: Compilation of General Comments and General Recommendations adopted by Human Rights Treaty Bodies, U.N. Doc. HRI\GEN\1\Rev.7 (May 12, 2004), pp. 127-128

Human Rights Committee, CCPR General Comment No. 06, *The Right to Life (Article 6)*, 16th Session, April 30, 1982, reprinted in: Compilation of General Comments and General Recommendations adopted by Human Rights Treaty Bodies, U.N. Doc. HRI\GEN\1\Rev.7 (May 12, 2004), pp. 128-129

Human Rights Committee, CCPR General Comment No. 07, *Torture or cruel, inhuman or degrading Treatment or Punishment (Article 7)*, 16th Session, May 30, 1982, reprinted in: Compilation of General Comments and General Recommendations adopted by Human Rights Treaty Bodies, U.N. Doc. HRI\GEN\1\Rev.7 (May 12, 2004), pp. 129-130

Human Rights Committee, CCPR General Comment No. 14, *Nuclear Weapons and the Right to Life (Article 6)*, 23rd Session, November 9, 1984, reprinted in: Compilation of General Comments and General Recommendations adopted by Human Rights Treaty Bodies, U.N. Doc. HRI\GEN\1\Rev.7 (May 12, 2004), p. 139

Human Rights Committee, CCPR General Comment No. 16, *The Right to Respect of Privacy, Family, Home and Correspondence, and Protection of Honour and Reputation (Article 17)*, 32nd Session, April 8, 1988, reprinted in: Compilation of General Comments and General Recommendations adopted by Human Rights Treaty Bodies, U.N. Doc. HRI\GEN\1\Rev.7 (May 12, 2004), pp. 142-144

Human Rights Committee, CCPR General Comment No. 23, *Rights of Minorities (Article 27)*, 50th Session, April 8, 1994, reprinted in: Compilation of General Comments and General Recommendations adopted by Human Rights Treaty Bodies, U.N. Doc. HRI\GEN\1\Rev.7 (May 12, 2004), pp. 158-161

Human Rights Committee, CCPR General Comment No. 24, *Issues relating to Reservations made upon Ratification or Accession to the Covenant or the Optional Protocols thereto, or in Relation to Declarations under Article 41 of the Covenant*, 52nd Session, November 4, 1994, UN Doc. CCPR/C/21/Rev.1/Add.6 (1994), reprinted in: Compilation of General Comments and General Recommendations adopted by Human Rights Treaty Bodies, U.N. Doc. HRI\GEN\1\Rev.7 (May 12, 2004), pp. 161-167

Human Rights Committee, CCPR General Comment No. 29, *Derogations during States of Emergency (Article 4)*, 72nd Session, August 31, 2001, UN Doc. CCPR/C/21/Rev.1/Add.11 (2001), reprinted in: Compilation of General Comments and General Recommendations adopted by Human Rights Treaty Bodies, U.N. Doc. HRI\GEN\1\Rev.7 (May 12, 2004), pp. 184-191

Human Rights Committee, CCPR General Comment No. 31, *The Nature of the General Legal Obligation Imposed on State Parties to the Covenant*, May 26, 2004, UN Doc. CCPR/C/21/Rev.1/

Add.13, reprinted in: Compilation of General Comments and General Recommendations adopted by Human Rights Treaty Bodies, U.N. Doc. HRI\GEN\1\Rev.7 (May 12, 2004), pp. 192-197

Human Rights Committee, *Concluding Observations on Cyprus*, UN Doc. CCPR/C/79/Add.88 (April 6, 1998)

Human Rights Committee, *Concluding Observations on Iraq*, UN Doc. CCPR/C/79/Add.84 (November 19, 1997)

Human Rights Committee, *Concluding Observations on Israel*, UN Doc. CCPR/CO/78/ISR (August 21, 2003)

Human Rights Committee, *Concluding Observations on Israel*, UN Doc. CCPR/C/79/Add.93 (August 18, 1998)

Human Rights Committee, *Concluding Observations on Peru*, UN Doc. CCPR/C/79/Add.8 (September 25, 1992)

Human Rights Committee, *Concluding Observations on the Federal Republic of Yugoslavia (Serbia and Montenegro)*, UN Doc. CCPR/C/79/Add.16 (December 28, 1992)

Human Rights Committee, *Concluding Observations on the Islamic Republic of Iran*, UN Doc. CCPR/C/79/Add.25 (August 3, 1995)

Human Rights Committee, *Concluding Observations on the Libyan Arab Jamahiriya*, UN Doc. CCPR/C/79/Add.101 (November 6, 1998)

Human Rights Committee, *Concluding Observations on the Netherlands*, U.N. Doc. CCPR/CO/72/NET/Add.1 (April 29, 2003)

Human Rights Committee, *Concluding Observations on the Russian Federation*, UN Doc. CCPR/C/79/Add.54 (July 26, 1995)

Human Rights Committee, *Concluding Observations on Yemen*, UN Doc. CCPR/CO/75/YEM (July 26, 2002)

Human Rights Committee, *Second Periodic Report of the State of Israel under the International Covenant on Civil and Political Rights*, UN Doc. CCPR/C/ISR/2001/2 (December 4, 2001)

Human Rights Committee, Summary Record of the 1675th Meeting (Israel), July 21, 1998, UN Doc. CCPR/C/SR.1675

Human Rights Committee, *Third Periodic Report of United States to Human Rights Committee*, U.N. Doc. CCPR/C/USA/3 (November 28, 2005)

Human Rights Committee, *Ann Maria Garcia Lanza de Netto v. Uruguay*, Communication No. 8/1977, UN Doc. CCPR/C/9/D/8/1977 (April 3, 1980)

Human Rights Committee, *C. v. Australia*, Communication No. 900/1999, UN Doc. CCPR/C/76/D/900/1999 (October 28, 2002)

Human Rights Committee, *Carlton Reid v. Jamaica*, Communication No. 250/1987, UN Doc. CCPR/C/39/D/250/1987 (August 21, 1990)

Human Rights Committee, *Daniel Monguya Mbenge v. Zaire*, Communication No. 16/1977, UN Doc. CCPR/C/18/D/16/1977 (March 25, 1983)

Human Rights Committee, *Delia Saldías de López, on behalf of her husband, Sergio Rubén López Burgos v. Uruguay*, Communication No. 52/1979, U.N. Doc. CCPR/C/13/D/52/1979 (July 29, 1981)

Human Rights Committee, *Eduardo Bleier v. Uruguay*, Communication No. 30/1978, UN Doc. CCPR/C/15/D/30/1978 (March 29, 1982)

Human Rights Committee, *Gordon C. Van Duzen v. Canada*, Communication No. 50/1979, UN Doc. CCPR/C/15/D/50/1979 (April 7, 1982)

Human Rights Committee, *Guillermo Ignacio Dermit Barbato and Hugo Haroldo Dermit Barbato v. Uruguay*, Communication No. 84/1981, UN Doc. CCPR/C/17/D/84/1981 (October 21, 1982)

Human Rights Committee, *Herrera Rubio v. Colombia*, Communication No. 161/1983, UN Doc. CCPR/C/31/D/161/1983 (November 2, 1987)

Human Rights Committee, *J. B. et al. (Alberta Union of Provincial Employees) v. Canada*, Communication No. 118/1982, U.N. Doc. CCPR/C/28/D/118/1982 (July 18, 1986)

Human Rights Committee, *Lilian Celiberti de Casariego v. Uruguay*, Communication No. 56/1979, UN Doc. CCPR/C/13/D/56/1979 (July 29, 1981)

Human Rights Committee, *Maria Fanny Suárez de Guerrero v. Colombia ("Camargo Case")*, Communication No. 45/1979, UN Doc. CCPR/C/15/D/45/1979 (March 31, 1982)

Human Rights Committee, *William Eduardo Delgado Páez v. Colombia*, Communication No. 195/1985, UN Doc. CCPR/C/39/D/195/1985 (August 23, 1990)

Inter-American Commission on Human Rights, *Areas in which Steps need to be taken towards full Observance of the Human Rights set forth in the American Declaration of the Rights and Duties of Man and the American Convention on Human Rights*, in: *Annual Report* (1986-1987), OEA/Ser.L/V/II.71, Doc. 9 Rev. 1 (September 22, 1987)

Inter-American Commission on Human Rights, *Armando Alejandre Jr., Carlos Costa, Mario de la Peña, and Pablo Morales v. Cuba ("Brothers to the Rescue")*, Case 11.589, Report No. 86/99 of September 29, 1999, in: *Annual Report* (1999), OEA/Ser.L/V/II.106 Doc. 6 rev. (April 13, 1999), Chapter III

Inter-American Commission on Human Rights, *Arturo Ribón Avilán v. Colombia*, Case 11.142, Report No. 26/97 of September 30, 1997, in: *Annual Report* (1997), OEA/Ser.L/V/II.98, Doc. 6 rev. (April 13, 1998), Chapter III

Inter-American Commission on Human Rights, *Bolivia ("Community of Caracoles")*, Case 7481, Report No. 30/82 of March 8, 1982, in: *Annual Report* (1981-1982), OAS Doc. OEA/Ser.L/V/II.57, Doc. 6, rev. 1 (September 20, 1982), pp. 36-40

Inter-American Commission on Human Rights, *Coard et al. v. United States (US military intervention in Grenada)*, Case 10.951, Report No. 109/99 (September 29, 1999), in: *Annual Report* (1999), OEA/Ser.L/V/II.106, Doc. 6 rev. (April 13, 1999), Chapter III

Inter-American Commission on Human Rights, *Disabled Peoples' International v. United States (US military intervention in Grenada, Richmond Hill Insane Asylum)*, Case 9213, Report No. 3/96 (March 1, 1996), in: *Annual Report* (1995), OEA/Ser.L/V/ II.91, Doc. 7 (February 28, 1996), Chapter III

Inter-American Commission on Human Rights, *Hugo Bustíos Saavedra v. Perú*, Case 10.548, Report No. 38/97 of October 16, 1997, in: *Annual Report* (1997), OEA/Ser.L/V/II.98, Doc. 6 rev. (April 13, 1998), Chapter III

Inter-American Commission on Human Rights, *Juan Carlos Abella v. Argentina ("La Tablada")*, Case 11.137, Report No. 55/97 of November 18, 1997, in: *Annual Report* (1997), OEA/Ser.L/V/II.98 Doc. 6 rev. (April 13, 1998), Chapter III

Inter-American Commission on Human Rights, *Masacre Las Hojas v. El Salvador*, Case 10.287, Report No. 26/92 of September 24, 1992, in: *Annual Report* (1992-93), OEA/Ser.L/V/II.83 Doc. 14, Corr. 1 (March 12, 1993), Chapter III

Inter-American Commission on Human Rights, *Monsignor Oscar Arnulfo Romero y Galdámez v. El Salvador*, Case 11.481, Report No. 37/00 of April 13, 2000, in: *Annual Report* (1999), OEA/Ser. L/V/II.106 Doc. 6 rev. (April 13, 1999)

Inter-American Commission on Human Rights, *Report on Terrorism and Human Rights*, OEA/Ser.L/V/II.116 Doc. 5 rev. 1 corr. (October 22, 2002)

Inter-American Commission on Human Rights, *Report on the Human Rights Situation in Chile*, OEA/Ser.L/V/II.66, Doc. 17 (September 27, 1985)

Inter-American Commission on Human Rights, *Riofrío Massacre (Colombia)*, Case 11.654, Report No. 62/01 of April 6, 2001, in: *Annual Report* (2001), OEA/Ser./L/V/II.111 Doc. 20 rev. (April 16, 2001)

Inter-American Commission on Human Rights, *Salas et al. v. United States (US military intervention in Panama)*, Case 10.573, Report No. 31/93 (October 14, 1993), in: *Annual Report* (1993), OEA/ Ser.L/V.85 Doc. 9 rev. (February 11, 1994), Chapter III

Inter-American Commission on Human Rights, *Status of Human Rights in Peru*, in: *Annual Report* (1993), OEA/Ser.L/V.85, Doc. 9 rev. (February 11, 1994), Chapter IV

Inter-American Commission on Human Rights, *Third Report on the Human Rights Situation in Colombia*, OEA/Ser.L/V/II.102, Doc. 9 Rev. 1 (February 26, 1999)

Inter-American Court of Human Rights, *"Other treaties" subject to the advisory jurisdiction of the Court (Art. 64 American Convention on Human Rights)*, Advisory Opinion No. OC-1/81 of September 24, 1982, Series A, No. 1

Inter-American Court of Human Rights, *Angel Manfredo Velásquez-Rodríguez v. Honduras*, Judgment of July 29, 1988, Series C, No. 4

Inter-American Court of Human Rights, *Asok Gangaram-Panday v. Suriname*, Judgment of January 21, 1994, Series C, No. 16

Inter-American Court of Human Rights, *Castillo-Páez v. Perú*, Judgment of November 3, 1997, Series C, No. 34

Inter-American Court of Human Rights, *Compulsory Membership in an Association Prescribed by Law for the Practice of Journalism (Arts. 13 and 29 American Convention on Human Rights)*, Advisory Opinion OC-5/85 of November 13, 1985, Series A, No. 5

Inter-American Court of Human Rights, *Efraín Bámaca-Velásquez v. Guatemala*, Judgment of November 25, 2000, Series C, No. 70

Inter-American Court of Human Rights, *Enforceability of the Right to Reply or Correction (Arts. 14(1), 1(1) and 2 American Convention on Human Rights)*, Advisory Opinion No. OC-7/86 of August 29, 1986, Series A, No. 7

Inter-American Court of Human Rights, *Fairén-Garbi and Solís-Corrales v. Honduras*, Judgment of March 15, 1989, Series C, No. 6

Inter-American Court of Human Rights, *Godínez-Cruz v. Honduras*, Judgment of January 20, 1989, Series C, No. 5

Inter-American Court of Human Rights, *Habeas corpus in Emergency Situations (Arts. 27(2), 25(1) and 7(6) American Convention on Human Rights)*, Advisory Opinion OC-8/87 of January 30, 1987, Series A, No. 8

Inter-American Court of Human Rights, *Interpretation of the American Declaration of the Rights and Duties of Man within the Framework of Article 64 of the American Convention on Human Rights.* Advisory Opinion No. OC-10/89 of July 14, 1989, Series A, No. 10

Inter-American Court of Human Rights, *Juan Humberto Sánchez v. Honduras*, Judgment of June 7, 2003, Series C, No. 99

Inter-American Court of Human Rights, *Las Palmeras v. Colombia (Preliminary Objections)*, Judgment of February 4, 2000, Series C, No. 67

Inter-American Court of Human Rights, *Proposed Amendments of the Naturalization Provisions of the Constitution of Costa Rica*, Advisory Opinion OC-4/84 of January 19, 1984, Series A, No. 4

Inter-American Court of Human Rights, *Restrictions to the Death Penalty (Arts. 4(2) and 4(4) American Convention on Human Rights)*, Advisory Opinion No. OC-3/83 of September 8, 1983, Series A, No. 3

Inter-American Court of Human Rights, *The Effect of Reservations on the Entry into Force of the American Convention on Human Rights (Arts. 74 and 75)*, Advisory Opinion OC-2/82 of September 24, 1982, Series A, No. 2

Inter-American Court of Human Rights, *The Right to Information on Consular Assistance in the Framework of the Guarantees of the due Process of Law*, Advisory Opinion OC-16/99 of October 1, 1999, Series A, No. 16

Inter-American Court of Human Rights, *The Word "Laws" in Article 30 of the American Convention on Human Rights*, Advisory Opinion OC-6/86 of May 9, 1986, Series A, No. 6

Inter-American Court of Human Rights, *Víctor Neira-Alegría, Edgar Zenteno-Escobar and William Zenteno-Escobar (El Frontón) v. Peru*, Judgment of January 19, 1995, Series C, No. 20

Inter-American Court of Human Rights, *Villagrán-Morales et al. v. Guatemala ("Street Children")* Judgment of November 19, 1999, Series C, No. 63

Inter-American Court of Human Rights, *Viviana Gallardo et al.*, Advisory Opinion No. G 101/81, Decision of November 13, 1981, Series A, No. G 101/81

International Court of Justice, *Anglo-Iranian Oil Co., United Kingdom v. Iran (Preliminary Objections)*, Judgment of July 22, 1952, I.C.J. Reports 1952, pp. 93-171

International Court of Justice, *Applicability of the Obligation to Arbitrate under Section 21 of the United Nations Headquarters Agreement of 26 June 1947*, Advisory Opinion of April 26, 1988, I.C.J. Reports 1988, pp. 12-64

International Court of Justice, *Application of the Convention of 1902 Governing the Guardianship of Infants, Netherlands v. Sweden*, Judgment of November 28, 1958, I.C.J. Reports 1953, pp. 55-156

International Court of Justice, *Application of the Convention on the Prevention and Punishment of the Crime of Genocide, Bosnia and Herzegovina v. Serbia and Montenegro*, Judgment of February 26, 2007 (not published yet), URL: <http://www.icj-cij.org/docket/files/91/13685.pdf> (last visited February 29, 2008)

International Court of Justice, *Application of the Convention on the Prevention and Punishment of the Crime of Genocide, Preliminary Objections, Bosnia-Herzegovina v. Yugoslavia*, Judgment of July 11, 1996, I.C.J. Reports 1996, pp. 595-624

International Court of Justice, *Application of the Convention on the Prevention and Punishment of the Crime of Genocide, Counter Claims, Bosnia-Herzegovina v. Yugoslavia*, Order of December 17, 1997, I.C.J. Reports 1997, pp. 243-261

International Court of Justice, *Application of the Convention on the Prevention and Punishment of the Crime of Genocide*, *Bosnia and Herzegovina v. Serbia and Montenegro*, Order of September 13, 1993, I.C.J. Reports 1993, pp. 325-465

International Court of Justice, *Barcelona Traction Light and Power Company, Limited, Second Phase*, Judgment of February 5, 1970, I.C.J. Reports 1970, pp. 3-357

International Court of Justice, *Case Concerning Armed Activities on the Territory of the Congo, Democratic Republic of Congo v. Uganda (new application of 2002)*, Judgment of December 19, 2005, (not published yet), URL: <http://www.icj-cij.org/docket/files/116/10455.pdf> (last visited February 27, 2008)

International Court of Justice, *Continental Shelf, Libyan Arab Jamahiriya v. Malta*, Judgment of June 3, 1985, I.C.J. Reports 1985, pp. 11-187

International Court of Justice, *Corfu Channel, Merits*, Judgment of April 9, 1949, I.C.J. Reports 1949, pp. 4-38

International Court of Justice, *East Timor, Portugal v. Australia*, Judgment of June 30, 1995, I.C.J. Reports 1995, pp. 90-106

International Court of Justice, *Elettronica Sicula S.p.A. (ELSI), United States of America v. Italy*, Judgment of July 20, 1989, I.C.J. Reports 1989, pp. 15-82

International Court of Justice, *Gabčíkovo-Nagymaros Project, Hungary v. Slovakia*, Judgment of September 25, 1997, I.C.J. Reports 1997, pp. 7-84

International Court of Justice, *Interpretation of Peace Treaties with Bulgaria, Hungary and Romania (Second Phase)*, Advisory Opinion of July 18, 1950, I.C.J. Reports 1950, pp. 221-254

International Court of Justice, *Kasikili/Sedudu Island, Botswana v. Namibia*, Judgment of December 13, 1999, I.C.J. Reports 1999, pp. 1045-1237

International Court of Justice, *Legal Consequences for States of the Continued Presence of South Africa in Namibia (South-West Africa) Notwithstanding Security Council Resolution 276 (1970)*,

Advisory Opinion of June 21, 1971, I.C.J. Reports 1971, pp. 12-345

International Court of Justice, *Legal Consequences of the Construction of a Wall in the Occupied Palestine Territory*, Advisory Opinion of July 9, 2004, I.C.J. Reports 2004, pp. 133-271

International Court of Justice, *Legality of the Threat or Use of Nuclear Weapons*, Advisory Opinion of July 8, 1996, I.C.J. Reports 1996, pp. 226-593

International Court of Justice, *Military and Paramilitary Activities in and against Nicaragua, Nicaragua v. United States of America*, Judgment (Merits) of June 27, 1986, I.C.J. Reports 1986, pp. 14-150

International Court of Justice, *North Sea Continental Shelf, Federal Republic of Germany v. Denmark; Federal Republic of Germany v. The Netherlands*, Judgment of February 20, 1969, I.C.J. Reports 1969, pp. 3-57

International Court of Justice, *Nottebohm, Preliminary Objections, Liechtenstein v. Guatemala*, Judgment of November 18, 1953, I.C.J. Reports 1953, pp. 111-125

International Court of Justice, *Oil Platforms, Islamic Republic of Iran v. United States of America*, Judgment (Preliminary Objections) of December 12, 1996, I.C.J. Reports 1996, pp. 802-900

International Court of Justice, *Reparation for Injuries Suffered in the Service of the United Nations*, Advisory Opinion of April 11, 1949, I.C.J. Reports 1949, pp. 174-220

International Court of Justice, *Reparation for Injuries Suffered in the Service of the United Nations*, Advisory Opinion of April 11, 1949, I.C.J. Reports 1949, pp. 174-219

International Court of Justice, *Reservations to the Convention on the Prevention and Punishment of the Crime of Genocide*, Advisory Opinion of May 28, 1951, I.C.J. Reports 1951, pp. 14-69

International Court of Justice, *South West Africa, Ethiopia v. South Africa and Liberia v. South Africa, second phase*, Judgment of July 18, 1966, I.C.J. Reports 1966, pp. 6-505

International Court of Justice, *Territorial Dispute, Libyan Arab Jamahiriya v. Chad*, Judgment of February 3, 1994, I.C.J. Reports 1994, pp. 6-41

International Court of Justice, *United States Diplomatic and Consular Staff in Tehran, United States of America v. Iran, Merits*, Judgment of May 24, 1980, I.C.J. Reports 1980, pp. 3-46

International Court of Justice, *Western Sahara*, Advisory Opinion of October 16, 1975, I.C.J. Reports 1975, pp. 12-82

International Criminal Tribunal for Rwanda (ICTR), *Prosecutor v. Jean-Paul Akayesu*, Case No. ICTR-96-4-T, Decision of September 2, 1998

International Criminal Tribunal for the Former Yugoslavia, *Prosecutor v. Zoran Kupreškić et al.*, Case No. IT-95-16-T, Judgment of January 14, 2000

International Criminal Tribunal for the Former Yugoslavia, *Prosecutor v. Zejnil Delalić* et al., Case No. IT-96-21-T ("Čelebići"), Judgment of November 16, 1998

International Criminal Tribunal for the Former Yugoslavia, *Prosecutor v. Tihomir Blaškić*, Case No. IT-95-14-T, ("Lasva Valley"), Judgment of March 3, 2000, reprinted in: 122 *International Law Reports* (2002), pp. 1-250 [*Int'l L.R.*]

International Criminal Tribunal for the Former Yugoslavia, *Prosecutor v. Dario Kordić and Mario Čerkez*, Case No. IT-95-14/2 ("Lasva Valley"), Judgment of February 26, 2001

International Criminal Tribunal for the Former Yugoslavia, *Prosecutor v. Pavle Strugar*, Case No. IT-01-42-T, Judgment of January 31, 2005

International Criminal Tribunal for the Former Yugoslavia, *Prosecutor v. Duško Tadić*, Case No. IT-94-1-A, Judgment of May 7, 1997, reprinted in: 112 *International Law Reports* (1999), pp. 1-285 [*Int'l L.R.*]

International Criminal Tribunal for the Former Yugoslavia, *Prosecutor v. Duško Tadić*, Case No. IT-94-1-AR72, Decision on the Defence Motion for Interlocutory Appeal on Jurisdiction of October 2, 1995, reprinted in: 105 *International Law Reports* (1997), pp. 419-648 [*Int'l L.R.*]

International Criminal Tribunal for the Former Yugoslavia, *Prosecutor v. Duško Tadić*, Case No. IT-94-1-A, Judgment (Merits Appeal) of July 15, 1999, reprinted in: 124 *International Law Reports* (2003), pp. 63-212 [*Int'l L.R.*]

International Criminal Tribunal for the Former Yugoslavia, *Prosecutor v. Jelisić*, Case No. IT-95-10-T, Judgment of December 14, 1999

International Military Tribunal (Nuremberg), Judgments and Sentences of October 1, 1946, reprinted in: 41 *American Journal of International Law* (1947), pp. 172-333 [*Am. J. Int'l L.*]

International Military Tribunal for the Far East (Tokyo), *In re Hirota* and others, Judgement of November 12, 1948, reprinted in: 15 *Annual Digest and Reports of Public International Law Cases* (1948), Case No. 118, pp. 356-376 [*Annual Digest*]

Permanent Court of International Justice, *Exchange of Greek and Turkish Populations*, Advisory Opinion of February 21, 1925, Series B No. 10 (1925), pp. 6-26

Permanent Court of International Justice, *Factory at Chorzów, Jurisdiction*, Judgment of July 26, 1927, Series A, No. 9 (1927), pp. 4-34

Permanent Court of International Justice, *Factory at Chorzów, Merits*, Judgment of September 13, 1928 Series A, No. 17 (1928), pp. 4-74

Permanent Court of International Justice, *Free Zones of Upper Savoy and the District of Gex*, Judgment of June 7, 1932, Series A/B No. 46 (1932), pp. 95-185

Permanent Court of International Justice, *Greco-Bulgarian "Communities"*, Advisory Opinion of July 31, 1930, Series B No. 17 (1930), pp. 4-36

Permanent Court of International Justice, *Jurisdiction of the Courts of Danzig*, Advisory Opinion of March 3, 1928, Series B No. 15 (1928), pp. 4-27

Permanent Court of International Justice, *Phosphates in Morocco, Preliminary Objections*, Judgment of June 14, 1938, Series A/B No. 74 (1938), pp. 10-30

Permanent Court of International Justice, *S.S. "Wimbledon"*, Judgment of August 17, 1923, Series A, No. 1 (1923), pp. 15-34

Permanent Court of International Justice, *SS "Lotus"*, Judgment of September 7, 1927, Series A, No. 10 (1927)

Permanent Court of International Justice, *Treatment of Polish Nationals and Other Persons of Polish Origin or Speech in the Danzig Territory*, Advisory Opinion of February 4, 1932, Series A/B No. 44 (1932), pp. 4-44

II. Arbitration Awards

Claim of the "Salvador Commercial Company", El Salvador v. United States of America, Award of May 8, 1902, in: *United Nations Reports of International Arbitral Awards* Vol. XV, pp. 465-479 [*RIAA*]

Claims of Italian Subjects Resident in Peru, Italy v. Peru, Awards of September 30, 1901, in: *United Nations Reports of International Arbitral Awards* Vol. 15, pp. 395-453 [*RIAA*]

Franco-Mexican Claims Commission, *Estate of Jean-Baptiste Caire (France) v. United Mexican States*, Award of June 7, 1929, in: *United Nations Reports of International Arbitral Awards*, Vol. V, pp. 516-534 [*RIAA*]

Italian-United States Conciliation Commission, *Flegenheimer*, Decision of September 20, 1958, in: *United Nations, Reports of International Arbitral Awards*, Vol. XIV, pp. 327-390 [*RIAA*]

Italian-United States Conciliation Commission, *Wollemborg*, Decision of September 24, 1956, in: *United Nations, Reports of International Arbitral Awards*, Vol. XIV, pp. 283-291 [*RIAA*]

Norwegian Shipowners' Claims, Norway v. United States of America, Award of October 13, 1922, in: *United Nations Reports of International Arbitral Awards*, Vol. I, pp. 307-346 [*RIAA*]

Rainbow Warrior, New Zealand v. France, Award of April 30, 1990, in: *United Nations Reports of International Arbitral Awards*, Vol. XX, pp. 217-284[*RIAA*]

The Créole (1855), in: Albert de Geouffre de La Pradelle; Nicolas Politis (eds.), *Recueil des Arbitrages Internationaux*, 2nd ed., Paris 1957, Vol. 1, pp. 704-705 [Les Éd. internationals]

Tinoco, United Kingdom v. Costa Rica, Award of October 18, 1923, in: *United Nations Reports of International Arbitral Awards*, Vol. I, pp. 371-399 [*RIAA*]

III. National Courts

Bosnia and Herzegovina, Human Rights Chamber for Bosnia and Herzegovina, *Josip, Božana and Tomislav Matanović v. Republika Srpska*, Case No. CH/96/1, Decision (Merits) of July 11, 1997,

URL: <http://www.hrc.ba/database/decisions/CH96-1%20Matanovic%20Merits%20E.pdf> (last visited February 19, 2008)

Bosnia and Herzegovina, Human Rights Chamber for Bosnia and Herzegovina, *Ratko Grgić v. Republika Srpska*, Case No. CH/96/15, Decision (Merits) of August 5, 1997, URL: <http://www.hrc.ba/database/decisions/CH96-15%20Grgic%20Merits%20E.pdf> (last visited February 19, 2008)

German Federal Administrative Court (Bundesverwaltungsgericht), Case No. 1 C 25/92 (Ausländische Staatsangehörigkeit i. S. des § 25 RuStAG), Judgment of September 28, 1993, in: 13 *Neue Zeitschrift für Verwaltungsrecht* (1994), pp. 387-389 [*NVwZ*]

German Federal Constitutional Court (Bundesverfassungsgericht), Case No. 1 BvR 357/05 (Lufsicherheitsgesetz/"Aviation Security Act"), Judgment of February 15, 2006, reprinted in: 59 *Neue Juristische Wochenschrift* (2006), pp. 751-761 [*NJW*]

German Federal Court of Justice (Bundesgerichtshof), Case No. 5 StR 306/03 (La Belle-Anschlag), Judgment of June 24, 2004, in: 57 *Neue Juristische Wochenschrift* (2004), pp. 3051-3057 [*NJW*]

Israel, District Court of Tel Aviv and Jaffa, *State of Israel v. Marwan Barghouti*, Criminal Case No. 092134/02, Judgment of December 12, 2002, English translation at URL: <http://www.mfa.gov.il/MFA/MFAArchive/2000_2009/2002/12/State%20of%20Israel%20vs%20Marwan%20Barghouti-%20Ruling%20by%20Jud> (last visited February 27, 2008)

Israel, Military Court Ramallah, *Military Prosecutor v. Omar Mahmud Kassem* et al., Case No. 4/69, Judgment of April 13, 1969, reprinted in: 42 *International Law Reports* (1971), pp. 470-483 [*Int'l L.R.*]

Israeli Supreme Court, *Affu v. Commander of the IDF Forces in the West Bank*, Israel High Court of Justice, judgment of April 10, 1988 (HCJ 785/87, "Deportation Orders"), reprinted in: 29 *ILM* (1990), pp. 139-181

Israeli Supreme Court, *Ajuri v. IDF Commander in the West Bank ("Assigned Residence")*, H.C.J. 7015/02, Judgment of September 3, 2002, English translation reprinted in: Israel Supreme Court, *Judgments of the Israel Supreme Court: Fighting Terrorism within the Law*, Jerusalem 2005, pp. 144-178 and 125 *International Law Reports* (2004), pp. 537-568 [*Int'l L.R.*]

Israeli Supreme Court, *Barakeh v. Prime Minister*, H.C.J. 5872/01, Judgment of January 29, 2002, in: 56 *Piskei Din* (2002), Issue 3, p. 1

Israeli Supreme Court, *Beit Sourik Village Council v. The Government of Israel* et al. *("Security Fence")*, H.C.J. 2056/04 (Petition for an Order Nisi), Judgment of June 30, 2004, English translation reprinted in: 43 *ILM* (2004), pp. 1099-1128

Israeli Supreme Court, *Physicians for Human Rights v. Commander of the IDF Forces in the Gaza Strip*, H.C.J. 4764/04, Judgment of May 30, 2004, English translation reprinted in: Israel Supreme Court, *Judgments of the Israel Supreme Court: Fighting Terrorism within the Law*, Jerusalem 2005, pp. 182-207

Israeli Supreme Court, *Public Committee against Torture in Israel v. Government of Israel*, H.C.J. 5100/94, Judgment of September 6, 1999, English translation reprinted in: Israel Supreme Court, *Judgments of the Israel Supreme Court: Fighting Terrorism within the Law*, Jerusalem 2005, pp. 25-58

Israeli Supreme Court, *The Public Committee Against Torture in Israel and LAW (Palestine Society for the Protection of Human Rights and the Environment) v. The State of Israel* et al. *("Targeted Killings" Merits)*, H.C.J. 769/02, Judgment of December 11, 2006, English translation reprinted in: 46 *ILM* (2007), pp. 375-408

Israeli Supreme Court, *The Public Committee Against Torture in Israel and LAW (Palestine Society for the Protection of Human Rights and the Environment) v. The State of Israel* et al., H.C.J. 769/02, Petition for a Conditional Order (Order Nisi) and for an Interim Order of January 24, 2002, URL: <http://www.stoptorture.org.il/eng/images/uploaded/publications/57.pdf> (last visited September 2, 2005)

Israeli Supreme Court, *The Public Committee Against Torture in Israel and LAW (Palestine Society for the Protection of Human Rights and the Environment) v. The State of Israel* et al. *("Targeted Killings" Admissibility II)*, H.C.J. 769/02, Decision of April 18, 2002

U.K. Military Court (Luneberg), *Trial of Joseph Kramer and 44 Others ("The Belsen Trial")*, Judgment of November 17, 1945, in: 2 *Law Reports of Trials of War Criminals* (1947), pp. 1-138

U.S. District Court for the Eastern District of Virginia, Alexandria Division, *United States v. Zacarias Moussaoui* (Superseding Indictment, June 2002), URL: <http://news.findlaw.com/hdocs/docs/

moussaoui/usmouss602supind.pdf> (last visited February 28, 2008)

U.S. Military Tribunal (Nuremberg), *U.S. v. Otto Ohlendorf* et al. (Einsatzgruppen Trial), Judgment of April 4, 1948, reprinted in: 15 *Annual Digest and Reports of Public International Law Cases* (1948), Case No. 217, pp. 656-668 [*Annual Digest*]

U.S. Military Tribunal (Nuremberg), *U.S. v. Wilhelm List* et al. (Hostage Trial), Judgment of February 19, 1948, reprinted in: 15 *Annual Digest and Reports of Public International Law Cases* (1948), Case No. 215, pp. 632-653 [*Annual Digest*]

U.S. Military Tribunal (Nuremberg), *U.S. v. Wilhelm von Leeb* et al. (German High Command Trial), Judgment of October 28, 1948, reprinted in: 15 *Annual Digest and Reports of Public International Law Cases* (1948), Case No. 119, pp. 376-398 [*Annual Digest*]

U.S. Supreme Court, *Brown v. United States*, No. 103, Judgment of May 16, 1921, 256 *U.S.* (1921), pp. 335-344

U.S. Supreme Court, *Dennis v. United States*, No. 336, Judgment of June 4, 1951, 341 *U.S.* (1951), pp. 494-517

U.S. Supreme Court, *Ex Parte Quirin* et al., Judgment of July 31, 1942, 317 *U.S.* (1942), pp. 1-48

U.S. Supreme Court, *Jacobellis v. Ohio*, Judgment of June 22, 1964, 378 *U.S.* (1964), pp. 184-204

U.S. Supreme Court, *Salim Ahmed Hamdan v. Donald H. Rumsfeld, Secretary of Defense,* et al., Case No. 05-184, Decision of June 29, 2006, reprinted in: 45 *ILM* (2006), pp. 1130-1203

U.S. Supreme Court, *Shafiq Rasul*, et al., *Petitioners v. George W. Bush, President of the United States*, et al.; *Fawzi Khalid Abdullah Fahad Al Odah*, et al., *Petitioners v. United States* et al., Judgment of June 28, 2004, 542 *U.S.* (2004), pp. 466-506

U.S. Supreme Court, *Yaser Esam Hamdi* and *Esam Fouad Hamdi* as next friend of *Yaser Esam Hamdi, Petitioners v. Donald H. Rumsfeld, Secretary of Defense,* et al., Judgment of June 28, 2004, 542 *U.S.* (2004), pp. 507-599

C. International Treaties and Conventions (by Date)

(1864-08-22) Convention for the Amelioration of the Condition of the Wounded in Armies in the Field, adopted at Geneva, Switzerland, on August 22, 1864, entry into force on June 22, 1865, reprinted in: Dietrich Schindler; Jiří Toman (eds.), *The Laws of Armed Conflicts: A Collection of Conventions, Resolutions and Other Documents*, 3rd ed., Dordrecht 1988, pp. 280-281

(1874-08-27) Project of an International Declaration Concerning the Law and Customs of War, Adopted by the Conference of Brussels, August 27, 1874 (Brussels Declaration), reprinted in: 1 *American Journal of International Law* (1907), Supplement, pp. 96-103

(1880-09-09) The Institute of International Law, *The Laws of War on Land*, Oxford, September 9, 1880 ("Oxford Manual" / "Manual d'Oxford"), reprinted in: Dietrich Schindler; Jiří Toman (eds.), *The Laws of Armed Conflicts: A Collection of Conventions, Resolutions and Other Documents*, 3rd ed., Dordrecht 1988, pp. 36-48

(1906-07-06) Convention for the Amelioration of the Condition of the Wounded and Sick in Armies in the Field, adopted at Geneva, Switzerland, on July 6, 1906, entry into force on August 9, 1907, reprinted in: Dietrich Schindler; Jiří Toman (eds.), *The Laws of Armed Conflicts: A Collection of Conventions, Resolutions and Other Documents*, 3rd ed., Dordrecht 1988, pp. 301-310.

(1907-10-18) Convention (IV) Respecting the Laws and Customs of War on Land, signed October 18, 1907 at The Hague, entry into Force January 26, 1910, reprinted in: James Brown Scott (ed.), *The Hague Conventions and Declarations of 1899 and 1907*, 3rd ed., New York (Oxford Univ. Press) 1918, pp. 100-127 (English translation by US Department of State, with minor corrections by J.B. Scott)

(1907-10-18) Convention (X) for the Adaptation to Maritime Warfare of the Principles of the Geneva Convention, adopted at The Hague, Netherlands, on October 18, 1907, entry into force on October 26, 1910, reprinted in: Dietrich Schindler; Jiří Toman (eds.), *The Laws of Armed Conflicts: A Collection of Conventions, Resolutions and Other Documents*, 3rd ed., Dordrecht 1988, pp. 314-318

(1907-10-18) Regulations Respecting the Laws and Customs of War on Land (1907 Hague Regulations), annexed to the 1907 Hague Convention (IV) Respecting the Laws and Customs of War on Land, signed October 18, 1907 at The Hague, entry into Force January 26, 1910, reprinted in: James Brown Scott (ed.), *The Hague Conventions and Declarations of 1899 and 1907*, 3rd ed., New York (Oxford Univ. Press) 1918, pp. 100-127 (English translation by US Department of State, with minor corrections by J.B. Scott)

(1923-02-19) Rules concerning the Control of Wireless Telegraphy in Time of War and Air Warfare, adopted at The Hague, Netherlands on February 19, 1923, reprinted in: Dietrich Schindler; Jiří Toman (eds.), *The Laws of Armed Conflicts: A Collection of Conventions, Resolutions and Other Documents*, 3rd ed., Dordrecht 1988, pp. 207-217

(1929-07-27) Convention for the Amelioration of the Condition of the Wounded and Sick in Armies in the Field, adopted at Geneva, Switzerland, on July 27, 1929, entry into force on September 24, 1931, reprinted in: Dietrich Schindler; Jiří Toman (eds.), *The Laws of Armed Conflicts: A Collection of Conventions, Resolutions and Other Documents*, 3rd ed., Dordrecht 1988, pp. 326-334

(1929-07-27) Convention relative to the Treatment of Prisoners of War, adopted at Geneva, Switzerland, on July 27, 1929, entry into force on December 19, 1930, reprinted in: Dietrich Schindler; Jiří Toman (eds.), *The Laws of Armed Conflicts: A Collection of Conventions, Resolutions and Other Documents*, 3rd ed., Dordrecht 1988, pp. 341-364

(1947-02-09) Inter-American Treaty of Reciprocal Assistance, also referred to as Rio Treaty, adopted by the Inter-American Conference for the Maintenance of Continental Peace and Security at Rio de Janeiro, Brazil on February 9, 1947, entry into force on March 12, 1948, *OAS Treaty Series*, Nos. 8 and 61

(1948-05-02) American Declaration of the Rights and Duties of Man, by the, O.A.S. Res. XXX (1948), adopted at the O.A.S. General Assembly, 9th Session March 30-May 2, 1948 in Bogotá, Colombia, OEA/Ser.L./V./II.23, doc. 21 rev. 6 (1948)

(1948-12-09) Convention on the Prevention and Punishment of the Crime of Genocide, adopted by the UN General Assembly on December 9, 1948, Resolution 260 (III) A, Annex, UN GAOR, 3rd Session, pp. 174-177, U.N. Doc. A/810 (1948), entry into force on January 12, 1951, reprinted in: 78 *UNTS* (1951), No. 1021, pp. 277-323

(1949-04-03) General Armistice Agreement, Israel and Jordan, signed at Rhodes, on April 3, 1949, reprinted in: 42 *UNTS* (1949), No. 656, pp. 303-325

(1949-04-04) North Atlantic Treaty, signed at Washington, D.C., on April 4, 1949, entry into force on August 24, 1949, reprinted in: 34 *UNTS* (1949), No. 541, pp. 243-255

(1949-08-12) Geneva Convention (I) for the Amelioration of the Condition of the Wounded and Sick in Armed Forces in the Field of 12 August 1949, adopted at Geneva, Switzerland, on August 12, 1949, entry into force on October 21, 1950, *Final Record of the Diplomatic Conference of Geneva of 1949*, Berne 1949, Vol. I, pp. 205-218 [Federal Political Department], reprinted in: 75 *UNTS* (1950), No. 970, pp. 31-83

(1949-08-12) Geneva Convention (II) for the Amelioration of the Condition of Wounded, Sick and Shipwrecked Members of Armed Forces at Sea of 12 August 1949, adopted at Geneva, Switzerland, on August 12, 1949, entry into force on October 21, 1950, *Final Record of the Diplomatic Conference of Geneva of 1949*, Berne 1949, Vol. I, pp. 225-236 [Federal Political Department], reprinted in: 75 *UNTS* (1950), No. 971, pp. 85-133

(1949-08-12) Geneva Convention (III) relative to the Treatment of Prisoners of War of 12 August 1949, adopted at Geneva, Switzerland, on August 12, 1949, entry into force on October 21, 1950, *Final Record of the Diplomatic Conference of Geneva of 1949*, Berne 1949, Vol. I, pp. 242-276 [Federal Political Department], reprinted in: 75 *UNTS* (1950), No. 972, pp. 135-285

(1949-08-12) Geneva Convention (IV) relative to the Protection of Civilian Persons in Time of War of 12 August 1949, adopted at Geneva, Switzerland, on August 12, 1949, entry into force on October 21, 1950, *Final Record of the Diplomatic Conference of Geneva of 1949*, Berne 1949, Vol. I, pp. 297-330 [Federal Political Department], reprinted in: 75 *UNTS* (1950), No. 973, pp. 287-417

(1950-11-04) European Convention on Human Rights, formally entitled "Convention for the Protection of Human Rights and Fundamental Freedoms", adopted at Rome, Italy, on November 4, 1950, entry into force on September 3, 1953, reprinted in: *Euro-*

pean Treaty Series No. 5 and 213 *UNTS* (1955), No. 2889, pp. 222-261

(1954-05-14) Convention for the Protection of Cultural Property in the Event of Armed Conflict, adopted at The Hague, Netherlands on May 14, 1954, entry into force on August 7, 1956, reprinted in: Dietrich Schindler; Jiří Toman (eds.), *The Laws of Armed Conflicts: A Collection of Conventions, Resolutions and Other Documents*, 3rd ed., Dordrecht 1988, pp. 747-768

(1966-12-16) International Covenant Economic, Social and Cultural Rights, adopted by the UN General Assembly on December 16, 1966, Resolution 2200 A (XXI), annex, UN GAOR, 21st Session, Supp. No. 16, pp. 49-60, at pp. 49-52, UN Doc. A/6316 (1966), entry into force on January 3, 1976, reprinted in: 993 *UNTS* (1976), No. 14531, pp. 3-106

(1966-12-16) International Covenant on Civil and Political Rights, adopted by the UN General Assembly on December 16, 1966, Resolution 2200 A (XXI), annex, UN GAOR, 21st Session, Supp. No. 16, pp. 49-60, at 52-58, UN Doc. A/6316 (1966), entry into force on March 23, 1976 for all provisions except those of Article 41, and on March 28, 1978 for the provisions of Article 41, reprinted in: 999 *UNTS* (1976), No. 14668, pp. 171-301 and 1057 *UNTS* (1977), p. 407 (corrigendum)

(1966-12-16) Optional Protocol to the International Covenant on Civil and Political Rights, adopted by the UN General Assembly on December 16, 1966, Resolution 2200 A (XXI), annex, UN GAOR, 21st Session, Supp. No. 16, pp. 49-60, at 59-60, UN Doc. A/6316 (1966), entry into force on March 23, 1976, reprinted in: 999 *UNTS* (1976), No. 14668, pp. 302-346

(1969-05-23) Vienna Convention on the Law of Treaties, adopted at Vienna, Austria, on May 23, 1969, entry into force on January 27, 1980, reprinted in: 1155 *UNTS* (1980), No. 18232, pp. 331-512

(1969-11-22) American Convention on Human Rights, also referred to as the "Pact of San José", adopted by the Inter-American Specialized Conference on Human Rights at San José, Costa Rica, November 22, 1969, entry into force on July 18, 1978, reprinted in: *OAS Treaty Series* No. 36 and 1144 *UNTS* (1979), No. 17955, pp. 123-212

(1973-12-14) (New York) Convention on the Prevention and Punishment of Crimes Against Internationally Protected Persons, Including Diplomatic Agents, adopted by the UN General Assembly on December 14, 1973, Resolution 3166 (XXVIII), Annex, UN GAOR 28th Sess., Supp. No. 30, pp. 146-149, UN Doc. A/RES/3166 (1973), entry into force on February 20, 1977, reprinted in: 1035 *UNTS* (1977), No. 15410, pp. 167-247

(1977-01-27) European Convention on the Suppression of Terrorism, adopted at Strasbourg, France on January 27, 1977, entry into force on August 4, 1978, *European Treaty Series* No. 90, reprinted in: 1137 *UNTS* (1979), No. 17828, pp. 93-111

(1977-06-08) Protocol Additional to the Geneva Conventions of 12 August 1949, and relating to the Protection of Victims of Non-International Armed Conflicts (Protocol II), adopted at Geneva, Switzerland, on June 8, 1977, entry into force on December 7, 1978, International Committee of the Red Cross, Protocols Additional to the Geneva Conventions of 12 August 1949, Geneva 1977, pp. 89-101; reprinted in: 1125 *UNTS* (1979), No. 17513, pp. 609-699

(1977-06-08) Protocol Additional to the Geneva Conventions of 12 August 1949, and relating to the Protection of Victims of International Armed Conflicts (Protocol I), adopted at Geneva, Switzerland, on June 8, 1977, entry into force December 7, 1978, International Committee of the Red Cross, Protocols Additional to the Geneva Conventions of 12 August 1949, Geneva 1977, pp. 3-87; reprinted in: 1125 *UNTS* (1979), No. 17512, pp. 3-608

(1979-03-26) Israel-Egypt Peace Treaty, signed in Washington, D.C. on March 26, 1979, reprinted in: 18 *ILM* (1979), p. 362

(1980-10-10) Convention on Prohibitions or Restrictions on the Use of Certain Conventional Weapons Which May be Deemed to be Excessively Injurious or to Have Indiscriminate Effects, adopted at Geneva, Switzerland on October 10, 1980, entry into force on December 2, 1983, reprinted in: Dietrich Schindler; Jiří Toman (eds.), *The Laws of Armed Conflicts: A Collection of Conventions, Resolutions and Other Documents*, 3rd ed., Dordrecht 1988, pp. 179-184

(1981-06-28) African Charter on Human and Peoples' Rights, adopted by the Organization of African Unity Summit at Nairobi, Kenya, on June 27, 1981, OAU Doc. CAB/LEG/67/3/Rev. 5, entry into force on October 21, 1986, reprinted in: 1520 *UNTS* (1988), No. 26363, pp. 217-292 and 21 *ILM* (1982), pp. 59-68, also known as the "Banjul Charter on Human and Peoples' Rights"

(1981-09-19) Universal Islamic Declaration of Human Rights, proclaimed by the Islamic Council in Paris, France on September 19, 1981, reprinted in: 4 *European Human Rights Reports* (1982), pp. 433-441

(1983-04-28) Protocol No. 6 to the Convention for the Protection of Human Rights and Fundamental Freedoms concerning the Abolition of the Death Penalty, adopted at Strasbourg, France on April 28, 1983, entry into force on March 1, 1985, *European Treaty Series* No. 114

(1984-09-01) International Law Association, *Minimum Standards of Human Rights Norms in a State of Emergency*, adopted on the conference from August 26 to September 1, 1984, in Paris, France, also referred to as "Paris Standards", reprinted in: 79 *American Journal of International Law* 1985, pp. 1073-1081 [*Am. J. Int'l L.*]

(1989-11-20) Convention on the Rights of the Child, adopted by the UN General Assembly on November 20, 1989, Resolution 44/25, Annex, UN GAOR 44th Session, Supp. No. 49, pp. 166-173, UN Doc. A/44/49 (1989), entry into force on September 2, 1990, reprinted in: 1577 *UNTS* (1990), No. 27531, pp. 3-177

(1989-12-15) Second Optional Protocol to the International Covenant on Civil and Political Rights, aiming at the Abolition of the Death Penalty, adopted by the UN General Assembly on December 15, 1989, Resolution 44/128, Annex, UN GAOR 44th Session, Supp. No. 49, pp. 207-208, UN Doc. A/RES/44/128 (1989), entry into force on July 11, 1991, reprinted in: 1642 *UNTS* (1991), No. 14668, pp. 414-471

(1990-06-08) Protocol to the American Convention on Human Rights to Abolish the Death Penalty, adopted at the 20th Regular Session of the OAS General Assembly at Asunción, Paraguay, by Res. 1042 of June 8, 1990, entry into force on August 28, 1991, *OAS Treaty Series* No. 73, reprinted in: 29 *ILM* (1990), pp. 1447-1448

(1993-09-13) Israel-PLO Declaration of Principles on Interim Self-Government Arrangements (Oslo I), finalized in Oslo, Norway on August 20, 1993 and signed at Washington, D.C., September 13, 1993, reprinted in: 32 *ILM* (1993), p. 1525

(1994-05-04) Israel-PLO Agreement on the Gaza Strip and the Jericho Areas (Cairo Agreement/Gaza-Jericho Agreement), Annex I – Protocol Concerning Withdrawal of Israeli Forces and Security

Arrangements, URL: <http://www.incore.ulst.ac.uk/services/cds/agreements/pdf/is22.pdf> (last visited August 30, 2005)

(1994-05-04) Israel-PLO Agreement on the Gaza Strip and the Jericho Areas (Cairo Agreement/Gaza-Jericho Agreement), signed at Cairo, Egypt on May 4, 1994, in: 33 *ILM* (1994), p. 626

(1994-08-29) Israel-PLO Agreement on the Preparatory Transfer of Powers and Responsibilities (Treaty of Erez), signed at Erez, Israel, on August 29, 1994, in: 34 *ILM* (1994), p. 455

(1994-10-26) Israel-Jordan Treaty of Peace, singed at the Arava/Araba Crossing Point, on October 26, 1994, in: 34 *ILM* (1994), p. 46

(1995-08-27) Israel-PLO Protocol on Further Transfer of Powers and Responsibilities, signed at Cairo, Egypt, on August 27, 1995

(1995-09-28) Israel-PLO Interim Agreement on the West Bank and Gaza Strip (Treaty of Taba/"Oslo II"), signed at Taba, Egypt on September 24, 1995 and countersigned at Washington, D.C., September 28, 1995, in: 36 *ILM* (1997), p. 557

(1995-09-28) Israel-PLO Interim Agreement on the West Bank and Gaza Strip (Treaty of Taba/"Oslo II"), Map No. 1, URL: <http://www.israel.org/NR/rdonlyres/479C928A-E9B3-498A-BE2C-22101CEEFF29/0/MFAJ01v30.jpg> (last visited December 1, 2007)

(1996-05-03) Protocol on Prohibitions or Restrictions on the Use of Mines, Booby Traps and Other Devices as amended on May 3, 1996 (Protocol II to the 1980 Convention as amended on 3 May 1996), entry into force December 3, 1998, U.N. Doc. CCW/CONF.I/16, Part I, Annex B (pp. 14-32), reprinted in: 35 *ILM* (1996), pp. 1209-1218

(1997-01-17) Israel-PLO Protocol Concerning the Redeployment in Hebron, signed at Jerusalem, on January 17, 1997, in: 36 *ILM* (1997), pp. 650-655

(1997-01-17) Israel-PLO Protocol Concerning the Redeployment in Hebron, "Hebron Redeployment Map", URL: <http://www.mfa.gov.il/NR/rdonlyres/47A2FEBB-27E6-4339-89EC-D06C2435361A/0/MFAJ00hl0.jpg> (last visited December 1, 2007)

(1998-06-09) Protocol to the African Charter on Human and Peoples' Rights on the Establishment of an African Court on Human and Peoples' Rights, adopted at Ouagadougou, Burkina Faso on June 9, 1998, entry into force on January 25, 2004, OAU Doc. OAU/

LEG/EXP/AFCHPR/PROT (III), reprinted in: 24 *Refugee Survey Quarterly* (2005), p. 152 (Extract) [*Refugee Surv. Q.*]

(1998-07-17) Rome Statute of the International Criminal Court, adopted at Rome, Italy, on 17 July 1998, entry into force on 1 July 2002, U.N. Doc. A/CONF.183/9 (1998), reprinted in: 2187 *UNTS*, No. 38544, pp. 90-158

(1998-08-23) Israel-PLO Wye River Memorandum ("Wye I"), signed at Washington, D.C., on August 23, 1998, in: 37 *ILM* (1998), p. 1251

(1998-11-01) Protocol No. 11 to the Convention for the Protection of Human Rights and Fundamental Freedoms, restructuring the control machinery established thereby, adopted at Strasbourg, France on May 11, 1994, entry into force on November 1, 1998, *European Treaty Series* No. 155

(1999-09-04) Israel-PLO Sharm el-Sheikh Memorandum on Implementation Timeline of Outstanding Commitments of Agreements Signed and the Resumption of Permanent Status Negotiations (Sharm el-Sheikh Memorandum/"Wye II"), signed at Sharm el-Sheikh, Egypt on September 4, 1999, in: 38 *ILM* (1999), p. 1465

(1999-12-09) International Convention for the Suppression of the Financing of Terrorism, adopted by the General Assembly of the United Nations on December 9, 1999, GA Res. 54/109, UN Doc. A/RES/54/109 (February 25, 2000), entry into force on April 10, 2002, reprinted in: 39 *ILM* (2000), pp. 270-280

(2000-11-4) Protocol No. 12 to the Convention for the Protection of Human Rights and Fundamental Freedoms, Introducing a General Prohibition of Discrimination, adopted at Rome, Italy on November 4, 2000, entry into force on April 1, 2005, *European Treaty Series* No. 177

(2001-12-05) High Contracting Parties to the Fourth Geneva Convention, 'Declaration on the Convention's Applicability to the Occupied Palestinian Territories', Geneva, 5 December 2001, in: 31 *Journal of Palestine Studies* (2002), 3, pp. 148-150

(2002-05-03) Protocol No. 13 to the Convention for the Protection of Human Rights and Fundamental Freedoms Concerning the abolition of the death penalty in all circumstances, adopted at Vilnius, Lithuania on May 3, 2002, entry into force on July 1, 2003, *European Treaty Series* No. 187

(2004-05-13) Protocol No. 14 to the Convention for the Protection of Human Rights and Fundamental Freedoms, Amending the Control System of the Convention, adopted at Strasbourg, France on May 13, 2004, not in force yet, *Council of Europe Treaty Series* No. 194

D. Other International Sources

African Union, *List of Countries which have Signed, Ratified / Acceded to the African Charter on Human and Peoples' Rights*, May 26, 2007, URL: <http://www.africa-union.org/root/au/Documents/Treaties/List/African%20Charter%20on%20Human%20and%20Peoples%20Rights.pdf> (last visited February 20, 2008)

Council of Europe, *Chart of Signatures and Ratifications of Protocol No. 13 to the Convention for the Protection of Human Rights and Fundamental Freedoms Concerning the abolition of the death penalty in all circumstances*, Status as of February 21, 2008, URL: <http://conventions.coe.int/Treaty/Commun/ChercheSig.asp?NT=187&CM=8&DF=2/21/2008&CL=ENG> (last visited February 22, 2008)

Council of Europe, *Chart of Signatures and Ratifications of Protocol No. 6 to the Convention for the Protection of Human Rights and Fundamental Freedoms concerning the Abolition of the Death Penalty*, Status as of February 21, 2008, URL: <http://conventions.coe.int/Treaty/Commun/ChercheSig.asp?NT=114&CM=8&DF=2/21/2008&CL=ENG> (last visited February 22, 2008)

Council of Europe, European Commission for Democracy through Law (Venice Commission), *Opinion on the possible Need for further Development of the Geneva Conventions*, Opinion No. 245 /2003, adopted by the Venice Commission on December 12-13, 2003, Doc. No. CDL-AD (2003) 18, URL: <http://www.venice.coe.int/docs/2003/CDL-AD(2003)018-e.pdf> (last visited May 9, 2007)

International Commission of Jurists, *The Berlin Declaration: The ICJ Declaration on Upholding Human Rights and the Rule of Law in Combating Terrorism*, adopted August 28, 2004, URL: <http://www.icj.org/IMG/pdf/Berlin_Declaration.pdf> (last visited February 17, 2008)

International Committee of the Red Cross, 'Fundamental Rules of Humanitarian Law Applicable in Armed Conflicts', in: 18 *International Review of the Red Cross* (1978), No. 206, pp. 247-249 [*Int'l Rev. Red Cross*]

International Committee of the Red Cross, 'The relevance of international humanitarian law in contemporary armed conflicts', Official Statement by ICRC President Jakob Kellenberger, September 14, 2004, URL: <http://www.icrc.org/Web/eng/siteeng0.nsf/html/66EMA9> (last visited December 28, 2007)

International Committee of the Red Cross, 'When is a war not a war? – The proper role of the law of armed conflict in the "global war on terror"', Official Statement by the Legal Adviser at the ICRC's Legal Division Gabor Rona (March 16, 2004), URL: <http://www.icrc.org/web/eng/siteeng0.nsf/html/5XCMNJ> (last visited February 29, 2008)

International Committee of the Red Cross, State Parties to the 1949 Geneva Conventions, URL: <http://www.icrc.org/ihl.nsf/Web Sign?ReadForm&id=375&ps=P> (last visited February 23, 2008)

North Atlantic Treaty Organization, Statement by the North Atlantic Council of September 12, 2001 (Invocation Article V – attacks on US), Press Release (2001) 124, URL: <http://www.nato.int/docu/pr/2001/p01-124e.htm> (last visited February 28, 2008)

Organization of American States, Convocation of the Twenty-Fourth Meeting of Consultation of Ministers of Foreign Affairs to Serve as Organ of Consultation in Application of the Inter-American Treaty of Reciprocal Assistance, OEA/Ser G, CP/RES. 797 (1293/01), September 19, 2001

Organization of American States, Twenty-Fourth Meeting of Consultation of Ministers of Foreign Affairs, *Resolution on Terrorist Threat to the Americas*, OEA/Ser.F/II.24, RC.24/RES.1/01 (September 21, 2001)

UN Commission on Human Rights, *Extrajudicial, Summary or Arbitrary Executions: Report of the Special Rapporteur Philip Alston*, UN Doc. E/CN.4/2005/7 (December 22, 2004)

UN Commission on Human Rights, *Human Rights in Chile*, UN Doc. E/CN.4/1983/9 (February 18, 1983)

UN Commission on Human Rights, *Question of the Violation of Human Rights in the Occupied Arab Territories, including Palestine – Report of the Human Rights Inquiry Commission established pursuant to Commission Resolution S-5/1 of 19 October 2000*, UN Doc. E/CN.4/2001/121 (March 16, 2001)

UN Commission on Human Rights, *Report on the Human Rights Situation in Iran by Special Representative Reynaldo Galindo Pohl*, UN Doc. E/CN.4/1987/23 (January 28, 1987)

UN Commission on Human Rights, *Report on the Situation of Human Rights in Kuwait under Iraqi Occupation*, UN Doc. E/CN.4/1992/26 (January 16, 1992)

UN Commission on Human Rights, Resolution 1982/7, UN Doc. E/CN.4/RES/1982/7 (February 19, 1982)

UN Commission on Human Rights, Resolution 1984/43, UN Doc. E/CN.4/RES/1984/43 (March 9, 1984)

UN Commission on Human Rights, Resolution 2002/8, *Question of the Violation of Human Rights in the Occupied Arab Territories, including Palestine*, UN Doc. E/CN.4/RES/2002/8 (April 15, 2002)

UN Commission on Human Rights, Sub-Commission on Prevention of Discrimination and Protection of Minorities, *Declaration on Minimum Standards*, adopted by a group of experts at a meeting in Turku/Åbo, Finland, December 1990, UN Doc. E/CN.4/Sub.2/1991/55 (August 12, 1991), reprinted in: 31 *International Review of the Red Cross* (1991), No. 282, pp. 328-336 [*Int'l Rev. Red Cross*]

UN Commission on Human Rights, *Summary or Arbitrary Executions: Report by the Special Rapporteur (S. Amos Wako)*, UN Doc. E/CN.4/1983/16 (January 31, 1983)

UN Economic and Social Council, Resolution 1984/50 (May 25, 1984), Annex, *Safeguards Guaranteeing Protection of the Rights of Those Facing the Death Penalty*, 1984 UN ESCOR, Supp. No. 1 (UN Doc. E/1984/84), p. 33

UN Economic and Social Council, Resolution 1989/65 (May 24, 1989), Annex, *Principles on the effective Prevention and Investigation of extra-legal, arbitrary and summary Executions*, 1989 UN ESCOR, Supp. No. 1 (UN Doc. E/1989/89), pp. 52-53

UN Economic and Social Council, Resolutions 2001/2 (July 24, 2001, *Situation of and assistance to Palestinian women*), UN Doc. E/RES/2001/2

UN General Assembly, Conference 144, *UN Basic Principles on the Use of Force and Firearms by Law Enforcement Officials*, UN Doc. A/CONF.144/28/Rev.1 (1990), pp. 112-116

UN General Assembly, Conference 183, *Report of the Preparatory Committee on the Establishment of an International Criminal Court*, UN Doc. A/Conf.183/2/Add.1 (April 14, 1998)

UN General Assembly, International Law Commission, *Commentaries to the Draft Articles on Responsibility of States for Internationally Wrongful Acts adopted by the International Law Commission at its fifty-third session (2001)*, UN GAOR, 56th Session, Supp. No. 10, UN Doc. A/56/10 (2001), pp. 43-58

UN General Assembly, International Law Commission, *Commentaries to the Draft Articles on Responsibility of States for Internationally Wrongful Acts adopted by the International Law Commission at its fifty-third session (2001)*, UN GAOR, 56th Session, Supp. No. 10, UN Doc. A/56/10 (2001), pp. 59-365

UN General Assembly, International Law Commission, *Eighth Report on State Responsibility (by Roberto Ago)*, UN Doc. A/CN.4/318 and UN Doc. A/CN.4/318/Add.1-4, reprinted in: *United Nations Yearbook of the International Law Commission* (1979), Vol. II, Part One, pp. 3-66 [*UN Yb. ILC*]

UN General Assembly, International Law Commission, *First Report on State Responsibility – Addendum 5 (by Special Rapporteur James Crawford)*, UN Doc. A/CN.4/490/Add.5 (July 22, 1998)

UN General Assembly, International Law Commission, Summary Records of the 683rd Meeting, reprinted in: *United Nations Yearbook of the International Law Commission* (1963), Vol. I, pp. 60-67 [*UN Yb. ILC*]

UN General Assembly, International Law Commission, Summary Records of the 685th Meeting, reprinted in: *United Nations Yearbook of the International Law Commission* (1963), Vol. I, pp. 73-79 [*UN Yb. ILC*]

UN General Assembly, Resolution 1514 (December 14, 1960), Declaration on the Granting of Independence to Colonial Countries and Peoples, UN GAOR 15th Sess., Supp. No. 16, U.N. Doc. A/4684 (1960), pp. 66-67

UN General Assembly, Resolution 181 (II) (November 29, 1947), *Future Government of Palestine ("Palestine Partition Plan")*, UN

GAOR, 2nd Session, Supp. No. 1, UN Doc. A/519 (1947), pp. 131-150

UN General Assembly, Resolution 2105 (December 20, 1965), *Implementation of the Declaration on the Granting of Independence to Colonial Countries and Peoples*, UN GAOR, 20th Session, Supp. No. 14, UN Doc. A/6014 (1966), pp. 3-4

UN General Assembly, Resolution 217 (III) A (December 10, 1948), *International Bill of Human Rights – Universal Declaration of Human Rights*, UN GAOR, 3rd Session, Part 1, UN Doc. A/810 (1948), pp. 71-77

UN General Assembly, Resolution 2444 (October 19, 1968), *Respect for Human Rights in Armed Conflicts*, UN GAOR 23rd Session, Supp. No. 18, UN Doc. A/7218 (1969), pp. 50-51

UN General Assembly, Resolution 2625 (October 24, 1970), Annex, *Declaration on Principles of International Law concerning Friendly Relations and Cooperation among States in accordance with the Charter of the United Nations*, UN GAOR 25th Session, Supp. No. 28, U.N. Doc. A/8028 (1971), pp. 121-124

UN General Assembly, Resolution 2675 (December 9, 1970), *Basic Principles for the Protection of Civilian Population in Armed Conflicts*, UN GAOR 25th Session, Supp. No. 28, UN Doc. A/ 8028 (1970), p. 76

UN General Assembly, Resolution 3103 (December 12, 1973), Basic Principles of the Legal Status of the Combatants Struggling against Colonial and Alien Domination and Racist Regimes, UN GAOR 28th Session, Supp. No. 30, UN Doc. A/9030 (1974), pp. 142-143

UN General Assembly, Resolution 3210 (XXIX) (October 14, 1974), *Invitation to the Palestine Liberation Organization*, UN Doc. A /RES/3210 (1974)

UN General Assembly, Resolution 3236 (XXIX) (November 22, 1974), *Question of Palestine*, UN Doc. A/RES/3236 (1974)

UN General Assembly, Resolution 3237 (XXIX) (November 22, 1974), *Observer Status for the Palestine Liberation Organization*, UN Doc. A/RES/3237 (1974)

UN General Assembly, Resolution 3246 (November 29, 1974), *Importance of the Universal Realization of the Right of Peoples to Self-Determination and of the Speedy Granting of Independence to Colonial Countries and Peoples for the Effective Guarantee and*

Observance of Human Rights, UN GAOR 29th Session, Supp. No. 31, UN Doc. A/9631 (1975), p. 87

UN General Assembly, Resolution 34/169 (December 17, 1979), *UN Code of Conduct for Law Enforcement Officials*, GA Res. 34/ 169, Annex, UN GAOR, 34th Session, Supp. No. 46, UN Doc. A /34/46 (1979), pp. 185-187

UN General Assembly, Resolution 35/172 (December 15, 1980), *Arbitrary or Summary Executions*, UN GAOR, 35th Session, Supp. No. 48, UN Doc. A/35/48 (1980), p. 195

UN General Assembly, Resolution 36/15 (October 28, 1981), *Recent developments in connexion with excavations in eastern Jerusalem*, UN GAOR, 36th Session, Supp. No. 51, UN Doc. A/36/51 (1981), p. 82

UN General Assembly, Resolution 36/22 (November 9, 1981), *Arbitrary or Summary Executions*, UN GAOR, 36th Session, Supp. No. 51, UN Doc. A/36/51 (1981), pp. 168-169

UN General Assembly, Resolution 57/269 (March 5, 2003), *Permanent sovereignty of the Palestinian people in the Occupied Palestinian Territory, including East Jerusalem, and of the Arab population in the occupied Syrian Golan over their natural resources*, UN. Doc. A/RES/57/269 (2003)

UN General Assembly, Resolution ES-10/2 (April 25, 1997), *Illegal Israeli Actions in Occupied East Jerusalem and the Rest of the Occupied Palestinian Territory*, UN Doc. A/RES/ES-10/2 (May 5, 1997)

UN General Assembly, Special Committee to Investigate Israeli Practices Affecting the Human Rights of the Palestinian People and other Arabs of the Occupied Territories, Report of October 21, 1992, UN Doc. A/47/509 (1992)

UN General Assembly, Third Committee (Social, Humanitarian and Cultural), *Government of the Netherlands proposal*, GAOR 10th Sess., Annexes (X), Agenda Item 28, Part I, p. 24, A/C.3/L.460 (September 20, 1955)

UN General Assembly, Third Committee (Social, Humanitarian and Cultural), UN GAOR 3rd Committee, 3rd Session, Part 1

UN General Assembly, Third Committee (Social, Humanitarian and Cultural), 12th Session (1957), UN Doc. A/C.3/L.644

UN General Assembly, Third Committee (Social, Humanitarian and Cultural), 12th Session (1957), UN Doc. A/C.3/L.654

UN General Assembly, Third Committee (Social, Humanitarian and Cultural), 12th Session (1957), UN Doc. A/C.3/L.653

UN High Commissioner for Human Rights, *Status of Ratifications of the Principal International Human Rights Treaties as of July 14, 2006*, URL: <http://www2.ohchr.org/english/bodies/docs/status.pdf> (last visited February 18, 2008)

UN Secretary-General *Kofi Annan*, Statement at the UN Headquarters, in: *Off the Cuff – Remarks to the Press and the Public*, March 22, 2004 (unofficial transcript), URL: <http://www.un.org/apps/sg/offthecuff.asp?nid=564> (last visited at December 28, 2007)

UN Secretary-General, *Report submitted in Accordance with General Assembly Resolution ES-10/2*, Report of June 26, 1997, 10th Emergency Special Session, Agenda Item 5, UN Doc. A/ES-10/6 (June 26, 1997)

UN Secretary-General, *Respect for Human Rights in Armed Conflicts*, Report of September 18, 1970, 25th Session, Agenda Item 47, UN Doc. A/8052 (September 18, 1970)

UN Secretary-General, *Respect for Human Rights in Armed Conflicts*, Report of November 20, 1969, 24th Session, Agenda Item 61, UN Doc. A/7720 (November 20, 1969)

UN Security Council, *Letter dated 19 April 1988 from the Permanent Representative of Tunisia to the United Nations addressed to the President of the Security Council*, UN Doc. S/19798 (April 19, 1988)

UN Security Council, Resolution 1368 (September 12, 2001), *Threats to International Peace and Security caused by Terrorist Acts*, U.N. Doc. S/RES/1368 (2001)

UN Security Council, Resolution 1373 (September 28, 2001), *Threats to International Peace and Security caused by Terrorist Acts*, U.N. Doc. S/RES/1373 (2000)

UN Security Council, Resolution 242 (November 22, 1967, *The Situation in the Middle East*), UN Doc. S/RES/242 (1967)

UN Security Council, Resolution 452 (July 20, 1979, *Territories occupied by Israel*), UN Doc. S/RES/425 (1979)

UN Security Council, Resolution 611 (April 25, 1988, *Israel-Tunisia*), U.N. Doc. S/RES/611 (1988)

UN Security Council, Resolution 904 (March 18, 1994, *on Measures to guarantee the Safety and Protection of the Palestinian Civilians in Territories occupied by Israel*), UN Doc. S/RES/904 (1994)

UN Security Council, Resolution 955 (November 8, 1994, *Establishing the International Tribunal for Rwanda, with Annexed Statute*), U.N. Doc. S/RES/955 (1994)

E. National Sources

Germany, *Dokumentation zu den Ereignissen und Entscheidungen im Zusammenhang mit der Entführung von Hanns Martin Schleyer und der Lufthansa-Maschine "Landshut"*, Presse- und Informationsamt der Bundesregierung, Bonn 1977

Germany, Federal Minister of the Interior *Otto Schily*, Interview, 'Wer den Tod liebt, kann ihn haben', in: *Der Spiegel* (2004), No. 18 (April 26, 2004), p. 44

Germany, Federal Minister of the Interior *Wolfgang Schäuble*, Interview, 'Es kann uns jederzeit treffen', in: *Der Spiegel* (2007), No. 28 (July 9, 2007), pp. 31-33

Germany, Federal Minister of the Interior *Wolfgang Schäuble*, Interview, 'We Could Be Struck at Anytime', in: *Spiegel Online* (July 9, 2007), URL: <http://www.spiegel.de/international/germany/0,1518,493364,00.html> (last visited February 2, 2008)

Israel Defence Forces, Casualties Since 29.09.2000, Updated 29.08.05, URL: <www1.idf.il/SIP_STORAGE/DOVER/files/7/21827.doc > (last visited August 30, 2005)

Israel, 'Declaration of the Establishment of the State of Israel', in: 1 *Laws of the State of Israel* (1948) 3 (Authorized Translation)

Israel, Incarceration of Unlawful Combatants Law (5762-2002), English translation reprinted in: 32 *Israel Yearbook on Human Rights* (2002), pp. 389-392

Israel, Military Proclamation No. 7 Concerning the Application of the Interim Agreement (West Bank), issued by the Military Commander on November 23, 1995

Israel, Ministry of Foreign Affairs, 'Israel, the Conflict and Peace: Answers to Frequently Asked Questions', November 2007, URL: <http://www.mfa.gov.il/MFA/MFAArchive/2000_2009/2003/11

/Israel-%20the%20Conflict%20and%20Peace-%20Answers%20to%20Frequen> (last visited February 26, 2008)

Israel, Ministry of Foreign Affairs, 'Targeting Terrorists', Background Paper (August 1, 2001), URL: <http://www.israel-mfa.gov.il/MFA/MFAArchive/2000_2009/2001/8/Targeting+Terrorists+-+Background.htm> (last visited February 10, 2008)

Jordan, *King Hussein of Jordan*, 'Address to the Nation' concerning the Disengagement from the West Bank and Palestinian Self-Determination, Amman, July 31, 1988, reprinted in: 28 *ILM* (1988), p. 1637

U.S. Attorney General *John Ashcroft*, Memorandum to President George W. Bush, February 1, 2002, URL: <http://news.findlaw.com/wp/docs/torture/jash20102ltr.html> (last visited February 23, 2008)

U.S. Council to the President *Alberto R. Gonzales*, 'Decision re Application of the Geneva Convention on Prisoners of War to the conflict with al Qaeda and the Taliban', Memorandum to President George W. Bush, January 25, 2002, URL: <http://msnbc.com/modules/newsweek/pdf/gonzales_memo.pdf> (last visited February 23, 2008)

U.S. Department of Navy, *Commander's Handbook on the Law of Naval Operations*, NWP 1-14M, Washington, D.C. 1995

U.S. Department of the Army, *The Law of Land Warfare*, Field Manual No. 27-10 (July 18, 1956), Washington, D.C. 1956

U.S. Department of the Army, *The Law of Land Warfare*, Field Manual No. 27-10, Change 1 (July 15, 1976), Washington, D.C. 1976

U.S. National Commission on Terrorist Attacks on the United States, *The 9/11 Commission Report*, Final Report, 2005, URL: <http://www.9-11commission.gov/report/911Report.pdf> (last visited September 11, 2007)

U.S. President *Abraham Lincoln*, General Order No. 100 of April 24, 1863, *Instructions for the Government of the Armies of the United States in the Field*, drafted by Francis Lieber ("Lieber Instructions"/"Lieber Code"), reprinted in: Dietrich Schindler; Jiří Toman (eds.), *The Laws of Armed Conflicts: A Collection of Conventions, Resolutions and Other Documents*, 3rd ed., Dordrecht 1988, pp. 3-23

U.S. President *George W. Bush*, 'Address Before a Joint Session of the Congress on the United States Response to the Terrorist Attacks of September 11', September 20, 2001, in: 37 *Weekly Compilation of Presidential Documents* (2001), No. 38, pp. 1347-1351 [*Weekly Comp. Pres. Doc.*]

U.S. President *George W. Bush*, 'Status of Detainees at Guantanamo', White House Fact Sheet of February 7, 2002, URL: <http://www.whitehouse.gov/news/releases/2002/02/20020207-13.html > (last visited February 27, 2008)

U.S. President *George W. Bush*, Memorandum of February 7, 2002, to Vice President Dick Cheney, *et al.*, URL: <http://www.cnn.com /2004/images/06/22/bush.memo.pdf> (last visited February 23, 2008)

U.S. President *Lyndon B. Johnson*, 'Proposal for A Nationwide War On The Sources of Poverty', Special Message to Congress, March 16, 1964, in: *Public Papers of U.S. Presidents, Lyndon B. Johnson, 1963-1964*, Washington, D.C. 1965, No. 1, pp. 375-380 [Government Printing Office]

U.S. Sharm el-Sheikh Fact Finding Committee, Final Report (2001), URL: <http://usinfo.state.gov/regional/nea/mitchell.htm> (last visited February 29, 2008)

United Kingdom, Ministry of Defence, *The Manual of the Law of Armed Conflict*, Oxford 2004 [Oxford Univ. Press]

United Kingdom, Permanent Representative to the United Nations (Sir Jeremy Greenstock, KCMG), Statement at the General Assembly Debate on Terrorism, October 1, 2001, in: UN General Assembly, 56th Session, 12th Plenary Meeting, Official Records, UN Doc. A/56/PV.12 (October 1, 2001), pp. 17-19

United Kingdom, The Geneva Conventions Act (First Protocol) Order 1998, *Statutory Instruments* (1998), No. 1754, made July 21, 1998, entry into force on July 28, 1998

F. Press

Amnesty International Press Release, 'Yemen/USA: Government must not sanction Extra-Judicial Executions', November 8, 2002, AI Index AMR 51/168/2002

B'Tselem, 'Activities of the Special Units in the Territories', Report of May 1992, URL: <http://www.btselem.org/Download/ 199205_ Undercover_Units_Eng.doc> (last visited November 24, 2007)

B'Tselem, 'Statistics: Fatalities 29.9.2000-31.12.2007', URL: <http://www.btselem.org/english/Statistics/Casualties.asp> (last visited January 21, 2008)

Bernstein, Richard, 'Biggest U.S. Terrorist Trial Begins as Arguments Clash', in: *New York Times*, January 31, 1995, p. A1

Croitoru, Joseph, 'Nach Liquidierung Scheich Jassins: Moraldebatte unter israelischen Philosophen', in: *Frankfurter Allgemeine Zeitung*, March 24, 2004 (No. 71), p. 43 [*FAZ*]

David, Steven R., 'The Necessity of Targeted Assassinations – The Israeli Reply to Terror is Moral and Appropriate', in: *Los Angeles Times*, July 25, 2002, p. 13

Dudkevitch, Margot, 'Sheikh Ahmed Yassin killed in Airstrike', in: *Jerusalem Post*, Online Edition, March 22, 2003, URL: <http://www.jpost.com/servlet/Satellite?pagename=JPost/JPArticle/Printer&cid=1079929443799&p=1006688055060> (last visited March 22, 2003)

Fischer, Dan/ Brodie, John M., 'Value of Israel's Assassination Policy Debated', in: *Los Angeles Times*, April 22, 1988, p. 1

Gabbai, Yoram, 'The American Way', in: *Israel's Business Arena*, October 7, 2001.

Hersh, Seymour M., 'Manhunt: The Bush Administration's new strategy in the war against terrorism', in: *New Yorker*, December 23 and 30, 2002, p. 66

Hirschberg, Peter, '"Pinpoint Liquidations" to Continue', in: *Irish Times*, August 3, 2001, p. 13

ITAR-Tass News Agency, 'ITAR-Tass News Digest' of September 27, 2002

Johnston, David/ Sanger, David E., 'Yemen Killing Based on Rules set Out by Bush', in: *New York Times*, November 6, 2002

Katz, Yaakov/ Stoil, Rebecca Anna, 'Peretz orders IDF to prepare for operations in Gaza', in: *Jerusalem Post*, January 29, 2007, URL: <http://www.jpost.com/servlet/Satellite?cid=1167467838057&pagename=JPost%2FJPArticle%2FShowFull> (last visited April 15, 2007)

MENA news agency, Cairo (in English), at 11.00 gmt, on March 15, 2001, according to *BBC Summary of World Broadcasts*, 'Palestinian Security Heads says Intifadah "Message of Peace"', March 17, 2001

Meyer, Josh, 'CIA Expands Use of Drones in Terror War', in: *Los Angeles Times*, January 29, 2006, p. A1

Neubach, Qeren, on Israel TV Channel 1, Jerusalem (in Hebrew), at 16.30 gmt, on June 20, 2001, according to *BBC Worldwide Monitoring*, June 20, 2001

O'Sullivan, Arieh, 'The Army Redefines the "Ticking Bomb"', in: *Jerusalem Post*, September 13, 2004, p. 2

Packer, George, 'Name Calling', in: *New Yorker*, August 8, 2005, URL: <http://www.newyorker.com/archive/2005/08/08/050808ta_talk_packer> (last visited February 17, 2008)

Pincus, Walter, 'U.S. Strike Kills Six in Al Qaeda', in: *Washington Post*, November 6, 2002, p. 1

Pinto, Jacques, 'Sharon's assassination policy sparks controversy in Israel', in: *Agence France Presse*, February 5, 2002

Radin, Charles A., 'In Israel, Support, Concerns on Attack some say that Nation must press the Fight', in: *Boston Globe*, July 25, 2002, p. A1

Risen, James, 'Threats and Responses: Hunt for Suspects – C.I.A. is reported to kill a Leader of Qaeda in Yemen', in: *New York Times*, November 5, 2002, p. 1

Rivkin, David B., Jr./ Casey, Lee A./ Bartram, Darin R., 'Suicide Attacks are War Crimes, Targeted Killings aren't', in: *Jerusalem Post*, November 7, 2002, URL: <http://www.jpost.com/servlet/Satellite?pagename=JPost/A/JPArticle/ShowFull&cid=1036644194377> (last visited January 20, 2003)

Schmitt, Eric, 'Senior Qaeda Commander Is Killed by U.S. Missile', in *New York Times*, February 1, 2008, URL: <http://www.nytimes.com/2008/02/01/world/asia/01qaeda.html> (last visited February 2, 2008)

Shapiro, Samantha M., 'Announced Assassinations', in: *New York Times*, December 9, 2001, p. 54

Sontag, Deborah, 'Israelis Track Down and Kill a Fatah Commander', in: *New York Times*, November 10, 2000, p. A1

Sontag, Deborah, 'Israelis, Suspecting Mortars, Raid Camp; 2 Arabs Die', in: *New York Times*, April 12, 2001

Stevenson, Richard W., 'President Makes it Clear: Phrase is "War on Terror"', in: *New York Times*, August 4, 2005, URL: <http://

www.nytimes.com/2005/08/04/politics/04bush.html> (last visited February 17, 2008)

Tempest, Matthew, 'UK condemns "unlawful" Yassin killing', in: *The Guardian*, March 22, 2004, URL: <http://politics.guardian.co.uk/foreignaffairs/story/0,11538,1175312,00.html> (last visited December 28, 2007)

Time Magazine, 'War on Terrorism', Vol. 110, No. 18 (October 31, 1977), front page, URL: <http://www.time.com/time/covers/0,16641,19771031,00.html> (last visited February 28, 2008)

Voice of Israel, Jerusalem (in Hebrew), at 8.00 gmt and 12.00 gmt, on February 2, 2002, according to *BBC Monitoring International Reports*, 'Israeli PM's Meeting with Palestinian Leaders had Arafat's Approval', February 2, 2002

Voice of Palestine, Ramallah (in Arabic), at 11.33 gmt, on August 20, 2001, according to *BBC Monitoring International Reports*, 'Palestine Minister slams Israeli "War Crimes", criticizes US role', August 20, 2001

Voice of Palestine, Ramallah (in Arabic), at 6.00 gmt, on March 7, 2002, according to *BBC Monitoring International Reports*, 'Palestinian Radio says death toll rises to 18', March 7, 2002

Whitaker, Brian/ Burkeman, Oliver, 'Killing Probes the Frontiers of Robotics and Legality', in: *Guardian*, November 6, 2002, URL: <http://www.guardian.co.uk/international/story/0,,834255,00.html> (last visited December 18, 2007)

Index

Max-Planck-Institut für ausländisches öffentliches Recht und Völkerrecht

Beiträge zum ausländischen öffentlichen Recht und Völkerrecht

Hrsg.: A. von Bogdandy, R. Wolfrum

Bde. 27–59 erschienen im Carl Heymanns Verlag KG Köln, Berlin (Bestellung an: Max-Planck-Institut für Völkerrecht, Im Neuenheimer Feld 535, 69120 Heidelberg); ab Band 60 im Springer-Verlag Berlin, Heidelberg, New York, London, Paris, Tokyo, Hong Kong, Barcelona

---

230 Roland *Otto*: **Targeted Killings and International Law.** 2012. XVIII, 661 Seiten. Geb. € 109,95

229 Nele *Matz-Lück*, Mathias *Hong* (Hrsg.): **Grundrechte und Grundfreiheiten im Mehrebenensystem – Konkurrenzen und Interferenzen.** 2012. VIII, 394 Seiten. Geb . € 89,95

228 Matthias *Ruffert*, Sebastian *Steinecke*: **The Global Administrative Law of Science.** 2011. IX, 140 Seiten. Geb. € 59,955 zzgl. landesüblicher MwSt.

227 Sebastian *Pritzkow*: **Das völkerrechtliche Verhältnis zwischen der EU und Russland im Energiesektor.** 2011. XXIV, 304 Seiten. Geb. € 79,95

226 Sarah *Wolf*: **Unterseeische Rohrleitungen und Meeresumweltschutz.** 2011. XXIII, 442 Seiten. Geb. € 94,95

225 Clemens *Feinäugle*: **Hoheitsgewalt im Völkerrecht.** 2011. XXVI, 418 Seiten. Geb. € 89,95

224 David *Barthel*: **Die neue Sicherheits- und Verteidigungsarchitektur der Afrikanischen Union.** 2011. XXV, 443 Seiten. Geb. € 94,95

223 Tilmann *Altwicker*: **Menschenrechtlicher Gleichheitsschutz.** 2011. XXX, 549 Seiten. Geb. € 99,95

222 Stephan *Bitter*: **Die Sanktion im Recht der Europäischen Union.** 2011. XV, 351 Seiten. Geb. € 84,95

221 Holger *Hestermeyer*, Nele *Matz-Lück*, Anja *Seibert-Fohr*, Silja *Vöneky* (eds.): **Law of the Sea in Dialogue.** 2011. XII, 189 Seiten. Geb. € 69,95 zzgl. landesüblicher MwSt.

220 Jan *Scheffler*: **Die Europäische Union als rechtlich-institutioneller Akteur im System der Vereinten Nationen.** 2011. XXXV, 918 Seiten. Geb. € 149,95

219 Mehrdad *Payandeh*: **Internationales Gemeinschaftsrecht.** 2010. XXXV, 629 Seiten. Geb. € 99,95

218 Jakob *Pichon*: **Internationaler Strafgerichtshof und Sicherheitsrat der Vereinten Nationen.** 2011. XXVI, 399 Seiten. Geb. € 89,95

217 Michael *Duchstein*: **Das internationale Benchmarkingverfahren und seine Bedeutung für den gewerblichen Rechtsschutz.** 2010. XXVI, 528 Seiten. Geb. € 99,95

216 Tobias *Darge*: **Kriegsverbrechen im nationalen und internationalen Recht.** 2010. XXXV, 499 Seiten. Geb. € 94,95

215 Markus *Benzing*: **Das Beweisrecht vor internationalen Gerichten und Schiedsgerichten in zwischenstaatlichen Streitigkeiten.** 2010. L, 846 Seiten. Geb. € 139,95

214 Urs *Saxer*: **Die internationale Steuerung der Selbstbestimmung und der Staatsentstehung.** 2010. XLII, 1140 Seiten. Geb. € 169,95

213 Rüdiger *Wolfrum*, Chie *Kojima* (eds.): **Solidarity: A Structural Principle of International Law.** 2010. XIII, 238 Seiten. Geb. € 69,95 zzgl. landesüblicher MwSt.

212 Ramin S. *Moschtaghi*: **Die menschenrechtliche Situation sunnitischer Kurden in der Islamischen Republik Iran.** 2010. XXIII, 451 Seiten. Geb. € 94,95

211 Georg *Nolte* (ed.): **Peace through International Law. The Role of the International Law Commission.** 2009. IX, 195 Seiten. Geb. € 64,95 zzgl. landesüblicher MwSt.

210 Armin *von Bogdandy*, Rüdiger *Wolfrum*, Jochen *von Bernstorff*, Philipp *Dann*, Matthias *Goldmann* (eds.): **The Exercise of Public Authority by International Institutions.** 2010. XIII, 1005 Seiten. Geb. € 149,95 zzgl. landesüblicher MwSt.

209 Norman *Weiß*: **Kompetenzlehre internationaler Organisationen.** 2009. XVIII, 540 Seiten. Geb. € 99,95

208 Michael *Rötting*: **Das verfassungsrechtliche Beitrittsverfahren zur Europäischen Union.** 2009. XIV, 317 Seiten. Geb. € 79,95

207 Björn *Ahl*: **Die Anwendung völkerrechtlicher Verträge in China.** 2009. XIX, 419 Seiten. Geb. € 89,95

206 Mahulena *Hofmann*: **Von der Transformation zur Kooperationsoffenheit?** 2009. XIX, 585 Seiten. Geb. € 99,95

205 Rüdiger *Wolfrum*, Ulrike *Deutsch* (eds.): **The European Court of Human Rights Overwhelmed by Applications: Problems and Possible Solutions.** 2009. VIII, 128 Seiten. Geb. € 59,95 zzgl. landesüblicher MwSt.

204 Niels *Petersen*: **Demokratie als teleologisches Prinzip.** 2009. XXVII, 280 Seiten. Geb. € 79,95

203 Christiane *Kamardi*: **Die Ausformung einer Prozessordnung sui generis durch das ICTY unter Berücksichtigung des Fair-Trial-Prinzips.** 2009. XVI, 424 Seiten. Geb. € 89,95

202 Leonie F. *Guder*: **The Administration of Debt Relief by the International Financial Institutions.** 2009. XVIII, 355 Seiten. Geb. € 84,95 zzgl. landesüblicher MwSt.

201 Silja *Vöneky*, Cornelia *Hagedorn*, Miriam *Clados*, Jelena *von Achenbach*: **Legitimation ethischer Entscheidungen im Recht.** 2009. VIII, 351 Seiten. Geb. € 84,95

200 Anja Katarina *Weilert*: **Grundlagen und Grenzen des Folterverbotes in verschiedenen Rechtskreisen.** 2009. XXX, 474 Seiten. Geb. € 94,95

199 Suzette V. *Suarez*: **The Outer Limits of the Continental Shelf.** 2008. XVIII, 276 Seiten. Geb. € 79,95 zzgl. landesüblicher MwSt.

198 Felix *Hanschmann*: **Der Begriff der Homogenität in der Verfassungslehre und Europarechtswissenschaft.** 2008. XIII, 370 Seiten. Geb. € 84,95

197 Angela *Paul*: **Kritische Analyse und Reformvorschlag zu Art. II Genozidkonvention.** 2008. XVI, 379 Seiten. Geb. € 84,95

196 Hans Fabian *Kiderlen*: **Von Triest nach Osttimor.** 2008. XXVI, 526 Seiten. Geb. € 94,95

195 Heiko *Sauer*: **Jurisdiktionskonflikte in Mehrebenensystemen.** 2008. XXXVIII, 605 Seiten. Geb. € 99,95

194 Rüdiger *Wolfrum*, Volker *Röben* (eds.): **Legitimacy in International Law.** 2008. VI, 420 Seiten. Geb. € 84,95 zzgl. landesüblicher MwSt.

193 Doris *König*, Peter-Tobias *Stoll*, Volker *Röben*, Nele *Matz-Lück* (eds.): **International Law Today: New Challenges and the Need for Reform?** 2008. VIII, 260 Seiten. Geb. € 69,95 zzgl. landesüblicher MwSt.

192 Ingo *Niemann*: **Geistiges Eigentum in konkurrierenden völkerrechtlichen Vertragsordnungen.** 2008. XXV, 463 Seiten. Geb. € 94,95

191 Nicola *Wenzel*: **Das Spannungsverhältnis zwischen Gruppenschutz und Individualschutz im Völkerrecht.** 2008. XXXI, 646 Seiten. Geb. € 99,95

190 Winfried *Brugger*, Michael *Karayanni* (eds.): **Religion in the Public Sphere: A Comparative Analysis of German, Israeli, American and International Law.** 2007. XVI, 467 Seiten. Geb. € 89,95 zzgl. landesüblicher MwSt.

189 Eyal *Benvenisti*, Chaim *Gans*, Sari *Hanafi* (eds.): **Israel and the Palestinian Refugees.** 2007. VIII, 502 Seiten. Geb. € 94,95 zzgl. landesüblicher MwSt.

188 Eibe *Riedel*, Rüdiger *Wolfrum* (eds.): **Recent Trends in German and European Constitutional Law.** 2006. VII, 289 Seiten. Geb. € 74,95 zzgl. landesüblicher MwSt.

187 Marcel *Kau*: **United States Supreme Court und Bundesverfassungsgericht.** 2007. XXV, 538 Seiten. Geb. € 99,95 zzgl. landesüblicher MwSt.

186 Philipp *Dann*, Michał *Rynkowski* (eds.): **The Unity of the European Constitution.** 2006. IX, 394 Seiten. Geb. € 79,95 zzgl. landesüblicher MwSt.

185 Pál *Sonnevend*: **Eigentumsschutz und Sozialversicherung.** 2008. XVIII, 278 Seiten. Geb. € 74,95

184 Jürgen *Bast*: **Grundbegriffe der Handlungsformen der EU.** 2006. XXI, 485 Seiten. Geb. € 94,95

183 Uwe *Säuberlich*: **Die außervertragliche Haftung im Gemeinschaftsrecht.** 2005. XV, 314 Seiten. Geb. € 74,95

182 Florian *von Alemann*: **Die Handlungsform der interinstitutionellen Vereinbarung.** 2006. XVI, 518 Seiten. Geb. € 94,95

181 Susanne *Förster*: **Internationale Haftungsregeln für schädliche Folgewirkungen gentechnisch veränderter Organismen.** 2007. XXXVI, 421 Seiten. Geb. € 84,95

180 Jeanine *Bucherer*: **Die Vereinbarkeit von Militärgerichten mit dem Recht auf ein faires Verfahren gemäß Art. 6 Abs. 1 EMRK, Art. 8 Abs. 1 AMRK und Art. 14 Abs. 1 des UN-Paktes über bürgerliche und politische Rechte.** 2005. XVIII, 307 Seiten. Geb. € 74,95

179 Annette *Simon*: **UN-Schutzzonen – Ein Schutzinstrument für verfolgte Personen?** 2005. XXI, 322 Seiten. Geb. € 74,95

178 Petra *Minnerop*: **Paria-Staaten im Völkerrecht?** 2004. XXIII, 579 Seiten. Geb. € 99,95

177 Rüdiger *Wolfrum*, Volker *Röben* (eds.): **Developments of International Law in Treaty Making.** 2005. VIII, 632 Seiten. Geb. € 99,95 zzgl. landesüblicher MwSt.

Printing: Ten Brink, Meppel, The Netherlands
Binding: Stürtz, Würzburg, Germany